ARTTALK

Fourth Edition

Rosalind Ragans, Ph.D.

Associate Professor Emerita
Georgia Southern University

Glencoe

New York, New York   Columbus, Ohio   Chicago, Illinois   Peoria, Illinois   Woodland Hills, California

About the Author

Rosalind Ragans

Rosalind Ragans is the author of Glencoe's senior high school art text, *ArtTalk*. She served as senior author on the elementary program *Art Connections* for the SRA division of McGraw-Hill, and was one of the authors of Glencoe's middle school/junior high art series, *Introducing Art*, *Exploring Art*, and *Understanding Art*. She received a B.F.A. at Hunter College, CUNY, New York, and earned a M.Ed. in Elementary Education at Georgia Southern University and a Ph.D. in Art Education at the University of Georgia. Dr. Ragans was named National Art Educator of the Year for 1992.

About Artsource®

 The materials provided in the *Performing Arts Handbook* are excerpted from *Artsource®: The Center's Study Guide to the Performing Arts,* a project of the Music Center Education Division. The Music Center of Los Angeles County, the largest performing arts center in the western United States, established the Music Center Education Division in 1979 to provide opportunities for lifelong learning in the arts, and especially to bring the performing and visual arts into the classroom. The Education Division believes the arts enhance the quality of life for all people, but are crucial to the development of every child. For additional information visit our Web site at **www.musiccenter.org/artsource**.

Performing Arts Handbook Contributors

Mark Slavkin
Vice President for Education
Music Center Education Division
The Music Center of Los Angeles County

Michael Solomon
Managing Director

Melinda Williams
Concept Originator and Project Director

Susan Cambigue-Tracey
Project Coordinator

Arts Discipline Writers:
Dance
  Susan Cambigue-Tracey
  Diana Cummins
  Barbara Leonard
  Carole Valleskey
  Melinda Williams
Music
  Ed Barguiarena
  Rosemarie Cook-Glover
  Connie Hood
  Barbara Leonard
Theatre
  Barbara Leonard

Copyright © 2005 by Glencoe/McGraw-Hill, a division of the McGraw-Hill companies. All rights reserved. Except as permitted under the United States Copyright Act, no part of this publication may be reproduced or distributed in any form or by any means, or stored in a database or retrieval system, without prior written permission of the publisher, Glencoe/McGraw-Hill.

Printed in the United States of America.

Send all inquiries to:
Glencoe/McGraw-Hill
21600 Oxnard Street, Suite 500
Woodland Hills, CA 91367

ISBN 0-07-830599-3 (Student Edition)

9 10 11 12 13 14   027   09 08 07

Editorial Consultants

Cris E. Guenter, Ed.D.
Specialist, Portfolio and
   Assessment
Professor, Arts
   Education/Curriculum
   and Instruction
California State University,
   Chico
Chico, CA

Marianne Hudz
Director of Career Services
Otis College of Art and Design
Los Angeles, CA

Holle Humphries, Ph.D.
Editorial Consultant
Austin, TX

Gloria McCoy
Administrator for Art
Spring Branch ISD
Houston, TX

Faye Scannell
K–12 Art Instructor
Bellevue Public Schools
Bellevue, WA

Contributors/Reviewers

Randy Hayward Jolly
Art Instructor
Warren Central High School
Vicksburg, MS

Joan Maresh
Digital Art Instructor
G. W. Carver High School
Houston, TX

Jack Schriber
Supervisor of Fine Arts
Evansville-Vanderburgh
   School Corporation
Evansville, IN

Nancy Shake
Art Instructor
Center Grove High School
Indianapolis, IN

Studio Project Contributors/Consultants

Acknowledgements: The author wishes to express her gratitude to the following art coordinators, teachers, and specialists who wrote and field-tested the Studio Projects and Digital Studio Projects with their students.

Jeanne P. Barefoot
Northwest School of the Arts
Charlotte, NC

Betsy Bridger
Albany High School
Albany, GA

Tina Burke
Providence High School
Charlotte, NC

Dorsey Chappell
Dr. Michael Krop Senior
   High School
Miami, FL

Gregg A. Coats
Whitehaven High School
Memphis, TN

Susan Cunningham
Chillicothe High School
Chillicothe, OH

Dan DeFoor
Lithia Springs High School
Lithia Springs, GA

Libby DeVine
Roswell High School
Roswell, GA

Karen Edwards
Robert E. Lee High School
Baytown, TX

Danise Egan
Sheldon High School
Sacramento, CA

Cheryl Evans
Ross S. Sterling High School
Baytown, TX

Barbi Fisher
Westover High School
Albany, GA

Paula Flohr
Sheldon High School
Sacramento, CA

Deborah George
Sheldon High School
Sacramento, CA

Carolyn Holmes
Stratford Senior High School
Houston, TX

Cindy Klingberg
Butler High School
Matthews, NC

Ron Marstall
Riverwood High School
Atlanta, GA

Bunyan Morris
South Effingham High School
Guyton, GA

Connie B. Nowlin
Myers Park High School
Charlotte, NC

Ted Oliver
Campbell High School
Smyrna, GA

Nikki Pahl
Sheldon High School
Sacramento, CA

Lori Phillips
Chattahoochee High School
Alpharetta, GA

Barbara Rosenberg
Crestwood High School
Sumter, SC

Jana Stiffel
Stratford Senior High School
Houston, TX

Shawn P. Sullivan
Sheldon High School
Sacramento, CA

Rhonda Test
Central High School
Memphis, TN

Pam Wittfeld
Myers Park High School
Charlotte, NC

The following students contributed exemplary artworks for Studio Projects, Digital Studio Projects, and the Student Art Portfolio features.

Figure 4.25A, Ashley Sehorn, Myers Park High School, Charlotte, NC; Figure 4.26A, Laura Beebe, Butler High School, Matthews, NC; Figure 4.27, Jonelly Muñoz, South Effingham High School, Guyton, GA; Figure 4.28, Kari Keziah, Butler High School, Matthews, NC; Figure 4.29, Leslie Canales, Dr. Michael Krop Senior High, Miami, FL; Figure 4.30, Cristina Ziegler, Central High School, Memphis, TN; Figure 4.31, Ryan Lawrence, Dr. Michael Krop Senior High, Miami, FL; Figure 5.35A, Travis Trentham, Stratford Senior High, Houston, TX; Figure 5.36A, Johnny Lyons, Whitehaven High School, Memphis, TN; Figure 5.37A, Aysha Shehim, Stratford Senior High, Houston, TX; Figure 5.38, Jomarcus Gipson, Whitehaven High School, Memphis, TN; Figure 5.39, Chris Hibler, Whitehaven High School, Memphis, TN; Figure 5.40, Jessica Gibson, Chattahoochee High School, Alpharetta, GA; Figure 6.30A, Christina Parkhurst, Chattahoochee High School, Alpharetta, GA; Figure 6.31A, Yoon Hwa Jang, Westover High School, Albany, GA; Figure 6.32A, Kevin Massoni, Sheldon High School, Sacramento, CA; Figure 6.33, Chloe Alexander, Roswell High School, Fairburn, GA; Figure 6.34, Wendy Rogers, Sheldon High School, Sacramento, CA; Figure 6.35, Zasha Hankins, Central High

School, Memphis, TN; Figure 6.36, Michael Gonzalez, Dr. Michael Krop Senior High, Miami, FL; Figure 7.16A, Meredith Curtin, Northwest School of the Arts, Charlotte, NC; Figure 7.17A, Elizabeth Oyer, Chillicothe High School, Chillicothe, OH; Figure 7.18A, Kate Castor, Sheldon High School, Sacramento, CA; Figure 7.19, Teasha Lockwood, Butler High School, Matthews, NC; Figure 7.20, Emily Spence, Central High School, Memphis, TN; Figure 7.21, Lorenzo Lattimore, Northwest School of the Arts, Charlotte, NC; Figure 7.22, Ariel Bérubé, Northwest School of the Arts, Charlotte, NC; Figure 8.21A, Haden Springer, Myers Park High School, Charlotte, NC; Figure 8.22A, Julie Kim, Riverwood High School, Atlanta, GA; Figure 8.23A, Eric Hann, Sheldon High School, Sacramento, CA; Figure 8.24, Anna McCarley, Myers Park High School, Charlotte, NC; Figure 8.25, Cynthia Ulysse, Dr. Michael Krop Senior High School, Miami, FL; Figure 8.26, Nkemjika Umenyiora, Roswell High School, Roswell, GA; Figure 8.27, Sherrie Williams, East High School, Memphis, TN; Figure 9.23A, Olivia Yun, Sheldon High School, Sacramento, CA; Figure 9.24A, Jahaziel Minor, Robert E. Lee High School, Baytown, TX; Figure 9.25A, Feifei A. Cao, Stratford Senior High School, Houston, TX; Figure 9.26, Brian

Hatem, Myers Park High School, Charlotte, NC; Figure 9.27, Ashley Noelle Stewart, Sheldon High School, Sacramento, CA; Figure 9.28, Javier Rangel, Robert E. Lee High School, Baytown, TX; Figure 9.29, Andrew Albert, Roswell High School, Roswell, GA; Figure 10.28A, Jessica Lamkin, Providence High School, Charlotte, NC; Figure 10.29A, Anton Prosyannikov, Dr. Michael Krop Senior High School, Miami, FL; Figure 10.30A, Myranda DeFoor, Lithia Springs High School, Lithia Springs, GA; Figure 10.31, Jeana Raquel McMath, Myers Park High School, Charlotte, NC; Figure 10.32, Nick Stevens, Providence High School, Charlotte, NC; Figure 10.33, Danielle Hopkins, Dr. Michael Krop Senior High School, Miami, FL; Figure 10.34, Ashley Crowley, Crestwood High School, Sumter, SC; Figure 11.24A, Christie Hartsfield, Albany High School, Albany, GA; Figure 11.25A, Rebecca Brunet, Campbell High School, Smyrna, GA; Figure 11.26A, Darrel Watson, Jr., Sheldon High School, Sacramento, CA; Figure 11.27, Emily Antoszyk, Myers Park High School, Charlotte, NC; Figure 11.28, Joshua Walls, East High School, Memphis, TN; Figure 11.29, Debbie Lurry, East High School, Memphis, TN; Figure 11.30, Theresa Wilbanks, Dr. Michael Krop Senior High School, Miami, FL.

TABLE OF CONTENTS

UNIT 1

The World of Art

▶ **Chapter 1**
Art in Your World   **4**

LESSON 1   What Is Art?   6

LESSON 2   Why Do Artists Create?   10
    Meet the Artist: Grant Wood   12

LESSON 3   The Language of Art   16

Art Criticism in Action
100 Cans by Andy Warhol   20

TIME ART SCENE **Virtual Art Tours**   22

CHAPTER 1 REVIEW   23

CREDIT ON PAGE 24.

CREDIT ON PAGE 4.

▶ **Chapter 2**
Art Criticism and
Aesthetic Judgment   **24**

LESSON 1   Art Criticism: Learning
from a Work of Art   26
    Meet the Artist: Georgia O'Keeffe   30

LESSON 2   Aesthetics: Thinking
About a Work of Art   31

LESSON 3   Art History: Learning
About a Work of Art   34

Art Criticism in Action
Headdress for Epa Masquerade
by the Yoruba people   36

TIME ART SCENE **Friendly Art Rivals**   38

CHAPTER 2 REVIEW   39

CREDIT ON PAGE 40.

UNIT 2
The Elements of Art

▶ **Chapter 4**
Line 68

LESSON 1 The Element of Line 70
    Looking Closely: Line Types
    and Variations 75

LESSON 2 The Expressive
Qualities of Line 77
    Meet the Artist: Jacob Lawrence 80

Studio Projects
▶ 4-1 Wire Jewelry 84
▶ 4-2 Nature Tapestry 86
  4-3 Digital Image Using Line 88

Student Art Portfolio 90

Art Criticism in Action
Plum Garden at Kameido by Andō Hiroshige 92

  TIME ART SCENE **What's My Line?** 94

CHAPTER 4 REVIEW 95

▶ **Chapter 3**
The Media and Processes of Art 40

LESSON 1 Two-Dimensional Media 42
    Meet the Artist: Winslow Homer 46

LESSON 2 Three-Dimensional Media 50

LESSON 3 Technological Media 57

Art Criticism in Action
Mirrored Room by Lucas Samaras 62

  TIME ART SCENE **The Art of Books** 64

CHAPTER 3 REVIEW 65

CREDIT ON PAGE 68.

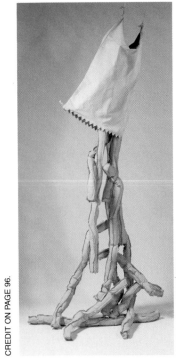

CREDIT ON PAGE 96.

▶ **Chapter 5**
Shape, Form, and Space   **96**

LESSON 1   Shapes and Forms   98

LESSON 2   Space   103
Meet the Artist: M. C. Escher   105

LESSON 3   How We Perceive Shape,
Form, and Space   108

LESSON 4   How Artists Create
Shapes and Forms in Space   111
Looking Closely: Identifying
Perspective Techniques   116

LESSON 5   What Different Shapes,
Forms, and Spaces Express   117

Studio Projects
▶ 5-1 Free-Form Clay Sculpture   122
▶ 5-2 Contrast Drawing   124
  5-3 Digital Genre Scene   126

Student Art Portfolio   128

Art Criticism in Action
Woodrow by Deborah Butterfield   130

TIME ART SCENE **Architectural Forms**   132

CHAPTER 5 REVIEW   133

▶ **Chapter 6**
Color   **134**

LESSON 1   Hue, Value, and Intensity   136

LESSON 2   Color Schemes   144

LESSON 3   Understanding the
Nature and Uses of Color   150
Meet the Artist: Elizabeth Murray   151
Looking Closely: Jumps in Color
Value Create Visual Movement   156

Studio Projects
▶ 6-1 Color Spectrum Star Book   158
▶ 6-2 Mood Painting   160
  6-3 Digital Color Collage   162

Student Art Portfolio   164

Art Criticism in Action
Father and Daughter by Miriam Schapiro   166

TIME ART SCENE **Seeing Colors in Art**   168

CHAPTER 6 REVIEW   169

CREDIT ON PAGE 134.

CREDIT ON PAGE 170.

▶ **Chapter 7**
Texture **170**

LESSON 1   Texture in Your Life   172
  Looking Closely: Visual Texture
  Combinations   176

LESSON 2   How Artists Use Texture   177
  Meet the Artist: Edgar Degas   181

Studio Projects
▶ 7-1 Self-Portrait Collagraph   184
▶ 7-2 Papier-Mâché Sculpture   186
  7-3 Layered Self-Portrait   188

Student Art Portfolio   190

Art Criticism in Action
Football Player by Duane Hanson   192

TIME ART SCENE **Textured Buildings** 194

CHAPTER 7 REVIEW   195

UNIT 3

The Principles of Art

▶ **Chapter 8**
Rhythm, Pattern,
and Movement   **198**

LESSON 1   Rhythm and Pattern   200
  Meet the Artist: Rosa Bonheur   201
  Looking Closely: Visual Rhythms
  Create Visual Movement   203

LESSON 2   Types of Rhythm and Pattern 205

LESSON 3   How Artists Use Rhythm
to Create Movement   211

Studio Projects
▶ 8-1 Found Objects Jewelry   214
▶ 8-2 Rhythm and Movement Painting   216
  8-3 Digital Rendering of Reflections 218

Student Art Portfolio   220

Art Criticism in Action
Nuestra Señora de la Selva by Alfredo Arreguin   222

TIME ART SCENE **Moving Art**   224

CHAPTER 8 REVIEW   225

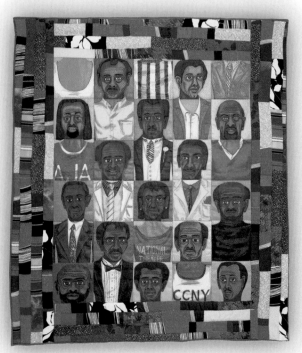

CREDIT ON PAGE 198.

CREDIT ON PAGE 226.

Chapter 10
Proportion 254

LESSON 1   The Golden Mean 256
   Looking Closely: Using the Golden
   Mean to Organize an Active Painting 258

LESSON 2   Scale 260

LESSON 3   How Artists Use
Proportion and Distortion 267
   Meet the Artist: Pablo Picasso 270

Studio Projects
▶ 10-1 The Golden Mean and Mixed Media 274
▶ 10-2 Symbolic Self-Portrait 276
  10-3 Digital Fantasy Creature 278

Student Art Portfolio 280

Art Criticism in Action
The Green Violinist by Marc Chagall 282

   TIME ART SCENE **Art and Politics** 284

CHAPTER 10 REVIEW 285

Chapter 9
Balance 226

LESSON 1   Visual Balance 228
   Meet the Artist: Diego Rivera 229

LESSON 2   Informal Balance 234

LESSON 3   The Expressive
Qualities of Balance 239
   Looking Closely: Using Formal
   Balance to Organize a Composition 239

Studio Projects
▶ 9-1 Ceramic Mask 242
▶ 9-2 Radial Balance Mandala 244
  9-3 Asymmetrical Balance Painting 246

Student Art Portfolio 248

Art Criticism in Action
Dla'ehl Interior House Post: Grizzly Bear Beneath Kolus.
by Arthur Shaughnessy 250

   TIME ART SCENE **Tipping the Balance** 252

CHAPTER 9 REVIEW 253

CREDIT ON PAGE 254.

CREDIT ON PAGE 286.

▶ Chapter 11
Variety, Emphasis, Harmony, and Unity   286

LESSON 1   Variety, Emphasis, and Harmony   288
   Looking Closely: Creating a Focal Point   293

LESSON 2   Unity   296
   Meet the Artist: Allan Houser   299

Studio Projects
▶ 11-1 Decorated Found Object   304
▶ 11-2 Multimedia High-Relief Collage   306
  11-3 Animation Movie Poster   308

Student Art Portfolio   310

Art Criticism in Action
Singing Their Songs, from *For My People* by Elizabeth Catlett   312

TIME ART SCENE **Artistic Roots**   314

CHAPTER 11 REVIEW   315

UNIT 4
Art Through the Ages

▶ Chapter 12
Art Traditions from Around the World   318

LESSON 1   Art of Earliest Times   320

LESSON 2   Art of Asia and the Middle East   326
   Meet the Artist: Katsushika Hokusai   330

LESSON 3   The Art of Africa   332

LESSON 4   Art of the Americas   339

Art Criticism in Action
Untitled by Jessie Oonark   346

TIME ART SCENE **Saving Africa's Art**   348

CHAPTER 12 REVIEW   349

CREDIT ON PAGE 318.

CREDIT ON PAGE 350.

▶ **Chapter 13**
Western Traditions in Art **350**

LESSON 1 The Beginnings
of Western Art Traditions 352

LESSON 2 The Beginnings
of Modern Art Traditions 356
   Meet the Artist:
   Michelangelo Buonarroti 357

LESSON 3 The Nineteenth Century 366

LESSON 4 Early Twentieth Century 374

LESSON 5 Art After 1945 378

Art Criticism in Action
Paul by Chuck Close 384

TIME ART SCENE **Meet Maya Lin** 386

CHAPTER 13 REVIEW 387

▶ **Chapter 14**
Careers in Art **388**

LESSON 1 Careers in
Two-Dimensional Art 390

LESSON 2 Careers in
Three-Dimensional Art and Education 398
   Meet the Artist: I. M. Pei 399

Art Criticism in Action
Book cover for *Duke Ellington: The Piano
Prince and His Orchestra* by Brian Pinkney 406

TIME ART SCENE **Designing Artist** 408

CHAPTER 14 REVIEW 409

CREDIT ON PAGE 388.

UNIT 5

Handbooks

▶ **Artsource®**
Performing Arts Handbook   **412**

Chapter 1 *(Theatre)*
Faustwork Mask Theater   413
Chapter 2 *(Dance)*
Martha Graham   414
Chapter 3 *(Dance)*
Merce Cunningham Dance Company   415
Chapter 4 *(Dance/Music)*
Ballet Folklorico de Mexico   416
Chapter 5 *(Dance)*
Lewitzky Dance Company   417
Chapter 6 *(Theatre)*
Joanna Featherstone   418
Chapter 7 *(Music)*
Paul Winter   419
Chapter 8 *(Music/Dance)*
African American Dance Ensemble   420
Chapter 9 *(Theatre)*
Eth-Noh-Tec   421
Chapter 10 *(Music)*
Eugene Friesen   422
Chapter 11 *(Music)*
Vocalworks   423
Chapter 12 *(Music/Dance)*
Korean Classical Music and
Dance Company   424
Chapter 13 *(Dance/Theatre)*
Kurt Jooss   425
Chapter 14 *(Music)*
John Ramirez   426

▶ **Technique Tips Handbook**   **427**

Drawing Tips
1. Making Contour Drawings   428
2. Making Gesture Drawings   428
3. Drawing Calligraphic Lines with a Brush   428
4. Using Shading Techniques   429
5. Using Sighting Techniques   429
6. Using a Viewing Frame   430
7. Using a Ruler   430
8. Making a Grid for Enlarging   431
9. Measuring Rectangles   431

Painting Tips
10. Mixing Paint to Change the Value of Color   431
11. Making Natural Earth Pigment Paints   432
12. Working with Watercolors   432
13. Cleaning a Paint Brush   432

Printmaking Tip
14. Making a Stamp Print   433

Sculpting Tips
15. Working with Clay   433
16. Joining Clay   433
17. Making a Pinch Pot   434
18. Using the Coil Technique   434
19. Papier-Mâché   434
20. Making a Paper Sculpture   435

Other Tips
21. Making Paper   435
22. Basic Embroidery Stitches   436
23. Weaving Techniques   437
24. Making a Coiled Basket   439
25. Making a Tissue Paper Collage   440

Display Tips
26. Making a Mat   441
27. Mounting a Two-Dimensional Work   442
28. Working with Glue   442

CREDIT ON PAGE 414.

▶ **Safety in the Art Room**　　**443**

▶ **Digital Media Handbook**　　**445**

Scanners　　446
Digital Cameras　　447
Graphics Tablets　　448
Paint Software　　449
Draw Software　　450
3-D Graphics Software　　451
Frame Animation Software　　452
Multimedia Presentation Software　　453
Page Layout Software　　454

Artists and Their Works　　455

Chronology of Artworks　　460

Glossary　　466

Glosario　　474

Index　　484

Photography Credits　　496

FEATURES

TIME ART SCENE

CHAPTER

1	Virtual Art Tours	22
2	Friendly Art Rivals	38
3	The Art of Books	64
4	What's My Line?	94
5	Architectural Forms	132
6	Seeing Colors in Art	168
7	Textured Buildings	194
8	Moving Art	224
9	Tipping the Balance	252
10	Art and Politics	284
11	Artistic Roots	314
12	Saving Africa's Art	348
13	Meet Maya Lin	386
14	Designing Artist	408

LOOKING CLOSELY

CHAPTER

4	Line Types and Variations	75
5	Identifying Perspective Techniques	116
6	Jumps in Color Value Create Visual Movement	156
7	Visual Texture Combinations	176
8	Visual Rhythms Create Visual Movement	203
9	Using Formal Balance to Organize a Composition	239
10	Using the Golden Mean to Organize an Active Painting	258
11	Creating a Focal Point	293

CREDIT ON PAGE 203.

Meet the ARTIST

CHAPTER

1	Grant Wood	12
	Andy Warhol	21
2	Georgia O'Keeffe	30
	The Yoruba People	37
3	Winslow Homer	46
	Lucas Samaras	63
4	Jacob Lawrence	80
	Andō Hiroshige	93
5	M. C. Escher	105
	Deborah Butterfield	131
6	Elizabeth Murray	151
	Miriam Schapiro	167
7	Edgar Degas	181
	Duane Hanson	193

CHAPTER

8	Rosa Bonheur	201
	Alfredo Arreguin	223
9	Diego Rivera	229
	Arthur Shaughnessy	251
10	Pablo Picasso	270
	Marc Chagall	283
11	Allan Houser	299
	Elizabeth Catlett	313
12	Katsushika Hokusai	330
	Jessie Oonark	347
13	Michelangelo Buonarroti	357
	Chuck Close	385
14	I. M. Pei	399
	Brian Pinkney	407

CREDIT ON PAGE 181.

Art Criticism *in Action*

CHAPTER

1	*100 Cans* by Andy Warhol	20
2	*Headdress for Epa Masquerade* by the Yoruba people	36
3	*Mirrored Room* by Lucas Samaras	62
4	*Plum Garden at Kameido* by Andō Hiroshige	92
5	*Woodrow* by Deborah Butterfield	130
6	*Father and Daughter* by Miriam Schapiro	166
7	*Football Player* by Duane Hanson	192
8	*Nuestra Señora de la Selva* by Alfredo Arreguin	222
9	*Dla'ehl Interior House Post: Grizzly Bear Beneath Kolus.* by Arthur Shaughnessy	250
10	*The Green Violinist* by Marc Chagall	282
11	*Singing Their Songs,* from *For My People* by Elizabeth Catlett	312
12	*Untitled* by Jessie Oonark	346
13	*Paul* by Chuck Close	384
14	Book cover for *Duke Ellington: The Piano Prince and His Orchestra* by Brian Pinkney	406

ACTIVITIES

Chapter 1

Learning to Perceive	7
Keeping a Sketchbook	15
Create a Symbol	16
Using Credit Line Information	19

Chapter 2

Aesthetic Theories	33

Chapter 3

Experimenting with Watercolor	47
Making a Printing Plate	49
Redesigning a Familiar Building	54
Traditional and Digital Media	60

Chapter 4

Analyzing Lines in Artworks	73
Using Line to Create Value	76
Using Imagination to Draw Lines Expressively	78
Contour Line Drawings	81
Creating Gesture Drawings	82
Calligraphic Lines	83

Chapter 5

Geometric and Free-Form Shapes	100
Creating Forms	102
Experimenting with Space	104
Using Three Dimensions	107
Shape and Point of View	108
Using Shading	112
Creating Depth	115
Active and Static Shapes	120

Chapter 6

Creating Values	142
Working with Intensity	143
Using Color Schemes	149
Mixing Colors	152
Using Color for Effect	157

Chapter 7

Creating Textures	174
Creating Contrasting Textures	175
Imagining Textures	183

Chapter 8

Analyzing Motifs and Patterns	204
Using Random Rhythm	206
Alternating Pattern	208
Progressive Rhythm	210

Chapter 9

Using Symmetry	231
Creating Radial Balance	233
Using Informal Balance	238
Identifying Balance	241

Chapter 10

Experimenting with Scale	261
Human Proportions	264
Drawing the Head	266
Distorting Proportions	273

Chapter 11

Variety and Contrast	289
Using Emphasis	295
Creating Unity	302

Chapter 12

Analyzing Ancient Art	325
Constructing a Mask	338
Sketching an Event	345

Chapter 13

Analyzing Architecture	353
The Gothic Style	355
Analyzing an Artwork	365
Analyzing a Style	373
Describing General Characteristics	381

Chapter 14

Practicing Logo Design	392
Critiquing Animation	396
Using Design for Display	400
Art in Your Life	405

LISTING OF STUDIO PROJECTS BY MEDIA

Clay
Free-Form Clay Sculpture   122
Ceramic Mask   242

Digital Technology
Digital Image Using Line   88
Digital Genre Scene   126
Digital Color Collage   162
Layered Self-Portrait   188
Digital Rendering of Reflections   218
Asymmetrical Balance Painting   246
Digital Fantasy Creature   278
Animation Movie Poster   308

Fibers
Nature Tapestry   86

Mixed Media
Nature Tapestry   86
Color Spectrum Star Book   158
Papier-Mâché Sculpture   186
Found Objects Jewelry   214
The Golden Mean and Mixed Media   274
Decorated Found Object   304
Multimedia High-Relief Collage   306

Other
Wire Jewelry   84
Found Object Jewelry   214

Paint
Mood Painting   160
Rhythm and Movement Painting   216
Asymmetrical Balance Painting   246
Symbolic Self-Portrait   276
Multimedia High-Relief Collage   306

Paper
Color Spectrum Star Book   158
Papier-Mâché Sculpture   186

Pencil, Pen, Charcoal, and Markers
Contrast Drawing   124
Radial Balance Mandala   244
Symbolic Self-Portrait   276

Printmaking
Self-Portrait Collagraph   184

The World of Art

"Church's content is idyllic and majestic—you feel he has frozen time at perfect moments, captured, and at times orchestrated, Nature's best at the best moment"

—Carter B. Horsley

Quick Write

Analyzing Context Clues. When a word is unfamiliar, you can often use its context—nearby words and phrases—to guess its meaning. Using context clues, try to determine the meaning of *idyllic* in the above quote. Then restate the quote in your own words.

◀

Frederic Edwin Church. *The Icebergs.* 1861. Oil on canvas. 163.8 × 285.8 cm (64½ × 112½"). Dallas Museum of Art, Dallas, Texas.

▲ **FIGURE 1.1** Artists speak to us, the viewers, through their works. Sometimes, they tell a story. At other times, as in this self-portrait, they express strong emotions. What emotion, or feeling, do you "read" in this artist's painting of herself? Does she appear happy? Sad? Explain your reaction.

Frida Kahlo. *Self-Portrait with Monkey.* 1938. Oil on Masonite. 40.6 × 30.5 cm (16 x 12"). Albright-Knox Art Gallery, Buffalo, New York. Bequest of A. Conger Goodyear, 1966.

CHAPTER 1

Art in Your World

The urge to create art is as old as humanity itself. Since the dawn of history, people have used art to communicate information, tell stories, and record events. Art is one of the deepest forms of personal expression.

In this chapter, you will:

- Identify the purposes of art.
- Compare and contrast sources to which artists turn for inspiration.
- Create visual solutions using direct observation and imagination.
- Compare and contrast the use of the elements of art in artworks.

Focus on **Art History** **Figure 1.1** is one of many self-portraits painted by the Mexican artist Frida Kahlo (1907–1954). Kahlo's tragic personal history was a driving force in her art. At the age of 6, she was stricken with polio, a crippling disease. Twelve years later, a bus accident broke nearly every bone in her body. She spent a year in a full-body cast and underwent 30 operations. Her self-portraits, which are highly expressive, seem to reflect a life of physical pain and emotional difficulties. She never appears smiling but, rather, always wears the expression appearing in Figure 1.1.

Compare and Contrast. Examine the work in Figure 4.23 on page 82. It is also a self-portrait of a twentieth-century artist. List similarities and differences in the subject and content between the two works.

What Is Art?

An **artwork** is *the visual expression of an idea or experience created with skill.* Visual art is more than paintings hanging on a wall. Visual art includes drawing, printmaking, sculpture, architecture, photography, film-making, crafts, graphic arts, industrial and commercial design, video, and computer arts.

Art Is Communication

When you talk to someone or write a letter, you communicate. You share your ideas and feelings by using words. You can also communicate through the arts. Art is a language that artists use to express ideas and feelings that everyday words cannot express. In order to experience art fully, you must do more than simply look at it with your eyes; you must develop the ability to perceive. To look is to merely notice and label an object with a name such as "chair" or "house." To **perceive** is *to become deeply aware through the senses of the special nature of a visual object.* Perception is the result of perceiving. To understand a work of art, you must train yourself to perceive. Try to perceive what Meyer Straus is expressing in his painting, *Bayou Teche* **(Figure 1.2).** If you concentrate on his image, you can feel the humid atmosphere of the Louisiana swamps and hear the mosquitoes buzzing. You can understand how it feels to be enclosed by branches dripping with Spanish moss. You can almost hear the water lapping at the boat.

▲ **FIGURE 1.2** Straus captured the feel of the bayou by including details such as the flowers in the foreground and the gray Spanish moss hanging from the limbs of the live oak trees. Look at the figures in the boat. The trees and swamp overwhelm them. What do you think the figures are doing? What atmosphere does the painting capture?

Meyer Straus. *Bayou Teche.* 1870. Oil on canvas. 76.2 × 152.4 cm (30 × 60"). Morris Museum of Art, Augusta, Georgia.

Illustrating Ideas from Direct Observation. Select an everyday object such as one that might be found in the classroom. Closely observe the object. Allow yourself two or three minutes to perceive the object. Then put the object where you can't see it and make a list of all the attributes of the object that you can think of. Look at the object again and add at least three more attributes or characteristics to your list. Use your list and your observations to illustrate an idea for an artwork.

The Purposes of Art

People created art to record ideas and feelings long before they had written words. They used art then as we use it today. The following are some of the most common functions of art:

- **Personal functions.** Artists create art to express personal feelings. Edvard Munch had a tragic childhood. His mother died when he was very young, and one of his sisters died when he was 14. His painting, *The Sick Child* **(Figure 1.3),** shocked viewers who were used to seeing happy paintings with bright colors. The work was meant to remind viewers of personal family tragedies. Perhaps the artist wanted to tell them to appreciate what they had. Often people who have suffered a loss remind

others to live each day as if it were their last. That is what Munch is saying with his striking image.

- **Social function.** Artists may produce art to reinforce and enhance the shared sense of identity of those in a family, community, or civilization (Figure 12.17, page 332). That is why many families commission or hire an artist or photographer to produce a family portrait. Art produced for this purpose also may be used in celebrations and displayed on festive occasions. Think of the many forms of visual art that might be seen in a parade—costumes, band uniforms, floats, and dances are all forms of visual art that might be included in the public celebration of a parade to commemorate an important holiday or event.

- **Spiritual function.** Artists may create art to express spiritual beliefs about the destiny of life controlled by the force of a higher power. Art produced for this purpose may reinforce the shared beliefs of an individual or

▶ **FIGURE 1.3** The child in the painting appears pale and calm. She is not looking at her mother. What is she staring at? Notice the exaggerated drooping of the woman's head. What has the artist done to focus your attention on the sick child?

Edvard Munch. *The Sick Child.* 1907. Oil on canvas. 118.7 × 121 cm (46³/₄ × 47²/₃). Tate Gallery, London, England. © 2003 Artists Rights Society (ARS), New York/BONO, Oslo

a human community. In *Pueblo Scene: Corn Dancers and Church* **(Figure 1.4),** the artists have created a three-dimensional representation of a religious festival that connects two cultures and two religions. Works of art have been created for religious purposes throughout history. Many experts believe that the prehistoric cave paintings of animals had ceremonial purposes, which means they were more than simple records of events. The Greek Temples were built to honor the ancient gods. During the Middle Ages in Europe, almost all art was created for the Catholic Church.

- **Physical functions.** Artists and craftspeople constantly invent new ways to create functional art. Industrial designers discover new materials that make cars lighter and stronger. Architects employ new building materials such as steel–reinforced concrete to give buildings more interesting forms. In **Figure 1.5,** notice how the artist has combined a variety of precious and semiprecious materials to create a unique necklace.

- **Educational function.** In the past, many people could not read and art was often created to provide visual instruction. Artists produced artworks, such as symbols painted on signs, to impart information. Viewers could learn from their artworks. In the Middle Ages, artists created stained-glass windows, sculptures, paintings, and tapestries to illustrate stories from the Bible or about rulers of a kingdom.

▲ **FIGURE 1.4** The figures and buildings for this scene were made by a family of artists. Look closely and you will notice that some of the figures are made of painted clay, while others have hair made from yarn and clothing made of fabric. What do the different figures appear to be doing? What does the procession in the foreground seem to be about?

Vigil Family, Tesuque Pueblo, New Mexico. *Pueblo Scene: Corn Dancers and Church.* c. 1960. Painted earthenware. Girard Foundation Collection at the Museum of International Folk Art, a unit of the Museum of New Mexico, Santa Fe, New Mexico.

 **FIGURE 1.5** This necklace is unusual because each unit is different. The repetition of rectangles and the repetition of materials and shapes on the different rectangles create a unified work.

Earl Pardon. Necklace 1057. 1988. Sterling silver, 14k gold, ebony, ivory, enamel, mother of pearl, ruby, garnet, blue topaz, amethyst, spinel, and rhodolite. 43.1 × 2.8 × .3 cm (17¼ × 1⅛ × ⅛"). National Museum of American Art, Smithsonian Institution, Washington, D.C. Renwick collection.

In addition, when we look at art from the past, we learn from it. Art from other places and other times can tell us what people did. Paintings such as *Anne of Cleves* **(Figure 1.6)** show us people from the past, what they wore, and how they looked.

Art as a Lifelong Pursuit

Art can be a part of your lifelong learning. You may choose to pursue a career in art or to explore art as an avocation, or hobby. Avocational opportunities in art include making art or craft projects at home, taking classes for personal enjoyment, and getting involved in community art programs.

In this book you will learn to analyze and evaluate artworks. You'll also find many opportunities to create artworks and discover the tools, materials, and techniques of various art media. There are many ways to make art a part of your life and education.

▲ **FIGURE 1.6** This portrait of Anne of Cleves, one of the wives of Henry VIII, shows what a royal person in the sixteenth century might have worn for special occasions. The portrait was created before the wedding because King Henry wanted to know what his intended wife looked like. He had never met her. Notice the unusual jewelry on her hat and the rich fabrics of her dress. How many different fabrics can you identify? How does her clothing indicate her social position?

Hans Holbein. *Anne of Cleves*. 1539. Tempera and oil on parchment. 65.1 × 48 cm (25⅝ × 18⅞"). The Louvre, Paris, France.

Check Your Understanding

1. What does it mean to *perceive?*
2. Name the five purposes of art.
3. Describe two of the purposes of art.

Why Do Artists Create?

Vocabulary

folk artists
artists
action painting

The urge to create is universal. Artists are driven by their sense of wonder and curiosity. The creative impulse is often suppressed if one becomes afraid of making mistakes. Artists exhibit the courage to take risks. They are able to see their surroundings in new and unusual ways. They are willing to work intensely for long periods of time to achieve their goals. *Artists who are self-taught and therefore have had little or no formal schooling in artistic methods* are called **folk artists**. Most artists learn skills and techniques from other artists. Eventually artists develop their own unique styles.

The impulses that drive artists to create vary. Both Leo Twiggs and Roger Brown created art in response to a devastating natural catastrophe: Hurricane Hugo. Twiggs, who lives in South Carolina and witnessed the hurricane, used strong lines to represent the force of the winds **(Figure 1.7)**. Brown, who lives in Chicago, responded to the same tragedy in a different way. He illustrated only the aftermath of the hurricane. He turned the event into a giant postcard in which he depicted the fury of the storm by showing the trees in neat rows, broken off at exactly the same level **(Figure 1.8)**.

▶ **FIGURE 1.7** Identify the door named in the title. Look at the dark shape near the center of the painting. How many figures are standing in the door? What part of this work tells you about the destructive force of the hurricane?

Leo F. Twiggs. *East Wind Suite: Door.* Hugo Series. 1989. Batik: Dyes and wax resist on cotton. 61 × 51 cm (24 × 20″). Private Collection.

Where Do Artists Get Ideas?

Artists are *creative individuals who use imagination and skill to communicate in visual form.* They use the materials of art to solve visual problems. Artists look to many sources for inspiration. Some look outward to their natural and cultural environment for ideas. Others look within themselves for creative motivation.

Nature

Sometimes artists look to their natural surroundings and record them. The first group of landscape artists in the United States was called the Hudson River School because most of them lived near that river in New York. They painted the world around them, paying meticulous attention to realistic detail. One Hudson River School artist, George Inness, lived in Newburgh, New York. His early work depicted the vast American landscape in a romantic manner **(Figure 1.9).**

◀ **FIGURE 1.9** This painting celebrates nature and industry, although the two are not necessarily compatible. If you look carefully, you can see the town of Scranton, Pennsylvania, accurately depicted in the distance. Why do you think the artist has included all the tree stumps in this painting? What symbols of industrialization has he used?

George Inness. *The Lackawanna Valley.* c. 1856. Oil on canvas. 86 × 127.6 cm (33⅞ × 50¼″). National Gallery of Art, Washington, D.C. © 1998 Board of Trustees. Gift of Mr. and Mrs. Huttleston Rogers.

American, 1892–1942

Grant Wood. *Self-Portrait.* 1932.
Oil on Masonite panel. 37.5 ×
31.4 cm (14³⁄₄ × 12³⁄₈″). Collection
of The Davenport Museum of Art,
Davenport, Iowa. © Grant Wood/
Licensed by VAGA, New York, NY.

Grant Wood grew up on a farm and drew with whatever materials could be spared. Often he used charcoal from the wood fire to sketch on a leftover piece of brown paper. He was only ten when his father died, and his mother moved the family to Cedar Rapids, Iowa, where Wood went to school. He studied part-time at the State University of Iowa and attended night classes at the Art Institute of Chicago. When he was 32, he went to Paris to study at the Académie Julian. In 1927, he traveled to Munich, Germany, where some of the most accomplished artists of the period were working. While there, he saw German and Flemish artworks that influenced him greatly, especially the work of Jan van Eyck. After that trip, his style changed to reflect the realism of those painters.

▶ **FIGURE 1.10** This painting has been used and parodied countless times. Because of this, it can be easy to overlook the message Wood intended. Symbols tell a story: the Gothic window represents the couple's European heritage, and the pitchfork stands for their determination. Can you identify other symbols in the painting and tell what they might mean?

Grant Wood. *American Gothic.* 1930. Oil on beaverboard. 74.3 × 62.2 cm (29¼ × 24½″). Friends of the American Art Collection. All rights reserved by the Art Institute of Chicago, Chicago, Illinois and VAGA, New York, New York. (1930.934).

People and Real World Events

Another artist, Grant Wood, captured the essence of the Midwestern American spirit during the Great Depression in his work, *American Gothic* **(Figure 1.10)**. The stern, small town citizens posed before their house. The couple's determination was meant to reassure those shaken by the stock market crash during the Great Depression.

Myths and Legends

Some artists borrow ideas from famous works of literature. Romare Bearden interpreted one part of an ancient Greek legend, *The Odyssey,* in his painting *Return of Ulysses* **(Figure 1.11)**. The Greek legend, written by the poet Homer, describes the adventures that befall a hero returning home from war. Bearden used his unique style to portray an important scene from this story.

Spiritual and Religious Beliefs

Visual artists in every culture use their skills to create objects and images to be used to express spiritual beliefs. Many non-Western cultures do not even have a word for "art." Those who create objects do the best work they can because it is important. The mask in **Figure 1.12** was made to be worn during ceremonial winter dances by the Yup'ik people who lived in northwestern Alaska.

Creative Techniques

Many artists founded new art movements and developed new techniques to create art. Jackson Pollock was a leader of the Abstract Expressionist movement. He studied painting in the 1930s with Thomas Hart Benton as his teacher. Benton was an American regionalist who painted realistic paintings and murals that celebrated American life (Figure 13.29, page 376). Pollock's earliest works were in the realistic style of his teacher. After 1947, he developed

▲ FIGURE 1.12 This bird mask was created for a dance ceremony. Notice how the artist has used natural earth pigments to color the wood, plus natural materials like feathers and sinew to decorate it.

Yup'ik. *Bird Mask.* 1988. Wood, feathers. Height: 64.7 cm (25½″). Robert H. Lowie Museum, University of California, Berkeley, California.

action painting, *the technique of dripping and splashing paint onto a canvas stretched on the floor* **(Figure 1.13** on page 14**).** The idea for this style of painting, which influenced many who came after him, came from within himself.

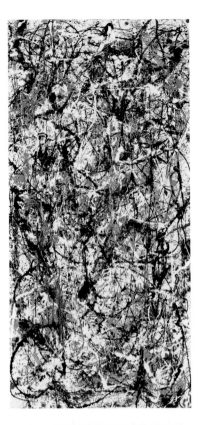

Artists of the Past

Art is not made in a vacuum. Artists of a particular time period often influence each other. Artists also learn from and build on the work of artists who came before them. Pablo Picasso based his 1957 painting, *Las Meninas* (after Velázquez) **(Figure 1.14),** on *Las Meninas (The Maids of Honor)* by Diego Velázquez **(Figure 1.15),** which was painted in 1656. Although Picasso changed the colors and used his own Cubist style, you can recognize some of the figures and objects that are in the realistic Velázquez painting. How many figures and objects can you find that appear in both works?

▲ **FIGURE 1.14** This painting is based on Diego Velázquez's *Las Meninas (The Maids of Honor)* (Figure 1.15). Similar figures and objects are present in both paintings—the artist, the easel with the unfinished painting, the child who appears to be the subject of the artwork in progress, the dog, and the figure in the door. Compare these objects with the ones depicted in Velázquez's work. What has Picasso done to make the work uniquely his own? Do you think he was exhibiting a sense of humor?

Pablo Picasso. *Las Meninas* (after Velázquez). 1957. Oil on canvas. 2 × 2.6 m (6' 6³⁄₄" × 8' 6³⁄₈"). Museo Picasso, Barcelona, Spain. © 2003 Estate of Pablo Picasso/Artists Rights Society (ARS), New York.

▶ **FIGURE 1.15** This painting was interpreted by Picasso, another Spanish artist, three centuries after Velázquez completed it. Explain what is happening in the painting. The princess, in white, has a regal bearing. She is clearly the center of attention. Do you see the king and queen in the picture? Who is the person in the doorway? Can you describe the roles of the other people in the painting?

Diego Velázquez. *Las Meninas (The Maids of Honor).* 1656. Oil on canvas. 3.18 × 2.8 m (10'5¼" × 9'3¾"). Museo del Prado, Madrid, Spain.

Ideas Commissioned by Employers

Many artists are hired by individuals or companies to create works of art. Graphic designers create corporate logos, brochures, and many other print materials. They may also design menus for restaurants. Fine artists, like sculptors and painters, are often commissioned to create artworks for display in public spaces and buildings.

Ideas for Your Own Artwork

In the coming chapters, you will need to come up with ideas of your own for original works of art. Like all other artists, you may at times find yourself at a loss for ideas. You can look to the sources listed in this lesson for inspiration. The work of your peers can also inspire you. See the Student Art Portfolio features in Chapters 4–11 of this book for a showcase of student artworks and visual art journal ideas. You will find that keeping a visual art journal or sketchbook can be an enormous help. In addition to recording images, you may jot down ideas that come to you after participating in other art events such as concerts, movies, and theatre productions. You will also find that a sketchbook can be used to practice skills and techniques you learn in class.

Activity Keeping a Sketchbook

Creating Visual Solutions Using Direct Observation. Artists develop perception and artistic skills by constantly sketching the world around them. Begin keeping a sketchbook of your own. Choose a notebook with unlined paper. Practice using direct observation to draw anything that catches your eye. The more you draw, the better you will "see" objects. Make written notes about your sketches, such as the quality of light or the colors you notice.

 Check Your Understanding

1. Define the word *artist*.
2. Identify four different sources for artistic ideas.
3. Why do artists keep sketchbooks?

The Language of Art

Vocabulary

symbol
elements of art
principles of art
subject
nonobjective art
composition
content
credit line
medium

People throughout the world speak many different languages. Spanish, Swahili, Japanese, Hindi, French, English, and Apache are just a few of the 3,000 different languages that are spoken. Each language has its own system of words and rules of grammar. To learn a new language, you need to learn new words and a new set of rules for putting those words together.

The language of visual art has its own system. All that you see in a work of art is made up of certain common elements. They are arranged according to basic principles. As you learn these basic elements and principles, you will learn the language of art. Being able to use the language of visual art will help you in many ways. It will increase your ability to understand, appreciate, and enjoy art. It will increase your ability to express yourself clearly when discussing art. It will even help you improve your ability to produce artworks.

The Elements of Art

A **symbol** is *something that stands for, or represents, something else.* In a spoken language, words are symbols. The word *chair* stands for a piece of furniture that has a seat, a back, legs, and sometimes arms. In the language of art, we use visual symbols to communicate ideas.

The *basic visual symbols in the language of art* are known as the **elements of art.** Just as there are basic kinds of words—such as nouns and verbs—there are basic kinds of art elements. These are *line, shape* and *form, space, color, value,* and *texture.* The elements are the visual building blocks that the artist puts together to create a work of art. No matter how a work is made, it will contain some or all of these elements.

When you look an image, it is difficult to separate one element from another. For example, when you look at **Figure 1.16,** you see a shiny, round bowl outlined with a thin yellow line filled with bumpy, red raspberries.

Activity — Create a Symbol

Creating Visual Solutions Using Experiences. In visual art, symbols can be concrete representations of abstract ideas, such as a heart standing for love. Create a visual symbol that represents something important to you. Elaborate on your experiences, such as an activity or club you are involved with. Share your symbol with your classmates. Can they identify what it represents?

Computer Option. Design a visual symbol using a computer application. Choose from the tools and menus to represent this idea with line, shape, or color. Hold down the Shift key when making straight lines or restricting shapes to circles or squares. Title, save, print, and display your best example. Include a short explanation about your symbol.

▲ **FIGURE 1.16**
Notice how the artist has used color and texture to direct the viewer's eye through this artwork. Look at the number of different surfaces she depicts. How many different textures can you identify? Although the shiny surfaces catch your attention, notice the matte, or dull, surfaces as well.

Janet Fish. *Raspberries and Goldfish.* 1981. Oil on canvas. 182.9 × 162.6 cm (72 × 64"). The Metropolitan Museum of Art, New York, New York. Purchase. The Cape Branch Foundation and Lila Acheson Wallace Gifts, 1983. (1983.171) © Janet Fish/Licensed by VAGA, New York, NY.

However, rather than seeing the elements of texture (shiny and bumpy), color (red), shape (round), and line (thin and yellow) separately, you see the bowl of raspberries as a whole. You visually "read" the elements together.

Sometimes the differences between the elements are not clear-cut. A line may be so wide that it looks like a shape, or an artist may manipulate light and dark values to indicate different surface textures. Look at the variety of textures Janet Fish has created in *Raspberries and Goldfish* (Figure 1.16).

When you first learned to read, you did not begin with a full-length novel. You learned by reading one word at a time. That is how you will start to read the language of art: one art element at a time.

The Principles of Art

After you have learned to recognize the elements of art, you will learn the ways in which the elements can be organized for different effects. When you learn a language, you learn the rules of grammar by which words are organized into sentences. Without these rules, people would find it difficult to communicate.

Visual images are also organized according to rules. The *rules that govern how artists organize the elements of art* are called the **principles of art.** They also help artists organize the art elements for specific effects. The principles you will learn about are *rhythm, movement, pattern, balance, proportion, variety, emphasis,* and *harmony.* When the elements and principles of art work together to create a sense of wholeness, *unity* is achieved. The elements and principles of art are often referred to as the *formal qualities* in artworks.

The Work of Art

In art, it is important to understand the three basic properties, or features, of an artwork. These are *subject, composition,* and *content.*

The Subject

The **subject** is *the image viewers can easily identify in a work of art.* The subject may be one person or many people. It may be a thing, such as a boat. It may be an event, such as a dance. What are the subjects in Gabriele Münter's painting, *Breakfast of the Birds* **(Figure 1.17)**?

Some artists choose to create nonobjective artwork. **Nonobjective art** is *art that has no recognizable subject matter* (Figure 1.13, page 14). In these types of works, the elements of art themselves become the subject matter.

The Composition

The second property of a work of art is the composition of the work. The **composition** is *the way the principles of art are used to organize the elements of art.* Notice how Münter has used the reds to separate indoors from outdoors, yet she ties the woman to the birds by using related colors. The woman is

▶ **FIGURE 1.17**
Gabriele Münter was one of the founders of modern German Abstract Expressionism. In 1911 she joined with other radical artists to form the group known as Der Blaue Reiter (The Blue Rider). She stayed in Germany through World War II but was forced to work in secret during the Nazi era, when German Expressionism was outlawed. Since this was painted in 1934, it is one of her "secret" paintings.

Gabriele Münter. *Breakfast of the Birds.* 1934. Oil on board. 45.7 × 55.2 cm (18 × 21¾"). The National Museum of Women in the Arts, Washington, D.C. Gift of Wallace and Wilhelmina Holladay.

placed with her back toward the viewer, so that the viewer looks in the same direction as the woman, toward the birds. As you learn more about the elements and principles of art, you will discover how to control the composition of your artwork.

The Content

The third property of a work of art is the content. The **content** is *the message the work communicates*. The message may be an idea or a theme, such as patriotism or family togetherness. It may be an emotion, such as pride, love, or loneliness. Sometimes you know what the intention of an artist might have been when he or she created the work, therefore the meaning of the work may be clear. However, at other times, you may not be certain of what the work might mean, and you have to consider all possibilities. Many artists can paint the same subject, a woman looking out a window, but each painting may have a different message. What do you think is the content of Münter's painting?

The Credit Line

Look at Figure 1.17. The credit line appears beneath the caption. A **credit line** is *a list of important facts about a work of art*. Every artwork in this book has a credit line.

Most credit lines contain at least six facts. They are as follows:

- **Name** of the artist.
- **Title** of the work. This always appears in italics.
- **Year** the work was created. Sometimes, in the case of older works, "c." appears before the year. This is an abbreviation for *circa*, a Latin word meaning "about" or "around."

- **Medium** used by the artist. This is *the material used to make art*. If more than one medium is used, the credit line may read "mixed media."
- **Size** of the work. The first number is always the height, the second number is the width, and if the work is three-dimensional, the third number indicates the depth.
- **Location** of the work. The location names the gallery, museum, or collection in which the work is housed and the city, state, and country. The names of the donors may also be included.

Activity — **Using Credit Line Information**

Applying Your Skills. Who is the artist of the work in Figure 1.9 on page 11? What is the title of the painting by Frida Kahlo (Figure 1.1, page 4)? Which work in this chapter was completed most recently? Which is the largest work in this chapter? Which works in this chapter are not housed in the United States?

 Check Your Understanding

1. List the elements and principles of art.
2. Compare and contrast the use of the elements of art in Figure 1.16 on page 17.
3. How do subject and composition differ?
4. Name the six facts most credit lines include.

Art Criticism
in Action

▲ **FIGURE 1.18**

Andy Warhol. *100 Cans.* 1962. Oil on canvas. 182.9 x 132.1 cm (72 x 52"). Albright-Knox Art Gallery, Buffalo, New York. Gift of Seymour H. Knox, 1963. © 2003 Andy Warhol Foundation for the Visual Arts/Artists Rights Society (ARS), New York/TM Licensed by Campbell's Soup Co. All Rights Reserved.

Critiquing the Artwork

Art criticism is a four-step process for using your perception skills to get deeply involved in a work of art. You will learn more about these four steps in Chapter 2.

▶ **1 DESCRIBE** *What do you see?*

During this step, you will collect information about the subject of this artwork.

● List all the information from the credit line.

● What is the subject of this work?

▶ **2 ANALYZE** *How is this work organized?*

This step deals with the work's composition or formal qualities. In it, you note the art elements used as well as the art principles that organize them.

● How are the shapes arranged in this work?

● What colors are used?

● How large is each can? (Note: Refer to the credit line to help you determine your answer.)

● Are the cans evenly spaced throughout? Explain.

● In what way is the bottom row of cans different from the others?

▶ **3 INTERPRET** *What message does this artwork communicate to you?*

This step focuses on the content of the work. In it, you make assumptions and guesses about the meaning.

● Why do you think the artist made the bottom row different?

● Why do you think the artist spaced the cans as he did?

● Form a conclusion about the meaning of depicting ordinary soup cans.

▶ **4 JUDGE** *What do you think of the work?*

In this step, you will tell whether you think the artwork is successful or not.

● Do you think this is a successful work of art? Why or why not?

Meet the ARTIST

Andy Warhol
1928–87

Andy Warhol. *Self-Portrait.* 1986. Acrylic screenprint on canvas. © 2003 Andy Warhol Foundation for the Visual Arts/Artists Rights Society (ARS), New York.

Andy Warhol was born in McKeesport, Pennsylvania, just outside of Pittsburgh. He began his career as a commercial artist in New York City. He was a painter, movie director and producer, and publisher. Warhol was a leader of the Pop art movement, an art style that celebrated images from contemporary culture, such as comic book characters and everyday objects, helping viewers to see them in a whole new light. Warhol's favorite subjects included celebrities and product packaging, as in **Figure 1.18.** When asked why he chose soup cans as his subject, he explained that he had soup for lunch every day for 20 years.

Virtual Art Tours

Museum Web sites offer interactive art experiences.

Imagine peeling back the layers of paint on a canvas to discover a "hidden" image underneath, or hearing the words of one of your favorite artists. You may not be able to do that on a visit to a museum. However, you may be able to do that on a visit to a museum's Web site! With a click of the mouse you can visit the "virtual" Louvre Museum in Paris, or museums closer to home. Museum officials hope that Web sites will get more people interested in art.

The interactivity of Internet technology allows people to explore art in a new, exciting way. They can get a taste of what the museum experience offers. For example, the Web site of the Metropolitan Museum of Art in New York City lets users move the cursor over the image of a piece of art. For each spot highlighted, users get an explanation of that feature's importance—the symbolism of a specific object in the painting, for example.

Visitors to the Web site of the Getty Museum in Los Angeles go behind the scenes to learn about research projects on some of the museum's artworks. The Frick Museum in New York City offers Web browsers a virtual tour of its exhibits, complete with audio histories of the paintings and the artists.

Of course, Web sites can't duplicate the experience of seeing artworks in person. But for many people, it's the next-best thing to being there!

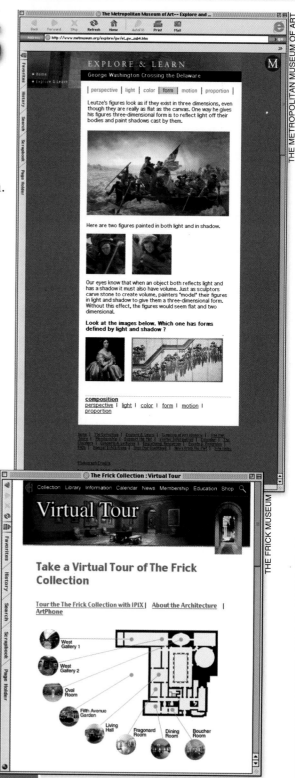

TOP: A page from the New York Metropolitan Museum of Art allows viewers to study a painting in depth. ABOVE: The Internet offers an online tour of the Frick Museum in New York City.

TIME to Connect

Using a search engine, locate an art museum or art gallery Web site that interests you. Analyze and evaluate the site. Then write a one-page critical analysis of the site.

- Analyze the features of the site. Which appeal to you? Which don't? How easy is it to navigate around the site?

- Describe any parts of the site you would change or improve. Evaluate the site's overall design, visual representations, and clarity of language.

- Evaluate the credibility of information represented on the site.

Building Vocabulary

On a separate sheet of paper, write the term that best matches each definition given below.

1. The visual expression of an idea or experience created with skill.
2. To become deeply aware through the senses of the special nature of a visual object.
3. Self-taught artists who have had little or no formal schooling in artistic methods.
4. Something that stands for, or represents, something else.
5. The basic visual symbols in the language of art.
6. The rules that govern how artists organize the elements of art.
7. Art that has no recognizable subject matter.
8. The way the principles of art are used to organize the elements of art.
9. A list of important facts about a work of art.
10. A material used to make art.

Reviewing Art Facts

Answer the following questions using complete sentences.

11. Describe the five purposes of art.
12. Name and describe four sources of inspiration for artists.
13. Explain the relationship between the elements of art and the principles of art.
14. Select a work of art in this chapter and identify the subject.
15. Read the credit-line information of an artwork from any chapter and list the figure number, the title, the year the work was created, and the medium.

Thinking Critically About Art

16. **Compare and Contrast.** Survey the avocational opportunities in art mentioned on page 9. Then research art classes and programs in your community. Compare and contrast these avocational opportunities to decide which one interests you the most. Consider such factors as time required, materials, training, and personal interest.
17. **Compare and Contrast.** Study Figures 1.14 on page 14 and 1.15 on page 15 to list their similarities and differences. Are light and dark values of colors used in the same places in each work?
18. **Historical/Cultural Heritage.** Review the Meet the Artist feature on page 12. Compare Grant Wood's American Gothic in Figure 1.10 to his self-portrait on the same page. Can you identify the theme of determination in each artwork? What else do these works have in common? Where does Grant Wood reveal part of his cultural heritage in his self-portrait?

Take a Web Museum Tour of the National Gallery of Art in Washington, D.C.

Click on the link at **art.glencoe.com.** Explore their online tour of still lifes to appreciate why this art genre is still popular.

Linking to the **Performing Arts**

Use the Performing Arts Handbook to discover the art of masks and the many ways this art form has been created and worn throughout the world's cultures. Faustwork Mask Theater presents the message of masks on page 413.

▲ **FIGURE 2.1** The goal of some artists is to imitate life. Their works are lifelike, down to the smallest detail. The goal of other artists is to create a mood or feeling. What do you think was the goal of the artist who created this work? Explain your reaction.

Red Grooms. *Ruckus Rodeo* (detail). 1975–76. Wire, celastic, acrylic, canvas, and burlap. 442 × 1539.2 × 746.8 cm (174 × 606 × 294″). Collection of the Modern Art Museum of Fort Worth, Fort Worth, Texas. Museum purchase and commission with funds from the National Endowment for the Arts and The Benjamin J. Tillar Memorial Trust, 1976.1.P.S. © 2003 Red Grooms/Artists Rights Society (ARS), New York.

CHAPTER 2

Art Criticism and Aesthetic Judgment

Have you ever seen—or skipped—a movie based on a friend's recommendation? We all make judgments about music, television, and other forms of culture. We share with others what we like and what we don't like. Making such *aesthetic judgments* about art is called *art criticism*.

In this chapter, you will:

- Learn the purpose of art criticism.
- Select and analyze artworks using the steps of art criticism to form precise conclusions.
- Explain the three aesthetic theories of art.
- Compare and contrast contemporary and historical styles, identifying themes and trends.

Focus on Art History In the second half of the twentieth century, a new form of three-dimensional art emerged on the scene. It was the *installation*. Installations are artworks made not to be walked *around* but walked *through* as one walks through a room. The installation in **Figure 2.1** is one of a series of creations by American Pop artist Red Grooms (b. 1937). Pop art is a style of art that explores everyday subjects and objects from contemporary culture. In Grooms's "Ruckus" series, the artist created life-sized environments such as Manhattan or a Texas rodeo and inhabited these fun, offbeat environments with cartoonlike characters.

Identify. Compare and contrast the contemporary styles in Figure 2.1 and Figure 2.6 on page 32 to identify the general themes of the works. Note that a theme could be revealed in the subject matter or as a concept communicated by the work.

Art Criticism: Learning from a Work of Art

Vocabulary

criteria
aesthetics
art criticism
aesthetic experience
description
analysis
interpretation
judgment

There are professional critics who appear on television or write reviews about new movies, plays, television shows, videos, books, art exhibits, and music. These critics describe their responses to various forms of art, and give you their assessment of the merits of the works. You may not always agree with their opinions because your **criteria,** or *standards of judgment,* may be very different from those of the professional critic. In this chapter you will learn about **aesthetics** (es-**thet**-iks), *the philosophy or study of the nature and value of art.* This will allow you to form your own intelligent opinions about works of art. You will also learn about art criticism. **Art criticism** is *an organized approach for studying a work of art.*

Why Study Art Criticism?

What do you think of when you hear the word *criticism?* Do you think it means saying something negative? This is not true. A criticism can be a positive statement. For example, when you shop for clothes, you try on many things. You act as a critic using personal criteria to determine which pieces of clothing look good on you and which pieces do not suit you. You have developed your own criteria for choosing clothing through personal experience.

When you look at Alma Thomas's painting, *Iris, Tulips, Jonquils, and Crocuses* **(Figure 2.2),** you may experience confusion. You may not have had enough experience to develop a set of criteria to judge a work that has no recognizable subject. If you are like most people who are new to art, you may not know what to say.

◀ **FIGURE 2.2** At first glance, this painting appears to consist of simple shapes and bright colors. The title of the work, however, should help you understand what the dabs of color represent. Notice how large the painting is. How big does that make each dab of color? Can you imagine the garden these flowers would grow in?

Alma Thomas. *Iris, Tulips, Jonquils, and Crocuses.* 1969. Acrylic on canvas. 152.4 × 127 cm (60 × 50″). The National Museum of Women in the Arts, Washington, D.C. Gift of Wallace and Wilhelmina Holladay.

Art criticism is not difficult. In fact, it can be a lot of fun. At the very least, it can make the study of art less mysterious and more logical. Art criticism is a sequential approach for looking at and talking about art.

Your own life experiences may also help you understand the meaning of each work of art. No one has done or seen exactly the same things you have, so no one will see exactly what you see in a work of art. No one can think exactly the way you think. You may see ideas in a work of art that were never dreamed of by the artist. This does not mean that you are wrong; it simply means that the work of art is so powerful that it has a special meaning for everybody.

Learning art criticism will help you interpret works of art. It will give you the confidence to discuss works of art without worrying about what other people might think. It will help you to organize your thoughts. You will develop the courage to speak your mind and make sound aesthetic judgments.

As you learn the language of art, you will be able to "dig deeper" into the layers of meaning of each art object. The deeper you dig, the more important your feelings for that work of art will become. This will make your **aesthetic experience,** or *your personal interaction with a work of art,* more meaningful and memorable. The work will then become a permanent part of your memory.

The Steps of Art Criticism

When you become involved in the process of art criticism, you learn *from* the work of art. Critiquing an artwork is like playing detective. You must assume the artist has a secret message hidden within the work. Your job is to find the message and solve the mystery.

In this chapter you will learn a special four-step approach that will help you find the hidden meanings in art. The four steps, which must be taken in order, are *description, analysis, interpretation,* and *judgment.* By following these steps you will be able to answer the following questions:

- What do I see? (*description*)
- How is the work organized? (*analysis*)
- What message does this artwork communicate? (*interpretation*)
- Is this a successful work of art? (*judgment*)

As you go through the steps of *description* and *analysis*, you will collect facts and clues. When you get to *interpretation,* you will make guesses about what message you think the artwork is communicating. Finally, during *judgment,* you will make your own decisions about the artistic merit of the work.

Step One: Description (What do I see?)

In the first step of art criticism, **description,** you carefully *make a list of all the things you see in the work.* These include the following:

- The size of the work, the medium used, and the process used.
- The subject, object, and details.
- The elements of art used in the work.

During the description step, notice the size of the work and the medium used. You will find these facts in the credit line. This information will help you visualize the real size and look of the work. Notice that Figure 2.4 on page 29 and Figure 2.6 on page 32 are about the same size as reproduced in this book. Read both credit lines and notice the difference in the actual size of each work.

Look at the painting by José Clemente Orozco called *Barricade* **(Figure 2.3).** Notice that the work is 55 inches tall. How does that compare to your own height? If this artwork were standing on the floor, would the figures be larger or smaller than you? What materials were used to create this work?

During the description step, you must be objective. In describing Orozco's painting, you can say that you see five people. You could not say they are all men. That would be a guess. You can describe the person crouched on the ground as wearing a blue shirt and holding a large knife. You can describe the tense muscles that are bulging on the other four figures, but at this point in the criticism process, you should not try to guess why they are tense.

Look again at Figure 2.3. Line and color are two of the art elements that play an important part in this work. Can you identify the other art elements used?

Look at Figure 2.2 on page 26. This is a nonobjective work. In nonobjective works, the art elements become the subject matter.

Step Two: Analysis (How is the work organized?)

During this step, you are still collecting facts about the elements and principles of art that are used in the artwork. In **analysis** you *discover how the principles of art are used to organize the art elements of line, color, value, shape, form, space, and texture.* You will learn how the artist has used these formal qualities to create the content of the art, which is known as the theme or the message. Look at *The Piper* by Hughie Lee-Smith **(Figure 2.4).** Notice the horizontal line that passes behind the boy's shoulders. Where are the darkest colors? Where are the lightest colors? Is the texture of the bricks on the wall the same as the texture of the plaster? As you learn more about the elements and principles, you will be able to collect more clues that you can use to interpret each work.

◀ **FIGURE 2.3** Orozco was one of the Mexican muralists who combined the solid forms of ancient Mexican art with the powerful colors of European Expressionism. This work depicts the peasants fighting for freedom during the Mexican Revolution in 1910. What could you do to find out more about the event this painting depicts?

José Clemente Orozco. *Barricade.* 1931. Oil on canvas. 139.7 × 114.3 cm (55 × 45″). The Museum of Modern Art, New York, New York. Given anonymously. © Estate of José Clemente Orozco/SOMAAP, Mexico/Licensed by VAGA, New York, NY.

▶ **FIGURE 2.4** Your interpretation of this work will depend on the clues you have collected during the first two steps of art criticism—description and analysis—plus your personal life experiences. People have different experiences which will produce a variety of interpretations, all of which could be acceptable.

Hughie Lee-Smith. *The Piper.* 1953. Oil on canvas. 55.9 × 89.5 cm. (22 × 35¼"). Detroit Institute of Arts, Detroit, Michigan. Gift of Mr. and Mrs. Stanley J. Winkelman. © Hughie Lee-Smith/Licensed by VAGA, New York, NY.

Step Three: Interpretation (What message does this artwork communicate to you?)

During this step, you will answer the question, "What message does this artwork communicate to me?" In **interpretation** you will *explain or tell the meaning or mood of the work.* It is here that you can make guesses about the artwork, as long as they appear to be supported by what you see in the work. Use your intelligence, imagination, and courage. Don't be afraid to make an interpretation that is different from someone else's. After all, you are different from other people. Your interpretation will be influenced by what you have experienced and seen in your life.

Your interpretation can be based on your feelings, but your feelings must be backed up by the visual facts and clues you collected during the first two steps.

When you look at Figure 2.4, you see a crumbling wall with the shadow of a neatly shaped modern building falling on it. Then you notice the boy standing between the modern building and the crumbling wall. He is playing a musical instrument. What is the meaning of the boy and his instrument? What message does this work communicate to you?

Step Four: Judgment (Is this a successful work of art?)

In this step you will judge whether or not the work is successful. In **judgment** you *determine the degree of artistic merit.* This is the time to make your own decisions. There are two levels of judgment to be made. The first is personal. Do you like the work? No one can ever tell you what to like or dislike. You must make up your own mind. To make a fair judgment, you must be honest with yourself. Only you know why you feel the way you do. Otherwise, you may close yourself off from experiencing different kinds of art. The second level of judgment you must make is also subjective, but it is somewhat different. At this point, you use aesthetics to help you decide whether the work is successful. A work can be very successful aesthetically, but you might not want to live with it.

From the time she was a child, Georgia O'Keeffe knew she was going to be an artist. She studied with several teachers. At age 29, she decided to focus totally on nature and she burned her earlier works in order to start fresh, emphasizing shapes and forms. The flower paintings that made her famous were begun at this time. She painted her flowers big so that they would take viewers by surprise. She continued following her own vision throughout her long life, never being pulled into any of the many movements that have dominated the American art scene during the twentieth century.

O'Keeffe loved to see "connections" in the shapes of ordinary things. After painting a shell and shingle many times, she painted a mountain. It was only later that she realized that she had given the mountain the same shape as the shell and the shingle. She saw beautiful forms everywhere, even in the most unusual places, such as the vast desert spaces and parched bones found near her home in New Mexico.

American, 1887–1986

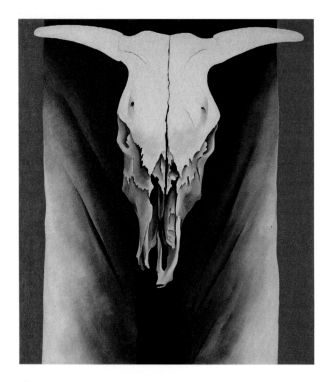

▲ **FIGURE 2.5** Georgia O'Keeffe loved the West. She shocked the public with paintings of objects from her environment that people were not used to seeing hanging on a wall. She painted *Cow's Skull: Red, White, and Blue* because she wanted to create something uniquely American. Do you think she succeeded?

Georgia O'Keeffe. *Cow's Skull: Red, White, and Blue.* 1931. Oil on canvas. 101.3 × 91.1 cm (39⁷/₈ × 35⁷/₈"). The Metropolitan Museum of Art, New York, New York. The Alfred Stieglitz Collection, 1952. (52.203). © 2003 The Georgia O'Keeffe Foundation/Artists Rights Society (ARS), New York.

To make a judgment, you must take your time. **Figure 2.5** is a painting by Georgia O'Keeffe. To judge this painting, first think about how you would describe the subject of the painting. Then consider how the artist has arranged the art elements according to the art principles in order to create the composition. Notice how she has used shading to make the skull look solid and the drapery look like a hanging banner. However, she has painted the red borders and the black shape behind the skull flat. Then, think about the feeling the painting gives you. By taking time to look at and describe, analyze, and interpret what you think the meaning of the painting might be, you will be able to make an intelligent judgment. Ask yourself, is this a work of artistic merit? Is it successful?

 *Check Your Understanding*

1. What is aesthetics?
2. Name and describe the four steps of art criticism in order.

Aesthetics: Thinking About a Work of Art

Vocabulary

literal qualities
formal qualities
expressive qualities
Imitationalism
Formalism
Emotionalism

Aesthetics is *a branch of philosophy concerned with the nature and value of art.* Physical beauty was once the only criterion for judging the quality of art. Today, artwork is judged by a different set of criteria and instead of being called "beautiful," a good work of art is called "successful." Some successful works of art may not look pretty, but they may be well-organized, and/or elicit emotional responses from viewers.

Aesthetic Theories and the Quality of Art

The aesthetic qualities that are discussed most often by *aestheticians* (specialists in aesthetics) are the literal qualities, the formal qualities, and the expressive qualities. These are directly related to the properties of art discussed in Chapter 1 on pages 18 and 19: subject, composition, and content. The **literal qualities** are *the realistic qualities that appear in the subject of the work.* For instance, if the artist depicts a realistic figure of a man on a horse, the literal qualities of the work are the images of a man on a horse. The **formal qualities,** or *the organization of the elements of art by the principles of art,* are found when you look at the composition of the work. Does it look balanced? Is there a rhythmic quality? Is there variety? Has the artist made a unified work of art? These are the types of questions one must ask to determine how well-organized a work is. The **expressive qualities,** or *those qualities that convey ideas and moods,* are those you notice when you study the content of a work. Is there something in the work that makes you feel a certain emotion or conveys an idea to you?

The three aesthetic theories of art criticism are most commonly referred to as Imitationalism, Formalism, and Emotionalism.

Imitationalism and Literal Qualities

Some critics think that the most important thing about a work of art is the realistic presentation of subject matter. It is their opinion that a work is successful if it looks like and reminds the viewer of what he or she sees in the real world. People with this point of view feel that an artwork should imitate life, that it should look lifelike, before it can be considered successful. This aesthetic theory, called **Imitationalism,** *focuses on realistic representation.*

Formalism and Formal Qualities

Other critics think that composition is the most important factor in a work of art. This aesthetic theory, called **Formalism,** *places emphasis on the formal qualities,* the arrangement of the elements of art using the principles of art.

Emotionalism and Expressive Qualities

This theory is concerned with the content of the work of art. Some critics claim that no object can be considered art if it fails to arouse an emotional response in the viewer. The expressive qualities are the most important to them. Their theory, called **Emotionalism,** *requires that a work of art must arouse a response of feelings, moods, or emotions in the viewer.*

Look at *Papiamento* by Julio Larraz **(Figure 2.6).** You may use the theory of Imitationalism to judge this work as successful because the artist has painted everything very accurately. You can recognize the texture of the freshly pressed, white cotton dress, the light flickering on the large, tropical leaves, the texture of the trunk of the palm tree, the palm fronds, the yellow sand of the beach, and the beautiful blue of the Caribbean waters. Someone else may choose the theory of Formalism to judge the work as successful because the artist has arranged the objects so that the foreground is in shadow and the background glows brightly with sunshine. A third person may choose the theory of Emotionalism because of the mysterious mood created by hiding the woman in the shadow of the tree, or because the painting may arouse in the viewer emotional associations with memories of a vacation on a Caribbean island.

You can judge art using just one aesthetic theory or more than one, depending on the type of art and your own purposes. If you limit yourself to using only one theory, however, you may miss some exciting discoveries in a work. Perhaps the best method is to use all three. Then you will be able to discover as much as possible about a particular piece of art.

▲ **FIGURE 2.6** Notice how the artist has blended the woman into the painting. You don't see her until you look carefully. What may have been the artist's reasons for doing this? The title of this work, *Papiamento,* is the name of a language spoken in the Antilles. What else could you find out about the work and its artist that might help you to understand it better?

Julio Larraz. *Papiamento.* 1987. Oil on canvas. 143.5 × 209.5 cm (56½ × 82½"). Courtesy of Nohra Haime Gallery, New York, New York.

Activity — Aesthetic Theories

Applying Your Skills. Select one large work of art in this book. Show the picture to at least three people outside of class. Ask them whether they like the work. Then ask them to tell you why they like or dislike the work. Classify their answers according to the three aesthetic theories of art: Imitationalism, Formalism, or Emotionalism.

Judging Functional Objects

You can use art criticism to make aesthetic judgments about functional objects such as cars, shoes, or fine china. The objects in **Figure 2.7** are an example. In criticizing functional objects, you follow the first two steps of art criticism—description and analysis—as described earlier. However, during the third step, interpretation, you must consider the purpose of the object as its meaning. In the last step, judgment, you must consider if the object works when it is used. That is, does it look like it will function properly? A chair may look beautiful, but if it is not comfortable to sit in, then it does not function properly. It is unsuccessful.

When you study a ceremonial object from a culture you are not familiar with, refer to the title and your observations during the first two steps of art criticism. During interpretation, you must imagine the function of the object and then judge it using one of the three aesthetic theories. Finally, research the object using the art history operations in the next lesson and refine your interpretation and judgment.

Judging Your Own Artwork

Art criticism will help you use critical thinking to analyze your own works of art. The four steps of art criticism will help you be as honest and unbiased as possible. When you apply all four of the steps of art criticism to your work, you should find out why your work either needs improvement or is a success.

☑ Check Your Understanding

1. What are the three aesthetic qualities most often discussed by art critics?
2. What is Imitationalism?
3. Compare and contrast Formalism and Emotionalism.
4. How does judging functional objects differ from judging fine art?

▲ **FIGURE 2.7** These chairs are appealing to the eye, but are they successful as functional objects? To find out, you will have to apply the steps of art criticism. Do they appear to be the right height for sitting? Would they provide enough back support? Is the padding thick enough for comfort?

John Dunnigan. *Slipper Chairs.* 1990. Purpleheart wood with silk upholstery. Left: 67.9 × 64.8 × 58.4 cm (26³/₄ × 25¹/₂ × 23″). Right: 110.5 × 66.7 × 61 cm (43¹/₂ × 26¹/₄ × 24″). © John Dunnigan. Renwick Gallery, National Museum of American Art, Smithsonian Institution, Washington, D.C.

Art History: Learning About a Work of Art

You can develop your appreciation for a work of art by gathering information about the artist and the time period in which the work was created. This is the historical and cultural context of the work. The **art history operations** are a *four-step approach for organizing the way you gather information about a work of art.* The names for the four steps of art history operations are the same as the four steps for art criticism: *description, analysis, interpretation,* and *judgment.* For art history operations, however, there are different definitions for the terms and different questions to be answered.

- **Description.** When, where, and by whom was the work done?
- **Analysis.** What is the style of the work and can the work be associated with an art movement?
- **Interpretation.** How did time and place affect the artist's style, in terms of subject matter, composition, and content?
- **Judgment.** Is the work considered to be significant in the history of art?

▲ **FIGURE 2.8** The objects in this work are easy to recognize—trees, mountains, and night sky—but the colors are not what you might expect. Why do you think the artist used these colors? What does he appear to be saying?

Ernst Ludwig Kirchner. *Winter Landscape in Moonlight.* 1919. Oil on canvas. 120.7 × 120.7 cm (47¹/₂ × 47¹/₂"). Detroit Institute of Arts, Detroit, Michigan. Gift of Curt Valentin in memory of the occasion of Dr. William R. Valentiner's 60th birthday.

Step One: Description

During this step you will look for information *about* the work of art. You want to know who did it, when, and where it was done. If you were looking at an original work of art, you would look for the artist's signature and the date on the work itself. In this book, because the works have been reduced to fit on the page, you will probably not be able to see the artist's signature or the date on the work. You will find that information in the credit line, however. If you look at the credit line for **Figure 2.8,** you will discover that this painting was created by the same artist who painted **Figure 2.9,** Ernst Ludwig Kirchner. Figure 2.9 was painted in 1907. Compare that date to Figure 2.8.

Which was painted earlier? To learn more about Kirchner, such as where and when he lived, you would need to do some further research.

Step Two: Analysis

During analysis, you examine the work and look for information about the artist's style. Style is like handwriting. No two people have exactly the same handwriting and no two artists have exactly the same style. **Individual style** is *the artist's personal way of using the elements and principles of art to express feelings and ideas.* To analyze the style of one artist, you will need to see several works by the same artist. When you look at Figure 2.8 and Figure 2.9, you can easily see the unique aspects of the artist's style: his unusual use of color and his exaggeration of shapes for expressive effect.

Step Three: Interpretation

In order to find the answers for this step you will have to do some research. You will discover that the artist was active in a group of young, adventurous artists in Germany who called themselves Die Brücke (The Bridge) and that their work was part of a larger movement known as German Expressionism. In order to interpret his work, you would need to find out what other artists influenced him, details about his life, and information about his surroundings.

Step Four: Judgment

Once again you must research to find out the importance of this work in the history of art. You must discover what different art historians have to say about Kirchner and use their assessments to help you shape your own. You can also

▲ **FIGURE 2.9** Spend a few moments describing this work. What is its most unusual feature? What is the subject matter? Then compare it to Figure 2.8, also by the same artist. What are the similarities and differences between the artworks? Can you draw any conclusions about Kirchner's individual style?

Ernst Ludwig Kirchner. *Seated Woman.* 1907. Oil on canvas. 80.6 × 91.1 cm (31³⁄₄ × 35⁷⁄₈"). The Minneapolis Institute of Arts, Minneapolis, Minnesota. The John R. Van Derlip Fund.

discover if Kirchner influenced other artists, which would help you judge his importance.

As you study the information in this book and learn more about the language of art, you will begin to acquire information from works of art. You will learn more about the artists who created the works. In Chapters 12 and 13, you will find a brief overview of art history. Refer to these chapters to learn more about art movements and time periods as you encounter them throughout the book.

 Check Your Understanding

1. What are the art history operations?
2. Describe each of the steps of art history operations.
3. What is individual style?

Art Criticism
in Action

▲ FIGURE 2.10

Yoruba people, Nigeria, Ekiti, Osi-Ilorin area. *Headdress for Epa Masquerade.* First half of the twentieth century. Carved wood and pigment. 127 × 50.8 × 45.7 cm (50 × 20 × 18″). Collection of the Birmingham Museum of Art, Birmingham, Alabama.

Critiquing the Artwork

Figure 2.10 is a mask-headdress. When it is worn, the performer's body is covered with fresh palm fronds.

▶ **1 DESCRIBE** *What do you see?*

Read the credit line for information about this work.

● List the information from the credit line.

● Do you recognize any objects or figures? Describe them.

● Based on its size and the materials used, do you think the work is heavy or light? Explain.

▶ **2 ANALYZE** *How is this work organized?*

This step deals with the formal qualities. It is a clue-collecting step. You will note the art elements used as well as the art principles that organize them.

● What shape is repeated on the horse's platform?

● Where do you find the same repeated shapes?

● What proportion of this sculpture is the helmet-mask?

▶ **3 INTERPRET** *What message does this artwork communicate to you?*

The third step is concerned with content. This is where you make guesses about the meaning of the work. Remember that you do not need to know what the artist meant. Instead, decide what this headdress communicates to you.

● From the measurements given in the credit line, do you think the helmet section is a hat or a mask?

● Why is this work decorated with painted patterns?

● On what type of occasion would you imagine the headdress is worn? By whom is it worn? Explain.

● What do you think it would feel like to have your body covered with palm fronds and the headdress on your head? How would you want to move?

● What do you think this headdress communicates? Write a brief story or poem about this mask-headdress.

▶ **4 JUDGE** *What do you think of the work?*

Now, you are ready to make an aesthetic judgment.

● Do you think this is a successful ceremonial work of art? Use one or more of the three aesthetic theories explained in this chapter to defend your judgment.

Meet the ARTIST
The Yoruba People

Court drummers of the Timi of Ede. Yoruba. Ede, southwestern Nigeria. Werner Forman Archive/Art Resource, NY.

The Yoruba people, who number over 12 million, live in southwest Nigeria and southern Benin. They are the most urban of all African groups. Their founding city, Ile-Ife, was the center of a successful city-state in the eleventh century. The masquerade, for which headdresses like this one are designed, is a multimedia event. It involves costumes, music, dance, drama, and poetry. The audience participates in it. This complex headdress is, thus, meant not only to be seen in a static setting but also to be worn in a performance. Imagine the play of light and shadow as a performer covered with palm fronds wears this headdress and moves in time with the music and the storytelling.

Friendly Art Rivals

Pablo Picasso and Henri Matisse did not always judge each other's work kindly.

Pablo Picasso and Henri Matisse, two leaders of the twentieth-century art world, were rivals. Each thought he was the better painter. Each was jealous of the other's fame. The two, however, respected and influenced each other's work. Picasso showed his respect for Matisse in a painting he created a year after Matisse's death in 1954. Like Matisse's *Red Interior Still Life on a Blue Table,* Picasso's *Studio of "La Californie"* shows the artist's workplace. But unlike Matisse's happy, colorful space, Picasso's studio is bleak and dark, with no bright colors.

These two paintings were part of an exhibit at the Tate Modern Museum in London that brought Picasso and Matisse "together" by hanging their canvases side by side. Visitors got a chance to compare similarities in the artists' styles. Both were interested in African art. Both were fascinated with collage, and with the female form. While Matisse was known for using bold colors and simple, yet energetic lines, he sometimes painted in the style of Cubism, a complex style invented by Picasso. Sometimes Picasso used bright colors and painted unusually dressed women. These characteristics are typically associated with Matisse.

Hanging the artists' works next to each other was an idea that would have made sense to Picasso. He said at the end of his life, "You've got to be able to picture side by side everything Matisse and I were doing at the time." Picasso added, "No one has looked at Matisse's paintings more carefully than I; and no one has looked at mine more carefully than him."

TOP: Henri Matisse's *Red Interior Still Life on a Blue Table.* ABOVE: Pablo Picasso's *Studio of "La Californie."*

TIME to Connect

Matisse and Picasso sometimes inspired each other in their work—even if it was in the form of competition.
• Write a personal narrative describing who inspires you to achieve your goals and to do your best. Be sure to include a brief character sketch of that person, supporting your story with specific examples of how the person inspired you.

Building Vocabulary

On a separate sheet of paper, write the term that best matches each definition given below.

1. Standards of judgment.
2. An organized approach for studying a work of art.
3. The art criticism step in which you make a list of all the things you see in a work of art.
4. The art criticism step in which you discover how the principles of art are used to organize the art elements of line, color, shape, form, space, and texture.
5. The art criticism step in which you explain or tell the meaning or mood of the work.
6. The art criticism step in which you determine the degree of artistic merit of the work.
7. The aesthetic theory that focuses on realistic representation.
8. The aesthetic theory that places emphasis on the formal qualities.
9. The aesthetic theory that requires that a work of art must arouse a response of feelings, moods, or emotions in the viewer.

Reviewing Art Facts

Answer the following questions using complete sentences.

10. What will learning the steps of art criticism help you develop?
11. Define the four steps of art criticism.
12. Describe the three aesthetic theories.
13. If the organization of an artwork is most important to an art critic, which aesthetic theory would he or she hold?
14. When criticizing functional objects, what must you consider during interpretation besides beauty?
15. In what ways are the steps of art criticism different from the steps of art history operations? In what ways are they similar?

Thinking Critically About Art

16. **Apply.** Select something from your home that is used solely for aesthetic purposes. Critique it using the four steps of art criticism. When you are finished, ask yourself if the object seems different than it did before. Has your opinion of the object changed?
17. **Analyze.** Find a movie critic's review of a current film in a newspaper or magazine. Read it carefully. Try to find statements that fit each of the four steps of art criticism.
18. **Historical/Cultural Heritage.** Learn about Georgia O'Keeffe's exploration of nature and natural objects in the Meet the Artist feature on page 30. Nature was a major theme in O'Keeffe's work. Compare and contrast her depiction of nature in the artwork on pages 316–317 with Ernst Kirchner's depiction of a similar scene in Figure 2.8 on page 34.

Museum curators need to be skilled in art criticism to select, analyze, and write about artworks for exhibitions. Visit **art.glencoe.com** to compare and contrast career opportunities in art.

Linking to the Performing Arts

Dance pioneer Martha Graham uses the aesthetic qualities in the development of her modern dances. See how Graham uses literal qualities, design qualities, and expressive qualities through the use of body movement on page 414.

▲ **FIGURE 3.1** This artist has developed new ways to use the process of glassblowing to create large sculptures and installations. He calls the objects in this window installation "flowers." Compare and contrast these glass flowers to the flowers painted by van Gogh in Figure 7.8 on page 178.

Dale Chihuly. *Malina Window* (detail). 1993. Handblown glass and steel. 4.87 × 4.87 m (16 × 16′). Detroit, Michigan.

CHAPTER 3

The Media and Processes of Art

Artists communicate with viewers through a variety of materials, tools, and techniques. Some artists "speak" with paint, others with marble. The artist responsible for the artwork in **Figure 3.1** communicates with handblown glass. What do the see-through forms, colors, and patterns of this artwork communicate to you?

In this chapter, you will:

- Compare and contrast the media used in drawing, painting, printmaking, and sculpting.
- Describe the media of crafts and architecture.
- Demonstrate the effective use of art media and tools in original works.
- Identify technological media.

Focus on **Art History** Traditionally, glass has been a medium of the craftsperson used to make small, decorative works of art. American artist Dale Chihuly (b. 1941) has revolutionized the process of glass-blowing to create monumental forms. His works appear in some 200 museums worldwide. His creations have been grouped into series. These include handblown glass baskets, sea forms, flowers, chandeliers, and huge installations, which include the 16-foot-square window in **Figure 3.1.** The window graces the lobby of a corporate headquarters. Its purpose, according to the artist, was to make "a difficult view beautiful." What do you think he meant by this statement? In other words, what do you think is the view outside this window?

Compare and Contrast. Examine Figure 6.2 on page 136. Like Figure 3.1, these windows were created by an artist renowned for his inventive and beautiful glass designs. Compare the work of Chihuly and Chagall to identify the general trend or style each work shows.

Vocabulary

medium/media
shading
printmaking
print
reproduction
edition

Two-Dimensional Media

Jackson Pollock dripped paint onto canvas in Figure 1.13 on page 14. Leo Twiggs used dyes and wax resist on cotton in Figure 1.7 on page 10. Each of these artists created a two-dimensional work of art using different materials. *Any material used to create art* is called a **medium.** The plural form of medium is **media.** A medium can be something as ordinary as a graphite pencil or as exotic as gold leaf gilding. In two-dimensional works, such as drawing and painting, artists use media such as crayons, paints, pastels, and pencils.

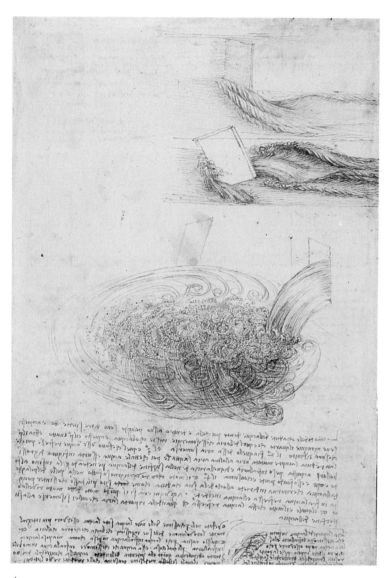

▲ **FIGURE 3.2** Da Vinci's observations of moving water were confirmed as accurate in this century when fast cameras could photographically freeze the action of the water. Da Vinci filled his notebooks with observational sketches and notes. His writing was backward and could only be read when held up to a mirror.

Leonardo da Vinci. Page from his sketchbook showing movement of water. Royal Library, Windsor Castle, London, England. The Royal Collection 1993, Her Majesty Queen Elizabeth II.

Drawing

In baseball, a pitcher throws warm-up pitches before facing a batter. Musicians tune their instruments or warm up their voices before a performance. Artists must also prepare before creating art. By drawing, artists become better at perceiving, or carefully noticing, the lines, shapes, and forms of an object.

Many artists use sketchbooks to record their surroundings and to produce studies of objects. Artists also record ideas for later use. The Renaissance artist Leonardo da Vinci filled more than 100 sketchbooks with his drawings and ideas. His sketchbooks included everything from perceptions of people, to his notations on the movement of water **(Figure 3.2),** to his plans for flying machines.

Drawing is usually the first step in producing artworks. Rough sketches, or studies, are often done before creating a work in another medium such as paint or clay. Fashion designers draw their ideas for new styles long before any fabric is cut. Stage designers, graphic designers, and architects must show presentation drawings for a client's approval. **Figure 3.3** is a costume design for a comic ballet, *The Devil's Holiday*. The designer modeled the costumes and stage designs based on the eighteenth-century paintings of Venice by the artist Canaletto.

Although drawings are often used as guides for other artworks, sometimes an artist's drawing *is* the finished artwork. One example of a drawing as a work of art is Canaletto's *Ascension Day Festival at Venice* **(Figure 3.4).**

Drawing Media

Drawing is the process of moving an instrument over a smooth surface to leave a mark, called a line. In drawing, line is the most important element of art. The characteristics of a line are determined, in part, by the medium used to draw it. The most popular drawing media are graphite pencils, colored pencils, crayons, colored markers, pens, pastels, and chalk. Pen and ink, pen and brush, and brushes with watercolors are also used to make drawings.

▲ **FIGURE 3.3** How does this sketch let you know that this character is in a comedy? What makes him look humorous?

Eugene Berman. *Vendeur de Chapeaux.* 1939. Gouache on paper. 31.8 × 24.8 cm (12¹/₂ × 9³/₄"). Wadsworth Atheneum, Hartford, Connecticut. Gift of Mr. and Mrs. James T. Soby. 1939.697.

◄ **FIGURE 3.4** Look closely at this meticulous drawing. Can you tell what city is depicted in this work? What helped you decide?

Canaletto. *Ascension Day Festival at Venice.* 1766. Pen and brown ink with gray wash, heightened with white, over graphite on laid paper. 38.6 × 55.2 cm (15³/₁₆ × 21³/₄"). National Gallery of Art, Washington D.C. © 1998 Board of Trustees. Samuel H. Kress Collection.

Each drawing medium has its own qualities. Chalk and crayon, for example, produce rough lines. Pens, by contrast, make smooth lines. **Figure 3.5** shows lines made with different drawing media.

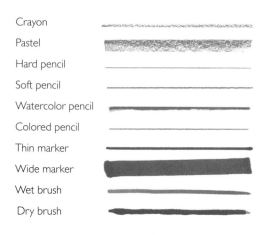

Crayon
Pastel
Hard pencil
Soft pencil
Watercolor pencil
Colored pencil
Thin marker
Wide marker
Wet brush
Dry brush

▲ **FIGURE 3.5** Drawing media.

Shading Techniques

Shading is *the use of light and dark values to create the illusion of form.* There are four main shading techniques:

- **Hatching.** This technique consists of drawing thin lines that run in the same direction. Find the forms in **Figure 3.6** that use hatching.

- **Crosshatching.** Shading created using crisscrossing lines is called crosshatching. Look at the forms in **Figure 3.6** that demonstrate this technique.

- **Blending.** Artists perform blending by changing the color value little by little. Find the forms in **Figure 3.6** that are shaded using blending.

- **Stippling.** Shading that creates dark values by means of a dot pattern is referred to as stippling. Locate the forms in **Figure 3.6** that show stippling.

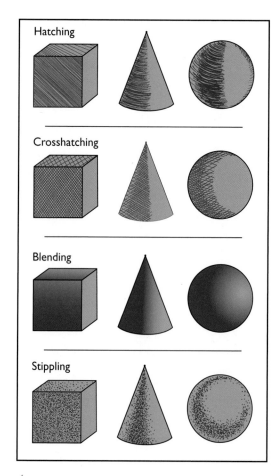

Hatching

Crosshatching

Blending

Stippling

▲ **FIGURE 3.6** Shading techniques.

Look at the drawing in **Figure 3.7.** Isabel Bishop used three different drawing media to create a drawing that has the look of three dimensions. The artist accomplished this through shading.

Which shading technique was used in Figure 3.4 on page 43?

Painting

Painting is the process of applying color to a surface using tools such as a brush, a painting knife, a roller, or even your fingers. The surface is the material to which the paint is applied. Canvas, paper, and wood are frequently used as surface materials.

◀ **FIGURE 3.7** Look at this drawing and identify the shading techniques Bishop used.

Isabel Bishop. *Head #5.* No date. Graphite, crayon, and chalk on paper. 29.8 × 22.4 cm (11¾ × 8¹³/₁₆"). Wadsworth Atheneum, Hartford, Connecticut. Gift of Henry Schnakenberg. 1953.217.

All paints have three basic ingredients:

- **Pigments.** Pigments are finely ground colored powders. Pigments come from natural or synthetic materials. Natural pigments include indigo, a vegetable, and the cochineal beetle, an insect. Natural pigments can also be made from minerals or clay. Synthetic pigments are artificially made from chemicals.

- **Binder.** A binder is a material that holds together the grains of pigment. The binder allows the pigment to stick to the painting surface. Egg yolks mixed with water have long been used as a strong binder for professional artist's tempera paints. Other binders are linseed oil and wax.

- **Solvent.** A solvent is a liquid that controls the thickness or the thinness of the paint. Different painting effects require different thicknesses of paint. Using thin watercolor paint gives a light, washed-out appearance; using thick watercolor paint produces a more intense appearance. Solvents are also used to clean paintbrushes and other applicators.

Winslow Homer is considered one of the artists who has captured the true feelings of the United States in his works. Homer developed an appreciation and love for the outdoors while growing up with his two brothers in Cambridge, Massachusetts. By the age of ten, his interest in art began and his talent for drawing became obvious. When he was 19, Homer was accepted as an apprentice at a large printing firm in Boston, even though he had little formal art training.

When his apprenticeship was over, Homer worked as a draftsman, specializing in woodblock engraving. Soon he began illustrating magazines. By the 1860s he was contributing regularly to *Harper's Weekly* magazine as an illustrator of events occurring in the Civil War. After the Civil War ended, Homer traveled to Europe. There, he was influenced by the works of French artists Édouard Manet and Gustave Courbet.

By the 1880s, Homer had begun painting the subject that was to become his trademark—the sea. He loved nature and spent hours outdoors. He felt at home on the sea although he knew its dangers as well. Because he was able to capture the elemental forces of nature, Homer is considered a Realist. His unique talent enabled him, as few others have done before him, to express the reality of the United States.

▶ **FIGURES 3.8 AND 3.9** One of these paintings was a sketch made at the scene, and the other was done in the studio based on the first work.

▶ **FIGURE 3.8**

Winslow Homer. *Sketch for 'Hound and Hunter.'* 1892. Watercolor. 35.4 × 50.8 cm (13¹⁵⁄₁₆ × 20"). National Gallery of Art, Washington, D.C. ©1998 Board of Trustees. Gift of Ruth K. Henschel in memory of her husband, Charles R. Henschel.

◀ **FIGURE 3.9**

Winslow Homer. *Hound and Hunter.* 1892. Oil on canvas. 71.8 × 122.6 cm (28¹⁄₄ × 48¹⁄₄"). National Gallery of Art, Washington, D.C. © 1998 Board of Trustees. Gift of Stephen C. Clark.

The look of a finished painting depends on the combination of media, tools, and the surface the artist chooses. In **Figures 3.8** and **3.9,** you can see how Winslow Homer has created two images that are almost exactly alike. However, he has used different media. Figure 3.8 is made with thin, wet, flowing watercolor on white paper. The white in this painting is the white of the paper showing through. Figure 3.9 is painted with thick, creamy oil paint on canvas. The white in this painting is opaque white paint.

Painting Media

As with drawing media, there are many different kinds of painting media, each with its own unique qualities. The artist chooses the paint based on personal preference and the purpose of the work.

Oil-Based Paint. First used in the 1400s, oil paint remains a popular medium today. True to its name, oil paint uses linseed oil as its binder. Its solvent is turpentine.

One advantage of oil paint is that it dries slowly. This allows the artist to blend colors right on the canvas. The work in Figure 3.9 is an oil painting. Notice how smoothly the colors blend.

Water-Soluble Paint. The most popular of water-based painting media, watercolor takes its name from its solvent, water. The binder is gum arabic. Compare the watercolor in Figure 3.8 with the oil painting in Figure 3.9. What differences do you see?

Tempera is another water-based paint. It dries more quickly than oil paint, and it has a more opaque finish than watercolor.

Acrylic paint, which first appeared in the 1950s, uses an acrylic polymer as a binder. The solvent used for acrylic paint is also water. However, once professional acrylic paint dries, it cannot be dissolved. School acrylics have been developed, however, that can be dissolved with soapy water after they dry.

Activity Experimenting with Watercolor

Demonstrating Effective Use of Art Media and Tools in Painting. Using watercolor paint, choose one bright color and paint several shapes on a dry sheet of watercolor paper. Then thoroughly brush water on both sides of a sheet of watercolor paper and repeat the process. If available, try using different types of natural and synthetic watercolor brushes. Share and compare your results with those of classmates.

Computer Option. Drawing with color on the computer is like drawing with light. Light as the computer's pigment can vary in opacity from opaque, like tempera paint, to transparent, like watercolors. Find the menu in the application you are using that controls opacity. Explore the settings. Remember, these qualities change as you paint on different surfaces. If available, investigate rough, smooth, or textured papers.

Printmaking

Printmaking is a *process in which an artist repeatedly transfers an original image from one prepared surface to another.* Paper is often the surface to which the printed image is transferred. *The impression created on a surface by the printing plate* is called a **print.** A print is not the same thing as a reproduction, although sometimes people confuse the two. A print is an original work of art. A **reproduction,** such as the artwork shown in this book, is *a copy of a work of art.*

The Basic Steps of Printmaking

While prints may be made using many different media, processes, and surfaces, all require three basic steps.

- **Creating the printing plate.** A printing plate is the surface on which the desired image is created. In producing a printing plate, the artist makes a mirror image of the final print. Letters and numbers must be made backward on the plate.

- **Inking the plate.** The artist applies ink to the plate. This is done with a *brayer,* a roller with a handle. For a multicolor print, one plate must be made for each color. The ink creates the image on the print.

- **Transferring the image.** The paper or other material is pressed against the inked plate, and the ink is transferred to the new surface. Sometimes this is done by hand. Other times a printing press is used.

Usually, more than one print is made from a single plate. Together, *all the prints made from the same plate, or set of plates,* form an **edition.** Each print in an edition is signed and numbered by the artist. The printmaker signs the work in the bottom margin and writes the title on each print of an edition as well as the number of each print. The number 10/200 indicates the tenth of 200 prints.

Printmaking Techniques

There are four main techniques artists use to make prints: relief, intaglio, lithography, and screen printing.

- **Relief printing.** In this method, the artist cuts away the sections of a surface not meant to hold ink. As a result, the image to be printed is raised from the background. In **Figure 3.10,** Elizabeth Catlett has controlled the light and dark areas of her linoleum-cut relief print by the amount she has cut away. Notice that the white lines are wider in the very light areas.

◀ **FIGURE 3.10** Catlett has devoted her artistic career to a socially conscious art that represents the struggles of African Americans.

Elizabeth Catlett. *Sharecropper.* 1970. Linoleum cut on paper. 45.2 × 43 cm (17¹³⁄₁₆ × 16¹⁵⁄₁₆″). The National Museum of American Art, Smithsonian Institution, Washington, D.C. © Elizabeth Catlett/Licensed by VAGA, New York, NY.

- **Intaglio** (in-**tal**-yo or in-**tal**-ee-o). This name comes from the Italian word meaning "to cut into." Intaglio is a process in which ink is forced into lines that have been cut or etched on a hard surface such as metal or wood. Then the plate's surface is wiped clean and the prints are made. You can actually feel the lines of raised ink on an intaglio print.

- **Lithography.** In lithography the image to be printed is drawn on limestone, zinc, or aluminum with a special greasy crayon or pencil. Ink is attracted to this material. When the drawing is completed, the areas that should remain blank are etched with a special solution that repels ink. Then, when the surface is inked, the greasy area alone holds the ink. Because the process is complicated, new materials are being developed to make lithography easier. There are kits for schools that use paper instead of limestone or zinc for the printing plate.

- **Screen printing.** This is the newest method for making prints. It uses a stencil and screen as the printing plate. The stencil is placed on a fabric screen stretched across a frame. The screen is placed flat on the printing surface. Ink is pressed through the fabric screen where it is not covered by the stencil. If more than one color is used, a separate screen is made for each color. Another term for screen printing is *serigraphy.*

Activity | Making a Printing Plate

Demonstrating Effective Use of Art Media and Tools in Printmaking. You can make your own relief printing plate. Begin by cutting a 4-inch square from a sheet of cardboard. Cut a variety of smaller geometric shapes from the same sheet. Arrange these on the surface of the square. Form an interesting design.

Glue the shapes in place. Let them dry overnight. Apply printing ink to the surface with a brayer. Lay a sheet of paper over your inked plate. Apply pressure evenly. Carefully peel back the print.

Computer Option. Explore the Shape and Line tools in your application. Change line thickness, color menus, gradients, and opacities. Arrange several shapes to make an interesting design. Print onto color transfer paper that is made for your printer. Remember to flip the image before printing if necessary because shapes and letters may be reversed. Follow the instructions on the printing paper package to transfer your design onto paper, cloth, or another surface. (An iron sets some transfer papers while others require more elaborate equipment.)

Check Your Understanding

1. Name four of the most popular media used in drawing.
2. What are the three ingredients found in every type of paint?
3. What are the three basic steps of printmaking?
4. Compare and contrast the media used in drawing, painting, and printmaking.

Three-Dimensional Media

Have you ever taken a lump of clay and formed it into a bowl or an animal? If so, you were working with a three-dimensional medium. These media make solid forms that have height, width, and depth.

Sculpture

Sculpture is *a three-dimensional work of art.* Sculpture is art that is made to occupy space. This is one way in which sculpture is different from other kinds of art. Although objects in a drawing or painting can look quite real, the work is flat, or two-dimensional. Artists who create sculpture are called sculptors.

The Media of Sculpture

Like other artists, sculptors use a wide variety of media in their work. Sculpting media include clay, glass, plastics, wood, stone, and metal. No matter what medium is used, a sculpture will be one of two types: sculpture in the round or relief sculpture.

▶ **FIGURE 3.11** How do the unusual colors and materials affect the expressive quality of this sculpture?

Luis Jimenez. *Vaquero.* Modeled 1980, cast 1990. Fiberglass and epoxy. Height: 5 m (16′6″). The National Museum of American Art, Smithsonian Institution, Washington, D.C. © Luis Jimenez/Artists Rights Society (ARS), New York.

- **Sculpture in the round.** This type of sculpture is surrounded *on all sides* by space. Another name for sculpture in the round is *freestanding* sculpture. You can walk around sculpture in the round or turn it over in your hands to see all sides. Sculptures in the round can be realistic representations of people or objects **(Figure 3.11).** Not all freestanding sculptures have recognizable subjects, however. (See Figure 5.6 on page 101).

- **Relief sculpture.** This type of sculpture projects into space from a flat background. Relief sculptures are designed to be viewed only from one side. **Figure 3.12** shows an example of a relief sculpture attached to a smooth, gently–rounded surface. You cannot see the back of the figure. The figure protrudes out into space from the smooth surface of the vase.

Sculpting Techniques

In addition to a wide array of media, sculptors use a variety of processes. The processes include modeling, carving, casting, and assembly.

▲ **FIGURE 3.12** Al Qoyawayma adds an architectural quality to his pottery by using relief elements that are forced from inside the pottery wall. He then carves details into the raised relief work.

Al Qoyawayma (Hopi). *Blanketed Figure Vase.* c. 1980. Clay pottery. Height: 27.9 cm (11″).

■ **Modeling.** In this process, a soft, pliable material is built up and shaped. Media such as clay, wax, and plaster are used in modeling. Because the sculptor gradually adds more material to build a form, modeling is referred to as an *additive* process.

■ **Carving.** In carving, the sculptor cuts, chips, or drills from a solid mass of material to create a sculpture. Material is removed until the sculpture is completed. Carving is therefore called a *subtractive* process. Wood and stone are the most common carving media.

■ **Casting.** In casting, molten metal or another substance is poured into a mold and allowed to harden. The artist duplicates a form originally molded with clay, wax, or plaster using a more permanent material. Just as in printmaking, an edition of sculptures can be made from the same

mold. Once the edition is complete, the mold is destroyed. This prevents the mold from being used again and safeguards the monetary value of the sculptures that were originally cast.

■ **Assembling.** In this process, also called *constructing,* a variety of different materials are gathered and joined together to make a sculpture. One assembly process involves welding metal, but media can be glued, sewn, or otherwise fitted together. Assembling is sometimes used along with other sculpting processes. A combination of casting and assembling was used to create *Zaga* **(Figure 3.13).**

▲ **FIGURE 3.13** Graves collected natural objects and cast them in bronze at a metal foundry. She then selected certain cast objects from her collection of thousands of objects and assembled them to make her sculpture.

Nancy Graves. *Zaga.* 1983. Cast bronze with polychrome chemical patination. 182.9 × 124.5 × 81.3 cm (72 × 49 × 32″). The Nelson-Atkins Museum of Art, Kansas City, Missouri. Gift of the Friends of Art (F84–27). © Nancy Graves Foundation/Licensed by VAGA, New York, NY.

Crafts

Before machines were invented, people made everything by hand. Today, artists are still creating one-of-a-kind items. Some objects are created for practical use, and others are made purely for decorative purposes. *Art made to be experienced visually* is called **fine art.** *Art made to be functional as well as visually pleasing* is called **applied art.** Today the distinction between fine art and applied art is fading.

Artists are currently creating both functional and decorative craft objects. Weavings are made from natural wool, linen, silk, cotton, and manufactured fibers. Quilts are stitched from fine fabrics to be hung on the wall like paintings. Baskets are woven from natural materials such as reeds and wood slats **(Figure 3.14),** as well as manufactured fibers. Pottery is made with clay from the earth. Handmade glass objects are formed by forcing air through a tube to shape globs of melted glass. Jewelry is crafted using expensive materials such as precious stones and gold, but it can also be made using paper. As wonderful as technology has become, we still appreciate having an object that is one-of-a-kind and made by hand.

The Media of Crafts

The most commonly used craft media are clay, glass, wood, fiber, and metal. Clay and glass can be used to make plates and cups, vases, and jars. Wood can be used to make furniture or containers. Fiber is used to weave cloth and to make baskets. Metal is used to make utensils and jewelry.

Each craft contains an almost unlimited number of choices. An artist using clay can choose stoneware, earthenware, or porcelain. A weaver can select natural

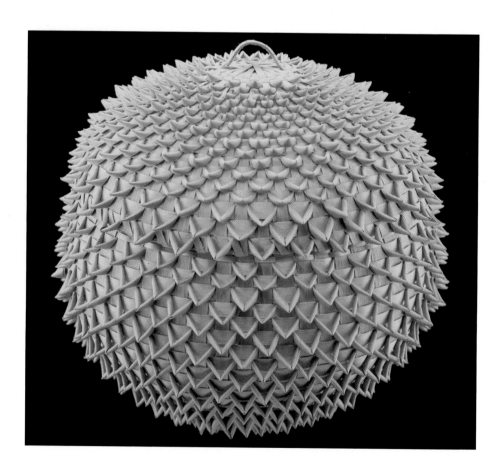

▶ **FIGURE 3.14** Imagine the skill it took to make this basket and lid perfectly round and to make each twist of the warp just the right size to create points in proportion to the shape of the basket. Notice that the points are smaller at the top and bottom and larger near the center.

Edith Bondie. *Porkypine Basket.* c. 1975. Wood. 20 × 21.6 × 21.6 cm (7⅞ × 8½ × 8½"). The National Museum of American Art, Smithsonian Institution, Washington, D.C.

▶ **FIGURE 3.15** This settee reminds us of an Asante stool from Africa because it incorporates animal totem forms into its structure.

Judy Kensley McKie. *Monkey Settee.* 1995. Walnut and bronze. 90.2 × 182.2 × 61 cm (35½ × 71¾ × 24"). Renwick Gallery, The National Museum of American Art, Smithsonian Institution, Washington, D.C.

fibers or synthetic fibers. A woodworker can choose among oak, ash, mahogany, rosewood, ebony, cedar, and pine.What media were used to create **Figure 3.15?**

The Processes of Crafts

The techniques and processes a craft artist uses depends on the media selected. Clay, for example, can be modeled, carved, and assembled. It can also be *thrown* on a potter's wheel. Clay is finished by firing it in a *kiln*, a furnace that reaches high temperatures.

Glass can be mold-made or blown. Blown glass requires a process in which the artist, using special tools, blows air into molten glass in order to shape it.

Wood is worked using techniques such as carving and assembling, turning, and bending. In turning, a piece of wood is rotated on a machine called a lathe. The machine may have a fixed tool that shapes the piece, or the artist may use a special tool. Bending is another shaping process. A piece of wood is soaked in water or another liquid to make it pliable. Then it is slowly manipulated into place.

Fiber can be woven into cloth or baskets. It can be embroidered, sewn, or quilted. Metal can be shaped in molds or it can be cut with special shears. Pliable metals can be hammered or filed into shape. Pieces can be assembled by linking them together or by soldering them together. Soldering is a process using a handheld tool called a soldering iron that melts small areas of the metal. When the metal cools, the pieces are joined. Assembling larger pieces of metal, a process called welding, requires a larger, more powerful tool with an open flame.

Architecture

Of all the arts, architecture has the greatest impact on our daily lives. The quality of the architecture we use for shelter, for gatherings, and for worship affects the quality of our lives. Architecture is the planning and creation of buildings. Because a well-designed building is a shelter as well as a work of art, architecture is considered both an applied art and a fine art. An artist who works in the field of architecture is an architect. To be certified, an architect studies engineering because a structure must be designed to hold its own weight and withstand the physical forces placed on it. An architect also studies the visual arts in order to create buildings that are well-proportioned and pleasing to the eye. Architects

design for individuals as well as for the public. The needs of each group must be considered and met before a building can be called a success.

The Media of Architecture

From the earliest times people have been creating shelters from materials found in their natural environment. Huts constructed from sticks and bark were covered with mud. Nomadic people constructed movable shelters from wood poles and covered them with animal skins. In the north, ice was cut and formed to make shelters. In the tropics, leaves and grasses were woven together. Gradually, people developed skills to make better use of available materials for permanent structures that were used for gathering as well as shelter. People learned to make bricks by firing clay to

---

Activity — Redesigning a Familiar Building

Demonstrating Effective Use of Art Media and Tools in Design. Architects are often hired to renovate an old structure. Look for a building in your community that you would like to see improved. Study it by making sketches from different points of view. Identify and list in your sketchbook the media that were used in the construction of the building you have selected. Think about the media you have just studied. List some that would harmonize with the surrounding buildings and the environment. Using pencil, draw one face of the building. Include the existing doors and windows. Then redesign the look of that side using the media that you believe will improve the look of the building. Use watercolors to indicate the colors of the new construction media.

Computer Option. Use a computer application to redesign the façade of a building in your community. Choose the Grids and Rulers option to guide your drawing so you can maintain scale and proportion. Consider how you can create harmony by repeating the materials, colors, or architectural features of other buildings in your community. Begin by drawing the front view. Hold down the Shift key to draw straight lines or restrict shapes. Use the copy and paste functions to make duplicates of features such as doors and windows. Save and title the line drawing. Then use your choice of brushes, textures, and gradients to simulate natural materials. Use the Save As option to retitle and save. Print and display your work.

make it hard. They stacked the bricks to build walls. Stonecutters develop methods for cutting stone so smoothly that one could be stacked on top of the next without anything to hold them in place **(Figure 3.16).** Others learned how to balance one long stone on top of two posts and developed the post-and-lintel method of construction. Today this is called post-and-beam construction because architects use wood or steel beams instead of stone lintels.

Later, architects learned to form an arch with stone. The arch carried the weight of walls and roofs without buckling. Arches led to vaults, or arched roofs that connect walls. Vaulted halls enabled architects to create more open space. A dome is a round roof, as if an arch had been extended into a full circle. Using more advanced construction techniques architects developed a pointed stone arch and supported it with buttresses. This allowed large openings to be made in the walls that were filled with stained-glass windows.

Wood was always a popular material, because it was plentiful. Balloon framing allowed builders to use heavy beams of wood to support thin walls. The truss supported a sloped roof. This technique is still being used today.

Technology has given us steel and reinforced concrete. Steel frames enabled us to cover the outside of skyscrapers with glass. The development of new materials has not eliminated the use of the older materials. New ways of

◀ **FIGURE 3.16** The builders of Tiwanaku in present-day Bolivia were excellent stone masons. They cut the stones to fit together so perfectly that the buildings have survived to this day without any mortar to hold the stones in place.

David Borsky. Wall from the Sunken Courtyard of Tiwanaku, Bolivia. A.D. 700. Photograph. Courtesy of the artist.

using them are always being developed. When Louis Sullivan built the Wainwright Building **(Figure 3.17),** he first created a large frame, or cage, made with steel beams. To cover the frame he used brick, which blended in with the surrounding buildings.

An architect is concerned with the environment into which the structure will be placed as well as the purpose of the building. The success of a building is the combination of the right media with good design. The Guggenheim Museum in Bilbao, Spain, by American architect Frank Gehry (Figure 14.1, page 388) is made of limestone, titanium, steel, and glass. The straight limestone blocks contrast with curved and bent titantium panels giving the building the look of a huge abstract sculpture.

Check Your Understanding

1 What are the two main types of sculpture?
2. What are the four basic sculpting methods?
3. Define *crafts*. Name three categories of functional crafts.
4. Define *architecture*.

▶ **Figure 3.17** This skyscraper echoes its internal steel frame in its exterior design. Sullivan emphasized the height of the skyscraper by stressing the vertical lines that move the viewer's eyes upward, and underplaying the horizontal elements in the window area.

Louis Sullivan. *Wainwright Building.* St. Louis, Missouri. 1890–91.

Technological Media

Vocabulary

photography
digital system
multimedia programs

Artists try to communicate ideas through their art, and as they do so, they constantly seek out new media. In recent times, technological advances have allowed artists to create new and exciting forms of art. In this lesson, you will learn about photography, film, video, and computer art.

Photography

Photography is *the technique of capturing optical images on light-sensitive surfaces.* Photographs are all around us. Newspapers, magazines, and books are full of them. Almost everyone has a collection of snapshots that they've taken. It is hard to imagine that photography started out as an expensive, difficult process only 150 years ago.

Although anyone can point a camera and click the shutter, photography as art requires more than simply recording images. As photographic media and processes have improved, some photographers have begun exploring photography's potential as art. They have gone beyond simply taking pictures of interesting images. Works by Dorothea Lange **(Figure 3.18)** and other photographers are carefully composed just as a painter composes an artwork. This artistic composition makes photography a fine art like painting or sculpting.

In recent years, some artists have combined painting and photography to create a new kind of visual expression. Look closely at **Figure 3.19** on page 58. Notice how the artist has modified a black-and-white photograph of an automobile in front of a house. The finished work combines familiar images from the real world altered according to the photographer's artistic vision.

▲ **FIGURE 3.18** Dorothea Lange did more than take a snapshot of this family. By moving her camera to get just the right angle and waiting for the right moment, her photograph reveals a lot about her subjects. What does the expression on the mother's face tell you? What emotions do the children convey with their body language?

Dorothea Lange. *Migrant Mother.* 20.3 × 25.4 cm (8 × 10″). Courtesy of the Library of Congress, Washington, D.C.

▶ **FIGURE 3.19** This work is based on a black-and-white photo taken by the artist. After printing it, she covered the areas she wished to stay black-and-white with rubber cement to protect them. Then she dipped the photo into an acid bath that changed the unprotected portions into tints and shades of brown. The final step was the addition of color, using paints designed for use on photographs.

Jessica Hines. *Dream Series.* Hand-colored black-and-white photograph. 40.6 x 50.8 cm (16 × 20"). Private Collection.

The Media of Photography

The idea of capturing an image on film is very old. Attempts to do so date back to the Renaissance, but the first permanent photograph was not made until the nineteenth century. L. J. M. Daguerre invented a process of creating silvery, mirrorlike images on a copper plate. This was called a *daguerreotype.* Daguerreotype was a time-consuming and very expensive process. In the 1850s, the wet plate method was invented. It used glass coated with chemicals to record the image, which was then transferred to paper or cardboard. As with contemporary photographs, the wet plate photos used *negatives*, the reverse image of the object photographed. Today, newer and better methods of making film have been invented. The process is simpler and less expensive. Photographers have many media and processes available to affect the look of a finished photograph.

Film

A movie, or motion picture, like any work of art is created for others to enjoy. However, when you watch a movie, you may not be aware of all the work that went into making it. Filmmaking is a collaborative process involving many different artistic and technical professionals.

The Media of Film

Filmmaking only became possible about 100 years ago, after photography began to catch on with amateur hobbyists and professional artists. This encouraged the development of different types of film and the invention of the film camera. Unlike still cameras, motion picture, or film, cameras have a mechanism that moves the film through the camera. The film is stopped very briefly to be exposed. Each frame of film is a still image. The illusion of image motion is created by a rapid succession of these still images or photographs. Early films suffered from jumpy action, flickering light, and other flaws. As cameras, film, film printers, and projectors improved, so did the visual quality of movies. Cinematographers—artists who use movie cameras—now have the ability to choose from many different film media and production processes to create visually exciting artistic films.

Video

Videotape records and stores images and sounds as magnetic impulses. Patterns of light beams and wavelengths of sound are translated into electric waves, which are then imprinted magnetically on the videotape. Video technology, however, is rapidly evolving. Today, videotape is being replaced by digital videotape and other digital systems. A **digital system** is *a system that processes words and images directly as numbers, or digits.* This is improving not only the flexibility of video but also the sound and image quality.

The Media of Video

Video is a remarkable development because, unlike film, it does not require special processing or printing. With a video camera, a person can record an event and immediately view the results. Video artists record the sights, sounds, and scenes of nature; or they create totally new environments with moving and still images and sound. This technology allows an artist to create a visual story or communicate a message, just like an artist who paints on canvas. Also, video can be combined with computer software and systems to create artwork never before possible. Amazing artistic results can be achieved when video images and sounds are edited and manipulated using computers.

Computers

Thanks to advances in digital technology, today's computers are becoming faster, smaller, and more versatile. Tiny computers, called *microprocessors,* can now operate computer programs that once required a computer the size of your classroom! These powerful computers are used by visual artists to create digital art.

Using Computers to Create Art

Computer programs, or software, are designed to instruct the computer to perform various functions. There are numerous programs available for artists. (For more information on software and hardware used in the art classroom, refer to the Digital Media Handbook, pages 445–454.) With paint or draw programs, artists can draw, paint, manipulate, and design images. The artwork in **Figure 3.20** was created with a software program. Other digital technologies, such as digital cameras and scanners, can be used with the computer to provide even more exciting ways to stimulate an artist's imagination.

When you use a computer to create art, the art images can be stored as files in the computer's memory or on different kinds of storage devices. Once saved, they may be opened in a new file and reworked. The advantage is that, while the original art is saved, you can try as many variations as you wish, saving each as a new file. This prevents you from losing the original work.

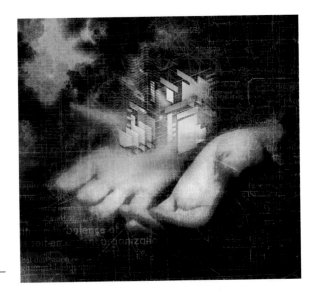

▶ **FIGURE 3.20** This artist has used digital technologies to combine several layers of images into a unified artwork. What ideas do you think he is expressing in this composition?

Jeff Brice. *Untitled.* Digital image.

Many computer applications exist to make the tasks of the artist more efficient. Some of these programs involve desktop publishing, word processing, image editing or manipulation, morphing or transforming images, and 3-D drawing and animation. To create digital drawings and paintings, there are two main types of programs: paint programs and draw programs.

- **Paint programs.** In paint programs, images are stored as bitmaps or a series of tiny dots called *pixels.* Images are made by filling in the dots using a variety of brush tools that imitate other media and drawing tools. An artist also has the ability to edit the image pixel by pixel.
- **Draw programs.** In draw programs, each line or curve drawn is stored as a separate object. An advantage of draw programs over paint programs are the crisp, sharp edges, which are excellent for fonts and straight line images. Because images are recognized as objects rather than individual pixels, they can be "resized"—made larger or smaller—without distortion.

Recently, the differences between paint and draw programs have begun to blur. Many paint programs today do jobs that were once performed only by draw programs and vice versa.

Computer Art Tools

In computer art, the physical tools that the artist actually handles are called *hardware.* Hardware includes equipment such as the monitor, keyboard, printer, and mouse. Along with these pieces of hardware, other external tools include the following:

- **Digital camera.** A digital camera works like a regular camera except that the images are recorded digitally. The camera usually has a viewer that allows you to see each picture you have taken. Most cameras store pictures on removable memory cards, which can be downloaded onto a computer. Pictures can then be printed out or they can be manipulated with special photo-editing software. The digital images can be altered and enhanced in unlimited ways, and each version can be saved as a separate file.

Activity — Traditional and Digital Media

Demonstrating Effective Use of Art Media and Tools in Drawing. Artists use computers as sketchbooks, design tools, and as painting and collage media because they can store and retrieve artwork quickly. Images can be easily combined and altered, which allows the artist to explore many ideas without wasting time or materials. First, try this with traditional media and tools such as drawing paper, pencil, brush, and watercolor. Draw a large rectangle or circle on the paper. Create a design based on a mood or feeling using the pencil and brush. Change length, thickness, and texture of the lines to create variety and make a pleasing composition. Choose a color scheme and add color.

Computer Option. Now, repeat the same activity using a computer paint program. Select a Shape tool, and draw a large open rectangle or circle on the page. Explore the Pencil and Brush tools. Consider a mood or feeling. Arrange a variety of lines, changing length, thickness, shape, and texture to match this mood. Use the Eraser and Zoom tool, if available, to eliminate unneeded marks. When you are satisfied, title and save your project. Now, choose a simple color scheme. Apply color with the Fill or Brush tool. Select the Save As command to retitle. Add a number behind the original title to indicate a new version.

Tool	Description	Type of Program
Zoom tool	Magnifies part of painting or drawing.	Paint or Draw
Brush tool	Paints lines of different thicknesses.	Paint
Pencil tool	Draws lines and curves.	Draw
Fill tool	Adds color to closed objects or shapes.	Paint or Draw
Selection tool	Selects objects.	Draw
Selection tool	Selects specific areas on screen.	Paint
Color picker	Selects colors.	Paint or Draw

◀ **FIGURE 3.21**
Common on-screen tools. Can you guess the purpose of the tools by their icons?

- **Stylus and graphics tablet.** A stylus and graphics tablet is the electronic equivalent of the pencil and paper. The stylus responds to pressure from the hand to make thick and thin lines—much like a real pencil, pen, or brush—and has an eraser on the end. Recent models are remote and programmable.
- **Scanner.** A scanner is a device that "reads" a printed image. It then translates the image into a language the computer can use to make an image on the screen or print with a printing device.

On-Screen Tools. These tools are located on-screen on a toolbar or pull-down menu. They mimic handheld tools used by conventional artists. On-screen tools include pencils, pens, assorted brushes, and erasers, but they vary from program to program. The table in **Figure 3.21** shows some common on-screen tools and the type of program in which each is found.

Multimedia Art

Combining technologies on the computer is made easier by the development of **multimedia programs.** These are *computer software programs that help users design, organize, and combine text, graphics, video, and sound in one presentation.* You can make reports, presentations, and art portfolios come alive. Multimedia art combines different media to create a new type of art. For example, an artist might scan a photograph into the computer to enhance it. The artist might also add sounds that help evoke a feeling. He or she could add text or quotations to add meaning. The artist might make the art appear to move (animate) or take different forms (morph) as the viewer watches. Multimedia art expands the boundaries of art by including more sensory experiences.

Check Your Understanding

1. What is photography?
2. How are motion picture cameras different from still cameras?
3. What advantage does video have over film?
4. Compare and contrast paint and draw programs.
5. What is the advantage of a multimedia program?

Art Criticism
in Action

▲ **Figure 3.22**

Lucas Samaras. *Mirrored Room.* 1966. Mirrors attached to a plywood frame with screws covered by glass balls. 243.8 × 243.8 × 304.8 cm (96 × 96 × 120″). Albright-Knox Art Gallery, Buffalo, New York. Gift of Seymour H. Knox, Jr., 1966.

Critiquing the Artwork

▶ **1** **DESCRIBE** *What do you see?*

What do you see when you look at this object? This is a clue-collecting step. If you are not sure of something, do not guess.

- List all the information in the credit line.

- Study the image carefully. Describe everything you see. *Hint:* There are four objects in the room that are not listed in the credit line. Two are solid, and two are reflections.

▶ **2** **ANALYZE** *How is this work organized?*

This step deals with composition or the formal qualities. In it, you will gather information about how the work uses the elements and principles of art. Even though you have not studied them yet, there are some obvious questions you can answer.

- What shapes make up the walls, floor, and ceiling of this room? How often are these shapes repeated?

- What other shapes can you find in the work?

▶ **3** **INTERPRET** *What message does this artwork communicate to you?*

In this step, you tell what feeling or mood the work creates. You make guesses about the meaning of the work.

- How do you think it would feel to sit or stand within this room? Write a brief paragraph or a poem that expresses how you would feel sitting on the mirrored chair surrounded by infinite reflections.

▶ **4** **JUDGE** *What do you think of the work?*

Now, you are ready to make an aesthetic judgment of the work.

- Do you think this is a successful work of art? Why or why not? Use one or more of the aesthetic theories from Chapter 2 to defend your decision.

Lucas Samaras. *Self-Portrait.* 1993. Reproduced courtesy of the artist and Pace Wildenstein, New York. © Lucas Samaras.

Lucas Samaras was born in Kastoria, Greece. In 1948, he moved to the United States with his family. Samaras attended Rutgers University. His works use unusual "art" materials such as glass, aluminum foil, and aluminum paint. Samaras's mirrored room series, which includes the installation in **Figure 3.22,** was created in the 1960s. These works, which are meant to be walked through, are remarkable for the precise positioning of the mirrors. They reflect the objects and viewer into infinity in all directions. All of Samaras's artworks are concerned with the distortion of visual space as seen in the *Mirrored Room.* He also creates distorted and decorated chairs and manipulated Polaroid photographs.

The Art of Books

Making your own books and book covers is a growing trend.

The art of bookmaking is becoming an increasingly popular craft and hobby. In this age of digital technology, people are looking back to the traditional arts of bookbinding and papermaking. Some of these new book artists create their works from scratch, including writing, designing, and binding. One book is made with fabric, paper, and beads and folds out like origami. Another one-of-a-kind work is an eyeglass case that holds a tale about Benjamin Franklin, taking a cue from his trademark glasses. Other bookmakers simply take existing books and give them a new look. They gut, paint, and design new covers for books that are in print.

While bookmaking has been around for centuries, current homemade works are straddling the line between books and art. By using bright colors and unusual designs, people are creating spines that will stand out on the shelf. Part of the enjoyment for many bookmakers is finding unique materials to make their books. This often leads to discoveries at flea markets, in attics, and at yard sales.

If these creative designs spark your interest, you can enroll in one of the many new workshops offered at craft stores and community centers.

MICHAEL L. ABRAHAMSON FOR TIME

ABOVE: A real accordion was used to make this book of accordion players. The artists combined the instrument with vintage photos.
LEFT: This colorful Mexican Day of the Dead festival book folds out. It is made of fabric and paper.

TIME to Connect

Design a book cover or interesting format for one of your favorite books. Keep these criteria in mind as you plan your design:

• What is the book about? How would your format and design summarize the book's theme, plot, or message?

• What details from the book could you use in your design to express the main theme?

• What materials would you use to create the new version of the book?

OSHIRO FOR TIME

Building Vocabulary

On a separate sheet of paper, write the term that best matches each definition given below.

1. Any materials used to create art.
2. The use of light and dark values to create the illusion of form.
3. A process in which an artist repeatedly transfers an original image from one prepared surface to another.
4. The impression created on a surface by a printing plate.
5. A copy of a work of art.
6. All the prints made from the same plate or set of plates.
7. A three-dimensional work of art.
8. The technique of capturing optical images on light-sensitive surfaces.
9. A system that processes words and images directly as numbers or digits.
10. Computer software programs that help users design, organize, and combine text, graphics, video, and sound in one presentation.

Reviewing Art Facts

Answer the following questions using complete sentences.

11. What is the difference between two- and three-dimensional art?
12. Describe the four shading techniques.
13. Name and define the three main ingredients of paint.
14. What are the three basic steps of printmaking?
15. What is the difference between sculpture in the round and relief sculpture?
16. Why are crafts called the applied arts?
17. How is videotape technology an improvement over cinematography?

18. What are the similarities and differences between paint and draw programs?

Thinking Critically About Art

19. **Compare and Contrast.** Study Figures 3.13 (page 51), 3.14 (page 52) and 3.15 (page 53). List the similarities and differences you find in all three artworks. In particular, compare and contrast the use of form in each work. How would you describe the form of each work?

20. **Historical/Cultural Heritage.** Review the Meet the Artist feature on page 46. Winslow Homer was influenced by the art trends of his time. Compare and contrast Figures 3.8 and 3.9 on page 46 with the work of another Realist, Édouard Manet in Figure 13.20 on page 369. Why are both artists considered Realists?

 How would you describe the differences between two- and three-dimensional media if you were blindfolded? Play this interactive game with your classmates after taking the **Web Museum Tour** of the Walker Art Center in Minneapolis, Minnesota. Just click on the link at **art.glencoe.com**.

Linking to the Performing Arts

Use the Performing Arts Handbook, page 415, to see how choreographer Merce Cunningham uses the computer and other technology to help him create his renowned ballets.

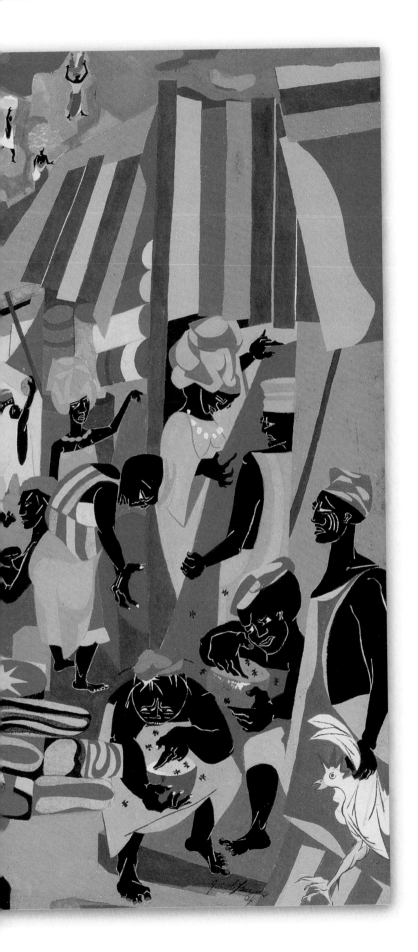

The Elements of Art

"My belief is that it is most important for an artist to develop an approach and philosophy about life—if he has developed this philosophy, he does not put paint on canvas, he puts himself on canvas."
—Jacob Lawrence (1917–2000)

Quick Write

Interpreting Text. Read and interpret the above quote. What does the artist mean? Write a brief interpretation of the quote in your own words. What have you learned about Jacob Lawrence from his painting and quote?

◀

Jacob Lawrence. *Street to M'bari.* 1964. Gouache with graphite on wove paper. 56.5 × 78.4 cm (22¹/₄ × 30⁷/₈"). National Gallery of Art, Washington, D.C. Gift of Mr. and Mrs. James T. Dyke. 1993.18.1.

▲ **FIGURE 4.1** Richly decorated interior settings, lit by the bright sunlight in south France, were a favorite theme of Henri Matisse. He transformed ordinary rooms into exotic settings full of energy. Matisse's use of line gives this painting a feeling of energy. Compare and contrast the variety of lines in this work.

Henri Matisse. *Interior with Egyptian Curtain*. 1948. Oil on canvas. 116.2 × 88.9 cm (45³/₄ × 35″). The Phillips Collection, Washington, D. C. © 2003 Succession H. Matisse, Paris/Artists Rights Society (ARS), New York.

CHAPTER 4

Line

When you, as a child, first picked up a crayon, a line might have been the first mark you made. You use lines to write numbers, symbols, and the letters of the alphabet. The lines on a map help you find the best route from one place to another. You use lines to draw pictures. Lines are everywhere.

In this chapter, you will:

- Compare and contrast the use of line in artworks.
- Identify the different kinds of lines and the ways lines can vary in appearance.
- Demonstrate how lines are used to change values.
- Analyze the expressive qualities or meanings of different lines in works of art.

Focus on Art History **Figure 4.1** was painted by Henri Matisse (1869–1954) in 1924. At this time, Matisse was well established in the European art world. He experimented with different styles throughout his long and varied career. Around the turn of the twentieth century, Matisse and a group of young French artists were shown together in a famous art exhibit. Their use of intense colors, bold designs, and energetic brushwork inspired a critic to name them the *Fauves*, or "Wild Beasts." Notice how the energetic lines in Figure 4.1 dance across the canvas and add decorative patterns to the fabrics and tree.

Compare and Contrast. This interior scene includes a still-life arrangement on a table. Figure 4.13 on page 74, painted 50 years later, also includes a still-life setup on a table. How are these works similar? How are they different?

Vocabulary

line
dimension
outline
implied lines
value
crosshatching

The Element of Line

L ines are everywhere. You can see lines in the grain of a piece of wood or in the cracks on a sidewalk. Lines are used to create words, numbers, and symbols. They are also used to create art. In drawing, **line** is *an element of art that is the path of a moving point through space.*

▲ **FIGURE 4.2** The artist has used the line of the highway to pull your eyes into and through this artwork. Compare and contrast the kinds of line the artist has used in this painting. How do they convey movement and rhythm?

Yvonne Jacquette. *Town of Skowhegan, Maine V.* 1988. Oil on canvas. 198.6 × 163 cm (78³/₁₆ × 64³/₁₆"). Courtesy DC Moore Gallery, NYC.

What Is Line?

Artists use line to lead your eyes through a work of art. This is because it takes movement to make a line. When you see a line, your eyes usually follow its movement. Lines can lead your eyes into, around, and out of visual images, as in the painting in **Figure 4.2.** Notice how the artist uses the line of the highway to pull your eyes into the artwork.

A line has width as well as length, but usually the width of a line is very small compared with its length. In fact, a line is thought of as being one-dimensional. Its one dimension is length. **Dimension** means *the amount of space an object takes up in one direction.* Two-dimensional objects have height as well as width. A painting is two-dimensional. Three-dimensional objects have height, width, and depth. A sculpture is three-dimensional. You will learn more about dimensions in the next chapter when you study shape, form, and space.

Artists create lines in many ways. A line can be drawn on paper with a pencil or scratched into wet clay with a stick. Of course, the world is full of lines that were not drawn with a tool. Some thin, solid objects look like lines. Examples are tree trunks, yarn, spiderwebs, and wires **(Figure 4.3).** These items look like lines because length is their most important dimension.

Some lines that we think we see in nature really do not exist. For instance, when you look at the edges of shapes, you think of lines. In the photo of the dogwood blossom **(Figure 4.4),** notice that there are no black lines around the outside of each petal. However, in a drawing of that same blossom in **Figure 4.5,** lines are used to show the edges of each shape. *A line that shows or creates the outer edges of a shape* is an **outline.**

Implied lines are *a series of points that the viewer's eyes automatically connect.* Implied lines are suggested rather than real lines. A series of dots or dashes, a line of machine stitches, or a trail of wet footprints can create an implied line. A group of shapes arranged in a row can also create an implied line. In **Figure 4.6** on page 72, Abrasha has created a Hanukkah menorah that holds nine cone-shaped candles. The round tops of the cones create an implied line that leads your eyes across the top of the menorah.

▲ **FIGURE 4.3** What lines do you see around you?

▲ **FIGURE 4.4** What edges do you see?

▲ **FIGURE 4.5** Student work. How have the edges on this picture been created?

LESSON 1 *The Element of Line* **71**

▶ **FIGURE 4.6** The artist has used implied line to create a sense of movement. How many sets of nine shapes can you find that create implied lines? Describe the lines.

Abrasha. *Hanukkah Menorah.* 1995. Fabricated stainless steel, silver, and gold. 17.5 × 43.8 × 7.3 cm (6⁷⁄₈ × 17¹⁄₄ × 2⁷⁄₈″). Renwick Gallery, National Museum of American Art, Smithsonian Institution, Washington, D.C.

Kinds of Lines

There are five basic kinds of lines: vertical, horizontal, diagonal, curved, and zigzag.

Vertical lines **(Figure 4.7)** move straight up and down—they do not lean at all. A vertical line drawn on a piece of paper is perpendicular to the bottom edge of the paper. It is also perpendicular to the horizon (the line where earth and sky seem to meet). When you stand up straight, your body forms a vertical line.

▲ **FIGURE 4.8** Horizontal lines lie parallel to the horizon.

Diagonal lines **(Figure 4.9)** slant. Diagonals are somewhere between a vertical and a horizontal line. Diagonals look as if they are either rising or falling. Imagine you are standing straight up; then, with your body stiff, you fall to the floor. At any point during your fall, your body forms a diagonal line.

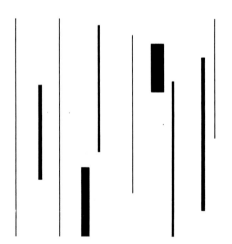

▲ **FIGURE 4.7** Vertical lines move straight up and down.

Horizontal lines **(Figure 4.8)** are parallel to the horizon. They do not slant. When you lie flat on the floor, your body forms a horizontal line.

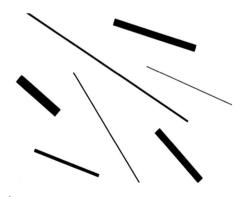

▲ **FIGURE 4.9** Diagonal lines slant.

Zigzag lines (**Figure 4.10**) are made from a combination of diagonal lines. The diagonals form angles and change direction suddenly.

▲ **FIGURE 4.10**   Zigzag lines are combinations of diagonals.

Curved lines (**Figure 4.11**) change direction gradually. When you draw wiggly lines, you are putting together a series of curves. Other kinds of curved lines form spirals and circles.

▲ **FIGURE 4.11**   Curved lines change direction gradually.

Activity	**Analyzing Lines in Artworks**

Applying Your Skills. Select and analyze one of the following paintings from this chapter: Figure 4.1, 4.12, 4.16, 4.18, or 4.19. Diagram the lines of the painting. Use green for verticals, blue for horizontals, red for diagonals, and violet for curves. Place your diagram on display. Can your classmates identify the painting you represented by looking at the colors?

Computer Option. Use the Line tool to create a series of drawings to illustrate each of the five line types. Vary the widths and lengths of your lines. You may also choose to vary patterns and colors. Label each drawing's line type.

Line Variation

Lines vary in appearance in five major ways:

- **Length.** Lines can be long or short.

- **Width.** Lines can be thick or thin.

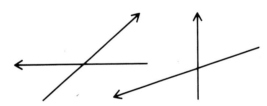

- **Texture.** Lines can be rough or smooth.

- **Direction.** Lines can move in any direction, such as vertical, horizontal, or diagonal.

- **Degree of curve.** Lines can curve gradually or not at all, become wavy, or form spirals.

These five variations can be combined in many, many ways. You can make long, wide lines; rough, short lines; and smooth, curved lines.

Georges Rouault. *The Italian Woman.*1938. Oil on panel. 79.4 × 63 cm (31¼ × 24¹³⁄₁₆"), Dallas Museum of Art, Dallas, Texas. Gift of Mr. and Mrs. Vladimir Horowitz. © 2003 Artists Rights Society (ARS), New York/ADAGP, Paris.

The media, tools, and surfaces used to make lines affect the way a line looks. As with the combination of various line types, a multitude of possible effects can be created. Some common materials used by artists to make lines are graphite, chalk, crayon, ink, and paint. The mate-rial is applied by using a tool. Some tools used for making lines include pencils, markers, pens, brushes, and scissors.

Artists use different tools and materi-als to create different types of lines. For example, a line drawn with chalk on a chalkboard looks smoother than a line drawn with chalk on a sidewalk. Some artists have discovered very unusual ways of using line, as shown in **Figures 4.12** and **4.13**. In **Figure 4.14**, the artist has used many line types and variations.

▲ **FIGURE 4.13** Although this painting is called a still life, it seems to have movement and activity. This is because of the artist's use of line. How many different line directions and line variations can you find in this painting? Describe them.

Alice Neel. *Still Life, Rose of Sharon.* 1973. Oil on canvas. 101.6 × 76.2 cm (40 × 30"). Collection of the Whitney Museum of American Art, New York, New York. Arthur M. Bullowa Bequest.

In this painting, the artist has used five different kinds of line and many line variations. Can you find other examples of line and line variation combinations?

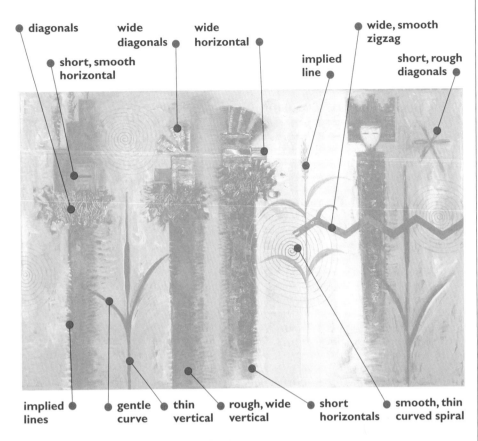

diagonals

short, smooth horizontal

wide diagonals

wide horizontal

implied line

wide, smooth zigzag

short, rough diagonals

implied lines

gentle curve

thin vertical

rough, wide vertical

short horizontals

smooth, thin curved spiral

◀ **FIGURE 4.14**

Dan Namingha. *Blessing Rain Chant.* 1992. Acrylic on canvas. 198 × 304.8 cm (78 × 120"). Niman Fine Art, Santa Fe, New Mexico.

Line and Value

Value is *the element of art that describes the darkness or lightness of an object*. Value depends on how much light a surface reflects. A surface has a dark value if it reflects little light. It has a light value if it reflects a lot of light. Every time you make a pencil mark on a piece of white paper, you are creating a line with a certain value. The harder you press, the darker the value. A series of closely placed lines can create areas of dark value. The lines may be parallel or they may cross one another. **Crosshatching** is *the technique of using crossed lines for shading.*

The values that line groups create depend on four factors: the number of lines, the size of the spaces between the lines, the media, and the tools. A soft pencil (2B, 4B) makes a wide, dark line. A hard pencil (2H, 4H) makes a thin, gray line. A crayon stroked over a rough surface makes a broken line. A crayon stroked over smooth paper makes a solid line.

Look at the Dürer drawing in **Figure 4.15.** Use a magnifying glass to study the way Dürer has used line combinations to create dark and light values.

▲ **FIGURE 4.15** The artist has used line to create this drawing. Identify the areas where the artist has used crosshatching to indicate shading. What kinds of line variation has Dürer used?

Albrecht Dürer. *An Oriental Ruler Seated on His Throne.* c. 1495. Pen and black ink. 30.6 × 19.7 cm (12 × 7³⁄₄″). National Gallery of Art, Washington, D.C. © 1998 Board of Trustees. Ailsa Mellon Bruce Fund.

Activity — Using Line to Create Value

Demonstrating Effective Use of Art Media and Tools in Drawing. Fold a sheet of white drawing paper into nine squares. In each square use a different combination of parallel or crosshatched lines to create a different value. Try a variety of pencils, from hard 2H to soft 4B lead. Try quill pens, ballpoint pens, and felt-tip pens. Think of some other tools and materials to use.

Computer Option. Use the Line tool to draw three diagonal lines (that are not parallel) from screen edge to screen edge. This will divide your screen into six or seven sections. Fill each section with lines. Vary the spacing of the lines by placing them close together in one section and farther apart in another. Lines can be crosshatched. You can choose the Patterns palette and fill the sections by using the Fill Bucket tool, or create your own patterns. Use only black and white. Notice that the value of the area darkens as lines are placed close together and lightens when lines are farther apart.

✓ Check Your Understanding

1. How is *line* defined in drawing?
2. What are the five basic kinds of lines?
3. Compare and contrast five ways that lines vary in appearance in artworks.
4. Describe the crosshatching technique.

The Expressive Qualities of Line

Vocabulary

contour line
gesture
calligraphy

Depending on its direction, a line can express different ideas or feelings. This is why line is an important element in the language of art. Vertical lines can make certain objects look taller. For example, vertical lines on wallpaper can make low ceilings seem higher. Clothing designers use vertical lines to make short people look taller and heavy people look thinner.

Line Movement

Vertical lines are static, or inactive. They appear to be at rest. For this reason, they express stability. Artists use them to show dignity, poise, stiffness, and formality, as in Figure 4.14 on page 75.

Horizontal lines are also static. They express feelings of peace, rest, quiet, and stability, as in **Figure 4.16.** They give a feeling of permanence or solidarity. Because we stand on solid horizontal ground, horizontal lines make us feel content, relaxed, and calm.

▲ **FIGURE 4.16**   Strong horizontal lines—such as the bands of black clouds, the horizon, and the railroad tracks—create a feeling of calm in this sunset scene. How do the verticals in this scene affect the meaning of the work?

Edward Hopper. *Railroad Sunset.* 1929. Oil on canvas. 71.8 × 121.3 cm (28¼ × 47¾″). Collection of the Whitney Museum of American Art, New York, New York. Josephine N. Hopper Bequest.

▲ **FIGURE 4.17** Notice the many different kinds of curves the artist used to create this luxurious gateway. Identify any straight lines. Follow them through the work. Do they stay straight? Can you think of adjectives to describe the many types of curves used in the artwork?

Albert Raymond Paley. *Portal Gates.* 1974. Forged steel, brass, copper, and bronze. 230.5 × 182.9 × 10.2 cm (90³⁄₄ × 72 × 4″). Renwick Gallery, The National Museum of American Art, Smithsonian Institution, Washington, D.C.

Because curved lines change direction, they express activity. How much activity they express depends on the type and direction of the curve. The less active the curve, the calmer the feeling. Spiral curves wind around a central point. They are hypnotic and draw the eye to their center. Curved lines are often used in decorative arts to suggest a feeling of luxury, as in **Figure 4.17.**

Diagonal lines express instability, tension, activity, and excitement, as shown in **Figure 4.18.** Since they can appear to be either falling or rising, they sometimes make a viewer feel uncomfortable. Artists use them to add tension or to create an exciting mood. However, when two diagonals meet and seem to support each other, as in the roof of a house, they appear more stable.

Zigzag lines create confusion. They are extremely active and may evoke feelings of excitement **(Figure 4.19, page 80)** and nervousness. The degree of intensity is indicated by the direction of the zigzag. Zigzags that move horizontally, such as those across the top of a picket fence, are less active than the irregular zigzags of a streak of lightning.

<table>
<tr><td>

Activity

</td><td>

Using Imagination to Draw Lines Expressively

</td></tr>
</table>

Applying Your Skills. Choose two words from the following list:

swimming	burning	praying
rocking	flowing	jumping
marching	running	growing
dancing	crawling	laughing
wagging	writing	flying

On separate sheets of paper, illustrate the words you have chosen by using line movement only. Do not draw objects.

Choose the medium you think will work best. When you are finished, write the words on the back of each paper. Ask your classmates to look at the lines and guess which words you have illustrated.

Computer Option. Use the Line tool to make two drawings using lines. Let one drawing illustrate quiet, calm piano music, and let the other illustrate loud rock music.

▲ **FIGURE 4.18** In this painting, every line that should be static is diagonal. Look at the window, the lamp, the rug, the floor planks, and the fiddler's bench. The diagonal lines fill the work with a sense of excitement. Not only the people but also every corner of the room seems to be alive and dancing to the music of the fiddler.

Thomas Hart Benton. *Country Dance.* 1929. Oil on gessoed canvas. 76.2 × 63.5 cm (30 × 25″). Private collection. © T. H. Benton and R. P. Benton Testamentary Trusts/Licensed by VAGA, New York, NY.

American, 1917–2000

Jacob Lawrence was born in Atlantic City, New Jersey, in 1917. When he was 12, his family moved to Harlem in New York City. The move would have a great impact on his growth as an artist.

The Harlem Renaissance of the 1920s had attracted many talented minority artists from all over the world, and many still remained in Harlem during the 1930s. These artists served as Lawrence's inspiration.

Lawrence sought every opportunity he could to learn about art. He listened to the Harlem artists as they talked in their studios. The 135th Street Public Library, which he visited often, always had pieces of African sculpture on display. His many trips to the Metropolitan Museum of Art gave him a strong background in art history.

Lawrence became fascinated with black history and its heroic figures. He took as his subjects such important people as Toussaint L'Ouverture, Harriet Tubman, and Frederick Douglass. Lawrence often found he could not express all he wanted to say in just a single picture. Therefore, he often made series of paintings to tell the whole story. In this way, he used his art to convey his ideas about the heritage of African Americans.

▲ **FIGURE 4.19** The artist has used line to show the movement of the children. Look at their arms, legs, and feet. What kinds of lines do you see? How has Lawrence used line to create a feeling of movement and excitement?

Jacob Lawrence. *Children at Play.* 1947. Tempera on Masonite panel. 50.8 × 60.9 cm (20 × 24″). Georgia Museum of Art, University of Georgia, Athens, Georgia. Eva Underhill Holbrook Memorial Collection of American Art, Gift of Alfred H. Holbrook.

Contour Drawing

A **contour line** *defines the edges and surface ridges of an object.* A contour line also creates a boundary separating one area from another. Learning how to contour draw will add to your drawing skills as well as to your ability to observe and understand objects. See the examples in **Figure 4.20** and **Figure 4.21**.

When drawing contours, let your eyes follow the contour of the object you are drawing. Move your pencil at the same speed as your eyes. Do not lift the pencil from the paper. The line should be continuous. Draw the line slowly and with care. Concentrate in order to draw accurately. See Technique Tip 1 on page 428 in the Handbook for help in making contour drawings.

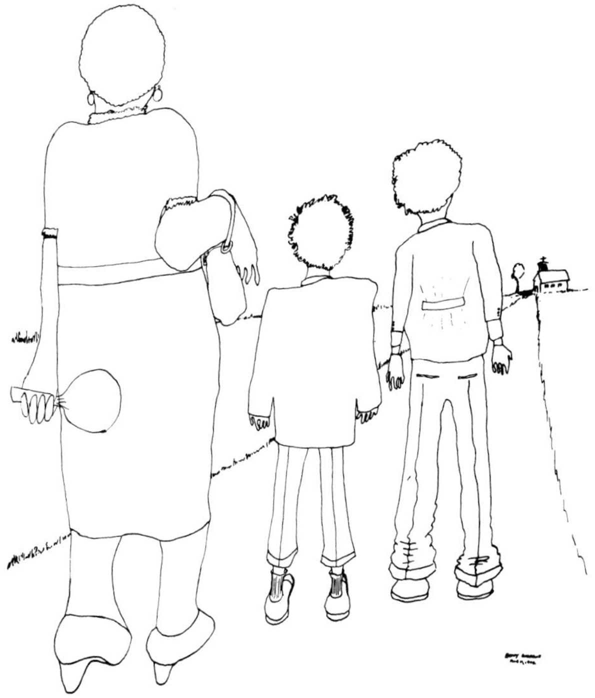

▲ **FIGURE 4.20** Andrews has used a contour line to draw a memory of his past. His mother insisted that the children dress up for Sunday church services. How does he use line to emphasize the ill-fitting clothes?

Benny Andrews. *Mom and Us.* 1972. Pen and ink drawing. 45.7 × 30.5 cm (18 × 12″). Collection of the artist.

◀ **FIGURE 4.21** Student work. Notice how the line flows through this hospital scene. Look at the difference between the busy zigzag lines that describe the wrinkles in the sheet and the few lines that define the person's face.

Activity — Contour Line Drawings

Creating Visual Solutions Using Direct Observation. Set up a group of three shoes in an interesting, overlapping composition. Arrange them at different angles so you can observe them sideways, head-on, from the top, and from the back. Use a black marker to do a contour line drawing of all the shoes. Use only line. Do not color or shade the drawing. Use line to add details such as laces, stitches, patches, and holes.

Computer Option. Sit at your computer, turn sideways, and look down. Use the Line tool to draw your feet, legs, and free hand. You may start at the feet and work your way up toward your lap, or vice versa. Use the mouse just as you would use a pencil. Be sure to start your drawing near the edge of your screen so you will have room for the entire picture.

Andrews captures the excitement of the jazz sounds of Thelonious Monk with gesture lines. Compare and contrast Andrews's use of line in this work to the lines in Figure 4.20.

Benny Andrews. *Thelonious at The Five Spot.* 1958. Pen and ink drawing. 27.3 × 20.6 (10³/₄ × 8¹/₈″). Collection of the artist.

Gesture Drawing

A **gesture** is *an expressive movement.* The purpose of drawing gestures is to capture the feeling of motion. A gesture drawing uses very little detail. (See **Figures 4.22** and **4.23**).

Lines showing gestures are drawn quickly. They should be sketched freely and loosely—even recklessly—in order to capture movement. (See Technique Tip 2 on page 428 in the Handbook.) Unlike contours, they represent the interior of an object. Your gesture drawings may look like scribbles at first, but this is acceptable. Concentrate on showing position and movement.

▶ **FIGURE 4.23**
The artist used a brush and paint to create this gesture oil sketch. Compare and contrast the use of line in this sketch with Figure 4.22. Describe the similarities and differences between the two works of art. Does this painting have more detail?

Audrey Flack. *Self-Portrait: The Memory.* 1958. Oil on canvas. 127 × 86.4 cm (50 × 34″). Miami University Art Museum, Oxford, Ohio. Gift of the artist.

Activity	Creating Gesture Drawings

Creating Visual Solutions Using Direct Observation. Make a series of gesture drawings. Classmates should take turns posing for one another. Start with thirty-second poses. Shorten the time by five seconds for each pose until the pose is held for only ten seconds. Have the model twist, turn, bend, and kick, trying to avoid doing the same thing twice.

Computer Option. Choose a round, medium-size Brush or Pencil tool. Sit at the computer station, turn sideways, and look at other students who are modeling for gesture drawing. They will be changing positions every 20 or 30 seconds. Try to capture the feeling of motion, not detail. Change color each time the model changes positions. Some of your drawings will overlap.

Calligraphic Drawing

The word **calligraphy** means *beautiful handwriting.* Calligraphy is often associated with Asian writing and art. In China and Japan, calligraphy is used to form *characters* that represent the language. However, characters are more than just a letter of the alphabet. They are like pictures. They can represent an idea, an object, or a verbal sound. The Chinese and Japanese use the same types of calligraphic lines and brushstrokes in their paintings **(Figure 4.24).** In fact, in the Chinese language, the words *writing* and *painting* are represented by the same character.

Calligraphic lines are usually made with brushstrokes that change from thin to thick in one stroke. To make a very thin line, use the tip of the brush. As you press on the brush and more of it touches the paper, the line becomes wider. (See Technique Tip 3 on page 428 in the Handbook.)

 Activity — Calligraphic Lines

Applying Your Skills. Practice making calligraphic lines with ink or watercolor paint. Use round, pointed brushes, both thin and thick. Also, try bamboo brushes. Next, use a watercolor brush and ink or watercolor paint to make a series of five calligraphic studies of one natural object, such as a leaf or a vegetable.

Computer Option. Research either Egyptian hieroglyphics or Southwestern pictographs to gain information about "picture writing." Create your own picture writing by making up symbols. Use any computer tools and options available. Remember that the Cut and Paste options are helpful when you want to repeat a symbol without redrawing it.

▲ **FIGURE 4.24** The long, flowing leaves of the orchid plant in the left corner of the painting are made with one flowing brushstroke. Where do you see other objects made with a single brushstroke?

Shitao. Qing Dynasty. c. 1700. *Orchids, Bamboo, and Rock.* Hanging scroll. Ink on paper. 72.4 × 51.1 cm (28½ × 20⅛"). Arthur M. Sackler Gallery, Smithsonian Institution, Washington, D.C. Gift of Arthur M. Sackler, S1987.206.

 Check Your Understanding

1. Select and analyze artworks in this lesson to form a conclusion about the meanings of vertical and horizontal lines.
2. How are contour drawings and gesture drawings different?
3. What type of artwork is often associated with calligraphy?

Wire Jewelry

▲ **Figure 4.25**

Iris Sandkühler. *Viking Net Chain Necklace.* 2001. Silver wire, malachite, and glass. 43.2 cm (17″) long. Private collection.

SUPPLIES

- Assortment of wire: steel, copper, brass, and color-coated wires of various gauges
- Needle-nose jewelry pliers and wire cutters
- Hammer and anvil block
- Sketchbook and pencils
- Jewelry findings: ear wires, pin backs, watch cord, etc.
- Jewelry files (half-round needle files)
- Steel wool and/or emery paper
- Brass and copper cleaner (optional)

Historical and Cultural Context

Iris Sandkühler is a San Francisco-based artist. The necklace in **Figure 4.25** is an example of Sandkühler's fine craftsmanship. Silver wires form an intricate net around hanging beads of colored glass and a rich, green mineral known as malachite.

Sandkühler was born in Bingen, West Germany, in 1958. Her family immigrated to Maine when she was seven years old. As a young adult, she attended Ohio State University. After obtaining a bachelor's degree in sculpture and glass, she went on to earn a master's degree in mixed media drawing and painting. After graduation, she honed her jewelry skills at the Jewelry Arts Institute in New York City. Her unique jewelry has been exhibited in Berlin, Tokyo, and in galleries throughout the United States.

Notice how the loops and lines of wire in the *Viking Net Chain Necklace* create implied lines. These lines lead the viewer's eyes across the necklace. The hanging glass forms also create an implied line that moves the eye rhythmically across the strand.

What You Will Learn

You will design and create a design for a practical application—a wearable piece of wire jewelry such as a pin, pendant, necklace, ring, hair ornament, bracelet, or pair of earrings. The wire may be bent, twisted, looped, and so on. However, only these "cold connections" are allowed—no solder or glue. You will be working with line in space. Your design may be nonobjective or represent an object, person, place, or thing.

Creating

Practice shaping a length of steel wire with a pair of pliers. What can you do with the wire? Try spiraling, coiling around a pencil, and flattening (forging) the wire with a hammer on an anvil block. An anvil is a flat-topped block of iron. Experiment with techniques for connecting wire pieces by twisting, weaving, wrapping, and linking.

After experimenting, sketch a series of five to ten line drawings of the type of object you wish to create, using the skills you were able to master during your practice session. Take into consideration any findings, or fasteners, that are necessary.

Step 1 Make a practice model in steel wire of your best design. Planning is the key to success. Solve all the problems that present themselves before beginning with the more expensive wires. For example, a fastener may need to be fashioned as part of the design for a necklace or bracelet.

Step 2 Carefully work with the pliers on the brass, copper, and color-coated wires, as these metals are softer and will scratch and scar more easily than the steel. All the scratches made during the construction will need to be removed with steel wool or emery paper to complete the project. Good craftsmanship, the care with which an object is completed, is an essential part of the finished project.

Step 3 Complete the project by sanding away any stains or scratches, rounding sharp ends with a file, and attaching findings such as ear wires, pin backs, and clasps.

Evaluating Your Work

▶ **DESCRIBE** What wire-forming techniques (wrapping, weaving, linking, forging, and so on) did you use in the creation of this object? If fasteners or jewelry findings were necessary, are they a part of the design? Is your piece representational or nonobjective? If it is representational, what object, animal, or person did you use in your design?

▶ **ANALYZE** Compare and contrast the different kinds of lines you used in your design. List them. How was working with line in three dimensions different from making the drawings in your sketchbook?

▶ **INTERPRET** What is the function of your wire jewelry? Interpret your artistic decisions. What idea, feeling, or mood does your work convey to the viewer?

▶ **JUDGE** Is your piece of jewelry aesthetically successful? Which of the three aesthetic theories would you use to judge your work? Is it a practical piece of jewelry? Is it comfortable to wear? Is it too heavy? Does any of the wire scratch skin or snag fabric?

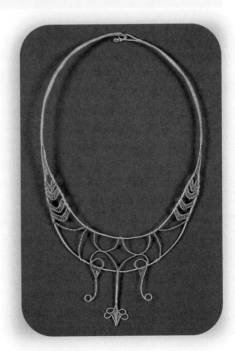

▶ **FIGURE 4.25A**

Student work.

Nature Tapestry

◀ **FIGURE 4.26**

Josep Royo. *Woman* (after Joan Miró). 1977. Wool and cotton tapestry. 10.5 × 6 m (34′ 7″ × 19′ 10″). National Gallery of Art, Washington, D.C. Gift of Collectors Committee and George L. Erion.

SUPPLIES

- Natural objects: flowers, shells, seedpods, plants, feathers, and so on
- Sheets of 6 × 8″ paper
- Pencils and markers or crayons
- Cardboard for loom, at least 8 × 14″
- Ruler and scissors
- A variety of fibers: yarns, embroidery floss, textured yarns, metallic thread, raffia, and so on
- Two 1 × 8″ strips of mat board
- Stitchery needle with large eye

Historical and Cultural Context

The wool and cotton tapestry in **Figure 4.26** is by Josep Royo, who was born in Spain in 1945. The work is based on—and is a tribute to—a painting by another Spanish artist and personal friend, Joan Miró. Miró was influenced by many different twentieth-century art styles. One style reflected in this work is Cubism. Cubism was an approach to art in which natural forms were broken down and reorganized to present a unique perspective. Notice the title of the tapestry in Figure 4.26. Can you find the outline of the woman in this abstract work? How many different shapes has the artist used in reassembling this figure? How many colors has he used?

What You Will Learn

You will design and weave a small tapestry using a cardboard loom. Your work will be an abstraction of an object from nature. You will begin by drawing the contour of one object. You will then divide the shape into an assortment of geometric and free-form shapes. You will create visual movement by using different colors for the resulting internal areas.

Creating

Collect and bring to class natural objects that have interesting lines and shapes, such as flowers, shells, feathers, and so on. Focus on the contour of each object. Choose one to draw.

Step 1 Using direct observation, make a contour drawing of your object. Divide the inner space of the object into geometric or free-form shapes of different sizes, as in **Figure 4.26A.** Make several such pencil drawings.

Step 2 Select your best drawing. Transfer it, using a marker or crayon, to a sheet of 6 × 8-inch paper. Choose a color scheme that will lead the viewer's eye around your object. Each shape should have a single color. You may repeat a color, but no shape should have the same color as its neighboring shapes.

Step 3 Make your loom. (See Technique Tips, pages 437–438.) Tape your completed design on the cardboard under the warp (vertical) threads, leaving 2¹⁄₂ inches at the bottom. Use a strip of mat board as a header at the bottom of the loom by weaving a tabby pattern (see page 438) starting over/under. Weave a second mat board strip, starting under/over, above the first one, creating a straight edge to begin.

Step 4 Weave ¹⁄₄ inch of plain tabby up to the design, using a color that will match the bottom of the design. Begin weaving the tapestry. Follow your design. Keep the outside finished edges straight by not pulling the weft (horizontal threads) tight. Do not stop or start new threads on the side edges. As you change yarns, leave 1¹⁄₂ inches of thread. When you are finished, use a stitchery needle to pull the thread tails through the weft along a warp thread.

Step 5 When the tapestry is complete, cut the warp threads and tie every two warp threads together securely by using an overhand knot. Pull the knots together close to the weaving.

Evaluating Your Work

▶ **DESCRIBE** Tell what object you chose as the basis for your tapestry. Explain how you made your loom and prepared it for weaving.

▶ **ANALYZE** Compare and contrast your use of lines and color. What type of lines did you use to divide the shapes? What colors did you choose? Did you vary the values of colors placed side by side?

▶ **INTERPRET** Give your tapestry a title that sums up what you think it expresses. Be prepared to justify why you have given it this title.

▶ **JUDGE** Were you successful in completing a tapestry that matched your original design? Which aesthetic theory would you use to judge your work? Explain.

▲ **FIGURE 4.26A**

Student work.

Digital Image Using Line

▲ **FIGURE 4.27**

Joaquin Torres-Garcia. *New York City: Bird's Eye View.* 1920. Gouache and watercolor on board. 33.6 × 48.6 cm (13¼ × 19⅛"). Yale University Art Gallery, New Haven, Connecticut. Gift of Collection Société Anonyme. © 2003 Artists Rights Society (ARS), New York/VEGAP, Madrid.

SUPPLIES

- Sketchbook and pencils
- Digital or conventional camera
- Scanner (optional)
- Computer equipped with advanced paint or photo-editing software
- Printer
- Photo quality paper (optional)

Historical and Cultural Context

The painting in **Figure 4.27** is by twentieth-century Uruguayan-born Spanish painter Joaquin Torres-Garcia. Torres-Garcia spent 40 years living in the United States and Europe before returning to Uruguay in 1934. This painting makes use of a style of art the artist termed *Constructive Universalism*. In it, a grid system is used for arranging symbols into compositions. Examine the painting, taking note of the vertical and horizontal lines. What symbols do you see? Do you think the lines symbolize anything? What do the diagonal and curved lines express?

What You Will Learn

In this lesson, you will create a digital image that emphasizes the expressive qualities of a particular line. You will begin by taking a photograph in which a single type of line dominates. The line may be horizontal, vertical, diagonal, or curved. Using computer painting tools, you will emphasize the expressive qualities of this line by altering its color, value, texture and/or width.

Creating

Review Lesson 2 briefly. Look around your environment for examples of lines that express a specific feeling or emotion. You might select the delicate curves on the petals of a flower or the graceful ripples on the surface of a pond. Make sketches of these and similar observations. Emphasize the line or lines that dominate.

Step 1 Take several digital photographs of settings similar to those described above. If a digital camera is not available, use a regular camera. Scan your images into the computer.

Step 2 Import your digital images, and view them. Select the one in which the lines are most evident and expressive. *Note:* Be sure to save or convert this file in a format that will permit it to open in your computer's paint or photo-editing application.

Step 3 Open the file. Crop any unnecessary edges or images that will detract from the expressive nature of the lines being emphasized.

Step 4 Use the Line Properties menu or tool to experiment with changing the color, value, texture and/or width of the line or lines. You may also select filters such as Emboss, as in the student artwork shown on this page. If a Preview feature exists in the software, use it to examine and calibrate the effect. (Usually, this is done by means of a slider indicating percentages.) Otherwise, simply use the Undo command to eliminate undesirable effects.

Step 5 When you are satisfied with the results, print a copy of your work.

Evaluating Your Work

▶ **DESCRIBE** What subject did you choose for your photograph? What type of camera did you use to take the photograph?

▶ **ANALYZE** Compare and contrast your use of line and emphasis. What type of line is emphasized in your photograph? What changes to these lines did you make?

▶ **INTERPRET** Were the lines in your photograph adequately expressive? What feelings or emotions do they express? How did you emphasize them? Give your digital image a title.

▶ **JUDGE** Were you successful in creating the feeling or emotion you wanted to emphasize? What would you do differently if you were to redo this assignment? Which of the three aesthetic theories would be best to judge your finished image?

▶ **FIGURE 4.27A**

Student work.

Line

As you have discovered in this chapter, there are many types and uses of line in art. Examine the student artworks on these pages to:

● Compare and contrast the use of line. How do the lines lead your eyes into, around, and out of the visual images?

● Select and analyze what media were used and how your peers created lines with these media.

Activity 4.28 **Implied line.** This artist has used implied line to lead your eyes to the central form in the weaving. What shape is this form? Identify the implied line.

Activity 4.29 **Line movement.** Compare the watercolor in Figure 4.29 to Figure 4.18 on page 79. Describe the similarities between the uses of line movement in both works.

▲ **FIGURE 4.28**

Student work. *Untitled.* Tapestry weaving made from fiber and embroidery floss.

▲ **FIGURE 4.29**

Student work. *Untitled.* Watercolor, pen and ink on paper.

Activity 4.30 **Line and pattern.**
Crisscrossed lines have been used to create a pattern in this artwork. Compare and contrast the use of line and pattern in this work with another work on these pages.

▲ **FIGURE 4.30**

Student work. *Sweet Kisses.* Acrylic on canvas.

Activity 4.31 **Interpreting line.**
The artist has included horizontal lines of text in this illustration. Identify other kinds of lines. Then interpret what idea or feeling the lines express.

▲ **FIGURE 4.31**

Student work. *Altered Expressions.* Watercolor, pen and ink on paper.

To view more student artworks, visit the Glencoe Student Art Gallery at **art.glencoe.com**.

For Your Portfolio

Evaluate Personal Artworks. As you add to your portfolio, include artworks that demonstrate use of the elements of art. Each entry in your portfolio should be marked clearly for identification. Make sure each piece includes your name and the date you completed the artwork. Any notes about the artistic decisions you made are valuable and should be kept with your artwork. Make it a point to use the names of the elements of art as you write about your artwork.

Visual Art Journal

A visual journal can be used to record your explorations and observations. As you study line, take notes and create sketches. For example, you may wish to record the various kinds of line you see as you ride in a car or on the bus.

Art Criticism
in Action

▲ **FIGURE 4.32**

Utagawa (Andō) Hiroshige. *Plum Garden at Kameido (Kameido Umeyashiki)* from *One Hundred Views of Edo, View 30*. 1857. Woodblock print. 33.9 × 22.5 cm (13¹/₃ × 8⁷/₈"). Gift of James A. Michener, 1991. Honolulu Academy of Arts, Honolulu, Hawaii.

Critiquing the Artwork

▶ **1** **DESCRIBE** *What do you see?*

Read the credit line.

● What media have been used to create this work of art?

● List everything you see in this work. To organize your thoughts, start with the objects that are closest to you and gradually work your way to the background.

▶ **2** **ANALYZE** *How is this work organized?*

This step deals with the composition or formal qualities of the work. This is a clue-collecting step about the elements of art.

● Compare and contrast the different kinds of line (vertical, horizontal, diagonal, curved, and zigzag) in this work. List at least one location for each line type you identify.

● Do you see any line variations—such as length, width, and texture—in this work? List at least one location for each variation you identify.

● Form a conclusion about which type of line dominates.

▶ **3** **INTERPRET** *What message does this artwork communicate to you?*

Now, you will combine the clues you have collected and your personal ideas to form a creative interpretation of the work.

● Why are the people so small? Why do you think they are separated from some of the trees by a fence?

● Analyze the meaning of this work. What does this work say about the relationship between people and nature?

● Write a brief paragraph or a poem that expresses the message you believe this print communicates.

▶ **4** **JUDGE** *What do you think of the work?*

Now, it is time to decide whether this is a successful work of art.

● What is your reaction to this work? Did it make you think?

● Do you think it is successful? Why or why not? Use one or more of the aesthetic theories of art explained in Chapter 2 to defend your judgment.

What's My Line?

Artist Al Hirschfeld (1903–2003) was famous for his line drawings and caricatures of famous people. In a TIME interview, he discussed his career and work habits.

Q. How old were you when you realized you could draw?

A. I don't remember doing anything else. I can't do anything else. That's one of my limitations.

Q. Why did you move toward drawing rather than becoming a painter, for example?

A. I started out as a sculptor, actually. And I found that it was impossible to make a living. So I became a painter and went to Paris.

Q. What turned you away from painting?

A. Line. I discovered line, and I fell in love with it. I still find it fascinating how a line can communicate. It expresses everything that I want.

Q. How would you describe your work habits?

A. I work seven days a week until around 5:00 P.M.

Q. Does drawing ever feel like work to you?

A. No, it's a luxury. Work is something you don't like to do.

TIME to Connect

Artists capture and express physical characteristics through drawing. Writers do the same with words. Choose a personality from the world of music, TV, sports, or film. Analyze photos of the person.

- Draft a descriptive paragraph so that a reader is able to "see" the person you are writing about.

- Edit your writing. Try to improve the wording and refine your style.

- Share your work with the class. Does your paragraph enable your classmates to picture the personality?

ABOVE: Elvis Presley in his blue suede shoes.
TOP: Al Hirschfeld, self-portrait at age 99.

Building Vocabulary

On a separate sheet of paper, write the term that best matches each definition given below.

1. An element of art that is the path of a moving point through space.
2. The amount of space an object takes up in one direction.
3. A line that shows or creates the outer edges of a shape.
4. A series of points that the viewer's eyes automatically connect.
5. The element of art that describes the darkness or lightness of an object.
6. The technique of using crossed lines for shading.
7. A line that defines the edges and surface ridges of an object.
8. An expressive movement.
9. A term meaning beautiful handwriting.

Reviewing Art Facts

Answer the following questions using complete sentences.

10. Give an example of an implied line.
11. How does a two-dimensional object differ from a three-dimensional object?
12. Compare and contrast the five basic kinds of lines.
13. Name five major ways in which lines can vary.
14. What are the four factors that affect the value of a group of lines?
15. Name the kind of line that conveys instability, tension, and action.

Thinking Critically About Art

16. **Analyze.** Study Figure 4.1 (page 68) Figure 4.14 (page 75), and Figure 4.19 (page 80). What is the common thread that links the three works?
17. **Compare and Contrast.** In what ways are Figure 4.20 (page 81) and Figure 4.22 (page 82) similar? In what ways are they different? Consider the element of line and the subject matter in your comparison.
18. **Historical/Cultural Heritage.** Review the Meet the Artist feature on page 80. Identify themes from Jacob Lawrence's cultural heritage shown in Figure 4.19.

Most fine artists use line to create their artworks. Fine artists range from sculptors to painters to installation artists. Visit art.glencoe.com to compare and contrast this art career with other career opportunities.

Linking to the Performing Arts

Explore the use of line in dance as shown in the performance of "Danza de la Reata" by Ballet Folklorico de Mexico in the Performing Arts Handbook on page 416. One example of the element of line is the use of the lariat, or lasso, during the performance. Identify other examples.

► **FIGURE 5.1** Without even looking at the title, you can identify this familiar object because of the shapes used. In what way is this work "larger than life"? If you are not sure of the answer, review the credit line below. Compare and contrast this work to another sculpture by the same artist on page 261. Can you draw any conclusions about the theme of his work from these two pieces?

Claes Oldenburg. *Shoestring Potatoes Spilling from a Bag.* 1966. Canvas, kapok, glue, and acrylic. 274.3 × 116.8 × 106.7 cm (108 × 46 × 42″). Walker Art Center, Minneapolis, Minnesota. Gift of T. B. Walker Foundation, 1966.

CHAPTER 5

Shape, Form, and Space

Y ou live in a world filled with objects. Each has a shape; some have form—or *depth*—and all inhabit space. As art elements, shape, form, and space are closely related to one another. Learning to "read" the meaning of these elements as well as how to use them effectively in artworks is very important as an artist.

In this chapter, you will:

- Compare and contrast the use of form and space in artworks.
- Create two- and three-dimensional works of art using direct observation and imagination.
- Interpret artistic decisions about using shapes, forms, and space in personal artworks.

Focus on **Art History** Up through the early twentieth century, the media of sculpting were fairly limited. Sculptors could choose from hard materials (marble, bronze) or softer ones (wood). Then a revolution in art occurred. "Anything goes" became the battle cry of experimental artists. One such artist is Swedish-born American sculptor Claes Oldenburg (b.1929). Oldenburg is a member of the Pop Art school. His art, like that of other Pop Artists, used everyday objects from American culture as a theme. Like **Figure 5.1**, however, the works are so large that the viewer can't help but notice them.

Compare and Contrast. Look at Figure 2.1 on page 24. This work shares the theme of contemporary Pop Art. Like Figure 5.1, this work uses unconventional materials. In what way does it go even further in breaking the traditional "rules" of three-dimensional art?

Shapes and Forms

Vocabulary

shape
geometric shapes
free-form shapes
forms

All objects are either shapes or forms. Rocks, puddles, flowers, shirts, houses, chairs, and paintings are all shapes and forms. The words *shape* and *form* are often used interchangeably in everyday language, but in the language of art, they have very different meanings.

Shape

A **shape** is *a two-dimensional area that is defined in some way.* A shape may have an outline or a boundary around it, or you may recognize it by its area. For instance, if you draw the outline of a square on a sheet of paper, you have created a shape. You could also create the same shape without an outline by painting the area of the square red.

You see many two-dimensional shapes every day. They are found in most designs, which in turn can be seen on many flat surfaces. Look for shapes on such things as floor coverings, fabrics, and wallpapers. Floors and walls are two-dimensional shapes; so are tabletops, book pages, posters, and billboards. The images you create with your computer and the images in the handheld and computer games you play may have the illusion of depth, but they are also two-dimensional shapes.

Geometric Shapes

All shapes can be classified as either *geometric* or *free-form.* **Geometric shapes** are *precise shapes that can be described using mathematical formulas* **(Figure 5.2).** The basic geometric shapes are the circle, the square, and the triangle. All other geometric shapes are either variations or combinations of these basic shapes. Some of the variations include the oval, rectangle, parallelogram, trapezoid, pentagon, pentagram, hexagon, and octagon.

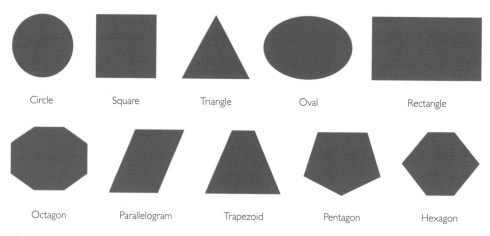

| Circle | Square | Triangle | Oval | Rectangle |
| Octagon | Parallelogram | Trapezoid | Pentagon | Hexagon |

▲ **FIGURE 5.2** Geometric shapes.

Geometric shapes are used for decoration, uniformity, and organization. Notice the decorative quality of the geometric shapes in the artwork shown in **Figure 5.3.** How many different simple and complex geometric shapes can you find in Biggers' painting?

Road signs are examples of uniformity. The same kind of sign must always have the same shape. Do you know the shape of a stop sign? Which shape is used for "Yield"? Which shape is used for TV screens? Why do you think ceiling tiles and window panes have geometric shapes?

Free-Form Shapes

Free-form shapes are *irregular and uneven shapes.* Their outlines may be curved, angular, or a combination of both. They often occur in nature. Another word that may be used to describe free-form shapes is *organic.* Organic is used when we talk about the shapes that are silhouettes of living things such as animals, people, or trees. Look at the difference between the decorative patterns of geometric shapes in Figure 5.3 and the free-form, organic shapes painted on the vases in **Figure 5.4.** Which looks more organized?

▲ **FIGURE 5.3** Biggers uses the women in this work to represent the African civilizations of Egypt, Benin, and Dogon. The crowns are symbols of these civilizations. The cloth on their laps represents the geometry that has brought order to each culture.

John Biggers. *Starry Crown.* 1987. Acrylic, mixed media on Masonite. 155 × 124.5 cm (61 × 49″). Dallas Museum of Art, Dallas, Texas. Museum League Purchase Fund.

◄ **FIGURE 5.4** Notice the free-form, organic qualities of the dragons and clouds that were painted on this matching pair of vases. Although the forms of the vases are perfectly matched, the paintings are not exactly alike. Look closely to find the differences between the two dragons.

Chinese, *Pair of Vases.* 1426–1435. Ming Dynasty (1368–1644). Porcelain with underglaze blue decoration. 55.2 × 29.2 cm (21¾ × 11½″). The Nelson-Atkins Museum of Art, Kansas City, Missouri. Purchase: Nelson Trust, 40-45/1,2.

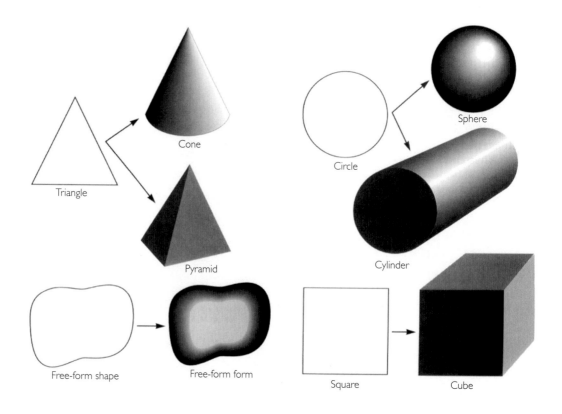

Triangle

Cone

Pyramid

Free-form shape

Free-form form

Circle

Sphere

Cylinder

Square

Cube

▲ **FIGURE 5.5** What kind of relationship do you see between the two-dimensional shapes and three-dimensional forms?

Activity

Geometric and Free-Form Shapes

Demonstrating Effective Use of Art Media in Design. Using the printed areas of a newspaper, make two cut-paper designs. Make one design by measuring and cutting precise geometric shapes. Make the second design by tearing free-form shapes. Arrange the shapes and glue them on a sheet of black construction paper. Use a white crayon to print the words *free-form* and *geometric* on the appropriate design. Try to make the letters for *geometric* look geometric, and the letters for *free-form* look free-form.

Computer Option. Use the Shape or Straight Line tools to draw four different geometric shapes. Do not overlap the shapes and space them apart so they can easily be selected and arranged later. Choose a color scheme and make each shape a solid color. Pick the Selection tool and then the Copy and Paste menu to repeat each of the shapes several times on the page. When the page is nearly full, choose a Brush or Pencil tool to draw free-form shapes in between the geometric shapes. Select the Bucket tool to fill these shapes with pattern.

Forms

Although the words *shape* and *form* are often used interchangeably in everyday language, they have different meanings in the language of art. **Forms** are *objects having three dimensions*. Like shapes, they have both length and width, but forms also have depth. *You are a three-dimensional form; so is a tree or a table.*

Two-dimensional shapes and three-dimensional forms are related **(Figure 5.5)**. The end of a cylinder is a circle.

One side of a cube is a square. A triangle can "grow" into a cone or a pyramid.

Like shapes, forms may be either geometric **(Figure 5.6)** or free-form **(Figure 5.7** on page 102**)**. Geometric forms are used in construction, for organization, and as parts in machines. Look around you. What forms were used to build your school, your church, your home? Look under the hood of a car. What forms were used to build the motor? Did you know that common table

▲ **FIGURE 5.6** The inspiration for this work came from Smith's studies of geometric crystalline forms in the early 1960s. The title, a pun on the insect it resembles, is based on the mythical beast of the same name in James Joyce's *Finnegan's Wake*. This is one of Smith's most complex sculptures. It took him eight years to see it to completion. The six separately constructed, geometric steel units were assembled on the museum's lawn in 1972.

Tony Smith, *Gracehopper.* 1971. Welded steel and paint. Height: 7 m (23′). The Detroit Institute of Arts, Detroit, Michigan. Founders Society Purchase with other funds.

▲ **FIGURE 5.7** An Inuit artist carved this free-form, organic sculpture of a polar bear from memories of personal experiences observing and hunting polar bears. Compare and contrast the forms of this sculpture from Inuit culture to the forms of Tony Smith's minimalist sculpture in Figure 5.6.

Ashevak Adla. *Walking Bear.* Serpentine stone. 14 × 34.3 × 13.3 (5½ × 13½ × 5¼"). Courtesy of Canadeau Gallery, Quebec, Canada.

salt is made of a series of interlocking cubes? You can see these cubes when you look at salt through a microscope.

Free-form forms are irregular and uneven three-dimensional objects such as stones, puddles, and clouds. Your own body and the bodies of animals and plants are free-form forms.

 Check Your Understanding

1. List three geometric shapes.
2. What is another word for *free-form* shapes?
3. Compare and contrast the use of form in the artworks in this lesson.

Activity | Creating Forms

Applying Your Skills. Make a flat sheet of construction paper into a three-dimensional paper sculpture by using cutting and scoring techniques. (See Technique Tip 20 on page 435 in the Handbook.) Give your sculpture a minimum of five different surfaces. Do not cut the paper into separate pieces. Use only slots and tabs if you wish to join any parts. Experiment with scratch paper before you make your final paper sculpture.

Computer Option. Use the Round Shape tool to draw a circle or oval on the screen. Choose the Airbrush to gently add shading around the edges to make the shape appear as a solid form. Draw a free-form shape. Apply shading with the airbrush to represent a form. Consider adding a surface for the three-dimensional forms to sit on and then apply shadows.

Space

Vocabulary

space
holograms

Space refers to both outer space and inner space. Rockets move through outer space to explore other planets. People move through the inner space of rooms and buildings. Space can be flat and two-dimensional, such as the space of a window. Space can also be three-dimensional, such as the space filled with water in a swimming pool.

Space and Its Relationship to Shape and Form

Shapes and forms exist in space. **Space** is *the element of art that refers to the emptiness or area between, around, above, below, or within objects.* All objects take up space. You, for example, are a living, breathing form moving through space.

Shapes and forms are defined by the space around and within them. They depend on space for their existence. This is why it is important to understand the relationship of space to shapes and forms.

Positive and Negative Spaces

In both two- and three-dimensional art, the shapes or forms are called the *positive space* or the *figure.* The empty spaces between the shapes or forms are called *negative spaces* or *ground.* Look at **Figure 5.8** and read the caption for an example of figure and ground. In a portrait, the image of the person is the positive space; the negative space is the area surrounding the person.

◀ **FIGURE 5.8** Do you see a vase or do you see two profiles of Picasso? Johns has deliberately organized this lithograph as a visual puzzle to confuse the viewer. One minute the faces are very clear and they seem to be the figure while the space between the profiles is the ground. The next moment the vase between the profiles becomes the figure and the space around the vase becomes the ground.

Jasper Johns. *Cups 4 Picasso.* 1972. Lithograph. 57.2 × 82 cm (22½ × 32¼"). Museum of Modern Art, New York, New York. Gift of Celeste Bartos. © Jasper Johns/Licensed by VAGA, New York, NY.

The shape and size of negative spaces affect the way you interpret positive spaces. Large negative spaces around positive spaces may express loneliness or freedom. When the positive spaces are crowded together, you may feel tension or togetherness **(Figure 5.9)**. The full meaning of a work depends on the interaction between the positive and negative spaces. It is not always easy to tell which are the positive spaces and which are the negative spaces in two-dimensional art. Sometimes it is difficult to identify the negative space. This is because some artists give equal emphasis to both the figure and the ground.

Sometimes artists even try to confuse the viewer. They create positive and negative spaces that reverse themselves while you are looking at them. These visual puzzles fascinate some viewers **(Figure 5.10)**.

▲ **FIGURE 5.9** In this sculpture, Brancusi uses the lack of space between the two figures to symbolize the concept of the togetherness, the unity, of a couple in love. Compare and contrast the ways these forms are balanced with the artwork in Figure 5.6 on page 101.

Constantin Brancusi. *The Kiss.* c. 1908. Stone. Height 50.2 cm (19 ³/₄″). Musée National d'Art Moderne, Centre Georges Pompidou, Paris, France. © 2003 Artists Rights Society (ARS), New York/ADAGP, Paris.

Activity   Experimenting with Space

Creating Visual Solutions Using Direct Observation. Select a group of objects to draw from direct observation. Make an arrangement with a variety of negative spaces between the shapes. Draw the arrangement lightly with pencil or chalk. Finish the work by (a) coloring only the negative spaces with crayons or paint, or (b) filling the negative spaces with closely drawn sets of parallel lines. Leave the positive spaces empty. What shapes did the negative spaces take?

Computer Option. Use the Rectangle shape tool to draw a solid rectangle approximately 3" x 4" in the center of the screen. Explore the different shapes of Selection tools to select and move parts of the rectangle away from the original shape. Continue selecting and moving until the rectangle has been broken into many smaller parts with varying spaces in between. Save and title your work when you have created an interesting composition by adding space within the form.

M. C.
ESCHER

Dutch, 1898–1972

Born in Leeuwarden, Holland, M. C. Escher (**esh**-ur) studied graphic art at Harlem's School of Architecture and Ornamental Design. He concentrated on illustrating his eccentric inner visions and his fascination with the laws of nature. In his lithographs, he explored a variety of visual jokes and trickery, such as optical illusions and distorted or impossible perspective.

Escher's works achieve their visual puzzles through his clever manipulation of positive and negative space. They skillfully switch forms into places where the viewer would logically expect space, or what appears to be the outer surface of an object reverses into an inner space.

Escher also created designs using positive and negative space to transform one object to another. A flock of birds on the left side of the picture becomes a school of fish on the right side. Each time a change takes place, the negative space becomes dominant and transforms into the new object.

▶ **FIGURE 5.10** At first this print looks normal. Water is falling to turn a water wheel. However, follow the water from the base of the fall. It runs uphill! Escher has created a visual puzzle using the mathematics of perspective.

M. C. Escher. *Waterfall.* 1961. Lithograph. © 1998 Cordon Art, Baarn, Holland. All rights reserved.

Space in Three-Dimensional Art

Over, under, through, behind, and *around* are words that describe three-dimensional space. Architecture, sculpture, weaving, ceramics, and jewelry are three-dimensional art forms. They all take up real space. You can walk around, look through, look behind, peer over, and reach into three-dimensional art.

Architects shape space. They design structures that enclose a variety of spaces for people. They create large spaces for group activities, such as the one you see in **Figure 5.11.** They also create small spaces for privacy. Landscape architects and city planners are also involved in planning spaces for people to use.

Negative areas in three-dimensional art are very real. Most three-dimensional works are meant to be *freestanding,* which means they are surrounded by negative space **(Figure 5.12).** The viewer must move through this negative space to see all of the different views of a three-dimensional work.

Relief sculpture is not intended to be freestanding. It projects out from a flat surface into negative space. You can find relief sculpture on ceramic pots and plaster ceilings. When the positive areas project slightly from the flat surface, the work is called *bas relief,* or *low relief* **(Figure 5.13).** When the positive areas project farther out, the work is called *high relief.*

Most jewelry is planned as relief sculpture to decorate human surfaces. The inside of a ring or the back of a pendant is smooth. It is not meant to be seen; it simply rests on the person's surface.

Today many artists are experimenting and changing traditional art forms. Printmakers are creating relief prints. Some printmakers are molding relief designs in handmade paper. Painters are adding a third dimension to the painted surface. Some painters are cutting or tearing real negative spaces in two-dimensional surfaces.

Weaving has also gone in new directions. It started as a practical craft, with weavers making two-dimensional fabrics for clothing, and has evolved into an art form. Today hand weavers are

▲ **FIGURE 5.11** The interior of this cathedral was designed so that the stained glass and the vertical columns would pull your eyes upward toward the heavens.

Reims Cathedral (interior). Reims, France. Begun c. 1225.

creating relief hangings and three-dimensional woven sculptures.

Photographers are creating **holograms,** *images in three dimensions created with a laser beam.* Sculptors are making *kinetic,* or moving, sculpture.

Activity | Using Three Dimensions

Applying Your Skills. Make a freestanding, three-dimensional design that projects into negative space on all sides. Using pieces of cardboard tubing and small boxes, join the design pieces with glue and tape. Paint the finished work in one color to emphasize its form.

Set up a spotlight on one side of your freestanding sculpture. In your sketchbook draw the contours of the sculpture and the shape of its shadow. Move the spotlight to another angle. Draw the sculpture and its shadow. Notice how the changing light changes the shadow's shape.

Computer Option. Draw a solid cube or rectangular form so the top, side, and front are visible. Add shading by filling each surface with a different value of a color, texture, or gradient. Remove an area within the form by using the Eraser or Selection tool. Explore adding shadows and lines to accurately depict the inner space you see.

 ## Check Your Understanding

1. Define *positive space* and *negative space.*
2. What words specifically describe three-dimensional art?
3. Compare and contrast the use of space in the artworks on this page.

◀ **FIGURE 5.12** This example of folk art from Peru is a freestanding sculpture. Look carefully and you can see forms peeking out from the back. To see them you would have to walk around to the back of the work.

Artist unknown. *Church Quinua,* Ayacucho, Peru. 1958. Painted earthenware. Girard Foundation Collection at the Museum of International Folk Art, a unit of the Museum of New Mexico, Santa Fe, New Mexico.

▲ **FIGURE 5.13** An example of low relief. Since the design was for the back of a chair, the relief has to be low relief or the chair back would be too uncomfortable to lean against.

Queen Ankhesenamun and King Tutankhamon. Egypt, Eighteenth Dynasty. Wood overlaid with gold, silver, semiprecious stones, and glass paste. Egyptian Museum, Cairo, Egypt. Scala/Art Resource, New York.

How We Perceive Shape, Form, and Space

Look up from this book to an object across the room to see if you can feel the movement of your eye muscles. If you didn't feel anything, try again until you become aware that your eyes are working to refocus.

You have just taken a trip through visual space. Your brain measured the amount of space between you and the object and sent a message to your eye muscles to adjust. The muscles then refocused your eyes so that you could clearly see the object.

Perceiving Depth

Your eyes and brain work together to enable you to see in three dimensions —*height*, *width*, and *depth*. Each eye sees an object from a slightly different angle. The brain merges these two separate and slightly different views into one, creating a three-dimensional image.

To see how this works try the following experiment. Close your right eye. Point to a specific spot in the room. Without moving your pointing finger, open your right eye and close your left eye. It will appear that you have moved your finger, even though you know you have not.

Point of View

The shapes and forms you see depend on your *point of view*. **Point of view** is *the angle from which the viewer sees an object*. Another viewer at another location will see the same shape or form differently. For example, a person looking down on a circle drawn on the sidewalk sees a round shape. If that person lies on the ground beside the circle and looks at it, the circle will appear to have an oblong shape. A person looking at the front end of a car will see a form different from the one seen by a person looking at the side of that same car. **Figure 5.14** shows three different views of a sculpture.

Activity | Shape and Point of View

Creating Visual Solutions Using Direct Observation. Look through magazines for three or more different views of one type of object. Look for TV sets, sofas, spoons, toasters, cars, or shoes. Cut out the objects and mount each one on a sheet of white paper. Observe and emphasize the changes in shape by drawing around each outline with a crayon or marker.

Computer Option. Divide the page into three equal sections. Use the Grids and Rulers menu to guide you if available. Choose an interesting but simple object such as a cup, a screw, pliers, a book, or a paint container. Observe and draw three views of the same object using the Pencil, small Brush, Crayon, or Marker tool. After drawing the contour or outer edges of the object, add shading to emphasize the form and surface from different views.

▶ **FIGURE 5.14** Notice how the feeling expressed by this sculpture changes as your point of view changes. You must view the sculpture from all angles to truly understand it.

Michael Naranjo. *Spirits Soaring.* 1985. Bronze. Height 50.8 cm (20″). Private collection.

Experiments in Point of View

You can learn about point of view by doing the following experiments. Place your hand flat on the desk and spread your fingers apart. The shape and form you see are the shape and form you would probably draw. They are part of the mental image you have of the object "hand." Now lift your hand and let your fingers relax. Notice how the shape and form of your hand change. Turn your hand and watch what happens. Your hand is still the same hand. Only its shape and form are different.

Next, look at a rectangular table. What shape does the top have when you are sitting at the table? Look at the top through a rectangular viewing frame. Are the edges of the table parallel to the edges of the frame? You know the top is a rectangle, but does it really look rectangular now? What shape does the top seem to take if you are sitting across the room from it? What would the shape look like if you viewed it from the top of a tall ladder? Do you think the shape you see will change if you lie on the floor directly under the table?

▲ **FIGURE 5.15** Grandma Moses is the professional name of Anna Mary Robertson Moses. She began to paint rural scenes from her memories in the 1970s. This painting depicts the many different aspects of making maple sugar. What point of view is she using? What effect does this point of view create for the viewer?

Grandma Moses. *Sugaring Off.* 1955. 50.8 x 63.5 cm (20 x 25"). © 1955 (renewed 1983) Grandma Moses Properties Company, New York, New York.

When you looked at your hand, your eyes stayed in the same place, but your hand moved. When you studied the table, it remained in one place, but you moved. In both cases, what you saw changed because your relationship to the object changed. Your point of view depends on where you are and where the object is. Look at **Figure 5.15.** Where is the artist's point of view in relation to the people in that picture?

 **Check Your Understanding**

1. What three dimensions are we able to see?
2. Define *point of view.*
3. Why may people who are looking at the same object see different shapes and forms?

How Artists Create Shapes and Forms in Space

Vocabulary

chiaroscuro
highlights
perspective

Shapes and forms can be classified as *natural* or *manufactured*. Natural shapes and forms are made by the forces of nature. For instance, animals, plants, and stones are natural forms. Manufactured forms are those created by people, whether mass-produced by the thousands in factories or made by hand.

Artists use many materials and techniques to make shapes. They concentrate on both outline and area. Some artists outline shapes in drawings and paintings. Others may paint shapes by placing brushstrokes together without using even a beginning outline. Some may cut shapes and print shapes and some may pour paint to create shapes **(Figure 5.16)**.

Like shapes, three-dimensional forms can be made in many ways. Artists model clay forms, mold metal forms, and carve forms from wood or stone. They use glass, plastic, bricks, and cement to create forms as well as shapes.

The Illusion of Form

Artists can create the illusion of three-dimensional form on a surface that is two-dimensional. They can give the impression of depth and solidity by using changes in value. **Figure 5.17** is an example of this illusion.

▲ **FIGURE 5.16** Frankenthaler is an action painter who creates shapes by pouring thinned acrylic paint onto a canvas that is placed flat on the floor.

Helen Frankenthaler. *The Bay*. 1963. Acrylic on canvas. 201.1 × 207 cm (79³/₁₆ × 81¹/₂″). Detroit Institute of Arts, Detroit, Michigan. Founders Society Purchase with funds from Dr. and Mrs. Hilbert H. DeLawter.

◀ **FIGURE 5.17** Artemisia Gentileschi was a Baroque artist who used the arrangement of contrasting light and dark to create a dramatic effect in her work. Notice how the light seems to be coming from a single candle.

Artemisia Gentileschi. *Judith and Maidservant with the Head of Holofernes*. c. 1625. Oil on canvas. 184.2 × 141.6 cm (72¹/₂ × 55³/₄″). Detroit Institute of Arts, Detroit, Michigan. Gift of Mr. Leslie H. Green.

◀ FIGURE 5.18 The artist has represented shadows and highlights with photographic reality. Notice how he has made the objects seem to look solid. The seats of the stools look round. The reflections on the metal ceiling indicate rounded form. How does he use light to create the effect of a cool, air-conditioned interior against a hot outdoor scene?

Ralph Goings. *Diner With Red Door*. 1979. Oil on canvas. 112.4 × 153.7 cm (44¼ × 60½"). Courtesy of OK Harris Works of Art, New York, New York.

The arrangement of light and shadow is called **chiaroscuro** (**kyah**-roh-**skoo**-roh). In Italian *chiaro* means "bright," and *oscuro* means "dark." Chiaroscuro was introduced by Italian artists during the Renaissance. Today, chiaroscuro is often called *modeling* or *shading*.

Look, for instance, at an object with angular surfaces, such as a cube. You will see a large jump in value from one surface of the cube to the next. One surface may be very light in value and the next very dark. Now look at an object such as a baseball. The curved surfaces of spheres and cylinders show gradual changes in value.

The area of a curved surface that reflects the most light is, of course, the lightest in a drawing. **Highlights** are *small areas of white used to show the very brightest spots.* Starting at the highlights, the value changes gradually from light values of gray to dark values of gray. The darkest values are used to show areas that receive the least light. An area that is turned completely away from a light source is almost black. Look at **Figure 5.18** to see the different ways an artist has created the illusion of form.

Activity

Using Shading

Applying Your Skills. Set up an arrangement of geometric forms. Use boxes, books, balls, and cylindrical containers. Study the way light reflects off the surfaces of the objects. Draw the arrangement. Give the shapes in your drawing the illusion of three dimensions by using the medium and shading technique of your choice. Use values that range from black to white, and employ many value steps in between.

Computer Option. To perfect your shading technique, experiment with the Pencil, Brush, Line, Gradient, and Airbrush tools. Several programs include a Smudge or Blending tool, which softens edges. The Pencil, Line, and small Brush tools can be used with shading techniques you use when working with pen and ink. To explore these options, draw a small square shape. Select, copy, and paste seven more copies of the square in a row across the screen. Then choose from a variety of tools, textures, and settings to create different values from light to dark in the squares.

The Illusion of Depth

In paintings, artists often create the illusion of depth. When you look at these paintings, you see objects and shapes, some of which seem closer to you than others. You seem to be looking through a window into a real place **(Figure 5.19)**. This idea—that a painting should be like a window to the real world—has dominated traditional Western art since the early Renaissance.

There are several terms that will help you as you talk about and create depth in a painting or drawing. The surface of a painting or drawing is sometimes called the *picture plane*. The part of the picture plane that appears nearest to you is the *foreground*. The part that appears farthest away is the *background*. The area in between is called the *middle ground*.

Perspective is *a graphic system that creates the illusion of depth and volume on a two-dimensional surface.* In the following pages you will learn techniques artists use to give their paintings and drawings perspective.

▲ **FIGURE 5.19** Panini excelled at capturing the interiors of famous buildings. Notice how he tries to focus your attention on the arch at the end of the hall by using converging lines. After reading about perspective on the following pages, try to find examples of each of the six perspective techniques in this painting.

Giovanni Paolo Panini. *Interior of Saint Peter's Rome.* 1746-54. Oil on canvas. 154.3 × 196.9 cm (60¾ × 77½"). National Gallery of Art, Washington, D.C. Ailsa Mellon Bruce Fund.

Overlapping. When one object covers part of a second object, the first seems to be closer to the viewer, as in **Figure 5.20.**

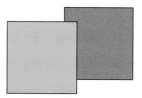

▲ **FIGURE 5.20**   Overlapping.

Size. Large objects appear to be closer to the viewer than small objects, as in **Figure 5.21.** The farther an object is from you, the smaller it appears. Cars far down the road seem to be much smaller than the ones close to you. If you stand at the end of a long hallway and raise your hand, you can block your view of a whole crowd of people. You know that each person is about your size, but at a distance the crowd appears to be smaller than your hand.

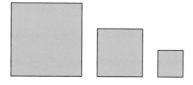

▲ **FIGURE 5.21**   Size.

Placement. Objects placed low on the picture plane seem to be closer to the viewer than objects placed near eye level. The most distant shapes are those that seem to be exactly at eye level **(Figure 5.22).**

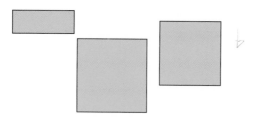

▲ **FIGURE 5.22**   Placement.

Detail. Objects with clear, sharp edges and visible details seem to be close to you **(Figure 5.23).** Objects that lack detail and have hazy outlines seem to be farther away. Look closely at your own hand. You can see very tiny lines clearly. Now look at someone's hand from across the room. You have trouble seeing the lines between the fingers. All the details seem to melt together because of the distance between you and what you are seeing.

▲ **FIGURE 5.23**   Detail.

Color. Brightly colored objects seem closer to you, and objects with dull, light colors seem to be farther away **(Figure 5.24).** This is called *atmospheric* perspective. The air around us is not empty. It is full of moisture and dust that create a haze. The more air there is between you and an object, the more the object seems to fade. Have you ever noticed that trees close to you seem to be a much brighter green than trees farther down the road?

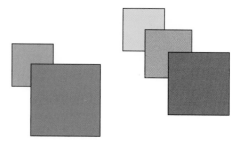

▲ **FIGURE 5.24**   Color.

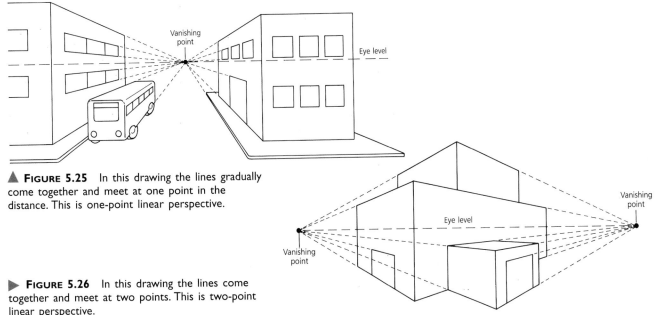

▲ **FIGURE 5.25** In this drawing the lines gradually come together and meet at one point in the distance. This is one-point linear perspective.

▶ **FIGURE 5.26** In this drawing the lines come together and meet at two points. This is two-point linear perspective.

Converging Lines. *Linear* perspective is one way of using lines to show distance and depth. As parallel lines move away from you, they seem to move closer together toward the horizon line **(Figure 5.25)**. When you look at the highway ahead of you, the sides of the road appear to move closer together. You don't worry, though, because you know this is an illusion. The sides of the road ahead of you are actually just as far apart as they are in your present position.

Sometimes lines appear to meet at a point on the horizon line called the *vanishing point.* In two-point linear perspective, different sets of parallel lines meet at different vanishing points **(Figure 5.26)**. Because two-point perspective creates more diagonal lines in a painting,

Activity	Creating Depth

Creating Visual Solutions Using Imagination. Create three different designs on three separate sheets of paper. Each design should contain five imaginary shapes. Use the same five shapes in each design as follows:

- Draw all of the items as close to the foreground as possible.
- Draw one item close to the foreground and make the others look as if they are slightly farther back.
- Draw one item close to the foreground, one far in the background, and the other three in the middle ground.

Computer Option. Use the Brush or Pencil tool to draw a landscape that includes a foreground, middle ground, and background. Draw several medium size trees in the middle ground. Draw at least one large tree in the foreground. This tree should touch two or three edges of the paper and overlap the smaller trees. It should display the most detail. Add other objects and details that might include plants, animals, water, and objects made by hand. Remember the methods for creating the illusion of depth that were discussed earlier in the chapter.

it seems more active. Renaissance artists used strict mathematical formulas to calculate perspective. Most of today's artists rely on visual perception rather than mathematical formulas. Notice the ways in which Doris Lee has used perspective to show depth in her busy kitchen scene **(Figure 5.27).**

Check Your Understanding

1. How are shapes and forms classified?
2. What effect does chiaroscuro create in artworks?
3. List and describe three techniques artists use to give their works perspective.

LOOKING CLOSELY

Identifying Perspective Techniques

In this painting about the preparations for an old-fashioned Thanksgiving feast, Doris Lee has used all six perspective techniques. The lines in the diagram of the painting indicate one example of each technique. Can you find more examples of the six techniques in the painting?

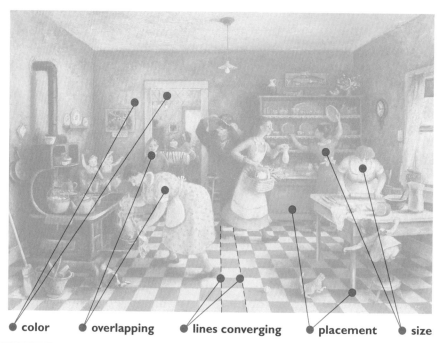

● color ● overlapping ● lines converging ● placement ● size

◀ **FIGURE 5.27**

Doris Lee. *Thanksgiving.* 1935. Oil on canvas. 71.1 × 101.6 cm (28 × 40″). The Art Institute of Chicago, Chicago, Illinois. Mr. and Mrs. Frank G. Logan Prize Fund (1935.313).

What Different Shapes, Forms, and Spaces Express

Shapes, forms, and spaces in art convey certain feelings. This is possible because you associate them with similar shapes, forms, and spaces in real life. When you see a certain shape or form in a work of art, you may think of an object from real life. Any feelings you have about that object will affect your feelings about the artistic work. Artists use this relationship between art and the environment to generate these feelings in the viewer.

Outline and Surface

The outline of a shape and the surface of a form carry messages. Artists often use free-form shapes and forms to symbolize living things. When they want to please and soothe viewers, they use shapes and forms with smooth, curved outlines and surfaces **(Figure 5.28).** Forms that remind us of well-worn river rocks or curled-up kittens tempt us to touch them. These forms are comfortable. They appeal to us through our memories of pleasant touching experiences.

Angular shapes with zigzag outlines and forms with pointed projections remind us of sharp, jagged things **(Figure 5.29).** We remember the pain caused by broken glass and sharp knives. We would never carelessly grab a pointed, angular form. If we were to touch it at all, we would do so very carefully.

◄ **FIGURE 5.28** The artist who created this horse used rounded forms to make it appealing to look at and to touch.

Haniwa Horse. Japan, Kofun Period, A.D. 300–550. Earthenware. 66 × 71.8 × 22.9 cm (26 × 28¼ × 9″). The Minneapolis Institute of Arts, Minneapolis, Minnesota. The John R. Van Derlip Fund and Gift of anonymous St. Paul Friends.

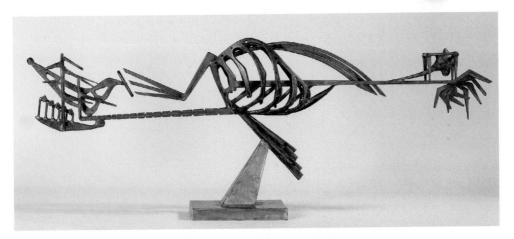

▲ **FIGURE 5.29** This sculpture is based on the skeleton of a prehistoric bird. How many bird body parts can you identify? How do the sharp points on its teeth, head, and tail make you feel about this work?

David Smith. *The Royal Bird.* 1947–48. Steel, bronze, stainless steel. 56.2 × 151.9 × 21.6 cm (22¹/₈ × 59¹³/₁₆ × 8¹/₂″). Walker Art Center, Minneapolis, Minnesota. Gift of T. B. Walker. Art © Estate of David Smith/Licensed by VAGA, New York, NY.

▲ **FIGURE 5.30** The artist has transformed a soft, feathered bird form into a dense, abstract, bronze form that represents the flowing movement of a bird.

Constantin Brancusi. *Bird in Space*. 1928. Bronze (Unique Cast). Height 137.2 cm (54"). Museum of Modern Art, New York, New York. © 2003 Artists Rights Society (ARS), New York/ADAGP, Paris.

Geometric shapes suggest mechanical perfection. It is impossible to draw a perfect circle freehand. The special appeal of geometric shapes and forms has been felt throughout the ages. Their lines, contours, and surfaces are clean and crisp. This appeals to people's sense of order.

As used by modern artists, geometric shapes and forms express less feeling than other types. They are unemotional; in fact, they may express a total lack of feeling. Geometric forms in artworks appeal to viewers' minds rather than to their emotions **(Figure 5.30).**

Density

The *density* or mass of an object refers to how compact it is. Dense materials are solid and heavy. Granite and lead, for example, are very dense. They are so solid and firm that you cannot make a dent on their surfaces when you press on them. Dense forms seem unyielding. They resist impact. For this reason, you may associate them with the idea of protection. In two-dimensional art, you can depict dense objects using shading techniques and hard-edge contours.

Soft, fluffy forms are less dense. When you press on them, you can make a dent. These forms have air inside them, and they look more comfortable than denser forms. In two-dimensional art, you can depict soft forms by using shading techniques and curved contours.

Openness

An open shape or form appears inviting. It seems to say, "Come in." You can see into or through it. An armchair is an open form that invites you to sit **(Figure 5.31).** An open door invites you to enter. An empty cup invites you to fill it. Transparent objects, such as a glass wall, invite you to look inside. When you extend your hand to invite someone to join you, the form of your outstretched hand is an open form.

Open spaces in sculpture invite your eyes to wander through the work. Weavers leave openings in fabrics and hangings to let you see through them. If you remove an oak table from a room and replace it with a glass table, the room will seem less crowded. Architects use glass walls to open small spaces. Windows open up a building and bring in the outdoors.

◀ **FIGURE 5.31** To Wright, form and function were inseparable, so a chair, which functions for sitting, should be considered along with the whole architectural environment.

Frank Lloyd Wright. *Armchair for the Ray W. Evans House,* made by Niedechen and Walbridge. c. 1908. Oak. 87 × 58.4 × 57.1 cm (34¼ × 23 × 22½"). The Art Institute of Chicago, Chicago, Illinois. Gift of Mr. and Mrs. F. M. Fahrenwald, 1970.435.

Closed shapes and forms look solid and self-contained. Windowless buildings look forbidding. Closed doors keep people out; closed drapes and shades keep light out. When you make a tight fist, your hand is a closed form that seems to say, "Keep away." Folding your arms tightly to your body closes you off from others. Open arms invite people to come closer to you. The plumed deity, or god, in **Figure 5.32** is a closed form. Even its feathers are pulled tightly against its body.

▲ **FIGURE 5.32** This carving represents Quetzalcoatl (Plumed Serpent), a highly revered god in Aztec culture. It is tightly knotted into a closed form. Notice the human head and the carefully carved quetzal bird feathers.

Aztec, Tenochtitlan (Mexico City), Mexico. *Sculpture in the form of the deity Quetzalcoatl.* Last half of the fifteenth century. 20.3 × 12.7 × 19.7 cm (8 × 5 × 7¾"). Birmingham Museum of Art, Birmingham, Alabama.

Activity and Stability

You have already learned about active and static lines. Shapes and forms, also, can look as if they are about to move or as if they are fixed in one place.

Active shapes and forms seem to defy gravity. They slant diagonally, as if they are falling or running. In **Figure 5.33** notice how the back of the wave and all the horse forms are arranged in diagonal, active positions.

Static shapes and forms are motionless, or stable. Their direction is usually horizontal **(Figure 5.34).** However, if two diagonal shapes or forms are balanced against each other, a static shape results. For instance, if an equilateral triangle rests on a horizontal base, the two diagonal edges balance each other.

Because static shapes and forms are firmly fixed in position, they evoke quiet and calm feelings. For instance, in landscape paintings the land forms are horizontal and the trees are vertical. They look very peaceful. This is probably why so many landscape paintings are chosen for people's homes.

Activity Active and Static Shapes

Demonstrating Effective Use of Art Media in Design. Make a simple design with geometric shapes. Lightly draw it with pencil on a sheet of watercolor paper. Repeat the same design on another sheet of watercolor paper of the same size. Next, paint the first design precisely. Use a pointed brush to make sure that all of the edges are clearly defined. Wet the second sheet of paper by sponging it with water. Using exactly the same colors, paint the second design while the paper is wet so that the edges of the shapes run and look soft. Mount the two designs, side by side, on a sheet of black paper. Label the first "hard-edged" and the second "soft-edged."

▶ **FIGURE 5.33** The diagonal push of the back of the wave creates an unstable, active feeling. The wave is caught at the moment before it will collapse.

Anna Hyatt Huntington. *Riders to the Sea.* 1912. Bronze. 47 × 61 × 53.3 cm (18½ × 24 × 21″). The Newark Museum, Newark, New Jersey. Gift of the estate of Mrs. Florence P. Eagleton, 1954.

Computer Option. Choose the Shape and Line tool to make a design that creates a static feeling. The Line tool on most applications can be constrained to draw straight horizontal, vertical, or diagonal lines by holding down the shift key while drawing with the mouse. Title and save the black line static design. Select a color scheme. Pick the Bucket tool to fill the spaces with solid colors. Use the Save As command to retitle the work by adding a number or letter after the original title. Open the original line design. Apply the same color scheme but explore the tools and menus, which create active flowing edges. Use the Save As command to retitle the active composition.

Check Your Understanding

1. What do angular shapes suggest?
2. What do geometric shapes suggest?
3. Define *density.*
4. List one example each of an open shape or form and a closed shape or form.

▲ **FIGURE 5.34** The strong horizontal shape of the orange wheat at the base of the work creates a calm, stable effect.

Jane Wilson. *Winter Wheat.* 1991. Oil on linen. 101.6 × 127 cm (40 × 50″). Photo courtesy of DC Moore Gallery, New York, New York. Private Collection.

Free-Form Clay Sculpture

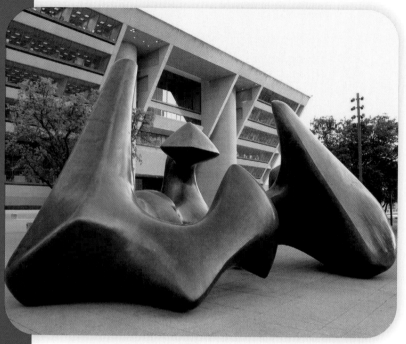

▲ **FIGURE 5.35**

Henry Moore. *Dallas Piece*. Bronze. Located in the plaza of the new City Hall, Dallas, Texas.

SUPPLIES

- Cotton cloth
- Plastic bag
- Clay rolling pin, dowel, heavy spoon
- Turntable
- Assorted clay tools
- Soft cloth
- Watercolor

Historical and Cultural Context

The twentieth-century British sculptor Henry Moore created works in stone, bronze, and marble. Most of these creations were abstractions of the human figure.

Moore did not design outdoor sculptures for specific sites. The original bronze casting shown in **Figure 5.35** consisted of three separate pieces. The present grouping was suggested by I. M. Pei, a Chinese-born American architect, who was commissioned to build a new city hall for Dallas. Pei liked this work but asked Moore to arrange the sculpture so that people could walk through it. Moore designed the pyramidal arrangement you see. Notice the careful balance between solid mass and an almost airy visual flow. Does your eye move in and around the smooth planes of the sculpture without interruption?

What You Will Learn

Using your imagination, you will create a nonobjective, free-form sculpture in clay. You will use the subtractive method of carving to demonstrate the effective use of media and tools in sculpture. Your work should have smooth planes with well-defined edges. The goal is to create visual flow, as in Figure 5.35. Decorate some small areas of emphasis in your work by carving small forms or creating textures. The completed sculpture must be freestanding and pleasing from all angles.

Creating

If you have not worked in clay before, take time to explore the properties of the medium. Clay must be *wedged*—or thumped on a surface—before use. Doing this removes any air bubbles. Keep the clay moist by covering it with a slightly damp cloth. Seal it in a plastic bag when not in use.

Step 1 Wedge seven to eight pounds of clay.

Step 2 Beat and shape the clay with various tools, such as a rolling pin, a two-inch dowel, or a large heavy spoon. Keep the form vertical rather than horizontal so you will have a standing sculpture.

Step 3 Place the resulting form on a turntable. Study it from all directions. Let the existing form of the clay guide you. Look for linear edges that flow through the form. Avoid looking for a recognizable object.

Step 4 Begin to carve the form you visualize, using large wire sculpture tools. Use smaller clay tools to refine the planes. Carve contrasting small areas of emphasis. One possibility to consider is adding texture with a fork

Step 5 Hollow the sculpture, leaving an outer shell no more than ³/₄ of an inch thick. If possible, hollow the sculpture from the bottom. Otherwise, carefully cut open the sculpture with a thin wire and remove the inside clay.

Step 6 Allow the sculpture to dry at room temperature until bone dry. Fire your work in a kiln.

Step 7 Using a soft cloth, apply stain by using a watercolor. Begin applying stain with a very light layer and end with a darker layer.

Evaluating Your Work

▶ **DESCRIBE** Did you use the media and tools effectively? Did you use only the subtractive method of sculpting? Did you hollow out the center so that your work dried properly? Describe the process you used to apply the finish. Is your sculpture vertical and freestanding?

▶ **ANALYZE** Did you create smooth planes with well-defined edges to develop a visual flow? Compare and contrast your own use of negative and positive space. Is your finished work nonobjective? Compare and contrast the areas of emphasis you carved or textures you created.

▶ **INTERPRET** What does your work express? Interpret your artistic decisions. Give your sculpture a title that reflects its form and mood.

▶ **JUDGE** Do you think this work is successful? Use one or more of the three aesthetic theories explained in Chapter 2.

▲ **FIGURE 5.35A**

Student work.

STUDIO PROJECT *Free-Form Clay Sculpture* | **123**

Contrast Drawing

▲ **FIGURE 5.36**

Rembrandt van Rijn. *Aristotle with a Bust of Homer.* 1653. 143.5 × 136.5 cm (56¹/₂ × 53³/₄″). The Metropolitan Museum of Art, New York, New York. Purchase, special contributions and funds given or bequeathed by friends of the Museum, 1961. (61.198).

SUPPLIES

- Charcoal, colored pencils (gray tones and black), or soft (4B) and medium (2B) pencils
- Tensor lamp or other strong light source
- Camera with black-and-white film
- Sketchbook and pencil
- White drawing paper
- Scrap paper

Historical and Cultural Context

Rembrandt van Rijn is one of the best-known artists of all times and is considered the greatest Dutch artist of the 1600s. He completed numerous portraits, including more than 100 self-portraits, in addition to landscapes and religious art. Rembrandt often used chiaroscuro for dramatic effect. The technique creates a high level of contrast between the subject and background. Sometimes, as in **Figure 5.36,** it almost appears as though the subject were illuminated by a spotlight. Notice how the light emphasizes the connection between the human figure—the philosopher Aristotle—and the bust of Homer, a great storyteller of the ancient world. Study Aristotle's face and body language. What do they tell you about his feelings toward this great author?

What You Will Learn

You will create a black-and-white drawing, using direct observation and a choice of drawing media: charcoal, gray to black colored pencils, or 4B and 2B graphite pencils. In your artwork, you will use chiaroscuro to create a sense of dramatic contrast and to emphasize some aspect of the subject.

Creating

Work in pairs in a darkened room, such as a closet, with a strong light source. Partners will take turns role-playing "model" and "artist." The model is to pose for a portrait. The artist should experiment with angling the light source on the subject to create dramatic contrast. The artist should take several black-and-white photographs. The artist and model should then switch roles.

Step 1 Select one photo that interests you most, and in your sketchbook, create a study for the work. A *study* is a preparatory sketch or painting. Your study can be either a contour or gesture drawing (see page 428). Make sure that you indicate areas of light and dark.

Step 2 Transfer your study onto a sheet of drawing paper. Do not worry if you are unable to capture your subject's exact likeness. Your chief goal is to make a dramatic statement through contrast. Decide which aspect of the subject you will emphasize through the use of light and dark.

Step 3 Apply shading techniques, using pressure, the edge of your medium, or both. (For more on shading effects, see page 429.) Start with the darkest areas and work toward the lightest areas. As you complete areas of the work, cover these with clean scrap paper to prevent smudging.

Step 4 As you work, stop periodically to assess your progress. Check to see that there is interplay between light and shadow, as in Figure 5.36.

Step 5 Use an art gum eraser to remove any stray marks or smudges. Mount your finished artwork. Give it a title that best describes the mood of the work.

Evaluating Your Work

▶ **DESCRIBE** What is the subject of your drawing? What drawing medium did you use? What shading techniques did you employ to create the light and dark areas in your drawing?

▶ **ANALYZE** Explain how you have used chiaroscuro in this particular drawing. Compare and contrast your use of light and dark values. Are there places where light gradually blends into darkness? Did you use the principle of emphasis?

▶ **INTERPRET** Can the viewer identify the mood that you have captured without glancing at the title? Does your work's title express the mood you feel the drawing conveys?

▶ **JUDGE** Do you consider your drawing successful? Evaluate your artistic decisions. Which aesthetic theory would you use to judge your artwork?

▲ **FIGURE 5.36A**

Student work.

STUDIO PROJECT 5-3

Digital Genre Scene

▲ **FIGURE 5.37**

Antonio Ruiz. *The Bicycle Race*. 1938. Oil on canvas. 33.3 × 43.2 cm (13$\frac{1}{8}$ × 17"). Philadelphia Museum of Art, Philadelphia, Pennsylvania. Purchased with the Nebinger Fund.

SUPPLIES

- Digital camera or scanner
- Computer
- Image-editing or paint program
- Printing paper
- Sketchbook and pencil
- Graphics drawing tablet (optional)

Historical and Cultural Context

The painting in **Figure 5.37** is by twentieth-century Mexican artist Antonio Ruiz. You don't need to look at the title of the work to know that it is a depiction of a bicycle race. What is unique about Ruiz's painting is the perspective of the event he shows us. We, the viewers, stand directly in the path of the leading cyclists as they bear down on the finish line!

Notice that Ruiz creates the illusion of deep space by using all six perspective techniques: overlapping of objects, size, placement, detail, color, and converging lines. Note also that, despite the crowds of people in the painting, Ruiz fills his composition with space and light by placing most of the people at the sides of the road.

What You Will Learn

In this project, you will create a digital genre scene that creates the illusion of deep space. A *genre scene* is an artwork depicting an event from everyday life—in this case, from your own. As in Figure 5.37, you will use as many of the six perspective techniques as you can. Using a digital or traditional camera, you will capture an ordinary, everyday scene or event. Then you will import or scan the images into an image-editing or paint application to experiment with perspective techniques.

Creating

Think for a moment about everyday experiences or places that have a special meaning for you. List them. Make notes and sketches in your sketchbook. Plan how you will draw from your experiences to create the visual solutions for your scene. Will there be one or more people in your scene? Will you place yourself in the scene? Apply perspective techniques to help you create the illusion of depth. Place larger, more vividly colored and detailed shapes in the foreground. Overlap some objects. Make the scene unique. Consider photographing the genre scene from a unique angle to take advantage of converging lines.

Step 1 List every person or object you will need to stage your scene. When everything is set up, take several images of your subject in its space from different angles.

Step 2 Download your digital images or scan your photos into the computer, and select your best composition. Get opinions from your classmates and teacher to help you select your strongest image.

Step 3 Save your best image. Be sure to choose a file format compatible with the image-editing program you will use and a resolution to match the printer's output.

Step 4 Using the tools available in your image-editing program, begin to paint, layer, distort, change lighting, and/or add text to your image. Experiment with various tools and controls.

Step 5 Study the final choice carefully, and make changes to your digital image, if necessary. When satisfied, save and print your work.

Evaluating Your Work

▶ **DESCRIBE** What experience did you draw from for your genre scene? Do people appear in the setting? Did you add extra objects? What were they? What kind of a camera did you use? How did you download the image into the computer? What software tools did you use to modify your digital image?

▶ **ANALYZE** Did you achieve the illusion of deep space in your image? Compare and contrast the perspective techniques you used to create deep space.

▶ **INTERPRET** Were you successful in expressing your feelings about the place or event? Give the image a title that sums up the feelings or mood you were trying to express.

▶ **JUDGE** Were you successful in staging your genre scene to achieve the illusion of depth? Use one or more of the three aesthetic theories to justify your judgment of this work.

▲ **FIGURE 5.37A**

Student work.

Shape, Form, and Space

The elements of shape, form, and space are closely related. Each is defined by the others. A square stretched into a third dimension becomes a cube. A pyramid squashed flat becomes a triangle. The area around and between these shapes and forms is space. As you examine the student works on this page:

- Compare and contrast the elements of shape, form, and space.
- Analyze the use of these formal qualities in artworks, forming precise conclusions about their relationships to one another.

Activity 5.38 **Geometric form.** What geometric form is used to create the hat in this portrait? Identify specific art techniques that were used to give depth to this and other forms.

Activity 5.39 **Positive and negative space.** Compare the artist's use of positive and negative space. Which objects in the work are figure, and which are ground? What mood is suggested by the interaction between the positive and negative space?

▲ **FIGURE 5.38**

Student work. *Gordon*. Pastel.

▲ **FIGURE 5.39**

Student work. *Thinking*. Charcoal and pencil.

Activity 5.40 **Identifying shape.**
What is the shape of this art object?
Is the shape geometric or free-form?

◀ **FIGURE 5.40**

Student work.

ART *Online*
To view more student artworks visit the Glencoe Student Art Gallery at **art.glencoe.com**.

For Your Portfolio

Select and Analyze Portfolios. As you begin to build your portfolio of artworks, it can be useful to evaluate the work of your peers and others. Work with your teacher to compile a collection of portfolios. Select and analyze these portfolios by peers and other artists to form precise conclusions about formal qualities (the elements and principles of art), historical and cultural contexts, intents, and meanings. Store your evaluations in your portfolio.

Visual Art ⟹ Journal

Shapes and forms are everywhere. They make up the environment. As you walk or ride through your community, keep an eye open for shapes and forms. Notice the space around them and how forms extend into three-dimensional space. Draw and label these shapes, forms, and spaces in your visual journal.

Art Criticism
in Action

▲ FIGURE 5.41

Deborah Butterfield. *Woodrow*. 1988. Bronze. 251.5 × 266.7 × 188 cm (99 × 105 × 74″). Walker Art Center, Minneapolis, Minnesota. Gift of Harriet and Edson W. Spencer, 1988.

Critiquing the Artwork

▶ **1** **DESCRIBE** *What do you see?*
List all the information found in the credit line.

- When was this work completed? Who is the artist?
- What object is depicted in this sculpture?
- What is unusual about the medium listed in the credit line?

▶ **2** **ANALYZE** *How is this work organized?*
This is a clue-collecting step about the elements of art.

- Is the work two- or three-dimensional? Geometric or free-form?
- Is this form open or closed? Active or static?
- Compare and contrast the use of form and space in this sculpture.

▶ **3** **INTERPRET** *What message does this sculpture communicate to you?*
Combine the clues you have collected to form a creative interpretation of the work.

- How do you think it would feel to walk around this sculpture? Would the horse appear the same from every viewpoint? Explain.
- The artist went to great lengths to imitate wood in cast bronze. Form a conclusion about her intent. Why didn't she simply use wood in the first place?
- What feeling about horses does the work communicate to you? Why?

▶ **4** **JUDGE** *What do you think of the work?*
Decide if this is a successful work of art.

- Do you think the artist constructed *Woodrow* with appropriate materials? Why?
- Do you think this is a successful work of art? Why or why not? Use one or more of the aesthetic theories you have learned to defend your decision.

ARCHITECTURAL FORMS

Frank Gehry's unusual buildings have forms that make people stop in their tracks.

L ike all architects, Frank Gehry deals with shape, form, and space when he designs buildings. But instead of creating buildings with pure box-like forms, Gehry's buildings curve, swoop, and tilt.

Frank Gehry was born in 1929 in Toronto, Canada. In 1947, he and his family moved to Los Angeles, where he studied architecture. Gehry liked the contemporary, nontraditional building styles he saw there. He was also introduced to the shapes and forms of sculpture. These sculptural forms influenced his building design. An office complex he designed in Prague, Czech Republic, has two towers that lean into one another. To some people, the towers seem to be dancing together. Gehry's Guggenheim Museum in Bilbao, Spain, resembles a spaceship that has landed in an ancient town (Figure 14.1, page 388).

One of Gehry's best-known works is the Experience Music Project in Seattle, Washington. The lines of this rock-and-roll museum twist and curve to look like parts of a giant smashed guitar. The walls are made of thousands of titanium and stainless steel panels. Each panel is cut in a different shape. Gehry used specially designed computer software to help fit the pieces together. Like most of Gehry's work, this building rocks!

DOUGLAS PEEBLES/CORBIS

ABOVE: The Experience Music Project in Seattle, Washington. BELOW: A Gehry building in Prague, Czech Republic, features two towers that remind some people of the dancers Fred Astaire and Ginger Rogers.

GETTY IMAGES

TIME to Connect

When Frank Gehry was a boy, he made models of buildings from scraps of wood. Architects make small models of buildings based on drawings. Models give them an idea of how the project will look when it is finished. The models are made to scale. For example, in a model, an inch may represent 10 feet of the actual building size.

- Design a two-story office building. Sketch the front view.

- Draw the front to scale on graph paper. Each box on the graph paper should represent a certain number of feet.

Building Vocabulary

On a separate sheet of paper, write the term that best matches each definition given below.

1. A two-dimensional area that is defined in some way.
2. Precise shapes that can be described using mathematical formulas.
3. Irregular and uneven shapes.
4. Objects having three dimensions.
5. The element of art that refers to the emptiness or area between, around, above, below, or within objects.
6. Images in three dimensions created with a laser beam.
7. The arrangement of light and shadow.
8. Small areas of white used to show the very brightest spots.
9. A graphic system that creates the illusion of depth and volume on a two-dimensional surface.

Reviewing Art Facts

Answer the following questions using complete sentences.

10. Name the two basic types of shapes and tell which is more often used in decoration.
11. What is the difference between shapes and forms?
12. Name the two kinds of space found in art.
13. Using a portrait as an example, name the kind of space the subject occupies.
14. Explain how the eyes and brain enable us to see in three dimensions.
15. Explain how an artist creates the illusion of three-dimensional form on a two-dimensional surface.
16. Name six devices for creating perspective.
17. Give an example of an active shape and tell what makes it look active.

Thinking Critically About Art

18. **Synthesize.** *The Kiss* (Figure 5.9, page 104) and *Bird in Space* (Figure 5.30, page 118) are two of Brancusi's abstract works. Make a list of the similarities and differences between them. Do you think his style has changed over the years? Explain and defend the conclusions you reach in a few paragraphs.

19. **Historical/Cultural Heritage.** Review the Meet the Artist feature on page 105. Compare and contrast Figure 5.10 by Escher with Figure 1.11 on page 13 by Romare Bearden. How do both works share a general theme in relation to the illusion of depth? How are they different?

Journey to the Dallas Museum of Art by clicking on the **Web Museum Tour** link at www.glencoe.com. Analyze how a group of Texas artists working in a variety of media have used shape, form, and space in their artworks. View these rich and diverse artworks, read about the artists, and then test yourself with questions prepared by the museum's curators.

Linking to the Performing Arts

Use Performing Arts Handbook page 417 to find out how dancer and choreographer Bella Lewitsky uses the elements of shape and form in dance to express her impressions of Henry Moore's art.

▲ **FIGURE 6.1** Notice the variety of colors used in this painting. Where in your environment do you find colors like these? Are these calming colors? If not, how would you describe them?

Wassily Kandinsky. *Tension in Red*. 1926. Oil on board. 66 × 53.7 cm (26 × 21⅛″). The Solomon R. Guggenheim Museum, New York, New York. Gift, Solomon R. Guggenheim, 1938. © 2003 Artists Rights Society (ARS), New York/ADAGP, Paris.

CHAPTER 6

Color

Color is everywhere. We see it in the blue of the sky and in the yellows, reds, and oranges of the changing autumn leaves. The expressive qualities of color are so powerful that they can create instant emotional reactions. The color green can be soothing; the color red, exciting.

In this chapter, you will:

- Identify hue, value, and intensity as the properties of color.
- Compare and contrast the use of color and value in different artworks.
- Demonstrate effective use of color art media in drawing, painting, and design.
- Analyze the use of color in the artworks of others to express meaning.

Focus on **Art History** **Figure 6.1** was painted by the Russian artist Wassily Kandinsky (1866–1944). Kandinsky was a founder of the "Der Blaue Reiter" (The Blue Rider) movement. The group followed the art style known as Expressionism. Its goal was to express raw emotion, mainly through composition. Kandinsky, an innovator, created abstract compositions at a time when most artists were producing lifelike subjects. He also stood out by using bold, brash colors as a unifying element.

Interpret. Study the bright colors and sharp, angular lines of Figure 6.1. Read the title. Do you think the title captures the mood of this work? Do you experience tension and unrest in this work, or do you find it peaceful and calm?

Vocabulary

color
color spectrum
hue
color wheel
value
tint
shade
intensity
complementary colors

Hue, Value, and Intensity

Color is the most expressive element of art. It shares a powerful connection with emotion. That relationship is why we hear people say, "I'm feeling blue," or, "She was green with envy." The connection of color to emotion is also illustrated in a question we often ask friends—"What's your favorite color?" Almost everyone has a favorite color. It might remind us of a favorite childhood toy or a piece of clothing that we love to wear. Our appreciation of color affects many of the choices we make.

In this lesson you will learn what color is and how you see it. You will learn the properties of color. You will also learn how to mix colors to create shades you might use in your artwork.

How We See Color

Color is *an element of art that is derived from reflected light.* You see color because light waves are reflected from objects to your eyes **(Figure 6.2).** White light from the sun is actually a combination of all colors.

When light passes through a wedge-shaped glass, called a prism, the beam of white light is bent and separated into bands of color, called the **color spectrum.**

▲ ▶ **FIGURE 6.2** Chagall has used many different tints and shades of blue. He has also used a few other colors for emphasis. Identify some of the objects he has emphasized this way. As the light outside changes throughout the day, how do you think the artwork changes? What if the day were stormy or rainy? How do you think the artist planned for this?

Marc Chagall. *The American Windows.* 1977. Stained glass. The Art Institute of Chicago, Chicago, Illinois. Gift of the Auxiliary Board of The Art Institute of Chicago in memory of Richard J. Daley, 1977. 938. © 2003 Artists Rights Society (ARS), New York/ADAGP, Paris.

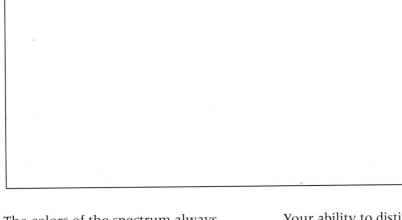

◀ **FIGURE 6.3** What color do you see when you shift your gaze from the red to the white area? Your eyes can fool you about color.

The colors of the spectrum always appear in the same order: red, orange, yellow, green, blue, and violet.

A rainbow is a natural example of a spectrum. Rainbows occur when sunlight is bent by water, oil, or a glass prism. You can find rainbows in the sky after a storm, in the spray from a garden hose, or in a puddle of oil.

We see color because objects absorb some of these light waves and reflect others. A red apple looks red because it reflects red waves and absorbs the rest of the colors. Special color receptors in your eyes detect the color of the reflected light waves. Another type of receptor detects the lightness or darkness of the color. Colors don't change.

Your ability to distinguish between them does. That is why your eyes have trouble seeing colors in dim light. Not enough light is reflected off of objects for you to see their color.

When you are looking at colors, your eyes can sometimes fool you. For instance, stare at the bright red shape in **Figure 6.3** for 30 seconds; then quickly shift your gaze to the white area below it. Did you see a green shape on the white surface? This is called an *afterimage*. It occurs because the receptors in your eyes retain the visual stimulation even after it has ceased. Your brain creates the afterimage as a reaction to the color you stared at originally.

LESSON 1   *Hue, Value, and Intensity*   **137**

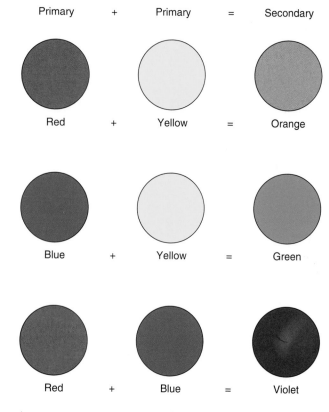

Primary	+	Primary	=	Secondary
Red	+	Yellow	=	Orange
Blue	+	Yellow	=	Green
Red	+	Blue	=	Violet

▲ **FIGURE 6.4** Primary and secondary hues.

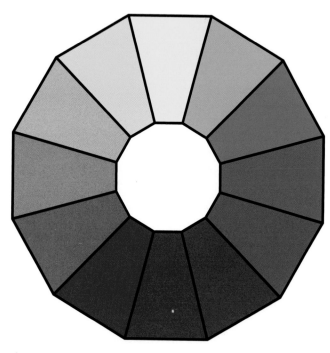

▲ **FIGURE 6.5** The color wheel.

The afterimage of a color is the opposite of that color. Green is the opposite of red. So the afterimage of green is the color red. The afterimage of black is white, and the afterimage of blue is orange. An afterimage isn't a strong color—it is only the ghost of a color. Some artists make use of the way your eyes work when they create optical illusions of color and movement.

Three properties of color work together to make the colors we see. These properties are *hue, value,* and *intensity.*

Hue

Hue is *the name of a color in the color spectrum,* such as red, blue, or yellow. Red, yellow, and blue are the *primary* hues. You cannot make primary hues by mixing other hues together. However, by combining the three primary colors and black and white, you can produce every other color.

The *secondary* hues are made by mixing two primary colors **(Figure 6.4).** Red and yellow make orange; red and blue make violet; and blue and yellow make green. Orange, violet, and green are the secondary hues.

The six *intermediate* colors are made by mixing a primary color with its secondary color. For example, red and orange make red-orange, red and violet make red-violet, blue and violet make blue-violet, and so on. You can make many additional variations by combining the intermediate colors.

A **color wheel** is *the spectrum bent into a circle.* It is a useful tool for organizing colors. The color wheel in **Figure 6.5** is a twelve-color wheel showing the three primary, three secondary, and six intermediate hues.

Other Color Systems

The three primary hues—red, yellow, and blue—are specifically the primary hues of pigment found in paints, pastels, or colored pencils. There are different color systems that apply to the colors seen on computer screens and those printed in magazines and photographs.

The primary colors of light, as on a computer screen, are red, green, and blue, commonly referred to as RGB. Because these colors are created by adding light, the pigment color system does not apply.

Another color system is used by printers—the CMYK color system. CMYK is short for the four primary colors of this system—cyan (also called process blue), magenta, yellow, and black. If you have worked with computer graphics software, you have probably seen references to CMYK color.

Value

Value is *the art element that describes the darkness or lightness of a color.* The amount of light a color reflects determines its color value. Not all hues of the spectrum have the same value. Yellow is the lightest hue because it reflects the most light. Violet is the darkest hue because it reflects the least light.

Black, white, and gray are *neutral colors* **(Figure 6.6).** When white light shines on a white object, the object reflects all of the color waves and does not absorb any. As a result, you see the color of all the light, which is white.

▲ **Figure 6.6** Neutral colors: black, gray, and white.

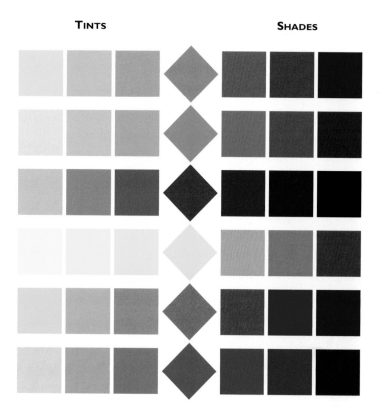

▲ **FIGURE 6.7** Color value scales.

A black object absorbs all of the color waves. Black reflects no light; black is the absence of light. Gray is impure white—it reflects an equal part of each color wave. The more light that gray reflects, the lighter it looks; the more it absorbs, the darker it looks.

You can change the value of any hue by adding black or white **(Figure 6.7)**. *A light value of a hue is called a* **tint,** *and a dark value of a hue is called a* **shade.** The term *shade* is often used incorrectly to refer to both tints and shades. A tint is created by adding white; a shade is created by adding black.

When artists want to show a bright, sunny day, they use tints **(Figure 6.8)**. Paintings having many tints are referred to as *high-key* paintings. Cassatt's *Margot in Blue* is an example of a high-key painting. *Low-key* paintings have shades,

▶ **FIGURE 6.8** Everything except Margot's eyes and hair are painted with tints of color. Even the shadow in the upper left corner of the picture has been softened with gray. The white highlights shimmer and create the effect of a sunny day.

Mary Cassatt. *Margot in Blue.* 1902. Pastel. 61 × 50 cm (24 × 19⅞"). The Walters Art Gallery, Baltimore, Maryland.

or dark values, which are used when the artist wants to represent dark, gloomy days, nighttime, and dusk. Dark values can add a feeling of mystery to a work. They can also be used to create a sense of foreboding or danger **(Figure 6.9)**.

If the change in value is gradual, the design produces a calm feeling. If the values take large leaps up and down the scale, from almost white to almost black, the artwork has an active, even nervous, effect.

◀ **FIGURE 6.9** The dark values in this work enhance its ominous mood. Every hue in this work has been darkened with the addition of black except one. Which hue has not been changed? Why?

Rufino Tamayo. *Girl Attacked by a Strange Bird.* 1947. Oil on canvas. 177.8 × 127.3 cm (70 × 50⅛″). Museum of Modern Art, New York, New York. Gift of Mr. and Mrs. Charles Zadok.

Demonstrating Effective Use of Art Media and Tools in Painting. Select a hue. Draw a row of three equal shapes. If you are using an opaque paint, such as tempera, add only a small amount of the hue to white with a brush or palette knife. Fill the first shape with the light value. Paint the second shape with the pure hue. Add a small amount of black to the hue to create a dark value, and paint this in the third shape.

If you are using a transparent watercolor paint, make a light value by thinning the paint with water to let more white paper show through. Make a hue darker by adding a small amount of black. Fill the three shapes as in the above directions.

Computer Option. Look at the color palette of your software program. Choose only the tints and shades of one hue to create a computer drawing of a simple cityscape or underwater scene. Colors do not have to be used realistically. Your software program will determine the number of tints and shades that you can use. If your software has the capabilities, mix your own tints and shades for use in this assignment.

Intensity

Intensity is *the brightness or dullness of a hue* (**Figure 6.10**). If a surface reflects only yellow light waves, for example, you see an intensely bright yellow. If a surface reflects other light waves, the color will appear duller. A pure or bright hue is called a *high-intensity color*. Dull hues are called *low-intensity colors*.

Complementary colors are *the colors opposite each other on the color wheel.* The complement, or opposite, of a hue absorbs all of the light waves that the hue reflects (**Figure 6.11**). Red and green are complements. Green absorbs red waves and reflects blue and yellow waves. (Blue and yellow waves combine to appear green.) Red absorbs blue and yellow waves and reflects red waves.

Mixing a hue with its complement dulls the hue, or lowers its intensity. The more complement you add to a hue, the duller the hue looks. Eventually, the hue will lose its own color quality and appear a neutral gray.

The hue used in the greatest amount in a mixture becomes dominant. For this reason, a mixture might look dull

▲ **FIGURE 6.10** Intensity scale. This scale shows how the intensity of one hue changes as you add its complement to it. The first box is pure, high-intensity green. Each time you add more red, the green becomes duller. Eventually the even mix of green and red creates an interesting, low-intensity gray.

orange or dull blue, depending on the amount of color used. Orange and blue mixtures usually yield brownish results.

Hue, value, and intensity do not operate independently. They rely on one another to create all of the colors that you see around you. When you observe colors, you will see dull tints and bright tints, dull shades and bright shades, light hues and dark hues. Knowing the three properties of color helps you to understand and use color.

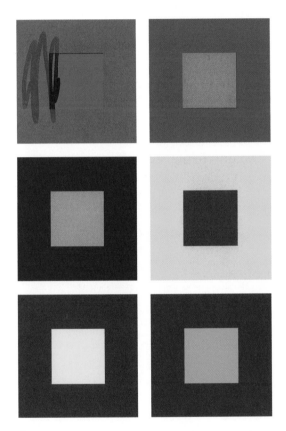

▲ **FIGURE 6.11** Sets of complements. The left column are sets of primary and secondary complements. The right column are sets of intermediate complements.

Activity	Working with Intensity

Applying Your Skills. Contrary to what you may have thought, tree trunks are not really brown. They reflect a variety of light and dark low-intensity grays. Draw seven or more bare trees on a large sheet of white paper. Use real trees as models, if possible; if not, find photographs. Combine varying amounts of one primary color and its complement as well as white and black to create a number of different, low-intensity light- and dark-valued colors. Then use these colors to paint each tree a different color.

Computer Option. Design a simple motif using only two solid colors. Use Copy and Paste options to make five copies of the motif. Fill each motif with one primary color or intermediate color and its complement. If your software has the capabilities, mix the two complements together to create a dull or low-intensity version of each. Label each set of complements and mixture sets.

 ## Check Your Understanding

1. What are the three properties of color?
2. Define *color wheel*. What does a color wheel show?
3. Describe the difference between tint and shade.
4. Compare and contrast the use of value in Figure 6.8 on page 140 and Figure 6.9 on page 141.

monochromatic
analogous colors

Color Schemes

Colors are like musical instruments. Each instrument has its own special sound. When you hear an instrument in an orchestra, the sound you hear is affected by the sounds of the other instruments. When the musicians tune up before a performance, you hear confusing, even unpleasant, noises. When they play together in an organized way, they can make beautiful sounds. In the same way, putting colors together without a plan can be confusing and unpleasant to your eyes. Color without organization can look like a visual argument. A plan for organizing colors is called a color scheme.

When two colors come into direct contact, their differences are more obvious. A yellow-green surrounded by a green looks even more yellow. A yellow-green surrounded by yellow, however, appears greener. Grayish-green will seem brighter when it is placed against a gray background. This effect is called simultaneous contrast **(Figure 6.12).**

A color scheme is a plan for organizing colors according to their relationship on the color wheel. By following a color scheme, you can avoid putting together colors in a confusing or unpleasant way. The following are some of the most frequently used color schemes.

▶ **FIGURE 6.12**
Your perception of any color is affected by the colors that surround it. This effect is called simultaneous contrast.

Monochromatic Colors

Monochrome means one color. A **mono-chromatic** color scheme is *a color scheme that uses only one hue and the tints and shades of that hue.* Because this is such a limited scheme, it has a strong, unifying effect on a design **(Figure 6.13).** It is very easy to organize furniture or clothing using monochromatic colors. The drawback to a monochromatic color scheme is that it can be boring.

Analogous Colors

Analogous colors are *colors that sit side by side on the color wheel and have a common hue* **(Figure 6.14).** Violet, red-violet, red, red-orange, and orange all have red in common. A narrow color scheme would be limited to only three hues, such as violet, red-violet, and red. An analogous color scheme creates a design that ties one shape to the next through a common color (see Figure 13.34 on page 380).

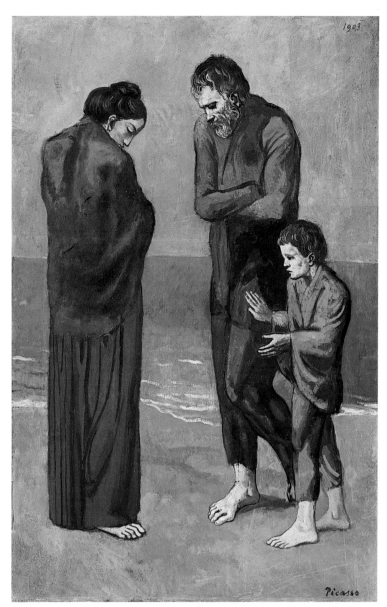

▲ **FIGURE 6.13** The artist has captured the sad mood of these people by using a monochromatic blue color scheme. He has kept it interesting by using the full range of tints and shades from white to black. Where are the whitest areas? Where are the blackest areas? Look at the title. Does the painting evoke this feeling?

Pablo Picasso. *The Tragedy.* 1903. Oil on wood. 105 × 69 cm (41½ × 27⅛"). National Gallery of Art, Washington D.C. © 1998 Board of Trustees. Chester Dale Collection. © 2003 Estate of Pablo Picasso/Artists Rights Society (ARS), New York.

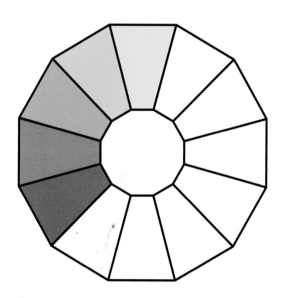

▲ **FIGURE 6.14** Analogous colors are related.

Complementary Colors

The strongest contrast of a hue is produced by complementary colors. When a pair of high-intensity complements are placed side by side, they seem to vibrate. It is difficult to focus on the edge where the complements touch. Some artists use this visual vibration to create special effects. They make designs that sparkle, snap, and sizzle as if charged with electricity **(Figure 6.15)**.

Complementary color schemes are exciting. They are loud, and they demand to be noticed. They are frequently used to catch the viewer's attention. How many ways do people use the red-and-green color scheme? Where else have you seen complementary color schemes used to grab attention?

Not all color schemes based on complements are loud and demanding. If the hues are of low intensity, the contrast is not so harsh. Changing the values of the hues will also soften the effect of the design.

Color Triads

A color triad is composed of three colors spaced an equal distance apart on the color wheel. The contrast between triad colors is not as strong as that between complements. The primary triad is composed of red, yellow, and blue. The secondary triad contains orange, green, and violet **(Figure 6.16)**.

A high-intensity primary triad is very difficult to work with. The contrast between the three hues is so strong that they might make people uncomfortable. A triad can be made more comfortable to the viewer by changing the intensity or values **(Figure 6.17)**. A triad of secondary colors is less disturbing.

▲ **FIGURE 6.15** Which set of complementary colors dominates this painting? Where is the contrast the strongest? Which area has the dullest contrast? Explain how the artist has done this?

Piet Mondrian. *Sun, Church in Zeeland*. 1910. Oil on canvas. 90.5 × 62.1 × 2.9 cm (35³⁄₈ × 24¹⁄₂ × 1¹⁄₈″). Tate Gallery, London, England. © Tate Gallery, London/Art Resource, NY. ARS, NY.

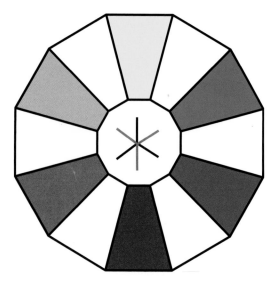

▲ **FIGURE 6.16** Color triads.

▲ **FIGURE 6.17** Even though this painting is based on the primary triad, it is very comfortable to view. How has the artist organized the colors to make this painting easy to look at?

Fritz Glarner. *Relational Painting, Tondo #40*. 1955–56. Oil on Masonite. Diameter: 111.8 cm (44"). Walker Art Center, Minneapolis, Minnesota. Gift of the T. B. Walker Foundation, 1956.

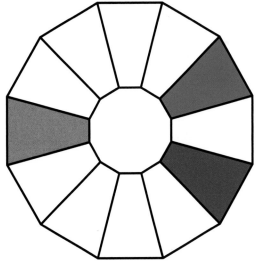

▲ **FIGURE 6.18** Split complement.

Split Complements

A *split complement* is the combination of one hue plus the hues on each side of its complement **(Figure 6.18).** This is easier to work with than a straight complementary scheme because it offers more variety. For example, start with red-orange. Check the color wheel to find its complement, blue-green. The two hues next to blue-green are blue and green. Red-orange, blue, and green form a split-complementary color scheme.

Warm and Cool Colors

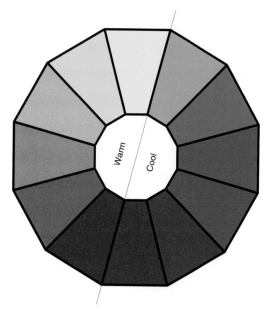

Sometimes the colors are divided into two groups, called *warm* and *cool* (**Figure 6.19**). Warm colors are red, orange, and yellow. They are usually associated with warm things, such as sunshine or fire (**Figure 6.20**). Cool colors are blue, green, and violet. They are usually associated with cool things, such as ice, snow, water, or grass (**Figure 6.21**). Warm colors seem to move toward the viewer and cool colors seem to recede, or move away.

▲ **FIGURE 6.19** Warm and cool colors.

▲ **FIGURE 6.20** Albizu is a Puerto Rican artist. Many of her paintings were commissioned by jazz musician Stan Getz to be used as covers for his record albums. Can you see how the small areas of black jump out from the warm colors to visually suggest music with a Latin jazz beat?

Olga Albizu. *Growth*. c. 1960. Oil on canvas. 127 × 107 cm (50 × 42⅛″). Lowe Art Museum, University of Miami, Miami, Florida. Gift of Esso Inter-American, Inc.

The amount of warmth or coolness is relative. Violet on a red background appears much cooler than violet alone. However, the same violet on a blue background seems much warmer than the violet alone.

▲ **FIGURE 6.21** The title for this work can be translated as "sad fact" or "sad figure" or even "metaphor for sadness." Examine the work to find a figure sitting in the center with legs and torso bent. The figure is surrounded by intersecting blue, black, and white shapes. Does the color scheme enhance the mood the artist intended to convey? Explain.

Francis Picabia. *Figure Triste*. 1912. Oil on canvas. 118.1 × 119.4 cm (46½ × 47″). Albright-Knox Art Gallery, Buffalo, New York. Gift of the Seymour H. Knox Foundation, Inc., 1968. © 2003 Artists Rights Society (ARS) New York/ADAGP, Paris.

Activity
Using Color Schemes

Demonstrating Effective Use of Art Media in Design. In your sketchbook, draw several squares. Arrange your initials or the letters of your name in a design in one of the squares. The letters must touch the four edges of the square. Do several different designs using the remaining squares. Play with the letters—turn them upside down, twist them out of shape, make them fat, or overlap them. Consider the letters as shapes. They do not have to be readable.

When you find a design you like, reproduce it on four squares of white paper. Now paint each design using one of the following color schemes: monochromatic, analogous, complementary, triad, split-complementary, warm, or cool. How do the color arrangements affect the design?

Computer Option. Create a design with the initials or letters of your name. The letters must touch the four edges of the screen. Experiment with the letters—make them different sizes and turn them upside down or twist them out of shape. They do not have to be readable.

When you find a design you like, save it. Use various tools to fill in all the shapes, lines, and spaces with each of the following color schemes: monochromatic, analogous, complementary, triad, split-complementary, warm, and cool.

When you finish all the color schemes, evaluate their effect on the basic design.

Check Your Understanding

1. Describe a monochromatic color scheme.
2. What types of colors, when placed side by side, seem to vibrate?
3. Compare and contrast the color schemes in Figures 6.20 and 6.21.

Vocabulary

pigments
binder
solvent
dyes

Understanding the Nature and Uses of Color

Artists use color to create special effects in art. Not only do they use color to depict objects the way they actually look, but artists also use color to express ideas and emotions **(Figure 6.22).** By experimenting with color, you will learn what it can do, and you will learn how to use it so that you achieve the results you want. Understanding the nature and uses of color allows you to express yourself artistically.

Paint

All paints used in art are made up of three basic ingredients: pigment, binder, and solvent. Artists' **pigments** are *finely ground, colored powders that form paint when mixed with a binder.* Pigment colors cannot match the purity and intensity of the colors of light. The **binder** is *a material that holds together the grains of pigment* in a form that can be spread over some surface. Linseed oil is the binder for oil paints. Wax is used for encaustic paint, gum arabic for watercolor paints, and acrylic polymer for acrylic paints. A chemical emulsion is used to make school tempera paint. Many professional artists use a traditional method of mixing pure pigments with egg yolk for a translucent tempera paint. These binders each give different qualities to the paint.

The **solvent** is *the liquid that controls the thickness or the thinness of the paint.* Turpentine is the solvent for oil paints. Water is the solvent for watercolors and tempera. Water or acrylic medium is the solvent for wet acrylic paints, but once acrylic paint dries, it is waterproof.

Paint pigments do not dissolve—they remain suspended in the binder. When applied, the pigments stay on top of the surface and dry there. *Pigments that dissolve in liquid* are called **dyes.** Dyes do not remain on the surface as paints do. Dyes sink into and color the surface by staining it.

Visual Effects of Paint

The pigment, the binder, the solvent, and the surface to which the paint is applied all affect the color you see. Wet colors look brighter and darker than dry ones. Tempera and watercolor paints look duller and lighter after they dry. Oil paints glow even when dry because of their oil binder. If diluted with turpentine, oil paints dry to a dull finish.

The color and density of the surface receiving the paint affects the way the light waves will be reflected back to your eyes. If you apply red paint to a colored surface and to a white surface, your eyes will perceive the red paint differently on each surface. The colored surface absorbs some light waves, whereas the white surface reflects all light waves.

Have you ever tried to match colors that are on two different surfaces? A brown leather bag can never truly match a fuzzy brown sweater. Dense surfaces always look brighter because they reflect more light.

American (b.1940)

Elizabeth Murray was born in Chicago in 1940. From an early age, she showed an interest in art, which her parents encouraged. In elementary school she sold drawings of elephants, cowboys, and stagecoaches to her classmates for 25 cents apiece. This early success kept her interest in art alive.

A high school teacher recognized her talent and created a scholarship for her at the Art Institute of Chicago. Murray took classes in figure drawing, landscape painting, and traditional techniques. She walked through the exhibit halls of the Art Institute museum. Surrounded by masterpieces, she was inspired to become a painter.

In the 1960s, she was told that painting was dead. Everything that could be done had been done. Murray refused to listen and kept painting. Through her perseverance, she developed a style that combines painting with sculpture. Murray is now considered a master of the shaped canvas.

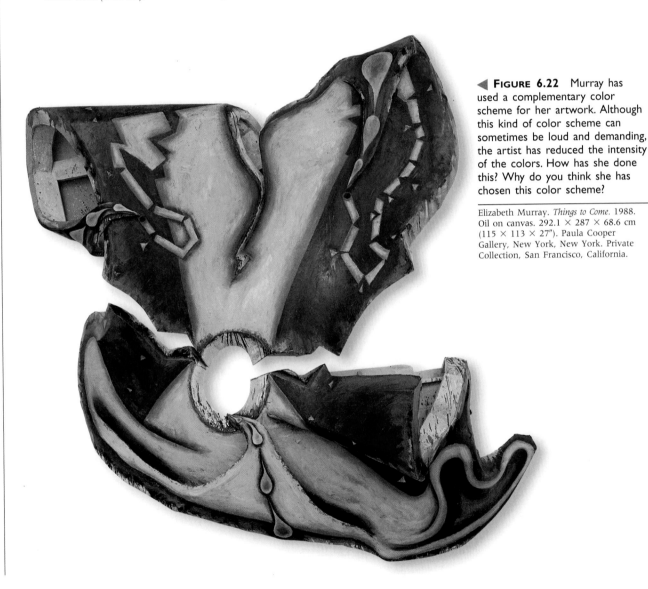

◀ **FIGURE 6.22** Murray has used a complementary color scheme for her artwork. Although this kind of color scheme can sometimes be loud and demanding, the artist has reduced the intensity of the colors. How has she done this? Why do you think she has chosen this color scheme?

Elizabeth Murray. *Things to Come.* 1988. Oil on canvas. 292.1 × 287 × 68.6 cm (115 × 113 × 27″). Paula Cooper Gallery, New York, New York. Private Collection, San Francisco, California.

Sources of Pigment

In the past, pigments came from animals, vegetables, and minerals. A kind of beetle and the root of a certain plant were both sources for red pigment. Another plant produced a deep, transparent blue. Ultramarine blue was made by grinding a semiprecious stone. The color ocher was created by using natural clay colored by iron rust.

Today, synthetic (artificially made) pigments have been developed by scientists. The synthetics are brighter and more permanent than natural pigments, but some artists still prefer to use natural colors **(Figure 6.23)**. Many weavers color their yarns with natural dyes. Some contemporary painters use only natural earth pigments.

▶ **FIGURE 6.23** Aboriginal bark paintings enjoy a long cultural tradition in Australia. Like this one, they are typically created by applying natural pigments to eucalyptus bark.

Yäma Mununggiritj. *Yellow Ochre Quarry.* 1961. Natural pigments on eucalyptus bark. 69.9 × 30.5 cm (27$\frac{1}{2}$ × 12"). The Kluge-Ruhe Aboriginal Art Collection of the University of Virginia, Charlottesville, Virginia.

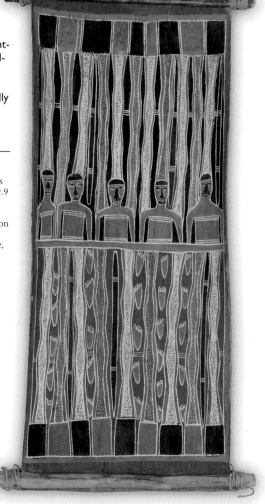

Activity	Mixing Colors

Applying Your Skills. Collect and grind three of your own earth pigments (see Technique Tip 11 on page 432 in the Handbook). Mix them with a binder and solvent and experiment with them. Try using a variety of brushes and surfaces. Finally, paint a design that shows all the colors you can obtain from the pigments.

Computer Option. Mixing colors with light on a computer is very different from mixing colors with pigment. If your computer software has the capabilities, practice making secondary and intermediate colors. Also mix tints, shades, and intensity changes. Fill a variety of geometric shapes with all the new colors you have made, and show off your work by filling your screen with repeated shapes.

The Expressive Effects of Color

Artists use color in the language of art. They use color to express thoughts, ideas, and emotions. There are many ways to use color to convey feelings, and realistic representation is only one of them.

Optical Color

Sometimes artists reproduce colors as they see them. Until the late nineteenth century, this was the way most Western artists painted. Artists would try to capture color as it actually appeared. As we saw earlier in the chapter, colors can change depending on their surroundings. For example, in an automobile dealer's showroom, the color of a blue car is affected by the light, the color of the floor and the walls, and even the colors of the other cars. The car may sparkle as it reflects the showroom lights. Shadows on the car may look dark blue or blue-violet. The red from the car next to it may cause a red-violet reflection on the blue surface.

A painter who is trying to show the car in its setting will use all the colors involved. He or she will make use of *optical color,* the color that results when a true color is affected by unusual lighting or its surroundings. Optical color is the color that people actually perceive. Compare the two paintings by Claude Monet in **Figures 6.24 and 6.25** to see how the time of day affects color.

The Impressionists were deeply involved with optical color and its relationship to light. They tried to express the sensation of light and atmosphere with their unique style of painting. They applied dots and dabs of colors from the spectrum. They did not mix black with any colors. They made gray, low-intensity colors by putting complements together instead of mixing just black and white. These low-intensity grays, such as dull blue and dull green, are much richer and look more natural in landscapes than do grays made by mixing black and white.

▲ **FIGURE 6.24** Monet was one of the first artists to paint outdoors. He realized that the colors of a scene changed as the sunlight changed; so he carried several canvasses to record the same scene at different times of the day.

Claude Monet. *Rouen Cathedral, West Façade.* 1894. Oil on canvas. 100 × 66 cm (39³⁄₈ × 25¹⁵⁄₁₆″). National Gallery of Art, Washington, D.C. Chester Dale Collection.

▲ **FIGURE 6.25** This is Monet's same view of the Rouen Cathedral façade painted in a different light than Figure 6.24. Compare and contrast this painting to Figure 6.24. Explain how the changes in color affect the mood of each work.

Claude Monet. *Rouen Cathedral, West Façade, Sunlight.* 1894. Oil on canvas. 100 × 66 cm (39³⁄₈ × 25¹⁵⁄₁₆″). National Gallery of Art, Washington, D.C. Chester Dale Collection.

Arbitrary Color

When artists use color to express feelings, they usually ignore the optical colors of objects. They choose the colors *arbitrarily,* that is, by personal preference. They choose arbitrary colors rather than optical colors because they want to use color to express meaning **(Figure 6.26).** In abstract art, color is teamed with the other elements to become the subject as well as the meaning of the work (see Figure 6.1 on page 134 and Figure 6.28 on page 156).

Colors affect feelings. Light, bright colors can create happy, upbeat moods. Cool, dark colors can express mysterious or depressing themes. Warm, low-intensity earth tones seem comfortable and friendly. They are often used to decorate rooms in which people gather. A unique, light value of red-orange has been used to soothe people and has even been successful in calming violent prisoners. Blue is also known for its soothing qualities. Bright yellow is stimulating and pure red excites.

▲ **FIGURE 6.26** Marc developed a personal theory of color symbolism. He believed that different hues symbolized different meanings. Yellow was a gentle, cheerful color, and for him, it symbolized women. He thought blue represented the spiritual and intellectual man. He said that red represented matter, and in this work, it symbolized the earth. Green served to complement the red.

Franz Marc. *Yellow Cow.* 1911. Oil on canvas. 140.7 × 189.2 cm (55³⁄₈ × 74¹⁄₂″). The Solomon R. Guggenheim Museum, New York, New York.

▲ **Figure 6.27** Look at the different objects on the table. Identify the number of colors used for each object. Notice how the artist has used dark blue lines to outline the fruit and make each piece stand out. Does this use of color make the objects seem real?

Paul Cézanne. *The Basket of Apples.* c. 1895. Oil on canvas. 65.5 × 81.3 cm (25¾ × 32″). The Art Institute of Chicago, Chicago, Illinois. Helen Birch Bartlett Memorial Collection. (1926.252).

Artists today have put their knowledge of color psychology to work to develop unusual methods for using color. Many of their choices are personal—they make color say what they wish to express.

Space

The placement of warm and cool colors can create illusions of depth. Warm colors advance toward the viewer, and cool colors seem to recede and pull away. The French artist Paul Cézanne painted a cool, blue outline around the shape of a warm, round orange. The fruit seemed to be pushed forward by the surrounding blue background **(Figure 6.27).**

Movement

Color can create a sense of movement. When the values in a work jump quickly from very high key to very low key, a feeling of excitement and movement is created **(Figure 6.28**, page 156). When all the values are close together, the work seems much calmer. Today's artists use color to create movement and depth in abstract art.

When you work with color to create movement, remember to use values of pure hues as well as those of tints and shades. You will need to remember, for instance, that the pure hue yellow is much lighter than red or blue.

Jumps in Color Value Create Visual Movement

This is one of Stuart Davis's first abstract works that celebrates his love for New York City. Davis has used strong jumps in value (from bright white, pale blue, and yellow to red, black, and orange) to make your eyes jump around the work. He wants you to feel the excitement and movement of the city. This diagram indicates some of the value jumps. Where can you find others?

Dark •   • Light   • Light   • Dark

• Dark • Light   • Light • Dark

◀ **FIGURE 6.28**

Stuart Davis. *Hot Still Scape for Six Colors–7th Avenue Style, 1940.* 1940. Oil on canvas. 91.4 × 113.9 cm (36 × 44⅞"). Museum of Fine Arts, Boston, Massachusetts. Gift of the William H. Lane Foundation and the M. and M. Karolik Collection, by exchange, 1983.120. © Estate of Stuart Davis/Licensed by VAGA, New York, NY.

Tonality

Sometimes an artist lets one color, such as blue, dominate a work. In such a case, the work is said to have a blue *tonality* **(Figure 6.29).** To have a certain tonality, the painting does not have to be monochrome. Other colors may be present. The overall effect of the work, however, will be of one color. Tonality has a unifying effect.

Check Your Understanding

1. All paints are made up of what three basic ingredients?
2. What is the difference between paint pigments and dyes?
3. Select and analyze two artworks from this lesson. What is the meaning of the color choices?

◀ **FIGURE 6.29** The blue tonality of this work conveys the cool impression of the water. The jellyfish are spots of contrast in the blue water. Although blue is the dominant color in this painting, other hues are used. What are they?

Childe Hassam. *Jelly Fish.* 1912. Oil on canvas. 35.8 × 43.8 cm (14$\frac{1}{8}$ × 17$\frac{1}{4}$"). Wichita Art Museum, Wichita, Kansas. The John W. and Mildred L. Graves Collection.

Color Spectrum Star Book

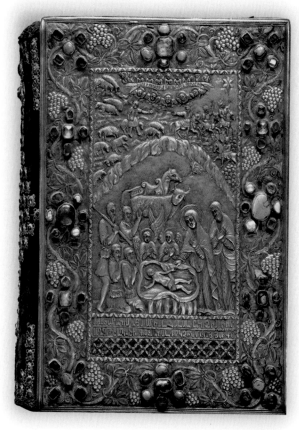

▲ **FIGURE 6.30**

Armenian. Front cover of *The Gospels*. Thirteenth century (binding fourteenth century). Carved and hammered silver, gilded, and enameled, and set with jewels. 26 x 18.7 cm (10¼ × 7⅜"). The Metropolitan Museum of Art, New York, New York. Gift of Mrs. Edward S. Harkness, 1916 (16.99).

SUPPLIES

- Sketchbook and pencil, ruler
- 2 sheets of 3 × 3" mat board
- White glue
- Heavy-duty aluminum foil
- Four sheets of 6 × 6" watercolor paper
- Watercolors and brushes
- Permanent nontoxic black marker
- Nontoxic rubber cement
- Two black ribbons ¼ × 8"

Historical and Cultural Context

The object in **Figure 6.30** is a book cover dating to the Middle Ages. It was carved and hammered from silver and then covered in gold leaf and studded with jewels. Notice the use of *relief,* positive areas extending from a negative, or flat surface. Observe how each grape along the border appears to jut out in space.

What You Will Learn

Today, the art of making books by hand has been revived. You will participate in this revival by making a star book with front and back covers. When opened, the pages will form a three-dimensional object. Aluminum foil will be used to simulate hammered and carved silver. Your book's cover will have both raised and etched areas. You will add radial balance using plant shapes, as in Figure 6.30.

Creating

Gather real plants and images of plant forms from print or online resources. Illustrate your ideas by directly observing these samples.

Step 1 Make line drawings of plants in your sketchbook. Using a ruler, divide a second page of your sketchbook into 1-inch squares. In these squares, make small drawings of plant parts—leaves, roots, stems, flowers, and so on.

Step 2 Transfer your drawing of an entire plant to the center of the sheet of mat board. Using white glue as your "drawing" medium, redraw the lines of your plant. Let glue dry.

Step 3 Lay a sheet of heavy-duty aluminum foil over the surface. Gently press the foil around the glue lines so that the lines appear raised. Smooth the foil down around the lines. Fold and glue any excess foil over the edges, taking care not to tear the foil.

Step 4 Place one of your plant-part drawings in the upper left corner. Using the drawing as a template, trace over the lines with your pencil to leave an impression in the foil.

Step 5 Repeat this step for each corner. Complete your cover by adding four more copies of your template, one along the center of each edge.

Step 6 Create the pages. Use watercolors to create washes of color on the four sheets of watercolor paper. Follow this sequence: (for page 1) yellow-green, yellow, yellow-orange; (for page 2) orange, red-orange, red; (for page 3) red-violet, violet, blue-violet; (for page 4) blue, blue-green, green.

Step 7 With pencil, transfer a plant-part drawing onto each of the four pages. Trace over the lines with black marker. Add color with watercolors.

Step 8 Fold and open each page top to bottom, side to side, diagonal to the left, and diagonal to the right. Notice that there is a front side and back side to the resulting three-dimensional object. Adorn each side with plant drawings and paint.

Step 9 With rubber cement, glue the pages and covers together, and attach ribbons.

Evaluating Your Work

▶ **DESCRIBE** Did you make two sketches, one of a complete plant, one of a plant part? Where does your whole plant appear on your finished cover? Where does the plant part appear? How many times does it appear?

▶ **ANALYZE** Does your cover have both raised and etched areas? Compare and contrast the use of color and the use of balance on the inside pages. What kind of balance is exhibited by the design of your finished cover?

▶ **INTERPRET** Does your book appear to be covered in silver? Does it suggest the ancient style of the book in Figure 6.30? What type of content would you expect to find inside a book with a color such as yours?

▶ **JUDGE** Would you judge your book cover to be a success? Why or why not? If you were able to redo your cover, what would you do differently next time? Evaluate your artistic decisions.

▲ **FIGURE 6.30AB**

Student work.

Mood Painting

▲ **FIGURE 6.31**

Kuna (Panama). *Mola: Our Environment.* 1995. Layered and cut fabric with stitchery. 106.7 × 167.6 cm (42 × 66"). Georgia Southern University, Statesboro, Georgia.

SUPPLIES

- Sketchbook and pencils
- Watercolors and assorted brushes
- Scrap paper
- Tape
- Heavy drawing paper
- Drawing board
- Chalk

Historical and Cultural Context

The colorful work in **Figure 6.31,** called a *mola,* was made by the Kuna people of Panama. Among the Kuna, the tradition of making molas is passed down through generations of the same family. The works are made by sewing together layers of colored fabric and adding decorative needlework to the top layer. Molas are made for the fronts and backs of blouses. Many of the designs are similar to those found on pre-Columbian pottery. (Pre-Columbian art predates the arrival on this continent of Christopher Columbus in 1492.) Take a moment to study Figure 6.31. Note the array of bright colors used for highly stylized figures and objects of nature. What mood does this work communicate to you?

What You Will Learn

You will create a painting that illustrates the mood of an event or experience in your life. You will create visual solutions by elaborating on your experience. The event or experience can be happy (for example, a memorable birthday) or sad (a time when your team lost a big game). As in Figure 6.31, your colors will be either bright and with high intensity to represent happy times or dull and low intensity for sad times. Figures and objects in your painting should be stylized. In other words, they should be easily identifiable but simple, almost childlike.

Creating

Brainstorm happy or sad moments in your life. Think about objects you associate with these events. List these on a page in your sketchbook. Sketch several ideas. Then begin thinking about colors that express the mood of this event. Choose your best idea.

Step 1 Using watercolors and sheets of scrap paper, practice mixing complementary colors to create low-intensity and high-intensity colors (see pages 144–149.) Think about which colors best fit the objects you have chosen and the mood you are attempting to communicate.

Step 2 Tape a piece of heavy drawing paper to a stiff drawing board. Using chalk, transfer the sketch of your best idea onto the painted surface. Make sure to include the contour lines of objects and figures. Add in details that will be outlined as well (like the fish scales in Figure 6.31).

Step 3 Begin painting. Use the colors you have chosen to express the mood of your artwork. Switch to a finer brush, as necessary, to complete fine details of your work. Allow your painting to dry thoroughly before displaying it.

Evaluating Your Work

▶ **DESCRIBE** Did you illustrate your ideas based on an experience or event? Identify the experience and all the objects and figures in your picture.

▶ **ANALYZE** Did you choose bright colors or dull colors? Are your figures and objects stylized?

▶ **INTERPRET** What mood were you trying to express through your painting? Give your work a title that sums up your feelings about the event.

▶ **JUDGE** Were viewers able to recognize the mood of your work? Could they pick out individual details? If you were to redo your painting, what, if anything, would you do differently?

▲ **FIGURE 6.31A**

Student work.

Digital Color Collage

▲ **FIGURE 6.32**

William H. Johnson. *Harbor Under the Midnight Sun.* 1937. Museum of American Art, Smithsonian Institution, Washington, D.C./Art Resource, NY.

SUPPLIES

- Digital camera (optional) and/or photograph or magazine picture
- Computer
- Scanner
- Sketchbook and pencil
- Image-editing or paint program
- Photo quality paper
- Printer

Historical and Cultural Context

Imagine taking a common scene—perhaps the one outside your bedroom window—and stripping it down to the bare essentials. What would you end up with? This is precisely the question asked and answered by early twentieth-century artist William H. Johnson in **Figure 6.32.** If you study the work for a moment, you notice a craggy mountain rising up to a deep, azure sky swirling with clouds. At the bottom of the picture is an expanse of water dotted with boats—a harbor.

When Johnson painted this work, his primary influence was the French Post-Impressionist Paul Cézanne. Like Cézanne, Johnson has reduced the objects in his work to flat planes of color. If in some places the colors appear a little too intense, note the title Johnson gave to this work. Could it be that the midnight sun casts a different type of light than the daytime sun?

What You Will Learn

You will create a digital landscape painting. Begin by selecting a view of an existing landscape; then capture the view with a camera. After your photograph has been imported into a paint program, you will divide the landscape into four geometric areas. By applying a different color filter or lighting effect to each area, the final image will depict the passage of time.

Creating

Choose a familiar setting that looks interesting. Notice the way changes in sunlight or the different seasons affect the setting. Make sketches in your sketchbook.

Step 1 Use a digital camera to capture a picture of the chosen landscape. If you are using a magazine image or a photograph as a picture source, scan the image into the computer. Use a format compatible with your image-editing or paint program. Save the image.

Step 2 Open your image-editing application. Go to the File menu, choose Open, and select a new document. Set up and save a document measuring 8 × 10 inches at a resolution of 72 dpi. Your orientation could be vertical or horizontal, depending on your image.

Step 3 Open your saved image in a separate file. Use the Freeform Selection tool to select about one fourth of the image. Copy and paste this section of the landscape into the corresponding area of your new document. Repeat this procedure for each of the remaining three quadrants of your landscape. Paste each selection into a new layer. Save the new document.

Step 4 Experiment with stretching, rotating, and overlapping the layers.

Step 5 Working with a layer at a time, experiment with enhancing and changing aspects of color, such as contrast/brightness, hue/saturation, and color balance. Try using one or more of the filters in your program to add texture and special effects. Concentrate on changes that will convey the mood and look of different seasons or times of day.

Evaluating Your Work

▶ **DESCRIBE** What was the original source of the landscape in your work? Which tools did you use to alter the image? Explain how you used each tool and on what area of the painting.

▶ **ANALYZE** Compare and contrast how you used colors to convey a sense of passing time. Identify how changes in mood, season, or time are shown in each part of the picture.

▶ **INTERPRET** What mood or feeling does your work communicate? What would be a fitting title for your work?

▶ **JUDGE** Which aesthetic theory does your landscape reflect? How would you improve or change your art?

▲ **FIGURE 6.32A**

Student work.

Color

Colors, as you have seen, can be warm or cool, dull or bright. These and other properties of color open up a world of possibilities for the artist. As you examine the student artworks on these pages:

● Compare and contrast the hues, values, and intensities of the colors used.

● Analyze them to form precise conclusions about the color scheme used.

Activity 6.33 **Color intensity.**
Compare and contrast the intensity of the two main colors used in this painting. Form a conclusion about which orange and which blue is most intense.

Activity 6.34 **Hue.** Analyze the hues this student artist has chosen. Which are optical colors, and which are arbitrary colors? Form a conclusion about the meaning of the work.

▲ **FIGURE 6.33**

Student work. *Spiders*. Acrylic.

▶ **FIGURE 6.34**

Student work. *Winds of Change*. Computer graphic.

▲ **FIGURE 6.35**

Student work. *Evening at the Rendezvous*. Acrylic.

Activity 6.35 **Color triads.**
The primary color triad—yellow, red, and blue—is used to color the shirt of the female figure in the background. Do you find this effective or distracting? Evaluate the use of this color triad.

Activity 6.36 **Color scheme.**
Evaluate and identify the color scheme used in this portrait. Explain how it is used to draw the viewer's eye to the subject.

▶ **FIGURE 6.36**

Student work. *Number 7*. Watercolor and colored pencil.

ART Online
To view more student artworks, visit the Glencoe Student Art Gallery at **art.glencoe.com**.

For Your Portfolio

Evaluate Personal Artworks. As you add to your portfolio, be sure to evaluate the artistic decisions you made in your works in terms of their use of color. In the second step of your evaluation (the *analyze* step), indicate the color scheme (monochromatic, complementary, and so on) and its role in unifying the work. Also, note the effective use of color properties, such as value and intensity, in your composition. Keep the evaluation with the work itself.

Visual Art ⟹ Journal

Survey the artworks on these pages or artworks in your classroom. Then select and analyze two of these peer artworks to form conclusions about historical and cultural contexts, intents, and meanings. If you are analyzing portraits, what can the clothing and/or hairstyles reveal about the historical context?

Art Criticism
in Action

▲ **FIGURE 6.37**

Miriam Schapiro. *Father and Daughter*. 1997. Acrylic and fabric on canvas. 182.9 × 175.3 cm (72 × 69″). Collection of Aaron and Marion Borenstein, Fort Wayne, Indiana.

Critiquing the Artwork

▶ **1** **DESCRIBE** *What do you see?*
List all the information found in the credit line.

- Describe the figures in this painting. Include details about their body language and clothing.
- What is the relationship of the figures?
- Describe the background.
- Which parts are painted, and which appear to be fabric?

▶ **2** **ANALYZE** *How is this work organized?*
This is a clue-collecting step about the elements of art.

- What hues do you see? Name and locate examples of each.
- Compare and contrast the use of tints, shades, and neutral colors.
- What expressive effects of color has the artist used in this work?

▶ **3** **INTERPRET** *What message or feeling does this artwork communicate to you?*
Combine the clues you have collected to form a creative interpretation of the work.

- Describe the relationship you sense between the father and daughter.
- How does color affect the mood of this work?
- What do you think the background represents?
- After your analysis, sum up what you believe the artist intended.

▶ **4** **JUDGE** *What do you think of the work?*
Decide if this is a successful work of art.

- Did the artist use the element of color to convey her message well?
- Do you think this is a successful work of art? Why or why not? Choose an aesthetic theory to defend your judgment.

Seeing Colors in Art

The visual arts may have been influenced by the paints and pigments available.

Philip Ball, an art historian and author of *Bright Earth,* claims that what artists paint isn't only influenced by their color sense and artistic tastes. It also has to do with the colors and paints available to them. Experts say that the ancient Greeks created somber paintings because they had only four colors: black, white, red, and yellow.

During the Middle Ages, artists had more colors to use. Natural pigments were discovered including malachite (green), azurite (blue), orpiment (yellow), and realgar (orange).

Then oil colors were discovered. This type of paint was made by binding pigments with linseed, poppy, and nut oils. With oil paints, masters such as fifteenth-century artist Jan van Eyck (Figure 9.8, page 231) could produce intense, layered colors.

In the 1700s, more colors appeared, thanks to the discovery of chemicals such as cadmium (orange and yellow), chrome (yellows and green), and cobalt (blues).

The discovery of new colors will continue to influence painting. With computers, artists today can use about 17 million colors. From Realism to Abstract Expressionism, new colors have steered artists in new directions.

TIME to Connect

Leonardo da Vinci wrote about the importance of observing color. He recognized that changing light plays an important role in how people perceive color. Test this yourself.

- Observe and then sketch the colors of an object under fluorescent and incandescent light. Then observe and sketch the colors of the object in natural light at different times of the day.

- Organize your sketches in a chart. In what ways did the colors change? What conclusions can you draw?

- Share your observations and conclusions with the class. Think about how light may affect the choice of colors an artist makes.

TOP: The mix of verdigris with resins sometimes reacted badly to light, turning foliage black, as in Pollaiuolo's *Daphne and Apollo.*
ABOVE: Modern artists boldly use pure pigments. Anish Kapoor let the colors of a 1981 sculpture spill onto the floor.

Building Vocabulary

On a separate sheet of paper, write the term that best matches each definition given below.

1. An element of art that is derived from reflected light.
2. Produced when light passes through a wedge-shaped glass, called a prism, and is bent and separated into bands of color.
3. The name of a color in the color spectrum.
4. A light value of a hue.
5. A dark value of a hue.
6. The brightness or dullness of a hue.
7. The colors opposite each other on the color wheel.
8. A color scheme that uses only one hue and the tints and shades of that hue.
9. Colors that sit side by side on the color wheel and have a common hue.
10. Finely ground, colored powders that form paint when mixed with a binder.
11. A material that holds together the grains of pigment.
12. The liquid that controls the thickness or thinness of the paint.

Reviewing Art Facts

Answer the following questions using complete sentences.

13. Explain how the eye sees color.
14. What is an afterimage? How is it produced?
15. Name the three components of color.
16. What is color value?
17. Name the different kinds of color schemes.
18. What are complementary colors? How do complementary colors affect each other?
19. What are synthetic pigments? How do they differ from natural pigments?
20. What is arbitrary color?

Thinking Critically About Art

21. **Synthesize.** Figure 6.20 on page 148 and Figure 6.21 on page 149 use very different color schemes. List the similarities and differences in their style and use of color.
22. **Interpret.** Look at Figure 6.9 on page 141. The artist has used a color scheme of dark values to create a specific mood. Study the lines and shapes in this work. How do they affect the feeling of the painting? Notice the areas of bright, intense color. How does this add drama? Does the title add to the mood?
23. **Compare and Contrast.** Examine Figures 6.15 on page 146, 6.22 on page 151, and 6.32 on page 162 to discuss the similarities and differences in the ways color is used to achieve a sense of balance.

ART Online

Understanding the properties of color and how to use color effectively is a job requirement of many careers in art. Interior designers and graphic designers, for example, create and work with color schemes on a daily basis. Go to **art.glencoe.com** to compare and contrast the job descriptions and requirements of these and many other art careers.

Linking to the Performing Arts

Read how Joanna Featherstone paints a picture with words as a professional storyteller in the Performing Arts Handbook on page 418. Like a painter, Joanna uses tonality, contrast, intensity, and movement to tap into the emotions that each color evokes.

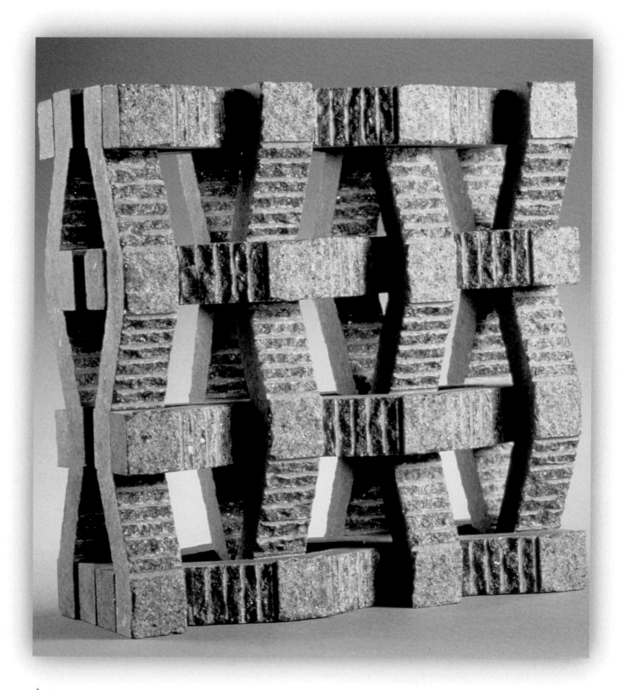

▲ **FIGURE 7.1** Notice the work's title. A playscape can be created with any playground equipment such as ladders and parallel bars. Why do you think this artist called this sculpture a playscape? Describe the way the surface of this sculpture appears to the touch.

Jesús Bautista Moroles. *Granite Weaving Playscape.* 1995. Fredericksburg granite. 45.7 × 45.7 × 17.8 cm (18 × 18 × 7″). The Getty Museum, Los Angeles, California.

Texture

Everything you touch has its own special feel, or texture. Polished glass feels slick; a bumpy road, rough. As an element of art, texture may be real, as in **Figure 7.1,** or it may be "suggested." The photo of Figure 7.1, for example, is smooth to the touch.

In this chapter, you will:

- Explain how texture is perceived through the senses.
- Compare and contrast different textures in personal artworks and in those of others.
- Create two- and three-dimensional artworks that explore texture.
- Analyze the use of texture in the artworks of others to express meaning.

Focus on **Art History**   American sculptor Jesús Bautista Moroles (b. 1950) draws inspiration from the past. His sculpture in Figure 7.1 was inspired by the art of the ancient Mayan civilization. Peaking around A.D. 800, this civilization occupied much of present-day Central America. The Mayans created towering structures from local stone (Figure 12.27, page 340). All were characterized by their deliberately rough-hewn textures and repeating geometric forms. These characteristics are also found in Moroles's sculptures. He has worked with many stone materials but prefers to use granite because it is such a challenge to work with and because of the textures he can create.

Describe. Examine Figure 7.1, the Olmec sculpture in Figure 12.26 on page 339, and the Buddha sculpture in Figure 12.14 on page 329. Describe general characteristics of these artworks from a variety of cultures.

Texture in Your Life

Texture is *the element of art that refers to how things feel, or look as if they might feel, if touched.* Textures play a role in decisions you make every day. Think about how fabric textures have influenced your clothing choices. Would you wear a shirt made of rough burlap against your bare skin? Probably not. Clothing manufacturers consider this when they decide what fabrics to use and how to make their clothes.

Think about the textures of food. Imagine the smoothness of ice cream, and consider how different it is from the angular roughness of tortilla chips. Would grilled steak taste the same if it were ground up in a blender? Textures are important to us in a variety of ways.

How You Perceive Texture

You perceive texture with two of your senses: touch and vision. Infants learn about their environment by touching objects and by putting them into their mouths. Toddlers are attracted to all objects that are within their reach. When you look at surfaces, you are able to guess their textures because you have learned how textures feel. Your eyes tell you what something would feel like if you were to touch it **(Figure 7.2).**

◀ ▲ **FIGURE 7.2** What textures are represented in these photographs?

When you actually touch something to determine its texture, you experience **tactile texture,** *the texture you feel.* When you look at a photograph of a texture, such as velvet, leather, concrete, or ice, you see surface patterns of light and dark that bring back memories of how those objects actually feel. When this happens, you are experiencing **visual texture,** *the illusion of a three-dimensional surface.* If you touch visual textures, you do not feel what your eyes told you to expect.

There are two kinds of visual texture: *simulated* and *invented.* Simulated textures imitate real textures. Plastic tabletops can be made to look like wood. Vinyl flooring can be made to look like ceramic tile or stone. Manufactured fabrics imitate natural leather and fur.

Artists can do the same. For example, painter Peggy Flora Zalucha simulates textures in her paintings so accurately that you think you might be looking at a photograph **(Figure 7.3).**

▲ **FIGURE 7.3** At first you might think you are looking at a photograph because the artist has simulated the textures of objects so realistically. This is actually a still-life painting of items associated with taking a road trip. The details of the map are so clear that if you recognized the area of the country, you could read the map. Zalucha has used white highlights to represent the brilliant reflections of light off the shiny surfaces of the glasses and keys. She has used more subtle changes of value to represent the textures found in nonreflective surfaces, such as the wrinkles on the map.

Peggy Flora Zalucha. *Map Still Life with Carnations, Keys, and Glasses.* 1989. Mixed watermedia. 76.2 × 111.8 cm (30 × 44"). Private Collection.

◆ FIGURE 7.4 In this painting, the artist has used a number of techniques to suggest texture. A variety of line types and shading techniques have been used. Can you identify the textures? Do they represent real textures or are they invented? The artwork clearly depicts two people and an elephant, but would you call it realistic? Why or why not?

Artist unknown. Deccan, Bijapur. *Stalling Elephant with Two Riders.* Mid-seventeenth century. Ink, gold, and watercolor on paper. 16.5 × 12.4 cm (6½ × 4⅞"). Brooklyn Museum of Art, Brooklyn, NY. Gift of Dr. Betram Shaffner.

Invented textures appear as two-dimensional patterns created by the repetition of lines or shapes. These patterns do not represent real surface qualities, but the patterns of light and dark suggest real texture. The purpose of invented texture is to create decorated surfaces that evoke memories of unusual textures **(Figure 7.4).**

Activity Creating Textures

Applying Your Skills. Make a collection of texture rubbings. To make a rubbing, place a sheet of thin paper against a rough object or surface. Hold the paper in place with one hand. Use the flat side of an unwrapped crayon or the side of a pencil lead to rub over the paper. Rub in one direction—away from the hand holding the paper. Rubbing back and forth can cause the paper or object to slip. Examine the rubbings closely, paying special attention to the lines, dots, shapes, and values.

Computer Option. Explore the textures on your computer application as well as those you can create. Begin with a Pencil, Brush, or Shape tool . Draw objects or shapes. Fill each shape with a different texture from available menus. Make some new textures by editing or adding textures. Use a variety of available tools and paper textures. Experiment with a blending tool to soften surfaces. Identify which objects look rough and which look smooth.

Texture and Value

The appearance of a surface depends on how it reflects light. Every surface displays a pattern of light and dark values. From the pattern of light and dark values, we can make a judgment about the texture of a surface or an object even if we cannot touch it.

Rough and Smooth Textures

The roughness or smoothness of a texture can be determined by looking at its light and dark values. A rough surface reflects light unevenly. It shows irregular patterns of light and shadow. Look at a shag rug, an orange, tree bark, or a patch of bare ground. Notice how the high places catch the light, casting shadows of different sizes and shapes.

A smooth texture reflects light evenly. Look at a sheet of paper, an apple, or a new, unmarked desktop. Your eyes glide across these objects, uninterrupted by shadows, just as your fingers would glide across them, uninterrupted by bumps and dents.

Matte and Shiny Textures

In addition to rough and smooth, textures can be matte or shiny. A **matte surface** is *a surface that reflects a soft, dull light.* It absorbs some light and reflects the rest. Matte surfaces, such as paper, denim, unfinished wood, and your skin, have a soft, dull look.

A shiny surface is the opposite of a matte surface. A shiny surface is a surface that reflects so much bright light that it seems to glow. Shiny surfaces also have highlights. Some surfaces reflect bright sunlight with such intensity that you have to squint your eyes to protect them from the glare. Window glass, a new car, a polished brass candlestick, and the surface of a calm pool of water are all examples of shiny surfaces.

Matte and shiny surfaces can be rough or smooth. Sandpaper is matte rough, and a freshly ironed pillowcase is matte smooth. Aluminum foil is shiny and smooth until it gets crumpled up; then it becomes shiny and rough. In **Figure 7.5** on page 176, Janet Fish has illustrated all of these texture variations.

Activity — Creating Contrasting Textures

Demonstrating Effective Use of Art Media in Drawing and Painting. Make a series of small drawings and paintings of objects that have different textures. Try to reproduce both smooth and rough textures. You may use a different medium for each drawing, but study the lights and shadows on each object before you choose the medium. For example, you might examine a hairbrush, an old work shoe, weathered wood, a wig, a fuzzy slipper, or a satin slip, then select a medium that would work best for each texture.

Computer Option. Make a series of small drawings and paintings of objects that have different textures, as in the preceding activity. Use the Pencil or Brush tool on the computer. First, sketch your shapes. Then reproduce the texture of each shape using dots, lines, and value blending. Concentrate on the shadows, lights, and highlights of each different texture.

Visual Texture Combinations

Janet Fish has used pastels to create the visual textures in this work. The diagram points out some areas where she has combined different kinds of visual texture, such as shiny-rough, shiny-smooth, and matte-smooth. Can you find more areas where she has created combinations of visual texture?

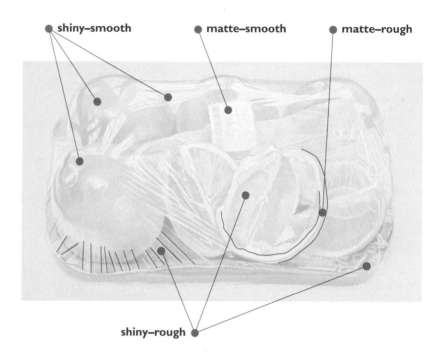

● shiny–smooth   ● matte–smooth   ● matte–rough

shiny–rough ●

◀ **FIGURE 7.5**

Janet Fish. *Oranges*. 1973. Pastel on sandpaper. 55.5 × 96.5 cm (21⁷/₈ × 38″). Allen Memorial Art Museum, Oberlin College, Oberlin, Ohio. Fund for Contemporary Art, 1974. © Janet Fish/Licensed by VAGA, New York, NY.

Check Your Understanding

1. Define visual texture.
2. Describe, in detail, the two types of visual texture.
3. Compare how rough and smooth textures reflect light.
4. Compare and contrast the use of textures in Figure 7.3 on page 173 and Figure 7.5 on this page.

How Artists Use Texture

Vocabulary

collage
frottage
grattage
decalcomania

The texture of surfaces is important in every form of visual art. Our minds are full of texture memories. Artists use both visual and real textures to make you remember those texture experiences.

Ivan Albright was a painter who loved to depict decaying, aging objects with meticulous precision. He painted the skin of the old gentleman in **Figure 7.6** to accent and exaggerate every tiny wrinkle. Look at the painting. How many different kinds of textures can you identify?

In contrast, Pierre-Auguste Renoir (ren-**wahr**) painted people with healthy, glowing complexions **(Figure 7.7).** How many different textures can you identify in this painting? Notice that both Albright and Renoir have imitated the texture of human skin. In each case, the artist has used texture to convey a feeling about the subject. In one painting the skin is appealing, in the other it is almost repulsive. Both artists have tried to control your reaction to the subject of the paintings through their use of visual texture.

▲ **FIGURE 7.6** Albright created this portrait for the movie called *The Picture of Dorian Gray*. The artist took over a year to create the textures that indicated extreme physical aging.

Ivan Albright. *The Picture of Dorian Gray.* 1943–44. Oil on canvas. 215.9 × 106.7 cm (85 × 42"). The Art Institute of Chicago, Chicago, Illinois.

▲ **FIGURE 7.7** Renoir started his career as an artist in a porcelain factory. He copied famous portraits of beautiful women onto porcelain plates. Notice the skin texture of the sisters in this work. Compare and contrast this painting to Figure 7.6.

Pierre-Auguste Renoir. *Two Sisters (On the Terrace).* 1881. Oil on canvas. 100.5 × 81 cm (39⁹/₁₆ × 31⁷/₈"). The Art Institute of Chicago, Chicago, Illinois. Mr. and Mrs. Lewis Larned Coburn Memorial Collection, 1933.455.

▶ **FIGURE 7.8** At times, van Gogh became so impatient with the progress of his work that he squeezed the paint directly from the tube onto the canvas. Then he used anything that was handy, including his fingers, to move and swirl the globs of paint around.

Vincent van Gogh. *Sunflowers.* 1888. Oil on canvas. 92 × 73 cm (36¼ × 28¾"). National Gallery, London, England.

Many painters use color and value patterns to produce the illusion of textures. Look, for instance, at the painting by Judith Leyster (Figure 10.4, page 257) or Rembrandt van Rijn (ryne) (Figure 5.36, page 124). These artists were experts at suggesting textures such as soft velvet, shiny satin, delicate lace, and fluffy feathers. When you look closely at their paintings, you discover that these artists do not paint every texture in photographic detail. They use a few brushstrokes to suggest the texture from a certain distance.

Instead of relying only on visual texture, many painters add real textures to their paintings. Vincent van Gogh (vahn **goh**) used such thick paint on his canvas that his swirling brushstrokes created a rough surface **(Figure 7.8)**. The surface ridges of the thick paint actually make the paint look brighter. The ridges catch more light and reflect brighter colors to the viewer. If you were to touch a van Gogh painting you would feel the texture you see. Even today, artists feel that such textural qualities enhance their work.

Joan Mitchell is one contemporary painter who brushes on paint and does not try to smooth out the brushstrokes **(Figure 7.9).**

Some painters add real textures to their work by attaching various materials to the work's surface. Some artists add sand and other materials to the paint. In some cases, artists create what is called a **collage** (kul-**lahzh**), or *an artwork created by pasting cut or torn materials such as paper, photographs, and fabric to a flat surface.* Although folk artists have used this technique for centuries, fine artists only began using collage in the last century. (The word wasn't even

◀ **FIGURE 7.9** Joan Mitchell remained an Abstract Expressionist throughout her entire painting career. This work refers to the snow and cold of her Chicago childhood. Notice how she has used the brushstrokes to show the excitement and tension of a snowy day in the city. What kinds of lines do you find in the brushstrokes?

Joan Mitchell. *Dirty Snow (Sale Neige).* 1980. Oil on canvas. 219 × 180 cm (86¼ × 70⅞"). National Museum of Women in the Arts, Washington, D.C. Gift of Wallace and Wilhelmina Holladay.

▶ **FIGURE 7.10**
Schapiro used pieces of embroidered, appliquéd, and crocheted fabrics that were created by women to add real textures to her work. In this way, she connected her work to the traditional women's arts of the past.

Miriam Schapiro. *In Her Own Image.* 1983. Acrylic and fabric on canvas. 152.4 × 254 cm (60 × 100″). Hunter Museum of American Art, Chattanooga, Tennessee. Museum purchase with funds provided by the Benwood Foundation and the 1983 Collectors' Group.

▲ **FIGURE 7.11** John Hoover is an Aleut sculptor. He uses the folklore of his people as subject matter, but he has developed a personal style that is not traditional. This work represents a female shaman. The circle around her face is made up of ravens that are escorting her on her journey.

John Hoover. *Shaman's Journey.* 2000. Cedar. Diameter: 81.3 cm (32″). Collection of the Artist.

invented until 1919.) Miriam Schapiro, an artist who uses collage, added bits of fabric, lace, and thread to her paintings to enrich the surface and to convey a message **(Figure 7.10).**

Sculptors must also be aware of texture because the tactile texture of each surface must fit the whole. Some sculptors imitate the tactile texture of skin, hair, and cloth; others create new textures to fit new forms. In **Figure 7.11,** the artist lets the texture of the cedar wood show through the natural pigments. In contrast, the sculptor of **Figure 7.12,** Edgar Degas, imitated tactile textures. He even added fabrics (a gauze skirt and a satin ribbon) to the figure to make it more realistic.

French, 1834–1917

Edgar Degas. *Self-Portrait.* c. 1862. Oil on canvas. 81 × 64.5 cm (31⁷⁄₈ × 25³⁄₈"). Musee d'Orsay, Paris, France.

Edgar Degas (day-**gah**) was born in Paris in 1834. His family, wealthy bankers, supported his ambition to become an artist. He was educated at the École des Beaux-Arts by a French Classicist who trained him in classical drafting. This expertise in drawing is a main element in Degas' work.

Around 1865, Degas fell under the influence of the Impressionist movement and abandoned academic, classical subject matter. He began painting contemporary subjects such as music halls, theatres, and cafés. Unlike the Impressionists with whom he is often associated, however, Degas was not interested in the use of light or in depicting nature on canvas. He worked in a studio and tried to capture his models in natural and spontaneous movements. He preferred women as his subjects and is best known for his studies of ballet dancers, although he also painted milliners (hatmakers) and laundresses.

In the 1860s, he began experimenting with unusual methods of composition, such as alternate perspectives, odd visual angles, asymmetrical balance, and accidental cut-offs. These methods of composition would inspire many modern artists. As he grew older, his eyesight began to fail and he turned to a new process: sculpture. In his sculpture, as in his painting, he tried to capture spontaneous movement and realistic poses.

▶ **FIGURE 7.12** What an unusual combination of textures! The figure of the young dancer is cast in bronze. Even the vest and the ballet shoes she wears are bronze. To that Degas added a skirt made of gauzelike fabric and a satin hair ribbon. Why do you think he added real textures to the metal figure?

Edgar Degas. *The Little Fourteen-Year-Old Dancer.* Model c. 1880, cast 1922. Bronze, slightly tinted, with gauze skirt and satin hair ribbon. Height: 104.5 cm (41¹⁄₈"). The Metropolitan Museum of Art, New York, New York. H. O. Havemeyer Collection, bequest of Mrs. H. O. Havemeyer, 1929. (29.100.370).

Architects are also aware of the importance of texture. They use stucco, brick, wood, stone, concrete, metal, and glass to create texture. Frank Lloyd Wright, one of the most influential architects of the twentieth century, believed that a building should develop out of its natural surroundings **(Figure 7.13)**. Because of this, he selected textures that related to the local environment. Interior designers select textures for rugs, drapes, furniture, and artworks that complement different wall surfaces. This gives a sense of cohesiveness, or unity, to a design.

In crafts, textures are essential. Potters manipulate textures by pressing different objects into wet clay. They can also change surfaces by applying glazes. Some glazes are shiny, while others are matte.

Some glazes result in a crackle finish that gives a rough texture to a piece of pottery. Weavers control texture through the use of fibers and weaving techniques. For example, rough wool fibers have a different texture than smooth cotton fibers. In addition, weavers use different techniques to create texture. By twisting fibers as they weave, they can create a rough texture. Other artisans also use texture. Jewelry makers work with different kinds of metal to create various textures. They might emboss or press a raised design into metal or facet a stone to give its surfaces a smooth, shiny appearance. Feathers, seashells, seeds, bones, and teeth have been used to make jewelry and hair ornaments, and decorate clothing and masks **(Figure 7.14)**.

▲ **FIGURE 7.13** The colors, forms, and textures of this building were planned so that Taliesin West would blend into the colors, forms, and textures of its desert setting. Wright believed that a building should be in harmony with its environment.

Frank Lloyd Wright. *Taliesin West.* Near Phoenix, Arizona.

▲ **FIGURE 7.14** Giant feathered masks like this one are worn by Tapirapé men as they run through the village in pairs shouting and causing a commotion. The other men of the village participate in a mock battle with the masqueraders.

Tapirapé People, Mato Grosso, Brazil. *Mask.* c. 1970. Glued and tied feather work, tropical bird feathers, mother-of-pearl, wood. 102.9 × 106.7 cm (40$\frac{1}{2}$ × 42"). Museum of International Folk Art, Museum of New Mexico, Santa Fe, New Mexico.

Artists also invent textures to enrich their works. Max Ernst used three unusual techniques—*frottage, grattage,* and *decalcomania*—to create his Surrealist fantasy paintings. In **frottage** (froh-**tahzh**), *designs and textural effects are created by placing paper over objects that have raised surfaces and rubbing the paper with graphite, wax, or crayon.* In **Figure 7.15,** Ernst combines frottage with painting techniques. The texture rubbings you made earlier in this chapter are another form of frottage. To create **grattage** (grah-**tahzh**) effects, *wet paint is scratched with a variety of tools, such as forks, razors, and combs.* In **decalcomania,** *paint is forced into random textured patterns. Paint is placed between two canvas surfaces. The canvases are then pulled apart.*

 **FIGURE 7.15** Compare and contrast the kind of texture used in this painting with the textures in Figure 7.14.

Max Ernst. *Age of Forests.* 1926. Oil on canvas. 91.8 × 59.7 cm (36⅛ × 23½″). Albright-Knox Art Gallery, Buffalo, New York. A. Conger Goodyear Fund, 1964. © 2003 Artists Rights Society (ARS), New York/ADAGP, Paris.

Activity Imagining Textures

Creating Visual Solutions Using Imagination. On a small piece of white paper, draw nine shapes of different sizes with a pencil or felt-tip pen. Some shapes should touch the edges of the paper. Fill each shape with sketches of a different texture. The textures should be imaginary. For instance, you could put lines of writing close together in one shape, or you could try repeating small shapes in another. Try line patterns, stippling, or smooth shadow.

Computer Option. Explore textures and effects that can be made with the Brush tool or other tools on the computer. Menus provide choices from thick, opaque oils to wet, transparent paint. Experiment. Save your results by applying your discoveries to objects, shapes, or scenes.

Check Your Understanding

1. Define *collage.*
2. Describe a form of frottage.
3. What is a grattage effect?
4. Select and analyze two artworks from this lesson to form a conclusion about the meaning of the textures used.

Self-Portrait Collagraph

Romare Bearden. *In the Garden*. 1974. Color lithograph on paper.
91.1 × 74.3 cm (35⅞ × 29¼″). Montgomery Museum of Fine Arts,
Montgomery, Alabama. Romare Bearden Foundation/Licensed by
VAGA, New York, NY.

SUPPLIES

- Heavy cardboard
- Found textured materials such as lace, nubby fabric, sandpaper, or aluminum foil
- Scissors
- White glue, white latex paint, or gloss/gel medium
- White and/or colored printing paper
- Water-based printing ink
- Tray and brayers
- Felt blankets
- Printing press
- Sponge, rag, or paper towels

Historical and Cultural Context

If asked, most artists would admit to loving their work. The work in **Figure 7.16** is a labor of love *in two ways*. First, it is a loving tribute to the sunny Caribbean. The artist, Romare Bearden, was so taken with this lush tropical setting that he moved there in 1973. Notice the dominance of warm colors.

To locate the second expression of love, find the rectangle in the center of the right side. Notice how it slices through one of the tall plants and continues into the woman's dress. Maybe the contents of this rectangle were meant to reflect a connection between the woman—the artist's grandmother—and her much-beloved garden.

What You Will Learn

Figure 7.16 is a *lithograph*, a type of fine art print that uses limestone for the printing plate. In this activity, you will create another type of print, a *collagraph*. You will glue items with different textures to different areas of your printing plate. This will give your collagraph both tactile *and* visual texture. You will demonstrate the effective use of printmaking media and tools in this project.

Creating

Sitting in front of a mirror, use direct observation to practice sketching self-portraits. If possible, angle a strong light source, such as a spotlight or unshaded lamp, so that it creates well-defined areas of dark and light. Shade areas of your drawing to reflect these contrasting values. Outline these areas with a pen.

Step 1 Choose your best drawing. Transfer it to a sheet of heavy cardboard. This will serve as the basis of your printing plate.

Step 2 Choose two found materials with different textures. Assign one material to the dark areas that you have highlighted. Cut out pieces of the material the size and shape of each such area. Glue the pieces of material in place. Follow the same procedure with the second textured material and the light areas of your self-portrait. Allow time for the printing plate to dry.

Step 3 Waterproof the printing plate by covering it with gloss medium or latex paint, and let it dry.

Step 4 Choose the paper for your print. Then choose a contrasting color of ink. Spray or soak your paper in water. Place the wet paper between towels and press to extract the excess water.

Step 5 Pour the ink into a tray, and roll the brayer through the ink to coat it. Carefully apply the ink to areas of the plate's surface that you want to print. Uninked areas will remain the color of the paper. Place the inked plate on the press. Carefully place the dampened paper over the plate. Put dry towels or felt blankets over the paper, and run the layers through the press.

Step 6 Place the print on a dry surface or a drying rack. When it is dry, sign the print in pencil directly under the image. Write the title on the left and your name and date on the right. Carefully wash off the front surface of the printing plate with a sponge, rag, or paper towel. Avoid wetting the back of the plate.

Evaluating Your Work

▶ **DESCRIBE** Did you create self-portrait sketches? Did you outline areas of light and dark value?

▶ **ANALYZE** Did you select textured items to suggest light and dark values? Compare and contrast your use of tactile and visual textures.

▶ **INTERPRET** Do the use of texture and sharp contrasts in values affect the mood of this work? If so, how? Does the title of the work express the same mood?

▶ **JUDGE** Were you successful using different textures to create contrast? Did you demonstrate the effective use of printmaking media and tools? Which of the three aesthetic theories would be best to judge your work?

▶ **FIGURE 7.16A**

Student work.

Papier-Mâché Sculpture

▲ FIGURE 7.17

Leo Sewell. *Penguin.* Atlanta Airport, Atlanta, Georgia.

SUPPLIES

- Found objects such as seashells, marbles, feathers, bottle caps, pieces of old toys, ribbons, scraps of fabric, and so on
- Sketchbook and pencils
- Cardboard, wire, or chicken wire
- Masking tape
- Nontoxic papier-mâché paste
- Bowls for mixing paste
- Newspaper
- Paper towels
- Acrylic paint
- White glue or hot glue gun

Historical and Cultural Context

Leo Sewell is a Philadelphia-based artist who grew up in Annapolis, Maryland. His home was near a junkyard belonging to the U.S. Navy. Sewell frequently visited the yard, collecting discarded items that interested him. These recycled materials became a driving force in his sculptures and *assemblages* (ah-sem-**blazh**). Assemblages are works created by simply combining existing objects into a meaningful whole.

Sewell's early works were functional objects such as a watchcase or a table. Today, they are decorative and complex creations. Study his penguin sculpture in **Figure 7.17.** How many different objects can you identify that have been integrated into the form of this bird?

What You Will Learn

You will design and create a papier-mâché sculpture of an animal or a fantasy creature. You will cover the sculpture completely with found items, some of which may relate to the sculpture. You will attach and layer the found materials to create interesting surface textures and a sense of unity.

Creating

Begin your sculpture by thinking about or examining pictures of animals or fantasy creatures. Once you have chosen an animal or creature, draw details of its limbs, body, and head in your sketchbook.

Step 1 Gather as many found materials as you can. Comb your neighborhood, your attic, and other places where you might find discarded materials. Set these aside for later.

Step 2 Combine your body part sketches into a unified whole. Practice drawing your creature from various viewpoints: top, sides, front, back, and underside. Try to make the drawings as consistent as you can.

Step 3 Create a skeletal frame for your animal out of cardboard, wire, chicken wire, or some other pliable material. Wrap and stuff paper around your base. Tape it together with masking tape to create your form. Continue wrapping and stuffing and connecting until you have completed the basic form of your animal's body, including limbs and head.

Step 4 Mix your papier-mâché paste, following directions on the package. Tear strips of newspaper, dip them in wheat paste, and smooth them over the body (see pages 434–435 of the Technique Tips Handbook.) Repeat two layers of newspaper and one final layer of paper towels over the entire structure. Let your sculpture dry completely.

Step 5 Paint the sculpture using acrylic paint for a base coat. Let the work dry.

Step 6 Choose objects from among your found materials that seem to fit the contours of the animal's body. Glue the objects to the form. Fill in every space. Continue gluing and layering your items until your animal is completely covered. Add facial features and details.

Step 7 Create a base for your creation, if necessary. Give your work a title to express the meaning or mood of your creature. Display your sculpture.

Evaluating Your Work

▶ **DESCRIBE** What animal did you create? What materials did you use to create your body form? What recycled items appear on your creation? How did you choose to display your creation?

▶ **ANALYZE** What basic shapes did you use to create your form? Did you select textured objects that were appropriate to the form? Compare and contrast your use of texture and unity.

▶ **INTERPRET** What mood were you trying to convey? Does the title you chose sum up the meaning of your work?

▶ **JUDGE** Were you successful in creating the specific animal or creature? Did it turn out how you imagined? Which aesthetic theory would be appropriate to judge your work?

▲ **FIGURE 7.17A**

Student work.

STUDIO PROJECT
7-3

Layered Self-Portrait

▲ **FIGURE 7.18**

Robert Silvers. *Wolf.* 2003. Photomosaic.

SUPPLIES

- Sketchbook and pencil
- Digital camera
- Computer
- Scanner
- Image-editing or paint program
- Printer

Historical and Cultural Context

Have you ever heard someone described as "not seeing the forest for the trees?" This expression might be applied to the work in **Figure 7.18.** If you study the work very closely, you will notice that it contains hundreds of tiny photographs, many of them of wolves and other animals. These images provide a clue to the overall "forest" made up of tiny "trees." Stand back, and you discover the work is a portrait of a wolf.

The unique type of digital art shown here is known as a *photomosaic.* Like traditional mosaics, it is made up of many tiny parts. Unlike traditional mosaics, the parts are photos. Digital artist Robert Silvers precisely selected each tiny photo for its colors.

What You Will Learn

You will create a digital portrait that depicts an individual and a unique background that reflects the subject's interests. After photographing the subject and objects that represent them, you will import all the images into a computer application. Then you will choose a color scheme and apply a variety of textures to communicate a mood or message about the individual.

Creating

Take a picture of yourself, a friend, or a celebrity with a digital or traditional camera. Import the image into the computer. Next, capture or find and scan additional pictures that show the subject's interests and accomplishments.

Step 1 Open your image-editing or paint program. In separate files, import and open the images that reflect the subject's interests and activities. Choose one image that is the most interesting or striking. Scale the image so that it measures 8 × 6 inches. Save the document.

Step 2 Identify interesting details from the remaining open images. Use the Rectangle tool, Circle tool, and other Selection tools. Choose details one at a time. As each one is copied and pasted into the saved document, assign each to a different layer.

Step 3 Open your portrait document. Select the image of the person. Copy and paste this image into the top layer of the document with the details.

Step 4 Explore menus and settings to enhance and change color, contrast/brightness, hue/saturation, and opacity. Consider the mood or the idea you want to express. Select a color scheme.

Step 5 Pick options from the Filter menu. Explore the endless choices for adding textures. These special effects can distort images as well as imitate other media such as watercolors, chalks, and brushstrokes. Preview the effects before applying them.

Step 6 Save three different solutions. Print the one whose mood best fits your subject.

Evaluating Your Work

▶ **DESCRIBE** Identify the person you picked as your subject. What are the subject's interests and accomplishments?

▶ **ANALYZE** Explain your choice of objects, colors, and special effects in the portrait. How many layers did you use? Compare and contrast the use of textures in your work.

▶ **INTERPRET** What mood or feeling does the portrait convey? Interpret your artistic decisions. What message does the image communicate about the person?

▶ **JUDGE** What do you like best about the artwork? What challenges did you overcome? Justify your artistic decisions in this work. Which aesthetic theory would you use to judge this work?

▲ **FIGURE 7.18A**

Student work.

Texture

Texture can be rough or smooth, shiny or dull. Texture can be tactile (experienced through touch) or visual (experienced through sight). As you examine the student artworks on these pages:

- Compare and contrast them in terms of their use of texture.

- Analyze the works, forming precise conclusions about whether each uses tactile or visual texture.

Activity 7.19 **Tactile texture.**
Describe how this tapestry might feel to the touch. What adjectives would you use to convey this sensation?

Activity 7.20 **Texture and value.**
Analyze this artist's use of visual texture in this painting. Where has this artist used light and dark values of a hue to suggest a glossy texture?

▲ **FIGURE 7.19**

Student work. *Untitled.* Weaving, embroidery floss, fiber:

▲ **FIGURE 7.20**

Student work. *Wishing.* Acrylic.

Activity 7.21 **Visual texture combinations.**
This artwork combines many different visual textures. Identify as many of these as you can. Match each texture with one or more objects that appear to have this surface.

▲ **FIGURE 7.21**

Student work. *Me.* Collagraph.

Activity 7.22 **Texture and unity.**
Compare and contrast the variety of textures in this student print with those in the print in Figure 3.10 on page 48. Does the textural variety in these works create a sense of unity? Explain your reaction.

▲ **FIGURE 7.22**

Student work. *Untitled.* Collagraph.

ART *Online* To view more student artworks, visit the Glencoe Student Art Gallery at **art.glencoe.com**.

For Your Portfolio

Select and Analyze Portfolios. Sharpen your visual awareness by evaluating the artworks of others. With your teacher's guidance, compile a collection of portfolios or find online portfolios. Select and analyze these portfolios by peers and others to form precise conclusions about formal qualities (the elements and principles of art), historical and cultural contexts, intents, and meanings. Store your evaluations in your portfolio.

Visual Art Journal

Every object has a texture. As you walk around your school or community, develop your awareness of texture. Touch objects such as stone walls, glass windows, and your own clothing. Practice capturing these tactile textures in visual form by sketching them in your visual journal.

Art Criticism
in Action

▲ FIGURE 7.23

Duane Hanson. *Football Player.* 1981. Oil on polyvinyl, clothes, helmet, Styrofoam cup. 109.9 × 76.2 × 80 cm (43¼ × 30 × 31½"). Lowe Art Museum, University of Miami, Miami, Florida. Museum purchase through funds from the Friends of Art and public subscription. © Estate of Duane Hanson/Licensed by VAGA, New York, NY.

Critiquing the Artwork

1 DESCRIBE *What do you see?*

List all the information found in the credit line.

- Judging from the media, do you think this artwork is a painting, photograph, or sculpture? Explain.

- Describe what you see.

2 ANALYZE *How is this work organized?*

This is a clue-collecting step about the elements of art.

- Which type of texture has the artist used, tactile or visual?

- Identify at least one example of rough, smooth, matte, and shiny texture. Compare and contrast their uses.

- Would you classify the form of this work as free-form or geometric?

3 INTERPRET *What feeling does this artwork communicate to you?*

Combine the clues you have collected to form a creative interpretation of the work.

- What mood do the facial expression and body language of this sculpture express?

- What do you imagine this person is thinking? Write his thoughts in a brief paragraph.

4 JUDGE *What do you think of the work?*

Now, it is time to decide whether this is a successful work of art.

- Do you think the artist used texture successfully in this work? Explain.

- Do you think this is a successful work of art? Why or why not? Use one or more of the three aesthetic theories to defend your judgment.

Meet the ARTIST

Duane Hanson
1925–1996

Duane Hanson was born in Alexandria, Minnesota, in 1925. He was always fascinated by the human figure. At age 13, he carved a wood version of Gainsborough's *Blue Boy* from a log. His "model" was a reproduction of the painting in an art history book. His early professional works use traditional painting and sculpting techniques. By the mid-1960s, he had begun using polyester resin and fiberglass to make castings of people. He painted these realistically with oils, adding hair and real clothing. The result is life-size sculptures so real that they are often mistaken for living people.

A ceramic bench in a Barcelona park. Gaudi designed the bench in 1914.

BELOW: The Sagrada Familia church

MACDUFF EVERTON/CORBIS

TEXTURED BUILDINGS

People are passionate about Antonio Gaudi's architecture.

Love it or hate it, most visitors react strongly to the bizarre architectural creations of Antonio Gaudi (1852–1926). Every year, visitors come to Barcelona, Spain, to admire—and even touch— his amazing buildings.

This Spanish architect combined a love of nature and of Gothic ornament in his design (Figure 13.7, page 355). That mixture produced buildings with shapes and textures so unusual, they still make people gasp. An apartment house completed in 1910 has curvy sides and a rough, grainy surface. Together, these textures create the effect of waves crashing on a beach. Gaudi used ceramics to decorate a public park. He embedded broken glazed ceramic tiles in a concrete bench and other structures to create fantastic colors and rich, varied textures. Gaudi's most famous work, the Sagrada Familia, is an unfinished church. The stone towers are so thickly decorated, they look to some people like trees in a rainforest. When Gaudi graduated from architecture school, one teacher said he was either a madman or a genius. Today, most people cast their vote for genius.

TIME to Connect

Climate, available materials, and the cultural backgrounds of the people often influence a nation's architecture. Use a map to locate these Spanish cities: Seville, Barcelona, and Granada. Using your school's media center to obtain photos and information, compare and contrast the architecture in those cities. Write a report including the following:

• **What are some landmark buildings in each of the cities? How are the styles alike or different? What types of materials were used to build these landmarks?**

• **Compare them with Gaudi's work. How are they similar? How are they different?**

Building Vocabulary

On a separate sheet of paper, write the term that best matches each definition given below.

1. The element of art that refers to how things feel, or look as if they might feel, if touched.
2. The illusion of a three-dimensional surface.
3. A surface that reflects a soft, dull light.
4. An artwork created by pasting cut or torn materials such as paper, photographs, and fabric to a flat surface.
5. A method of producing textures by placing paper over objects that have raised surfaces and rubbing the paper with graphite, wax, or crayon.
6. The technique of scratching into wet paint with a variety of tools to create texture.
7. A technique of creating random textured patterns by applying thick paint to two surfaces, pressing them together, and then pulling them apart.

Reviewing Art Facts

Answer the following questions using complete sentences.

8. With what senses is texture perceived?
9. What is the difference between tactile and visual texture?
10. What is the difference between simulated and invented texture?
11. Name the four types of texture.
12. Name two ways in which painters may add real texture to their paintings.
13. In what ways do sculptors create texture in their works?
14. Describe the similarities and differences in frottage, grattage, and decalcomania.

Thinking Critically About Art

15. **Describe.** Look at the photographs in Figure 7.2 on page 172. Describe them without naming any of the objects shown. Describe only the lines, shapes, spaces, values, and textures in the photographs. From your description, have classmates guess which photograph you are describing.

16. **Historical/Cultural Heritage.** Review the Meet the Artist feature on page 181. The dancer in Figure 7.12 is depicted in a spontaneous, natural manner. This reflected the general trend toward capturing natural scenes in art at that time. Compare and contrast the historical style shown in Figure 7.12 with Figure 5.9 on page 104 and identify the general trend in art at the time Figure 5.9 was created.

Learn more about the amazing textures in the sculptures of Jesús Moroles. Take part in an interactive online exhibition and discussion of his works at the J. Paul Getty Museum Web site. Click on the **Web Museum Tour** link at **art.glencoe.com.**

Linking to the Performing Arts

Use the Performing Arts Handbook page 419 to find out how Paul Winter captures the texture of the sounds of nature through his music.

The Principles of Art

"The fundamental thing in art is freedom! In art, there are millions of paths—as many paths as there are artists."

—*Rufino Tamayo (1899–1991)*

Quick Write

Identifying Connotations. In the above quote, the artist refers to paths. He was not using the word in its strict dictionary sense. Tell what you think he meant by restating the quote in your own words.

◄

Rufino Tamayo. *Fruit Vendors.* 1952. Oil on canvas. 150.8 × 200.8 cm (59³/₈ × 79¹/₁₆"). Albright-Knox Art Gallery, Buffalo, New York. Gift of Seymour H. Knox, Jr., 1954.

▲ **FIGURE 8.1** The quilt shown here is unique in that the images in the center have been painted by hand. Can you find a pattern in this quilt? What objects or figures are repeated?

Faith Ringgold. *The Men: Mask Face Quilt #2.* 1986. Acrylic on canvas with fabric borders. 177.8 × 157.5 (70 × 62"). © 1986 Faith Ringgold.

CHAPTER 8

Rhythm, Pattern, and Movement

Life is full of rhythmic events and patterns. Think about the yearly cycle of the seasons. The regular routines or patterns of daily life create a sense of stability and security.

In this chapter, you will:

- Identify rhythms and patterns occurring in the world around you.
- Observe the relationship of motif to pattern.
- Compare and contrast the use of the art principles rhythm and pattern to organize the art elements in artworks.
- Create visual solutions that use the principles of rhythm and pattern.

Focus on **Art History** Faith Ringgold (b. 1930) is known for her colorful painted story quilts **(Figure 8.1).** She grew up in a close-knit family in Harlem, New York. Her early oil paintings focused on civil rights issues of the 1960s. Then in 1980, she was invited to make a quilt for a special exhibit. Her mother, who was a seamstress, helped her make *Echoes of Harlem,* a quilt of painted faces and fabrics. She has been creating quilts that combine storytelling and painting ever since. Her story quilts have also been used as illustrations in children's books that focus on the achievements of African Americans.

Analyze. Look again at Figure 8.1 to form a conclusion about the use of pattern. Can you find a repeated pattern in this quilt? Explain your answer.

Rhythm and Pattern

Vocabulary

rhythm
visual rhythm
pattern
motif
module

Rhythm is *the principle of art that indicates movement by the repetition of elements or objects.* The principle of rhythm is found in all the arts: music, dance, poetry, and theatre. In music, rhythm is created by the measure of time between musical sounds. Beats are followed by rests. In poetry, the repetition of words, sounds, and phrases creates rhythm. The visual arts combine repetition and pauses to create rhythm.

Visual Rhythm

Visual rhythm is *rhythm you receive through your eyes rather than through your ears.* Visual rhythm is created by repeated positive shapes separated by negative spaces. Everywhere you look you can see visual rhythms. Books lined up in a bookcase and cars in a parking lot are examples of visual rhythms. A line of people in the cafeteria has visual rhythm. Each person is a positive shape, and the space between each person is a negative space.

In **Figure 8.2,** Chief Black Hawk has used visual rhythm to suggest the movements of a dance ceremony. The repeated images of the six Crow men are the major beats, or positive shapes, of the rhythm. The spaces between the men are the rests, or negative spaces, in the rhythm.

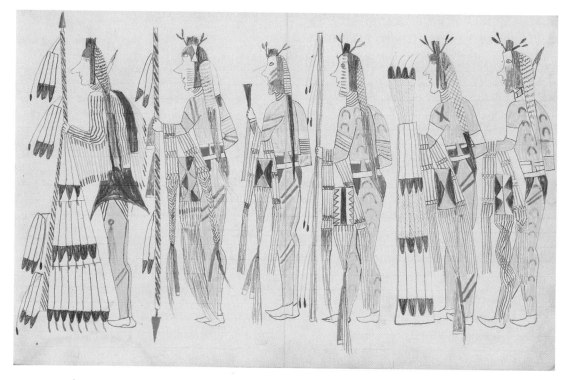

▲ **FIGURE 8.2** In the winter of 1880–81, Chief Black Hawk, a Lakota man, supported his family by selling drawings to a trader on the reservation. He was unknown until 1994, when a book of his drawings emerged on the auction market. Chief Black Hawk's book shows natural history drawings, hunting and ceremonial activities of the Lakota, and many pictures of Crow ceremonies.

Chief Black Hawk. *Crow Men in Ceremonial Dress.* 1880–81. Ink and pencil on paper. 26 × 41.9 cm (10¼ × 16½"). Thaw Collection, Fenimore Art Museum, Cooperstown, New York.

Rosa Bonheur (**roh**-zah bah-**nur**) was born in Bordeaux, France in 1822. When she was seven years old, her family moved to Paris. Her father, Raymond Bonheur, was a landscape artist and painting teacher. He trained Rosa and her three siblings. As a member of the religious group called Saint-Simonians, he believed in the equality of women. This attitude allowed Rosa Bonheur to develop unrestrained by traditional women's roles.

When she was ten years old, she refused to be apprenticed to a dressmaker, preferring instead to sketch animals in nearby woods and to draw scenes from the balcony of the family apartment. This lifelong love of animals would inspire her later art. She painted huge compositions in which horses and other animals played a major role. She visited slaughterhouses to learn the anatomy of animals. She also traveled to livestock markets. *The Horse Fair* (**Figure 8.3**) is a painting that depicts one of these scenes. Bonheur became a famous, well-known artist. In 1865, she became the first woman to be awarded the Grand Cross of the Legion of Honor.

▲ **FIGURE 8.3** Bonheur, a lifelong animal lover, often created large-scale artworks with horses and other animals as the subject matter. In this painting Bonheur has used the horses as a motif. The rhythm the horses create pulls your eyes through the painting. Where does the movement start? From which direction does the viewer get drawn through the art?

Rosa Bonheur. *The Horse Fair*. 1853–55. Oil on canvas. 244.5 × 506.7 cm (96¼ × 199½″). The Metropolitan Museum of Art, New York, New York. Gift of Cornelius Vanderbilt, 1887. (87.25).

▲ **FIGURE 8.4** In this unusual night view of New York City, you can see examples of rhythms made by the buildings and the lit windows. Notice how the value changes also create a sense of rhythm.

Berenice Abbott. *The Night View.* 1936. Photograph. Museum of the City of New York, New York. Gift of Mr. Todd Watts.

▶ **FIGURE 8.5** There are two major motifs in this design. One is a solid blue square set on its point. The alternating motif is bordered with a light blue band and divided in the center into four smaller squares.

Annie M. Peachey. *Four in Block Work Quilt.* 1925–35. Cotton, rayon, and synthetics. 216 × 184 cm (85 × 72½"). Collection of the Museum of American Folk Art, New York, New York. Gift of Mr. and Mrs. William B. Wigton.

In visual rhythm, a beat may be one element or a combination of elements. Look at the photograph in **Figure 8.4.** The strongest beats are the big, tall buildings. The lighted windows are secondary rhythms. The streets and the spaces between the buildings create negative, empty space—the rests between the beats.

Visual rhythms create a sensation of movement. Rhythms cause the viewer's eyes to follow the visual beats through a work of art. Visual movement is different from real action, which involves a physical change in position. For example, a ball bouncing across a room is real action. Visual movement simply suggests movement. In an artwork, round shapes separated by negative spaces can create the visual sensation of the movement of a ball. Your eyes bounce from one round shape to the next. In **Figure 8.6** on page 203, the artist has used rhythm to pull your eyes through the work. Notice how the curved figures and the slanted hoes give a sensation of visual movement.

Pattern

Pattern *is the principle of art that is concerned with decorative surface design.* It is usually a two-dimensional visual repetition. Blue stripes on a shirt are a pattern. Ten blue striped shirts arranged in a store window create a visual rhythm that in turn creates visual movement.

The unit that is repeated in visual pattern is called a **motif.** Sometimes, every motif is an exact duplicate of the first unit; sometimes, the repetitions vary from the original **(Figure 8.5).** Look around, and you will find examples of patterns created by the repetitions of one or more motifs. You can discover patterns in furniture, rugs, clothing, or the line of lockers in the hallway.

Woodruff has used many random visual rhythms in this work to create the feeling that the workers are singing and working to the rhythm of the song as they hoe the cotton. In the diagram you can see how he has used repeated shapes to move your eyes through the work. How many visual beats can you find in this painting?

◀ **FIGURE 8.6**

Hale Woodruff. *Poor Man's Cotton.* 1944. Watercolor on paper. 77.5 × 57.2 cm (30½ × 22½″). The Newark Museum, Newark, New Jersey.

▲ **FIGURE 8.7** This elevator grille is a delicate pattern of lines and round forms. It was once part of a large bank of elevators in the 1893 Chicago Stock Exchange. The building was torn down in 1972, but parts of it, such as this grille, have been saved and housed in various museums.

Louis Sullivan. *Grille of Elevator Enclosure Cage from the Chicago Stock Exchange Building.* 1893–94. Painted cast and wrought iron and bronze. 185.4 × 78.7 cm (73 × 31″). High Museum of Art, Atlanta, Georgia. Virginia Carroll Crawford Collection, 1982.291.

In sculpture and architecture *a three-dimensional motif* is sometimes called a **module.** Modular furniture is composed of standard matching units.

A pattern of lines can decorate a piece of fabric or wallpaper. **Figure 8.7** shows a pattern decorating an elevator grille. These are decorative patterns meant to be visually appealing. Other patterns are functional. A bricklayer places bricks in a certain pattern in order to build a sturdy, durable wall. The bricklayer may make the pattern more complex in order to create a finished work that is very decorative, but the main purpose is still functional.

Activity   **Analyzing Motifs and Patterns**

Comparing and Contrasting the Use of Pattern. Make a collection of decorative patterns. You may use photographs, clippings from magazines, scraps of fabric, and original drawings. Compare and contrast the use of pattern in your work and identify the motif in each pattern by drawing a circle around one. Organize your pattern collection into a poster, a bulletin board, a booklet, or some other type of presentation.

Computer Option. Start with a rectangle and design a simple motif. Use three colors or three original textures in black and white. Create a variety of pattern with that motif. Print your patterns. If your printer is black and white, you can add color with other media such as colored pencil after the design is printed out.

✓ *Check Your Understanding*

1. Define *rhythm.*
2. What is visual rhythm?
3. What is pattern? How do motifs relate to pattern?

Types of Rhythm and Pattern

Arranging beats or motifs and space in different ways creates different visual rhythms and patterns. There are many ways to combine beats or motifs and space. Each combination gives a different character to the rhythm or pattern depicted.

Random

A motif repeated in no apparent order, with no regular spaces in between, creates a random rhythm. One example is autumn leaves that cover the ground. Cracks in mud and splashes of paint are also examples of random rhythm.

Crowds of people often create random rhythms —think of holiday shoppers, rush-hour commuters, and students in the halls between classes. A large group of people pushing onto a bus is full of rhythm. The beat is one person. Every person is different, and the space between and around each person is slightly different.

Philip Moulthrop, the creator of the *White Pine Mosaic Bowl* in **Figure 8.8,** is an artist and craftsman. He uses a machine called a lathe to create the form of his wooden bowls. At the beginning of the twentieth century, wood turning was considered an industrial activity since lathes had been used to

◀ **FIGURE 8.8** To create this random rhythm of round shapes on the surface of his turned bowl, Moulthrop placed white pine branches in a specific arrangement and embedded them in a black resin mixture.

Philip Moulthrop. *White Pine Mosaic Bowl.* 1993. White pine, resin, lathe-turned. 23.5 x 29.8 x 29.8 cm (9¼ × 11¾ × 11¾"). Mint Museum of Craft + Design, Charlotte, North Carolina.

▲ **FIGURE 8.9** This building was the first office building to rise above 1,000 feet. Notice how the pairs of windows form a regular beat both vertically and horizontally. The negative spaces between them are the rests between the beats.

William van Alen. *Chrysler Building,* New York, New York. Completed in 1930.

mass-produce furniture. Gradually, the turners became accepted as craftspeople. They believed that the finding of a piece of wood with specific qualities led to the quality of the finished piece of work. In Figure 8.8, the pieces of wood create a beautiful random pattern. Today, you will find turned-wood vessels in crafts museums around the world.

Regular

Regular rhythms and patterns have identical beats or motifs and equal amounts of space between them **(Figure 8.9).** Regular rhythm has a steady beat. Regular repetitions are used to organize objects. Parking spaces are laid out with regular rhythm. Stores organize merchandise into regular stacks and rows. This makes it easier for you to find things, and it also makes the displays more attractive than if items were arranged in a random fashion.

◀ **FIGURE 8.10**
While doing research for this project, Maya Lin stumbled on a photo of the "Stokes Wave" that occurs naturally on the open sea. She transformed something that was liquid and moving into a solid sculpture in the landlocked, Midwestern landscape.

Maya Lin. *The Wave Field.* 1995. Shaped earth. 30.5 × 30.5 m (100 × 100'). University of Michigan, Ann Arbor, Michigan.

A grid is based on regular rhythm. It is a regular arrangement of parallel lines. A football field is laid out in a grid, as is a checkerboard. Windows form a grid pattern on the side of a building. Maya Lin used a grid to lay out her *Wave Field* in **Figure 8.10.** It is a series of 50 grass waves in eight rows. The texture of the grasses and curved forms engage the viewer. The field was built with a combination of soil and sand and covered with green sod. The crest of each wave is three feet high. Lin has created an interesting space for relaxing, studying, or playing.

The tunic in **Figure 8.11** was woven to be part to the formal dress of the ancient Peruvian people known as the Huari. It was worn at court and placed on the body for burial. Another strong example of regular rhythm is Figure 1.18 on page 20.

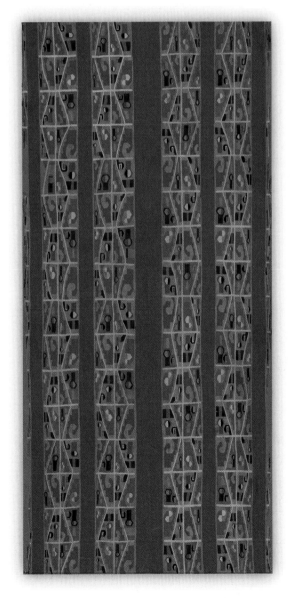

▶ **FIGURE 8.11** Look closely at the designs in the repeated geometric shapes. They are stylized eyes and mouths with fangs that symbolize powerful feline deities.

Peru, Huari. Tunic. c. A.D. 800–1000. Cotton and wool. Height: 210.8 cm (83"). Detroit Institute of Arts, Detroit, Michigan. Founders Society Purchase with funds from Lee and Tina Hills.

▲ **FIGURE 8.12** Notice how this artist has switched the direction of every other column so that the designs seem to reverse as you look across the row of designs.

Upper Orinoco River, Venezuela. Yekuana *muaho* (woven beaded apron). Early twentieth century. 25.1 × 33.7 cm (9⅞ × 13¼"). Courtesy National Museum of the American Indian, Smithsonian Institution, Washington, D.C.

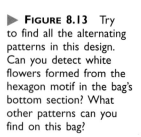 **FIGURE 8.13** Try to find all the alternating patterns in this design. Can you detect white flowers formed from the hexagon motif in the bag's bottom section? What other patterns can you find on this bag?

Ojibwe. Bandolier Bag. Beaded cloth. 108 × 33.7 cm (42½ × 13¼"). Courtesy National Museum of the American Indian, Smithsonian Institution, Washington, D.C.

Alternating

Alternating rhythm and pattern can be created in several ways. One way is to introduce a second beat or motif. Another way is to make a change in the placement or content of the original beat or motif. A third way is to change the spaces between the beats or motifs. Sometimes, alternation is created simply by changing the position of the motif. For example, the motif may be turned upside down. The native Venezuelan artist used alternation to make the beaded apron in **Figure 8.12** more interesting. The Ojibwe Native American who sewed the beads on the bandolier bag in **Figure 8.13** made the design interesting by alternating the colors of the beaded flowers.

Flowing

Flowing rhythm is created by repeating wavy lines. Curved shapes, such as rolling hills or ocean waves, create

Activity	Alternating Pattern

Demonstrating Effective Use of Art Media in Design. Using a pen or pencil, draw a checkerboard grid on a sheet of white paper. Create an alternating pattern using one motif. Turn the motif upside down in every other box. Next, draw a checkerboard grid and create an alternating pattern using two motifs.

Computer Option. Design two motifs using the tools of your choice. Use the Select tool and the Copy and Paste options to create an alternating pattern using both motifs. On a new screen, create an alternating pattern using only one motif. In this design, you can change the placement of the motif—for example, turn it upside down, or change the spaces between the motifs. Label and save both designs.

flowing rhythms. In **Figure 8.14,** the artist was able to capture the flowing movement of the waterfall as it rolled over the rocks. Your eyes follow the curving path as it changes direction gradually. There are no sudden breaks in the line. In **Figure 8.15,** the artist has used flowing rhythm to arrange the heads of the singers to create the mood of the flowing melody coming from the harp.

Flowing rhythm is created using upward swells and downward slides. You might think of the upward moves as the beats and the downward moves as the rests. Allan Houser has used flowing rhythms symbolically in his sculpture, *Coming of Age* **(Figure 8.16).** The work expresses the symbolic union of nature and femininity. The thick, rhythmically flowing strands of hair suggest motion and the act of running. They also suggest the movement of the wind, of water, or even the blazing motion of flames.

▲ **FIGURE 8.14** Borsky captured the white flow of this waterfall in his photograph by increasing the amount of time he exposed the film to light.

David Borsky. *Waterfall.* Photograph. Courtesy of the artist.

▲ **FIGURE 8.15** This sculpture was inspired by the song *Lift Every Voice and Sing,* which was a popular song among African Americans in the 1930s. This is a cast-iron souvenir version of the original sculpture, a 16-foot plaster work exhibited at the 1939 World's Fair.

Augusta Savage. *Lift Every Voice and Sing.* 1939. Cast iron. 27.6 × 23.5 × 11.4 cm (10⅞ x 9¼ x 4½″). Countee Cullen Collection, Hampton University Museum, Hampton, Virginia.

▲ **FIGURE 8.16** This sculpture was created to celebrate feminine youth and beauty. The upturned head symbolizes the girl's desire to run to the four directions of the earth. The small shape above her forehead represents an abalone shell, a fertility symbol. The feather in her hair signifies a long life.

Allan Houser. *Coming of Age.* 1977. Bronze, edition of 12. 19.2 × 39.4 × 17.8 cm (7½ × 15½ × 7″). Denver Art Museum, Denver, Colorado.

Progressive

In *progressive* rhythm, there is a change in the beat each time it is repeated. The change is a steady one. Each time the beat appears, it is slightly different **(Figure 8.17).** A progressive rhythm may start with a square. The size of the square may be changed by making it slightly smaller each time it is repeated, or each square may be made a different color of the spectrum or a different step on the value scale each time it is repeated. Shapes can be progressively changed. The sides of a square can be gradually rounded until the square becomes a circle.

▲ **FIGURE 8.17** In this etching, Escher creates a progressive rhythm of reptiles climbing out of a flat drawing and evolving into fully formed creatures. The progression ends with a fully three-dimensional reptile standing on the polygon, steam blowing from its nostrils. Then the reptile reenters the two-dimensional drawing.

M. C. Escher. *Reptiles.* 1943. Lithograph. 33.3 × 40 cm (13⅛ × 15¾″). © 2003 Cordon Art, Baarn, Holland. All rights reserved.

✓ Check Your Understanding

1. Explain the difference between random and regular rhythm and pattern.
2. In what ways can an alternating rhythm and pattern be created?
3. Compare and contrast the use of pattern in Figures 8.12 and 8.13 on page 208.

How Artists Use Rhythm to Create Movement

Vocabulary

visual movement
kinetic

Artists use rhythm in a work of art just as they use the elements and other principles of art—to convey feelings and ideas. Rhythm, which can be comforting and predictable, can also be monotonous, symbolic, or graceful, depending on the artist's goals. Rhythm can also create visual movement.

Visual Movement

Visual movement is *the principle of art used to create the look and feeling of action and to guide the viewer's eyes throughout the work of art.* In **Figure 8.18,** the artist has used visual movement to tell her story. Xiong has arranged the figures and objects in her art using visual rhythm to create the sense of movement. The main beat is Xiong's family. Notice how the figures change slightly from one appearance to the next. Is the rhythm random, alternating, or progressive?

◀ **FIGURE 8.18** This story cloth tells the story of the artist's flight from Laos, across the Mekong River, to an American refugee camp in Thailand. The story starts in the upper right corner. Can you follow the family as it moves toward safety?

Chaing Xiong. *Hmong Story Cloth.* 1987. Pieced and embroidered polyester, cotton blend. 140.3 × 145.4 cm (55¼ × 57¼"). Wadsworth Atheneum, Hartford, Connecticut. Florence Paull Berger Fund.

▲ **FIGURE 8.19** What kind of rhythm does Stella use to create this celebration of movement and light at the Coney Island Amusement Park? Which elements does he use to create his rhythms?

Joseph Stella. *Battle of Lights, Coney Island, Mardi Gras.* 1913–14. Oil on canvas. 1.9 × 2.2 m (6′4″ × 7′1″). Yale University Art Gallery, New Haven, Connecticut.

One group of artists tried to do more than control the way in which viewers looked at works of art. This group of artists, called the *Futurists,* used rhythm to capture the idea of movement itself. The Futurists used the word *dynamism* to refer to the forces of movement. They believed that nothing was solid or stable and that art should show such dynamism. In their artworks, the dynamic movement of forms is shown by slanting and overlapping shapes. In **Figure 8.19,** the artist, Joseph Stella, captures the excitement and movement of the Amusement Park at Coney Island. A frenzy of movement is created through the use of rhythms and patterns of colors and shapes. Can you find indications of amusement park rides such as a Ferris wheel and a roller coaster? Do you recognize any other rides? Can you find indications of people?

◀ **FIGURE 8.20**
Look closely at the places where the rods are joined by a carefully planned set of loops. Calder's works are so carefully balanced that the slightest movement of air will set the sculpture in motion. Watching a Calder sculpture is like watching a graceful dancer.

Alexander Calder. *Untitled.* c. 1942. Painted aluminum sheet, steel sheet, and steel wire. 147.3 × 182.9 × 114.3 cm (58 × 72 × 45″). Amon Carter Museum, Fort Worth, Texas. 1999.6. © 2003 Estate of Alexander Calder/Artists Rights Society (ARS), New York.

You can also see movement in the visual art of Alexander Calder. He was a mechanical engineer who believed in what the Futurists were doing. In his work he repeated abstract shapes and put them into real motion. He did this using the real forces of air currents and gravity. Calder's creations were dubbed **kinetic** sculpture, because they *actually move in space* **(Figure 8.20).** Artist Marcel Duchamp gave Calder's moving sculptures another name, *mobiles.* Moving sculptures of this kind have been called mobiles ever since.

 Check Your Understanding

1. Define *visual movement.*
2. Which group of artists used rhythm to capture the idea of movement itself?
3. Describe a kinetic sculpture.
4. Compare and contrast the use of rhythm in Figure 8.18 on page 211 and Figure 8.19 on page 212.

Found Objects Jewelry

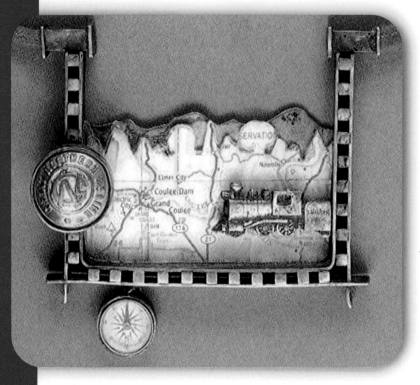

▲ **FIGURE 8.21**

Ramona Solberg. *Cracker Jack Choo Choo.* 1995. Cast and forged silver, compass, map, button, Lucite, leather. 66 cm long, 8.2 × 10.2 cm (26″ long, 3¹/₄ × 4″). Collection of Jean Anderson.

SUPPLIES

- Assorted found objects

- Sketchbook and pencil

- Small piping cord for wire coiling and/or hanging neck pieces

- Scrap or precut metal shapes, such as copper

- Wire (copper, brass, nickel silver) in a variety of gauges

- Wire cutters, needle nose pliers, screwdrivers

- Jeweler's saw and blades

- Hand files and/or abrasive papers

- Drill and bits

- Super-strength adhesives

- Pin backs, chain, or cord for necklaces

Historical and Cultural Context

Jewelry is the making or use of objects for body adornment and decoration. Among ancient peoples, the wearing of jewelry was often limited to royalty and/or tribal leaders. Materials were specific to the environment of the craftsperson. These might include bone, stone, shell, claws, hair, plant fibers, ceramic, metal ores, and semiprecious gems. As trade between cultures increased, so did the availability of materials. Jewelry began to show more variety and became available to commoners.

The necklace pendant in **Figure 8.21** was crafted by Ramona Solberg, a contemporary jewelry maker, but bears resemblances to jewelry crafted long ago. Not the least of the similarities is the use of found objects. Notice the title. What do you think was the source of the found object central to this work?

What You Will Learn

You will create a jewelry design for practical application using found objects, alternative materials, and simple cold connection techniques. Cold connections are usually wire, loops, glue, or any means of connection without the use of a torch or heat. Your work will make use of visually compatible or related objects organized in a balanced composition. The arrangement of your chosen design-related components will make use of random, regular, alternating, or flowing rhythm.

Creating

Brainstorm with classmates about materials and sources for found objects appropriate to this project. Locate items at home, make a trip to a local hardware store, or acquire materials from donated sources. Share extra parts and items not needed with classmates. This creates a wider variety of materials from which to choose. (*Note:* This activity is not about restringing broken necklace beads or buttons.)

Step 1 Select approximately seven items of similar shape, color, or texture. This will help establish a sense of rhythm and unity in your arrangement.

Step 2 Experiment with arranging your found items in interesting ways. Attempt to "view" a grouping that might be suitable for a pin or a suspended neckpiece. Make sketches of arrangements that appeal to your design sense. Determine whether additional items are needed to complete an idea for which you are missing components.

Step 3 Choose your best design.

Step 4 Problem-solve ways to attach your items. Possible solutions might include drilling holes and "sewing" with wire, super-strength adhesives, wire jump rings, and so on. Be flexible if an idea is not successful, and rethink your strategy. (*Note:* If using super-strength adhesives, you might try putting a small amount on a scrap of mat. Then you can apply the glue with a toothpick.)

Step 5 Attach a pin back or cord to present your piece when finished.

Evaluating Your Work

▶ **DESCRIBE** Identify the objects you used in your art object. How were these objects connected in the final work?

▶ **ANALYZE** Compare and contrast the use of color, texture, and form to create rhythm in your work. Describe how balance was used in your composition.

▶ **INTERPRET** What feeling is conveyed by the materials, use of rhythm, and composition of your piece? Give your piece a title. What type of person might enjoy wearing this piece? Explain your answer.

▶ **JUDGE** What aesthetic theory is best applied to your work? Are you satisfied with your finished art object? What might you change if you were to do this activity again? Explain your answer.

▲ **FIGURE 8.21A**

Student work.

Rhythm and Movement Painting

▲ **FIGURE 8.22**

Jacob Lawrence. *Harriet Tubman Series Number 4.* 1939–40. Casein tempera on gessoed hardboard. 30.5 × 45.4 cm (12 × 17⁷/₈″). Hampton University Museum, Hampton, Virginia.

SUPPLIES

- Sketchbook and drawing pencils
- Scissors
- 12 × 8″ watercolor paper
- Watercolor paints
- Watercolor brushes
- Colored pencils

Historical and Cultural Context

Some art captures a moment in time. Jacob Lawrence, the artist who painted the work in **Figure 8.22,** captured many moments—all in the life of one person. That person was Harriet Tubman, the heroic African American who led countless fellow enslaved persons to freedom via her "Underground Railroad." Take a look at the figures in this painting. Notice their body language and facial expressions. Can you sense what point they are at in their long journey to freedom?

What You Will Learn

The success of Lawrence's painting depends on the use of two art principles—rhythm and movement. In this activity, you will do the same. You will create a mixed-media work using active figures organized in a repeated rhythm to express visual movement. A secondary rhythm of background shapes will be painted in a color scheme that contrasts with that of the main figures.

Creating

Working in groups of at least five, brainstorm ideas for poses from activities that have strong movement. Possibilities include sports, cheerleading, dance, and running. Each group member is to take turns doing an action pose. Others in the group will meanwhile make gesture drawings of the model, trying to get the proportions as accurate as possible (Technique Tips Handbook, page 428). Each group member should end up with at least five sketches.

Step 1 Select at least two drawings to use multiple times. Cut the figures out. Then plan how you will arrange the repeated shapes on a sheet of watercolor paper. When you are satisfied with a figure's placement, lightly trace around the shape with pencil. Remember to emphasize a flowing, rhythmic movement that pulls the viewer's eyes throughout the composition.

Step 2 Divide the background into shapes that create a secondary rhythm. Leave about a quarter of an inch of white space between the shapes.

Step 3 Choose a color to paint the main figures. Proceed with the painting.

Step 4 While the paint is drying, plan a background color scheme that will contrast harmoniously with the figures you painted. Once the paint is dry, paint the background shapes.

Step 5 Plan an alternating pattern using lines and shapes that can be used throughout the unpainted areas. Select two shades of colored pencil that are reflected in the background color scheme. Using these, apply alternating patterns. Place your lines and shapes close together when creating your pattern. Fill all the white areas.

Evaluating Your Work

▶ **DESCRIBE** What action poses are represented in your finished painting? Tell why you chose the poses you did.

▶ **ANALYZE** Did you use rhythm and repetition in arranging the active figures? Does the background show a secondary rhythm? Compare and contrast the use of color and line organized by the principles of rhythm and pattern. Does your work seem to convey visual movement?

▶ **INTERPRET** What kind of mood does your work express? Name a song you know that would fit the mood of your work.

▶ **JUDGE** How well do you feel your artwork shows rhythm and visual movement? If you were to do it over again, how would you improve your work? Which of the three aesthetic theories would you use to judge this work?

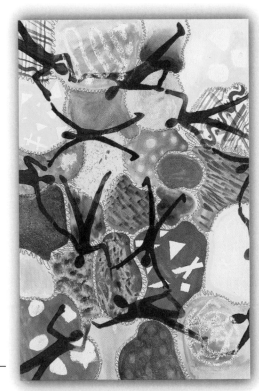

▶ **FIGURE 8.22A**

Student work.

STUDIO PROJECT 8–3

Digital Rendering of Reflections

▲ **FIGURE 8.23**

M. C. Escher. *Day and Night.* 1938. Woodcut in black and gray, printed from two blocks. 39.1 × 67.7 cm (15²/₅ × 26²/₃″). © Cordon Art, Baarn, Holland.

SUPPLIES

- Sketchbook and pencils
- Computer
- 3-D modeling program
- Scanner (optional)
- Color printer

Historical and Cultural Context

The unusual image in **Figure 8.23** is by twentieth-century Dutch graphic artist M. C. Escher. It is one of many the artist did in which one set of objects or shapes gradually changes—or metamorphoses—into another. In this case, the objects undergoing this transformation are two flocks of birds, one white and one black. Notice how the figures (the birds) on one side of the image little by little become the ground (the land) for the other side. In fact, the two sides of the work are mirror images of each other. At least they would be if it weren't night on one side and day on the other.

What You Will Learn

You will create a complex image using repeated reflections of the same objects within the artwork. You will use a 3-D modeling program (Digital Media Handbook, page 451). Your composition is to be arranged such that there is progressive rhythm throughout the work.

Creating

Think of as many highly reflective objects as you can, such as mirrors, puddles, sunglass lenses, and chrome bumpers. Sketch several of these items.

Step 1 Choose your two best sketches. These forms will be the basis of your artwork.

Step 2 Using a 3-D modeling program, model these forms, using basic geometry. You may, if you like, scan in your sketches. Make sure you name all of the surfaces, especially the areas that will have the reflection properties applied to them. Be sure to save your work often.

Step 3 Once you have modeled and named each surface, import the forms into the program's layout area.

Step 4 Arrange and angle multiple instances of one or both forms into a composition in which each is reflected at least once. There should a minimum of nine reflections altogether. At least some of the images should be reflected in such a manner as to show progressive rhythm.

Step 5 Set your surface properties for each surface area to Maximum Reflection. Then set your Lighting by determining the type of light (for example, Spotlight, Diffused Light), how many lights you will use, and from what direction each light source will be coming. You cannot have reflection if you have no light to reflect.

Step 6 Save your layout of the scene. Then test render the scene. Repeat steps 4 through 6 as needed until you are satisfied with your output.

Step 7 Once satisfied, set the antialiasing to low, and render your final picture.

Evaluating Your Work

▶ **DESCRIBE** Tell what objects you modeled for your artwork. Explain how you modeled your objects and arranged them in layout.

▶ **ANALYZE** Compare and contrast your use of form and rhythm. Did your forms change at all with each reflection, and if so, how? Did you create a natural progressive rhythm?

▶ **INTERPRET** What mood does your artwork express? Give a title to your work that sums up the feelings you are trying to express in your work.

▶ **JUDGE** Were you successful at creating a work of art using progressive rhythm? Evaluate and justify your artistic decisions.

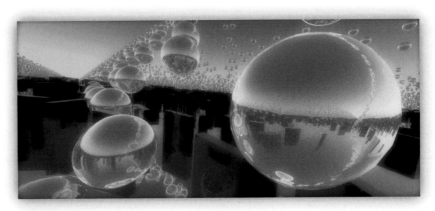

▲ **FIGURE 8.23A**

Student work.

Rhythm, Pattern, and Movement

Rhythm in art, as in music, gives stability to a composition. By repeating a visual "beat" or motif, the artist creates movement and interesting patterns. As you examine the student artworks on these pages:

- Compare and contrast them in terms of their use of rhythm, pattern, and movement.

- Analyze the works, forming precise conclusions about the type of rhythm or pattern each displays.

▲ **FIGURE 8.24**

Student work. *Untitled.* Black and white yarn woven on copper frame with beads and metal nuts.

Activity 8.24 **Visual rhythm.**
Analyze this student artwork to form a conclusion about pattern. Which objects carry the visual "beat"? Describe the repeating pattern of these objects.

▲ **FIGURE 8.25**

Student work. *The Culture of Salt.* Watercolor and ink.

Activity 8.25 **Regular rhythm.**
Compare the rhythm in this painting and Figure 4.18 (page 79). Identify the repeated lines or shapes that contribute to the movement in each.

Activity 8.26 Pattern.

Analyze the motif that is repeated in this painting. Would you describe the repetition as regular or random? Explain.

▲ **FIGURE 8.26**

Student work. *Butterflies*. Acrylic.

Activity 8.27 Repetition and motif.

This artwork illustrates how direct observation of rhythms in everyday objects can form the basis of art. Evaluate the main focus of the work. How many motifs can you find? Explain.

▲ **FIGURE 8.27**

Student work. *Glasses*. Color pencil.

For Your Portfolio

Select and Analyze Exhibitions. Add a critical review to your portfolio. With your teacher's guidance, organize class exhibitions at your school. Select and analyze these peer exhibitions to form conclusions about formal qualities, historical and cultural contexts, intents, and meanings. Compile your critical analysis into a four-part report that you can add to your portfolio.

To view more student artworks, visit the Glencoe Student Art Gallery at **art.glencoe.com.**

Visual Art → Journal

Become a "student" of visual rhythms in the world around you. Illustrate ideas for artworks by directly observing objects that you handle on a daily basis, such as paper money. Find motifs on these objects. Notice the type of repetition each pattern uses. Practice sketching various rhythms in your visual journal, noting their types.

Art Criticism
in Action

▲ **FIGURE 8.28**

Alfredo Arreguin. *Nuestra Señora de la Selva.* 1989. 182.9 × 121.9 cm (72 × 48"). Collection of the artist.

Critiquing the Artwork

▶ **1** **DESCRIBE** *What do you see?*

List all the information found in the credit line.

- What do you see in the foreground?

- What do you see in the background?

▶ **2** **ANALYZE** *How is this work organized?*

During this step you will collect information about the way the elements of art are organized using the principles of rhythm, pattern, and movement. This is still a clue-collecting step, so do not make guesses.

- What geometric shapes can you find in this painting? Identify them.

- Where do you see patterns? What kinds of repetition do they show? What relationship can you find between the patterns on the floor and the woman's skirt?

- Where do you see visual rhythms that create visual movement?

▶ **3** **INTERPRET** *What message does this artwork communicate to you?*

Combine the clues you have collected to form a creative interpretation of the work.

- Form conclusions about the meaning of this work. What do the floor tiles in the foreground represent? What does the background represent?

- Notice that the woman stands behind the tile floor but in front of the nature scene. What does this mean?

▶ **4** **JUDGE** *What do you think of the work?*

Decide if this is a successful work of art.

- Did the artist use the principles of rhythm and pattern successfully?

- Do you think the artist has successfully expressed his beliefs in this painting? Why or why not? Defend your opinion using one or more of the aesthetic theories.

Meet the ARTIST

Alfredo Arreguin
(b. 1935)

Alfredo Arreguin was born in Mexico. As a child, Arreguin loved to explore the tropical forests of Mexico. In the summer of 1955, he met an American family. A strong friendship grew between them. Arreguin's new friends invited him to visit them at their home in Seattle. He remained to study at the University of Washington, ultimately settling in Seattle. Many of his paintings, like Figure 8.28, express his concern for natural conservation in an age of industrialization.

MOVING ART

With *The Lion King*, director Julie Taymor brings the movement of art to theater.

Julie Taymor had a challenge. She was hired to turn the animated movie *The Lion King* into a play with real actors. Luckily, Taymor, a renowned theater director, is a wizard at puppetry, costumes, and illusion. She put a jungle full of animals onstage without using a single live beast.

In the stage version of *The Lion King*, actors use puppets and masks to portray animals. A headpiece and four stilts turn an actor into a long-legged giraffe. A cheetah prowls the stage, pushed by an actor behind the puppet. Life-size elephants, moved by actors in each leg, lumber down the aisles of the theater. By having the actors recreate the movements of these animals, Taymor brought an African habitat to life.

Taymor uses different types of movements to create emotions, moods, and settings. When the lionesses cry over the death of their leader, they show tears by pulling ribbons of fabric from their eyes. Actors shake long lengths of blue silk to make a rushing waterfall. These visual movements serve the purpose of theater: they create visual effects that transport the audience into another world.

BRYAN-BROWN/MARCUS/TIME PICTURE COLLECTION

Actors portraying animals join with puppets to create graceful stage movements.

JOAN MARCUS/TIME PICTURE COLLECTION

By using movement and donning a mask, an actor transforms into a lion.

TIME to Connect

Theater and film directors often ask actors to use body language and movement to communicate ideas and feelings.

- Watch a television show or a movie and notice how the actors communicate through gestures, movements, and body language. Then write a critical review of the show, discussing the acting, writing, directing, costumes, and sets.

- As part of your review, include your reaction to the nonverbal techniques the actors use to express meaning. Is the "unspoken" as powerful as the "spoken"? Can movements speak louder than words?

Building Vocabulary

On a separate sheet of paper, write the term that best matches each definition given below.

1. The principle of art that indicates movement by the repetition of elements and objects.
2. Rhythm you receive through your eyes rather than through your ears.
3. The principle of art concerned with decorative surface design.
4. A unit that is repeated in visual rhythm.
5. A three-dimensional motif.
6. The principle of art used to create the look and feeling of action and to guide the viewer's eyes throughout the work of art.
7. A work of art that actually moves in space.

Reviewing Art Facts

Answer the following questions using complete sentences.

8. In general, how is visual rhythm created?
9. How does rhythm add a sense of movement to a work of art?
10. How are different rhythms and patterns created?
11. What is the difference between a module and a motif?
12. Name and describe four types of rhythm and pattern.
13. What is *dynamism* and with what group is it associated?

Thinking Critically About Art

14. **Compare and Contrast.** Study the subject matter of the *Poor Man's Cotton* (Figure 8.6 on page 203) and *Hmong Story Cloth* (Figure 8.18 on page 211). List the similarities and differences you find. Are the themes of the two works similar or different? Explain your answer.

15. **Historical/Cultural Heritage.** Read about Rosa Bonheur's lifelong love of animals in the Meet the Artist feature on page 201. Animals and their relationship to humans were a major theme in Bonheur's work. Compare and contrast her depiction of man's attempt to dominate animals in Figure 8.3 on page 201 with the depiction of a similar scene in Figure 7.4 on page 174. How did both artists use movement in their works?

ART Online Pattern is used in many everyday materials and objects. Fabric designers are responsible for creating fabric patterns. Their designs can be found in everything from rugs and sheets to high-fashion clothing. Visit art.glencoe.com to compare and contrast career opportunities in art.

Linking to the Performing Arts

Explore rhythm and movement with Chuck Davis and the African American Dance Ensemble in the Performing Arts Handbook on page 420.

▲ **FIGURE 9.1** This art object, a painted portable scroll, uses different kinds of balance. There is a border at the top of the scroll that is balanced by one at the bottom. Likewise, the four large circles are balanced side by side and top and bottom. Compare and contrast the balance used in the images within the four largest circles.

Central Tibet, Tsang (Ngor Monastery), Sakya order. *Four Mandalas of the Vajravali Series.* c. 1429–56. Thangka, gouache on cotton. 88.9 × 73.7 cm (35 × 29″). Kimbell Art Museum, Fort Worth, Texas.

CHAPTER 9

Balance

Have you ever lost your balance, perhaps while skating or bicycling? Maintaining your balance in such situations is critical to your well-being. Balance is important, not only to life but also to art. It is used by artists to bring a sense of wholeness, or *unity,* to their works.

In this chapter, you will:

- Describe types of balance and why balance is important in a work of art.
- Compare and contrast the use of different types of balance in artworks.
- Create visual solutions using direct observation and imagination to explore the art principle balance.
- Analyze the expressive qualities of balance in artworks.

Focus On **Culture**

Figure 9.1 dates to the fifteenth century. It is a *thangka,* a portable scroll. It was used during the 1400s for meditation by followers of Vajrayana (**vahj**-ree-ah-na) Buddhism. Also known as the Diamond Path to spiritual knowledge, Vajrayana was the main Buddhist sect in the Asian country Tibet. The four large circles on this thangka are *mandalas.* In Hindu and Buddhist religion, a mandala is seen as a symbolic map of the spiritual universe. It is believed that worshippers actually entered this mystic realm during prayer.

Describe. Examine an art object from another culture and time in Figure 9.9 on page 232. Describe the general characteristics of the artworks in Figures 9.1 and 9.9.

Visual Balance

Vocabulary

balance
central axis
formal balance
symmetry
radial balance

A work of art must contain balance. **Balance** is *the principle of art concerned with equalizing visual forces, or elements, in a work of art.* Visual balance causes you to feel that the elements have been arranged well.

If visual balance creates a feeling that the elements have been arranged just right, visual imbalance creates the opposite feeling. It causes a feeling of uneasiness. It makes you feel that something is not quite right. The Leaning Tower of Pisa **(Figure 9.2)** attracts attention because it is out of balance. It had tilted into a danger zone and was closed to the public in January 2000. Engineers corrected the tilt by $17^1/_2$ inches. (See page 252 for more details.)

In order to know whether two objects are of equal weight—that is, if they balance—a balance scale can be used. In the visual arts, however, balance must be *seen* rather than weighed. The art elements become the visual forces, or weights, in an art object. A **central axis** is *a dividing line that works like the point of balance in the balance scale.* Many works of art have a central vertical axis **(Figure 9.3)** with equal visual weight on both sides of the dividing line. Works of art can also have a horizontal axis. In this case, the visual weight is balanced between top and bottom **(Figure 9.4).**

► **FIGURE 9.2**
This building is known throughout the world, not because of its beauty or because the architect is well known, but because it leans— it is off balance. The many diagonal lines tell the viewer that this building must either straighten up or fall down.

Bell Tower of the Cathedral at Pisa (The Leaning Tower of Pisa). Begun in 1174.

◄ **FIGURE 9.3**
With a vertical axis, there is equal visual weight on both sides.

◄ **FIGURE 9.4**
With a horizontal axis, there is equal visual weight above and below.

Diego Rivera, the son of two teachers, was born in 1886 in the small town of Guanajuato, Mexico. As a young man, Rivera received a government grant to study art in Spain. He also studied with Picasso in France and traveled to Italy to study the works of Raphael and Michelangelo.

When he returned to Mexico, he decided to paint only Mexican subjects. He used the simplified forms of pre-Columbian art in his work. His concern for the workers, the poor, and the illiterate influenced all of his art. He painted many murals with political themes, considering them a way to teach people who could not read. In his art, he combined the techniques of European painters with the history of Mexico to create a new way to portray his ideas about the people and culture of Mexico.

Mexican, 1886–1957

Diego Rivera. *Self-Portrait.* 1941. Oil on canvas. 61 × 43.2 cm (24 × 17″). Smith College Museum of Art, Northampton, Massachusetts.

▶ **FIGURE 9.5** Rivera used his art to show his serious concern for the Mexican working people. Many of his works depicted the labors of the Mexican peasants. His work reflects the style of the solid-looking, pre-Columbian artwork of the Mayans.

Diego Rivera. *Flower Day.* 1925. Oil on canvas. 147.3 × 120.7 cm (58 × 47½″). Los Angeles County Museum of Art, Los Angeles, California. Los Angeles County Fund. Reproducción autorizada por el Instituto Nacional de Bellas Artes y Literatura.

Formal Balance

One type of balance is called formal balance. **Formal balance** occurs *when equal, or very similar, elements are placed on opposite sides of a central axis.* The axis can be vertical or horizontal. It may be a real part of the design, or it may be an imaginary line, as in Figures 9.3 and 9.4. Formal balance is the easiest type of balance to recognize and to create **(Figure 9.5).** After you find the axis, all you have to do is place similar objects on each side, equally distant from the center.

Symmetry

Symmetry is *a special type of formal balance in which two halves of a balanced composition are identical, mirror images of each other.* Another term for this is *bilateral* symmetry **(Figure 9.6).**

Symmetry appeals strongly to us, probably because of the bilateral symmetry of the human body. Objects closely associated with our bodies, such as clothing and furniture, are usually symmetrical. Most traditional architecture, especially public architecture, is symmetrical **(Figure 9.7).**

◄ **FIGURE 9.6** This urn shows a young man wearing a headdress depicting his guardian spirit, the goddess Quetzal, an unforgettably beautiful bird. The artist who created this urn used symmetry to emphasize the seriousness of this work.

Mexican, Zapotec (from Monte Alban). *Figural Urn.* A.D. 500–700. Painted earthenware. 63.5 × 63.5 × 31.8 cm (25 × 25 × 12¹/₂"). Nelson-Atkins Museum of Art, Kansas City, Missouri. Purchase: Nelson Trust 61-16.

▲ **FIGURE 9.7** This view of the White House expresses the dignity and importance of the home of the president of the United States. The use of symmetry makes the building appear secure and stable.

James H. Cromartie. *View of the White House, South Portico.* 1980. Acrylic on canvas. 50.8 × 76.2 cm (20 × 30"). Private Collection.

Activity   Using Symmetry

Creating Visual Solutions Using Direct Observation. Arrange a symmetrical still life. Carefully observe the arrangement before making a pencil drawing on a small sheet of paper. Then rearrange or change the objects slightly to create approximate symmetry. Make a drawing of the second arrangement. Mount the drawings side by side on a sheet of construction paper and label each drawing. Which one do you prefer? Survey your friends to find out their preferences.

Computer Option. If available, use the Symmetry menu and Brush or Pencil tool to create a symmetrical landscape. Vary the Brush shape, thickness, pattern, and color. If the Symmetry menu is not available, determine the central axis or line of symmetry. Draw half of the scene. Use the Select tool and Copy, Paste, and Flip commands to make the matching second half. Title and save the work. Try rearranging the shapes in your scene so that it is not perfectly symmetrical. Compare the two drawings. Which do you prefer?

▲ **FIGURE 9.8** Van Eyck used approximate symmetry to depict this wedding portrait. The halves of the picture are not quite the same. However, the work still has the dignity of perfect symmetry, only the composition is more interesting and less monotonous than if he had used perfect symmetry.

Jan van Eyck. *The Arnolfini Wedding.* 1434. Oil on panel. 83.8 × 57.2 cm (33 × 22.5"). National Gallery, London, England.

Symmetry can be very stiff and formal. Artists use it to express dignity, endurance, and stability. Because formal balance is so predictable, however, it can be dull. Many artists avoid boring the viewer by using approximate symmetry, which is *almost* symmetrical.

Approximate symmetry has the stability of formal balance **(Figure 9.8).** Some small differences make it more interesting than perfect symmetry. If you look carefully in a mirror, you may discover that your face has approximate symmetry. The two sides do not match perfectly.

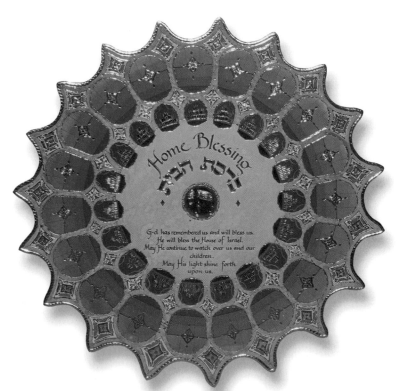

Radial Balance

Radial balance occurs *when the forces or elements of a design come out (radiate) from a central point.* The axis in a radial design is the center point. In almost all cases, the elements are spaced evenly around the axis to form circular patterns **(Figure 9.9).**

Radial balance is a complex variation of symmetry. While symmetry requires only two matching units, designs with radial balance usually involve four or more matching units. In **Figure 9.10,** notice that the center of the design is the family shield surrounded by a blue circle of zigzag lines. Four petal-like shapes and four bars radiate from the center of the bowl to its rim. On the rim, wide blue and thin gold lines continue to form a circular design. Notice how all the blue line designs resemble Arabic writing but do not form any real letters.

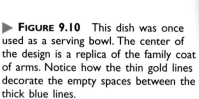 **FIGURE 9.9** The use of radial balance adds to the decorative quality of this design. This print is based on the stained-glass dome found in the main synagogue of Szeged, Hungary.

N. Anderson, Israel. *Blue Dome–House Blessing.* 1995. Etching. 43.2 × 43.2 cm (17 × 17″). Private Collection.

▶ **FIGURE 9.10** This dish was once used as a serving bowl. The center of the design is a replica of the family coat of arms. Notice how the thin gold lines decorate the empty spaces between the thick blue lines.

Valencia, Spain. Dish c. 1430. Tin-glazed earthenware painted in cobalt blue and lustre. Height: 6.7 cm (2⅝″); diameter of mouth: 48.2 cm (19″). Hispanic Society of America, New York, New York.

Radial balance occurs frequently in nature. Most flower petals are arranged around a central axis and radiate outward. Many plants follow radial patterns of growth. For instance, if you cut an apple in half horizontally, you will see a radial star design. Cut an orange the same way and you will notice the radial pattern of segments.

You can find many examples of radial balance in architecture. Domes are designed on the principle of radial balance. Manufactured items such as gears, wheels, tires, dials, and clocks are also radial in structure. Radial designs are used by many potters to decorate the surfaces of their work because they adapt well to the rounded forms of pottery **(Figure 9.11).**

Activity — Creating Radial Balance

Creating Visual Solutions Using Imagination. Draw on your creativity to design five objects that exhibit radial balance. Make a drawing of each imaginary object, using pen or pencil. Emphasize the radial balance of each object, using line, form, and color.

Computer Option. Choose from a variety of Shape tools. Determine the center of the computer page. Use a dot, an X, an addition sign (+), or other shape to mark this spot. Copy and Paste a shape four times around the center point. Continue to add and arrange shapes to maintain radial balance. Try a variety of sizes to add interest but make sure each set of four shapes is identical. Title and save your work. Now explore a more complex radial design. Combine lines and shapes and use more than four repeated combinations to complete the design.

Check Your Understanding

1. What is a central axis?
2. What is the easiest type of balance to recognize and create?
3. Which type of balance can be found frequently in nature and in architecture?
4. Compare and contrast the use of balance in Figure 9.6 on page 230 and Figure 9.10 on page 232.

 FIGURE 9.11 Torivio, a Native American potter, has developed her own style for decorating her pots. She repeats the designs in radial patterns. The motif starts out small at the top rim and then expands to the widest part of the vessel.

Dorothy Torivio. *Vase.* c. 1984. Clay. Height about 20.3 cm (8"). Heard Museum Collection, Phoenix, Arizona.

Informal Balance

Informal balance gives the viewer the same comfortable feeling as formal balance, but in a much more subtle way. **Informal balance,** or asymmetry, involves *a balance of unlike objects.* While informal balance can express dignity, endurance, and stability, these qualities are less pronounced. Informal balance seems more realistic because it is closer to what appears in your everyday environment. It does not consist of two equal or nearly equal halves or sides. Instead, it relies on the artistic arrangement of objects to *appear* balanced.

Using Informal Balance in Art

Informal balance creates a casual effect **(Figure 9.12).** Although it seems less planned than formal balance, it is not. What appears to be an accidental arrangement of elements can be quite complicated. Symmetry merely requires that elements be repeated in a mirror image. Informal balance is more complex. Artists must consider all the visual weight factors and put them together correctly. Many factors influence the visual weight, or the attraction, that elements in a work of art have to the viewer's eyes.

▲ **FIGURE 9.12** Pippin balanced the large, simple form of the log cabin near the center of the work with a complex shape formed by two trees and a shed near the edge of the work.

Horace Pippin. *Cabin in the Cotton.* Mid-1930s. Oil on panel. 46 × 84.1 cm (18¹/₈ × 33¹/₈″). The Art Institute of Chicago, Chicago, Illinois. In memoriam: Frances W. Pick from her children Thomas F. Pick and Mary P. Hines, 1996.417.

▲ **FIGURE 9.13** The objects in this painting appear balanced because the complex shape of the creature on the right is counteracted by the large, thin spiral shape on the left. Also, the background space is informally balanced by the areas of orange and brown.

Joan Miró. *Landscape (The Hare).* Autumn 1927. Oil on canvas. 129.5 × 194 cm (51 × 76³/₈″). The Solomon R. Guggenheim Museum, New York, New York. © 2003 Artists Rights Society (ARS), New York, ADAGP/Paris.

Size and Contour

A large shape or form appears to be heavier than a small shape. Several small shapes or forms can balance one large shape.

An object with a complicated contour is more interesting and appears to be heavier than one with a simple contour. A small, complex object can balance a large, simple object **(Figure 9.13)**.

Color

A high-intensity color has more visual weight than a low-intensity color. The viewer's eyes are drawn to the area of bright color. What does this mean in terms of balance? It means that a small area of bright color is able to balance a larger area of a dull, neutral color **(Figure 9.14)**.

▲ **FIGURE 9.14** The bright red color of the cloth wrapped around the child helps it stand out against the larger, low-intensity color of the enlarged head and the neutral colors of the forms on the ground.

David Alfaro Siqueiros. *Echo of a Scream.* 1937. Enamel on wood. 121.9 × 91.4 cm (48 × 36″). Museum of Modern Art, New York, New York. Gift of Edward M. M. Warburg (633.193a). © Estate of David Alfaro Siqueiros/Licensed by VAGA, New York, NY/SOMAAP, Mexico City.

Warm colors carry more visual weight than cool colors. Red appears heavier than blue, and yellow/orange appears heavier than green **(Figure 9.15)**.

Value

The stronger the contrast in value between an object and the background, the more visual weight the object has **(Figure 9.16)**. Black against white has more weight than gray against white. Dark values appear heavier than light values. A dark red seems heavier than a light red.

Texture

A rough texture, with its uneven pattern of light highlights and dark, irregular shadows, attracts the viewer's eye more easily than a smooth, even surface does. This means that a small, rough-textured area can balance a large, smooth surface. In a poster or advertisement, a block of printed words has the quality of rough texture because of the irregular pattern of light and dark. Graphic designers must keep this in mind when balancing words with other visual elements.

◀ **FIGURE 9.16** Elijah's white beard is the lightest area in the illustration. The use of this bright, light color emphasizes Elijah, who otherwise might blend in with the neutral, dull colors of the background. Compare and contrast this use of color and balance with Figure 9.15 on page 236.

Jerry Pinkney. Illustration from *Journeys with Elijah*.

Position

Children playing on a seesaw quickly discover that two friends of unequal weight can balance the seesaw by adjusting their positions. The heavier child moves toward the center; the lighter child slides toward the end. The board is then in balance **(Figure 9.17).**

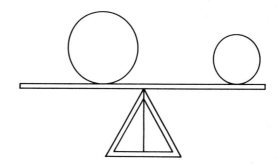

▲ **FIGURE 9.17** Does the seesaw look balanced?

▲ **FIGURE 9.18** In the foreground, two dancers placed side by side create a busy, large shape that draws the viewer's attention. How do the four small dancers in the distance create balance with the dancers in the foreground?

Edgar Degas. *Before the Ballet.* 1890/1892. Oil on canvas. 40 × 88.9 cm (15¾ × 35″). National Gallery, Washington, D.C. Widener Collection.

Activity	Using Informal Balance

Demonstrating Effective Use of Art Media in Design. Create small designs using cut paper and/or fabric shapes to illustrate five weight arrangements that create informal balance. In each design keep all of the elements as alike as possible. Vary only the weight factors. For example, to illustrate differences in size, a large red circle could be balanced by several small red circles.

Computer Option. Use the drawing tools of your choice to make a series of small compositions that show informal balance. Use both lines and shapes. Explore changes in size, color, texture, value, contour, and position to create these asymmetrical compositions. Make several of each kind. Title, save, and print your best examples. Display them and compare with your classmates.

In visual art, a large object close to the dominant area of the work can be balanced by a smaller object placed farther away from the dominant area **(Figure 9.18)**. In this way, a large, positive shape and a small, negative space can be balanced against a small, positive shape and a large, negative space.

 Check Your Understanding

1. What is the effect of informal balance?
2. Name the six factors that influence the visual weight of an object.
3. Which has a heavier visual weight, an object with a simple contour or one with a complicated contour?

The Expressive Qualities of Balance

The type of balance an artist uses to organize a work of art affects the feeling expressed by that work. Artists choose balance based on the feeling they wish to convey. An artist who wants to present a calm arrangement will use formal balance. Formal balance can be used to present a person in a dignified portrait **(Figure 9.19).**

LOOKING CLOSELY

Using Formal Balance To Organize A Composition

Frida Kahlo has used formal balance to organize this painting to give it a sense of dignity and importance. In the diagram you can see that if the painting were folded in half along the vertical axis the shapes would match. Notice, however, that there are a few small variations. They would not match perfectly because she has used approximate symmetry. Can you find any matching shapes that were not included in the diagram?

vertical axis

◀ **FIGURE 9.19**

Frida Kahlo. *Self-Portrait Dedicated to Leon Trotsky.* 1937. Oil on Masonite. 76.2 × 61 cm (30 × 24″). National Museum of Women in the Arts, Washington, D.C. Gift of the Honorable Clare Boothe Luce.

◀ **FIGURE 9.20** Ferdinand Hodler used formal balance to create a stiff, stable portrait of his friend. The line from the sculptor's nose through the line in his shirt divides the portrait vertically into almost perfectly matching halves.

Ferdinand Hodler. *James Vilbert, Sculptor.* 1907. Oil on canvas. 65.4 × 66.4 cm (25¾ × 26⅛″). The Art Institute of Chicago, Chicago, Illinois. Helen Birch Bartlett Memorial Collection, 1926.212

Formal balance can also be used in religious paintings to evoke feelings of dignity and endurance. In the past, paintings used as altarpieces in churches were designed to fit in with the formal balance of the church altar. The artist Ferdinand Hodler developed a personal aesthetic theory called Parallelism that relied on symmetry and repetition to create images that expressed stability **(Figure 9.20).**

Many government buildings, hospitals, and office buildings are designed using formal balance. One purpose of this type of balance is to imply that the business conducted in these buildings is serious and solemn.

With approximate symmetry, artists express the same sense of calm stability, but they avoid the rigid formality of pure symmetry. Georgia O'Keeffe used approximate symmetry in her paintings of large close-ups of flowers. This impresses the viewer with feelings about the importance of the natural world. The use of approximate symmetry lends dignity to the flowing curves and alternating pastel colors of her painting, *White Rose with Larkspur, No. 2* **(Figure 9.21).**

Radial design, on the other hand, is almost purely decorative. It appears in architecture, jewelry, pottery, weaving,

◀ **FIGURE 9.21** How has O'Keeffe arranged the shapes in this painting to create approximate, not absolute, symmetry? Would you like the painting more if it were perfectly symmetrical? Why or why not?

Georgia O'Keeffe. *White Rose with Larkspur, No. 2.* 1927. Oil on canvas. 101.6 × 76.2 cm (40 × 30″). Museum of Fine Arts, Boston, Massachusetts. Henry H. and Zoe Oliver Sherman Fund, 1980.207. © 2003 The Georgia O'Keeffe Foundation/Artists Rights Society (ARS), New York.

▶ **FIGURE 9.22** Notice how Carr has used informal balance by placing most of the raven to the right of center in this landscape. She made many trips to the Northwest Coast of Alaska to record images of the Native American villages. This work was made in her studio based on sketches she had done on her trip to Queen Charlotte Island. The Haida village had been deserted and the large carving of the raven remained. She has balanced the raven, flowers, and trees near the foreground against the blue mountain in the distance.

Emily Carr. *Cumshewa.* c. 1912. Watercolor over graphite on wove paper. 52 × 75.3 cm (20¹/₂ × 29⁵/₈″). National Gallery of Canada, Ottawa, Ontario, Canada.

and textile design. It is not often used by painters in its pure form. You can, however, find loose arrangements of radiating lines in many paintings. Artists use this technique to focus attention on an important part of an artwork.

Informal balance has a more natural look. When you look around your natural environment, you seldom find objects arranged with formal balance. To capture this natural quality in their works, artists use informal balance in arranging landscapes or groups of people **(Figure 9.22).**

Architects are using informal balance in many modern structures (see Figure 14.16, page 399). Single-family suburban homes have become the symbol of casual living. These houses are often designed using informal balance.

Check Your Understanding

1. What feeling does formal balance convey?
2. What kind of buildings use formal balance? Why?
3. Why might an artist prefer approximate symmetry over pure symmetry?

Ceramic Mask

▲ **FIGURE 9.23**

Zaire, Kuba Culture. *Mukenga Mask.* Wood, animal fur, raffia cloth, cowrie shells, glass beads, string. 49.5 × 43.2 × 55.8 cm (19¹/₂ × 17 × 22″). Virginia Museum of Fine Arts, Richmond, Virginia. The Arthur and Margaret Glasgow Fund.

SUPPLIES

- Sketchbook and pencil
- Newspaper
- Clay (can be self-hardening)
- Clay modeling tools
- Acrylic paint and brushes
- Raffia
- Thin wire
- Beads
- Fabric scraps
- Glue

Historical and Cultural Context

Did you recognize the object in **Figure 9.23** to be a mask? This mask is one of three that tells the story of the Kuba culture. The Kuba are an indigenous people of the Democratic Republic of Congo (formerly Zaire). According to Kuba legend, royalty descended from divine beings. The face on this object is meant to represent a king named Woot, who founded the kingdom. Different aspects of this mask are hints to the status of the figure depicted. The elephant-trunk shape with its patterns of beads and shells refers to a king's commanding power. The animal fur covering his face and the raffia encircling his neck signify a king's strength. The cowrie-shell collar signifies a king's wealth and power.

Notice that the mask is organized by means of symmetrical balance. The elements of color and visual texture are used to suggest this symmetry.

What You Will Learn

You will create a symmetrical ceramic mask representing a real or imaginary leader. You will add textures and patterns around the facial features, using clay. To add these facial features, you will demonstrate the effective use of sculpting media and tools. The mask is to be embellished, using paint and other decorative materials including raffia, wire, beads, and fabric.

Creating

List in your sketchbook the qualities you want your leader to show. Draw preliminary sketches that illustrate these qualities. Plan how you will use texture and color to organize your work according to the principle of symmetrical balance.

Step 1 Crumple newspaper into a tight ellipse (oval). Roll a slab of clay about 3/8-inch thick, and drape the clay over the newspaper bundle. Form a face by modeling the clay. Cut away unneeded clay from around the edges.

Step 2 Using your modeling tools, add clay and sculpt the features of the face. (See Technique Tips Handbook, pages 433–434.) Cut holes into the clay in order to attach the wire, beads, or other decorative materials later. Add textures to the face by adding small pieces of clay or by carving gently into the slab. (Remember to score and moisten the clay before joining two pieces.)

Step 3 Allow the clay to dry completely before it is fired in the kiln.

Step 4 Using a No. 2 pencil, lightly sketch your designs on the face, especially the forehead and cheeks. Create simple patterns of repeating shapes. Again, arrange these symmetrically to echo the overall symmetric organization of your object. Use acrylic paint to color the patterns. Allow the paint to dry.

Step 5 Attach the raffia, if desired, by tying it through the holes you cut in the clay. Using wire, string beads over and around the face. These may also be tied through the same holes. Additional beads can be glued on the surface. Fabric strips, which you could fringe, could also be glued along the underneath edge to add more layers of texture.

Evaluating Your Work

▶ **DESCRIBE** List and describe the characteristics of the leader portrayed in your mask. How did you symbolize these characteristics? What materials did you use to embellish the mask?

▶ **ANALYZE** Explain how you used symmetry in creating the form of the face. Compare and contrast how you used texture and color to reinforce the symmetrical balance of the design.

▶ **INTERPRET** What does your mask say about the person represented? Give your mask a title. Interpret your artistic decisions.

▶ **JUDGE** Did you demonstrate the effective use of clay and clay modeling tools in sculpting the face? Which aesthetic theories would you use to judge this work? Are there any improvements you would make to your design?

▲ **FIGURE 9.23A**

Student work.

Radial Balance Mandala

▲ **FIGURE 9.24**

Himachal Pradesh. *Chamba Rumal.* India. Early nineteenth century. Cotton with colored embroidery (silk). 66 cm (26") diameter. Philadelphia Museum of Art, Philadelphia, Pennsylvania.

SUPPLIES

- Sketchbook and pencil
- Vellum finish bristol paper or heavy white drawing paper
- Compass
- Protractor
- Colored pencils
- Clean scrap paper
- Fixative (optional)

Historical and Cultural Context

The Himalayas in Asia are known as home to the planet's highest mountain, Mount Everest. To the people of India, however, the range holds an additional significance. Deep within the mountains is the village of Chamba, which for the past thousand years has been turning out exquisite examples of a native art form known as the *rumal* (roo-**mall**). Created by the women of the village, rumals are richly intricate paintings embroidered with fine needlework. Traditionally, they were used as ceremonial handkerchiefs or scarves.

The rumal in **Figure 9.24** is typical. Note that this object exhibits radial balance. The design begins with the small red circle at the center. A pattern of flower petals radiates out from this central point, each petal pointing to a circle of male and female figures that are notable in Hindu tradition. An interlacing pattern of flower petals continues the design along the outer border.

What You Will Learn

You will illustrate ideas for a mandala design from personal experiences. In Hindu writing, mandala is the word for circle. The basic pattern of a mandala is a circle with a center. Like the rumal in Figure 9.24, the mandala will exhibit radial balance. Your mandala will use three symbols. One should be a symbol of your personal heritage—something with special meaning to your family or cultural group. A second should be a personal symbol of your everyday life (for example, a schoolbook or symbol of a sport or activity you enjoy). The third should be a symbol of art, such a paintbrush. You will layer and blend colors in your work to create gradual changes in value.

Creating

Think about the three symbols you will use. You may want to talk with family members about the cultural symbol. Make visual and verbal notes in your sketchbook. Produce several thumbnail sketches. Select your best sketches.

Step 1 On a sheet of drawing paper, draw a circle approximately 9 inches in diameter, using a compass. Line up a protractor over the center point, and divide the circle into three equal wedges. In each third, enlarge one of your three symbol sketches.

Step 2 Decide on a color scheme. For each color moving outward from the center, select a color that is one step warmer or lighter or one step cooler or darker. The object ultimately is to layer and blend these colors together to create gradual changes in value. Choose colored pencils to match each color you will use in your design.

Step 3 Begin coloring your mandala. Keep a sheet of clean scrap paper beneath your hand as you work. This will prevent your hand from smearing your work.

Step 4 When you have finished your mandala, spray it with fixative—if your teacher provides it—to keep the colors from smearing. *Safety note:* Do the spraying outside or in a well-ventilated area.

Evaluating Your Work

▶ **DESCRIBE** Describe the three symbolic images you have chosen. Identify the meaning of each.

▶ **ANALYZE** Did you use radial balance? What color scheme did you use? Compare and contrast your use of value. Is there a gradual progression from the center out?

▶ **INTERPRET** What does your personal mandala express about you as a person? Write a brief paragraph or a poem expressing the meaning of your work.

▶ **JUDGE** Which aesthetic theory would you use to judge this work? If you were to do another mandala, what, if anything, would you change?

▲ **FIGURE 9.24A**

Student work.

STUDIO PROJECT *Radial Balance Mandala*   **245**

STUDIO PROJECT 9-3

Asymmetrical Balance Painting

▲ **FIGURE 9.25**

Katsushika Hokusai. *Shichiri Beach in Sagami Province* from *Thirty-Six Views of Mount Fuji.* 1823–31. Woodblock print. 26.4 x 38.4 cm (10³/₈ × 15¹/₈″). Honolulu Academy of Art, Honolulu, Hawaii. Gift of James A. Michener. 1985.

SUPPLIES

- Digital camera
- Image-editing or paint program
- Computer
- Printer
- Sketchbook and pencil
- Large sheets of heavy white paper
- Acrylic, tempera, or watercolor paints
- Brushes, water containers, and towels

Historical and Cultural Context

Figure 9.25 is a woodblock print created by nineteenth-century Japanese artist Katsushika Hokusai. The print is from one of Hokusai's best-known series, *Thirty-six Views of Mount Fuji.* In this asymmetrical composition, your eye is first drawn to one of the blue areas, perhaps in the lower right corner. From there, your gaze drifts diagonally to the snow-capped peak, Mount Fuji. You might expect a work so designed to be terribly lopsided, but this composition is not. The intense blue areas are neatly balanced by the large amount of water on the left.

What You Will Learn

In this lesson, you will create a digital image that has asymmetrical balance. The central figures in the work (the positive space) are to be a person and one or two pieces of furniture or objects from nature. There will be a large, open, negative space, as in Figure 9.25, that creates asymmetrical balance. Photograph the staged composition using a digital camera. After importing the images into a computer paint program, alter the work—selecting among the tools and menus. Print the image. Then create a painting based on the digital print. (See Digital Media Handbook, page 449.)

Creating

Using direct observation, sketch settings in and around your school that include one or two large objects, such as a bench, a tree, or a staircase. Use a classmate as a model. Have your model pose near—not necessarily in front of—the objects you have selected. Try to visualize a composition that includes just the person and the objects against a backdrop of negative space. Attempt to achieve asymmetrical balance.

Step 1 Place the model in the setting you have selected. Take several pictures of the scene from different angles and distances. Pick arrangements that emphasize asymmetrical balance.

Step 2 Import the digital images into a computer. Open the images in a paint program. Select and save the best composition.

Step 3 Use the paint program's tools and menus to improve the composition by selecting and moving the figure or objects. Crop the work, if needed, to emphasize asymmetrical balance.

Step 4 Explore and adjust the color settings. Increase color saturation; increase the contrast and change the settings to emphasize foreground images. Alter some colors. Although these changes will give the image a flatter appearance, like a woodcut, many striking, colorful, and unusual effects can be achieved on the computer that are otherwise not possible.

Step 5 Save and print your image.

Step 6 Select a paint medium. Make a freehand painting based on your digital image.

Step 7 When the paint is dry, mat and display both artworks.

Evaluating Your Work

▶ **DESCRIBE** What settings did you record in your sketchbook? What objects appear in your work? What software tools did you use to change your original digital image? What media did you choose to create your painting?

▶ **ANALYZE** How are objects arranged in the digital image and the painting to show asymmetrical balance? What contributes to the asymmetrical balance created between positive and negative space? Describe how camera angle, position of objects, and cropping support this kind of balance.

▶ **INTERPRET** What feelings does your finished work express? Give your painting a title that reflects these feelings.

▶ **JUDGE** Do both artworks show asymmetrical balance? If you were to redo any part of the work, what would you do differently to improve the work? How would a different color scheme affect the work? Evaluate and justify your artistic decisions.

▲ **FIGURE 9.25A**

Student work (photograph).

▲ **FIGURE 9.25B**

Student work (painting).

Balance

Whether balance is symmetrical, radial, or informal, it is essential to an artwork's success. Formal balance can add dignity; informal balance, excitement. As you examine the student artworks on these pages:

- Compare and contrast them in terms of their use of the principle of balance.

- Analyze the works, forming precise conclusions about the type of balance used.

▲ **FIGURE 9.26**

Student work. *Untitled.* Copper wire, coiled copper, rubber, electronic armature.

Activity 9.26 **Type of balance.**
Analyze the balance used in this art object. Form a conclusion as to whether it is formal or informal. Does the object appear to have a practical use, or is it purely decorative?

▲ **FIGURE 9.27**

Student work. *Untitled.* Stoneware, beads, wire, raffia.

Activity 9.27 **Expressive qualities of balance.**
What feeling or idea does this mask communicate through its use of balance? Explain.

▲ **FIGURE 9.28**

Student work. *Earth Wheel.* Soil, flowers, sand.

Activity 9.28 **Type of balance.**
Describe the type of balance used in this earth artwork. How are textures and colors used to reinforce balance?

▲ **FIGURE 9.29**

Student work. *Bear.* Acrylic.

Activity 9.29 **Comparing balance.**
Compare and contrast the use of balance in this student work with Figure 12.30 on page 343. What other differences and similarities can you detect?

To view more student artworks, visit the Glencoe Student Art Gallery at **art.glencoe.com**.

For Your Portfolio

Analyzing Peer Artworks. Many art students nowadays maintain online or digital art portfolios. With your teacher's guidance, organize online exhibitions of student artworks. You may also research online exhibitions of student art at other high schools. Select and analyze these peer exhibitions to form conclusions about formal qualities, historical and cultural contexts, intents, and meanings. Compile your analysis into a four-part report that you can store in your portfolio.

Visual Art Journal

One way to sharpen your skills at perceiving balance is to tour your city. Notice the buildings and type of balance used in their designs. Make notes and sketches about these and other objects. See whether you can find at least one example of each of the following types of balance: radial, symmetrical, approximate symmetrical, and informal.

Art Criticism
in Action

▲ **FIGURE 9.30**

Arthur Shaughnessy, Native American, Dzawada'enuxw. *Dla'ehl Interior House Post: Grizzly Bear Beneath Kolus.* c. 1907. Red cedar, and paint. 457.2 × 335.3 × 86.4 cm (180 × 132 × 34″). The Seattle Art Museum, Seattle, Washington. Gift of Mr. John H. Hausberg.

Critiquing the Artwork

▶ 1   **DESCRIBE** *What do you see?*

List all the information found in the credit line.

- Describe the general characteristics of this house post. Provide as many visual details as you can.

▶ 2   **ANALYZE** *How is this work organized?*

During this step you will collect information about the way the elements of art are organized using the principle of balance. This is still a clue-collecting step, so do not make guesses.

- Is this a two- or three-dimensional object? Explain.

- What kind of balance has the artist used to organize this house post? Compare and contrast examples of how and where this balance is used.

- Where do you see patterns? Where do you see visual movement caused by repeated rhythms?

▶ 3   **INTERPRET** *What message does this artwork communicate to you?*

Combine the clues you have collected to form a creative interpretation of the work.

- How do the forms, shapes, and colors on this post make you feel? Explain your reaction.

- What do you think is the purpose of this post?

- Write an imaginary dialogue between these creatures that explains the legend of their creation.

▶ 4   **JUDGE** *What do you think of the work?*

Decide if this is a successful work of art.

- Did the artist use the principles of rhythm and balance to organize the elements of art to communicate a feeling or an idea? Explain.

- Do you think this is a successful work of art? Why or why not? Use one or more of the aesthetic theories to defend your judgment.

Meet the **ARTIST**

Arthur Shaughnessy
(1884–1945)

The Dzawada'enuxw (duh-**zuh**-wah-dah-ee-noocks-wa) are a native people of the Pacific Northwest. This totem pole was one of four decorative house posts carved by Arthur Shaughnessy around 1907. Such carvings were traditionally done to dedicate new homes built for families of stature. The posts, which carry the family's history, were viewed as spiritual in nature. In 1966, a collector purchased the weather-beaten posts and had them restored. He donated them to the Seattle Art Museum. In 1992, the posts were rededicated in a ceremony led by the descendants of the original owners.

Tipping the *BALANCE*

Balance is more than an important characteristic in art. For a world-famous building, maintaining its balance means preserving the past.

DAVID BUFFINGTON/GETTY IMAGES

In 1989, visitors climbed the 294 steps to the top of Italy's Leaning Tower of Pisa. They could look out from the famous tilting tower at the surrounding countryside that has inspired so many artists. Not all was well, though.

Experts warned that the off-balance tower, which began leaning soon after it was built in 1173, had leaned too far. The tower is built directly on an ancient riverbed of soft, sandy soil, and the foundation is too shallow for a structure that weighs 32 million pounds. By 2009, it could fall.

So engineers spent $25 million—and took 12 years—setting the 192-foot tower a bit straighter. Not, of course, entirely in balance. That would have destroyed its appeal. It was made straight enough, however, to keep it stable for another 300 years.

Nearly 2 million pounds of lead weights were placed on one of the tower's sides. A giant belt was looped around the tower and connected to large weights a block away. These two steps stopped the tilting. Two million pounds of soil were removed from around part of the foundation. This created cavities into which the tower could settle. When it was all over, Pisa had gone from an angle of 5.5 degrees back to an even 5 degrees. That's where it was 200 years ago. By 2001, tourists were climbing to the top to enjoy the sight as well as the tilt.

TIME to Connect

The Leaning Tower of Pisa tilts because it was built on sandy soil. What other environmental factors can change a building over time? Using your school's media center or the Internet, investigate an engineering marvel—such as the pyramids of Egypt or Mexico, the Acropolis in Greece, or the Taj Mahal in India. Write a brief report, including the following data and information:

• What materials were used to build the structure?

• What natural and human-made factors—such as weather, geological events, and pollution—are affecting the structure? To what degree has the structure been damaged by these factors?

• What efforts, if any, are taking place to preserve the structure?

Building Vocabulary

On a separate sheet of paper, write the term that best matches each definition given below.

1. The principle of art concerned with equalizing visual forces, or elements, in a work of art.
2. A dividing line that works like the point of balance in the balance scale.
3. The type of balance that results when equal, or very similar, elements are placed on opposite sides of a central axis.
4. A special type of formal balance in which two halves of a balanced composition are identical, mirror images of each other.
5. When the forces or elements of a design come out (*radiate*) from a central point.
6. A balance of unlike objects.

Reviewing Art Facts

Answer the following questions using complete sentences.

7. Why is balance important to a work of art?
8. What are the visual forces, or weights, in art?
9. What is the difference between symmetry and approximate symmetry?
10. What factors in a work of art influence the visual weight of the art elements?
11. Which carry more weight, warm or cool colors?
12. How can value affect visual weight?
13. What does a formally balanced building express?

Thinking Critically About Art

14. **Research.** The Zapotec people, a pre-Columbian civilization in Mexico, left behind some interesting artifacts, as shown in Figure 9.6 on page 230. Using online or print resources, write a one-page research report on whether or not the use of symmetry is common in Zapotec architecture and art.
15. **Historical/Cultural Heritage.** Analyze the painting of Mexican peasants in Figure 9.5 on page 229. After reading the Meet the Artist feature on Diego Rivera on the same page, identify the general theme of this artwork. Then compare and contrast Rivera's style with Figure 9.14 on page 235 by David Alfaro Siqueiros. Describe the differences between the works of the two Mexican contemporaries.

ART Online

Like other fine artists, sculptors need to consider balance as they design their sculptures. Try your hand at creating a balanced sculpture design at the education Web site of the Smithsonian Institution. Simply follow the **Web Museum Tour** link at **art.glencoe.com.**

Linking to the Performing Arts

Turn to the Performing Arts Handbook on page 421 to learn how Eth-Noh-Tec uses a balance of music, movement, and words to present their unique style of theatre and storytelling.

▲ **FIGURE 10.1** This painting is a *fresco*. Italian for "fresh," fresco is an art technique in which paint is applied to a fresh, or wet, plaster surface. Examine the size of the figures depicted in this fresco. Is this depiction always realistic?

Diego Rivera. *The Making of a Fresco Showing the Building of a City*. 1931. Fresco. 6.9 x 9 m (22′7″ × 29′9″). Located at the San Francisco Art Institute, San Francisco, California. Gift of William Gerstle.

CHAPTER 10

Proportion

You may be taller than some students in your art class, shorter than others. Distinctions like these involve proportion, or relative size. As an art principle, proportion can direct the viewer's eye to a specific area or object in an artwork.

In this chapter, you will:

- Explain and recognize the Golden Mean.
- Identify scale and proportion in artworks.
- Create visual solutions using direct observation to reflect correct human proportions.
- Compare and contrast the use of proportion in personal artworks and those of others.

Focus on Art History **Figure 10.1** was painted by the Mexican artist Diego Rivera (1886–1957). At age 21, Rivera went to study art in Europe, where he met Paul Cézanne and Pablo Picasso. Returning to Mexico in 1921, Rivera rejected what he had learned. He chose instead to imitate the simplified forms of his pre-Columbian ancestors in Mexico. Rivera also became a champion of the rights of the working class. Social themes inspired him to create large mural paintings. His murals, which adorn the walls of public buildings, all have political or historical themes.

Analyze. The mural in Figure 10.1 shows scenes of urban construction. Notice the large male figure in the center. Form a conclusion about the meaning and historical context of this figure. Who or what does he represent?

The Golden Mean

Through the ages, people have sought an ideal of harmony and beauty. One way they have tried to capture this ideal is through correct proportion. **Proportion** is *the principle of art concerned with the size relationship of one part to another.* Artists and architects have looked for a ratio (a mathematical comparison of sizes) that would produce an ideal form for figures and structures.

The ancient Greek philosopher Pythagoras found that he could apply mathematical equations to both geometric shapes and musical tones. If this was so, he thought, there must also be a way to explain other things—even the universe—in mathematical terms.

Euclid, a Greek mathematician, discovered what he considered a perfect ratio, or relationship of one part to another. He called this ratio the Golden Section, or **Golden Mean,** *a line divided into two parts so that the smaller line has the same proportion, or ratio, to the larger line as the larger line has to the whole line* **(Figure 10.2).** With this ratio, the ancient Greeks felt they had found the ideal proportion. It was used to control the relationship of parts in their sculpture, architecture, and pottery. In math, this ratio is written 1 to 1.6 or 1:1.6.

▲ **FIGURE 10.2** The ratio of the Golden Mean is 1 to 1.6.

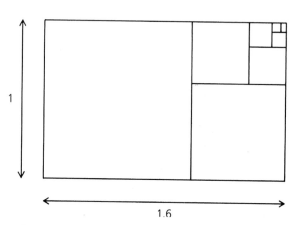

▲ **FIGURE 10.3** The Golden Rectangle is interesting to study. If you divide it into two shapes, one of which is a square, the remaining shape will always be a smaller Golden Rectangle. This new Golden Rectangle can be divided again and again.

The Golden Rectangle **(Figure 10.3)** had sides that matched this ratio. The longer sides were a little more than one and a half times as long as the shorter sides. This ratio was thought to be the most pleasing to the eye. If you look closely at Leyster's *The Concert* **(Figure 10.4),** you can see that the wall and the two figures on the right side of the work is a square, while the wall and the single figure on the left is the smaller section of the Golden Rectangle.

The Golden Mean is also related to the human figure. If you divide the average adult male body horizontally at the navel, the two body measurements that result (head to navel = a and navel to toes = b) have a ratio of 1 to 1.6 **(Figure 10.5).**

▲ **FIGURE 10.4** Judith Leyster has used the proportions of the Golden Mean to organize this painting. Look at the line dividing the back wall. The section on the right forms a perfect square. The section on the left is a Golden Rectangle. It can be divided just like the smaller section of the diagram in Figure 10.3.

Judith Leyster. *The Concert.* c. 1633. Oil on canvas. 109.2 × 167.6 cm (43 × 66″). The National Museum of Women in the Arts, Washington, D.C. Gift of Wallace and Wilhelmina Holladay.

The secret of the Golden Mean was forgotten with the fall of Ancient Greece. The ratio was rediscovered, however, during the Renaissance, and a book was written about it. This time the ratio was called the Divine Proportion, and it was thought to have magical qualities.

Since that time, some artists have chosen to use the Golden Mean as the basis for their compositions. Others, unaware of the mathematical ratio, used the Golden Mean just because that arrangement of parts looked good. Most artists now reject the idea that only this one rule can define the "correct" proportions for all works of art. The ratio, however, is found in visual art so often that it is hard to ignore its importance (**Figure 10.6,** on page 258).

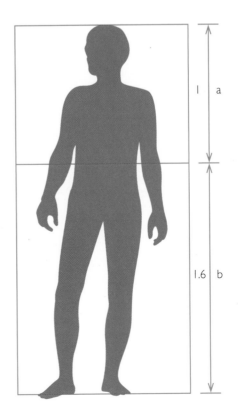

◀ **FIGURE 10.5** The relationship of the Golden Mean to the human body. Section a extends from head to navel and section b extends from navel to toes.

Notice how Bellows has used the Golden Rectangle and the diagonal of the square in the rectangle to give this action painting stability. He has used the vertical line for his standing figure and the diagonal line to help him place the leaning figure. Can you find the square in the small rectangle? Can you find any other artworks that use the Golden Mean? Many of them are very subtle and hard to notice.

◄ **FIGURE 10.6**

George Bellows. *Both Members of This Club.* 1909. Oil on canvas. 115 × 160.3 cm (45^{1}/$_{4}$ × 63^{1}/$_{8}$"). National Gallery of Art, Washington, D.C. © 1998 Board of Trustees. Chester Dale Collection.

▲ **FIGURE 10.7** Le Corbusier has been called the poet of the apartment house. This building has many of the features of a resort, such as a kindergarten and nursery, a roof garden, children's swimming pool, gymnasium, and snack bar. Lead sheets were placed between the walls to soundproof the apartments.

Le Corbusier. *Unité d'Habitation*. Marseille, France. 1947–52.

Many people looked to the human body as a source for perfect proportions. Artists during the Golden Age of Greece believed that the human body was the true expression of order. Statues created during that time were not realistic portraits of real people. The artists of the period showed the ideal form rather than the real form (see Figure 13.3, page 353).

In the first century B.C., Vitruvius, a Roman writer, determined typical ratios for human proportion. These were later used by Leonardo da Vinci and other Renaissance artists. The twentieth-century architect Le Corbusier (luh-kor-**boo**-see-ay) applied human dimensions to architecture and city planning **(Figure 10.7).**

 Check Your Understanding

1. What is the Golden Mean?
2. Describe the Golden Rectangle.
3. What is the ratio of the Golden Mean?
4. How does the Golden Mean apply to the body?

Scale

Vocabulary

scale
hierarchical
 proportion
foreshortening

Scale is much like proportion, but there is a difference. Proportion refers to the relationship of one part to another. **Scale,** on the other hand, refers to *size as measured against a standard reference,* such as the human body. A 7-foot basketball player may not look tall next to other basketball players. The player will look tall, however, when you see him in scale—that is, compared with a crowd of people of average height.

In art there are two kinds of scale to consider. One is the scale of the work itself. The other is the scale of objects or elements within the design.

The pyramids of Egypt are of such large scale that people are overwhelmed by their size. These pyramids were designed to be large to express the eternal strength of Egypt.

Wall paintings inside a pyramid depict important people in a larger scale than less important people. The tomb painting *Nakht and Wife* **(Figure 10.8)** depicts stories about the priest Nakht and his wife. They watch their busy servants hunting, fishing, and farming on the priest's land. In the painting, the figures of the priest and his wife are much larger than the servants. *When figures are arranged in a work of art so that scale indicates importance,* the artist is using **hierarchical proportion.** This arrangement disregards the actual size of figures and objects in order to indicate rank in a society. Use of scale to emphasize rank appears in the art of many cultures (see Figure 10.10, page 262).

Actual works of art are usually much larger or much smaller than they appear to be when you look at photographs of them. You may have seen photos with a human hand or a human figure added for the purpose of showing the size of the objects in relation to human scale. Without some sort of measure, no illustration in any book can convey the effect of the scale of a work of art.

Some works that seem monumental are really quite small in size. This is why the dimensions are always listed in the credit line of the work. Try to visualize the size of a work in relation to your size. Imagine how it would look if it were in the room with you.

▲ **FIGURE 10.8** The servants in this painting are not all the same size. Two figures are as large as the priest and his wife, some are half their size, and some are even smaller. The painting uses hierarchical proportion. The more important figures are larger than the less important figures.

Egyptian, Thebes. *Nakht and Wife.* Copy of a wall painting from the Tomb of Nakht. c. 1425 B.C. 2 × 1.5 m (6.5 × 5′). Egyptian Expedition of The Metropolitan Museum of Art, New York, New York. Rogers Fund, 1915 (15.5.19 e).

▶ **FIGURE 10.9** An ordinary clothespin takes on a whole new meaning when it is 45 feet tall and installed in a plaza in front of the Philadelphia City Hall.

Claes Oldenburg. *Clothespin.* 1976. Cor-Ten Steel. Height: 13.7 m (45'). Centre Square, Philadelphia, Pennsylvania.

Claes Oldenburg often uses scale to make you look at ordinary objects with a new perspective. He created a 45-foot-tall pair of binoculars, a soft saxophone that is 69 inches tall, and a 45-foot-tall clothespin **(Figure 10.9).** Can you imagine what it would feel like to stand in front of a clothespin that is over eight times taller than you?

Variations in scale within a work can change the work's total impact. For example, interior designers are concerned with the scale of the furniture that is to be placed in a room. The designer considers the scale of the space into which the furniture will be placed. The needs of the people who will use the space must also be considered. An oversized, overstuffed sofa would crowd a small room with a low ceiling. However, the same sofa would fit comfortably in a large hotel lobby with a four-story ceiling. The large scale of the lobby would make the size of the sofa look right.

Activity | Experimenting with Scale

Applying Your Skills. Create a small collage scene using magazine cutouts of people, furniture, and hand-held objects such as books, combs, pencils, hair dryers, and dishes. Arrange the cutouts on a small sheet of paper using realistic, accurate scale. All of the objects in the scene should be in scale with the people, and all of the people should be in correct proportion to each other. Use perspective techniques and arrange things in depth to create an accurate scale. Draw a background environment for the scene using water-base markers, colored pencils, or crayons.

Computer Option. Use digital hardware such as a camera, scanner, or video camera and accompanying software to capture a variety of photographs of people and objects. Use the Selection tool and Copy and Paste commands to assemble a computer collage that shows unrealistic scale. Apply the tools of your choice to manipulate the images. Images can be selected from many other sources such as a CD-ROM or the Internet. If you do not have these capabilities, use the drawing and painting tools of your choice to create a surrealistic scene.

▲ **FIGURE 10.10** In the art of the Benin people, symbolic proportions were used. Notice how large the head of the Oba (in the center of the work) is in proportion to the rest of his body.

Nigeria, Edo. Court of Benin. *Mounted King with Attendants.* Sixteenth to seventeenth centuries. Brass. Height: 47.9 cm (18⁷/₈″). The Metropolitan Museum of Art, New York. Gift of Mr. and Mrs. Klaus G. Perls, 1990. (1990.332).

▲ **FIGURE 10.11** Wilt Chamberlain, an NBA star, was a seven-time consecutive winner of the NBA scoring title from 1960 to 1966. He retired in 1974. Willie Shoemaker, an American jockey, won 8,833 races in his career and is considered the best rider in thoroughbred racing history. Chamberlain is over 7 feet tall, while Shoemaker is approximately 5 feet tall.

Annie Liebovitz. *Wilt Chamberlain and Willie Shoemaker.* Photograph.

Drawing Human Proportions

In Western art, realistic representation of people has been the dominant style from the Renaissance to the twentieth century. However, many artists around the world use symbolic proportions rather than representational accuracy. To the Benin people of West Africa, the head represented life and intelligence. The prosperity of the Benin people depended on the head of the Oba, the divine ruler. In **Figure 10.10** the head of the Oba is one third of the whole body. This demonstrates its symbolic importance.

Figures

People come in a variety of sizes and shapes. Categories for clothes sizes—husky, petite, tall—are just one indication of the many different shapes and sizes of people.

Although they vary in height and width, most people do not vary with regard to proportion. Many basketball players, such as Wilt Chamberlain, are tall. Jockeys, such as Willie Shoemaker, are usually small and light. In **Figure 10.11,** notice that Chamberlain's arms, legs, and torso have the same proportions as those of Shoemaker. Body proportions cannot be defined in inches or centimeters. They can only be defined in ratios of one part of the body to another.

The unit usually used to define the proportions of an individual figure is the length of the head from the chin to the top of the skull. The average adult is seven and one-half heads tall **(Figure 10.12);** a young child is five or six heads tall; and an infant is only three heads long. Many artists use adult proportions when drawing an infant, and the painting looks strange because the head is small in relation to the rest of the body. In Giotto's (**jot**-toe) painting *Madonna and Child* **(Figure 10.13),** the child looks like a miniature adult because of proportion.

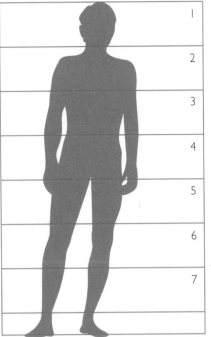

◀ **FIGURE 10.12**
Average body proportions.

◀ **FIGURE 10.13** Giotto was the first artist to make a flat surface appear three-dimensional by using shading. He was the first to attempt realism. The child in this painting looks awkward, like a little adult. This is because Giotto used incorrect proportions to depict the child.

Giotto. *Madonna and Child.* 1320–30. Paint on wood. 85.5 × 62 cm (33⅝ × 24⅜"). National Gallery of Art, Washington, D.C. © 1998 Board of Trustees. Samuel H. Kress Collection.

FIGURE 10.14 Siqueiros used foreshortening in this painting to dramatically exaggerate his reach. It is as if the artist wants to grab everything he can. His hand becomes a burst of superhuman energy.

David Alfaro Siqueiros. *Self-Portrait (El Coronelazo).* 1945. Pyroxylin on Masonite. 91 × 121 cm (35¹³/₁₆ × 47⁵/₈″). Museo de Arte Moderno, Mexico City, Mexico. © Estate of David Alfaro Siqueiros. Licensed by VAGA, New York, NY/ SOMAAP/Mexico City.

Heads and Faces

As you read this section, look in a mirror or at a classmate to check the examples discussed.

The front of the head is approximately oval. No one has a head that is perfectly oval—some people have narrow chins, and some have square jaws.

A face is approximately symmetrical. It has a central vertical axis when viewed from the front **(Figure 10.15)**. If the face turns away from you, the axis curves over the surface of the head. You can divide the head into four sections along the central axis. This is done by drawing three horizontal lines that divide the axis into four equal parts, as shown in Figure 10.15.

Sometimes an artist may purposely distort proportion to make a drawing look more realistic. If a person is pointing at you, the arm from the fingertips to the shoulder will look shorter than it actually is. In a painting, an artist will use a technique to visually shorten the arm. **Foreshortening** is *to shorten an object to make it look as if it extends backward into space* **(Figure 10.14)**.

Activity — Human Proportions

Applying Your Skills. Use the length of your head (from the bottom of your chin to the top of your skull) as a unit against which to measure the rest of your body. In this way you can calculate the relationship, or ratio, of all parts of your body to your head. You may need a friend to help you obtain accurate measurements. Determine the number of head lengths that each of the following represents: total height, chin to waist, waist to hip, knee to ankle, ankle to bottom of bare heel, underarm to elbow, elbow to wrist, wrist to tip of finger, and shoulder to tip of finger. Record the ratios and create a diagram or chart to show your findings. Compare your findings with those of your classmates. Find averages for the class, because the ratios will not be exactly alike.

Computer Option. Use video digitizing software and a video camera or a scanner to capture a variety of photographs of people and objects. Clip art and CD-ROMs can also be used. If you do not have these capabilities, use the drawing tools of your choice to create your images. Use the Selection tool and the Copy and Paste options to assemble a computer collage using unrealistic scale. Use the tools of your choice, such as Resize, to manipulate the images. Create a surrealistic scene.

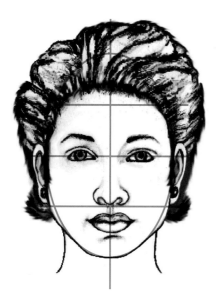

▲ **Figure 10.15** Facial proportions.

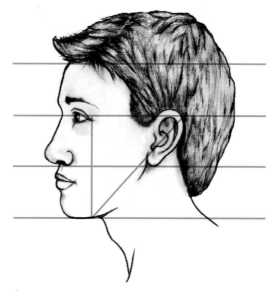

▲ **Figure 10.16** Profile proportions.

The top fourth of the head is usually full of hair. The hair may start above the top horizontal line, or it may fall below it if the person wears bangs.

The eyes usually appear on the central horizontal line. They are at the center of a person's head. Notice the width of the space between the eyes. How does it relate to the width of one eye? The bottom of the nose rests on the lowest horizontal line, and the mouth is closer to the nose than to the chin. Use the sighting technique to determine other relationships, such as nose width, mouth width, and ear placement.

When you view a head in complete profile, or from the side, all of the vertical proportions remain the same as in the front view. However, both shape and contour change. Try to discover the new ratios **(Figure 10.16).** Notice the relationship between the distance from the chin to the hairline and the distance from the front of the forehead to the back of the head. Can you find a ratio to help you locate the ear in profile? Study the contour of the front of the face. Which part protrudes the most? Notice the jawline from the chin to the ear and the relationship of the neck to the head. In **Figure 10.17,** the artist has drawn

▲ **Figure 10.17** The center face in this drawing is a young woman whom Gauguin painted on his first visit to Tahiti. These serene faces with blank eyes look like ancient stone heads sculpted in Egypt or Mexico. The local Tahitian people were the inspiration for many of Gauguin's paintings.

Paul Gauguin. *Tahitians.* c. 1891–93. Charcoal on laid paper. 41 × 31 cm (16¹/₈ × 12¹/₄"). The Metropolitan Museum of Art, New York, New York. Purchase, The Annenberg Foundation Gift. 1996. (1996.418).

both the front and two profile views of a woman's head.

Notice that the facial proportions of infants are different, as shown in the print by Bonnard **(Figure 10.18)**.

▲ **FIGURE 10.18** Even though Bonnard has flattened and simplified this work, the differences in the proportions between the profile of the father and the infant are easily measured. The skull of the infant is very large, and the baby's features seem to be squeezed down into the lower part of the head.

Pierre Bonnard. *Family Scene.* From an album of *L'Estampe Originale.* 1893. Color lithograph on heavy cream wove paper. 31 × 17.8 cm (12¼ × 7"). The Metropolitan Museum of Art, New York, New York. Rogers Fund, 1922. (22.82.1-3). © Artists Rights Society (ARS), New York/ADAGP, Paris.

Activity Drawing the Head

Creating Visual Solutions Using Direct Observation. Improve your observation skills. Look through magazines for large photographs of heads. Look for adults, children, and babies. Remember that a head is not flat, and when it is turned, the central axis moves and curves around the shape of the head. You can always find the axis because it goes through the center of the nose, lips, and between the eyes. Draw the central axis and the three horizontal dividing lines on each face. What are the proportional differences among the faces of adults, children, and infants?

Computer Option. Gather some pictures of the faces of adults, children, and babies. Notice that facial proportions change with age. Use the drawing tools of your choice to draw a human face using average facial proportions. Save your work. Use the Selection tool and the Copy and Paste options to duplicate the first face you drew. To experiment with the size of facial features, use the Selection tool to select the features of the face but not the outline of the head itself. Use the Resize option to create the correct feature size for a young child. Save your work. Reduce the size even more to create the correct feature size for an infant. The features need to be small and in the lower third of its face. If possible, save all three faces on the same screen. Finally, compare the three faces you have created.

 Check Your Understanding

1. What is scale?
2. What are the two kinds of scale present in a work of art?
3. Describe hierarchical proportion.
4. How does the credit line help you understand the scale of an artwork?
5. Explain foreshortening.

How Artists Use Proportion and Distortion

Vocabulary

exaggeration
distortion

Many artists use correct proportions in their work. They want every viewer to recognize the person, place, or thing being shown. These artists use correct proportion to create illusions of reality. This ability to show objects as though they were real seems magical to many viewers. Other artists choose exaggeration and distortion to create works with unusual expressive qualities.

Realistic Proportion

During the Renaissance in Italy, there was a renewed interest in art and literature. Ancient Greek and Roman sculptures were discovered, and artists were inspired to create works with the realistic proportions of the ancient masters. To better understand the human body, the artists Leonardo da Vinci and Michelangelo Buonarroti dissected cadavers in secret because dissection was illegal at that time.

Michelangelo's statue of *David* is an outstanding example of Renaissance proportional accuracy. The artist was asked to create a bigger than life size figure of *David* (**Figure 10.19**) for the façade of the Cathedral in Florence. When it was finished, the people decided that it was too important to be placed high up on the cathedral. Instead, it was placed in the main square and became a symbol of the city of Florence.

▲ **FIGURE 10.19** One unusual feature of Michelangelo's *David* is the fiery intensity of the young man's facial expression. He is staring at an enemy, the giant Goliath. What do you think David is thinking?

Michelangelo. *David (detail).* 1501–1504. Marble. Galleria dell' Accademia, Florence, Italy.

Before the invention of photography, artists were hired to paint portraits to record accurate information about real people **(Figure 10.20).** A contemporary American artist, Marisol, painted in the Pop style in the 1960s. In **Figure 10.21,** she has used an unusual combination of materials, yet she still uses accurate proportions for all of the figures.

Exaggeration and Distortion

Some artists use exaggeration and distortion rather than realistic proportion to convey their ideas and feelings. **Exaggeration** and **distortion** are *deviations from expected, normal proportions.* They are powerful means of expression. Artists can lengthen, enlarge, bend, warp, twist, or deform parts or all of the human body. By making these changes, they can show moods and feelings that are easily understood by viewers. The exaggeration used by the artist in **Figure 10.22** lets us know how the woman feels.

▲ **FIGURE 10.20** Vigée-Lebrun painted this wealthy princess without indications of her material wealth so that she could emphasize her subject's beauty. Do the facial and body proportions of the princess seem realistic?

Marie-Louise-Élisabeth Vigée-Lebrun. *Portrait of Princess Belozersky.* 1798. Oil on canvas. 81.3 × 66.7 cm (32 × 26¹/₄″). National Museum of Women in the Arts, Washington, D.C.

▲ **FIGURE 10.21** This mixed-media work is based on a photograph that Marisol found among waste papers near her studio. She uses realistic painting on the flat surfaces of rectangular solids and recycled doors, and combines it with carved wooden forms to create a realistic portrait of the unknown family. Notice the different accurate proportions in this work. Use a ruler and you will see that the head-to-body ratio is appropriate for each figure.

Marisol. *The Family.* 1962. Painted wood and other materials in three sections. 209.6 × 166.4 × 39.4 cm (82¹/₂ × 65¹/₂ × 15¹/₂″). Collection, Museum of Modern Art, New York, New York. Advisory Committee Fund. © Marisol Escobar/Licensed by VAGA, New York, NY.

◀ FIGURE 10.22
The proud anxiety of the mother is expressed through the exaggerated stretch of her arms and body. She encourages her daughter to walk, yet she is ready to catch her if she falls.

Napachie Pootoogook. *My Daughter's First Steps.* 1990. Lithograph. 55.8 × 85.8 cm (22 × 33³/₄"). Permission courtesy of the West Baffin Eskimo Co-operative Limited.

In the past, movie stars of the silent screen had to exaggerate facial expressions and body language to convey meaning without words. If you have ever seen an old silent movie, you have probably laughed at the exaggerated eyelid movements used to express meaning.

It takes study and skill to use exaggeration and distortion effectively. Before an artist can distort a person or an object, he or she must study perception drawing and anatomy of the human figure. It takes knowledge to know what to exaggerate and how to distort images effectively.

In *Single Family Blues* **(Figure 10.23),** Twiggs has used exaggeration to express the feeling of "the blues" that engulf this family. Notice that the hand is twice the size of the child's blue head or the mother's blue-purple, or violet, face. This distortion allows the viewer to see how dominant "the blues" are in this family.

▲ FIGURE 10.23 Twiggs uses exaggeration to emphasize the hand playing the blues for this family.

Leo Twiggs. *Single Family Blues.* 1996. Batik on cotton. 26.7 × 34.3 cm (10¹/₂ × 13¹/₂"). Courtesy of the artist.

Pablo Picasso (**pah**-bloh pee-**cah**-so) was born in Malaga, Spain, in 1881. One day his father, a painter and teacher, came home to a surprise. His son had finished a portrait. After examining the work, Pablo's father gave the boy all his art materials. So great was Picasso's work that his father vowed never to paint again. Picasso was just eight years old.

He went to Paris in 1904. There he met other artists and writers. The creative climate encouraged him to develop a new style, which he called Cubism. Combining his appreciation of African art with his interest in geometrical forms, he created a unique and innovative form. His aim was to shock viewers into visual awareness. His intensity drove him to experiment with all media, discovering new forms and new ideas. He painted Cubist works as well as realistic representations of people. He also created prints and collages throughout his long and full life.

▶ FIGURE 10.24 Picasso exaggerates the thinness of this old man, elongates his limbs, and places him in an impossibly angular position to create a painting that expresses sympathy for his condition. How does the contrast between the thin, angular man painted in blue and the warm brown, rounded guitar affect the meaning of this work?

Pablo Picasso. *The Old Guitarist.* 1903. Oil on panel. 122.9 × 82.6 cm (48³/₈ × 32¹/₂″). The Art Institute of Chicago, Chicago, Illinois. Helen Birch Bartlett Memorial Collection. © 2003 Estate of Pablo Picasso/Artists Rights Society (ARS), New York.

Picasso was also a master of distorting proportion to express an idea or feeling. The works he painted during the early twentieth century are known as his "Blue Period." During this time he painted poor and tragic people. Despite the sorrowful condition of the figures, there seems to be a sense of optimism in the works. In *The Old Guitarist* (**Figure 10.24**), the grotesquely thin old man seems unaware of his condition. His head is bent toward the instrument as if nothing matters but the beautiful sound of his music.

▲ **Figure 10.25** This watercolor represents a design for a backdrop commissioned by a Moscow theatre. The backdrop was used as scenery for a play by the famous Russian nineteenth-century writer Gogol.

Marc Chagall. *Homage to Gogol.* 1917. Watercolor on paper. 39.4 × 50.2 cm (15¹/₂ × 19³/₄"). Museum of Modern Art, New York, New York. Acquired through the Lillie P. Bliss Bequest. Licensed by SCALA/Art Resource, NY. © 2003 Artists Rights Society (ARS), New York/ADAGP, Paris.

In his painting *Homage to Gogol* **(Figure 10.25),** Chagall used exaggeration and distortion to emphasize his love of the theatre. Some say that the huge black figure who is stretched and twisted into an exaggerated bow is Chagall himself. He is holding a laurel wreath in one hand and balancing a church on his foot while bowing to Gogol. Chagall greatly admired Nikolay Vasilyevich Gogol, a nineteenth-century author of plays, short stories, and novels that stand out as masterpieces of Russian literature. A message in Russian, "To Gogol from Chagall," is incorporated into the design.

Artists can create feelings of great stability and calm by placing a small head on a large body. A monumental, or large and imposing, quality results. The monumental quality of Gaston Lachaise's *Walking Woman* **(Figure 10.26** on page 272) is created through exaggerated proportions rather than through large scale.

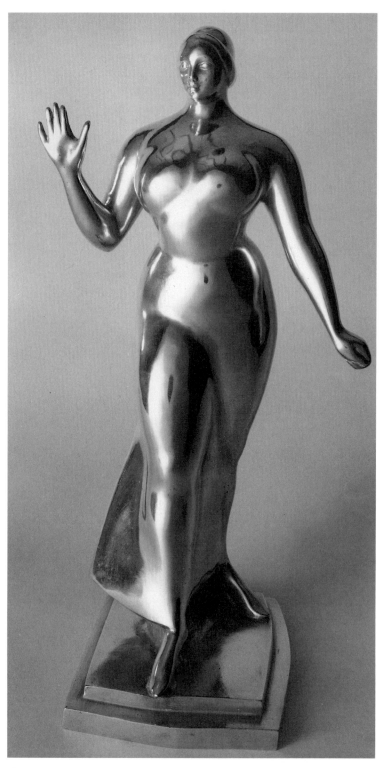

Another use of exaggeration can be seen in the features of a mask. Masks have been used in all societies, from early primitive tribes to our modern computer age **(Figure 10.27).** A mask allows a person to hide his or her real self and become someone, or something, else.

Masks are used in many cultures as part of religious ceremonies and rituals. In many cases the features of the mask are exaggerated for expressive purposes. Each culture has specific traditions and procedures that are followed for making and using masks. Sometimes the mask appears to the person in a dream. Sometimes the mask is part of a cultural tradition. In most cases the mask is intended to aid efforts in communicating with the spirit world.

Cartoons are another way in which exaggeration can be used. Editorial cartoonists use this technique to make caricatures of famous people. (See page 284 for more about how cartoonists use exaggeration.) The caricatures emphasize unusual facial features. Similarly, characters in comic strips are often made by using proportions that are larger than life. The most distorted comic-strip characters are often the funniest ones.

▲ **FIGURE 10.26** This sculpture is only 19¼ inches (48.8 cm) high and yet it has a monumental quality because Lachaise has made the head small in comparison to the body.

Gaston Lachaise. *Walking Woman.* 1922. Bronze. 48.8 × 26.9 × 18.9 cm (19¼ × 10⅝ × 7½"). Hirshhorn Museum and Sculpture Garden, Smithsonian Institution, Washington, D.C. Gift of Joseph H. Hirshhorn, 1966.

▶ **FIGURE 10.27** Imagine sitting in the dark around a fire when a mysterious figure jumps out of the dark into the dim flickering light wearing one of these masks. How would you feel? How does exaggeration and distortion affect the expressive qualities of these masks?

(right) George Walkus. *Secret Society Mask. (Four Headed Cannibal Spirit)* 1938. Wood; cedar bark, shredded; string. 53.3 × 129.5 cm (21 × 51″). Denver Art Museum, Denver, Colorado.

(bottom right) New Ireland, South Pacific Islands. *Mask.* c. 1920. Wood, paint, fiber, seashells. Height: 38.1 cm (15″). Milwaukee Public Museum, Milwaukee, Wisconsin.

Activity	**Distorting Proportions**

Applying Your Skills. Cut two ovals about 9 inches long from any color of construction paper. Using parts cut from magazines, create one face using accurate proportions. On the second oval, create a distorted face.

Computer Option. Use the drawing tools of your choice to draw a human face using average facial proportions. Use the Select tool and the Copy and Paste options to make four or five copies of the head and face on the same screen. Use the Select tool to experiment with the whole head and with individual facial features. Resize, Distort, Rotate, and Bend are some options that may prove useful to you. If your software does not have these options, draw the changes with the drawing tools of your choice. Save your work. Compare the faces you have distorted and changed. How does the distortion affect the way you would use each face in a piece of artwork?

 Check Your Understanding

1. How do exaggeration and distortion affect proportion?
2. Why do artists use distortion?
3. How can artists create monumental qualities without using a large scale?
4. Compare and contrast the proportion of the heads in Figure 10.19 on page 267 and Figure 10. 26 on page 272.

The Golden Mean and Mixed Media

Historical and Cultural Context

In his painting *Both Members of This Club* **(Figure 10.28),** turn-of-the-twentieth-century American artist George Bellows brings us ringside to view the action of a boxing match. Take a moment to study this work. Notice in particular the straining muscles of the fighters. Observe the bloodied face of the boxer on the left. The viewer is almost able to feel, as much as see, the impact of the blows in this contest of brute strength.

One particularly important device worth noting is the artist's use of the Golden Mean to organize the composition. (See Figure 10.6, page 258.) By breaking up the two-dimensional space using this classical mathematical formula, the composition is stabilized. The fighters and spectators—both real and in the painting—are locked in an intense moment of time. Which member of the club will break the clinch? Only time will tell.

▲ **FIGURE 10.28**

George Bellows. *Both Members of This Club.* 1909. National Gallery of Art, Washington, D.C.

SUPPLIES

- Sketchbook and pencil
- Ruler
- Large sheet of heavy drawing paper
- Tissue paper, light to medium values
- Diluted white school glue or matte medium adhesive
- Black permanent felt-tip markers, thick and thin point
- Tray or palette for color mixing
- Acrylic paints and assorted brushes

What You Will Learn

You will create a nonobjective tissue paper collage, following the proportions of the Golden Mean (see page 256). You will then make a contour drawing of a student model in a classroom studio setting that includes furniture and objects. The drawing is intended to convey the atmosphere of an art classroom studio. You will unify the composition by adding acrylic glazes in a color scheme related to the collage colors.

Creating

Members of the class are to take turns modeling. Other students are to position the model and suggest different poses. Do several quick gesture drawings in your sketchbook of various poses. Set aside the sketch you like best. Decide on the mood your work will convey. Jot down the names of colors that suggest this mood.

Step 1 Choose a horizontal or vertical format for your paper. Using a ruler, divide your paper using the 1 to 1.6 ratio of the Golden Mean. Decide where your figure will be placed. Make a light pencil mark at the focal point of your figure.

Step 2 Gather sheets of tissue paper according to your color scheme. Tear varying shapes and sizes of paper. Use these to create a composition that leads the eye to the focal point. Overlap shapes and glue these down using matte medium or diluted white glue that dries clear. (See Technique Tips Handbook, pages 440–441.)

Step 3 When the glue has dried, transfer your sketch to the collage. The center of your figure should be at the focal point. Using a fine-tipped marker, reinforce the contour lines of your figure as well as important details. Add elements of the environment, such as furniture.

Step 4 Select one of the colors in the tissue paper collage. Using acrylic paint, glaze over portions of the background in order to define the figures and unify the composition. Keep the paint thin and transparent. Do not cover the entire surface. Vary the values. There should be a balance between the drawn and painted areas of the composition.

Evaluating Your Work

▶ **DESCRIBE** Tell what objects are depicted in your work. Point to areas of your work that are nonobjective.

▶ **ANALYZE** Explain and describe how you used the Golden Mean in your composition. Compare and contrast the use of color, proportion, and unity in your artwork.

▶ **INTERPRET** Does the composition create a mood that represents the art studio and the model? Does the color scheme fit the mood you were trying to create? Give your work a title that sums up the expressive quality of your work.

▶ **JUDGE** Is there anything you would change to make the work more successful? Which of the three aesthetic theories would you use to judge your work?

▲ **FIGURE 10.28A**

Student work.

Symbolic Self-Portrait

▲ **FIGURE 10.29**

Gustav Klimt. *Portrait of Joseph Pembaur.* 1890. Oil on canvas. 69 × 55 cm (27¹/₈ × 21²/₃"). © Erich Lessing/Art Resource, NY. Tiroler Landesmuseum Ferdinandeum, Innsbruck, Austria.

SUPPLIES

- Sketchbook and pencil
- Soft eraser
- Mirror
- Hot press watercolor paper or heavy white paper
- Masking tape
- Drawing board
- Watercolors, brushes, and water jars
- Fine-line, nontoxic black ink pen

Historical and Cultural Context

When you first look at **Figure 10.29,** you almost mistake the work for a photograph. This work is an example of *photorealism,* art created with the precision found in photographs. Note that the work was created in the late 1800s, just as photography was coming into its own right.

Take a moment to study this painting. It is more than a simple portrait. It is a tribute to a musician. You can tell from the symbols in the painting—which include Apollo, the god of music, who is depicted standing on a column. The golden lyre behind the main subject also represents Apollo. What other objects can you find that appear to have symbolic value?

What You Will Learn

You will paint a realistic self-portrait. You will add symbolic images that reflect aspects of your personality, interests, culture, and/or dreams for the future. You will enhance the realistic quality of your work by using watercolor and pen-and-ink techniques to create values and textures.

Creating

In your sketchbook write a list of words you would use to describe yourself, your personality, your interests, and so on. Choose the words that fit you best, and think of symbols to represent those words. Be creative.

Step 1 Select three to five ideas from your list. Practice drawing the symbols you have thought of, using pen-and-ink shading techniques. (See Technique Tips Handbook, page 429.) When drawing your symbolic objects, try to work from direct observation.

Step 2 Using a mirror, practice drawing self-portraits in your sketchbook in pencil. See pages 264–265 for specific directions for drawing heads and faces in correct proportions.

Step 3 Begin planning a composition that combines your portrait with the symbols you have selected. Make small rough drawings in your sketchbook, trying different arrangements of the head and symbols. Think about the focal point and the use of negative space in your composition. Choose your best rough sketch for your final work.

Step 4 Tape a sheet of drawing paper onto your drawing board. Draw the composition you have selected. Fill the page. Use a very light pencil line that will not show through the watercolors. Draw your symbols.

Step 5 Switching to watercolors and brush, start painting your face. Continue using the mirror to help you see the hues and values of your face. Start with the lightest colors first. Gradually add the darker colors. You will need to work in layers, letting one layer dry before adding the next. Use value to make your face as three-dimensional as possible. You can always make a watercolor area darker, but it is almost impossible to make it lighter.

Step 6 Next, paint the symbols and background.

Step 7 Once the paint has dried, add pen-and-ink details.

Evaluating Your Work

▶ **DESCRIBE** What symbolic imagery did you use? What does each symbol represent about you? Does your work bear a likeness to you?

▶ **ANALYZE** Did you paint your portrait using accurate proportions? Did your use of watercolor and pen and ink enhance the portrait? Did you include light and dark values to give the face three dimensions? Does your face dominate the composition or do the symbols dominate?

▶ **INTERPRET** What does your painting tell about you? What do the symbols reveal? Give your painting a title that sums up what you were trying to express about yourself.

▶ **JUDGE** If you were to do this painting over, what changes would you make? Justify your artistic decisions.

▲ **FIGURE 10.29A**

Student work.

STUDIO PROJECT
10–3

Digital Fantasy Creature

▲ **FIGURE 10.30**

Salvador Dali. *The Elephants (Design for the Opera La Dama Spagnola e il Cavaliere Romano).* 1961. Indianapolis Museum of Art, Indianapolis, Indiana. © 2003 Salvador Dali, Gala-Salvador Dali Foundation/ Artists Rights Society (ARS), New York.

SUPPLIES

- Sketchbook and pencil
- Magazines, clip art, or original photographs
- Computer
- Scanner
- Paint or image-editing program
- Graphics tablet, optional

Historical and Cultural Context

The early-twentieth-century art movement known as Surrealism took the unreal and made it plausible. One of the masters of this movement was Salvador Dali, who drew the unworldly creatures in **Figure 10.30.** These fantastic elephants are relatively ordinary compared to Dali's other creations. Many of his works, rendered with photorealistic quality, present a nonsensical world where anything goes—where up is down, night is day, and so on.

One recent art development that is similar in spirit to Surrealism is digital fine art. It, too, draws on a world that defies the laws of nature, and where anything is possible.

What You Will Learn

Using your imagination, you will create a fantasy creature with exaggeration and distortion. You will combine different insect, animal, and human body parts to produce a new, imaginary creature with the help of a paint or image-editing program. (See Digital Handbook, page 449). You will then create an environment in which to place this creature.

Creating

Start by drawing an image of a person or an animal in your sketchbook. Consult nature magazines or other art resources for ideas. Experiment with exaggerating or distorting various physical features such as arms and legs. Try lengthening, shortening, thickening, thinning, and multiplying body parts. Find unexpected combinations of shapes.

Step 1 Use a paint or image-editing program to recreate the insect, animal, or human figure. Use the software's drawing tools or a graphics tablet (see Digital Handbook, page 448), if one is available. If you like, combine your drawing or painting with scanned images from magazines, clip art, or original photographs.

Step 2 Experiment with copying and pasting different parts of your creature. Use the program's tools to stretch, shrink, or otherwise alter these parts. Try changing and distorting the proportions. Save your work frequently.

Step 3 If filters or special effects menus and tools are available, continue to alter your image. Add contrasting textures, shapes, and colors. Zoom in occasionally to clean up any rough lines, stray pixels, or other mistakes.

Step 4 Once you are satisfied with the imaginary creature, create a surprising and illogical background for it. Once again, choose the tools available in the software program to add interest to the setting you design. If your software offers Layering, create multiple layers. You can create the illusion of depth and atmospheric perspective using layers.

Step 5 After you have saved your final composition, print it. Prepare your final copy for display.

Evaluating Your Work

▶ **DESCRIBE** What animal, insect, or human part(s) did you use to create your imaginary figure? Identify the features you have distorted and exaggerated. Describe the things you have added to create an illogical background. List, in order, the specific hardware and software you used.

▶ **ANALYZE** Explain how you used exaggeration and distortion to create your creature. Describe the colors and textures you used to enhance the creature and background.

▶ **INTERPRET** Describe the mood, theme, or idea you have created. Is your creature funny? Frightening? Give your work a descriptive title that sums up the feeling or mood it conveys.

▶ **JUDGE** Have you successfully combined, exaggerated, and distorted the features of your creature to emphasize an idea or mood? Is there anything you would change? What aesthetic theory would you use to judge this artwork?

▶ **FIGURE 10.30A**

Student work.

Proportion

You wouldn't think twice if a car drove by. You might do a double take, however, if the car were 90 feet long. Proportion in art, as in life, can command your attention. As you examine the student artworks on these pages:

- Compare and contrast them in terms of their use of the principle of proportion.

- Analyze the works, forming precise conclusions about the type of proportion used.

- Analyze the works, forming precise conclusions about the artist's intent.

Activity 10.31 **Form and proportion.**
Notice how this artist has used circular forms of varying sizes. Compare and contrast the forms in this art object. Which ones receive the most emphasis?

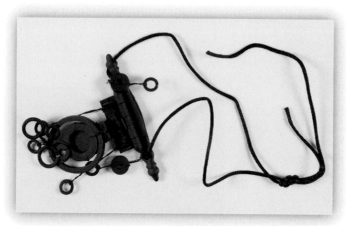

▲ **FIGURE 10.31**

Student work. *Untitled.* Cabinet hinge, lock washers, rubber disks, and wire connectors on a satin cord, spray-painted black. 88.9 x 101.6 mm (3¹/₂ × 4").

Activity 10.32 **Golden Mean.**
Compare and contrast this artwork with Figure 9.19 on page 239. Analyze each artist's use of the proportions of the Golden Mean.

▲ **FIGURE 10.32**

Student work. *Red and Blue Figure Study.* Monoprint. 22.9 × 304.8 mm (9 × 12").

Activity 10.33 **Scale.** Analyze this student artwork, noting its actual size. Compare the scale of these facial features with those of a life-size face. Form conclusions about the artist's intent.

Activity 10.34 **Exaggeration and distortion.** Evaluate this sculpture in terms of the artist's probable intent. Do you think the student artist's goal was to achieve realism? Explain.

▲ **FIGURE 10.33**

Student work. *Portions of Me.* Pen and ink, watercolor. 457.2 × 457.2 mm (18 × 18").

▲ **FIGURE 10.34**

Student work. *All Alone in the Moonlight.* Clay, acrylic, mixed media. 127 x 177.8 x 76.2 mm (5 × 7 × 3").

ART *Online*

To view more student artworks visit the Glencoe Student Art Gallery at **art.glencoe.com.**

For Your Portfolio

Analyze Personal Artworks. As you build your art portfolio, compare and contrast the use of proportion in your artworks. Make sure to include some human figure drawings. These will reflect your understanding of the Golden Mean. Be sure to attach notes that detail the principles used in an artwork's design. Also, identify the art elements that these principles organize.

Visual Art Journal

Evaluate the portfolios of other artists and keep these notes in your art journal. Work with your teacher to gather a collection of artists' portfolios. Select and analyze the portfolios to form conclusions about formal qualities, historical and cultural contexts, intents, and meanings. Add sketches to your evaluations to illustrate your conclusions.

Art Criticism
in Action

▲ **FIGURE 10.35**

Marc Chagall. *The Green Violinist.* 1923–24. Oil on canvas. 198 × 108.6 cm (78 × 42³/₄″). The Solomon R. Guggenheim Museum, New York, New York. Gift, Solomon R. Guggenheim, 1937. © 2003 Artists Rights Society (ARS), New York/ADAGP, Paris.

Critiquing the Artwork

▶ **1 DESCRIBE** *What do you see?*

List all the information found in the credit line.

- Describe the main figure in this painting. Do the man's feet appear to be touching the ground? Explain.

- Can you find any other figures or objects in the work? Describe everything that you see.

▶ **2 ANALYZE** *How is this work organized?*

This is a clue-collecting step about the elements and principles of art.

- Compare the artist's use of bright colors for some objects and pale colors for others. Explain why he has used the element of color in this fashion.

- Compare and contrast the artist's use of color and form and the art principle of proportion.

▶ **3 INTERPRET** *What message does this artwork communicate to you?*

Combine the clues you have collected to form a creative interpretation of the work.

- Notice that the violinist cradles his violin almost as though it were a baby. What does this tell you about his feelings toward the violin? About the music that he makes?

- Does everyone in the painting seem to hear the music? Explain.

▶ **4 JUDGE** *What do you think of the work?*

Decide if this is a successful work of art.

- After analyzing this work, form a conclusion about the artist's intent. Did he intend to create a lifelike work of art? Which aesthetic theory would be most applicable to this work? Explain your answer.

Meet the ARTIST

Marc Chagall
(1887–1985)

Marc Chagall was born in a small town in Russia to a poor, Jewish family. He studied art in St. Petersburg, and moved to Paris upon graduation. In 1914, he returned to Russia for a visit but was unable to leave when World War I broke out. In 1918, he was appointed Commissar of Art. After the war, Chagall returned to Paris. His subject matter ranges from personal experiences and folklore to Biblical stories. In addition to his painting, he is noted for his mosaics and stained-glass windows. Some of his murals hang in the Metropolitan Opera House in New York City.

Art and Politics

Political cartoonists draw the world as they see it—just off center.

Q. What is a political cartoon?

A. It's a drawing that comments—often in a humorous way—on people, events, and ideas in the news. Political cartoonists have to amuse their readers and address complicated issues using just ink and a few words.

Q. How do political cartoonists create their humor?

A. One way is by exaggerating the physical features or proportions of the people they draw—a technique called caricature. For example, a political cartoonist may take the symbols of the American political parties, the donkey and the elephant, and draw them the size of a person, complete with coat and tie. Or a cartoonist may poke fun at politicians by shrinking them down to the size of a baby.

Q. How does a political cartoonist get started?

A. Signe Wilkinson draws cartoons for the Philadelphia *Daily News* and other newspapers. Her career began with doodling—something she started doing as a child. Her first job was reporting for a newspaper in Pennsylvania. Wilkinson began drawing the people she was supposed to be writing about. Back in the newsroom, she fine-tuned her doodles and convinced some editors to publish her work. "I realized that I liked drawing more than writing," Wilkinson says. She also realized that cartooning combined her interests in art and politics. "[We] take a topic, like gun control, and express how we feel through our drawings."

the THOROUGHLY MODERN MEDICAL SCHOOL

WELCOME TO BASIC ANATOMY CLASS!

HMO RULES & REGULATIONS Vol. 1

covered
uncovered
slip covered
will cover if seen on '60 Minutes'

claims forms
referral forms
appeals forms
unappealing forms
re-imbursement schedule
re-imbursement complaint forms
re-imbursement if complaint is seen on '60 Minutes'

TOMORROW:
MEDICARE
FRIDAY:
INTRO TO MALPRACTICE LAW

SIGN WILKINSON

Signe Wilkinson takes on the medical profession and health insurance companies in this political cartoon. What examples of exaggeration can you find in her drawing?

SIGNE WILKINSON

Self-portrait of Wilkinson at work.

TIME to Connect

Using your school's media center or the Internet, find political cartoons that were published during one of these significant points in American history: World War II, the Vietnam War, and the corporate scandals of 2002.

• What was the significance or importance of each of the events and/or people shown in the cartoons? Where were they originally shown? What are the points of view of the cartoonists regarding the subject, event, or politician?

• As a class, create a display that shows copies of the cartoons, organizing them by subject matter and time period. Discuss the cartoonists' points of view.

Building Vocabulary

On a separate sheet of paper, write the term that best matches each definition given below.

1. The principle of art concerned with the size relationship of one part to another.

2. A line divided into two parts so that the smaller line has the same proportion, or ratio, to the larger line as the larger line has to the whole line.

3. Size as measured against a standard reference.

4. Figures arranged in a work of art so that scale indicates importance.

5. To shorten an object to make it look as if it extends backward into space.

6. Deviations from expected, normal proportions.

Reviewing Art Facts

Answer the following questions using complete sentences.

7. What is the Golden Mean ratio?

8. Explain the difference between scale and proportion.

9. What was the name for the geometric form that had sides matching the ratio of the Golden Mean?

10. What are the two kinds of scale in art?

11. What unit is usually used to define the proportions of any individual figure?

Thinking Critically About Art

12. **Extend.** Do some library research to determine how hierarchical proportions have been used in the art of different cultures. Photocopy examples to show and report your findings to the class.

13. **Compare and Contrast.** Siqueiros's painting, *Self-Portrait* (Figure 10.14, page 264) uses a distortion called foreshortening to create a symbolic proportion. The Oba figure (Figure 10.10, page 262) also uses symbolic proportion. Compare the two works. List the similarities and differences. Explain what the distortion conveys in each artwork.

14. **Historical/Cultural Heritage.** Review the Meet the Artist feature on Pablo Picasso on page 270. Picasso both initiated and followed many art trends throughout his long career. Compare and contrast Figure 10.24 on page 270 with Figure 6.26 on page 154. These artworks were created within a ten-year span of each other. Identify the general trend that both paintings reflect in their use of color and proportion.

ART Online

Fashion designers need to understand the rules of human body proportions. These artists illustrate their designs with figure drawings. Not only must the illustrations reflect realistic human proportions but also their clothing must fit the human body. Visit **art.glencoe.com** to compare and contrast career opportunities in art.

Linking to the Performing Arts

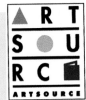

Use the Performing Arts Handbook on page 422 to discover how Eugene Friesen explores the elements of exaggeration and distortion of human proportions through the use of masks in his performance of "Cello Man".

▲ **FIGURE 11.1** Notice how the variety of colors and patterns in this painting create a harmonious whole. Observe how the artist emphasizes the baby's head by surrounding it with white and placing it at the top of the canvas.

Gustav Klimt. *Baby (Cradle)*. 1917. Oil on canvas. 111 × 110 cm (43⅝ × 43⅓"). National Gallery of Art, Washington, D.C. Gift of Otto and Franziska Kallir with the help of the Carol and Edwin Gaines Fullinwider Fund.

CHAPTER 11

Variety, Emphasis, Harmony, and Unity

Art principles such as balance, rhythm, and proportion do not operate in isolation. They work as a team. In the pages ahead, you will learn about three additional principles: *variety, emphasis,* and *harmony.* You will also learn about *unity,* or "oneness." Unity is achieved when the elements and principles are used together to create a sense of wholeness.

In this chapter, you will:

- Describe variety, emphasis, harmony, and unity in your environment and in art.
- Compare and contrast the use of the art principles emphasis and unity in artworks.
- Explain how artists create unity through effective use of the elements and principles of art.
- Use variety, emphasis, and harmony to create unified artworks.

Focus on **Art History** Austrian painter Gustav Klimt (1862–1918) was a leader of the Art Nouveau school. Art Nouveau was a highly ornate, or decorative, art style. It found expression in both the fine arts and crafts such as glassmaking. Klimt's earliest works, theatrical murals, received little critical attention. He is best known for his portraits. Like his other mature works, these reflect an emphasis on rich patterns of curving lines. Notice the abundance of curved patterns in **Figure 11.1.**

Interpret. Notice that Figure 11.1 has two titles. Why do you think the artist gave the work a second title? Which title do you think best captures the main focus of the work?

Variety, Emphasis, and Harmony

Vocabulary

variety
emphasis
focal point
harmony

Variety is a principle of art that adds interest to an artwork. Emphasis is a principle of art that enhances variety because it creates areas that draw your attention. The eye-catching, or dominant, area is usually a focal point that first attracts the attention of the viewer. The viewer then looks at the less dominant, or subordinate, areas. Harmony makes variety and emphasis work together in a piece of art. Variety and harmony complement one another in the same way that positive and negative spaces complement each other. Variety adds interest to an artwork while harmony prevents variety from causing chaos.

Variety

People need variety in all areas of their lives. Imagine how boring it would be if daily routines were exactly the same every day of the week for a whole year. Imagine how visually boring the world would be if everything in it—everything—were the same color.

People put a great deal of time and effort into creating variety in their environment. They may buy new furniture or paint the walls, not because the furniture is old or the paint is peeling, but simply because they need a change. They add variety to other aspects of their lives as well. New clothes, new foods, new friends—people make endless changes to relieve the sameness or add interest to life.

Just as people must add variety to their lives to keep it interesting, so must artists add variety to their works. **Variety** is *the principle of art concerned with difference or contrast.*

◀ **FIGURE 11.2** The artist has used only one shape (an isosceles triangle) and two colors to create this print. How has he used variety to change these two elements of art into an interesting design that has the illusion of three dimensions?

Miroslav Sutej. *Ultra AB.* 1966. Color silkscreen. 49.2 × 45 cm (19¹/₃ × 17³/₄"). Library of Congress, Washington, D.C. Pennell Fund, 1970.

A work that is too much the same can become dull and monotonous. For example, a work composed of just one shape may be unified, but it will not hold your attention. Variety, or contrast, is achieved by adding something different to a design to provide a break in the repetition **(Figure 11.2).** When different art elements are placed next to each other in a work of art, they are in contrast **(Figure 11.3).** This type of contrast, or variety, adds interest to the work of art and gives it a lively quality.

Almost every artist uses contrasting elements to balance unifying elements. Wide, bold lines complement thin, delicate lines. Straight lines contrast with curves. Free-form shapes differ from geometric shapes. Rough textures add interest to a smooth surface. Colors can contrast in limitless ways. The degree of contrast may range from bold to subtle. The amount of difference between the elements depends on the artist's purpose.

▲ **FIGURE 11.3** Which elements of art has Pereira used to create variety in this painting? Which element of art do you think shows the strongest contrast?

Irene Rice Pereira. *Pillar of Fire*. 1955. Oil on canvas. 145.7 × 94.9 cm (57³/₈ × 37³/₈″). San Antonio Museum of Art, San Antonio, Texas. Purchased with funds provided by Charles M. Knipe by exchange; 95.3.

Activity — Variety and Contrast

Applying Your Skills. Look through *ArtTalk* and find works of art that show bold contrast of line, shape, color, value, and texture. List one work for each kind of contrast. Explain how the contrast was created.

Computer Option. Make a simple design using five or six shapes. Overlap some shapes. Choose the Selection tool and Copy and Paste commands to make five copies of the design on the same page. Leave the original design unchanged but alter the rest to show a type of variety. Change color schemes, contrasts, and value as well as line thickness and textures. Use the Bucket fill or Selection tool to make changes quickly.

Emphasis

Have you ever underlined an important word or phrase several times in a letter? Have you ever raised the volume of your voice to make sure the person you were talking to understood a key point? These are just two ways that people use emphasis to focus attention on the main points in a message.

▲ **FIGURE 11.5** This artist has used value contrast to create a strong focal point. Compare and contrast the use of emphasis in this work to Rembrandt's painting, Figure 5.36 on page 124.

Cecilia Beaux. *Ethel Page (Mrs. James Large).* 1884. Oil on canvas. 76.2 × 63.8 cm (30 × 25¹/₈″). National Museum of Women in the Arts, Washington, D.C.

In advertisements, music, news stories, your lessons at school, and your day-to-day communications, you see and hear certain ideas and feelings being emphasized over others.

Emphasis is *the principle of art that makes one part of a work dominant over the other parts.* Artists use emphasis to unify a work of art. Emphasis controls the sequence in which the parts are noticed. It also controls the amount of attention a viewer gives to each part.

There are two major types of visual emphasis. In one type, an *element of art* dominates the entire work. In the other type of emphasis, an *area* of the work is dominant over all the other areas.

Emphasizing an Element

If the artist chooses to emphasize one element, all the other elements of the work are made *subordinate,* or less important. The *dominant,* or most important, element affects the viewer's perception of the total work. This element also affects the way in which all the separate items and elements in the work are perceived.

Sometimes the dominant element is so strong that the whole work seems to be drenched in that element. Rauschenberg's *Red Painting* **(Figure 11.4)** is saturated with the color red. Even though he has used a variety of textures to create different areas, the redness takes on a meaning all its own. It affects the viewer's perception of the painting as a whole. It also affects the viewer's perception of the separate parts of the work.

Emphasizing an Area

Sometimes a specific area in a work of art is emphasized. This area, called the **focal point,** is *the first part of a work to attract the attention of the viewer.* The other areas are subordinate to the focal point. Beaux used value like a spotlight to emphasize one important area—a focal point—in her painting *Ethel Page* **(Figure 11.5).**

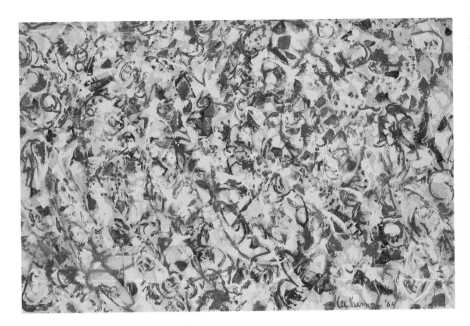

▲ **FIGURE 11.6** In this painting the artist used three different greens, three values of brown, and white to make a net of colors. She used thick and thin brushstrokes as well as curves, lines, and dots squeezed straight from the tube. No one color or line advances toward the viewer. All are equal in importance.

Lee Krasner. *The Springs*. 1964. Oil on canvas. 109.2 × 167.6 cm (43 × 66″). National Museum of Women in the Arts, Washington, D.C. Gift of Wallace and Wilhelmina Holladay. © 2003 Pollock-Krasner Foundation/Artists Rights Society (ARS), New York.

It is possible for a work of art to have more than one focal point. Artists must be careful about this, however. Too many focal points cause the eye to jump around and will confuse the viewer. Artists must also determine the degree of emphasis needed to create a focal point. This usually depends on the purpose of the work.

Of course, a focal point is not necessary. Many artists don't create a focal point in their works **(Figure 11.6).** When artists do create focal points, they are usually careful not to over-emphasize it. They make certain that the focal point is unified with the rest of the design.

Artists use several techniques to create a focal point in a work of art. Following are some examples of these techniques.

Contrast. One way to create a focal point is to place an element that contrasts with the rest of the work in that area. One large shape, for example, will stand out among small ones. One angular, geometric shape will be noticed first among rounded, free-form shapes. A bright color will dominate low-intensity colors, while a light area will dominate a dark design **(Figure 11.7).** An object with a smooth texture becomes a focal point in a design filled with rough textures.

◀ **FIGURE 11.7** Rubens has created contrast between the light, smooth skin of Daniel against the dark rocks and the rough fur of the lions. Daniel sits in a closed position while the lions growl and stretch in active poses.

Peter Paul Rubens. *Daniel in the Lions' Den*. c. 1615. Oil on linen. 224.3 × 330.4 cm (88¼ × 130⅛″). National Gallery of Art, Washington, D.C. © 1998 Board of Trustees. Ailsa Mellon Bruce Fund.

Isolation. Artists sometimes use isolation to create a focal point and thereby emphasize one part of their work. They do this by putting one object alone, apart from all the other objects **(Figure 11.8).** This draws the viewer's eye to the isolated object.

Location. Location is another method used to create a focal point for emphasis. A viewer's eye is normally drawn toward the center of a visual area. Thus, something near this center will probably be noticed first. Because the exact center is a predictable location, most artists place the objects they wish to emphasize a bit off center. They select a location a little to the left or right of center and a little above center **(Figure 11.9).**

◀ FIGURE 11.9 The 12-year-old subject looks as if she were standing in the center of the painting. If you measure, you will find that the artist, Anguissola, has placed most of the face and body left of the center of the work.

Sofonisba Anguissola. *Portrait of the Infanta Isabella Clara Eugenia.* c. 1578. Oil on canvas. 115.9 × 101.9 cm (45⁵/₈ × 40¹/₈″). Prado Museum, Madrid, Spain.

Convergence. When many elements in a work seem to point to one item, that item becomes the focal point. This technique, called convergence, can be created with a very obvious radial arrangement of lines. It can also be achieved through a more subtle arrangement of elements **(Figure 11.10)**.

LOOKING CLOSELY   Creating a Focal Point

Many lines lead your eyes toward the brightly lit, yellow area of the café. Notice the ruts in the cobblestones, the edge of the awning, and the top of the blue door frame all point to the yellow area. How many more objects can you find that point to that area?

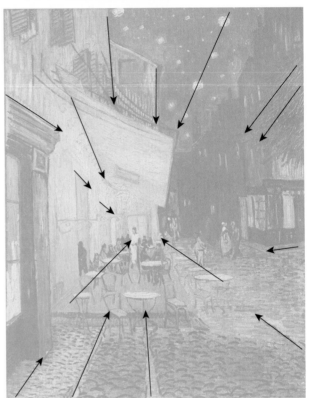

◄ **FIGURE 11.10**

Vincent van Gogh. *Café Terrace at Night.* 1888. Oil on canvas. 81 × 65.5 cm (31⅞ × 25¾"). Rijksmuseum Kroller-Muller, Otterlo, the Netherlands.

▲ **FIGURE 11.11** At first glance, you might think you are looking at an ordinary painting of a Mexican figure. The clothes are depicted with realistic pleats and folds. The smooth skin of the hands and woven texture of the sombrero are also painted realistically. However, when you look at the face, it seems to be wearing a wooden Olmec mask. The mask is the unusual focal point of this work.

The Unusual. In a work of art, an object that is out of the ordinary can become the focal point **(Figure 11.11)**. In a row of soldiers standing at attention, the one standing on his head will be noticed first. The unexpected will always draw the viewer's attention.

Harmony

Harmony is *the principle of art that creates unity by stressing the similarities of separate but related parts.* In musical harmony, related tones are combined into blended sounds. Harmony is pleasing because the tones complement each other. In visual harmony, related art elements are combined. The result looks pleasing because the elements complement each other.

Used in certain ways, color can produce harmony in a work of art. Repetition of shapes that are related, such as rectangles with different proportions, produces harmony **(Figure 11.12)**. A design that uses only geometric shapes appears more harmonious than a design using both geometric and free-form shapes. Even space used in a certain way can produce harmony. If all the parts in a work of art are different sizes, shapes, colors, and textures, the space between the parts can be made uniform to give the work a sense of order.

 **Check Your Understanding**

1. Describe the principle of variety.
2. What is a focal point?
3. Name the five ways emphasis can be created.
4. What is harmony?
5. Compare and contrast the use of emphasis for the central figure in Figure 11.7 on page 291 and Figure 11.8 on page 292.

▲ **Figure 11.12** Scully has used related shapes and colors to create harmony in this work. What has he done to introduce variety?

Sean Scully. *White Robe.* 1990. Oil on linen. 243.8 × 304.8 cm (96 × 120"). High Museum of Art, Atlanta, Georgia. Purchase in honor of Richard A. Denny, Jr., President of the Board of Directors, 1991–94, with funds from Alfred Austell Thornton Sr. in memory of Leila Austell Thornton and Albert Edward Thornton Sr. and Sarah Miller Venable and William Hoyt Venable, 1992.5 a-b.

Activity | Using Emphasis

Creating Visual Solutions Using Imagination. Draw from your imagination to make a series of small designs with strong focal points. Use each of the following: contrast of shape, contrast of color, contrast of value, contrast of texture, isolation, location, convergence, and the unusual.

Computer Option. Use the drawing tools of your choice to create a series of small designs with strong focal points, using each of the following: contrast of shape, contrast of color, contrast of value, contrast of texture, isolation, location, convergence, and the unusual.

You will be able to transform some designs to others by using the Fill Bucket tool. Others can be changed by using the Selection tool and rearranging the shapes. See if you can create all seven designs by starting with only three designs and making alterations to them. Save your work.

Unity

Unity is oneness. It brings order to the world. Without it, the world would be chaotic.

Countries made up of smaller parts are political unities: the United States is such a country. Its 50 states are joined by a single federal government. As a unit, the United States is a world power far stronger than the combined power of the separate states **(Figure 11.13).**

A tree is an example of unity in nature. It is composed of roots, trunk, bark, branches, twigs, and leaves. Each part has a purpose that contributes to the living, growing tree. An electric lamp is a manufactured unit composed of a base, electric wire, sockets, bulbs, shades, and so on. The parts of the lamp work together as a unified whole to provide light. If any part does not work, the unity of the lamp is impaired.

Creating Visual Unity

In art, **unity** is *the quality of wholeness or oneness that is achieved through the effective use of the elements and principles of art.* Unity is like an invisible glue. It joins all the separate parts so that they look as if they belong together.

Unity is difficult to understand at first because it is not easily defined. It is a quality that you feel as you view a work of art **(Figure 11.14).** As you study an artwork, you may think that you would not change one element or object. You are receiving an impression that the work is a unified whole.

▶ **FIGURE 11.13** Johns combines the loose brushwork of Abstract Expressionism with the commonplace objects of American Realism. His map of the United States could be pulled apart by the wild action painting, but it is unified by the harmonious, limited color scheme of a primary triad.

Jasper Johns. *Map*. 1961. Oil on canvas. 198.2 × 312.7 cm (78 × 123⅛″). Collection, Museum of Modern Art, New York, New York. Gift of Mr. and Mrs. Robert C. Scull. © Jasper Johns/Licensed by VAGA, New York, NY.

◀ **FIGURE 11.14** The title of this work does not tell the viewer that the three children and two adults are related, but the artist reveals this in his use of line, form, color, and unity. The clothing and skin of all five figures are divided into similar, unusual free-form shapes. The children's bodies fit within the outlines of the adults. The woman's large, clapping hands are the focal point of the work. How do her hands add to the sense of unity?

Robert Gwathmey. *Children Dancing.* c. 1948. Oil on canvas. 81.2 × 101.6 cm (32 × 40″). The Butler Institute of American Art, Youngstown, Ohio. © Estate of Robert Gwathmey/Licensed by VAGA, New York, NY.

Unity helps you concentrate on a visual image. You cannot realize how important this is until you study a work that lacks unity. Looking at a work that lacks unity is like trying to carry on a serious discussion while your little sister is practicing the violin, your brother is listening to the stereo, and your mother is running the vacuum cleaner. It would be difficult to concentrate on your conversation with all these distractions. It is the same with a work of art that lacks unity. You can't concentrate on the work as a whole, because all the parts demand separate attention.

To create unity, an artist adjusts the parts of a work so they relate to each other and to the whole work. A potter plans decorations for ceramic ware to complement the shape, size, and purpose of the work. Notice the birdlike decoration in the center of the vase in **Figure 11.15.** This creature, the phoenix, was often used to symbolize rebirth in Buddhism. It is assumed that the vase was one of a set of altar vases in a Buddhist temple. Clothing designers

▲ **FIGURE 11.15** The designs for this vase were first outlined with a trail of raised slip, filled in with glaze, and then fired. Overglaze enamels were added, and a second, lower temperature firing was done. What art elements did the artist use to create unity?

China, Shanxi or Henan Province. *Jar.* Late fifteenth century, Ming Period. Stoneware with trailed slip under glaze and overglaze enamels. Height 35.2 cm (13⅞″), diameter 30.2 cm (11⅞″). Asia Society, New York: Mr. and Mrs. John D. Rockefeller 3rd Collection.

▶ **FIGURE 11.16** The Kuba men cut thin strips from raffia palm leaves and wove the basic cloth. Women embroidered the black plush designs onto the cloth. The finished cloth is as flexible and soft as silk. Sometimes, two or more finished cloths are sewn together to make a ceremonial skirt.

Kuba Group, Western Kasai Province, Congo. *Ceremonial Robe.* 1950–75. Cut pile and linear embroidery on plain-weave raffia palm. 58.4 × 64.8 cm (23 × 25¹/₂″). Museum of International Folk Art, Museum of New Mexico, Santa Fe, New Mexico.

choose fabrics that complement the design and purpose of each outfit. Artists adjust the elements in a work to each other. A "busy" work with a variety of shapes and textures can be unified with a limited color scheme, for example **(Figure 11.16)**.

Simplicity

Another way to create unity is through *simplicity.* Simplicity is not easy to achieve. An artist must plan carefully to create a good, simple design. This is done by limiting the number of variations of an element. The fewer variations the artist uses, the more unified the design will seem **(Figure 11.17)**.

A painting in which the entire surface is covered with a single, even layer of one hue will appear strongly unified. A sculpture of a single unit expresses a simple unity **(Figure 11.18)**.

▲ **FIGURE 11.17** Johnson used simplification by limiting the materials for his *Water Garden* to concrete and water. He also limited the forms of the structure to geometric forms.

Philip Johnson. *Water Garden.* 1976. 17,000 cubic yards of concrete, 19,000 gallons of water. Fort Worth, Texas (downtown).

Allan Houser created contemporary Apache sculpture. As a child, he listened to his father's stories about the adventures of Chief Geronimo. This gave him a deep attachment to his ancestral background, an attachment that is shown in his artwork. Houser studied at the Indian School in Sante Fe, New Mexico, and then remained in Sante Fe, where he worked as a freelance artist. During World War II, he traveled to California, where he became interested in the media of sculpture. He created works in a variety of styles and mastered bronze, metal, and stone sculpture. Houser's designs are modern, yet firmly rooted in the special tradition of his Native American forefathers. He drew inspiration from both past and present, but like all successful artists, his sculpture transcends race and language. The sculpture *Reverie* **(Figure 11.18)** shows a distinct Native American influence, but it can be appreciated by anyone, regardless of his or her background.

▶ **Figure 11.18** Notice how the artist has used simple lines and few details to create this artwork. The simplicity serves to emphasize the faces of the mother and child, which become focal points. The unity of the design shows the connection between mother and child. What feeling does this piece evoke?

Allan Houser. *Reverie.* 1981. Bronze, edition of 10. 63.5 × 58.4 × 33 cm (25 × 23 × 13"). Collection of the Duke and Duchess of Bedford. The Glen Green Galleries, Santa Fe, New Mexico. Copyright Allan Houser Inc.

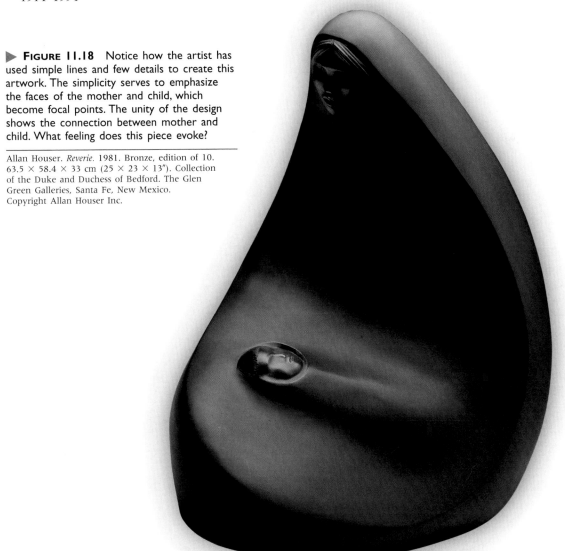

Repetition

The repetition of objects and elements can be an effective way to unify a work of art. Louise Nevelson's assemblages are good examples. She collects objects that are not alike. This presents a problem of unity, which she solves in one or more ways. Often, she places the objects in a series of boxlike containers **(Figure 11.19)**. The boxes help to unify the work. She sometimes paints the entire structure the same color. Sometimes she repeats both container shape and color to unify her assemblages.

Most architects are concerned with unity. Their goal is to design structures

▲ **FIGURE 11.19** The artist has collected different found objects and assembled them together. What has the artist done to unify this work and make the objects look like they belong together? Can you identify any of the found objects?

Louise Nevelson. *Dawn.* 1962. Wood painted gold. 323 × 240 × 19 cm (127 × 94½ × 7½″). The Pace Gallery, New York, New York. © 2003 Estate of Louise Nevelson/Artists Rights Society (ARS), New York.

that blend with the surroundings **(Figure 11.20)**. They may use materials that repeat the colors and textures found in the structure's environment. They may also use materials that reflect the surroundings. For instance, mirrored outside walls have been used on skyscrapers. The mirrors reflect the shapes and colors of the clouds and sky, and the buildings seem to blend with their surroundings and the atmosphere.

Proximity

Proximity, or closeness, is another way of unifying very different shapes in a work **(Figure 11.21)**. This is achieved by limiting the negative space between the shapes. Clustering the shapes in this way suggests unity and coherence. The sense of unity can be made even stronger if the cluster of unlike items is surrounded by an area of negative space.

▲ **FIGURE 11.20** Wright was a genius who dared to be different. In 1936 he was asked to design a house close to this waterfall. Instead, he placed the house right over the falls. Concrete terraces hang suspended over the running water. The stones that make up the walls come from the building site, which ties the house more closely to its surroundings.

Frank Lloyd Wright. *Fallingwater House.* Bear Run, Pennsylvania. 1936. Photography by Sandak, Inc., Stamford, Connecticut. © 2003 Frank Lloyd Wright Foundation/ Artists Rights Society (ARS), New York.

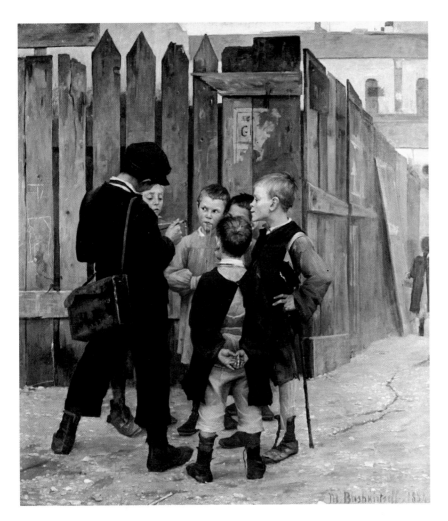

◀ **FIGURE 11.21** The artist has used proximity by grouping the children close together. What do the children appear to be doing? What kind of meeting are they having?

Marie Bashkirtseff. *A Meeting.* 1884. Oil on canvas. 190.5 × 172.2 cm (75 × 67³/₄″). Musée d'Orsay, Paris, France. Art Resource, New York, New York.

Demonstrating Effective Use of Art Media in Design. Suppose you have been hired to create a window display for a gift shop that sells many unrelated objects. From magazines, cut out photographs of 15 unrelated objects that represent the merchandise to be displayed. Use as many unifying techniques as you can to create the display. Using pencil and then darkening with a black, felt-tip marker, draw the window and the design for the display. Glue the cutouts where the objects would be placed in the design.

Computer Option. Arrange three or four different objects close together on a table. Use the Pencil or small Brush tool to draw the outline of all the objects using a continuous line. Another option is to draw the objects as individual shapes but extend the lines into the background. Select, copy, and repeat a few of the shapes but vary their sizes. Arrange the shapes to emphasize a focal point. Add a simple background. Now, choose and apply a limited color scheme with no more than four or five colors. Title, save, and print your work.

How Artists Use Variety, Emphasis, and Harmony to Enhance Unity

As you know, artists use variety, emphasis, and harmony to make their works more interesting and appealing. If carried to extremes, however, these principles can destroy the unity of a visual work. This means that artists must be careful to balance contrasting qualities of variety and emphasis with harmonizing and unifying techniques to create a unified work.

Jane Wilson has successfully balanced the harmonizing and varying devices in *Tempest* **(Figure 11.22).** The entire work is composed of waves of color. Although a contrasting color scheme of cool and warm colors is used, the work is unified by simple wavelike forms. The bright yellow streaks of sunlight are the focal point.

▶ **FIGURE 11.22** Wilson has created a unified composition, using several techniques. What has she simplified, and what has she repeated?

Jane Wilson. *Tempest.* 1993. Oil on linen. 177.8 × 177.8 cm (70 × 70″). Courtesy DC Moore Gallery, New York.

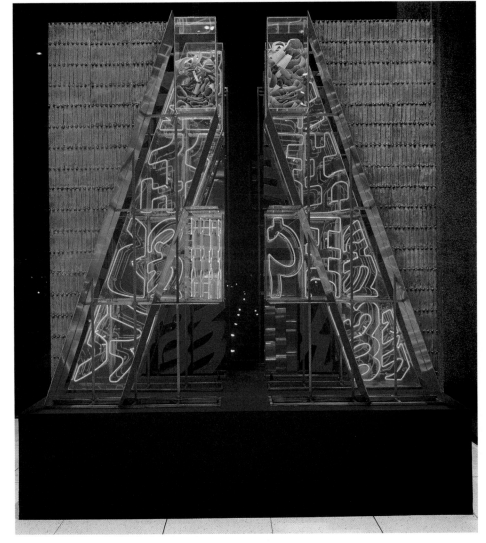

▲ **FIGURE 11.23** Why do you think Chryssa used the letter *A* as a form to contain all her active lines, shapes, and forms?

Chryssa. *The Gates to Times Square.* 1966. Welded stainless steel, neon, and Plexiglas. 3.04 × 3.04 × 3.04 m (10 × 10 × 10'). Albright-Knox Art Gallery, Buffalo, New York. Gift of Mr. and Mrs. Albert List, 1972.

Look closely at the work in **Figure 11.23.** The artist, Chryssa, left her home in Greece when she was 20 to study art. She arrived in New York City in the 1950s and was inspired by the materials of modern technology—especially the flashing neon signs in Times Square.

Within the letter *A* form in Figure 11.23, Chryssa has placed different kinds of shapes transformed from letters of the alphabet. Some are neon outlines. Others are flat metal. Everything is colored with blue light except the two Plexiglas rectangular forms near the top. They contain wiggly curved forms that are a very pale, low-intensity orange.

What do you think the different parts represent? Which art principles has she balanced to give this work unity?

Check Your Understanding

1. Define *unity.*
2. What is simplicity?
3. How is proximity used to create unity?
4. Compare and contrast the use of unity in Figure 11.14 on page 297 and Figure 11.19 on page 300. What art elements were used to create unity?

Decorated Found Object

▲ FIGURE 11.24

Julia Russell. *Jaguar Chair.* 2002. Back 106.7 cm (42″) tall, seat 48.3 × 48.3 × 43.2 cm (19 × 19 × 17″). Gessoed linen, acrylic paint, polymer glaze. Private Collection.

SUPPLIES

- Any ordinary, old, or worn object with a paintable surface
- Sketchbook and pencils
- Sandpaper, medium and fine
- Colored pencils or crayons
- Acrylic paints and a variety of paintbrushes
- Kraft paper
- Chalk
- Spray acrylic (gloss or matte) finish (optional)

Historical and Cultural Context

All art is meant to appeal to the eye, to delight. Some art goes beyond that requirement, serving a practical function as well. An example is the object in **Figure 11.24**. Its practical function is to provide a place to sit. The artist, Julia Russell, transformed an ordinary chair into a one-of-a-kind art object by giving it a new "skin." Notice the variety of lively colors and shapes. The artist has depicted tropical foliage, a jaguar, a butterfly, and a monkey—images common to Central American cultures. Do you find your eye moving over and around the chair covering? Observe that no matter where your eye begins its journey, it always ends with the soft-eyed monkey grasping a flower. What feelings does this painting-within-a-chair evoke?

What You Will Learn

You will create a design for a practical application. You will revive an old, worn, functional object by painting it with a variety of images and designs typical of a particular culture, past or present. Research your chosen culture and study its distinctively unique designs in art books, your school's media center, and the Internet. Make both visual and verbal notes in your sketchbook of the images, designs, and colors that are distinctive of that culture.

Creating

Sketch your object from different points of view. In a small group, brainstorm cultures that you have learned about in art or other classes. Select a culture that might be appropriate for this project. Your object itself may suggest a culture. Do outside research, as needed, finding pictures and descriptions of typical designs, images, and colors.

Step 1 Begin, if necessary, by sanding the surface of your object to remove any finish and to make it smooth.

Step 2 Incorporate images or individual art elements—such as lines, forms, and shapes—into the sketchbook drawings of your object. Vary the placement of objects by size or shape to add visual interest and variety.

Step 3 Choose a color scheme typical of your culture. Using colored pencils or crayons, add color to your final sketchbook designs.

Step 4 On large pieces of kraft paper, practice painting your designs and patterns with acrylic paint. Experiment with different brushes. Decide on a base (background) color. Choose a color that will unify the images or designs to be painted over it. Using a broad brush, apply the base color to all visible surface areas. Allow the paint to dry.

Step 5 Using soft pencil or chalk, draw the contours (outlines) of the images from your sketch on the dried base coat. Working with one color at a time, paint your images and designs.

Step 6 When your object is completely dry, apply a protective spray acrylic finish if your teacher provides it. This will protect the new "skin" you have added to your found object. *Safety Note:* Spray outside or in a well-ventilated area.

Evaluating Your Work

▶ **DESCRIBE** What found object did you use for your project? What is its primary function? What cultural style did you select for your design? Describe the different images you used in your overall design.

▶ **ANALYZE** Compare and contrast the use of line, form, and color in your art object. Were your colors consistent with those of the culture you had selected? Did you use variety to make your work interesting? Explain.

▶ **INTERPRET** Describe the theme of your project. Does your design complement the object, or is it a surprising design that one wouldn't expect to see on the object? Give your work a title that sums up its meaning.

▶ **JUDGE** Did your painted design transform or enhance the expressive quality of the original object? Justify your artistic decisions. If you were starting over, what would you do differently?

▲ **FIGURE 11.24A**

Student work.

Multimedia High-Relief Collage

▲ **FIGURE 11.25**

Missionary Mary L. Proctor. *Like a Butterfly.* 1999. Acrylic, leather, hot glue, painted on wood. 22.9 × 30.5 cm (9 × 12"). Collection of Ted and Ann Oliver.

SUPPLIES

- Sketchbook and pencil

- Unusual found objects: beads; old and/or broken jewelry; holiday decorations; buttons; fibers; ribbons; fabrics; screws; washers; computer parts; mosaiclike pieces of broken china, glass, or pottery

- Mat board, canvas panels, or a scrap of plywood

- Acrylic or house paint

- Scissors

- Glue

- Permanent markers or paint pens

Historical and Cultural Context

An old riddle asks "When is a door not a door?" For contemporary artist Mary Proctor, the riddle might be rephrased "When is a door *more* than a door?" To her, a door is a symbol. It represents a passage from one moment of life to the next and to the opportunities and challenges that may lie on the other side. Her obsession with painting doors began when her grandmother, who raised her, died in a fire, trapped by a door that would not open.

The work in **Figure 11.25** is a mixed-media collage by Mary Proctor. Like the many doors she has painted, this collage carries a message of hope. What do you think lies beyond the "door" in this work of art?

What You Will Learn

You will design and create a *high-relief* collage—one that stands out vividly in three-dimensional space. Your collage will express your visual interpretation of an inspirational line from a favorite poem, song, or saying. As in Figure 11.25, the words must be incorporated into the design. You will unify the different materials and letters, using the principles of variety, emphasis, and harmony.

Creating

In small groups, brainstorm ideas from poetry you have studied, lines from songs you like, and famous sayings. Choose one line or phrase that is most meaningful to you. Write it in your sketchbook. Make rough sketches of images that you feel illustrate these words. In each sketch, work at incorporating the words themselves into the design. Select your best idea.

Step 1 Collect unusual materials that you think you can use in your collage. A piece of mat board, canvas panel, or a scrap of plywood is to serve as the base.

Step 2 Using acrylic or house paint, add a layer of background color to your base. Allow the paint to dry before continuing.

Step 3 Switching to pencil, transfer the large shapes from your sketches to your backdrop in their relative positions. Plan to use found objects to fill each shape. Think about variety, emphasis, and harmony as you select colors and textures. Think also about what sense the materials themselves convey. What feelings do you associate, for example, with discarded jewelry? With holiday decorations such as tinsel? With broken glass or ceramic?

Step 4 Fill in the collage shapes by gluing in your found materials. Once the glue is dry, print your inspirational line of text.

Evaluating Your Work

▶ **DESCRIBE** What line of text served as the inspiration for your collage? What objects did you choose? Why did you choose these? How was the use of words incorporated into the overall design?

▶ **ANALYZE** Compare and contrast your selection of colors and textures to create variety and emphasis in your work. Is your design harmonious? If so, how? Do the found objects in your collage stand out in high relief?

▶ **INTERPRET** Does your collage reflect the meaning of the words you have chosen? Give your work a short title, other than the words included within the image, that expresses your feelings about the work.

▶ **JUDGE** Were you successful in unifying the words and objects in your image? Which aesthetic theory would be best to judge your work?

▲ **FIGURE 11.25A**

Student work.

STUDIO PROJECT 11–3

Animation Movie Poster

▲ **FIGURE 11.26**

David Feiss. *Thrown for a Curve.* 1998. Cartoon Network.

SUPPLIES

- Sketchbook and pencil
- Fine-tip black marker
- Computer
- Scanner
- Any computer paint program
- Color printer
- Mat board

Historical and Cultural Context

David Feiss (b. 1959) is an award-winning American animator. He started his professional career as an animator with Hanna-Barbera Studios in 1978. Since then, he has worked with various studios as an animator, storyboard artist, director, and producer on television series, feature films, and commercials.

Look closely at **Figure 11.26,** titled *Thrown for a Curve.* This is a cel, a single sheet of celluloid that is drawn on and colored to make animated cartoons. The repetition of curves dominates the composition and creates harmony, which unifies the layout of the cel. Notice the repetition of curves that radiate from the pitcher's knee: the edges of the stadium, the signs atop the stadium, the swirl above the pitcher's head, and the curve of the batter's body and bat. The clouds and the placement of each ballplayer also mirror the curved path of the ball as it moves toward the catcher's glove.

What You Will Learn

Using a computer paint program (Digital Media Handbook, page 449), you will create a poster for an animation movie. Create visual unity in your poster by arranging and drawing the movie's characters, using any or all of the unifying devices of harmony, simplicity, repetition, or proximity.

Creating

Plan and write the outline for the movie. In your outline, introduce, name, and describe each character. Describe the main conflict, the climax, and the resolution of your story. This outline will help you plan your movie poster.

Step 1 Using your sketchbook and a pencil, draw rough sketches of the characters, including their names and notes describing their characteristics.

Step 2 Create rough sketches of different layouts for your poster, using as many of the unifying devices (harmony, simplicity, repetition, and proximity) as possible.

Step 3 Select your best layout drawing. Ink the lines in this drawing. Then scan the inked drawing into a computer.

Step 4 Open your scanned image in a paint program. Insert the scanned image into your working file, but save the original in a different file so that you can go back to it later, if necessary.

Step 5 Add a layer to your file. Use a line tool to trace the original drawing onto this new layer. Make sure all areas to be painted are enclosed by solid lines.

Step 6 Using various paint tools—such as paintbrush, paint bucket, or airbrush—you can begin coloring your poster. Make sure that the color stays within the lines of character. Most paint programs have a gradient option for coloring. By applying gradient values to your colors, your characters will look more three-dimensional in form.

Step 7 Add the movie's title to your poster. When finished, save, print, and mat your poster for display.

Evaluating Your Work

▶ **DESCRIBE** Explain the concept or story of your movie. Describe the characters in your layout. What type of paint program and which tools did you use?

▶ **ANALYZE** How many unifying devices (harmony, simplicity, repetition, and proximity) did you use in your poster? Compare and contrast how you used the various elements of your poster to create a sense of visual unity.

▶ **INTERPRET** Does your poster express the mood of the movie? Does it tell what type of movie it is? Do the images and title express the same message about the characters and story?

▶ **JUDGE** Were you successful in creating a sense of visual unity? Does your poster represent the concept or story of the movie? Which of the three aesthetic theories would you use to judge this work?

▶ **FIGURE 11.26A**

Student work.

Variety, Emphasis, Harmony, and Unity

Variety is not only the spice of life but of art. Along with emphasis, harmony, and unity, this principle gives works visual interest. As you examine the student artworks on these pages:

- Analyze them to form precise conclusions about their use of variety, emphasis, and unity.

- Compare and contrast them in terms of their use of color, form, or line to achieve unity.

Activity 11.27 **Variety.**
Analyze this item of found-object jewelry in terms of variety. Describe which art elements the student artist has varied to add visual interest.

▲ **FIGURE 11.27**

Student work. *Untitled.* Copper and brass coiled wire on paint can opener with aluminum can ring snap and other components. 12.1 × 8.9 cm (4³⁄₄ × 3¹⁄₂″).

Activity 11.28 **Harmony and unity.**
Compare the use of art elements. Which element contributes to a sense of harmony and unity? Analyze the details in this peer artwork to form a conclusion about its historical or cultural context.

▶ **FIGURE 11.28**

Student work. *Even the Kitchen Sink.* Oil pastel and graphite. 30.5 × 45.7 cm (12 × 18″).

Activity 11.29 Emphasis.

Analyze this student artwork, to form a conclusion about how the artist has used the formal qualities to emphasize the subject. What art elements contribute to the emphasis on the subject?

◀ **FIGURE 11.29**

Student work. *Leah.* Oil pastel. 30.5 × 45.7 cm (12 × 18″).

Activity 11.30 Harmony and variety.

Compare the way harmony and variety have been used to balance each other in this student artwork.

▶ **FIGURE 11.30**

Student work. *Untitled.* Watercolor, pen and ink. 25.4 × 35.6 cm (10 ×14″).

To view more student artworks, visit the Glencoe Student Art Gallery at **art.glencoe.com**.

For Your Portfolio

Evaluate Personal Artworks. The principles you have studied in this chapter can be found in any successful artwork. Review artworks that you have added to your portfolio previously in terms of these principles. Evaluate the artistic decisions you made to achieve unity. Unity is the goal of most artists. Be sure that your notes are attached to the works.

Visual Art Journal

Sketch or photograph two different rooms in your home or school. Number the sketches or photos 1 and 2. Next, divide a page of your art journal into three columns. Label one column *Variety,* one *Emphasis,* and one *Harmony.* Write an analysis of each picture in terms of the three art principles. Note which art elements contribute in each case.

Art Criticism
in Action

▲ **FIGURE 11.31**

Elizabeth Catlett. *Singing Their Songs,* from *For My People.* 1992. Color lithograph on paper.
40 × 35 cm (15³/₄ × 13³/₄"). National Museum of Women in the Arts, Washington, D.C.
© Elizabeth Catlett/Licensed by VAGA, New York, NY.

Critiquing the Artwork

▶ **1** **DESCRIBE** *What do you see?*

This is a clue collecting step. If you are not sure of something, do not guess.

● Describe what you see in this fine art print.

▶ **2** **ANALYZE** *How is this work organized?*

This step deals with the formal qualities. You will gather information about how the principles of art are used to organize the elements of art.

● How has the artist used variety in organizing this print?

● Is one part of the work emphasized over the others?

● What has the artist done to harmonize the separate but related parts?

● What unifies this work?

▶ **3** **INTERPRET** *What message does this artwork communicate to you?*

Combine the clues you have collected to form a creative interpretation of the work.

● What kind of sound do you think you would hear from each person? Explain your reaction.

● What emotion is expressed on each face?

● Write a sentence or two that you think each person is expressing.

▶ **4** **JUDGE** *What do you think of the work?*

Now, you are ready to make an aesthetic judgment of the work.

● Do you think the artist has organized the elements and principles of art to achieve a unified composition? Explain.

● Is this a successful work of art? Why or why not? Use one or more of the aesthetic theories to defend your decision.

Meet the **ARTIST**

Elizabeth Catlett
b. 1915

Elizabeth Catlett was born in Washington, D.C. She studied painting and design at Howard University. She became the first person to receive an MFA degree from the University of Iowa in 1940. Grant Wood was her painting teacher. Wood encouraged his students to focus on subjects they knew best and to experiment with different media. Catlett spent the rest of her career following his advice. Her subjects have been almost exclusively African American women. She has made lithograph and linoleum prints as well as sculptures from wood, stone, clay, and bronze. She won a grant to study printmaking in Mexico in 1946. Since then, she has divided her time between her studios in New York City and Cuernavaca, Mexico.

ARTISTIC ROOTS

A Southwestern artist celebrates his heritage.

Luis Jimenez is a Texas-born sculptor and artist whose colorful work in a variety of media celebrates Chicano life and history. Raised in El Paso, Jimenez worked in his father's sign shop. It was there that he first came in contact with fiberglass—a lightweight material that Jimenez later used for some of his large-scale figurative sculptures.

As a young boy, Jimenez read art books and visited art museums. He also traveled to Mexico, where he was inspired by the Mexican people and the huge murals about Mexican history.

As an adult, Jimenez first studied architecture but then switched to sculpture, drawing, and painting. His works emphasize the Southwest and working class Mexican-Americans, subjects that are close to his geographic and cultural roots. His art celebrates the contributions of Mexican-Americans to American history. Mexican cowboys, Native Americans, farmers, and even rodeo queens are some of his favorite subjects.

Jimenez continues to live in the Southwest, where the region and its people inspire him.

Howl, a color lithograph completed in 1977.

©SMITHSONIAN AMERICAN ART MUSEUM, WASHINGTON, DC/ART RESOURCE, NY

Jimenez created *Fiesta Jarabel*, a fiberglass sculpture, in 1986.

TERRY GUGLIOTTA

TIME to Connect

How have famous Americans been depicted in painting, sculpture, photographs, and other media?

• Choose and research an important figure from American history. What was he or she famous for? What contribution to United States history or society did the person make?

• What symbols would you include to emphasize the person's contributions to history? Why did you choose the symbols you did? Incorporate them into a collage to create a unified design.

• Share your work with the class.

Building Vocabulary

On a separate sheet of paper, write the term that best matches each definition given below.

1. The principle of art concerned with difference or contrast.
2. The principle of art that makes one part of a work dominant over the other parts.
3. The first part of a work to attract the attention of the viewer.
4. The principle of art that creates unity by stressing the similarities of separate but related parts.
5. The quality of wholeness or oneness that is achieved through the effective use of the elements and principles of art.

Reviewing Art Facts

Answer the following questions using complete sentences.

6. Why do artists use variety in artworks?
7. Name the two major types of visual emphasis.
8. What is the most important part of an artwork called?
9. Name and describe the five ways in which artists create a focal point.
10. Name and describe three techniques that artists use to create unity in a work of art.
11. What can happen if variety, emphasis, or harmony is carried to an extreme in an artwork?

Thinking Critically About Art

12. **Compare and contrast.** Notice the variety used in Figure 11.2, page 288. Compare this with the variety used in Figure 11.3, page 289. Explain how each artist used variety and point out the similarities and differences between the two works.
13. **Analyze.** Look through the other chapters of this book to find three examples of works in which the artist has emphasized one element, making all the others subordinate to it. List the works and explain which element has been emphasized.
14. **Historical/Cultural Heritage.** Read the Meet the Artist feature on Allan Houser on page 299. Analyze Houser's sculpture in Figure 11.18 to identify the general theme. Then compare and contrast Figure 11.18 with another contemporary artwork in Figure 4.20 on page 81. Do they share a similar theme? Explain.

ART Online

Now that you have mastered the principles of variety, emphasis, harmony, and unity, challenge yourself with an interactive composition game. Simply follow the **Web Museum Tour** link at **art.glencoe.com** to visit the Montreal Museum of Fine Arts in Canada.

Linking to the Performing Arts

Read how the "Vocalworks Radio Hour" presents variety and harmony in the re-creation of a live radio broadcast from the 1930s era. Showcasing swing music, comedy, and drama programs, Vocalworks swings us back to the past in the Performing Arts Handbook on page 423.

Art Through the Ages

"I found I could say things with color and shapes that I couldn't say any other way—things I had no words for."

—*Georgia O'Keeffe (1887–1986)*

Quick Write

Interpreting Text. Read the quote above. What do you think the artist means when she writes that using elements of art enabled her "to say things she had no words for"? Write your interpretation of the ideas she is expressing.

◄

Georgia O'Keeffe. *Back of Marie's No. 4*. 1931. Oil on canvas. 40.6 × 76.2 cm (16 × 30"). The Georgia O'Keeffe Museum, Santa Fe, New Mexico. Gift of The Burnett Foundation © 2003 The Georgia O'Keeffe Foundation/Artists Rights Society (ARS), New York.

▲ **FIGURE 12.1** This complex sculpture, composed of curved forms and intricate patterns, is only 12¼″ tall. Observe closely the precise detail and craft that went into the making of this elegant art object. Describe the type of balance that organizes this object.

Kashmir or Northern Pakistan. *Crowned Buddha Shakyamuni.* Eighth century. Brass with inlays of copper, silver, and zinc. Height: 31.1 cm (12¼″). Mr. and Mrs. John D. Rockefeller 3rd Collection. Asia Society: New York.

CHAPTER 12

Art Traditions from Around the World

Art is more than just objects and images. It is a visual story of a people and their culture. It reveals their feelings, views, and beliefs. In a sense, art history mirrors the history of the world. It is a window on the past and the many cultures that enrich our lives.

In this chapter, you will:

- Describe general characteristics in artworks from a variety of cultures.
- Compare and contrast historical styles, identifying trends and themes.
- Describe art traditions from cultures around the world.

Focus on **Art History**

Figure 12.1 is an ancient object of worship from Kashmir or Northern Pakistan. The subject is Buddha Shakyamuni, spiritual leader of the Shakya clan of Buddhism. His hands are positioned in the gesture of teaching as he sits peacefully on a lotus flower rising above the water on a thick stem. To the right and left of the base are small female and male figures. Art historians believe that these figures represent the donors of the sculpture.

Compare and Contrast. Compare the Buddha Shakyamuni to a religious sculpture from another culture and time (Figure 13.5, page 354.) What similarities and differences can you find in the style and theme of the two works?

Art of Earliest Times

Vocabulary

Paleolithic period
Neolithic period
megaliths
cuneiform
ziggurats
pharaohs
dynasty

The artworks produced many thousands of years ago tell us a great deal about the earliest cultures and civilizations of our world. These ancient people left no written records. What we know of them has been learned from the objects and the art that they left behind.

Prehistoric Art

Prehistoric means before history, or before written records were kept. The objects made by people during this period are all that remain to tell us about the people who lived long ago.

Figure 12.2 is one of many cave paintings left by cave dwellers in Europe during the Paleolithic period. The **Paleolithic** (pay-lee-oh-**lith**-ik) **period,** or *Old Stone Age, began about two million years ago, and ended with the close of the last ice age about 13,000 B.C.* It was a time when people began using stone tools. In these cave paintings, the colors are so bright and the animals so realistic that, for a long time, scholars refused to believe they had been created by prehistoric people.

To this day no one knows the purpose of the paintings. Found deep inside caves, far from the entrances and living areas, they probably were not created for decoration. Some scholars believe the paintings were part of a hunting ritual. A shaman, or medicine man, may have created the image of the animal, believing that it would help hunters capture the animal. The paintings may also have been visual prayers for animals to appear during the next hunt. According to another theory, cave dwellers created the paintings to celebrate a successful hunt.

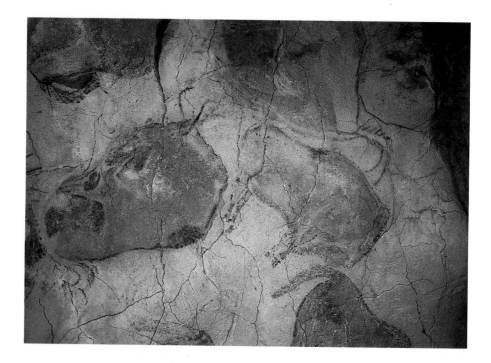

▶ **FIGURE 12.2** An amateur archaeologist excavated in this low-roofed cave for four years. One day his daughter, who was small enough to stand up straight in the cave and look up, discovered these paintings of sleeping, galloping, and crouching animals.

The Hall of the Bulls. c. 15,000 B.C. Altamira Caves, Spain.

Prehistoric Builders

Eventually prehistoric people moved out of caves and began constructing their own shelters. Small communities developed, and some hunters gave up their nomadic life and settled down, becoming farmers. After some time, small tribal groups grew into organized villages surrounded by cultivated fields and domesticated animals.

During the Neolithic period, people built structures of stone. The **Neolithic** (nee-uh-**lith**-ik) **period,** or *New Stone Age, is a prehistoric period stretching roughly from 7000 B.C. to 2000 B.C.* During this time, humans developed agriculture, and stone tools were refined. Ancient structures from this period, called megaliths, have been found throughout Europe, Asia, and even North America. **Megaliths** (**meg**-uh-liths) are *large monuments created from huge stone slabs.* As early as 4000 B.C., circular arrangements of huge, rough-hewn stones were created in Western Europe. The most famous of these is Stonehenge in England. Built around 2000 B.C., it consists of a series of four concentric rings. Builders used an ancient building method that we now call *post-and-lintel construction.* Upright slabs, called posts, support horizontal slabs, called lintels. More than half of the original stones still stand. The tallest measures 17 feet and weighs more than 50 tons. Scholars are uncertain how prehistoric people, working with primitive tools, were able to cut these huge stones, transport them many miles, and then raise them into position. The purpose of Stonehenge has also baffled scholars for many centuries. In the past, people believed a great magician created it. Today, Stonehenge is thought to have served as a kind of observatory, enabling people to practice a type of astronomy and serve as an accurate calendar.

As prehistoric peoples learned to herd animals and grow crops, they also learned to live in harmony with their surroundings. This peaceful balance was upset by population growth. Small tribes began to fight over grazing land and soil suitable for growing crops. They were forced to band together into more organized groups for protection and also to be able to produce more food. By around 3000 B.C. four major civilizations had developed at different points on the globe. The ancient civilizations of Mesopotamia, Egypt, India, and China emerged at this time.

Ancient River Valleys

The ancient civilizations of Mesopotamia, Egypt, India, and China, are referred to as river valley civilizations. Each of these civilizations was ruled by a monarchy, practiced a religion based on nature, and achieved great skill in art and architecture.

Mesopotamia

The area of Mesopotamia included the cultures of many people within an extensive region. The region was the fertile crescent of land between the Tigris and Euphrates rivers in the Middle East. The people lived in city-states, and each city was ruled by a monarch. Today, this land is shared by Syria and Iraq.

The Sumerians were the first dominant group in the area. They were the first people to have a system of writing (using symbols to represent spoken language). **Cuneiform** (kyoo-**nee**-uh-form) was *the Sumerian writing system made up of wedge-shaped characters.* These characters stood for concepts and ideas. Because paper was not yet developed, clay tablets were used. Some of these still exist.

This figure was placed in the temple to represent the worshiper. The wide eyes, hands folded in prayer, and attention to detail are typical of Sumerian sculpture.

Statua di Donna. c. 2700–2600 B.C. Marble. The Iraq Museum, Baghdad, Iraq.

Sumerian artists depicted figures in a lifelike and realistic way. Look at **Figure 12.3.** This small sculpture shows precise details of dress and facial features. Sumerians also built structures known as **ziggurats** (**zig**-uh-rats), or *stepped mountains made of brick-covered earth* **(Figure 12.4).** These temples had exterior staircases. A temple honoring the god of the city was placed at the top. Does it resemble other buildings that you have seen?

In time, the Sumerian civilization merged with that of Akkad, its northern neighbor, giving rise to the civilization of Babylonia (around 750 B.C.). Babylonian art and architecture resembled Sumerian to a great extent. Another Mesopotamian civilization, called Assyria, emerged after the decline of Babylonia. A distinct Assyrian artistic style began to emerge around 1500 B.C. Assyrian artists created precise, detailed stone reliefs, which they painted using many colors. They depicted royal events, hunts, wars, and animals, especially horses and lions. Human figures were given less emphasis, although they were still depicted in a realistic and detailed way.

◀ **FIGURE 12.4** A temple honoring the god of the city was placed at the top of the ziggurat. This structure was built in 2100 B.C. What other art and architecture was being created throughout the world at that time?

Ziggurat. Ur, Iraq. c. 2100 B.C.

Egypt

The culture of ancient Egypt developed along the banks of the Nile River more than 3,000 years before the birth of Christ. Religion influenced every part of Egyptian life. The **pharaohs,** or *Egyptian rulers, were worshiped as gods and held complete authority over the kingdom.* Egyptians believed in life after death and preserved the bodies of the pharaohs in preparation for the afterlife. The famous pyramids were built as the tombs of the pharaohs.

Egyptian artists decorated temples and tombs according to very strict rules set forth by the priests. The rules required that each part of the body be shown from the most visible angle. Look at **Figure 12.5.** The heads, arms, legs, and feet are shown in profile. The shoulders and eyes, however, are shown from a frontal view.

The paintings found on the walls inside the tombs reveal a great deal about life in Egypt. Scenes from the life of the person buried in the tomb were intended to remind the spirit of life on earth.

India

In the Indus River Valley, the ancient civilization of India arose. Only in recent times have historians realized the age of Indian culture. For many centuries, no one knew that a civilization had flourished on the banks of the Indus River in northwest India. Then in 1865, railroad workers uncovered a hill of crumbling, fired-clay bricks near the city of Harappa (in present-day Pakistan). The bricks were found to be thousands of years old, dating back to 2500 B.C.

In 1922, a second city was discovered in the same area. Called Mohenjo-Daro (moh-hen-joh dahr-oh), meaning "Hill of the Dead" **(Figure 12.6),** the city was

◄ **FIGURE 12.5**
What symbols or features make these figures seem important? Observe the shapes in the boxes along the top border. These are hieroglyphs, an early form of picture writing. They give information about the painted scene.

Egyptian. *The Goddess Hathor Places the Magic Collar on Sethos I.* Thebes, Nineteenth Dynasty. c. 1303–1290 B.C. Painted bas-relief. 226.5 cm (89⅛"). The Louvre, Paris, France.

▲ **FIGURE 12.6** Experts believe the city of Mohenjo-Daro was abandoned because the climate changed. The ancient Indians built with fire-baked bricks, which meant they had ready access to timber. The area is a desert today.

Mohenjo-Daro, India. c. 2500 B.C.

once home to about 35,000 people. Architectural remains indicate that it served as a major commercial center. Wide, open streets divided the city into large blocks. The city featured multi-storied houses made from fired brick and wood, and elaborate, sophisticated drainage systems.

At this archeological site, workers discovered a number of small relief carvings in soapstone **(Figure 12.7).** These carvings are the earliest known examples of Indian art. As you can see, several unusual lines and shapes are incised above the animals. These are characters from the ancient Harappan system of writing.

Over 70 cities, towns, and villages have been discovered in the Indus valley, as well as evidence of an organized kingdom with a central government that existed about 4,500 years ago.

China

The Yellow River valley became the site of the ancient Chinese civilization, a civilization that retains many of its ancient traditions today. Beginning 4,000 years ago, it is the oldest continuous culture in the history of the world.

As their civilization developed, the Chinese gained skill and knowledge in many different areas. They invented paper, porcelain (a type of ceramic), and

▲ **FIGURE 12.7** The designs on these seals "belonged" to their owners. Seals were pressed into soft clay to secure a container or document.

Soapstone seals from Mohenjo-Daro (Indus Valley culture). Karachi Museum, Karachi, Pakistan.

woodblock printing as well as the compass and gunpowder. Until modern times, emperors ruled China. Its historical periods were divided into dynasties, which were named after ruling families. A **dynasty** is *a period of time during which a single family provided a succession of rulers.* Bronze vessels found in ancient graves reveal that Chinese artisans cast bronze as early as the first imperial Chinese dynasty, the Shang dynasty, which began in 1766 B.C. The ritual wine vessel shown in **Figure 12.8** is an example of the intricate work done at that time. Abstract motifs and spirals cover the vessel. Experts believe the spirals stand for clouds, rain, or water. Such images reveal an ancient Chinese regard for nature. Many early bronze vessels show extraordinary technical mastery— evidence of the centuries of development required before such artworks could be created.

◀ **Figure 12.8** This vessel was used in a ceremony to ensure harmony with the spirits of deceased ancestors. Notice the large eyes and beak of an owl on the lower part of the vessel. Can you find other animals in the designs that cover this container?

Ancient China. *Ritual Wine Container.* Shang dynasty. Thirteenth century B.C. Bronze. 30.1 × 12.2 × 12.5 cm (11^{7}/$_{8}$× 4^{3}/$_{4}$ × 4^{7}/$_{8}$″). Arthur M. Sackler Gallery, Smithsonian Institution, Washington, D.C. Gift of Arthur M. Sackler, s1987.23a-b.

Activity | **Analyzing Ancient Art**

Selecting and Analyzing Exhibitions. Research exhibitions of ancient art online or at art museums in your community. Select early artworks from the cultures listed in this lesson. Analyze the exhibitions to form conclusions about formal qualities, or how these cultures used the elements and principles of art. Also, form conclusions about historical and cultural contexts. What was the role or significance of the artworks or art objects in these ancient cultures?

Check Your Understanding

1. For what purpose might cave paintings have been created?
2. What is a ziggurat?
3. Why and for whom were the pyramids built?
4. Define the word *dynasty.*
5. Describe general characteristics of artworks from the Paleolithic period, Ancient Egypt, and Ancient China.

Art of Asia and the Middle East

The cultures of India, China, Japan, and the Middle East have all produced exciting art forms, some very different from European art. The art of Asia and the Middle East reflects different philosophies and religious beliefs from those in Western art.

India

The art of India has been strongly influenced by the Hindu and Buddhist religions. Hinduism is one of the world's oldest religions. It began in ancient India around 2000 B.C. It is not one religion but a group of many related sects. Buddhism began as a Hindu reform movement, and had a strong influence over the country from the third century B.C. to the sixth century A.D. Among the earliest, and most important, examples of modern Indian architecture are **stupas** (**stoop**-uhs), which are *beehive-shaped domed places of worship*. These were built by Buddhist architects to house relics of Buddha, their religion's founder. Each stupa was reached through four gates covered with relief sculptures **(Figure 12.9)**.

After the fifth century, Hinduism rose again in popularity because it was encouraged by the monarchs of the period. Hindu temples and sculptures of the Hindu gods were created. Hinduism combined several different beliefs and practices that developed over a long period of time. In Hinduism there are three primary processes in life and in the universe: creation, preservation, and destruction. The three main Hindu gods reflect this belief system.

▶ **FIGURE 12.9** Domes such as this were often erected over holy places, burial mounds, and holy relics. What is the purpose of preserving such things?

Great Stupa. Sanchi, Madhya Pradesh, India. c. first century B.C.

They are Brahma, the Creator; Vishnu, the Preserver; and Siva, the Destroyer **(Figure 12.10)**. In Hinduism, both humans and animals are believed to have souls that undergo reincarnation. Reincarnation is a purification process in which the soul lives in many bodies in many lifetimes until it becomes one with Brahma, the great soul.

India exported its religions to the rest of Asia. In Cambodia many temples were built of stone in the Indian style. The temple at Angkor Wat **(Figure 12.11)** was originally a Hindu temple built between A.D. 1113 and 1150. Dedicated to Vishnu by its builder, it represents the Hindu view of the universe.

▶ **FIGURE 12.10** The Hindu god Siva is called the Destroyer. This sculpture is rich in symbolism. Notice what the figure is standing on. The objects he holds are a drum that symbolizes creation and a flame that symbolizes destruction. How is destruction related to creation?

Unknown, India, Tamil Nadu. *Siva as Lord of the Dance.* c. 950. Copper alloy. 76.2 × 57.1 × 17.8 cm (30 × 22½ × 7″). Los Angeles County Museum of Art, Los Angeles, California, given anonymously.

◀ **FIGURE 12.11** The layout of this temple was designed to create a solar calendar by which the summer and winter solstices and the spring and fall equinoxes could be fixed. Why was this important in an agricultural society?

Southeast Asia. Temple at Angkor Wat, Cambodia. 1113–50.

China

China adopted Buddhism during the Han Dynasty, which lasted from 206 B.C. to A.D. 220. Buddhism was easily adopted in China because, like other Chinese religions, it stressed the harmony of human beings with nature. An important part of Buddhism is meditation, focusing one's thoughts on a single object or idea. Chinese artists found that long periods of meditation enabled them to perceive the beauty of an object or a scene with greater clarity. This enabled them to more effectively

capture the beauty of the subject in their paintings. Chinese art of the last 2,000 years has been greatly influenced by Buddhism and meditation.

The Chinese were the first people to consider "picture painting" a valuable endeavor. This was because many artists were also scholars who wrote poems in beautiful writing (called calligraphy) using brushes that could make thick and thin lines. They used these same brushes and line techniques to paint pictures.

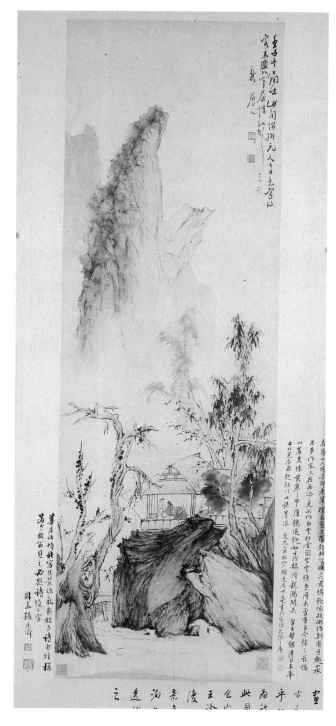

▲ **FIGURE 12.12** Notice how small the people are in relation to the landscape. The hut blends in with the natural setting. The calligraphy bordering the drawing is an important part of the picture. Notice how it echoes the shapes of the leaves. How might the calligraphy be part of the "conversation"?

Hua Yen. *Conversation in Autumn.* 1762. Ink and color on paper. 115.3 × 39.7 cm (45⅛ × 15⅝"). The Cleveland Museum of Art, Cleveland, Ohio. The John L. Severance Fund.

They painted fans, pages of books, and scrolls **(Figure 12.12). A scroll** is *a long roll of parchment or silk.* Some were hung on walls, while others were meant to be unrolled a little at a time and read like a book.

The earliest Chinese paintings were filled with images illustrating the beliefs that people should live together peacefully and be respectful of their elders. With the influence of a new religion, Buddhism, the focus of painting began to shift away from humans and toward nature. By around A.D. 1100, the landscape was the main theme of Chinese painting.

The Chinese also produced sculpture for religious purposes and to honor the dead. During the Sung **(soong)** Dynasty (A.D. 960–1279), artists first produced ceramic objects of porcelain made from a fine-grained white clay called kaolin (**kay**-uh-luhn). Work in porcelain reached its highest point during the Ming Dynasty (A.D. 1368–1644). Today, collectors especially prize porcelain from this dynasty (see Figure 5.4, page 99).

Japan

In A.D. 552 the ruler of a kingdom in nearby Korea sent the Emperor of Japan a gift. The gift was a bronze figure of the Buddha, the founder of Buddhism. Along with the sculpture came priests to spread Buddhist teachings. Eventually many of the people of Japan accepted this new religion. They also learned about new styles of art. For the next 250 years, Japanese art would show strong traces of Korean, Chinese, and other Asian styles.

The first important Japanese art objects of "modern times" were started in A.D. 594. These were magnificent Buddhist temples that were built throughout the country. Since the islands of Japan are made of volcanic rock, the Japanese could not use stone to build their temples. Instead, they made them from wood. In the process, they elevated the architecture of wooden structures to new levels.

Japanese temples are intricately assembled and richly decorated. They are carefully fitted together with special joints. Because Japan suffers frequent earthquakes and violent storms, the buildings had to be durable. One of the most interesting features of early Japanese temples was the **pagoda** (puh-**gohd**-uh). This is *a tower several stories high with roofs curving slightly upward at the edges* (**Figure 12.13**).

The Japanese also created monumental sculptures, often of the Buddha. Such a sculpture can be seen in **Figure 12.14,** the Great Buddha at Kamakura. It was cast in bronze in A.D. 1252. It is situated outdoors in a grove of trees, which seems an appropriate setting for this contemplative Buddha.

▲ **FIGURE 12.13** This pagoda stands as the oldest wooden structure in the world. Its purpose is to preserve relics.

Pagoda from the Temple Complex at Horyuji, near Nara, Japan. c. A.D. 616.

◀ **FIGURE 12.14** The Great Buddha was once housed in a temple, but the temple was destroyed by a tidal wave. What effect does its current location have on this artwork?

Great Buddha. 1252. Bronze. Height: 10.68 m (35'). Kamakura, Japan.

Hokusai was an artist who changed his name as often as he changed residences. At the age of 37, he began to call himself Hokusai, the name he is known by today. He often combined it with other names. The most unusual one was Gakyojin Hokusai: A Man Mad About Painting, Hokusai.

In eighteenth- and early nineteenth-century Japan, printmakers specialized in one area of the printing process. They were designers, woodcarvers, or printers. Artisans did not usually cross from one skill to another. Hokusai, however, mastered all the skills. In 1831, he published the landscape series *Thirty-six Views of Mount Fuji,* using the Zen Hokusai Iitsu name. In 1833, three major print series were published: *A Tour of Japanese Waterfalls; Imagery of the Poets;* and his *Nature* series, which included flowers, birds, and insects. In 1834, *Rare Views of Famous Bridges,* a series of 11 prints, was published.

Hokusai had endless energy, a tremendous ego, a restless imagination, and extraordinary talent. In fact, he produced most of his masterpieces after the age of 70. On his deathbed he begged for ten more years of life so that he could become a true artist.

▶ **FIGURE 12.15** The gust of wind blows away the papers and clothing of the human figures. Mount Fuji stands white and stable, unmoved by the wind or the human drama.

Katsushika Hokusai. *Ejiri in Suruga Province,* from *Thirty-six Views of Mt. Fuji.* 24.6 × 37.9 cm (9²⁄₃ × 15″). Honolulu Academy of Arts, Honolulu, Hawaii. James A. Michener Collection, 1991.

In A.D. 784, Japan entered its golden age of art. During this period, Japanese artists developed a painting style called *Yamato-e* (yah-**mah**-toh-ay), or "pictures in the Japanese manner." Paintings done in this style were the first examples of pure Japanese art, meaning that they did not show the influence of other Asian cultures. Yamato-e screen paintings were often made in sections and were used to brighten the dimly lit interiors of temples and homes as a temporary wall to divide a room.

Another new Japanese style of art was called Ukiyo-e (oo-**kee**-yoh-ay), meaning "pictures of the floating world," which depict different aspects of the pleasures of life. The demand for artworks in this new style was great. To meet this demand, artists turned to a new technique, **woodblock printing.** This is *making prints by carving images in blocks of wood.* Using this technique, artists could produce many inexpensive prints of one image **(Figure 12.15).**

Art of Islam

In A.D. 570, an event took place that had a major effect on both the religious beliefs and the art of the Middle East and much of Asia. Muhammad was born in Mecca. He grew up and became a merchant, following the tradition of his family. However, he believed he received personal revelations that challenged him to change the religion of his people, the Arabs, who worshiped many idols. Muhammad taught that there was only one god, called Allah. After his death, his teachings were assembled into the Koran, a holy scripture. Islam was the name given to the religious faith of people who followed Muhammad. Worshippers are called Muslims.

Islamic art (art of the Muslim world) was characterized by the use of ornate line, shape, and pattern. The interior of **mosques,** *Muslim places of worship,* were decorated with calligraphy, geometric patterns, and stylized plants and flowers. Art depicting people or animals was not permitted in mosques. Such art was prohibited early in the history of the Islamic religion and was meant to prevent Muslims from worshiping images when they should instead be worshiping the idea of Allah.

Book illustrators, however, were not limited by the same restrictions. They depicted people and animals in everyday scenes. They filled their illustrations with beautiful decorative patterns.

The religion of Islam, and its influence on art, also spread to the East. Muslims conquered Delhi in India and converted many Indians to Islam. **Figure 12.16** shows a famous building, the Taj Mahal, which was built by an Indian Muslim leader as a memorial to his wife. The building is an outstanding example of Islamic architecture and is considered one of the most beautiful structures in the world. The building emphasizes formal balance and harmony with its surroundings. Its cool marble walls and placid lake evoke a response of serenity and tranquility in those who visit.

Check Your Understanding

1. What is a stupa?
2. What medium did the Chinese often paint on that could be hung on walls or read like a book?
3. Compare and contrast the historical styles in Figure 12.12 on page 328 and Figure 12.15 on page 330. Identify the general trends in art.

The Art of Africa

Throughout Africa, in both the past and the present—even within the context of modern nation-states—the visual arts are well integrated with other art forms, including music, dance, and drama. The art of Africa was an integral part of the daily lives and religious rituals of the people.

The Role of Art in African Cultures

The huge continent of Africa has a population of millions that is sub-divided into about 1,000 cultural groups. The peoples of Africa have long-established, highly developed cultures that have been producing sophisticated art forms for centuries. The arts are as varied as the peoples.

Everything is made with great care, whether for rituals or everyday use. Art addresses not only the concerns of the living, their ancestors, and those yet to be born, but also those of the spirits of nature. A great deal of African art emphasizes important events of life and forces of nature that influence the lives of individuals and communities.

Dominant themes in African art include birth and death; the roles of men, women, and children; coming of age; sickness and healing; the importance of food and water; and the human relationship with nature. Artworks are often linked to celebrations and rituals, both nonreligious and sacred. Westerners are fascinated with objects from these cultures and have put them in museums. It is important to understand the original context in which these objects were made and used.

▶ **FIGURE 12.17** The vertical lines on the face of this figure probably represent ornamental scars made to indicate ancestry and to enhance physical beauty. How did the artist use the principles of art in creating this portrait of a king?

Portrait of a King. Ife, Nigeria. Copper alloy. Eleventh–fifteenth century. H: 36.2 cm (14¹/₄″). Museum of Mankind, London, England.

Ancient Ife

For the Yoruba (**yaw**-ruh-buh)people of Nigeria, the city of Ife (**ee**-feh) is the place where life and civilization began. Yoruba cities developed between the years A.D. 800 and 1000. By A.D. 1100, artists of Ife had developed a highly refined, lifelike sculptural style to create portraits of the first Yoruba kings and queens. The display of royal portraits, with their composed, balanced facial features, added a sense of stability in periods of political transition between rulers, or following the death of a ruler **(Figure 12.17)**.

According to Yoruba beliefs, the world consists of two realms: the real world that can be seen and touched; and the supernatural world of ancestors, gods and goddesses, and spirits. Works of art created for the real, or visible, world tend to be realistic, whereas works of art created for the supernatural, or invisible, world tend to be more abstract.

As memorial portraits of Yoruba royalty, these sculptures celebrate the lives and accomplishments of individuals. Like Yoruba poems, which record family history and personal deeds, these refined works of art encourage living generations to strive for perfection. They encourage the living to match or surpass the cultural accomplishments of previous generations.

The Empire of Mali

Works of art made centuries ago in Ife and elsewhere in West Africa document the rise of city-states throughout the region. The terra-cotta sculptures of cavalrymen and foot soldiers from the Inland Niger Delta, near the ancient city of Jenne, date back to the early thirteenth century, when the empire of Mali was founded by a powerful military leader and king named Sundiata.

These figures reveal proud profiles, with jutting chins and heads held high atop sturdy necks. Their bodies appear straight and tall whether shown standing or seated upright on stallions **(Figure 12.18)**. The figures represent members of the well-outfitted and well-organized army described in an epic that recounts Sundiata's life history.

▲ **FIGURE 12.18** Because wet clay is soft, artists can easily add texture to the overall forms of clay sculptures. How many different kinds of texture can you identify in this work?

Inland Delta Region, Mali. Equestrian figure. c. thirteenth century. Ceramic. 70.5 cm (27¾"). National Museum of African Art, Smithsonian Institution, Washington, D.C. Museum purchase, 86–12–2.

▶ **FIGURE 12.19** This solid iron figure shows the strong vertical lines that characterize Mali sculpture.

Bamana peoples, Mali. Bamana iron figure. Iron, string, cowrie shells. Indiana University Art Museum, Bloomington, Indiana. Gift of Ernst Anspach.

▶ **FIGURE 12.20** Notice that the proportions of these figures are expressive rather than realistic.

Seated Man and Woman. Dogon people, Mali. Wood. 76.2 cm (30"). Photograph © 1993 by the Barnes Foundation, Merion Station, Pennsylvania.

The strength of Sundiata's great cavalry and army of foot soldiers enabled him to gain political power. Under his leadership, the empire of Mali became one of the largest and wealthiest kingdoms the world has ever known. The epic story of the rise of Sundiata is passed on by **griots** (**gree**-oh), *oral historians who are also musicians and performers,* throughout West Africa to this day.

The city of Jenne is the oldest city in sub-Saharan Africa. In the art and architecture from this city there is an emphasis on vertical elements **(Figure 12.19).** This can be seen in the corner pinnacles of house facades, which are made tall and straight.

The sculpture shown in **Figure 12.20,** made by the Dogon (**doh**-gahn) people of Mali, conveys a sense of harmony and balance. As images of the first man and woman described in Dogon myths of creation, this sculpture serves as an inspiration to living generations. These figures are seated on a stool with a circular support that symbolizes the link between the earth below and the spirit world above. Carved from a single piece of wood, the interlocking forms effectively convey Dogon ideas regarding the interdependence of men and women and their complementary social roles.

The Kingdom of Benin

The Benin (**buh**-neen) kingdom, situated in what is now southern Nigeria, was a society of many class levels, with an oral tradition that goes back seven or eight centuries. The kingdom reached the peak of its power in the sixteenth century. Like earlier artists in nearby Ife, Benin artists excelled in creating metal sculptures using a copper alloy possessing many of the same qualities as bronze.

Among the most ambitious of the Benin castings are the high-relief sculptures that once covered the walls and pillars of the royal palace. One of these contains the figure of the *oba* (**oh**-bah), or king, flanked by two chiefs bearing shields, sword bearers, and palace attendants **(Figure 12.21).**

Here four social ranks are depicted. The king, or *oba* is placed in the center and is the largest figure. The two chiefs are almost as large as the king. Two sword bearers, one a child, are even smaller. Three tiny figures, one supporting the king's foot and two in the top corners, represent the least powerful members of the court.

The *oba* wears a patterned wrapper, or waist cloth, a six-ringed necklace, and sits side-saddle on a horse. In Benin culture, horses are symbols of political power.

The Asante Kingdom

The Akan people lived in central and coastal Ghana. In the first half of the eighteenth century, these people joined together to form a powerful

◄ **FIGURE 12.21** In Benin art the most politically powerful person is represented as the largest figure. This representation reflects the central organization of the kingdom. Less powerful individuals are smaller.

Kingdom of Benin, Edo people, Nigeria. *Mounted King with Attendants.* c. sixteenth–seventeenth century. Brass. 49.5 × 41.9 × 11.3 cm (19½ × 16½ × 4½″). The Metropolitan Museum of Art, New York, New York. The Michael C. Rockefeller Memorial Collection. Gift of Nelson A. Rockefeller, 1965. (1978.412.309)

▲ **FIGURE 12.22** Works of art made using the lost-wax casting technique often show finely textured details. What elements of art are especially important in this work?

Akan people, Asante Kingdom, Ghana. *Necklace.* Nineteenth century. Gold. 2.5 × 40 cm (1 × 15³⁄₄″). Virginia Museum of Fine Arts, Richmond, Virginia. The Adolph D. and Wilkins C. Williams Fund.

confederation of states that included many cultural groups. The largest of these groups was the Asante (ah-**sahn**-tee).

Gold was the measure of wealth for the Asante and their kings, who tightly controlled its use. Items fashioned from the precious metal were made to be worn by these kings as a sign of their divine authority and absolute power.

Asante necklaces, bracelets, and anklets were crafted by stringing cast-gold beads with gold nuggets, glass and stone beads, and other items. In **Figure 12.22,** a pendant in the form of a land crab is used. This necklace was probably designed for a queen mother, because the land crab was widely recognized by the Asante as a symbol for a person of this rank.

The work of goldsmiths in Kumase, the Asante capital, was regulated by the king. He allowed people to commission works of art from these highly skilled craftsmen. Items obtained through the king's court included gold ornaments, staffs, and swords.

▶ **FIGURE 12.23** Weavers of Kente cloth have invented many different patterns. These patterns often have names that are immediately recognized by members of Akan societies. What elements of art have been used to create the patterns on this cloth?

Asante people, Ghana. Man's cloth (Kente cloth). Rayon. L: 314 cm (123⅜″), W: 217 cm (85⁷⁄₁₆″). UCLA Fowler Museum of Cultural History, Los Angeles, California. Anonymous gift.

The Asante king also controlled the use of special cloth. During the 1600s, weavers created the first *Kente* (**ken**-tee) *cloth,* a brilliantly colored and patterned fabric that became the royal cloth. Kente cloth is woven in narrow strips that are then stitched together to form large pieces with complex patterns **(Figure 12.23).** By the 1720s, Asante weavers were unraveling imported silk fabrics and reweaving them into cloths featuring their own unique designs. Silk cloths woven with special symbolic patterns were reserved exclusively for kings.

The Bwa People

Although wood is the most common material used to carve face masks and headdresses, African masks were constructed in different ways using a wide variety of materials. For example, the Bwa people of Burkina Faso made masks of leaves, plant fibers, porcupine quills, and feathers. Leaf masks were made at the end of the dry season, before the rains that marked the beginning of the next agricultural cycle. The Bwa people considered leaf masks the most ancient mask form and closely associated them with nature **(Figure 12.24).**

The Bwa people also produced wooden masks that were used during village ceremonies or harvest festivals. The music of flutes, drums, and gongs accompanied the dancers wearing these masks, which took different forms—animal, human, and abstract. All were painted with black, white, and red geometric patterns. Plank masks were among the most abstract of all mask forms made by the Bwa people **(Figure 12.25,** page 338**).**

▲ **FIGURE 12.24** African masks are generally more than just a face covering. Imagine wearing a leaf mask like this one. How would you feel?

Bwa people, Burkina Faso, village of Boni. Detail of a leaf mask. 1985.

▲ **FIGURE 12.25** Though large and cumbersome, plank masks are made of lightweight wood. To help steady the mask, the performer holds a stick between his teeth. This stick projects through rim holes at the back of the mask. What elements of art are emphasized in these masks?

Bwa people, Burkina Faso, village of Pa. Plank masks entering performance area, harvest celebration.

Activity Constructing a Mask

Demonstrating Effective Use of Media and Tools in Design. What happens when you cover your face with a mask? Can you hide your identity from others? Design your own mask using thin cardboard, construction paper, paint, or other media and tools. In choosing your design and materials, think about what you want your mask to represent.

 ## Check Your Understanding

1. What beliefs are reflected in the terra-cotta and bronze sculptures of the Yoruba people?
2. What are griots?
3. How do artists of the Benin kingdom signify the importance of figures in their artworks?
4. What is Kente cloth, and what is it used for?
5. Describe general characteristics of sculptures from the Ife, Dogon, and Edo cultures of Africa.

Art of the Americas

Many archaeologists believe that the first visitors to North America were groups of Asian hunters who crossed an ancient land bridge across the Bering Strait. They began to arrive in what is now Alaska between 20,000 and 40,000 years ago. Gradually these people spread out to cover all parts of North and South America. In this lesson, you will study the contributions of Native peoples of the Americas.

Art of Mesoamerica and South America

The term **pre-Columbian** refers to *the time period before the arrival of Christopher Columbus in the Americas in 1492.* Art historians use the term to refer to the art of the Indian civilizations of early Mexico, Central America, and South America. However, archaeologists are discovering that many of these pre-Columbian civilizations were highly sophisticated and created magnificent works of art and architecture.

Olmec Culture

Olmec (**ol**-mek) culture is often called the "mother culture" of Mexico because the artifacts found in the region are the most ancient. The Olmec civilization dates from 1200 B.C. to A.D. 500. The artifacts left by the Olmec had an influence on all the civilizations that were to follow. They carved altars, pillars, sarcophagi (sahr-**kah**-fuh-guy) (stone coffins), and statues. Among the most interesting of the Olmec creations are four huge human heads carved from volcanic rock **(Figure 12.26)**. These were discovered at La Venta, a center for religious ceremonies. These sculptures weigh up to 40 tons and stand 8 feet tall. Notice the childlike features on this giant face. The full lips, which seem almost to be pouting, are typical of the Olmec style.

▶ **FIGURE 12.26** This monumental sculpture depicts a simple, stylized face. The stone was quarried and transported over many miles of swampland before reaching its destination. What does this indicate about the technology of the Olmec people?

Olmec. Colossal Head. 1200 B.C.–A.D. 500. Basalt. 243.8 cm (8′) high. Anthropology Museum, Veracruz, Mexico.

Mayan Culture

By around A.D. 800 the Mayan (**my**-uhn) empire covered the Yucatán peninsula, modern Belize, Guatemala, and Honduras. The Maya were gifted mathematicians. They had the most accurate calendar of any people in history and had developed the most advanced hieroglyphic writing in Mesoamerica. They were also great builders. The Maya erected huge temples and cities with tools of wood, stone, and bone. In the late 1800s, scientists discovered an ancient city in northern Guatemala. This Mayan city, Tikal (tih-**kahl**), is known to have covered an area of 50 square miles. The city is thought to have been home to some 55,000 people **(Figure 12.27).**

The surviving works of Mayan civilization range from the smallest objects to great temples covered with relief carvings. Among the smallest artworks of the Maya are many beautifully designed clay figures only a few inches high. However, most of the Mayan sculpture that has survived consists of relief carvings on buildings and monuments. In the early stages of the Mayan civilization, these carvings were mostly simple and realistic. In some later temples, a more complex, geometric style came to be the rule.

Aztec Culture

The largest of the cultures of ancient Mexico and Central America was the Aztec. This civilization emerged sometime between A.D 1200 and 1325. The Aztecs were a warlike people. Like other pre-Columbian peoples, they were very religious. When their god told them to leave their comfortable homeland and settle where they saw an eagle perched on a cactus, they obeyed. There, they built a magnificent city, which they called Tenochtitlán (tay-noch-teet-**lahn**). A collection of tiny islands, this Aztec city was connected by a network of canals. In the fifteenth century, the Aztecs embarked on an aggressive military campaign to force other groups in Mexico to pay them tribute. They reached the height of their power and domination less than a century before the arrival of the Spanish. By the time Spanish conquerors arrived in 1519, their island city covered over 25 square miles. Today we know the city, which is no longer surrounded by water, as Mexico City.

The Aztecs adopted many of the ways of making art from the people they conquered. They created a type of painted book called a codex. Such painted books told the stories of mythological or historical events. Like Mayan art, Aztec art was greatly influenced by religion.

▶ **FIGURE 12.27**
The Mayan city Tikal included temples and other stone and stucco structures. The pyramids here are 230 feet high.

Maya. Great Plaza of Tikal, general view. A.D. 150–700. Tikal, Guatemala. Vanni/Art Resource, New York.

◀ **FIGURE 12.28**
Machu-Picchu
was built on a
mountainside to
discourage would-
be attackers. The
city has withstood
five centuries of
earthquakes.

Machu-Picchu, Peru.

The Aztecs also built temples and shrines, some carved directly into the mountains. Highly stylized and elaborately ornamented sculptures depicted gods and religious symbols in bold, dramatic style.

Inca Empire

The Inca civilization flourished between the thirteenth and fifteenth centuries, and their empire stretched more than 2,500 miles from north to south. It included present-day Peru plus parts of Ecuador, Chile, Argentina, and Bolivia. In acquiring such a large territory, the Inca Empire absorbed many cultural and religious influences from neighboring groups and from civilizations that had flourished before it. Although governing such an immense territory required a vast administration and bureaucracy, the Incas managed to govern without the benefit of a written language. They made calculations and kept records using pieces of knotted string of different colors, called *quipu* (**kee**-poo). The Incas' ability with numbers is reflected in their art. Inca artifacts were made with great mathematical precision.

The Incas were masters of shaping and fitting stone. They were also highly skilled urban planners. Proof of both talents can be found in the walled city of Machu-Picchu (**mahch**-oo **peek**-choo) **(Figure 12.28).** The stones of its buildings were so carefully matched that a knife blade cannot be slipped between any two.

Native American Art

When Christopher Columbus reached North America in 1492, he thought his ship had landed on the east coast of India. He referred to the natives he found living there as Indians. Today these first settlers are called Native Americans.

Some groups became hunters while others turned to growing crops as a way to survive. Artifacts found in these regions show that all of these people created art of some kind. These works have given us insight into the cultures of these peoples. Native American art and traditions are still being practiced today by these cultural groups.

The Arctic Region

The Inuit (**in**-yuh-wuht) people inhabited present-day Canada and Alaska from the earliest times. Although they are often called Eskimos, they refer to themselves as the Inuit.

Inuit society is loosely organized into family groups that rely on hunting and fishing for survival. The images created by Inuit artists reveal the importance attached to the animals they relied on for food—seal, walrus, fish, whale, and caribou. Other animals such as the fox, wolf, and bear were also represented in their art. The human figure was shown in the masks and dolls that they created.

Figures are also found on the engravings done on walrus ivory. In these engravings, Inuit artists used a kind of pictorial writing that described various activities and events associated with everyday life. In one such engraving on an ivory pipestem, a series of lively drawings record the activities associated with the daily quest for food. Since the surface of this pipestem is less than one inch wide, the engraving takes the form of tiny, decorative circles and miniature figures. Despite their small size, the artist still managed to present an easy-to-read account of the hunt. To accent the engraved lines used in works like this, artists filled them in with color or made them dark with soot.

Frequently, Inuit art was created to serve the religious needs of the people. The mask representing a moon goddess in **Figure 12.29** is an example. An Inuit shaman, or medicine man, wore such a mask during ceremonial dances. While dancing, he would go into a trance and act as a messenger between the world of the living and the mysterious world of spirits.

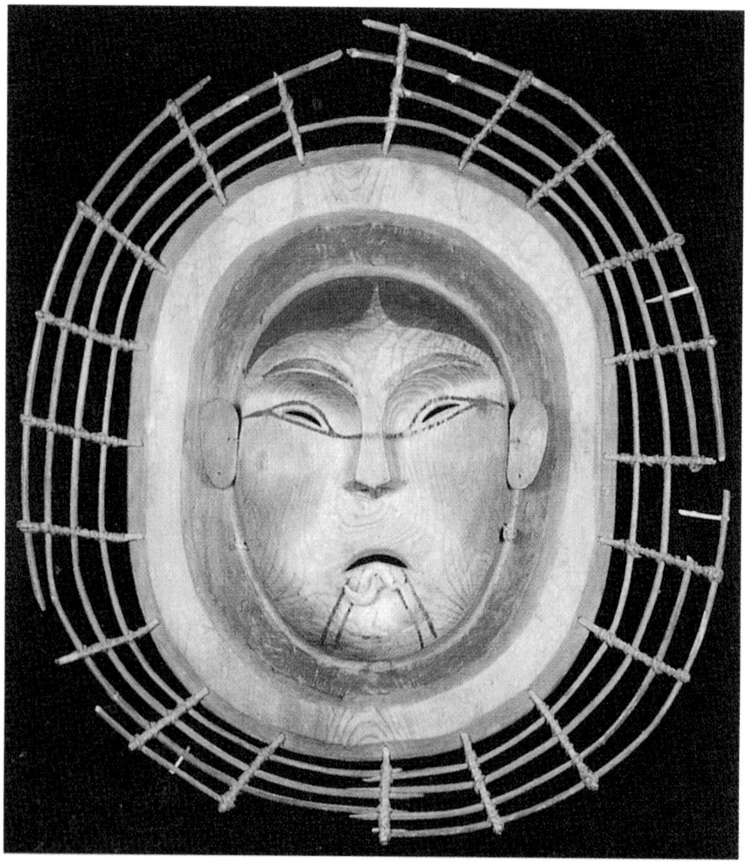

The Northwest Coast Region

The Northwest Coast Region refers to an area rich in natural resources that runs from southern Alaska to northern California. Native cultural groups in this region, including the Haida (**high**-duh), Tlingit, and the Kwakiutl (kwa-kee-**yoo**-tul), developed a complex culture in which art played a prominent role.

Like other people, the Kwakiutl held annual rituals to initiate new members, reinforce the status of old members, and

◀ **FIGURE 12.29** A mask of this kind was worn only by a shaman during ceremonial dances. How do you think the purpose of this mask is reflected in its design? What feelings do you think the mask evoked in viewers?

Inuit. Mask of Moon Goddess. Lower Yukon or Northwest Bering Sea. Before 1900. 64.1 cm (25¼") high. Hearst Museum of Anthropology, The University of California at Berkeley, Berkeley, California.

demonstrate their magical powers. Ceremonial masks and dramatic costumes were created for these rituals. Look at the Secret Society Mask pictured in Figure 10.27 on page 273. It is composed of several hinged pieces that moved. This movement was intended to add surprise and drama to the ritual. Often after a Kwakiutl ceremony, or to celebrate another important event, people gathered to enjoy a *potlatch*. This event enabled the members of one clan to honor those of another, while adding to their own prestige.

Native Americans of the Northwest Coast lived in large family groups. Each family group traced descent from a mythological animal or human-animal, from which they took their name. In order to symbolize their association with this mythic ancestor, they carved totem poles. **Totem poles** are *tall posts carved and painted with a series of animal symbols associated with a particular family or clan* **(Figure 12.30).**

The Southwest Region

The Native American groups of the southwestern United States include the Pueblo (**pweb**-loh) and the Navajo (**nav**-uh-hoh). Early Spanish explorers used the term *pueblo,* meaning village, to describe groups of people living in large, highly organized settlements. Ancient Pueblo dwellings were built with adobe, or sun-dried clay, walls.

The Pueblo were especially skillful in creating painted pottery. Each community developed its own distinctive shapes and painted designs. In the Rio Grande Valley of New Mexico, for example, Pueblo potters used black outlines and geometric shapes to create bold designs over a cream-colored base **(Figure 12.31).**

◀ **FIGURE 12.30** Totem poles are similar to a European family's coat of arms and were erected in front of a dwelling as a means of identification and a sign of prestige.

Haida totem pole. Prince of Wales Island. c. 1870. Originally 16.2 m (53') high. Taylor Museum of the Colorado Springs Fine Arts Center, Colorado Springs, Colorado.

▶ **FIGURE 12.31** The materials and techniques used in this water jar identify it as a Pueblo work. What elements of art can you identify in this design?

Water jar. Santo Domingo Pueblo, New Mexico. 1910. Ceramic. 24.1 cm (9½") high × 24.45 cm (9⅝") diameter. Denver Art Museum, Denver, Colorado.

The Navajo, another Southwestern cultural group, learned the art of weaving from the Pueblo. Male Pueblo weavers taught the Navajo weavers, who were women, to make cloth with looms at the beginning of the eighteenth century. As Spanish and Mexican settlers moved into the Southwest, they introduced new designs and patterns, which the Navajo adopted. By the first half of the nineteenth century, the Navajo were using European dyes and Spanish wool to create weavings that matched the work produced by the best looms in Europe. A blanket once owned by the Civil War general Philip Sheridan **(Figure 12.32)** exhibits many of the qualities associated with the finest Navajo weavings. These include the closeness of the weave, rich, vibrant colors, and bold design.

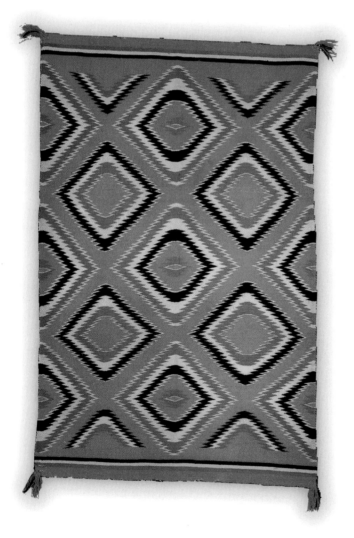

Great Plains Region

The Native Americans of the Great Plains followed the huge herds of bison that roamed the broad grasslands of central North America. The different cultural groups of the Plains—including Blackfeet, Crow, Cheyenne (shy-**ann**), and Sioux (soo)—were highly skilled in the preparation of skins used for clothing, footwear, shields, and various kinds of containers. These were then painted or embroidered with porcupine quills and, later, glass beads.

Because they were nomadic hunters, they created the *tepee* (**tee**-pee). This was a portable shelter made of buffalo hide stretched over poles that were lashed together in an upright position. The hides were covered with designs symbolizing the forces of nature and telling stories of heroic events. At its base, a tepee could range anywhere from 12 to 30 feet in diameter. A large tepee contained about as much space as a standard living room of today.

These artisans also created ceremonial headdresses for chieftains, which were worn during ritual dances. The elaborate headdress shown in **Figure 12.33** was created with natural materials found in the surrounding environment.

◀ **Figure 12.32** This saddle blanket, created for everyday use, is now on display in a museum. How are the principles of harmony and variety used in this design? How is rhythm suggested?

Saddle blanket. Navajo weaving. c. 1890. Wool. 129.5 × 83.8 cm (51 × 33″). Denver Art Museum, Denver, Colorado.

Woodlands Region

The Woodlands made up the largest cultural group of Native Americans east of the Mississippi River. The Woodlands people combined hunting and gathering with simple farming. The Iroquois (**ear**-uh-kwoi), made up of six different Woodlands groups, combined to form the highly organized Iroquois nation.

Expert wood carvers, the Iroquois created wooden masks that were usually painted and decorated with horse hair. The best known masks were created for a society of healers known as the False Faces because of the masks they wore. These False Face masks were thought to be sacred and represented the spirits who gave healers the magic they needed to treat illnesses. Because they were considered to be so powerful, these masks were hidden away when not in use so they would not cause accidental injuries. The masks were considered sacred and were not intended to be seen by nonbelievers.

Activity Sketching an Event

Applying Your Skills. Native Americans of the Great Plains painted tales of their battles on skins. Look through a newspaper or magazine for coverage of an important event in your city or in the world. On a sheet of paper, sketch the story behind the event.

Check Your Understanding

1. What does the term *pre-Columbian* refer to?
2. Which culture created huge heads carved from volcanic rock?
3. Which culture created the walled city of Machu–Picchu?
4. What were totem poles used for?

Art Criticism
in Action

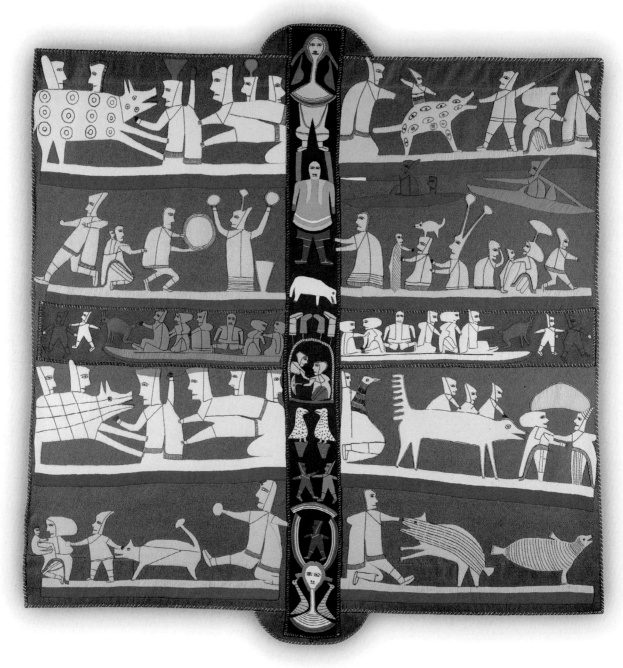

▲ **FIGURE 12.34**

Jessie Oonark. *Untitled.* c. 1973. Duffle wool, felt, embroidery floss, and thread. 186 × 181 cm (73¼ × 71¼″). National Gallery of Canada, Ottawa, Ontario, Canada. Gift of the Department of Indian Affairs and Northern Development, 1989.

Critiquing the Artwork

Meet the ARTIST

Jessie Oonark
(1906–1986)

▶ **1**   **DESCRIBE** *What do you see?*

This is a clue collecting step.

- What media were used to create this work? What is the size of the work?

- What objects and figures are shown in the work?

▶ **2**   **ANALYZE** *How is this work organized?*

In this step you will form conclusions about the formal qualities in this artwork.

- What pattern emerges in the use of colors chosen for this work?

- What kind of balance has the artist used to organize the hanging?

- Describe the use of proportion.

- How has the artist used harmony and variety to unify this large work?

▶ **3**   **INTERPRET** *What is the artist trying to communicate?*

Combine the clues you have collected to form a creative interpretation of the work.

- Do the people in this work appear to be inhabitants of a large, modern city? If not, how would you describe them? Explain your reaction.

- Why do you think the artist used proportion as she did?

- The artist left this work untitled. Give it a title that fits your interpretation.

▶ **4**   **JUDGE** *What do you think of the work?*

Now, you are ready to make an aesthetic judgment of the work.

- Do you think this is a successful work of art? Why or why not? Use one or more of the aesthetic theories to defend your decision.

Jessie Oonark was born northwest of Hudson Bay to an Inuit family. She was taught traditional Inuit beliefs and essential skills: childcare, preparing skins, and making clothing. After becoming a widow at age 40, Oonark fell on hard times. The next 19 years were filled with many hardships. After being rescued from near-starvation, she was taken to a hospital at Baker Lake. It was there that she discovered art. Her works are mostly wall hangings and prints based on memories of her earlier life. Her use of bold, flat areas of color makes her style unique.

SAVING AFRICA'S ART

Africa's treasures are prized by collectors all over the world, but this popularity isn't all good news.

For at least 2,000 years, various cultures in Africa have been creating sculptures, busts, and masks from ivory, terra-cotta, soapstone, and metals. The continent's rich artistic output has long influenced Western artists including Henri Matisse, Pablo Picasso, and Georges Braque.

African art is prized by collectors and museums for its intrinsic beauty and artistic merit. In fact, the art has become so valued that thieves have been stealing grave markers, pottery, masks, and sculptures. Some of these items are being dug up from ancient burial sites in villages in East and West Africa. Other works are stolen from African museums. All are sold illegally to collectors in Europe and the United States. The pricetag for the illegal African art trade: about $45 million each year.

Fighting Back

Now Africans are fighting back. "These objects of art are the relics of our history—why must we lose them?" asks Omotoso Eluyemi, director general of Nigeria's National Commission for Museums and Monuments. His group is in charge of maintaining Nigeria's museums and landmarks.

Nigeria and other African countries, including Benin, Mali, and Kenya, are cutting down on the looting of an important part of Africa's heritage. Now art dealers from around the world are asking questions if someone is selling a piece of ancient African art. Villagers and police are on the lookout for thieves who are digging up art treasures. Governments are using the Internet to track down missing pieces of art. This has helped reduce the looting. That's good news for the many Africans who want to hold on to their art and cultural history.

A sixteenth-century bust of Queen Idia is one of the most famous images in African art.

SHERIDEN/AAA COLLECTION

TIME to Connect

Look at a map of Africa, choose one nation, and research a traditional art form, dance form, type of music, or storytelling tradition. Use your school's media center or the Internet for background information.

• Write a report reflecting the cultural importance of the art form to the tribe or the nation as a whole. Be sure to include the origins of the form, symbolism (if any), and how the form has evolved over time.

• Share your report with the class. Are there any similarities or differences in the traditional forms of music, art, dance, and storytelling from nation to nation? How can you explain these similarities or differences?

Building Vocabulary

On a separate sheet of paper, write the term that best matches each definition given below.

1. Large monuments created from huge stone slabs.
2. The Sumerian writing system made up of wedge-shaped characters.
3. Stepped mountains made of brick-covered earth.
4. Egyptian rulers who were worshiped as gods and held complete authority over the kingdom.
5. A period of time during which a single family provided a succession of rulers.
6. Beehive-shaped domed places of worship.
7. A tower several stories high with roofs curving slightly upward at the edges.
8. Muslim places of worship.
9. Tall posts carved and painted with a series of animal symbols associated with a particular family or clan.

Reviewing Art Facts

Answer the following questions using complete sentences.

10. During what time period did people begin to build structures of stone?
11. Describe the rules that Egyptian artists were required to follow when painting or sculpting a relief figure.
12. What influenced the style of Chinese "picture painting"?
13. What art technique did Japanese artists perfect to meet the demand for artworks?
14. Describe the differences between the art used in Islamic mosques and the art used in Islamic book illustration.
15. What do the images created by Inuit artists reveal about what they valued as a culture?

Thinking Critically About Art

16. **Explain.** For what reasons did people of African and Native American cultures create art? How does this differ from more recent European or American art that you find in a museum?
17. **Analyze.** Visit art museums online or in your community. Select and analyze exhibitions of non-Western cultures to form conclusions about formal qualities, historical and cultural contexts, intents, and meanings.
18. **Historical/Cultural Heritage.** Review the Meet the Artist feature on page 330. Compare Hokusai's print in Figure 12.15 to Figure 4.32 on page 92 by Hiroshige. Hiroshige was inspired by the work of Hokusai. By examining both works, determine one of the general trends in art during this historical time period.

ART Online

Understanding and appreciating the arts from many cultural traditions enriches the work of all artists. Art directors for film and television often do extensive research into the cultural artifacts and art of the time period and people being depicted in movies and shows. Visit **art.glencoe.com** to compare and contrast career opportunities in art.

Linking to the Performing Arts

Explore the classical and folk traditions of Korean music and dance on page 424 of the Performing Arts Handbook.

▲ **FIGURE 13.1** This painting is a *genre* (**zhan**-ruh) scene. It focuses on an activity that was part of everyday life. Notice how the artist has focused as much on the surroundings as on the human subjects. How would you describe the mood of this scene?

Jan Vermeer. *The Concert.* c. 1658–60. Oil on canvas. 72.4 × 64.8 cm (28¹/₂ × 25¹/₂″). Isabella Stewart Gardner Museum, Boston, Massachusetts.

Western Traditions in Art

The term *Western art* refers to art of the western hemisphere, specifically western Europe and North America. Western art includes the rich traditions of Ancient Greek and Roman architecture up through the groundbreaking movements and styles of Modern art.

In this chapter, you will:

- Identify historical and cultural events that have shaped Western art.
- Describe general characteristics in artworks from a variety of Western cultures.
- Compare and contrast historical and contemporary styles of Western art, identifying trends and themes.

Focus on **Art History** **Figure 13.1** is a painting by the Dutch artist Jan Vermeer (1632–1675). Vermeer was born in Delft, Holland. During his life he traveled little, and his paintings were largely unknown. Vermeer is now considered one of the greatest Dutch painters. In seventeenth century Holland, painters mainly created their artworks for the working class. Vermeer and his contemporaries chose everyday subjects as they were recognizable and appreciated by this class. As in Figure 13.1, the style of these works is very precise and realistic, and the mood is hushed and serious.

Compare and Contrast. Compare and contrast Vermeer's use of color and value to create an area of emphasis. Where is the focal point in this artwork?

The Beginnings of Western Art Traditions

Vocabulary

Byzantine art
Romanesque
Gothic

Greece was the birthplace of Western civilization. The influence of ancient Greek culture can still be seen today. Almost every city in our country has at least one building with features that resemble the architecture of the classic Greek temple.

The Art of Greece and Rome

The Greeks built temples in honor of their gods. The most outstanding example is the Parthenon in Athens **(Figure 13.2).** The columns slant slightly inward to prevent a top-heavy look. Inside was a huge statue of the goddess Athena created of ivory and gold. The relief sculpture that covered the area under the roof is missing. Many of the missing pieces are in foreign museums. The Greeks worked to create a logical, harmonious world. They sought perfect proportions in buildings, sculpture, and music by following the guidelines of mathematical proportion. Their artists produced statues that represented the Greek ideal of the perfect body. According to one story, athletes used these statues, like the one shown in **Figure 13.3,** as inspiration for developing their own muscle strength and tone.

▲ **FIGURE 13.2** Although partially destroyed, you can see that the Parthenon was designed to look harmonious. Architects used mathematical formulas to make the temple look balanced and beautiful.

Parthenon. Temple of Athena. Fifth century B.C. Acropolis, Athens, Greece.

When they were new, Greek temples and statues were not the pure white we see today. The Greeks loved color, and they painted their buildings and sculptures various hues. Time has since worn the paint away.

Even though the Romans conquered Greece in 146 B.C., they did not conquer Greek culture. Instead, the Romans adopted Greek culture, modifying it to suit their own needs. Greek sculptors, painters, architects, philosophers, and teachers exerted a great influence on the culture of the Roman Empire.

Earlier, the Romans had absorbed the culture of the Etruscans in Italy. Two outstanding Etruscan developments that the Romans adopted included a system of drainage and an improved use of the arch in the construction of buildings. What we call Roman art is a blend of the ideal Greek and the practical Etruscan arts.

The Romans added much to what they adopted. They used the arch and concrete to build large-scale structures, including huge vaulted and domed inner spaces. Engineers constructed a network of roads to connect all parts of the Roman Empire. The Romans also developed beautiful interior decoration and created realistic rather than idealized portrait sculpture (Figure 13.4).

◀ **FIGURE 13.3** Look at the proportions and detail of this athlete. Notice the idealized muscles and facial features. What does such a sculpture reveal about Greek culture? What features of the human body were admired by them and important to them?

Myron. *Discobolus (Discus Thrower).* c. 450 B.C. Roman copy of a bronze original. Life-size. Italy. Palazzo Vecchio, Florence, Italy.

◀ **FIGURE 13.4** Unlike the Greeks, the Romans did not seek to depict idealized human forms. The expression on the boy's face seems haughty or proud, but notice how his features have been shown realistically. For example, his ears stick out from his head.

Roman. *Portrait Statue of Boy.* Late first century B.C.–early first century A.D. Julio-Claudian. Bronze. Height: 123.2 cm (48¹/₂″). The Metropolitan Museum of Art, New York, New York. Rogers fund, 1914 (14.130.1).

Activity — Analyzing Architecture

Illustrating Ideas for Artworks Using Direct Observation. Find a building in your community in the Greek or Roman style. Write the location, the culture from which the style was adopted, the purpose of the building, and anything else you can find out about it. Using direct observation, make a sketch of the building in your sketchbook. Name the ancient culture and describe the features that match the style of the ancient culture.

Byzantine art expressed a solemn, devotional mood. Notice how the infant Christ in this ivory sculpture is presented as a miniature man. He holds a scroll in one hand and blesses the viewer with the other.

Byzantine, Constantinople. *Virgin and Child.* Mid-tenth to eleventh century. Ivory. 23.4 × 7 × 1.3 cm (9³/₁₆ × 2³/₄ × ¹/₂″). The Metropolitan Museum of Art, New York, New York. Gift of J. Pierpont Morgan, 1917. (17.190.103).

▶ **FIGURE 13.6**
This church was built in the Romanesque style. Identify the rounded arches.

Church of San Clemente. Tahull, Spain. Twelfth century.

The Art of the Middle Ages

The Middle Ages began with the conquest of Rome in A.D. 476 by invaders from the north and lasted about 1,000 years. This period of time was also called the *Age of Faith* because the Christian religion exerted such an important influence. Monasteries, or buildings that housed people who had made religious vows, grew in number. The monks who lived in them created finely decorated religious manuscripts. Churches grew in size, number, and political importance, reflecting the status of the Christian religion during this period.

Byzantine Art

In the eastern part of the former Roman Empire, a new style of art developed during the Middle Ages. This style thrived around the city of Constantinople (now Istanbul, Turkey) and spread to towns such as Ravenna in Italy. Constantinople, built on the site of the ancient city of Byzantium, served as the capital of the Byzantine Empire. **Byzantine art** *featured very rich colors and heavily outlined figures that appeared flat and stiff.* Constantinople was close to Asia as well as to Greece, and because of this proximity, Greek, Roman, and Asian art and culture all influenced Byzantine artists **(Figure 13.5).**

Romanesque Style

At the beginning of the Middle Ages, many new churches were built in western Europe in a style of architecture similar to ancient Roman buildings. It was called **Romanesque** and *featured buildings of massive size; solid, heavy walls; wide use of the rounded Roman arch; and many sculptural decorations.*

Churches, castles, and monasteries were all built in the Romanesque style **(Figure 13.6).** Architects building Romanesque structures could not include many windows because they weakened the structure of the walls and could cause the heavy stone roofs to collapse. As a result, Romanesque buildings were dark and somber inside.

Gothic Style

In Europe in the twelfth century, increasing numbers of people moved from the countryside into towns. Workers such as stone carvers and carpenters organized into craft guilds (or unions), and apprentices learned their crafts from the masters in these guilds. A wealthy new merchant class, pride in the growing cities, and religious faith led to the building of huge cathedrals. Two developments in architecture—the pointed arch and the flying buttress—brought about changes in how buildings were built, and how they looked. The flying buttress removed the weight of the roof from the walls, allowing for higher walls and many more windows than had been possible in Romanesque structures. This new style, called **Gothic,** *featured churches that seemed to soar upward, used pointed arches, and included stained-glass windows,* like the cathedral shown in **Figure 13.7.**

By using stained-glass windows, Gothic builders changed the light that entered the churches into rich, glowing color. Gothic sculptors and painters sought more realistic ways to depict subject matter. Religious scenes were painted on church altarpieces with egg tempera paint and gold leaf.

▲ **Figure 13.7** This cathedral was built in the Gothic style. Notice the pointed arches and stained-glass windows. Compare this to Figure 13.6. Describe the similarities and differences between the two churches.

Chartres Cathedral, Chartres, France. Twelfth to sixteenth century.

Check Your Understanding

1. How did the Greeks represent the human form?
2. Describe general characteristics of Greek, Roman, and Byzantine art.
3. Identify two features of Romanesque buildings.
4. What two developments of the Gothic period allowed builders to place many openings in walls and to build churches taller?

Activity	The Gothic Style

Applying Your Skills. Research cathedrals built in the Gothic style. List the names of and sketch three of the cathedrals in your sketchbook. Write down where and when they were built.

The Beginnings of Modern Art Traditions

At the beginning of the fifteenth century, the Middle Ages began drawing to a close. The invention of the printing press and the European exploration of the Americas and the Pacific Ocean expanded knowledge and contributed to the dawn of a new era. As the culture changed, so did the art. During the Middle Ages, most art had been made for religious reasons. Even artworks made for wealthy people, such as illuminated books, most often depicted religious subject matter. During the next period, artists continued to paint religious subjects but also expanded their repertoire to include mythological and secular, or nonreligious, themes.

Renaissance

Renaissance (**ren**-uh-sahns) is a French word for "rebirth." **Renaissance** is *the name given to the period at the end of the Middle Ages when artists, writers, and philosophers were "re-awakened" to art forms and ideas from ancient Greece and Rome.* The Renaissance did not happen all at once, nor did it spread to all parts of Europe at the same time. Rather, it dawned gradually, first in Italy, then spreading through northern Europe, finally reaching France and England. Along with a new appreciation of classical antiquity, social structures also changed. Kings and popes, who had always been extremely powerful, had competition from bankers and merchants, whose wealth also equaled political power. The authority of the Catholic Church was challenged by Renaissance scholars and artists who sought to understand the natural world through science and reason.

Italian Renaissance

An architect named Filippo Brunelleschi (fee-**leep**-poh brew-nell-**less**-key) developed linear perspective, a graphic system that creates the illusion of depth and volume on a flat surface. Linear perspective provided a set of guidelines that allowed artists to depict figures and objects in space on a two-dimensional surface. This system made the placement of objects, and the depiction of their volume or form, measurable and exact, which gave an exciting illusion of reality to works of art. Italian artists sought to create realistic and lifelike works. They studied the classical art of Greece and Rome and meticulously observed and recorded the world around them.

Michelangelo Buonarroti (my-kel-**an**-jay-loh bwon-nar-**roh**-tee), an Italian artist, was a master of poetry, painting, sculpture, and architecture. However, he always thought of himself primarily as a sculptor. One of his most famous works is **Figure 13.8**, *Pietà*. A pietà is a work showing Mary mourning over the body of Christ.

Born in a small village near Florence, Italy in 1475, Michelangelo was apprenticed to a painter when he was 13. While still a teen, he joined the Medici household, a powerful ruling family. There he met many prominent Florentine citizens, artists, and philosophers. In 1494, the Medici family was overthrown and Michelangelo was forced to flee. He traveled to Rome, where many classical statues and buildings were being discovered. He eagerly studied their formal qualities and proportions:

Michelangelo created many masterpieces, mostly on a grand scale. When Pope Julius II asked Michelangelo to design a tomb for him, Michelangelo devised a design calling for 40 sculptures, only a few of which were completed before Pope Julius decided not to spend any more money. Instead, he asked Michelangelo to paint the ceiling of the Sistine Chapel in the Vatican. The chapel had a rounded ceiling high above the floor. Michelangelo was insulted at being asked to paint a ceiling, which was not considered a very prestigious assignment. He also did not know how he could paint a ceiling so far off the ground. However, the pope insisted and Michelangelo gave in. He built a high scaffold and lay on it to paint the wet ceiling plaster. He created nine different sections on the ceiling, each telling a Biblical story, including the creation of the world.

▶ **FIGURE 13.8** Notice the proportions of the two figures in this sculpture. Mary is much larger than her son. Michelangelo did this on purpose so that she would not seem overwhelmed by her son's body. What feeling does this proportion convey?

Michelangelo. *Pietà.* c. 1500. Marble. 174 cm (5′8½″) high; base 195 cm (6′4⅘″) high. Vatican, St. Peter's Basilica, Rome, Italy.

Like Michelangelo, Leonardo da Vinci (lay-oh-**nar**-doh da **vin**-chee) studied and mastered a broad range of disciplines, including mathematics, physics, geography, and painting. Although he had many ideas, Leonardo often left paintings and sculptures unfinished because he was not happy with them. A page from one of his sketchbooks is shown in Figure 3.2 on page 42.

Women first achieved fame as artists during the Renaissance. They had to overcome political, social, and economic obstacles to achieve artistic success. One of them, Sofonisba Anguissola, was the first Italian woman to gain wide recognition as an artist. The oldest of seven children, her father encouraged her to pursue art and allowed her to study with local artists. He even wrote to Michelangelo to tell him about Sofonisba's skills. Michelangelo responded with kind words of encouragement and

a drawing for her to copy and study as part of her training. Much of her early work consisted of portraits of her family and herself **(Figure 13.9)**. She also painted religious subjects. As her fame spread, the king of Spain asked her to join his court, where she painted many portraits and enjoyed respect and admiration as a court painter.

Northern Renaissance

The changes that took place during the Renaissance in Italy later filtered into northern European countries such as Flanders (a region in Belgium) and Germany. Flemish artists (those from Flanders) began to use oil rather than egg to bind their pigments. This new medium allowed artists more versatility than ever before.

Northern artists had little interest in recreating the classical art of Greece and Rome. They placed greater emphasis on

▲ **FIGURE 13.9** Notice the dramatic use of color in this painting. Observe the detail of the dresses the sisters are wearing. What does this tell you about them and their social status?

Sofonisba Anguissola. *A game of chess, involving the painter's three sisters and a servant.* 1555. Oil on canvas. 72 × 97 cm (28¹/₂ × 38¹/₅″). Muzeum Narodove, Poznan, Poland.

◀ **FIGURE 13.10** At first, this portrait of a well-to-do woman appears to be a realistic portrayal. If you look closely, however, you will see that her waist, as indicated by the red band, is about the same size as her head. Her head is elongated, which is emphasized by the severely pulled back hair. Do you think these odd proportions are natural? Why would the artist paint her this way if she did not look like this?

Rogier van der Weyden. *Portrait of a Lady.* c. 1460. Oil on panel, painted surface. 34 × 25.5 cm (13³/₈ × 10¹/₁₆″). National Gallery of Art, Washington, D.C. © 1998 Board of Trustees. Andrew W. Mellon Collection.

depicting the accurate and precise details such as an intricate design on clothing or the details of the environment. Symbolism became even more important. Images in art conveyed more than just one meaning.

The art of Jan van Eyck (**yahn** van **eyek**) and his successors made Flanders the center of the Northern art world. Like other Northern painters, Jan van Eyck emphasized precision and accuracy. Look at Figure 9.8 on page 231. Notice the attention to detail, such as the lace on the woman's headcovering and the carpet under the bed. The picture includes many symbols. For example, the wedding couple is shown

barefoot to symbolize that they are standing on holy ground. The burning candle indicates the presence of God. The little dog stands for loyalty.

The work of Jan van Eyck influenced another important Northern Renaissance painter, Rogier van der Weyden (roh-**jehr** van duhr **vy**-duhn). Like van Eyck, he paid meticulous attention to detail. Look at **Figure 13.10.** Notice the pins in the subject's veil and the intricate design on her belt buckle.

As is often the case, changes in society brought about changes in artistic expression. In the mid-sixteenth century, religious reformers challenged the authority of the Catholic Church, causing conflict

and turmoil. Great artists like Leonardo and Michelangelo had died, leaving behind a vacuum in artistic inspiration and innovation. Artists began showing the tension and struggle they experienced during this period of crisis in their art. The result was an artistic style called **Mannerism,** which *featured highly emotional scenes and elongated figures.* The style was developed by certain artists to be a deliberate shift away from the ideals and perfect forms of Renaissance art. If Renaissance artists preferred balance and harmony, Mannerists preferred imbalance and dynamic movement.

One of the most famous Mannerist artists was El Greco (el **greh**-koh). His name means "the Greek," for his birthplace on the Greek island of Crete. Because of his unusual style, El Greco found it difficult to secure patronage. In 1577, he traveled to Toledo, Spain, where he spent the rest of his life. There he gained a reputation as a superior artist. **Figure 13.11** shows the intense emotionalism and strong sense of movement characteristic of El Greco's work.

The Seventeenth and Eighteenth Centuries

A reform movement known as the Protestant Reformation, which began in the sixteenth century, caused many people to depart from the teachings of the Catholic Church. In order to gain them back, the Church started its own reform movement, known as the Counter-Reformation, in the seventeenth century. Art was an important part of this movement. Catholic Church authorities called upon artists to create works that would inspire renewed religious feelings in viewers.

▲ **FIGURE 13.11** Notice the dreamlike quality of the background. It causes the viewer to focus on the two figures in the foreground. What appears to be happening in this painting?

El Greco. *Saint Martin and the Beggar.* 1597/1599. Oil on canvas; wooden strip added at bottom. 193.5 × 103 cm (76¹/₈ × 40¹/₂″). National Gallery of Art, Washington, D.C. © 1998 Board of Trustees. Widener Collection.

Baroque Art in Italy

A new art style developed as a result of the Counter-Reformation. **Baroque** (buh-**rohk**) is *an art style emphasizing dramatic lighting, movement, and emotional intensity.* The leader of the Baroque style in Italy, a young painter named Michelangelo Merisi da Caravaggio (my-kel-**an**-jay-loh mah-**ree**-see dah kar-uh-**vah**-jyoh), depicted light in a daring new way. *The Conversion of St. Paul* **(Figure 13.12),** shows only St. Paul, his horse, and an attendant. The figures fill the canvas. Nothing distracts the viewer from the scene. Although the religious meaning may not be apparent at first, Caravaggio's mysterious use of light dramatizes the scene. This dramatic use of light and dark is also evident in the art of one of his followers, Artemisia Gentileschi (see Figure 5.17 on page 111).

Dutch Art

Dutch Protestants did not want religious paintings and sculptures in their churches. Dutch artists had to turn to

◀ **FIGURE 13.12** Notice the use of light in this picture. It is not a natural light. Where does it come from? What mood is created by it?

Caravaggio. *The Conversion of St. Paul.* c. 1601. Oil on canvas. Approx. 228.6 × 175.3 cm (90 × 69″). Santa Maria del Popolo, Rome, Italy.

ordinary people and places for their subject matter. The demand for landscapes, portraits, and still lifes grew as wealthy merchants surrounded themselves with art that depicted scenes of everyday life. The greatest Dutch artist of this period was Rembrandt van Rijn (**rem**-brant van **reyn**). Like other Dutch artists, he painted ordinary people and everyday events. He was somewhat unusual, however, in that he also continued painting religious subjects. He was especially interested in the psychological character of the people he portrayed, suggested by his use of light and shadow to create atmosphere. *Aristotle with a Bust of Homer* (Figure 5.36, page 124) is considered one of the grandest Rembrandts because of its rich use of color and texture. The texture of the gold chain is depicted in three-dimensional relief because of the thickness of the paint.

Jan Vermeer (yahn vair-**meer**) is another important Dutch artist. For several hundred years, his artwork remained unappreciated, but in the second half of the nineteenth century critics recognized his artistic genius. Vermeer is best known for his use of light and texture. **Figure 13.13** shows his talent in using dark and light values to express a feeling or evoke a mood.

▶ **FIGURE 13.13**
This portrait depicts an ordinary woman engaged in an everyday activity. How does Vermeer add interest to the painting? What mood or feeling does it evoke?

Jan Vermeer. *Girl with the Red Hat.* c. 1665/1666. Oil on panel. 23.1 × 18.1 cm (9¹/₈ × 7¹/₈″). National Gallery of Art, Washington, D.C. © 1998 Board of Trustees. Andrew W. Mellon Collection.

Rococo Style

As the seventeenth century ended and the eighteenth century began, France emerged as the strongest, wealthiest nation in Europe. Paris, its capital, became the center of the art world. When pleasure-loving King Louis XIV assumed the throne, a new style of art influenced by his lighthearted personality arose. Called **Rococo** (ruh-**koh**-koh), it is *an art style that expresses free, graceful movement, playful use of line, and delicate colors.*

One of the first painters working in the Rococo style was Antoine Watteau (an-**twahn** wah-**toh**). His paintings depict an idealized world filled with happy, carefree people **(Figure 13.14).**

In England, artists modified the Rococo style. They used its delicate, light-washed techniques but rejected artificial subject matter. One of the most famous English painters of this period, Thomas Gainsborough (**gainz**-bur-roh), began his artistic career as a landscape painter but later became a famous portrait painter for members of English high society.

▲ **FIGURE 13.14** Describe the dress and manners of these people. Notice how the colors and shapes blend together for a dreamlike, misty quality. Is this a happy occasion? How do you know?

Antoine Watteau. *Embarkation for Cythera.* 1717–19. Oil on canvas. 1.3 × 1.9 m (4′ 3″ × 6′ 4¹/₂″). The Louvre, Paris, France.

▶ **FIGURE 13.15** The most
striking element of this painting is
the use of color. What does the
background depict? Do you think
it is important to the painting?

Thomas Gainsborough. *The Blue Boy.*
c. 1770. Oil on canvas. 177.8 × 121.9
cm (70 × 48″). The Huntington Library,
Art Collections, and Botanical Gardens,
San Marino, California.

Figure 13.15, Gainsborough's most
famous painting, resulted from a professional rivalry. A rival painter gave a lec-
ture at the Royal Academy of Art and
stated that blue, a cool color, should
always be used in the background,
never in the main part of a picture.
When Gainsborough heard this, he considered it a challenge and painted a portrait of a boy dressed entirely in blue.

In Spain, Francisco Goya (frahn-
seese-koh **goh**-ya) transformed Rococo
art. Early in his career, Goya achieved
considerable fame and fortune painting in
the Rococo style. However, this changed
after he suffered a serious illness and,
later, a grave accident. He lost his hearing
and endured other physical setbacks.
A war in Spain made him aware of the
suffering of others. He found he was
no longer comfortable painting in the
decorative Rococo fashion.

Goya's art reflected his bitterness and
disillusionment. One of his most famous
paintings shows the ugliness and brutal-
ity of war **(Figure 13.16).**

▲ **FIGURE 13.16** The figures are arranged in this painting so that they seem in opposition to each other. Which is the most important figure in this composition? How has the figure been made to stand out? What is the feeling or mood of the piece?

Francisco Goya. *The Third of May, 1808.* 1814. Oil on canvas. Approx. 2.64 × 3.43 m (8'8" × 11'3"). Museo del Prado, Madrid, Spain.

Activity **Analyzing an Artwork**

Selecting and Analyzing Artworks for Historical and Cultural Contexts. Select one work of art from the Renaissance or Baroque periods. Use the four steps of the art history method discussed in Chapter 2 to form conclusions about the historical or cultural context of the work. You may need to research the work or art and the artist in an encyclopedia, art history books, or online resources. Write your analysis in your sketchbook.

Check Your Understanding

1. What is linear perspective?
2. What medium used by Flemish artists revolutionized painting in the Renaissance?
3. Compare and contrast the historical styles in Figure 13.10 on page 359 and Figure 13.11 on page 360. Identify the general trends in art.
4. What style of painting is characterized by contrast and variety?
5. List the characteristics of Rococo art.

Vocabulary

Neoclassicism
Romanticism
Impressionism
Post-Impressionism

The Nineteenth Century

In the late eighteenth century, disruption in European society, including the French Revolution, caused artists to abandon the Rococo and Baroque styles, which mirrored the life of the aristocracy. In the nineteenth century, many artists wanted to create art that reflected the world they saw.

Neoclassicism

At the end of the eighteenth century, some European artists developed a new kind of art called **Neoclassicism** ("new classicism"), *an approach to art that borrowed subject matter and formal design qualities from the art of Greece and Rome*. Neoclassicism emphasized realism, minimized emotionalism, and featured epic or heroic events. The French artist Jacques-Louis David (**zjahk** loo-**ee** dah-**veed**) was the major artist working in this style. His work *The Death of Socrates* (**Figure 13.17**) depicts the last moments of the life of the great philosopher, who was tried for religious heresy and

▲ **Figure 13.17** This painting has a formal, dignified feeling to it. Even if you did not know the title, you would realize that the artist has depicted a serious and solemn occasion. What in the artwork tells you this? What do the different figures appear to be doing?

Jacques-Louis David. *The Death of Socrates.* 1787. Oil on canvas. 129.5 × 196.2 cm (51 × 77¼"). The Metropolitan Museum of Art, New York, New York. Catharine Lorillard Wolfe Collection, Wolfe Fund, 1931. (31.45)

sentenced to death. Although his friends and students appealed to the authorities to prevent the sentence from being carried out, Socrates willingly drank the cup of poison hemlock given to him.

Romanticism

At the dawn of the nineteenth century, the struggle to impose a new democratic political and social order continued. People grew anxious in response to ongoing political turmoil and uncertainty. Many did not want to be reminded of the events surrounding them, but instead wanted to be distracted. A new art style evolved as a reaction to contemporary events. **Romanticism,** as it was called, is *a style of art that found its subjects in the world of the dramatic and in cultures foreign to Europe. It emphasized rich color and high emotion.* Romantic artists disliked the cool colors, stiffness, and subdued emotion in Neoclassicism.

Eugéne Delacroix (oo-**zhen** del-uh-**kwah**) demonstrated a mastery for capturing action in foreign locales. **Figure 13.18** shows one of his famous works.

▲ **FIGURE 13.19** This painting is very different from traditional pictures of ships at sea. Describe the mood created by the swirling colors. What feeling do you experience when viewing this artwork?

Joseph M.W. Turner. *Snowstorm: Steamboat off a Harbours Mouth.* 1842. Oil on canvas. 92 × 122 cm (36¼ × 48″). Clore Collection, Tate Gallery, London, Great Britain.

Joseph M. W. Turner emerged as England's most dramatic Romantic painter. Turner expected his viewers to use their imaginations. For him, the depiction of light and atmosphere was the most important part of a painting. In **Figure 13.19,** he portrayed nature at its most violent. Instead of using precise detail, he suggests this violence by using loose brushwork to apply bright color and light values in swirling patterns.

Realism

One group of artists grew dissatisfied with both Neoclassicism and Romanticism. They felt that artists should portray political, social, and moral issues, but without glorifying the past or presenting romantic views of the present. Their art movement, called Realism, presented familiar scenes as they actually appeared. Édouard Manet (ay-doo-**ahr** mah-**nay**), an artist who participated in the Realist movement, discovered that the new style of art required new techniques. Therefore, he became more interested in *how* to paint rather than *what* to paint.

In *The Railway* **(Figure 13.20),** Manet painted a simple, common scene. A woman sits with a puppy in her lap. She is reading and has glanced up. A young girl faces away, watching the steam from a train. Manet avoided painting precise detail because he wanted to capture what a person would see with a

◀ **FIGURE 13.20** The artist uses line to unify this composition. Identify the different lines in the work and describe them. Do other elements or principles work to unify this painting? What are they?

Édouard Manet. *The Railway.* 1873. Oil on canvas. 93.3 × 111.5 cm (36³/₄ × 43⁷/₈″). National Gallery of Art, Washington D.C. © 1998 Board of Trustees. Gift of Horace Havemeyer in memory of his mother, Louisine W. Havemeyer.

▶ **FIGURE 13.21** This photo depicts a civil war battle. The photographer was a journalist who reported on the war. Do you think this photograph is art? Why or why not? On what criteria do you base your judgment?

Mathew Brady. *Civil War.* c. 1865. Photograph. National Archives, Washington, D.C.

quick glance. Rosa Bonheur, a very successful artist of the time, combined the drama of Romanticism with the accuracy of Realism (see Figure 8.3, page 201).

Photography

In the mid-nineteenth century, photography was invented as a method for recording people and events on film. It was exciting for artists interested in realism. Early versions of the photographic process were very expensive and time-consuming, but by the 1850s, several new methods were introduced that made the process easier and less expensive. Because of this, artists could record news events in the second half of the nineteenth century. A famous Civil War photographer, Mathew Brady, documented a battle that took place around 1865 **(Figure 13.21).** Photography introduced a new kind of realism to art.

▲ **Figure 13.22** Notice that the woman is not the focal point of the painting. Instead, she is depicted as simply a part of the whole garden.

Claude Monet. *Gladioli.* c. 1876. Oil on canvas. 60 × 80 cm (23⅝ × 31½″). Detroit Institute of Arts, Detroit, Michigan. City of Detroit Purchase.

Photographs were more realistic than drawings could be. They preserved a visual record of an event in a single moment in time with more detail and precision than a painter ever could. Photography influenced the development of painting for many years to come.

Impressionism

The Realists had taken a hard look at the real world. This interest in the world outside the studio influenced another group of artists who did much of their painting outdoors. Their style, which came to be known as **Impressionism,** *featured everyday subjects and emphasized the momentary effects of light on color.* Impressionist painters concentrated on the play of light over objects rather than on the shape of objects themselves. These artists broke up solid shapes and blurred the edges of objects by applying paint to the canvas in small dabs of pure color. When viewed from a distance, the dabs blend together visually. If you stand too close to an Impressionist painting, all you will see are colorful brushstrokes of paint. You have to step back to allow your eyes to perform the work of blending the colors.

One of the first artists working in the Impressionist style, Claude Monet (**klohd** moh-**nay**), painted many different series of landscapes, seascapes, and cityscapes that depicted the quality of light at various times of day, and in different seasons of the year (see Figures 6.24 and 6.25 on page 153). In **Figure 13.22,** Monet has achieved the effect of a hot summer day with brushstrokes that make the gladioli flowers appear to shimmer in the light.

Post-Impressionism

Eventually, some artists felt that Impressionism was not suited to the way they wished to depict the world. These artists began working in a variety of styles that came to be called **Post-Impressionism,** *a more individual approach to painting, unique to each artist working at this time.* The term for this period is Post-Impressionism because these works appeared after Impressionism. The word *post* means *after.* Some of the most outstanding Post-Impressionist artists were Paul Cézanne (say-**zahn**), Paul Gauguin (goh-**gan**) and Vincent van Gogh (van **goh**).

Paul Cézanne, who had originally painted in the Impressionist style, felt that the blurred shapes of Impressionism did not depict the solidity of the world. He wanted to create an art that emphasized form more than light. Cézanne did this by laying down interlocking blocks of color rather than dots and dabs of paint. He joined these patches of color together as if they were pieces of a puzzle. In this way, Cézanne strengthened the underlying structure in his compositions, giving the images a feeling of permanence and solidity. In **Figure 13.23,** the trees look almost as solid as the buildings, and the hills across the gulf look like geometric forms.

▲ **FIGURE 13.23** Cézanne was interested in the structure of objects. He used small brushstrokes like building blocks to make forms look like geometric solids. Notice how the trees look almost as solid as the buildings. How does Cézanne's technique affect the appearance of this scene?

Paul Cezanne. *The Gulf of Marseilles Seen from L'Estaque.* c. 1885. Oil on canvas. 73 × 100.3 cm (28³/₄ × 39¹/₂″). The Metropolitan Museum of Art, New York, New York. Bequest of Mrs. H. O. Havemeyer, 1929 (29.100.67).

Paul Gauguin turned to the use of color and shape to create daring, unconventional works depicting far-off lands and people. Giving up his job as a stockbroker, he traveled around the world to learn about art and experience different artistic traditions. He finally settled in Tahiti, where he produced most of his famous works. Notice the simple shapes and brilliant colors in **Figure 13.24.** Gauguin used arbitrary color in most of his paintings.

Vincent van Gogh, like the other Post-Impressionists, was initially dazzled by Impressionist works but later felt that Impressionism was limited in what it could express. Van Gogh was not interested in achieving visual accuracy.

▶ **FIGURE 13.24**
Notice how color is the dominant element in this painting. Shape and form are also important. How do these elements create a dreamy quality?

Paul Gauguin. *Faaturuma (Melancholic)*. 1891. Oil on canvas. 94 × 68.3 cm (37 × 26⁷/₈″). The Nelson-Atkins Museum of Art, Kansas City, Missouri. Purchase: Nelson Trust, 38-5.

▲ **Figure 13.25** Notice van Gogh's unusual use of color, texture, and line to depict rhythm and movement. He uses the elements to make the stars swirl and the trees dance as if all of nature was alive.

Vincent van Gogh. *The Starry Night.* 1889. Oil on canvas. 73.7 × 92.1 cm (29 × 36¹/₄″). The Museum of Modern Art, New York, New York. Acquired through the Lillie P. Bliss Bequest.

Instead, he explored ways to convey his feelings about a subject. To do so, he used expressive elements in his paintings such as twisting lines, rich colors, and complex textures.

Van Gogh's art was rejected and he only sold one painting during his lifetime. His brother supported him financially. Toward the end of his life, he painted *The Starry Night* (**Figure 13.25**). He executed it using quick brushstrokes to create the dark trees that resemble flames. The stars in the sky seem to be alive with movement. He expressed the violent energy and creative force of nature in this painting. Today, we regard this artwork as one of van Gogh's greatest because it reflects his passion and originality in creating an energetic and forceful image.

Activity Analyzing a Style

Selecting and Analyzing Exhibitions for Intents and Meanings. Find an exhibition of Impressionist art in your community or online. List at least four Impressionist works of art, each one painted by a different artist. Select one of the four works to analyze. What conclusions can you form about the meaning of the work and the artist's intent?

 Check Your Understanding

1. Describe Neoclassicism.
2. What was Realism a reaction to?
3. What was emphasized in Impressionist painting?

Early Twentieth Century

Vocabulary

Expressionism
Cubism
Surrealism
Regionalists

During the first half of the twentieth century, artists responded to rapid changes in technology, world politics, and culture by creating a variety of approaches to artistic expression. One style replaced another with bewildering speed. With the invention and spread of photography, artists no longer functioned as recorders of the visible world. They launched a quest to redefine the characteristics of art.

Trends in the arts changed rapidly because increased travel and new ways of communication helped artists to compare ideas. One individual or group could easily influence another. It no longer took years for one art movement or style of art to catch on in other areas. In fact, some artists who lived long lives, such as Henri Matisse and Pablo Picasso, changed their own styles several times during their careers.

European Art

In general, European artists assumed one of three different directions in artistic expression: self-expression, composition, or imagination. Each direction emphasized a different aspect of art.

In Germany, artists began working in a style later called **Expressionism,** *a style that emphasized the expression of innermost feelings.* The German Expressionists did not think the purpose of art was to make pretty pictures. Instead, because they experienced the terrible economic and social conditions in Germany before and after World War I, they wanted to express their feelings about these conditions. Their emotional subjects ranged from fear and anger to a preoccupation with death. Käthe Kollwitz (**kah**-teh **kohl**-vits), an Expressionist concerned with poverty and war, created many moving images of mothers grieving for dead children. She based her work on personal experience: she lost her eldest son during the first weeks of World War I **(Figure 13.26).**

In France, a group of artists created works that focused on the formal qualities. Some of these artists created **Cubism,** *a style that emphasizes structure and design.* Three main concepts influenced the Cubists.

▲ **FIGURE 13.26** Describe the person that you see here. Identify the elements of art that the artist used. How does Kollwitz view herself? Is this a person you would be interested in meeting? Why or why not?

Käthe Kollwitz. *Self-Portrait.* 1921. Etching. 21.6 × 26.7 cm (8½ × 10½"). National Museum of Women in the Arts, Washington, D.C. Museum Purchase: The Members' Acquisition Fund. © 2003 Artists Rights Society (ARS), New York/VG Bild-Kunst, Bonn.

The first concept was that shapes in nature are based on geometric forms. The second concept, based on a scientific discovery, showed that all matter is made up of atoms that are constantly in motion. The third concept, based on art from other cultures (African sculpture had recently been displayed in Paris), revealed that shape and form could be simplified and rearranged to increase the expressive qualities of an artwork. Pablo Picasso and Georges Braque pioneered the movement. In **Figure 13.27,** you can see how Picasso visually translated the human body into geometric shapes. He tried to paint three-dimensional objects as if they could be seen from many different points of view at the same time.

A third group of artists relied on fantasy to create art that expressed personal feelings. They explored the psychology of the mind as subject matter in their work. **Surrealism** emphasized *art in which dreams, fantasy, and the subconscious served as inspiration for artists.* Surrealists painted very realistic, almost photographic, images but combined objects that didn't belong together. The work of the Surrealists appears strange and dreamlike. Surrealist paintings can be funny or mysterious and frightening. **Figure 13.28** reflects the Surrealist belief in the power of dreams. René Magritte places the external environment, a cloudscape, within the eye.

▲ **FIGURE 13.27** Near the bottom of this work, Picasso places a musical staff and a treble clef near the song title *Ma Jolie*. This, along with the title, suggests the presence of a figure playing music.

Pablo Picasso. *"Ma Jolie" (Woman with a Zither or Guitar).* 1911–12. Oil on canvas. 100 × 65.4 cm (39³⁄₈ × 25³⁄₄″). Museum of Modern Art, New York, New York. © 2003 Estate of Pablo Picasso/Artists Rights Society (ARS), New York.

◀ **FIGURE 13.28** Magritte has combined the realistic depiction of a human eye with a surreal sky reflected in the eye's iris. Interpret the meaning of this work's title.

René Magritte. *The False Mirror.* 1928. Oil on canvas. 54 × 81 cm (21¹⁄₄ × 31⁷⁄₈″). Museum of Modern Art, New York, New York. © 2003 Herscovici, Brussels/Artists Rights Society (ARS), New York.

North American Art

In the United States in the beginning of the twentieth century, a group of young artists turned to the harsh realities of the city for subject matter. They called themselves The Eight and organized an exhibition in 1908. Their original name was soon forgotten when critics immediately labeled them the Ashcan School. Critics expressed displeasure at the subject matter of their work: stark tenement buildings, crowded city streets, poor working people, and ragged children.

Although this realism shocked unwary viewers, the Armory Show of 1913 exerted an even greater impact on the American art world. This show introduced Americans to the work of European artists. Most Americans felt confused by what they saw. The art on display did not fit into their traditional understanding of the nature and purpose of art. However, the show energized many American artists, who responded to the challenge posed by the daring exhibition and took their first steps toward making modern art in the United States.

Alexander Calder, a sculptor, ranks among these twentieth-century innovators. Most sculptors at this time worked with traditional materials and methods. A few experimented with the new materials of modern industry. Calder created a new form of sculpture by arranging wire and sheet metal into balanced arrangements that stayed in motion (Figure 8.20 on page 213). He called these moving sculptures mobiles (**moh**-beels).

As a reaction against the infusion of European styles into American art, some artists decided to focus on strictly American themes. Called **Regionalists,** these artists *painted the farmlands and cities of the United States in an optimistic way.* Each artist had a slightly different style, but all of them portrayed upbeat messages in their work. They focused on the vast expanse, beauty, productivity, and abundance of the United States and depicted happy, hardworking people. **Figure 13.29** is an example of Regionalism.

▶ **FIGURE 13.29** Benton modifies the backbreaking nature of the work by placing the workers in an idyllic setting. He created a flowing rhythm by repeating the gentle curves of the hills, trees, clouds, and bundles of wheat.

Thomas Hart Benton. *Cradling Wheat.* 1938. Oil on board. 78.7 × 96.5 cm (31 × 38″). The Saint Louis Art Museum, St. Louis, Missouri. © T. H. Benton and R. P. Benton Testamentary Trusts/Licensed by VAGA, New York, NY.

▶ **FIGURE 13.30** Wright designed the ramp from the main gallery to the upper level, using a gentle curve. The slope and curve allow the customer to look down on the objects on display. Notice how the wall and the upstairs gallery create harmony through repetition of flowing rhythms.

Frank Lloyd Wright. Xanadu Gallery, San Francisco, California. 1949.

In this painting, Thomas Hart Benton celebrates the work of farmers harvesting wheat. He portrays their labor in a dignified, graceful style.

Another American artist working at the same time showed a different side of the American experience. African-American artist Jacob Lawrence used bright, flat areas of color in a geometric style to create his art (see Figure 4.19 on page 80). His series paintings tell the stories of historical African-American figures, as well as describe the struggles of African-Americans moving from the South to the North in the early twentieth century.

The twentieth century also saw vast changes in architecture. New materials and technology and new demands for commercial space led to the development of skyscrapers. Architects designed functional structures with steel frames that emphasized simplicity of form to replace heavy, decorated structures. One famous modern architect, Frank Lloyd Wright, believed that form should follow function, meaning that the look of a building should be based on its use **(Figure 13.30)**. He also designed buildings that blended harmoniously with the landscape around them (Figure 11.20, page 301).

Like France in the late eighteenth century, Mexico at the beginning of the twentieth century experienced deep social and political unrest. The tension erupted into the Mexican Revolution. Some Mexican artists felt the need to develop new approaches to art that would express their feelings about the plight of the people. These Mexican artists were referred to as the Mexican muralists, because they covered walls and ceilings with murals about Mexican history, the suffering of the peasants, and the immoral behavior of the ruling class. Artists such as Diego Rivera (Figure 9.5, page 229) and David Alfaro Siqueiros (Figure 10.14, page 264) combined the solid forms of ancient, pre-Columbian Mexican art with the powerful colors and bold lines of Cubism and Expressionism.

 Check Your Understanding

1. Define *Expressionism*.
2. Name the three main influences on Cubism.
3. Compare and contrast the historical styles in Figure 13.28 on page 375 and Figure 13.29 on page 376 to identify the general themes of each style.

Art After 1945

Vocabulary

Abstract
 Expressionism
Minimalism
Super-Realism
Post-Modernism

After World War II ended in 1945, the European art world was in disarray. Paris was no longer the center of artistic creativity. The war displaced many people. A number of artists who had fled Nazi Germany settled in New York City. They began teaching there and by the 1950s, they and their students established a new center for the arts. New York City became the new capital of the art world.

In the years since World War II, artists have created many changes in artistic approaches, styles, and techniques. A variety of art forms once considered minor, such as printmaking, weaving, ceramics, and jewelry making, have come to be considered art forms equal to painting and sculpture. New digital media, such as graphics programs and digital cameras, have had a powerful impact on the world of art.

▲ **FIGURE 13.31** Hofmann, who was inspirational to the Abstract Expressionist style that grew in New York, is best known for his use of brilliant colors and textures. What does the artist appear to be expressing here? What is the mood or feeling of this work?

Hans Hofmann. *Flowering Swamp.* 1957. Oil on wood. 122 × 91.5 cm (48⅛ × 36⅛"). Hirshhorn Museum and Sculpture Garden, Smithsonian Institution, Washington, D.C. Gift of the Joseph H. Hirshhorn Foundation, 1966. © 2003 Estate of Hans Hofmann/Artists Rights Society (ARS), New York.

Abstract Expressionism

Abstract Expressionism, the first new style to arrive on the scene in New York in the years following World War II, *emphasized abstract elements of art rather than recognizable subject matter, and also stressed feelings and emotions.* Following in the tradition of German Expressionism, Abstract Expressionist artists believed that art should function as a spontaneous expression of emotion, and they did not necessarily rely on planned structure to organize the design of their paintings. Look at **Figure 13.31.** It is called *Flowering Swamp,* but you cannot see any realistically depicted flowers or swamps. If you use your imagination, however, you can see how the two rectangles seem to float over a background that suggests water and flowers.

Pop and Op Art

During the early 1960s, artists turned to the mass media, and especially to advertising, for subject matter. Pop art portrayed images of popular culture, such as soda bottles, soup cans, soap boxes, giant hamburgers, and comic strips, in a variety of art forms (Figure 1.18, page 20). Pop artists made people take a new look at everyday objects.

FIGURE 13.32 The comic book quality of this painting is captured in its strong black lines, limited use of color, and bold shapes. Lichtenstein calls what he does "quotation." What do you think he means by that?

Roy Lichtenstein. *Blam*. 1962. Oil on canvas. 172.7 × 203.2 cm. (68 × 80″). Yale University Art Gallery, New Haven, Connecticut. Gift of Richard Brown Baker, B. A. 1935.

They often used bright colors and cartoonish graphics to depict their subject matter. **Figure 13.32** is an example of Pop art. Artist Roy Lichtenstein (**lick**-ten-steyn) used a strong sense of design, a limited color scheme, and bold shapes to create a painting that was based on a comic strip.

Another style of art popular in this period took advantage of people's fascination with visual illusions. Op art, or optical art, uses scientific knowledge about vision to create optical illusions of movement. Op art relies on the special arrangement of the art elements such as the precise arrangement of lines, or the placement of complementary colors next to each other to create the illusion of movement. If you look at **Figure 13.33,** you will notice the unusual orange color of the background. The blue-green dots seem to be placed in no apparent order, but in fact the artist carefully planned their arrangement. If you look at the dots for a few moments, they appear to vibrate because the after-image causes a visual response that creates the illusion of movement.

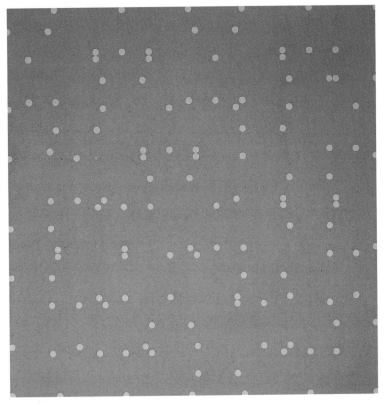

FIGURE 13.33 This piece of Op art is intended to cause a visual effect. Do you think the artwork has another purpose or meaning? Why or why not?

Larry Poons. *Orange Crush*. 1963. Acrylic on canvas. 203.2 × 203.2 cm (80 × 80″). Albright-Knox Art Gallery, Buffalo, New York. Gift of Seymour H. Knox, 1964. © Larry Poons/Licensed by VAGA, New York, NY.

Color-Field Painting

As artists experimented with a variety of new styles, they occasionally selected just one element of art to focus on in their work. An example, Color-Field painting, is art created using only flat fields of color. It is created without the precision of Op art and also without its interest in illusion. It is color for the pure sensation of color. Look at the example by Mark Rothko in **Figure 13.34.** His color areas have hazy edges that seem to float in space.

Minimalism

Some artists sought absolute simplicity in their art. This focus came to be known as **Minimalism,** or *art that uses a minimum of art elements.* Minimalists emphasized either color or shape as the dominant element in painting. In sculpture, they used the fewest possible geometric forms. They depicted art at its most austere, arranging only the simplest art elements. Minimalist painters who placed importance on the crisp, precise edges of the shapes in their paintings came to be known as Hard-edge painters. Frank Stella **(Figure 13.35),** used different canvas shapes for his works and created art on a large scale. He relied on thin white lines to set off colors, define shapes, and unify the work.

▲ **FIGURE 13.34** Rothko controlled the visual effect of his work by limiting the number of colors. Standing in front of this painting, which is over 7' tall, the viewer has an intense visual experience. Why do you think Rothko tried to evoke this kind of experience?

Mark Rothko. *Ochre and Red on Red.* 1954. Oil on canvas. 2.3 × 1.7 m (7'6″ × 5'9″). The Phillips Collection, Washington, D.C. © 1988 Kate Rothko Prizel and Christopher Rothko/Artists Rights Society (ARS), New York.

▶ **FIGURE 13.35** Notice the outlines of this painting. It is not a traditional rectangular shape. Observe how the red border ties the work together. How has Stella used repetition and contrast to further unify the painting?

Frank Stella. *Agbatana III.* 1968. Acrylic on canvas. 304.8 × 457.2 cm (120 × 180″). Allen Memorial Art Museum, Oberlin College, Oberlin, Ohio. Ruth C. Roush Fund and National Foundation for the Arts and Humanities Grant, 1968. © 2003 Frank Stella/Artists Rights Society (ARS), New York.

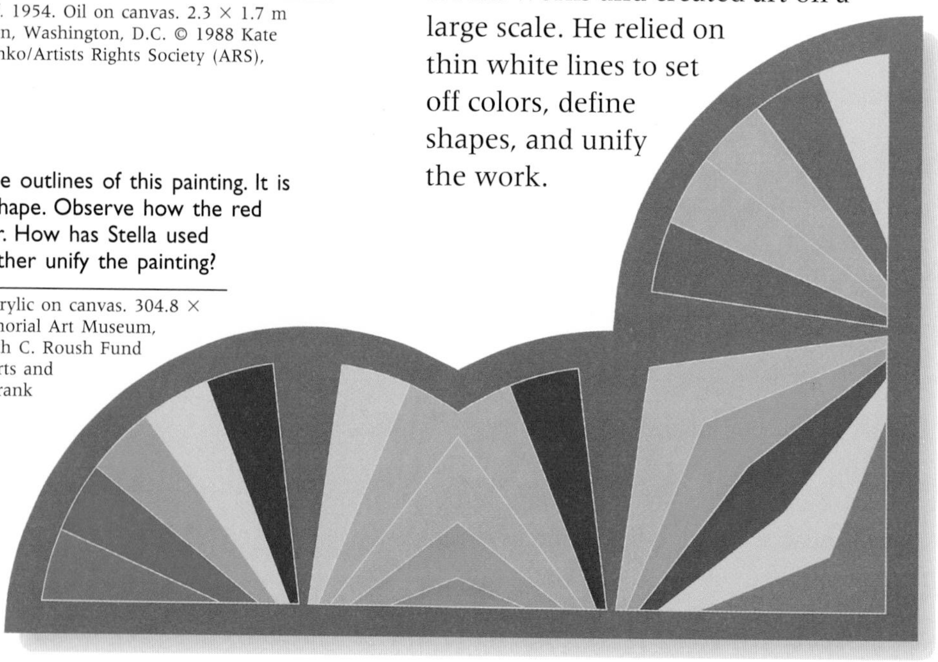

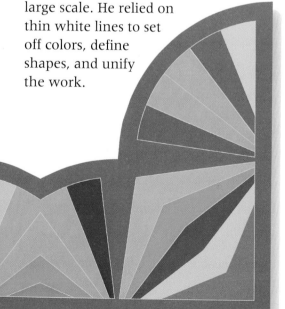

New Forms of Realism

Although modern American artists have created many abstract and non-objective artworks, Americans harbor a love for realism. Many American artists continue to portray subjects in a realistic style. This sculpture made by Duane Hanson (**Figure 13.36**) appears so life-like that it once fooled a gallery security guard. The guard thought that one of Hanson's motionless, seated figures looked ill and called for an ambulance. The painting in **Figure 13.37** looks so accurate in visual detail that a casual observer could easily mistake it for a photograph. This is how the style earned one of its names: Photo-Realism. It is also called Hyper-Realism and Super-Realism. **Super-Realism** is *art that depicts objects as precisely and accurately as they actually appear.*

Activity	Describing General Characteristics

Applying Your Skills. Look through this book to find five paintings from a variety of Western cultures. Select artworks created after 1950. For each, list the name of the artist, the title of the work, the style in which the work was painted, and other general characteristics.

Architecture

After World War II, architects developed the International Style of architecture, a plain, austere building style. Its origins could be traced back to the work of Frank Lloyd Wright and Louis Sullivan, who both designed buildings before

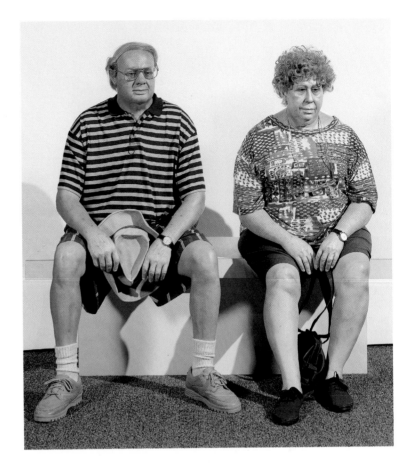

▲ **FIGURE 13.36** These figures are made of bronze painted to look lifelike. They are dressed in real clothes and accessories. If you walked up to them, do you think they would fool you? Why or why not?

Duane Hanson. *Old Couple on a Bench.* 1995. Bronze and mixed media with accessories. Life size. Collection of Palm Springs Desert Museum, Palm Springs, California. Purchased with funds provided by Muriel and Bernard Myerson. © Estate of Duane Hanson/ Licensed by VAGA, New York, NY.

▲ **FIGURE 13.37** This street scene seems almost like a photograph although it is a painting. How does the artist create this illusion? What is the purpose of painting such an illusion when one could simply take a photograph?

Richard Estes. *Paris Street Scene.* 1972. Oil on canvas. 101.6 × 152.4 cm (40 × 60″). Virginia Museum of Fine Arts, Richmond, Virginia. Gift of Sydney and Frances Lewis. © Richard Estes/Licensed by VAGA, New York, New York/Courtesy Marlborough Gallery, New York.

This simple design, called International Style, appealed to architects as a reaction to the highly ornate Art Deco style that was popular in the 1920s and 1930s. Can you easily identify the purpose of the building? What is its purpose?

Ludwig Mies van der Rohe and Philip Johnson. *Seagram Building.* New York, 1958. © 2003 Artists Rights Society (ARS), New York/VG Bild-Kunst, Bonn.

World War II. In their Seagram Building, the architects Ludwig Mies van der Rohe (ludd-**vig** meez van der **row**) and Philip Johnson created a simple geometric glass box that exemplifies van der Rohe's favorite saying, "Less is more" **(Figure 13.38).**

Architects of the 1960s looked to the future as well as to the past. **Figure 13.39** shows an apartment complex that looks futuristic in its design but actually echoes the Pueblo apartment complexes built by Native Americans hundreds of years ago. The interlocking apartment units are designed to give occupants a sense of openness and space. Because the units are not lined up next to each other as in traditional apartment complexes, each apartment has plenty of windows that allow sunlight to enter and give the illusion that each apartment is a separate house.

Post-Modern Art

We are currently in a period of art that is rapidly evolving. Some say we are at the end of the modern era. Others insist that we have already entered the postmodern era. The subject is being hotly debated in artistic circles, but the answer is something that only time can judge.

► **FIGURE 13.39** This apartment complex uses space efficiently. Do you find the complex attractive? Why or why not? What are some of the personal touches the residents have added?

Moshe Safdie. *Habitat.* Montreal, 1967.

The term post-modernism first appeared in reference to architecture. **Post-Modernism** is *an approach to art that incorporates traditional elements and techniques while retaining some characteristics of modern art styles or movements.* Post-Modern architecture was a reaction to the plain glass boxes of the International Style. It incorporates decorative elements from the past and takes advantage of the flexibility of new materials (See Figure 14.1 on page 388.)

The Rock-and-Roll Hall of Fame and Museum (Figure 14.16 on page 399), designed by I. M. Pei, is an example of architecture's break from the modern glass box. The museum contains a concert hall, a film and video display center, several sound chambers, and a party area as well as the usual glass display cases for showing off costumes, instruments, sheet music, and the personal belongings of famous musicians. The architect designed a building that reflects the freedom of rock-and-roll, but also functions as a museum to house its memorabilia.

Other Post-Modern artists are breaking traditional restrictions. Painters are creating three-dimensional paintings and sculptors are adding paint to their works. **Figure 13.40** is an example of a Post-Modern work with some identifiable subject matter. Is it a painted sculpture or a three-dimensional painting?

No one knows what will happen next in the art world. The acquisition of images from the past, and the incorporation of them into new works with new meanings, is only one facet of this new era. We have entered a time in art in which the diversity of ideas reflects the diversity of contemporary life.

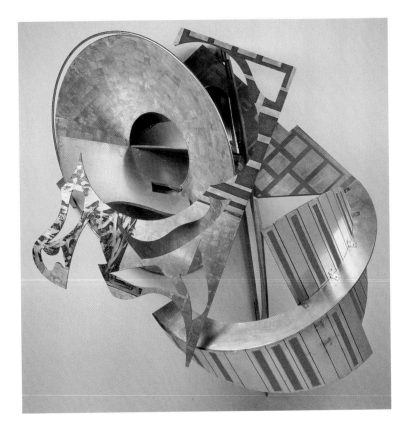

▲ **FIGURE 13.40** This sculpture represents several musical instruments. Can you identify what these instruments are? Notice how big the sculpture is. Why do you suppose the artist chose to make it so large?

Frank Stella. *St. Michael's Counterguard (Malta Series).* 1984. Mixed media on aluminum and fiberglass honeycomb. 396.2 × 342.9 × 274.3 cm (156 × 135 × 108″). Los Angeles County Museum of Art, Los Angeles, California. Gift of Anna Bing Arnold. © Frank Stella/Artists Rights Society (ARS), New York.

 *Check Your Understanding*

1. What is the subject matter of Pop Art?
2. How is Color-Field painting different from Op art?
3. Why is Super-Realism sometimes called Photo-Realism?
4. Describe Post-Modern architecture.
5. Compare and contrast the contemporary styles in Figure 13.32 on page 379 and Figure 13.37 on page 381 to identify general art trends.

Art Criticism
in Action

▲ **FIGURE 13.41**

Chuck Close. *Paul.* 1994. Oil on canvas. 259.1 × 213.4 cm (102 × 84″) Philadelphia Museum of Art, Philadelphia, Pennsylvania. Purchased with funds from the gift of Mr. and Mrs. Cummins Catherwood, the Edith H. Bell Fund, and others.

Critiquing the Artwork

▶ **1 DESCRIBE** *What do you see?*

Read the credit line for information about the artwork.

- What do you see when you look at this painting up close? When you look at it from a distance?

▶ **2 ANALYZE** *How is this work organized?*

This step deals with the composition of the work. This is a clue-collecting step about the elements of art.

- Which art elements do you think play the biggest role in the eye's ability to form a picture out of seemingly random shapes? Explain.

- Compare and contrast the artist's use of balance and harmony to unify this work. Describe his use of variety.

▶ **3 INTERPRET** *What message is this artwork communicating to you?*

Now you will combine the clues you have collected and your personal ideas to form a creative interpretation of the work.

- This work is 8½′ tall. How do you think it would feel to stand close to it?

- Give this work a new title that sums up your reactions to it.

▶ **4 JUDGE** *What do you think of the work?*

Now it is time to decide if this is a successful work of art.

- Do you think this is a successful work of art? Why or why not? Which aesthetic theory best supports your judgment?

MEET MAYA LIN

A sculptor and architect communicates tremendous emotion through her work.

LAYNE KENNEDY/CORBIS

Artists and architects often create memorials to honor the memory of important people or historic events. These works challenge visitors to reflect on the past and to think about the future. One such artist is Maya Lin, a sculptor, architect, and craftswoman. Every year, more than one million people are moved by the simple beauty of her most famous work: the National Vietnam Veterans Memorial in Washington, D.C. It is inscribed with the names of the American soldiers who died in the Vietnam War. Lin designed the memorial when she was a 21-year-old student at Yale University's School of Architecture.

Thousands more have been moved by another monument that Lin has created in Montgomery, Alabama. It honors people of all colors and religions who were killed fighting for civil rights in the 1950s and 1960s.

The monument is composed of a sheet of water running over a granite table. The slick table is inscribed with words from a speech by Martin Luther King Jr. As with Lin's Vietnam Memorial, it reminds visitors of past struggles. It also honors those who worked to make this world a better place.

Maya Lin

The Civil Rights Memorial is made of organic materials to create a soothing work of art. It honors those who have died in the fight for civil rights.

...UNTIL JUSTICE ROLLS DOWN LIKE WATERS
AND RIGHTEOUSNESS LIKE A MIGHTY STREAM

MARTIN LUTHER KING JR

TODD A. GIPSTEIN/CORBIS

TIME to Connect

Sculptors and architects connect with viewers by conveying common emotions. Writers do the same by conveying emotions with words.

• Write a personal essay about an emotional event in your life—a special celebration or an argument with a friend. What do you want to convey about that moment in time?

• Using powerful language, including descriptive adjectives and vivid verbs, re-create your emotions on paper. Start by prewriting (jotting down all your thoughts and feelings on paper), then write a first draft. Proofread your draft for style and use of proper grammar. You may wish to present your finished paper to the class.

Building Vocabulary

On a separate sheet of paper, write the term that best matches each definition given below.

1. A style of architecture in which churches soared upward, used pointed arches, and had stained-glass windows.

2. The period at the end of the Middle Ages when artists, writers, and philosophers were "re-awakened" to art forms and ideas from ancient Greece and Rome.

3. An art style that borrowed subject matter and formal design qualities from the art of Greece and Rome.

4. An art style that featured everyday subjects and emphasized the momentary effects of light on color.

5. An art style that emphasized the expression of innermost feelings.

6. A style of art in which dreams, fantasy, and the subconscious served as inspiration for artists.

7. Artists who painted the farmlands and cities of the United States in an optimistic way.

Reviewing Art Facts

Answer the following questions using complete sentences.

8. Why was the Middle Ages also called the *Age of Faith*?

9. What social changes was Mannerism a response to?

10. Identify the characteristics of Romanticism.

11. Name one similarity and one difference between the artworks created by the Realists and the Impressionists.

12. Describe the subject matter chosen by the Mexican Muralists.

13. Define Op art.

Thinking Critically About Art

14. **Explain.** In this chapter, you learned how political and social events can shape art movements. You also learned how advances in technology can influence art styles. What social and political events, along with technological advances, paved the way for the Renaissance movement?

15. **Historical/Cultural Heritages.** Compare the famous historical sculpture by Michelangelo in Figure 13.8 on page 357 to the contemporary sculpture by Allan Houser in Figure 11.18 on page 299. Identify the general theme of these works.

ART Online

Would you like to know more about the richness and variety of modern art? Explore the online exhibits of the collections at the world famous Museum of Modern Art in New York. Simply follow the **Web Museum Tour** link at **art.glencoe.com** to discover more about the diverse artists and philosophies of the twentieth century.

Linking to the Performing Arts

A R T
S O U
R C ▪
ARTSOURCE

Read about one of the most performed dance works created in the twentieth century. The classic "The Green Table", presented by choreographer Kurt Jooss, is featured on page 425 of the Performing Arts Handbook.

▲ **FIGURE 14.1** This interesting building was designed by Frank Gehry, a well-respected and prolific contemporary architect. Note the use of form in this structure. Gehry often designs buildings in a free-form sculptural style.

Frank O. Gehry. The Guggenheim Museum, Bilboa, Spain. 1997.

Careers in Art

In centuries past, artists learned their craft by apprenticing—assisting established artists. Many of the greatest painters and sculptors served apprenticeships. Today, you can develop art skills by taking courses in high school. After high school you can study art at community colleges, technical training programs, four-year colleges with art departments, or art colleges. The range of career possibilities for artists is greater than ever.

In this chapter, you will:

- Compare and contrast career opportunities in art.
- Identify skills and media used in careers involving art and design.
- Describe the difference between vocational and avocational opportunities in art.
- Identify your own areas of interest in the field of art.

Focus on **Art History** Canadian-born architect Frank O. Gehry (b. 1929) designed the unique structure in **Figure 14.1** in 1997. Gehry studied art and architecture at the University of Southern California and Harvard. He began his career designing conventional commercial structures. In the late 1970s, he began listening to an inner artistic voice. Drifting away from convention, Gehry started creating architectural designs that were part sculpture, part building. Some consider his creations functional sculpture.

***

Evaluate. Frank Gehry's architectural style has been described as "deconstructed" or "exploded." Evaluate Figure 14.1 in terms of those descriptions.

Careers in Two-Dimensional Art

Vocabulary

graphic designer
logos
illustrators
photojournalists
animators
storyboards

You are probably beginning to consider ideas about your future. If you have art abilities and you enjoy art, this chapter will introduce you to some exciting career possibilities. In addition to the major categories mentioned here, there are many careers within each field. Countless possibilities exist; so plan to explore art careers further. As you read, think about each career, and keep those that interest you in mind. You will be surprised at how your skills might fit many different art-related jobs.

Today, the business world needs art specialists in many areas. Trained artists design company reports, publications, and advertising. Company employees develop some of this design work. Other, more complex projects are assigned to outside designers or advertising firms with many different kinds of artists on staff. Plenty of opportunities are available for self-employed (or freelance) artists and salaried employees with art ability and training **(Figure 14.2)**.

Technology and Careers in Art

Computers have changed the way many people perform their work, including artists. Work done by hand in the past, including creating maps and charts, is now done with computers. Most art-related careers now require computer skills as well as artistic ability. Using computers, designers can create images that can be moved, changed, erased, duplicated, reduced, enlarged, colored, patterned, textured, animated, and otherwise manipulated. They scan images created using traditional methods (painting and drawing) and materials (including pencil, paint, and charcoal) into the computer. Designers work with devices such as stylus and graphics tablets. Software programs let the artist compare different variations of their work, changing size, color, and/or type style. There are also computer-aided design

▶ **FIGURE 14.2**
Artists who work for advertising agencies may be asked to design ads for display in magazines, on billboards, or even on the side of a bus.

► **Figure 14.3** Assistive technology helps artists with disabilities to meet their full potential in the visual arts.

programs to be used for other art tasks, such as planning and drafting a building or designing the interior of a room. Voice-recognition software and other types of *assistive technology* can help artists with physical disabilities design images **(Figure 14.3)**. With all these digital tools, designers can create any type of artwork needed.

Once the artwork is completed, computers can also be used to send images by disk or e-mail to customers all over the world. These capabilities also allow collaborations among artists over distances and allow designers to work with manufacturers by sending images electronically instead of shipping actual samples.

With the use of computers, jobs often cross over from one field to another. For example, look at the directional signs in an airport. They are an example of environmental graphics, combining space design, typography, and information delivery. In almost every area of art-related employment, artists use computers and other technology to aid them in their jobs.

Graphic Design

The early Christian monks who illustrated religious writings were also artists **(Figure 14.4)**. After the invention of the printing press in the fifteenth century, the craftspeople who arranged type and illustrations were what we now call graphic artists. They had to plan the layout, the way items are arranged on the page, before a page could be printed. It was slow work because it all had to be done by hand.

▲ **Figure 14.4** Manuscript illuminators were fine artists. After the introduction of the printing press, craftspeople learned to create and arrange type and illustrations.

Artist unknown. *Missal (The Calling of Saints Peter and Andrew)*. 1389–1404. Tempera colors, gold leaf, and gold paint on vellum in a medieval, blind-stamped binding. 33 x 24 cm (13 x 9⁷/₁₆"). The J. Paul Getty Museum, Los Angeles, California.

LESSON 1 *Careers in Two-Dimensional Art* | **391**

▶ **FIGURE 14.5** Graphic designers plan every detail of a book or magazine page, including the selection of the size and kind of typeface or font.

Graphic Designer

A **graphic designer** *translates ideas into images and arranges them in appealing and memorable ways*. Graphic designers use computers to *produce* the art but still rely on fundamental design principles to *create* it. Graphic designers use line, shape, form, space, color, value, and texture to communicate and to motivate **(Figure 14.5)**. Your first job as a graphic artist might include designing company letterheads, greeting cards, CD covers, or invitations.

Newspaper, magazine, and book publishers employ graphic designers. A designer, sometimes called a publication or production designer, created the look of this book. The designer carefully planned the size of the type, the font style **(Figure 14.6)**, the length of the lines, the layout of the text and artwork, and the length of the columns. The designer had to make sure the book was visually appealing while at the same time easy for students to use. Writers typed the manuscript into a computer, and the information was stored on a disk. An editor proofread the manuscript to ensure that the content was clear and concise. The manuscript was then given to the designer. Lastly, the printer followed the design plan provided by the book designer. Often, the book designer and printer work together very closely.

COMMENCEMENT CEREMONY

Commencement Ceremony

Commencement Ceremony

Commencement Ceremony

Commencement Ceremony

▲ **FIGURE 14.6** Which of these fonts would you choose for your high school graduation announcement?

Activity	Practicing Logo Design

Demonstrating Effective Use of Art Media in Design. Design a logo for your school, your favorite club, or your community. Pick an object or image that can serve as the basis for your design, such as the school mascot or a letter (or letters) in the name of the school, club, or community. Use the school or organization colors, if possible. Use colored pencils or markers to draw your design by hand. Also, create a digital version on the computer. Begin with either a simple geometric shape or a font that creates an interesting logo.

Advertising Designer

Graphic artists also design promotional material for companies. They may be employed by outdoor advertising agencies to create billboards or by traditional advertising agencies to work on ad campaigns. When graphic artists apply their skills to promotional work, they are called advertising designers. Advertising designers create **logos,** or *symbols or trademarks that are immediately recognizable.*

Advertising agencies employ teams of artists who work under the supervision of an art director. They often collaborate with copywriters and managers—all of whom may have different ideas and visions; so teamwork and communication skills are essential **(Figure 14.7)**.

Illustration

Many businesses hire **illustrators** to *create the visual images that complement written words.* Illustrations, or visual images that clarify or decorate a text, can be found in magazines, books, television, film, and online. Illustrations are used for advertising, editorial, informational, and educational purposes.

Commercial Illustrator

In addition to the type and the artwork you see in this book, there are drawings by commercial illustrators. Most illustrators specialize in one area—such as fashion, medical, or technical illustration—while a few work in several areas **(Figure 14.8)**. They might work with an author to create drawings for a children's book. Some illustrators work for one company while others prefer to freelance. Freelance artists are self-employed and do many different jobs for many different companies.

▲ **FIGURE** 14.8 A technical illustrator specializes in drawing diagrams and product illustrations.

Cartoonist

Cartoonists produce distinctive, entertaining drawings meant to provoke thought and laughter **(Figure 14.9)**. They submit their work for publication in magazines and newspapers. They may choose to draw single cartoons or comic strips. They usually try to make a humorous point about human nature. Editorial cartoonists, who are interested in politics and current events, present complex ideas in simple, humorous drawings. Editorial cartoonists try to make people think about current issues. They may also try to influence public opinion.

Cartoonists also create comic books and other publications. Several famous cartoonists have created comic books that deal with serious issues such as war and disease. They try to illuminate social problems for people to be aware of and understand. Some cartoonists work in animation, creating moving cartoons such as those that entertain children (and adults) on Saturday mornings.

▲ **FIGURE 14.9** Although much cartooning is now done using digital media, artists still use traditional methods as well.

Photography, Film, and Multimedia

Artists and designers interested in photography, film/video, and multimedia can find employment in many fields including publishing, advertising, and entertainment. Hard work, persistence, talent, and some special training are necessary for all these fields.

Photographer

Photographers work in studios and on location to provide photographs for books, magazines, and other resources. Fashion, product, and food photography, architectural photography, and fine art photography are all growing specialties **(Figure 14.10)**. Photographers also work for advertising agencies and corporations to create visual images that help sell a product. Some photographers sell their photographs to stock photography houses (also called image banks), which sell them to the public.

Digital cameras, which allow artists to record images digitally, are becoming more and more important in the field. Digital cameras do not require special processing labs. The pictures can be viewed and printed immediately or stored and manipulated using computer software.

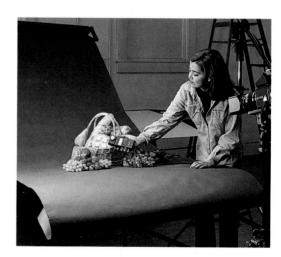

▲ **FIGURE 14.10** Photographers are skilled artists who use their cameras to create artwork.

Film and Video

Photographers also work in film and video. Moving picture photography for movies and television, or cinematography, is one behind-the-scenes career many photographers find appealing **(Figure 14.11)**. Although these fields are not always easy to break into, plenty of aspiring artists eventually achieve success in them. Videographers make documentaries, create visual presentations for corporations and other institutions, and record special events or celebrations such as weddings and anniversaries.

Photojournalist

Photojournalists are *visual reporters*. They work for newspapers and magazines and tell stories through their photographs. Photojournalists must understand design, know how to develop and print their own work, and have an eye for what is interesting to look at. Photojournalists often travel to where the news is happening.

Animator

Animators, or *artists who create moving cartoons,* use their skills in movies, television, and for the Internet. The field of animation is growing faster than any other art career area.

When artists create an animated film, they first select a story. They decide what styles of architecture and dress fit the story. Then they develop the story by drawing **storyboards**, *a series of still drawings that show the story's progress.* They draw approximately 60 sketches for each board **(Figure 14.12)**. A short film needs three storyboards, and a full-length film may require more than 25. Storyboards look like comic strips. They provide the outline for the development of the film.

Layout artists are responsible for the overall look of the animation. Background artists paint the settings from the layout artist's sketches. To create

◀ **FIGURE 14.11**
Cinematographers operate movie cameras. They are trained in using light, color, and composition.

action, animators draw the major poses of each character, then *in-betweeners* fill in the many drawings required to complete each movement. Each second of film requires 24 drawings to make the movement look smooth. As you can imagine, creating the more than 125,000 drawings required for a 90-minute movie is a very expensive and time-consuming process. Your career in animation may begin as a background artist, character designer, or in-betweener.

◀ **FIGURE 14.12**
Animators use magazines and books as visual references when making sketches for storyboards.

Today, many animation production companies use computers to fill in many of the images necessary to create the illusion of movement. An artist creates the main drawings and the important actions and scans these drawings into the computer. Then using mathematical models, the computer determines how to make the drawings appear to move. The artist uses the computer to manipulate the images. This is a much less expensive and less time-consuming process than creating all the images by hand.

Special Effects Designer

Special effects designers plan the stunts and illusions in movies in order to make them look real. Training for this field may require attending a college with an art department offering specialized technology courses.

Special effects artists require the skills of a painter, sculptor, and engineer. These artists have the ability to imagine and create fantasy scenes or imaginary creatures that look real **(Figure 14.13)**. They can make you believe you are watching a dinosaur driving a car or a battle scene in outer space. Special effects artists need to know how to draw realistically and usually use computers to create believable settings and action.

Multimedia Designer

Multimedia designers combine text, graphics, sound, and interactive devices into visually appealing presentations. These presentations are used by companies to acquire clients. Multimedia designers also create interactive CD-ROMs and software for business, education, and entertainment. This requires a team approach. One person is usually responsible for the overall concept while others create the images and text and still others put all the parts together.

Activity	Critiquing Animation

Applying Your Skills. Watch several animated programs on television. Notice the differences in quality. Then list the programs you have watched in order from best to worst. How did the backgrounds compare? Describe the quality of the movement. Did the programs with the best movement have the best backgrounds?

▲ **FIGURE 14.13** Digital effects help us believe movie characters are in faraway places.

Web Designers

As the Internet continues to grow and expand as a center for information and commerce, businesses need to attract visitors to their Web sites. Web artists design the individual Web pages that make up the Web site, which may include text; photos; three-dimensional, or moving graphics; sound; and interactive devices. The Web artist must make the page visually appealing but easy to use. Because it can take a long time for the viewer's computer to process images, the Web artist must balance beauty with function. If it takes too long to get information, a viewer will leave the page. A confusing or poorly laid out Web page will cause Internet users to look elsewhere.

Web artists also make Web movies and organize Internet broadcasts of current affairs or events of special interest that broadcast television networks do not cover.

Computer, Arcade, and Video Game Designers

Game designers plan and create all aspects of computer, arcade, and video game design (**Figure 14.14**). They create the background renderings and the animated figures and objects. They work with computer programmers to design visually appealing and exciting games. Because the game experience is a multimedia experience, the designer must have a special sensitivity to sound, story, and other aspects of game production. This field grows each year as the game industry expands.

Computer game designers also create virtual reality or three-dimensional worlds that gamers, or game players, enjoy experiencing. As these technologies have become more sophisticated, companies and even branches of the military have begun using computer-aided simulators when training.

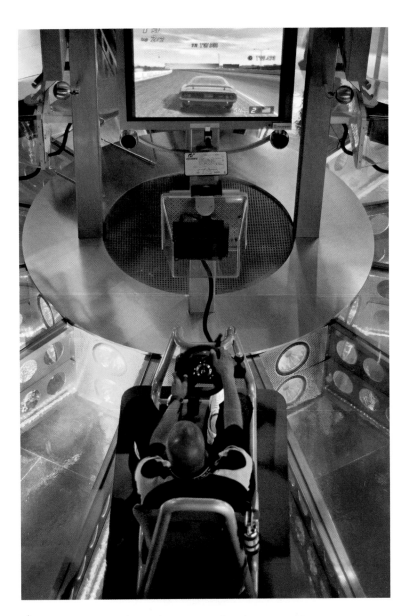

▲ **Figure 14.14** Game designers need to keep up with advances in digital and mechanical technology to make their games more exciting and realistic.

 Check Your Understanding

1. What does a graphic designer do?
2. Compare and contrast the art careers of graphic design and photography.
3. What two elements must Web designers balance?

Careers in Three-Dimensional Art and Education

Vocabulary

architect
interior designer
package designer
museum curators

Designing three-dimensional spaces, or environments, is called environmental design. The first environmental designers were prehistoric cave dwellers who eventually moved out of their caves and into the countryside. They learned to build huts for protection and, thus, became the first architects. Today, there are many kinds of designers who plan environmental spaces. Their careers involve making homes, workspaces, and the surrounding landscape attractive and functional.

Architecture

An **architect** must *design buildings that are well constructed, aesthetically pleasing, and functional.* To function properly, a building must do what it was designed to do. Private houses and apartments must serve as comfortable homes for people. Office buildings, schools, and factories must also be comfortable, safe, efficient, and pleasant to look at. The aesthetic effect of a building is extremely important. The structure must fit into its environment and enhance or complement the community. Because modern construction technology is so complex, architects usually specialize in particular types of buildings, such as skyscrapers, shopping malls, or homes **(Figure 14.15)**.

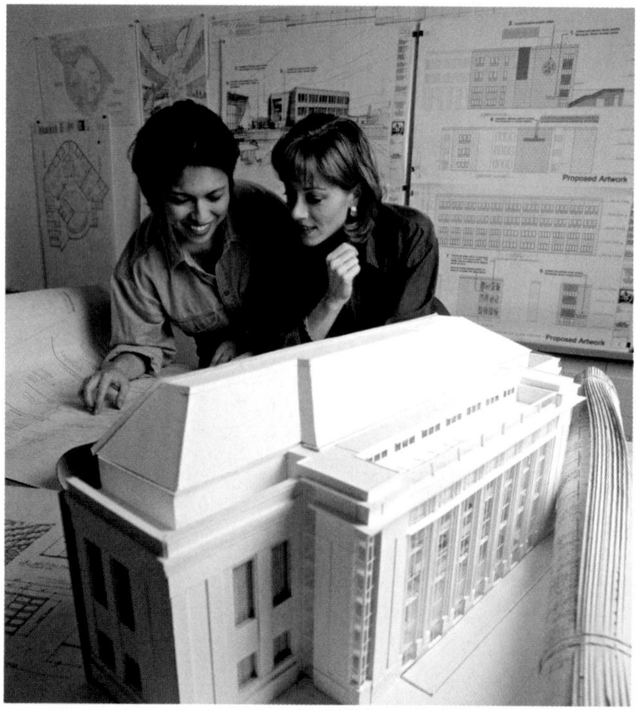

▲ **FIGURE 14.15** Architects must be able to show their client models and full color renderings of a building before it is actually built.

Architects must be knowledgeable about building materials, ventilation, heating and cooling systems, plumbing, stairways, and elevators. They must know basic engineering concepts so that they do not plan structures that are impossible to build. In addition, architects must be creative, be able to make accurate mechanical drawings using a computer, have a strong background in mathematics and drafting, and be able to communicate with clients. Many architects are certified by the American Institute of Architects, or A.I.A. Entry-level jobs in architecture often include drafting and model-making.

Chinese-American, (b. 1917)

If you have ever visited the Rock-and-Roll Hall of Fame in Cleveland, Ohio, or seen a picture of the pyramid entrance to the Louvre in Paris, you will be familiar with the work of the famous architect I.M Pei. Pei was born in Guangzhou (Canton), China, on April 26, 1917. When he was 18, he immigrated to the United States, where he studied architecture at the Massachusetts Institute of Technology and Harvard University. After World War II, he taught at Harvard for several years.

In 1956, he started his own firm, I. M. Pei & Partners. Soon, he and his company were in great demand, not just in the United States but all over the world. Pei has designed some of the largest constructions of the twentieth century.

Pei is known for approaching design problems with an innovative flair. Many of the buildings he is asked to design must meet multiple functions, such as the Rock-and-Roll Hall of Fame **(Figure 14.16)**. This structure reflects the spirit of rock and roll while housing memorabilia, sound chambers, a concert hall, a film-and-video display center, an event room, and numerous other features.

▲ **FIGURE 14.16** This building must hold an extensive collection of artifacts while expressing the spirit of rock-and-roll. Do you think it serves its purpose?

I. M. Pei. *Rock-and-Roll Hall of Fame and Museum,* Cleveland, Ohio. 1995.

Urban Planning

Urban planners are professionals concerned with the care and improvement of city environments. Every major American city has an urban planner (sometimes called a city planner). This person helps control the growth and development of a city. Some of the responsibilities of the urban planner are land use; urban renewal; and the development of harbors, city parks, and shopping malls. A good urban planner meets the needs of the community while keeping it attractive and appealing.

▲ **FIGURE 14.17** Landscape architects consider texture as an element of their designs.

Landscape Architecture

Landscape architects design playgrounds, parks, and outdoor areas around buildings and along highways. They work closely with architects and urban planners to use and improve the natural setting so that it is easy to maintain and beautiful to look at. They create designs using flowers, plants, trees, shrubs, rivers, ponds, lakes, walks, benches, and signs, as shown in **Figure 14.17**. Landscape architects work with architectural firms, government agencies, individual homeowners, and facilities such as golf courses.

▲ **FIGURE 14.18** Interior designers show their clients color swatches and other design samples.

Interior Design

An **interior designer** *plans the design and decoration of the interior spaces in homes and offices.* Successful designers use styles and materials that blend with the architecture and that please the client. They must understand decorating styles and materials. They must be able to look at an empty room and visualize the finished area. They must know the latest trends and developments in wall coverings, carpets, furniture, appliances, and lighting **(Figure 14.18)**.

Because interior designers spend as much time with clients as they do at the drawing board or computer, they must have patience and good communication skills. Some designers work for individual homeowners while others plan and coordinate the interiors of department stores, offices, and hotels.

Exhibit and Display Design

Exhibit designers plan presentations of collections, temporary exhibits, and traveling shows of all types. They work for trade shows, department stores, showrooms, art galleries, and museums. They decide how objects should be arranged and lit.

Display designers, also called visual merchandisers, arrange merchandise to attract customers and persuade them to buy products or services. A display designer is an important member of a

Activity	**Using Design for Display**

Creating Designs for Practical Applications. Create a bulletin board display promoting an upcoming event at school. Work with the coordinators of the event to determine the important information about the event and an appropriate color scheme.

sales team. Display designers coordinate storewide color schemes, design banners, and even create shopping bags.

Industrial Design

Industrial design is the planning of the products of industry **(Figure 14.19)**. All objects—such as tools, home appliances, furniture, toys, and automobiles—must be carefully designed. These artists work closely with engineers who develop the products. Sometimes, industrial designers are asked to work on things as simple as tamper-proof caps for medicines. At other times, they are asked to work on projects as complicated as space vehicles. Industrial designers plan products based on three requirements. First, it must do

▲ **FIGURE 14.19** Industrial designers create new versions of household appliances.

the job for which it was designed. Second, it must look like it can do the job. Third, it must be visually pleasing.

Product Designer

Product designers usually specialize in one industry or product such as machinery, furniture, medical equipment, toys, or cars. Designers work in teams. For instance, planning a new automobile requires many different types of designers.

Special designers plan the outer form or body of the car. Then textile designers and plastic specialists create new interiors to go with the body. They must be certain that human needs are met, such as comfort and ease of movement. Designers must make sure that controls are within reach of the driver, without the dashboard becoming crowded or confusing. Computers help ensure that all the parts fit together correctly. This way, potential problems are identified before the vehicle goes into production.

The concept car for the redesigned Volkswagen Beetle **(Figure 14.20)** was developed by J Mays, who studied automotive design at Art Center College of Design in California. This design received the Harvard Design School annual Excellence in Design Award. Artists and engineers worked together to determine that the curves in the design help make this small car safer. Safety features include energy absorbing crush zones, pretensioning front safety belts, front and rear headrests, daytime running lights, dual airbags, and front seat-mounted side airbags. Each of these features was designed by a team who considered both the aesthetics and function of the feature and how they fit into the car as a whole. The Beetle was also designed to be an affordable passenger and commuting car. The next time you get into a car, look at the number of features that need to be accessible to the driver.

▲ **FIGURE 14.20** The curved body structure of this car is aerodynamic and provides additional headroom for all passengers.

Using computer programs, designers can translate their line drawings into three-dimensional pictures, or *renderings*. Computers are also used now to produce physical models from drawings. This enables product designers to meet the requirements of industrial design more quickly and efficiently.

Package Designer

A **package designer** *produces the containers that attract consumers.* They make boxes, tubes, bottles, shopping bags, and other kinds of containers. They use shape, color, and graphics to make packages unique and appealing. Package designers must consider package function. For example, when pill bottles first came on the market, the caps were so easy to remove that children were able to open them. Designers had to invent a cap that was childproof but could be opened by an adult. It requires imagination and ingenuity to combine the visual, functional, and safety criteria needed to design for consumers.

Fashion Designer

Fashion designers plan and create clothing, hats, handbags, shoes, and jewelry **(Figure 14.21)**. They must know the appropriate materials to use for the articles being designed. They must also consider comfort and the way the human body moves when creating fashion designs. High-fashion designers create very expensive, one-of-a-kind originals. Fashion designers also work for manufacturers who make affordable, mass-produced clothes. Pattern makers, cutters, tailors, technical designers, and factory workers complete the team. Graduates from college-level fashion design programs enter the industry as assistant designers or fashion illustrators.

Art Director

In film, television, and theater, an art director works with set, costume, and lighting directors, as well as makeup artists and hairstylists, to bring the visual elements of the show together **(Figure 14.22)**. Art directors should know art history as well as the special techniques of their craft. If a film or play is set in the past, the setting, furniture, costumes, and hairstyles must correctly reflect that time period.

◀ **FIGURE 14.21** Fashion designers work year round to create new looks. Anyone considering a career in this area must be comfortable working creatively under tight deadlines.

A set or stage designer is an artist who is responsible for planning the backdrops and many of the props for a production. He or she oversees a team of artists who prepare the stage or set for the production. The set designer works with the prop master, who supplies everything the actors use during the production. The costume designer helps tell the story, creating clothing that is appropriate to the time and setting of the production **(Figure 14.23)**. For productions that travel, the work of the art director and set designer may include how to design sets that can be taken apart, moved, and rebuilt. They may consult with engineers and architects and work with property designers and location planners. Art directors and set designers often begin their careers as production assistants.

▲ **FIGURE 14.23** Can you tell the historical period for which these costumes were designed?

Art Education

Some art-related careers combine an interest in art with an interest in education. Teachers, art therapists, and museum curators and designers all use their training in different ways. Artistically inclined people who want to help others may find careers in education rewarding and fulfilling.

Art Teacher

Art teachers share their artistic knowledge and skills with students. They work in elementary, middle, or high schools as well as colleges. Art teachers help students learn to make aesthetic judgments and to develop their artistic skills and talents. Some teachers specialize in art history and help students learn about art. Many art teachers spend time outside the classroom in their own studios. Teaching art in public schools requires a college degree, advanced training, and often a teaching certificate.

Art Therapist

Art therapists use art to help people with emotional and physical problems. They help physically challenged children and adults learn to explore the senses of vision and touch through artistic play and creation. An art therapist might help someone with limited use of their hands learn to mold and model clay, using special adaptive equipment. He or she might help a child with sensory problems learn what different textures feel like and how to tolerate them.

Art therapists also help patients with mental and emotional problems change their behavior in a positive way. They show them how to express themselves in a constructive way through art **(Figure 14.24)**.

Art therapists may have physical therapy or psychological training and usually work with professionals in these fields. They work in medical and psychiatric hospitals, community centers, physical rehabilitation programs, drug and alcohol treatment centers, schools, and prisons.

Museum Curator and Designer

Museums house collections of paintings, sculpture, crafts, costumes, books, jewelry, and artifacts. **Museum curators,** who are usually trained in art history, *oversee the operations of museums.* They organize the collections and are responsible for recommending artwork that fits in with the theme or focus of the museum **(Figure 14.25)**. Museum designers assemble and display these museum collections. Some museums publish books that contain photographs of the objects in their collections, which requires the help of the curator and designers.

▲ **FIGURE 14.24** Art therapists help children explore their emotions through creative expression.

▲ **FIGURE 14.25** Museum curators guide students through museum exhibitions.

Fine Artists

Some artists choose to work independently as painters, sculptors, printmakers, weavers, or jewelers **(Figure 14.26)**. Such artists create art on their own terms or are paid (commissioned) to create a certain piece of art. Some artists find public or private grants to fund their work. Many fine artists need a second job to help pay their living expenses. Some fine artists work in commercial art fields to supplement their income. Many teach in schools and colleges. Some, like Jacob Lawrence (Figure 4.19 on page 80), continue teaching even after they have become financially successful because they feel that the ongoing interaction with art students enhances their creative thinking.

Thinking About an Art or Design Career

Are you suited for a career in the art world? It may be too soon for you to make a final decision about your future. However, art can be pursued and enjoyed throughout your life as either a career or as an avocational interest. *Avocational* means not related to a job or career. Studying or creating art as a hobby can provide many rewards. Learning about art in school or at museums enriches your life. Making art projects, such as paintings or pottery, can be fun and relaxing.

If you decide you want a career in art, you should begin working toward that goal while in high school. Practice your skills. Study the great artists. Experiment with art-related computer programs. Talk with your art teacher or guidance counselor for advice. Some colleges offer summer programs for high school students. Research the different options you can pursue after high school. Look for schools that offer a specific area you are interested in, such as fine art, industrial design, or fashion design.

◀ **FIGURE 14.26**
The work of artists is usually classified as either fine art or applied art. Fine art, such as painting, is created to be viewed and appreciated. Applied art, such as ceramics or other craft objects, is created to be used.

Activity Art in Your Life

Comparing Career and Avocational Opportunities in Art. From the visual art fields listed in this book, choose one that interests you. Art can be pursued as an avocation, or hobby, and as a career. Research the art field to compare and contrast ways to pursue it as an interest and as a career. Which one is best for you?

 Check Your Understanding

1. Compare and contrast the art careers of architecture and landscape architecture.
2. What three requirements must a product of industrial design meet?
3. What type of artist or designer plans presentations of collections?
4. What do art therapists do?

Art Criticism
in Action

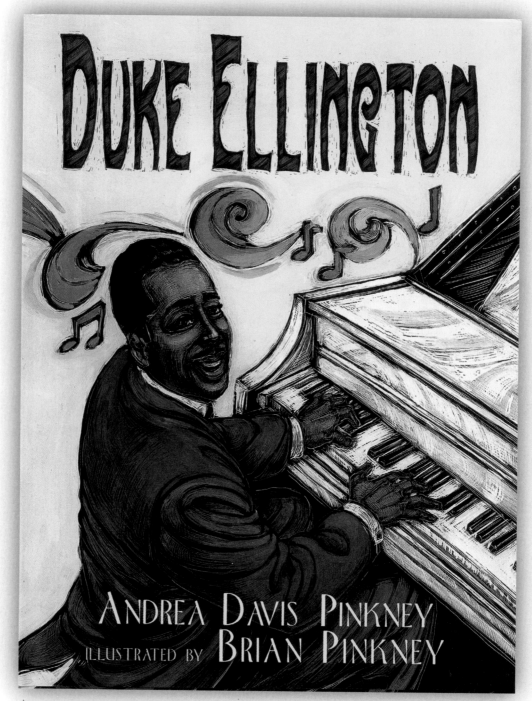

▲ **FIGURE 14.27**

Brian Pinkney. Book cover for *Duke Ellington: The Piano Prince and His Orchestra* by Andrea Davis Pinkney. Hyperion Books for Children. 1998.

Critiquing the Artwork

▶ **1** **DESCRIBE** *What do you see?*

Read the credit line for information about the artwork.

● Describe the subject matter of this work.

● Judging from the words in this artwork, what function would you guess the work was meant to serve? Explain your answer.

▶ **2** **ANALYZE** *How is this work organized?*

This step addresses the formal qualities. You will gather information about how the principles of art are used to organize the elements of art.

● Compare and contrast the types of lines used in this work.

● Where has the artist used rhythm and pattern?

● How has he achieved unity in this work?

▶ **3** **INTERPRET** *What does this artwork communicate to you?*

Combine the clues you collected to form a creative interpretation of the work.

● How do you think the color scheme affects the appeal of this work?

● What do the green swirls floating out of the piano tell you about Duke Ellington's music?

● What mood is suggested by the colors of this work? How do you think the artist feels toward his subject? Explain your reaction.

▶ **4** **JUDGE** *What do you think of the work?*

Now, you are ready to make an aesthetic judgment of the work.

● Do you think this is a successful book cover design? Why or why not? Use one or more of the aesthetic theories to defend your decision.

Meet the **ARTIST**

Brian Pinkney
(b. 1961)

Prior to beginning his career as a commercial artist, Brian Pinkney taught art. His favorite medium is scratchboard. Pinkney begins by covering a white board in black ink. He then scratches or scrapes off the areas that are to appear white. He finally colors these areas with dyes, gouache, and/or oil paints. Jerry Pinkney, Brian's father, is a celebrated children's book illustrator. Brian's mother is a children's book writer as is his wife, Andrea Davis Pinkney. Brian has illustrated some of her books, including the tribute to Duke Ellington featured in Figure 14.27.

Designing Artist

Designer Karim Rashid has made a career of making ordinary objects look extraordinary.

Karim Rashid in his studio.

ROBERT CLARK/TIME PICTURE COLLECTION

Karim Rashid wants people to pay more attention to the way everyday objects are designed. Rashid is an award-winning industrial designer. What he enjoys best about his work is making everyday objects look special—from manhole covers on city streets to garbage bins, chairs, and plastic pens.

Rashid has developed a unique style. He creates objects that have energy and humor. For example, Rashid's glassware looks like a forest floor, with mushroom bowls and vases shaped like lilies.

Rashid wants his creations to have more than one use. "Every new object should replace three," he says. His packaging for a perfume is a plastic envelope that can be used as a purse. His children's chair doubles as a toy chest.

His most popular products are made of plastic. Nearly 2 million North Americans throw rubbish into the plastic trash receptacles he designed. More than 750,000 people sit in his inexpensive Oh chairs. The chairs got that name because "Oh" is what people supposedly say when they relax in one.

Thanks to Rashid's talent, people just may be starting to pay more attention to the design of everyday objects—especially his!

TIME to Connect

Karim Rashid analyzed his skills and his passions and chose a career in industrial design. Think about what interests you and what careers match those interests.

- Think critically about yourself. On a sheet of paper, list your talents, your strengths, and the activities you enjoy.

- Then write a one-page persuasive letter in business format to a prospective employer. Present yourself, your skills, and your career objective or goals. Proofread your work. Exchange letters with a classmate and critique each other's work.

KARIM RASHID, INC (2)

This chair and chess set are two of Rashid's popular designs.

Building Vocabulary

On a separate sheet of paper, write the term that best matches the definition given below.

1. An artist who creates and arranges images in an appealing and memorable way.
2. Symbols or trademarks that are immediately recognizable.
3. One who creates visual images that complement written words.
4. Photographers who are visual reporters.
5. Creator of moving cartoons.
6. A series of still drawings that show a story's progress.
7. Designer of buildings which are well constructed, aesthetically pleasing, and functional.
8. One who plans the design and decoration of the interior spaces in homes and offices.
9. Designer who plans and produces attractive containers.
10. One who oversees the operations of museums.

Reviewing Art Facts

Answer the following questions using complete sentences.

11. Why is technology important in art-related fields?
12. When did the field of graphic design begin? What invention made it possible?
13. For what purposes are illustrations used?
14. What training do special effects designers need?
15. What does an urban planner do?
16. What three requirements must industrial designers plan for?
17. What elements of art do package designers use to make every package unique and appealing?

Thinking Critically About Art

18. **Analyze.** Find a copy of a book you enjoyed reading, preferably one that has an interesting cover design. Look at the design, and think about how it relates to the content of the book. Then write a few paragraphs describing the cover design, the meaning of any symbolism the designer used, and your opinion of whether the cover illustrates the story appropriately. Don't forget to justify your opinion by providing examples.

19. **Historical/Cultural Heritage.** Review the Meet the Artist feature on page 399. Then examine architect I. M. Pei's Rock-and-Roll Hall of Fame in Figure 14.16. Compare and contrast the contemporary style of Figure 14.16 with Figure 14.1 by Frank Gehry. What general trends in architecture do these two buildings exhibit?

There are many areas of specialization for illustrators and other art careers. Medical illustration is just one. Visit **art.glencoe.com** to compare and contrast the many specialized areas of visual art careers.

Linking to the Performing Arts

Explore the art of a storyboard artist. Use the Performing Arts Handbook on page 426 to discover the work of animator John Ramirez.

Handbooks

"If we study Japanese art, we see a man who is undoubtedly wise, philosophic, and intelligent, who spends his time doing what? In studying the distance between the earth and the moon? No— he studies a single blade of grass."

—*Vincent van Gogh (1853–1890)*

Quick Write

Drawing Inferences. Carefully examine the quote above by Post-Impressionist painter Vincent van Gogh. Based on this quote, what can you infer about Van Gogh's feelings toward Japanese art? Explain your reaction in a sentence or two.

◀

Suzuki Kiitsu. *Reeds and Cranes* (one of a pair of screens). Edo period (nineteenth century). Color on gilded silk. 1.76 × 3.89 m (5′ 9¹/₂″ × 12′ 9¹/₄″). Detroit Institute of the Arts, Detroit, Michigan. Founders Society Purchase with other funds.

$\mathbf{T}$he following pages were excerpted from *Artsource®: The Center's Study Guide to the Performing Arts,* developed by the Music Center Education Division, an award-winning arts education program of the Music Center of Los Angeles County.

The following artists and groups are featured in the *ARTTALK Performing Arts Handbook.*

Table of Contents

Theatre	Faustwork Mask Theater	**413**
Dance	Martha Graham	**414**
Dance	Merce Cunningham Dance Company	**415**
Dance/Music	Ballet Folklorico de Mexico	**416**
Dance	Lewitzky Dance Company	**417**
Theatre	Joanna Featherstone	**418**
Music	Paul Winter	**419**
Dance/Music	African American Dance Ensemble	**420**
Theatre	Eth-Noh-Tec	**421**
Music	Eugene Friesen	**422**
Music	Vocalworks	**423**
Music/Dance	Korean Classical Music and Dance Company	**424**
Dance/Theatre	Kurt Jooss	**425**
Music	John Ramirez	**426**

Faustwork Mask Theater

Faustwork Mask Theater. "The Mask Man." Robert Faust, artistic director. Photo: Craig Schwartz, © 1993.

Robert Faust is an actor, athlete, dancer, choreographer, mask-maker, and the artistic director of his company, Faustwork Mask Theater. Born and raised in New Orleans, he experienced the color and pageantry of the Mardi Gras celebration throughout his youth and college years. Through his studies he came to realize that the carnival characters that annually paraded the streets of his hometown were actually works of art rooted in theatrical traditions. His one-man show, "The Mask Man," provides insights into the artistic, psychological, and historical aspects of masks. In his performance, Faust transforms himself into more than 20 different characters. Some characters speak, wearing *commedia dell'arte* style half-masks. Other characters are created with full masks worn on top of the head or on the back of the head. These masks can transform the performer into creatures on all fours or create distortions that baffle or surprise. Masks, found in many cultures throughout the world, are worn at festivals, celebrations, and rituals. In whatever ways they are used, masks have the power to transform an ordinary person into someone or something else.

■ Discussion Questions

1. The photo on this page shows Robert Faust with masks from "The Mask Man." Study the expression of the masks. What kinds of personalities are being shown? What can you tell about the character's age, culture, and personality traits from the mask alone?

2. The first Greek masks were used in plays to impersonate gods. What Greek gods and goddesses can you name? What were their attributes or symbols?

■ Creative Expression Activities

LANGUAGE ARTS. Read Greek myths such as "Theseus and the Minotaur" or "The Golden Fleece." How might masks be used in these works?

ART. Create a two-sided mask showing contrasting feelings on each side. You might choose happy and sad or good and evil. Think of movements to go with your mask to express each emotion.

"Lamentation," 1930. Choreography and costume by Martha Graham. Performed by Janet Eilber. Photo: © Max Waldman. Max Waldman Archives.

PERFORMING ARTS HANDBOOK

Martha Graham

"No matter what you say, you reveal yourself. Movement does not lie." These words, spoken to Martha Graham by her father when she was just a young girl, would hold great meaning for her later in life. Renowned for her contributions to the art of modern dance, Graham established a new way of communicating through the use of the body. Graham redefined the modern dance form by using movement to express emotion. She developed a vocabulary of movements to describe emotion in physical rather than verbal language. Exploring emotional moves that come from the center of the body, she based her movement system on the "contraction" or folding in of the torso that happens when you sob or laugh, and the "release" that happens when you inhale and unfold. "Lamentation" was created by Graham to represent the essence of grief and became her signature solo piece. Graham continued creating dances until her death, at the age of 96.

◼ Discussion Questions

1. What is body language? How might body language be exaggerated and developed into a dance form?

2. Graham said that the movement of the torso called a contraction comes from where you laugh or cry. Think of other emotions that a person might feel. How are these emotions expressed by the body?

3. How do you think the costume in the picture could help in depicting movements that are the essence of grief or sorrow?

◼ Creative Expression Activities

SCIENCE. Many of the movements in Graham's technique are based on contraction and release. The action that triggers or generates the contraction and release of muscles is breathing. Taking in the breath was a "release," pressing it out was a "contraction." Research the muscles involved in breathing and explore the action of your own breathing, trying to match it to the Graham idea of contraction and release.

Merce Cunningham Dance Company

Members of the **Merce Cunningham Dance Company** in *CRWDSPCR* (Crowdspacer). Photo: Lois Greenfield.

Merce Cunningham recounts four events that have led to important discoveries in his work: 1) his initial collaboration with composer John Cage in the late 1940s, when they began to separate the music and the dance; 2) his use of chance operations in his choreography; 3) his use of video and film as a medium to choreograph works specifically for the camera; 4) and his use of dance computer software in the 1990s. With the computer tool known as the Sequence Editor, one can create movements, store them in memory, and eventually create a movement sequence. It is possible to vary the timing so that you can see the body change from one shape to another in slow motion. Even if the computer produces positions and transitions that are not possible for humans to perform, it opens up new possibilities to explore. The film *CRWDSPCR* (Crowdspacer) documents the choreographic process in which Cunningham and the dancers experiment and adapt the movement sequences derived from the computer.

■ Discussion Questions

1. Study the dancers' positions in the photograph. Discuss similarities or differences from partnering or "lifts" that you have seen in ballet, ice skating, or gymnastics.

2. Look at the group of dancers in the photograph. Can you visually pinpoint a "center of balance" within the group? Is it in the exact center of the group or not? Explain why or why not.

3. Describe how the costumes affect your impression of the dancers and the dance shown in this photograph.

■ Creative Expression Activities

TECHNOLOGY. Learn more about Merce Cunningham's ongoing creative work and the activities of the Merce Cunningham Dance Company on the Internet. Research the company's touring schedules to countries and cities around the world.

SOCIAL STUDIES. Select one particular visual or performing artist from the 1950s and 1960s and find out what events during that period might have influenced their work.

DANCE/MUSIC

ARTSOURCE

Ballet Folklorico de Mexico

Ballet Folklorico de Mexico, "Danza de la Reata." Amalia Hernández, artistic director. Courtesy of Ballet Folklorico de Mexico.

Amalia Hernández, director of Ballet Folklorico de Mexico, decided at the age of eight to make dance her life's work. Her parents made her dream possible, and her training and experiences inspired her artistic vision. For over 30 years she has researched the roots of Mexican folklore and traditions. Her intention has been to create a contemporary show based on Mexican themes, and to convey the heart and spirit of the Mexican people. From the time of the Olmec Indians to the birth of modern Mexico, more than thirty distinct cultures have influenced Mexican culture. The Spanish brought horses to Mexico and introduced the caballero, or rancher, lifestyle. The dance shown in this photo is called "Danza de la Reata" and celebrates the beauty and harmony of life on the ranchero, or Mexican ranch.

■ Discussion Questions

1. Look closely at the photo of the male and female dancers inside the lariat, or lasso. Describe the costumes and what you think the dance is about.

2. What do you know about Mexican culture and dance? Can you think of any other styles of Mexican dance? Describe the costumes and movements.

3. What dances, songs, or paintings can you think of that refer to the work of a group of people, or to a specific culture?

■ Creative Expression Activities

LANGUAGE ARTS. Look at the photo on this page and use your imagination to write a description about what is taking place. Describe the relationship between the two people and the types of movements that would be done.

SOCIAL STUDIES. The Spanish brought horses and the Catholic religion to the indigenous people of Mexico and taught them a new way of life. The word "Mestizo" is used to refer to the unique blend of European and native cultures and races that make up the majority of the Mexican people of today. Research what other European cultures influenced the people of Mexico.

Lewitzky Dance Company

Lewitzky Dance Company. Bella Lewitzky, director. "Impressions #1 (Henry Moore)." Featured dancers: Jennifer Handel, Nancy Lanier, Laurie McWilliams, Theodora Fredericks, Deborah Collodel, Claudia Schneiderman. Photo: Vic Luke.

Bella Lewitzky has been a modern dance performer, choreographer, and dance educator for over 60 years. During her career, Bella realized that sculpture and other works of art could be used as a source of inspiration for dance movements. In particular, she focused on the work of sculptor Henry Moore. Since it was impossible to bring his sculptures into her studio, she and her dancers worked from photos found in books. They observed that his sculptures have massive physical weight and bulk and they also have two or three balance points, or places where the sculpture touches the ground. There are also holes, or negative spaces, that encourage the viewer to look through the sculptures, which alters the perspective. These observations and movement explorations evolved into a dance work called "Impressions #1 (Henry Moore)."

■ Discussion Questions

1. Look at the photo of the dancers on this page. Use the elements of line, shape, form, and texture to describe what you see.

2. Can you think of other artists who were inspired by an existing work of art and used it as a point of departure for a new work?

3. Use art books to locate a sculpture by Henry Moore. Observe it in terms of size, negative and positive space, form, and the number of balance points. Discuss how these concepts might be communicated through movement.

■ Creative Expression Activities

THEATRE/MOVEMENT. Working with partners, sketch out a few human *sculptures* of your own. Join with other pairs of students and position yourselves in relationship to each other to make more complex forms. Present your forms to the class.

DANCE. Dancers use the movements of their bodies to express action as it relates to weight, flow, space, and time. Explore ways to show the following eight actions using dance movements: press, flick, punch, float, slash, glide, wring, and dab.

SCIENCE. Select an object and answer the following questions: Is it light or heavy? How does it move or balance? How many points are touching the ground? What is the object's shape? Observe it from different perspectives (for example, upside down, and so on).

Joanna Featherstone

Joanna Featherstone. Photo: Craig Schwartz, © 1998.

Theatre artist and storyteller Joanna Featherstone has been "dancing with words" for as long as she can remember. A shy child who taught herself to read by studying cereal boxes, Featherstone read and memorized everything she could get her hands on, including boxes of baking soda, the Bible, and shopping catalogs. She discovered poetry at the age of 10 through a church reading of *Creation,* a work written by African American poet James Weldon Johnson (1871–1938). Featherstone memorized that poem too, although it wasn't until she was in college that she learned that it was the work of a writer of color, a man respected for his work in collecting and preserving much of the early poetry written by African Americans. An accomplished actress, Featherstone has performed on Broadway and off-Broadway stages, as well as for audiences in Europe and in West Africa. She has worked with award-winning string quartets, dancers, jazz musicians, and the New York Philharmonic. However, the performances in which she recites the work of early African American poets such as James Weldon Johnson, Paul Laurence Dunbar (1872–1906), and Phillis Wheatley (1753–1784) are where Featherstone finds her "dance of words" to be most fulfilling and complete.

■ Discussion Questions

1. Do you think it is possible for a solo storyteller or performer to move an audience by just using words? What other "tools" do they need to make an audience feel an emotion?

2. Featherstone taught herself to read by using cereal boxes. How did you learn to read? Have you ever helped someone else improve his or her reading skills? How many times each day do you use your reading skills?

■ Creative Expression Activities

LANGUAGE ARTS. Poetry is normal, everyday speech that has been "heightened" through the use of rhyming words, rhythmic patterns, and strong images. Think of a poem or song lyric that you know well and admire; write it down. Now translate it into normal speech, replacing or moving all rhyming words, changing rhythmic patterns, and turning the word images into less descriptive phrases. How does this "deconstruction" change the impact of the message the original writer tried to convey? Does the altered speech still contain a strong emotional impact?

Paul Winter

Paul Winter. Photo courtesy of Paul Winter.

The music of Paul Winter includes the voices of animals from all around the world, including whales, wolves, elk, buffalo, eagles, tigers, and elephants. Paul listens to their songs, cries, and howls and adds melodies from his saxophone. In 1968, he heard the songs of the humpback whales, which strongly influenced his music and life. The humpback songs appear on some of his albums, which he considers a highlight in his musical career. The sounds of nature and animals help Paul create what he calls, "living music." Paul has recorded his music in the Grand Canyon, Yellowstone, and Glacier National Parks, and has visited the homes of many creatures throughout the world. These experiences are the foundation of his respect and concern for all living things. Paul views our planet as one big community and has received numerous awards in recognition of his musical efforts for endangered species and the environment, including two Grammy Awards. Paul lives in Connecticut and continues to pursue his love of music, nature, and community.

■ Discussion Questions

1. What is your favorite animal? What does this animal have in common with you?

2. What ecological or environmental issues are important to you, and how can they be reflected in your daily life?

■ Creative Expression Activities

SOCIAL STUDIES. Describe as many communities as you can—cultural, social, intellectual, spiritual, artistic, etc. Which communities are you a part of now or would like to be a part of in the future? How does nature and the environment fit within your definition of community?

LANGUAGE ARTS. Imagine human history with a greater understanding of nature and the environment. How would human progress be changed? What kinds of societies would be created and how would they coexist with nature? How would world relations be affected? Would we have a need for technology?

DANCE/MUSIC

African American Dance Ensemble

African American Dance Ensemble. Chuck Davis, founder and artistic director. *African Roots in American Soil.*

Chuck Davis, a towering African American dancer and choreographer, came from a background that was poor financially but rich in love. His first dance break came when he substituted for an injured member of the Richardson Dancers in Washington, D.C. In 1959, he joined the Klara Harrington Dancers and studied and performed with a number of modern, jazz, Afro-Cuban, and African dance companies. With disdain for the way black people were being portrayed in the media, he set out to present the truth about black culture through dance. "I have gone to Africa and I have sat at the feet of elders and I have listened as their words poured like raindrops onto and into my being. I have danced on the dusty earth and the sound of my feet pounding against the earth brought the rhythms of life into my blood," states Davis. After two decades of building his company in New York, he returned to North Carolina to start a second company, the African American Dance Ensemble, which he currently directs. Through dance, he works energetically to bring *all* people his message of "peace, love, and respect for everybody."

■ Discussion Questions

1. Look carefully at the photo on this page and describe the mood, costumes, and actions you observe. What clues do these give you about the style of dance and what is being communicated?

2. What popular dance styles do you think have their roots in traditional African cultural dances?

■ Creative Expression Activities

LANGUAGE ARTS. In many African ethnic groups, it is believed that wise people deliver proverbs. Read the following proverbs, then think of English equivalents: "Rain beats a leopard's skin, but it does not wash out the spots" (Asante); "When spider webs unite, they can tie up a lion" (Ethiopia); "Cross the river in a crowd and the crocodile won't eat you" (Kenya).

Eth-Noh-Tec

Eth-Noh-Tec. Robert Kikuchi-Yngojo and Nancy Wang, artistic co-directors. Photo: Allen Nomura.

Eth-Noh-Tec, an Asian American Company based in San Francisco, uses a synthesis of music, movement, and words to present their unique style of theatre and storytelling. Their work is characterized by rhythmic dialogue, tightly choreographed poses, comic facial expressions, extensive hand gestures, and body postures with low centers of gravity. The Eth-Noh-Tec performance style reflects ancient Asian theatre styles such as Chinese opera (highly moral stories about the lives of common people) and Japanese Kyogen (comic plays written in everyday language). Company founders Robert Kikuchi-Yngojo and Nancy Wang present stories drawn from centuries-old Asian legends and modern-day experiences of Asian-Americans. The musical sounds of *ditze* (Chinese flute) and *taiko* (Japanese drums) add excitement, color, and punctuation to their performance. The mission of Eth-Noh-Tec is to create a fusion of cultures with a weaving (tec) together of distinctive cultural elements (eth) to create new possibilities (noh).

■ Discussion Questions

1. Look at the photo and discuss the stylized posture, costumes, and facial expressions of these performers. How does this differ from other plays, dances, or films you have seen?

2. One of the stories presented by Eth-Noh-Tec, *The Long Haired Girl,* is about the heroic acts of a young woman who brings water to her village. This ancient story is still being lived out today. Describe some examples of courageous acts done by people who wanted to help others.

■ Creative Expression Activities

HISTORY/SOCIAL STUDIES. There are universal values shared by all cultures in the world. Values such as the importance of family and friendship, respect for bravery, helping others, protecting our homes, and sharing our experiences (storytelling) are common to most cultures. Make a list of other shared values that you think exist in many of our world's cultures.

PERFORMING ARTS HANDBOOK

Eugene Friesen

Eugene Friesen. "Cello Man." Photo: Craig Schwartz, © 1998.

Eugene Friesen has created a unique voice among the cellists of the world. Drawing on a childhood filled with the great masterworks of Western music as well as the influences of hymn, ethnic, and popular music, Eugene uses cello and voice to create new music that is accessible and personal. At age eight Eugene began playing the cello, pulling it in a little red wagon to school for orchestra practice. In high school and college, Eugene played in school and community orchestras and began experimenting in rock and blues styles on an amplified cello. A graduate of the Yale School of Music, Eugene takes the cello out of its traditional classical realm, propelling it forward as an exciting instrument with immense powers of free expression. "Cello Man," featured in the photo, is a solo performance created in collaboration with Faustwork Mask Theater. In the show, Eugene weaves a spellbinding fabric with stories, songs, masks, and inventive techniques on cello and electric cello. The repertoire for "Cello Man" features Friesen's original music in a variety of styles: blues, contemporary, folk, electronic, and pop, and includes a duet with the recorded song of a humpback whale. The use of masks designed and created by director Robert Faust adds a dramatic element to the performance. During segments of the show, Eugene transforms himself with masks and costumes, integrating each character with the music he is playing.

■ Discussion Questions

1. Look at the photo and identify the animal depicted by the mask Eugene is wearing. Can you imagine the characteristics of the music Eugene might play based upon that animal?

2. Do you know how a cello is played? Can you describe the sound a cello makes?

3. Can you name any other instruments in the string family?

■ Creative Expression Activities

LANGUAGE ARTS. Write a story that has a musical instrument as a main character. The instrument's character may be personified, employing human traits and emotions, or it may appear as a key element in the story's plot. Think about the materials used in making the instrument you have selected to write about. Your story could begin with the tree from which a cello was made or the gourd from which a shaker was fashioned.

Vocalworks

Vocalworks. Bruce Cooper, Michael Geiger, Debbie and Tim Reeder, and Dave Eastly perform "Vocalworks Radio Hour." Photo: Richard Hines, © 1998.

Since 1983, Bruce Cooper, Michael Geiger, Debbie and Tim Reeder, and Dave Eastly of Vocalworks have brought the music of the 1930s and 1940s to audiences throughout the United States and abroad. Singing the music of the swing era, they are proud to note that Vocalworks has lasted longer than the swing era itself. In the "Vocalworks Radio Hour," the group re-creates a live radio broadcast from the period when home entertainment meant gathering around the radio in the living room to hear news, music, drama, or comedy programs. The Depression and World War II were very difficult times for the American people. They were concerned about their future and what would become of their country. Swing music was a wonderful escape that allowed people to lift their spirits and forget their troubles for awhile. Vocalworks shows the importance of music in that role and how it can still function in the same way today.

■ Discussion Questions

1. Improvisation is one of the characteristics of swing jazz. Look at the photo on this page. Identify the instruments. Which one is improvised?

2. Swing music was characterized by its positive message during the Depression in the 1930s and during World War II in the 1940s. Swing dance and music has had a resurgence today. How do you account for its renewed popularity?

■ Creative Expression Activities

LANGUAGE ARTS. Read about the Harlem Renaissance and its influence on jazz musicians and poets. Working in groups, present a choral verse reading of one of the following Langston Hughes poems to show how he was influenced by jazz: "The Weary Blues," "The Negro Speaks of Rivers," or "Afro-American Fragment."

SOCIAL STUDIES. Each of three groups will research one of the following periods: 1930–1935, 1936–1940, 1941–1945. Use the group period as a title and divide the paper into three sections: World, United States, and Swing Music. Group members should fill in the significant dates, people, and events during that time period.

MUSIC/DANCE

Korean Classical Music and Dance Company

Korean Classical Music and Dance Company. Dong Suk Kim, artistic director. Photo: © Craig Schwartz.

Much of Korean folk music can be traced back more than 2,000 years. These rich traditions were passed down from person to person, rather than taught formally, and have remained a part of everyday village life. A childhood interest in Korean folk music developed into a rewarding career for Dong Suk Kim, director of the Korean Classical Music and Dance Company. At the age of 12 he began to study the music and dance of his birthplace, Korea. His studies eventually led him to a membership in a Korean government-sponsored troupe, which performed the music and dances of their country on a world tour. As part of the tour, Mr. Kim visited the United States and decided to make it his new home, eventually settling in southern California. In 1973, he founded a school for the study of Korean music and dance. The Korean Classical Music and Dance Company repertoire includes folk as well as ancient formal court music and dance.

■ Discussion Questions

1. Look at the photo on this page and describe the details of the costumes the dancers are wearing. How might the costumes enhance the performance?

2. What other cultures can you think of that preserve their history, traditions, and dances by passing the knowledge from one generation to the next?

■ Creative Expression Activities

DANCE. Do some research on a traditional Korean folk dance and an ancient Korean formal court dance. Describe how these two styles of dance are similar or different from one another.

SOCIAL STUDIES. Both China and Japan have dominated Korea throughout its history. Do some research to find out how either China or Japan has contributed to Korean culture and traditions.

Kurt Jooss

The Joffrey Ballet of Chicago performing "The Green Table," Kurt Jooss choreographer. Photo: © Herbert Migdoll, 1998.

The curtain rises on a rectangular green table with ten gentlemen in morning coats and spats. They posture and disagree until pistols emerge, a shot is fired, and war is declared. The scene goes black. Next we see the figure of Death. In the scenes that follow, soldiers are called to fight, battles rage, refugees comfort one another, a profit-maker preys on the miseries of his fellow man, and a lone soldier holds watch. Through every scene, Death stalks the stage, claiming victim after victim, warrior and citizen alike. In the end the scene returns to the table, where the Gentlemen in Black start it up all over again.

"The Green Table," created by choreographer Kurt Jooss in 1932, is a compassionate and humanistic dance drama about the horrors of war. The mysterious figure of Death is a constant companion, simultaneously strong and sensitive, sinister and soothing. Ultimately he comes to each character, slipping into their lives and claiming them. Some victims he takes swiftly and surely, others slowly and gently. Some resist, some welcome him. Through the movement vocabulary, we see each character meeting Death in their own way, just as we all will. Productions of "The Green Table" are given by dance companies almost every year all over the world, making it probably the most performed of all dance works created in the twentieth century.

■ Discussion Questions

1. What do you think a dance theatre or dance drama is? How might it be different from dance pieces you have seen before?

2. Why do you think the gentlemen at the table wear masks?

3. Ballet or dance is, for the most part, made familiar to audiences through the world of myths, fairies, and mechanical dolls. Should dance pieces confront disturbing issues? Can they do so successfully?

■ Creative Expression Activities

LANGUAGE ARTS. There is a theory that dance cannot compete with the complexity offered by the spoken word. Can dance works take on complex intellectual arguments? Discuss these ideas using "The Green Table" as an example. Write a play, a narrative, or a poem based on the characters in "The Green Table." Read or perform it. Compare it with the ballet/dance work you are familiar with.

MUSIC

ARTSOURCE

John Ramirez

John Ramirez, "Every Picture Tells a Story." Photo: © Craig Schwartz, 1998.

Animator John Ramirez likes to mix art with music. Working with professional musicians such as Paul Tracey, he draws storyboards that bring music and words to life. Ramirez has worked as a storyboard artist for both Walt Disney Feature Animation and Warner Brothers Feature Animation. He loved to draw when he was growing up, especially trains, and felt very proud when his mother would make copies of his work. Eventually, he began to create his own comic strips—a form of storyboarding—and later his own animated films. For every animation project a team of highly creative people come together. The process might begin with the storyboard artist listening to the selected music many times, working with the images that come to mind, and then developing them into a rough storyboard sequence. Ramirez then explains the story line and describes the characters to the other members of the creative team. The storyboard artist then goes back to the drawing board and incorporates the new ideas. This process is repeated over and over until the work is refined. Only then does the animation process begin, usually taking about two years to complete a feature film.

■ Discussion Questions

1. Describe in your own words the basic process required in the making of an animated film.

2. Technology has had a great impact on animated films by enabling animators to produce very complex moving images, such as those seen in *Toy Story,* or *Finding Nemo*. What else can you think of that has been enhanced by technology? How has technology affected communication, work, and personal relationships?

3. What about animated films do you find the most intriguing? Why?

■ Creative Expression Activities

LANGUAGE ARTS/ART. Think of a specific topic, such as airplanes, cars, animals or people. Look in magazines to identify all the photos you can find that relate to this theme. Create a simple storyboard, then write a simple storyline which describes or sells an idea or product.

ART. Take a pad of unlined paper or make one by stapling 25 to 50 pages together to make a flip book. Choose a simple idea like a bouncing ball or a flower growing. Create a series of pictures in the right hand bottom corner that will show action when you flip through the pages.

Table of Contents

Drawing Tips

1	Making Contour Drawings	428
2	Making Gesture Drawings	428
3	Drawing Calligraphic Lines with a Brush	428
4	Using Shading Techniques	429
5	Using Sighting Techniques	429
6	Using a Viewing Frame	430
7	Using a Ruler	430
8	Making a Grid for Enlarging	431
9	Measuring Rectangles	431

Painting Tips

10	Mixing Paint to Change the Value of Color	431
11	Making Natural Earth Pigment Paints	432
12	Working with Watercolors	432
13	Cleaning a Paint Brush	432

Printmaking Tip

14	Making a Stamp Print	433

Sculpting Tips

15	Working with Clay	433
16	Joining Clay	433
17	Making a Pinch Pot	434
18	Using the Coil Technique	434
19	Papier-Mâché	434
20	Making a Paper Sculpture	435

Other Tips

21	Making Paper	435
22	Basic Embroidery Stitches	436
23	Weaving Techniques	437
24	Making a Coiled Basket	439
25	Making a Tissue Paper Collage	440

Display Tips

26	Making a Mat	441
27	Mounting a Two-Dimensional Work	442
28	Working with Glue	442

Safety in the Art Room — 443

DRAWING TIPS

1. Making Contour Drawings

When you make a contour drawing, your eye and hand must move at the same time. You must look at the object, not at your drawing. You must imagine that your pencil is touching the edge of the object as your eye follows the edge. Don't let your eye get ahead of your hand. Also, do not lift your pencil from the paper. When you move from one area to the next, let your pencil leave a trail. If you do lift your pencil accidentally, look down, place your pencil where you stopped, and continue.

a. To help you coordinate your eye-hand movement, try this: First, tape your paper to the table so it will not slide around. Then, hold a second pencil in your nondrawing hand and move it around the edges of the object. With your drawing hand, record the movement.

b. If you have trouble keeping your eyes from looking at the paper, ask a friend to hold a piece of stiff paper between your eyes and your drawing hand so the drawing paper is blocked from view. You might also place your drawing paper inside a large paper bag turned sideways. A third method is to put the object on a chair and place the chair on a table. When you are standing, the object should be at your eye level. Then, place your drawing paper on the table directly under the chair. In this way you will be unable to see the paper easily.

c. When you draw without looking at the paper, your first sketches will look strange. Don't be discouraged. The major purpose of blind contour drawing is to teach you to concentrate on directions and curves. The more you practice, the more accurate your drawings will become.

d. As you develop your skills, remember that in addition to edges, contours also define ridges. Notice the wrinkles you see at the joints of fingers and at a bent wrist or bent elbow. Those wrinkles are curved lines. Draw them carefully; the lines you use to show these things will add the look of roundness to your drawing.

e. After you have made a few sketches, add pressure as you draw to vary the thickness and darkness of your lines. Some lines can be emphasized and some can be made less important through the right amount of pressure from your hand.

2. Making Gesture Drawings

Unlike contour drawings, which show an object's outline, gesture drawings show movement. They should have no outlines or details.

a. Using the side of a piece of unwrapped crayon or a pencil, make scribble lines that build up the shape of the object. Do not use single lines that create stick figures.

b. Work very quickly. When drawing people, do the head, then the neck, and then fill in the body. Pay attention to the direction in which the body leans.

c. Next, scribble in the bulk of the legs and the position of the feet.

d. Finally, add the arms.

3. Drawing Calligraphic Lines with a Brush

Mastering the technique of drawing with flowing, calligraphic lines takes practice. You will need a round watercolor brush and either watercolor paint or ink. First, practice making very thin lines.

a. Dip your brush in the ink or paint and wipe the brush slowly on the side of the ink bottle until the bristles form a point.

b. Hold the brush at the metal ferrule so the brush is vertical rather than slanted above the paper. Imagine that the brush is a pencil with a very sharp point—if you press down, you will break the point (Figure T.1).

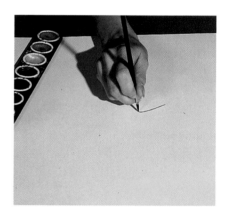

▲ **FIGURE T.1**

c. Touch the paper lightly with the tip of the brush and draw a line.

d. When you are able to control a thin line, you are ready to make calligraphic lines. Start with a thin line and gradually press the brush down to make the line thicker. Pull up again to make it thinner (Figure T.2, page 429). Practice making lines that vary in thickness.

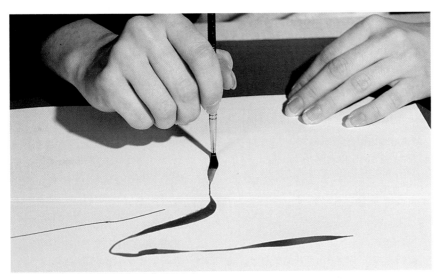

▲ FIGURE T.2

lines or dots far apart and bring them closer together. (Figure T.3.)

5. **Using Sighting Techniques**
   Sighting is a method that will help you determine proportions.
   a. Hold a pencil vertically at arm's length in the direction of the object you are drawing. Close one eye and focus on the object you are going to measure.
   b. Slide your thumb along the pencil until the height of the pencil above your thumb matches the height of the object (Figure T.4, page 430).
   c. Now, without moving your thumb or bending your arm,

4. **Using Shading Techniques**
   The following techniques help create shading values.
   - **Hatching:** Use a series of fine parallel lines.
   - **Crosshatching:** Use two or more intersecting sets of parallel lines.
   - **Blending:** Use a smooth, gradual application of an increasingly dark value. Pencil lines may be blended.
   - **Stippling:** Create shading with dots.

   To be effective in forming the shaded areas, your lines and strokes must follow the form of the object. Use lines to show the surface of a flat surface. Let the lines run parallel to one edge of the surface. To show a curved surface, draw a series of parallel curved lines to give the illusion of roundness. The lines should follow the curve of the object.

   Lines or dots placed close together create dark values. Lines or dots spaced farther apart create lighter values. To show a gradual change from light to dark, begin with

Hatching

Crosshatching

Blending

Stippling

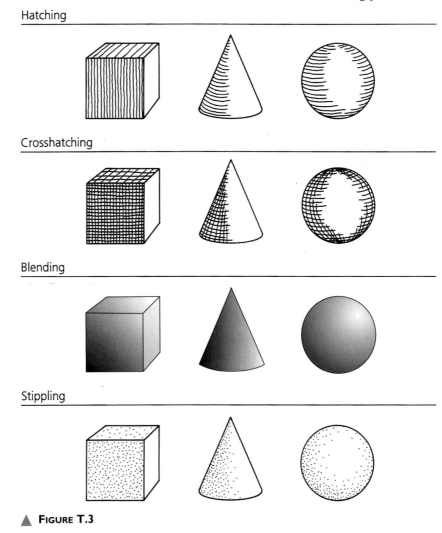

▲ FIGURE T.3

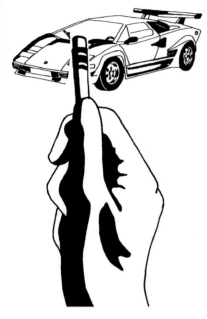

▲ **FIGURE T.4**

subject. Imagine that the opening represents your drawing paper.

c. You can decide how much of the subject you want to include in your drawing by moving the frame up, down, or sideways.

d. You can also move the frame closer or farther away to change the focus of your drawing.

7. Using a Ruler

There are times when you need to draw a crisp, straight line.

a. Hold the ruler with one hand and the pencil with the other.

b. Place the ruler where you wish to draw a straight line.

c. Hold the ruler with your thumb and first two fingers. Be careful that your fingers do not stick out beyond the edge of the ruler.

d. Press heavily on the ruler so it will not slide while you're drawing.

e. Hold the pencil lightly against the ruler.

f. Pull the pencil quickly and lightly along the edge of the ruler. The object is to keep the ruler from moving while the pencil moves along its edge.

hold the pencil parallel to the widest part of the object. Compare the height of the object with its width. You can determine the ratio of height to width by seeing how many times the smaller measure fits into the larger measure. This method can be applied either to different parts of the same object or to two or more different objects. Use one measurement as a base measurement and see how the other measurements relate to it.

6. Using a Viewing Frame

A viewing frame helps you to zero in on an area or object you intend to draw. To make a viewing frame, do the following:

a. Cut a rectangular hole in a heavy sheet of paper (Figure T.5).

b. Hold the frame at arm's length and look through it at your

▲ **FIGURE T.5**

8. Making a Grid for Enlarging

Sometimes you must take a small drawing and enlarge it. To do this, you must first measure the size that the large, finished drawing will be. Then, using proportional ratios, reduce that size to something you can work with.

a. For example: If you want to cover a wall 5 feet high and 10 feet wide, let 1 inch equal 1 foot. Then make a scale drawing that is 5 inches high and 10 inches wide. You may work either in inches or centimeters.

b. After you have completed your small drawing, draw vertical and horizontal grid lines 1 inch apart on the drawing. Number the squares (Figure T.6).

c. On the wall, draw vertical and horizontal grid lines one foot apart.

d. Number the squares on the wall to match the squares on the paper and enlarge the plan by filling one square at a time.

9. Measuring Rectangles

Do you find it hard to create perfectly formed rectangles? Here is a way of getting the job done:

a. Make a light pencil dot near the long edge of a sheet of paper. With a ruler, measure the exact distance between the dot and the edge. Make three more dots the same distance in from the edge. (See Figure T.7.)

b. Line a ruler up along the dots. Make a light pencil line running the length of the paper.

c. Turn the paper so that a short side is facing you. Make four pencil dots equally distant from the short edge. Connect these with a light pencil rule. Stop when you reach the first line you drew.

d. Do the same for the remaining two sides. Erase any lines that

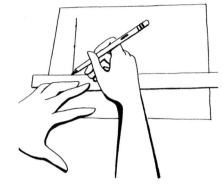

▲ **Figure T.7**

may extend beyond the box you have made.

e. Trace over the lines with your ruler and pencil. The box you have created will be a perfectly formed rectangle.

PAINTING TIPS

10. Mixing Paint to Change the Value of Color

You can better control the colors in your work when you mix your own paint. In mixing paints, treat opaque paints (for example, tempera) differently from transparent paints (for example, watercolors).

a. *For light values of opaque paints.* Add only a small amount of the hue to white. The color can always be made stronger by adding more of the hue.

b. *For dark values of opaque paints.* Add a small amount of black to the hue. Never add the hue to black.

c. *For light values of transparent paints.* Thin a shaded area with water. This allows more of the white paper to show through.

d. *For dark values of transparent paints.* Carefully add a small amount of black to the hue.

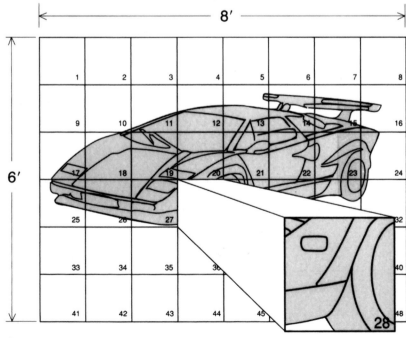

▲ **Figure T.6**

11. Making Natural Earth Pigment Paints

Anywhere there is dirt, clay, and sand, you can find natural earth pigments.

a. Collect as many different kinds of earth colors as you can find (Figure T.8).

▲ FIGURE T.8

b. Grind them as finely as possible. If you can, borrow a mortar and pestle from the science lab (Figure T.9). Regardless of the method you use, your finished product will still be a little gritty. It will not have the smooth texture of commercial pigment.

c. For the binder, use one part white glue to one part water. Put a few spoons of pigment into a small container and add some of the binder. Experiment

▲ FIGURE T.9

with different proportions of pigment and binder.

d. When you have found the best proportion, apply the mixture to paper with a variety of brushes. Do not allow the brushes you use to dry before you wash them, because the glue will solidify.

e. Keep stirring your paint as you work to keep the pigment from settling. The pigment will keep indefinitely. Mix a fresh batch each time you paint, because the mixed paint is difficult to store for more than a few days.

12. Working with Watercolors

Here are some tips to control watercolor paints.

a. If you apply wet paint to damp paper, you create lines and shapes with soft edges.

b. If you apply wet paint to dry paper, you create lines and shapes with sharp, clear edges.

c. If you dip a dry brush into damp paint and then brush across dry paper, you achieve a fuzzy effect.

d. School watercolors come in semi-moist cakes. Before you use them, place a drop of water on each cake to let the paint soften. Watercolor paints are transparent. You can see the white paper through the paint. If you want a light value of a hue, dilute the paint with a large amount of water. If you want a bright hue, you must dissolve more pigment by swirling your brush around in the cake of paint until you have dissolved a great deal of paint. The paint you apply to the paper can be as bright as the paint in the cake.

13. Cleaning a Paint Brush

Rinsing a paint brush under running water will not clean it completely. Paint will remain inside the bristles and cause the brush to lose its shape. Use the following procedure to help your brushes last a long time.

a. Rinse the thick paint out of the brush under running water.

b. Do not use hot water. Gently "paint" the brush over a cake of mild soap or dip it into a mild liquid detergent (Figure T.10).

c. Gently scrub the brush in the palm of your hand to work the soap into the center of the brush. This will remove paint that you did not realize was still in the brush (Figure T.11).

d. Rinse the brush under running water while you continue to scrub your palm.

e. Repeat steps b, c, and d.

▲ FIGURE T.10

▲ FIGURE T.11

▲ **Figure T.12**

f. When your brush is thoroughly rinsed, shape it into a point with your fingers (Figure T.12).

g. Place the brush in a container with the bristles up so it will keep its shape as it dries.

PRINTMAKING TIP

14. Making a Stamp Print

A stamp print is an easy way to make repetitive designs. The following are a few suggestions for making a stamp and printing with it. You may develop some other ideas after reading these hints. Remember, printing reverses your design, so if you use letters, be certain to cut or carve them backward.

- Cut a simple design into the flat surface of a rubber eraser with a knife that has a fine, precision blade.
- Glue yarn to a bottle cap or a jar lid.
- Glue found objects to a piece of corrugated cardboard. Make a design with paperclips, washers, nuts, leaves, feathers, or anything else you can find. Whatever object you use should have a fairly flat surface. Make a handle for the block with masking tape.
- Cut shapes out of a piece of inner tube material. Glue the

shapes to a piece of heavy cardboard.

There are several ways to apply ink or paint to a stamp:

- Roll water-base printing ink on the stamp with a soft brayer.
- Roll water-base printing ink on a plate and press the stamp into the ink.
- Apply tempera paint or school acrylic to the stamp with a bristle brush.

SCULPTING TIPS

15. Working with Clay

To make your work with clay go smoothly, always do the following:

a. Dip one or two fingers in water.

b. Spread the moisture from your fingers over your palms.

Never dip your hands in water. Too much moisture turns clay into mud.

16. Joining Clay

Use these methods for joining clay.

a. First, gather the materials you will need. These include clay, slip (a creamy mixture of clay and water), brush, a scoring tool (such as a fork), and clay tools.

b. Rough up or scratch the two surfaces to be joined (Figure T.13).

c. Apply slip to one of the two surfaces using a brush or your fingers (Figure T.14).

d. Gently press the two surfaces together so the slip oozes out of the joining seam (Figure T.15).

e. Using clay tools and/or your fingers, smooth away the slip that has oozed out of the seam (Figure T.16). You may wish to smooth out the seam as well,

▲ **Figure T.13**

▲ **Figure T.14**

▲ **Figure T.15**

▲ **Figure T.16**

Technique Tips | **433**

or you may wish to leave it for decorative purposes.

17. Making a Pinch Pot

To make a pot using the pinch method, do the following:

a. Make a ball of clay by rolling it between your palms.

b. Set it on the working surface and make a hole in the top by pushing both thumbs into the clay. Stop pushing before your thumbs reach the bottom.

c. Begin to pinch the walls between your thumb and fingers, rotating the pot as you pinch.

d. Continue pinching and shaping the walls of the pot until they are an even thickness and the pot is the desired shape.

18. Using the Coil Technique

Collect all the materials you will need. These include clay, a cloth-covered board, slip and brush, scoring tool, small bowl of water, and pattern for a circular base.

a. Make a base by flattening a piece of clay to about ½ inch thick. Using the pattern, cut the base into a circle.

b. Begin a clay coil by shaping a small ball of clay into a long roll on the cloth-covered board until the roll is about ½ inch thick (Figure T.17). Your hands should be damp so the clay remains damp.

▲ **FIGURE T.17**

c. Make a circle around the edge of the clay base with the roll of clay. Cut the ends on a diagonal and join them so the seam does not show. Using scoring and slip, join this first coil to the base.

d. Make a second coil. If you want the pot to curve outward, place the second coil on the outer edge of the first coil. Place coil on the inner edge for an inward curve. Use proper joining techniques for all coils.

19. Papier-Mâché

Papier-mâché is a French term that means mashed paper. It refers to sculpting methods that use paper and liquid paste. The wet paper and paste material are molded over supporting structures such as a wad of dry paper or crumpled foil. The molded paper dries to a hard finish. Following are three basic methods for working with papier-mâché.

Pulp Method

a. Shred newspaper, paper towels, or tissue paper into tiny pieces and soak them in water overnight. (Do not use slick paper as it will not soften.)

b. Mash the paper in a strainer to remove the water or wring it out in a piece of cloth.

c. Mix the mashed paper with prepared paste or white glue until the material is the consistency of soft clay. Use the mixture to model small shapes.

d. When papier-mâché is dry, it can be sanded, and holes can be drilled through it.

Strip Method

a. Tear paper into strips.

b. Either dip the strips in a thick mixture of paste or rub paste on the strips with your fingers. Decide which method works best for you.

c. Use wide strips to cover wide forms. Very thin strips will lie flat on a small shape.

d. If you do not want the finished work to stick to the support structure, first cover the form with plastic wrap or a layer of wet newspaper strips. If you are going to remove the papier-mâché from the support structure, you need to apply five or six layers of strips. Rub your fingers over the strips so that no rough edges are left sticking up (Figure T.18). Change directions with each layer so that you can keep track of the number. If you are going to leave the papier-mâché over the support structure, then two or three layers may be enough.

Sheet Method

a. Brush or spread paste on a sheet of newspaper or newsprint (Figure T.19). Lay a second

▲ **FIGURE T.18**

▲ **FIGURE T.19**

▲ **FIGURE T.20**

sheet on top of the first and smooth out the layers. Add another layer of paste and another sheet of paper. Repeat this process until you have four or five layers of paper. This method is good for making drapery on a figure (Figure T.20).

b. If you let the layers dry for a day until they are leathery, they can be cut and molded any way you wish. Newspaper strips dipped in the paste can be used to seal any cracks that may occur.

Support Structures

a. Dry newspaper can be wadded up and wrapped with string or tape (Figure T.21).
b. Wire armatures can be padded with rags before the outside shell of papier-mâché is added.
c. Found materials such as boxes, tubes, and plastic

▲ **FIGURE T.21**

bowls, can be arranged and taped together to form a base (Figure T.22).

d. For large figures, a wooden frame covered with chicken wire makes a good support. Push and pinch the wire into the shape you want.

▲ **FIGURE T.22**

20. Making a Paper Sculpture

Another name for paper sculpture is origami. The process originated in Japan and means "folding paper." Paper sculpture begins with a flat piece of paper. The paper is then curved or bent to produce more than a flat surface. Here are some ways to experiment with paper.

• **Scoring.** Place a square sheet of heavy construction paper on a flat surface. Position a ruler on the paper so that it is close to the center and parallel to the sides. Holding the ruler in place, run the point of a knife or a pair of scissors along one of the ruler's edges. Press down firmly but take care not to cut through the paper. Gently crease the paper along the line you made. Hold your paper with the crease facing upward. You can also score curved lines, but you must do this with gradually bending curves or wide arcs. If you try to make a tight curve, such as a semicircle, the

paper will not give. For a tight curve you will have to make cuts to relieve the tension.

• **Pleating.** Take a piece of paper and fold it 1 inch from the edge. Then fold the paper in the other direction. Continue folding back and forth.

• **Curling.** Hold one end of a long strip of paper with the thumb and forefinger of one hand. At a point right below where you are holding the strip, grip it lightly between the side of a pencil and the thumb of your other hand. In a quick motion, run the pencil along the strip. This will cause the strip to curl back on itself. Don't apply too much pressure, or the strip will tear. (See Figure T.23.)

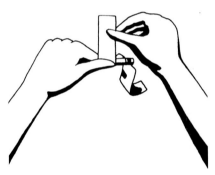

▲ **FIGURE T.23**

21. Making Paper

Papermaking is a process in which fibers are broken down and reformed as a sheet. In order to make paper, collect all the materials you will need. These include a food blender, two matching stretcher frames approximately 9 x 12 inches each, a rustproof window screen slightly larger than the stretchers, staple gun, duct tape, Handi Wipes towels, a large pan 5 to 8 inches deep, newspapers, assorted papers, and water.

a. Make the mold by stretching the screen over the frame, stapling it at the edges, and covering the rough edges with duct tape. The second frame is the deckle, the frame that keeps the pulp in place on the mold.

b. Tear paper into 1-inch squares. Put 4 cups water and $1/2$ cup paper scraps into the blender and blend for several minutes until the mixture is the consistency of watery cooked oatmeal.

c. Pour pulp into pan. Continue making pulp until there is about 4 inches of pulp in the pan. Additional water may be added to aid in the papermaking process.

d. Make a pad of newspapers $1/4$ inch thick. Unfold Handi Wipes towels and lay one on the pad; this is the blotter.

e. Align deckle on top of mold. Stir pulp to suspend paper fibers. Scoop mold and deckle under surface of water and shake to align fibers. Lift to drain excess water.

f. Remove the deckle and flip the mold and pulp onto the blotter, pulp side down against the Handi Wipes towel. Blot back of molds with a sponge to remove excess water and to compress the fibers. Remove the mold, using a rocking motion.

g. Lay another Handi Wipes towel on top of the sheet of paper and add more newspapers. Repeat the layering process.

h. Let paper dry slowly for 1–3 days. When dry, peel off the Handi Wipes.

i. To clean up, drain pulp through the mold or a sieve. Squeeze excess water from pulp and save pulp in a plastic bag for one to three days or discard it.

22. Basic Embroidery Stitches
The charts below and on the next page show the most common embroidery stitches.

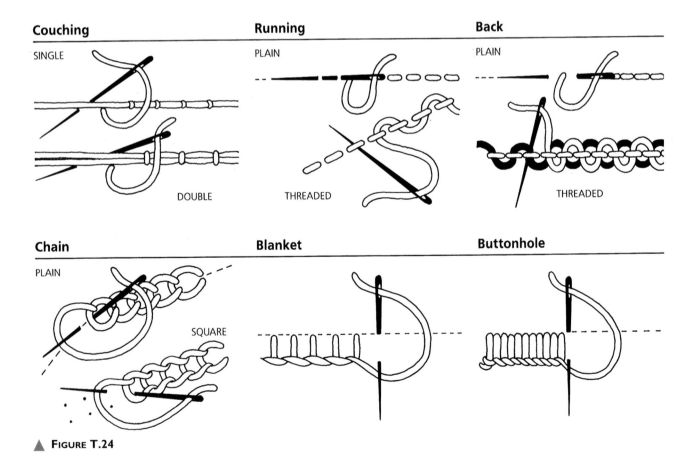

Couching
SINGLE
DOUBLE

Running
PLAIN
THREADED

Back
PLAIN
THREADED

Chain
PLAIN
SQUARE

Blanket

Buttonhole

▲ **FIGURE T.24**

Feather

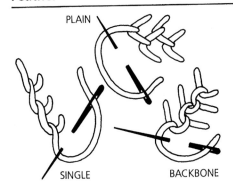

PLAIN

SINGLE

BACKBONE

Outline

Satin

Cross

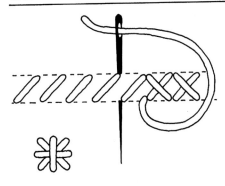

Knotted

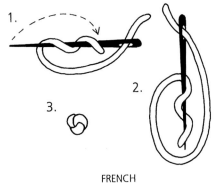

1.

2.

3.

FRENCH

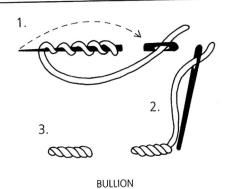

1.

2.

3.

BULLION

▲ **FIGURE T.24 (CONTINUED)**

23. Weaving Techniques

To make a cardboard loom, gather the materials you will need. They include cardboard, ruler, pencil, scissors, strong, thin yarn for warp, various yarns and fibers for weft, tapestry needle, comb, and dowel.

a. Measure and cut notches ¹/₄ inch apart and ¹/₂ inch deep on opposite sides of the cardboard.

b. Tape warp thread to back of loom. Bring it to the front through the top left notch. Pull it down to the bottom of the loom and pass it through the bottom left notch to the back. Move one notch to the right and continue until you reach the last notch. Then tape the end of the warp thread to the back. (Figure T.25)

c. Start to weave at the bottom of the loom, using a thin yarn. The weft yarns are the horizontal yarns; the easiest way to pull the weft yarn through the warp threads is to use an over-one-under-one motion. At the end of the row, reverse directions. (Figure T.26)

d. Do not pull the weft threads too tight. Let them balloon, or curve slightly upward (Figure T.27).

▲ **FIGURE T.25**

▲ **FIGURE T.26**

▲ **FIGURE T.27**

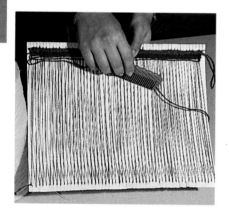

▲ **FIGURE T.28**

e. After weaving several rows, pack the weft threads with a comb (Figure T.28). The tighter the weave, the stronger it will be.

f. After there is about 1 inch of tight weave, begin varying weave and materials (Figure T.29). End the process with another inch of thin, tight weave.

g. Before removing the fabric from the loom, weave in the loose ends. Cut the warp threads from the loom carefully and tie two at a time so they will not unravel.

h. Tie or sew the finished fabric to a dowel.

▶ **FIGURE T.29**

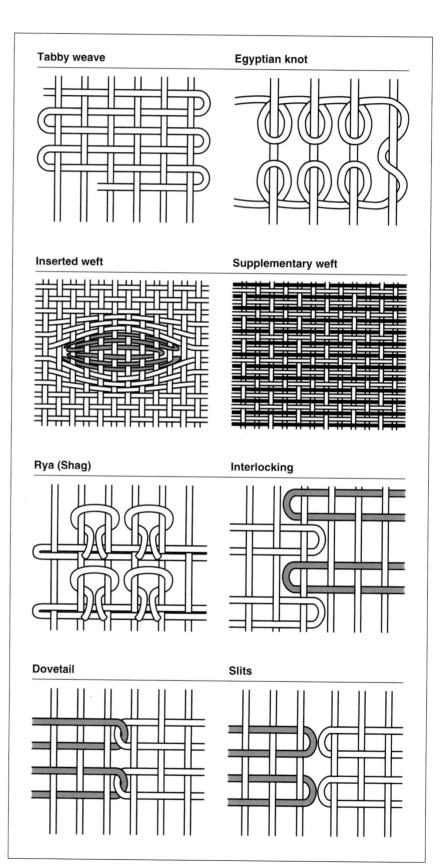

24. Making a Coiled Basket

Mastering the technique of making a coiled basket takes practice. You will need *core* material (such as heavy cord), *weft* wrapping materials (such as yarns and fibers), a tapestry needle, scissors, and tape.

Coiling is a stitching technique in which the continuous coils of the *core* material are stitched together with a binding material called the *weft*. The first time you try this your binding and stitches probably will not look neat. Undo the work and begin again. You want to cover the core material completely, and all your weft binding and stitches must be even and tight.

a. Trim the end of the core so it tapers. Thread the tapestry needle with a 3-foot length of weft. Using the loose weft end, begin to wind it around the core starting about 2 inches from the end. Overlap the end as you wind to anchor it. Wind the weft to about ¹/₂ inch from the tapered end of the core (Figure T.30).

b. Bend the core, catch the tapered end, and make a loop (Figure T.31).

c. Continue winding for about 2 inches, being sure that the tapered core is attached securely to the solid section of core material. Push the tapestry needle through the center of the loop (Figure T.32).

d. Bend the core to form a coil and bring the weft between the core and the coil. (Figure T.33) Begin winding the weft around the core from front to back. You are now ready to begin the Lazy stitch.

e. Wind the weft around the core from front to back four times.

Then, bringing the weft from behind and over the core, push the needle into the center of the coil (Figure T.34). Pull tightly and hold. Continue to wrap the weft four times around the core and pull the fifth stitch into the center until you complete two coils. Hold them flat between your fingers while you work.

f. As the coiling progresses, you may wrap the weft more than four times between stitches. After the first two coils, you will no longer bring the stitch back to the center; just take it over two coils (Figure T.35). Always insert the needle from the front. This way you can see exactly where you are placing the needle. If you want to create a pattern of long stitches, this is essential.

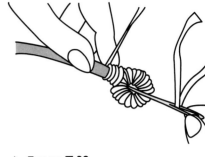

▲ **FIGURE T.32**

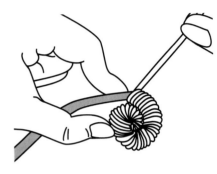

▲ **FIGURE T.33**

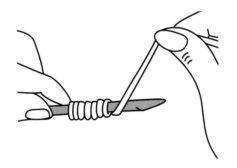

▲ **FIGURE T.30**

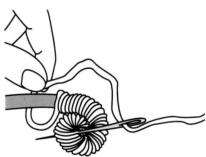

▲ **FIGURE T.34**

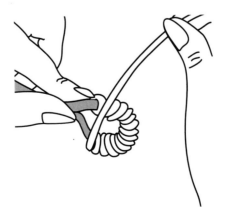

▲ **FIGURE T.31**

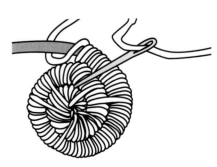

▲ **FIGURE T.35**

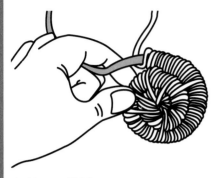

FIGURE T.36

g. Hold the coil with your left hand with the core material coming from the left, and wind the weft with your right hand so you do not tangle it with the core (Figure T.36). If you are left-handed, reverse the process. Always pull the weft very tight.

h. You will need to splice, or invisibly join, the ends of separate materials. To splice the core, taper the cut on the old and the new piece. Before working the weft, secure the spliced ends of the core by wrapping them with sewing thread or tape. Always hold the spliced area carefully until it is wrapped with the weft. Splice the weft during the wrapping, not during the stitching. Hold the tail ends of the old and the new weft together against the core as shown in Figure T.37. Wrap the new weft at least once before making a long stitch.

i. When the base is the desired size, it is time to begin making the sides of the basket. If the side is to be perpendicular to the base, lay the first foundation coil directly on top of the last coil. If you want the basket to curve outward, place each new coil on the outer edge of the one below. To make an inward curve, place each coil on the inner edge of the previous coil. Use pressure from the nonstitching hand to keep the coils in place.

j. The best way to finish the basket is to taper the core and make several stitches around the last coil and the tapered coil. Then run the needle back through the wrapping stitches for about an inch and pull the weft thread through. Cut off the excess weft.

k. If you want to make a handle, simply wrap the end of the core until it is as long as you wish.

Then attach it to the other side of the top of the basket following the instructions from Step j.

25. Making a Tissue Paper Collage

For your first experience with tissue, make a free design with the tissue colors. Start with the lightest colors of tissue first and save the darkest for last. It is difficult to change the color of dark tissue by overlapping it with other colors. If one area becomes too dark, you might cut out a piece of white paper, glue it over the dark area carefully, and apply new colors over the white area.

a. Apply a coat of adhesive to the area where you wish to place the tissue.

b. Place the tissue down carefully over the wet area (Figure T.38). Don't let your fingers get wet.

c. Then add another coat of adhesive over the tissue. If your brush picks up any color from the wet tissue, rinse your brush

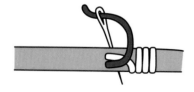

FIGURE T.37

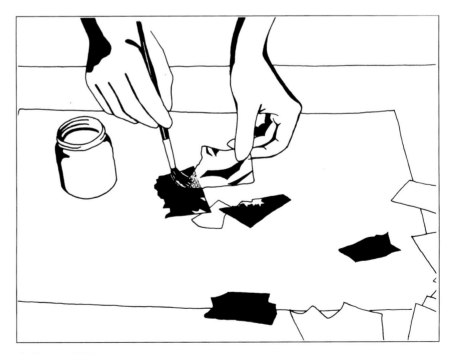

FIGURE T.38

in water and let it dry before using it again.

d. Experiment by overlapping colors. Allow the tissue to wrinkle to create textures as you apply it. Be sure that all the loose edges of tissue are glued down.

26. Making a Mat

You can add appeal to an artwork by making a mat, using the following steps.

a. Gather the materials you will need. These include a metal rule, a pencil, mat board, cardboard backing, a sheet of heavy cardboard to protect your work surface, a mat knife with a sharp blade, and wide masking tape.

b. Wash your hands. Mat board should be kept very clean.

c. Measure the height and width of the work to be matted. Decide how large a border you want for your work. (A border of approximately 2$\frac{1}{2}$ inches on three sides with 3 inches on the bottom is aesthetically pleasing.) Your work will be behind the window you will cut.

d. Plan for the opening, or window, to be $\frac{1}{4}$ inch smaller on all sides than the size of your work. For example, if your work measures 9 by 12 inches, the mat window should measure 8$\frac{1}{2}$ inches (9 inches minus $\frac{1}{4}$ inch times two) by 11$\frac{1}{2}$ inches (12 inches minus $\frac{1}{4}$ inch times two.) Using your metal rule and pencil, lightly draw your window rectangle on the back of the board 2$\frac{1}{2}$ inches from the top and left edge of the mat. (See Figure T.39). Add a 2$\frac{1}{2}$-inch

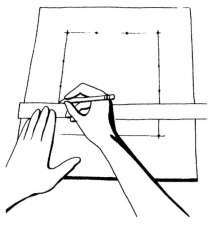

▲ **Figure T.39**

border to the right of the window and a 3-inch border to the bottom, lightly drawing cutting guidelines.

Note: If you are working with metric measurements, the window should overlap your work by 0.5 cm (centimeters) on all sides. Therefore, if your work measures 24 by 30 cm, the mat window measures 23 cm (24−[2 x 0.5]) by 29 cm (30 − [2 × 0.5]).

e. Place the sheet of heavy, protective cardboard on your work surface. Place the mat board, pencil marks up, over the cardboard. Holding the metal rule firmly in place, score the first line with your knife. Always place the metal rule so that your blade is on the inside of the frame. (See Figure T.40.) In case you make an error you will cut into the window hole or the extra mat that is not used for the frame. Do not try to cut through the board with one stroke. By the third or fourth stroke, you should be able to cut through the board easily.

f. Working in the same fashion, score and cut through the board along all the window lines. Be careful not to go

beyond the lines. Remove the window.

g. Cut a cardboard backing for your artwork that is slightly smaller than the overall size of your mat. Using a piece of broad masking tape, hinge the back of the mat to the backing. (See Figure T.41.) Position your artwork between the backing and the mat and attach it with tape. Anchor the frame to the cardboard with a few pieces of rolled tape.

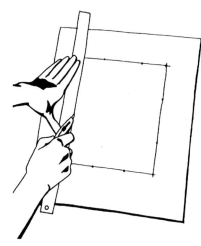

▲ **Figure T.40**

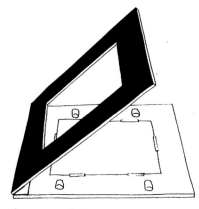

▲ **Figure T.41**

27. Mounting a Two-Dimensional Work

Mounting pictures that you make gives them a professional look. To mount a work, do the following:

a. Gather the materials you will need. These include a yardstick, a pencil, poster board, a knife with a very sharp blade, a sheet of newspaper, and rubber cement.

b. Measure the height and width of the work to be mounted. Decide how large a border you want around the work. Plan your mount size using the work's measurements. To end up with a 3-inch border, for example, make your mount 6 inches wider and higher than your work. Record the measurements for your mount.

c. Using your yardstick and pencil, lightly draw your mount rectangle on the back of the poster board. Measure from the edges of the poster board. If you have a large paper cutter available, you may use it to cut your mount.

d. Place the sheet of heavy cardboard on your work surface. Place the poster board, pencil marks up, over the cardboard. Holding the yardstick firmly in place along one line, score the line with your knife. Do not try to cut through the board with one stroke. By the third try, you should be able to cut through the board.

e. Place the artwork on the mount. Using the yardstick, center the work. Mark each corner with a dot. (See Figure T.42)

▲ **Figure T.42**

▲ **Figure T.43**

f. Place the artwork, face down, on a sheet of newspaper. Coat the back of the work with rubber cement. (Safety Note: Always use rubber cement in a room with plenty of ventilation.) If your mount is to be permanent, skip to Step h.

g. Line up the corners of your work with the dots on the mounting board. Smooth the work into place. Skip to Step i.

h. After coating the back of your artwork, coat the poster board with rubber cement. Be careful not to add cement to the border area. Have a partner hold your artwork in the air by the two top corners. Once the two glued surfaces meet, you will not be able to change the position of the work. Grasp the lower two corners. Carefully lower the work to the mounting board. Line up the two corners with the bottom dots. Little by little, lower the work into place (Figure T.43). Press it smooth.

i. To remove any excess cement, create a small ball of dry rubber cement. Use the ball of rubber cement to pick up excess cement.

28. Working with Glue

When applying glue, always start at the center of the surface you are coating and work outward.

- When gluing papers together don't use a lot of glue, just a dot will do. Use dots in the corners and along the edges. Press the two surfaces together. Keep dots at least $1/2$ inch in from the edge of your paper.

- Handle a glued surface carefully with only your fingertips. Make sure your hands are clean before pressing the glued surface into place.

- Note: The glue should be as thin as possible. Thick or beaded glue will create ridges on your work.

Many artists, both students and teachers, come into daily contact with dangerous, possibly deadly materials. The unfortunate truth is that many art supplies contain high levels of chemicals, such as hexane, lead, toluene, and asbestos, and many people are unaware of the danger that these substances pose, both to art students and to teachers. In fact, the danger to art teachers, who are often exposed to toxins for several hours a day for many years, is often greater than to the students. Therefore, it is essential that all art teachers and students become aware of the potential hazards in using art materials.

Many art supplies contain materials that can cause acute illness (that is, a severe sudden illness that can be caused by a single exposure to a toxic substance and result in permanent disability or death). Long-term exposure to materials in many other art supplies can cause chronic illness (which develops gradually after repeated exposure) or cancer. Other chemicals in art supplies are sensitizers, causing allergies, particularly in children. Lead, for example, is acutely toxic and can be found in such commonly used supplies as stencil paint, oil paint, some acrylics, gessoes, ceramic glazes, copper enamels, and automotive paint in spray cans. Many highly toxic hydrocarbon-based solvents, including methyl alcohol, are used in school art programs. Other widely used art materials, such as preservatives, formaldehyde, epoxy glues, and dichromates, can contain dangerous chemicals like cadmium, nickel, silica, and pesticides.

There are three ways in which such chemicals can enter the body: absorption, inhalation, and ingestion. They can be absorbed through the skin from cuts or scrapes, resulting in burns or rashes, or into the bloodstream, moving to and damaging other parts of the body. Chemical irritants can be inhaled, causing lung problems like bronchitis and emphysema. Inhaling small particles, like the free silica in clay dust, can cause pulmonary fibrosis or asthma. Chemicals can be ingested through touching the mouth with the hands or fingers while working with supplies or unconsciously placing tools like paint brushes in or near the mouth. Since hazardous substances can easily enter the body, it is extremely important to make sure that the materials used are safe and that they are used safely.

Labeling

Labeling can provide information on any potentially dangerous art supplies, but teachers need to be aware of what various labels mean. The label *nontoxic*, for example, does not guarantee a product's safety. According to federal regulations, toxicity means that a single exposure can be fatal to adults. The effect on young people, who are more likely to be harmed by dangerous substances, is not considered in this definition. Also, the chance of developing chronic or long-term illnesses is not addressed by the legal definition of toxicity. Repeated exposure to nontoxic materials is not always safe. Many dangerous substances, such as asbestos, can legally be defined as nontoxic. Also, some art supplies, particularly those manufactured by small or foreign companies, may be improperly labeled as nontoxic.

Not all products whose labels provide chemical components, but have no warnings or list no information at all, are safe to use. Since manufacturers are not required to disclose ingredients, products without this information or warnings are potentially hazardous.

For more complete information on the presence of hazardous substances in art supplies, teachers may request a Material Safety Data Sheet (OSHA Form 20) from the manufacturer. This sheet provides information on potential heath and fire hazards, a list of chemicals that might react dangerously with the product, and a list of all ingredients for which industrial standards exist. The manufacturer should supply this sheet on request, and a local public health

SAFETY

official or poison control center technician can help interpret the information.

Art teachers can also take advantage of voluntary labeling standards developed by the art materials industry. The Art and Creative Materials Institute (ACMI) administers a voluntary testing and labeling program that helps to insure the safety of those who work with art materials. This system uses the labels AP and CL. AP (Approved Product) labels are used mainly on products designed for younger children, while CL (certified to be properly labeled) is used on products intended for older students and adults. Products labeled AP or CL are certified in a program of toxicological evaluation by a medical expert to contain no materials in sufficient quantities to be toxic or injurious to humans or to cause acute or chronic health problems. Products labeled AP, in addition, meet specific requirements of material, workmanship, working qualities, and color. CL means that the product is certified to be properly labeled in a program of toxicological evaluation by a medical expert. The Art and Creative Materials Institute makes available a list of certified products. For a copy, or for more information on the institute's certification program, teachers can write to:

The Art and Creative Materials Institute, Inc.
P. O. Box 479
Hanson, MA 02341-0479

Safety Rules

There are certain guidelines to be followed in selecting and using art supplies. Perhaps the most important is to know what the materials are made of and what potential hazards exist. If a material is improperly labeled, or if adequate information cannot be obtained about it, don't use it. The following rules are also helpful:

- Be sure that all materials used by younger students (ages 12 and under) have the AP label and that materials used by older students and adults are marked CL.
- Don't use acids, alkalies, bleaches, or any product that will stain skin or clothing.
- Don't use aerosol cans because the spray can injure lungs.
- Use dust-producing materials (such as pastels, clays, plasters, chalks, powdered tempera, pigments, dyes, and instant papier-mâché, except the premixed cellulose type) with care in a well-ventilated area (or better yet, don't use them at all).
- Don't use solvents (including lacquers, paint thinners, turpentines, shellacs, solvent-based inks, rubber cement, and permanent markers) in the art room.
- Don't use found or donated materials unless the ingredients are known.
- Don't use old materials. Many art supplies formerly contained highly dangerous substances, such as arsenic, or raw lead compounds, or high levels of asbestos. Older solvents may contain chloroform or carbon tetrachloride.

Working conditions in the art room also affect safety. A disorderly art room leads to unsafe conditions, particularly when there are many people working close to each other. Controlling the buildup of litter and dust, insuring that tools are in good condition, and keeping workspace reasonably organized not only help prevent common accidents but also make it easier to recognize and eliminate other hazards. An orderly art room is absolutely essential to the students' and teacher's safety.

Table of Contents

Scanners. **446**

Technology Notes: Resolution

Digital Cameras. **447**

Technology Notes: Storage

Graphics Tablets. **448**

Technology Notes: Ergonomics

Paint Software. **449**

Technology Notes: Bitmap File Formats

Draw Software. **450**

Technology Notes: Color Models

3-D Graphics Software **451**

Technology Notes: Rendering

Frame Animation Software. **452**

Technology Notes: Sound

Multimedia Presentation Software **453**

Technology Notes: Executable Files

Page Layout Software **454**

Technology Notes: Style Sheets and Libraries

Using Scanners

Whether you need to manipulate an artwork or insert a photo into a report, a scanner can be a useful tool. Scanners allow you to convert documents, illustrations, or photographs into digital image files on your computer. Once stored in a computer, these scanned files can be altered in an image-editing program.

Technology NOTES

Resolution

Resolution is the fineness of detail that can be distinguished in an image. A basic rule of thumb is the finer the detail, the better the quality. In a high-quality image, even the smallest details can be distinguished. The resolution of a scanned image is measured in dpi (dots per inch). On a computer monitor, these dots are referred to as pixels. The more dots or pixels per inch, the better the quality. The recommended settings of dpi depend on the final output. For an image that will be seen on screen via e-mail or the Web, select a dpi between 72 and 96. For printing, the recommended settings vary depending on the type of image. Below are some typical settings which will vary depending upon the printer:

▶ **Color photo**   300 dpi

▶ **Text**   400 dpi

▶ **Text with images**   400 dpi

▶ **Line art**   300 to 3200 dpi

Scanner Basics

Scanners come in a variety of shapes and sizes—from small, hand-held devices to full-scaled, professional-quality drum scanners. Flatbed scanners are the most common household or schoolroom models. These machines include a flat, glass panel called the document table glass that is usually large enough to accommodate an 8½ x 11″ image. Many scanners also come with film adapters to let you scan slides and negative or positive filmstrips.

Although individual makes and models will vary, there are some basic guidelines for using a flatbed scanner:

- Clean the glass to make sure there are no smudges or dirt.

- Open a host application on your computer—the program into which you plan to import the scanned image or document.

- Place the image facedown on the glass. Align with the appropriate corner markings.

- Adjust the settings in your host application program to specify the document source, image type, destination, resolution, and desired image size.

Always read the manual that came with your scanner for specific instructions and troubleshooting information.

Working with Digital Cameras

Digital cameras combine the features of the analog, or conventional, camera and the scanner. Like scanners, digital cameras allow you to download images to your computer's hard drive. Unlike scanners, digital cameras are cordless. They allow you to capture live images. Also, because the images are digital, you never need to buy film.

How Digital Cameras Work

Taking pictures with a digital camera is simple. If it is set on automatic focus, you just aim at your subject and click the shutter. Once you have taken a picture, you can download it to your computer. There, it can be edited, imported into a document, printed, or e-mailed.

Digital cameras vary widely in terms of features. One of the most important features is memory, or storage. The more memory the camera has, the more pictures you can take in a single session. (See "Technology Notes" for more on storage.) Other important features to look for include:

- **Software.** Most cameras come with software for downloading and manipulating images. Some lower-end cameras may not include software. Also, the quality of this software varies. Make sure the output file format is compatible with image-editing programs already installed on your computer.

- **Image quality.** Think about how you intend to use the camera. If you plan to take high-resolution pictures (pictures with very fine detail), you will need a better camera. For most art tasks and other student needs, medium resolution is usually fine.

Technology NOTES

Storage

Storage is where your digital camera maintains digitized versions of the pictures you take. The least expensive models of digital cameras come with built-in *flash memory*. This type of storage cannot be upgraded. Flash memory can hold up to 25 images. These must be downloaded to your computer or erased before you can take more pictures.

The next step up in storage solutions is the *smart card*. A little like a floppy disk, a smart card is a removable flash memory module. The camera comes with one card, but you can buy additional cards as needed.

Top-of-the-line cameras have built-in hard disks that hold up to a gigabyte of data. Some newer cameras even come with writable CDs and DVDs.

Understanding Graphics Tablets

A graphics tablet is a high-tech version of drawing paper or a painter's canvas. Instead of brushes or other conventional media, you draw or "paint" on the tablet with an electronic pen. The image appears simultaneously on the computer screen. If you are unhappy with any pen stroke, you can simply select "Undo" from an on-screen menu. That portion of the drawing will disappear without a trace.

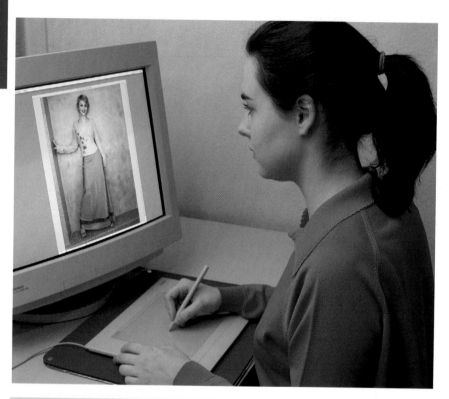

Tablet Fundamentals

Graphics tablets are as easy to install as they are to use. The tablet is plugged into the computer's USB (universal serial bus) or serial port. There is no need to attach the pen, which is cordless. Once the accompanying software is installed, you are ready to draw. Graphics tablets may be used with all major paint and draw applications.

Tablets come in a range of sizes to suit different tasks. The smallest, which measure around 4 × 5″, are often used for sketches or to add objects to larger artworks. The largest tablets, at around 12 × 18″, are the size of a standard sheet of drawing paper. They can be used to create complete artworks.

The electronic pen is pressure sensitive. As with a conventional pen or brush, the harder you press, the darker and thicker the line. Some models boast as many as 1,024 levels of pressure sensitivity. Pressure sensitivity not only controls line thickness, but transparency and color as well. The higher the pressure sensitivity, the more natural your pen and tablet will feel.

Technology NOTES

Ergonomics

The term *ergonomics* refers to the application of science to the design of objects and environments for human use. In recent years, ergonomic engineers have been at work, developing computer tools that reduce the risk of repetitive stress injury. This is a type of injury affecting the nerves in the wrist and forearm.

Recent ergonomic developments include the cushioned electronic pen. The cushioned pen has a softer surface and weighs less than earlier pens. These features have been shown to reduce grip effort by up to 40 percent. The cushioned pen, thus, is more comfortable and safer to use.

Using Paint Software

Paint software programs offer new conveniences and capabilities to artists. Traditional paints require drying time before a painting is finished or can be retouched. Not only is there no drying necessary with digital paints, but paint mixing is a mathematical process. A digital artist has billions of colors in his or her palette. Previously used colors can be duplicated with ease and precision. Also, as with all art software, a painting can be easily erased and altered.

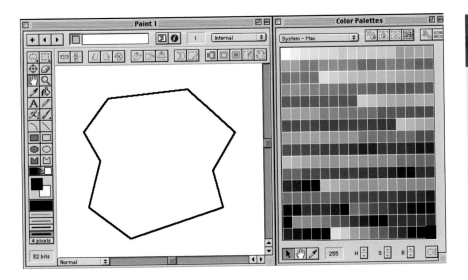

Paint Software Basics

In digital paint programs, images are created and stored as *bitmaps*. These are files made up of tiny dots called *pixels*. Since photographs downloaded to the computer have a similar format, paint programs do double duty as photo editors. A paint program can be used to brighten a dark photo, enhance its contrast, and so forth.

The main features of a paint program are:

● **A menu bar.** The menu bar contains file management commands (such as <u>O</u>pen and <u>S</u>ave), edit commands (such as <u>U</u>ndo and <u>R</u>edo), and view commands (for example, <u>Z</u>oom).

● **The toolbox.** The toolbox contains art tools, such as brushes and pens, and image manipulation tools. These allow you to flip or rotate an image among many other options.

● **Palettes.** These are separate windows that allow you to control colors, brush tip sizes, line thickness, and the like.

Most paint programs also come with a variety of filters. These add special effects to an image or photo. One example is "feathering," which gives an image a wispy, cloudlike look.

Examining Draw Software

A cousin to paint software, draw software shares many of the same art tools and menus. Although draw programs lack some of the editing capabilities of paint programs, they are ideal for creating original artworks. They are especially well suited for creating logos, book or CD covers, and other art that combines images and text

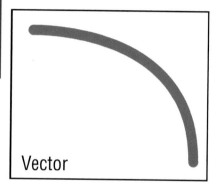

Vector

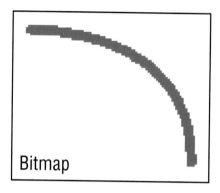

Bitmap

Draw Software Fundamentals

In draw programs, images are stored as mathematical formulas called *vectors*. These formulas carry information about the lines and curves that make up a particular drawing. Vector-based formats allow images to be *resized*—shrunk or enlarged—without distortion. This is one advantage of draw programs over paint programs. Paint programs produce images that cannot easily be resized without some loss of image quality.

Every object created by an artist using a draw program contains editable points and handles. By moving or dragging these elements, the artist can alter or smooth out shapes and curves with ease and precision. Digital illustrators often scan and import sketches into draw programs.

This allows them to trace over the sketch with a mouse or stylus. They can then refine and color the sketch creating a digital illustration.

In addition to pens and brushes, the toolbox in a typical draw program contains assorted shape tools. For example, once shapes have been drawn, they can then be extended into three dimensions using an *extrude* command. Draw programs may include a selection of vector-based images that can be manipulated and used in other illustrations.

Recent draw software enhancements enable artists to work with bitmap images. Some sophisticated programs now come with filters, similar to the filters found in paint programs. These filters can be used for adding special effects to bitmap images.

Technology NOTES

Color Models

Draw programs today allow users to select from more than 4 billion colors. Before you can choose colors, however, you need to decide on a *color model*. Color models are systems for arranging the colors of the visible spectrum so that they appear as the user intended when the image is viewed. The standard printing color model is CYMK. The letters are short for cyan (a greenish blue), yellow, magenta, and black. Most draw software comes preset for CYMK. Some artists instead work with the RGB (red, green, blue) model. For example, Web designers use the RGB model because their work is viewed on computer monitors. On monitors all the colors of the spectrum are created with only red, green, and blue.

Examining 3-D Graphics Software

Creating art in three dimensions is nothing new. Creating *digital* art in three dimensions *is* relatively new. The ability to give form to computerized objects only became a reality some 15 years ago. That was when the first 3-D modeling programs arrived on the market. Since that time, the capabilities of these programs have been expanded dramatically. Today, digital artists can create entire animated movies using a single 3-D software package.

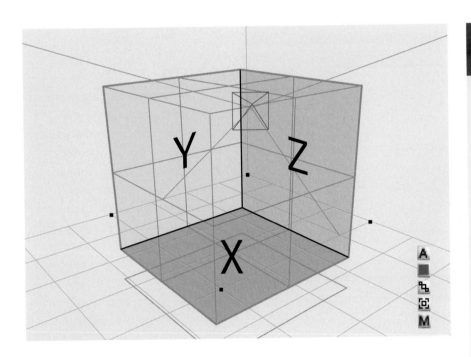

How 3-D Software Works

There are many types of 3-D graphics programs. Some are designed specifically for creating and editing 3-D images for use on Web sites and CD-ROMs, or print materials. Other 3-D modeling programs are designed for architects and engineers. These programs are used to create complex digital blueprints for buildings and other structures.

Like draw and paint programs, 3-D programs include tools for creating objects. Once created, objects are placed on a *stage*. The stage is similar to the *work area* in draw and paint programs. The stage has three surfaces, or *planes*—one for width (X), height (Y), and depth (Z). Each plane includes grid lines that allow the user to place objects at exact locations in space.

Similar to movies, 3-D programs include *lighting* and *camera* controls. Lighting allows the user to adjust the intensity and direction of the light source. The camera control determines the view and angle from which the object is seen.

Technology NOTES

Rendering

When you see a movie on the big screen, you don't see the lighting, cameras, or film crew. The same is true of 3-D modeling and animation programs. The final product is the *rendered* scene or movie. *Rendering* is a process by which the program mathematically assigns shading, texture, and other art features to one or more bitmaps. Behind-the-scenes details do not appear in the rendered scene or movie.

Rendering can take anywhere from an hour to a day or more, depending on the resolution. If you are previewing a scene or movie, choose a low resolution. Make sure to allow ample rendering time for the final "cut."

Understanding Frame Animation Software

In comic strips, the action occurs frame by frame. It is precisely this principle that is at work in frame animation software. Using this software, the digital artist is able to animate words and images quickly and easily. The programs even provide tools for "publishing" the finished movie on the Internet.

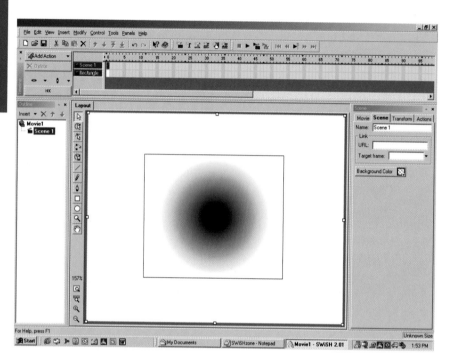

Frame Animation Basics

The first step in creating a frame animation is choosing your "actors." Objects, created in other graphics programs or by hand, may be imported. Frame animation software also includes tools for creating original simple objects and text.

Once the "cast" has been established, objects are placed on the timeline. This is series of numbered frames beginning at zero. An object's position on the timeline determines the point at which it enters or exits the scene.

The third step in an animation is to create movement. An object can be made to move by means of one of the following:

● **A preset effect.** Animation software comes with a number of preset actions. These include *fade in, fade out, blur,* and *transform.* The last of these controls an object's size, angle, and so on.

● **A motion path.** The software also permits the user to create original motion paths. These tell an object where and how to move at any given moment.

Technology NOTES

Sound

Animation software allows the addition of sounds and music to accompany the action. Sound files may be recorded using the computer's microphone. Another source of sounds is clip art Web sites, many of which offer free sound clips. Since sound files tend to be large, they can increase the size of the movie, possibly causing the action to pause. There are two ways of avoiding this:

► Looping sounds. This is having a single sound file, such as background music, repeat over and over.

► Using compressed sound files. AVI sound files tend to be larger because they are not compressed. Choose MPEG-3 files whenever possible. These require far less memory.

Using Multimedia Presentation Software

Imagine viewing an exhibition of your own portfolio. With multimedia presentation software, there is no need to imagine. These remarkable programs allow you to create digital slideshows right on your computer. You can even add narration, background music, and special visual effects to your presentation.

Technology NOTES

Executable Files

Some multimedia presentation programs allow you to turn your shows into *executable files*. An executable file is a self-contained program that will open and run when double-clicked. All the icons on your system's desktop are executable files.

Executable files may be e-mailed or burned onto a CD or other portable medium. This permits viewers to run your slide show even if they do not have presentation software installed on their computers.

Multimedia Presentation Software Basics

The chief building block of the multimedia presentation is the *slide*. This is an individual screen containing a combination of multimedia *objects*. Objects are digital files that are *embedded*—contained within—a larger file. Sound, image, and animation files are all potential objects in a presentation.

In some multimedia presentation packages, objects can be added to a slide simply by dragging them from an *object bar*. In other programs, you use menus to embed objects.

Once you have created all the slides for your presentation, you are ready to *produce* your show. During the production phase, you attend to details such as the following:

- **Transitions**. *Transitions* are special effects between slides that add visual interest to your show. Known in some packages as "wipes," transitions include *dissolve* (one slide fading into another) and *explode* (a slide appearing to burst apart, revealing the next).

- **Timing.** This is the amount of time any given slide appears on the screen. Timing is one of the most important aspects of a multimedia presentation. If slides change too quickly, your viewers will not have a chance to appreciate each artwork fully. If a slide appears on the screen too long, the presentation may drag.

DIGITAL MEDIA HANDBOOK

Using Page Layout Software

The page you are reading right now was produced using page layout software. In the last two decades, this type of software has replaced earlier manual methods of page layout. It has revolutionized the process whereby printed materials are created.

Page Layout Software Basics

Page layout software is one of the chief digital tools of the graphic artist. When the application is opened, a blank text page appears surrounded by panes. Panes are windows containing the tools used to manage and arrange text. The text is imported from a word processing program.

The first step in the layout process is to set specifications for the printed page. These include the number of columns, the size of margins, and whether the page will be vertical (portrait) or horizontal (landscape).

Next, the graphic artist adds frames to the page. Frames are blank rectangles with dotted outlines used to hold either text or pictures. In the simplest layout, the artist creates a single text frame and "pours in" the text file. This type of layout is used for novels and other books that consist entirely of running text. For more complex page layouts, several frames of different sizes may be added. The page you are looking at right now contains a picture box and several different text boxes.

The typeface, or font, used for a particular block of text is chosen from a list of typefaces in the text pane. The text pane also allows the artist to control such features as paragraph indents and line spacing.

Technology NOTES

Style Sheets and Libraries

Page layout programs contain several powerful features that further streamline the graphic artist's work. Among these are *style sheets* and *libraries*. Style sheets are sets of user-defined instructions for how to treat a particular block of text or heading. They will include information including the font name, size and color, and the amount of vertical space above and below each line of text.

Libraries contain design elements like logos, and special features that are used repeatedly throughout the document. The artist simply drags a copy of the item from the library window into position on the page.

ARTISTS AND THEIR WORKS

A

Abbott, Berenice, American, b. 1898, photographer
The Night View, 202

Abrasha, Dutch-American, b. 1948, jewelry designer, goldsmith
Hanukkah Menorah, 72

Adla, Ashevak, Canadian, Inuit, sculptor
Walking Bear, 101, 102

Albizu, Olga, Puerto Rican, b. 1924, painter
Growth, 148

Albright, Ivan, American, 1897–1983, painter
The Picture of Dorian Gray, 177

Andrews, Benny, African American, b. 1930, painter, printmaker
Mom and Us, 81
Thelonious at The Five Spot, 82

Anguissola, Sofonisba, Italian, 1527–1625, painter
A Game of Chess, Involving the Painter's Three Sisters and a Servant, 358
Portrait of the Infanta Isabella Clara Eugenia, 292

Arreguin, Alfredo, Mexican American, b. 1935, painter
Nuestra Señora del la Selva, 222–223

B

Bashkirtseff, Marie, Russian, 1860–1884, painter
A Meeting, 301

Bearden, Romare, American, 1914–1988, painter, printmaker
In the Garden, 184
Return of Ulysses, 12, 13

Beaux, Cecilia, American, 1863–1942, painter
Ethel Page (Mrs. James Large), 290

Bellows, George, American, 1882–1925, painter, printmaker
Both Members of This Club, 258, 274

Benton, Thomas Hart, American, 1882–1975, painter
Country Dance, 78, 79
Cradling Wheat, 376–377

Berman, Eugene, Russian American, 1899–1972, painter, stage designer
Vendeur de Chapeaux, 43

Biggers, John, American, b.1924, painter
Starry Crown, 98, 99

Bishop, Isabel, American, 1902–1988, painter
Head #5, 44, 45

Black Hawk, Chief, Native American, 19th century, draftsman
Crow Men in Ceremonial Dress, 200

Bonheur, Rosa, French, 1822–1899, painter
The Horse Fair, 201, 369

Bonnard, Pierre, French, 1867–1947, painter, graphic artist
Family Scene, 266

Borsky, David, American, contemporary, photographer
Wall from the Sunken Courtyard of Tiwanaku, Bolivia, 55
Waterfall, 209

Brady, Mathew, American, 1823–1896, photographer
Civil War, 369

Brancusi, Constantin, Romanian, 1876–1957, sculptor
Bird in Space, 118
The Kiss, 104

Brice, Jeff, American, contemporary, computer artist
Untitled, 59

Brown, Roger, American, b. 1941, muralist
Hurricane Hugo, 10–11

Butterfield, Deborah, American, sculptor
Woodrow, 130–131

C

Calder, Alexander, American, 1898–1976, sculptor
Untitled (c. 1942), 213

Canaletto, Italian, 1697–1768, painter
Ascension Day Festival at Venice, 43

Caravaggio, Michelangelo Merisi da, Italian, 1573–1610, painter
The Conversion of St. Paul, 361

Carr, Emily, Canadian, 1871–1945, painter
Cumshewa, 241
A Rushing Sea of Undergrowth, 236

Cassatt, Mary, American, 1845–1926, painter
Margot in Blue, 140

Catlett, Elizabeth, African American, b. 1915, printmaker, sculptor, painter
Sharecropper, 48–49
Singing Their Songs, 312–313

Cézanne, Paul, French, 1839–1906, painter
The Basket of Apples, 155
The Gulf of Marseilles Seen from L'Estaque, 371

Chagall, Marc, Russian, 1887–1985, painter, stained glass artist
The American Windows, 136
The Green Violinist, 282, 283
Homage to Gogol, 271

Chihuly, Dale, American, b. 1941, glass artist
Malina Window, 40, 41

Chryssa, Greek American, sculptor, painter
The Gates to Times Square, 303

Church, Frederic Edwin, American, 1826–1900, painter
The Icebergs, 2–3

Close, Chuck, American, b. 1940, painter
Paul, 384–385
Self-Portrait, 385

Cromartie, James H., American, painter
View of the White House, South Portico, 230

D

Dali, Salvador, Spanish, 1904–1989, painter
The Elephants (Design for the Opera La Dama Spagnola e il Cavaliere Romano), 278

David, Jacques-Louis, French, 1748–1825, painter
The Death of Socrates, 366

da Vinci, Leonardo. see Leonardo da Vinci

Davis, Stuart, American, 1894–1964, painter
Hot Still Scape for Six Colors-7th Avenue Style, 1940, 154–156
Degas, Edgar, French, 1834–1917, painter, sculptor
Before the Ballet, 238
The Little Fourteen-Year-Old Dancer, 180, 181
Self-Portrait, 181
Delacroix, Eugène, French, 1798–1863, painter
Arabs Skirmishing in the Mountains, 367
Dunnigan, John, American, 20th century, furniture designer
Slipper Chairs, 33
Dürer, Albrecht, German, 1471–1528, painter, printmaker
An Oriental Ruler Seated on His Throne, 76

E

El Greco, Spanish, 1541–1614, painter
Saint Martin and the Beggar, 360
Ernst, Max, German (in America after 1941), 1891–1976, painter
Age of Forests, 183
Escher, M. C., Dutch, 1898–1972, printmaker
Day and Night, 218
Portrait of M. C. Escher, 105
Reptiles, 210
Waterfall, 105
Estes, Richard, American, b. 1932, painter
Paris Street Scene, 381

F

Feiss, David, American, b. 1959, animator
Thrown for a Curve, 308
Fish, Janet, American, b. 1939, painter
Oranges, 175, 176
Raspberries and Goldfish, 16–17
Flack, Audrey, American, b. 1931, painter, sculptor
Self-Portrait: The Memory, 82
Frankenthaler, Helen, American, b. 1928, painter
The Bay, 111

Gainsborough, Thomas, English, 1727–1788, painter
The Blue Boy, 364
Gaudi, Antonio, Spanish, 1852–1926, architect
ceramic park bench *(Barcelona, Spain),* 194
Sagrada Familia (church), 194
Gauguin, Paul, French, 1848–1903, painter
Faaturuma (Melancholic), 372
Tahitians, 265–266
Gehry, Frank, American, b. 1929, architect, sculptor
The Experience Music Project (Seattle, Washington), 132
Guggenheim Museum (Bilbao, Spain), 56, 132, 388, 389
Office complex, two towers (Prague, Czech Republic), 132
Gentileschi, Artemisia, Italian, c. 1597–after 1651, painter
Judith and Maidservant with the Head of Holofernes, 111
Giotto di Bondone, Italian, c. 1266–1337, painter
Madonna and Child, 263

Glarner, Fritz, Swiss American, 1899–1972 painter
Relational Painting, Tondo #40, 147
Goings, Ralph, American, b. 1928, painter, sculptor
Diner With Red Door, 112
Goya, Francisco, Spanish, 1746–1828, painter
The Third of May, 364–365
Grandma Moses, American, 1860–1961, painter
Sugaring Off, 110
Graves, Nancy, American, b. 1940, sculptor
Zaga, 51
Grooms, Red, American, b. 1937, installation artist
Ruckus Rodeo, 24, 25
Gwathmey, Robert, American, 1903–1988, painter
Children Dancing, 297

H

Hanson, Duane, American, b. 1925, sculptor
Football Player, 192–193
Old Couple on a Bench, 381
Hassam, Childe, American, 1859–1935, painter, printmaker
Jelly Fish, 157
Hines, Jessica, American, contemporary, photographer
Dream Series, 57, 58
Hiroshige, Utagawa (Andō), Japanese, 1797–1858, printmaker
Plum Garden at Kameido Umeyashiki, 92–93
Hirschfeld, Al, American, 1903–2003, illustrator
Elvis Presley, "Blue Suede Shoes," 94
Self-Portrait at 99, 94
Hodler, Ferdinand, Swiss, 1853–1918, painter
James Vilbert, Sculptor, 240
Hofmann, Hans, German (born in America), 1880–1966, painter
Flowering Swamp, 378
Hokusai, Katsushika, Japanese, 1760–1849, printmaker, painter
Ejiri in Suruga Province, 330
Shichiri Beach in Sagami Province, 246
Holbein, Hans, German, 1465–1524, painter
Anne of Cleves, 9
Homer, Winslow, American, 1836–1910, painter
Hound and Hunter, 46
Sketch for 'Hound and Hunter,' 46
Hoover, John, Native American, Aleut, b. 1919, sculptor
Shaman's Journey, 180
Hopper, Edward, American, 1882–1967, painter
Railroad Sunset, 77
Houser, Allan, Native American, 1914–1994, sculptor
Coming of Age, 209
Reverie, 298, 299
Hua Yen, Chinese, c. 1682–1765
Conversation in Autumn, 328
Huntington, Anna Hyatt, American, 1876–1973, sculptor
Riders to the Sea, 120

I

Inness, George, American, 1825–1894, painter
The Lackawanna Valley, 11

J

Jacquette, Yvonne, American, b. 1934, painter
Town of Skowhegan, Maine V, 70
Jimenez, Luis, American, b. 1940, sculptor
Fiesta Jarabel, 314
Howl, 314
Vaquero, 50
Johns, Jasper, American, b. 1930, painter
Cups 4 Picasso, 103
Map, 296
Johnson, Philip, American, b. 1906, architect
Seagram Building (with Mies van der Rohe), 382
Water Garden, 298
Johnson, William H., African American, 1901–1970, painter
Harbor Under the Midnight Sun, 162

K

Kahlo, Frida, Mexican, 1907–1954, painter
Self-Portrait Dedicated to Leon Trotsky, 239
Self-Portrait with Monkey, 4, 5
Kandinsky, Wassily, Russian, 1866–1944, painter
Tension in Red, 134, 135
Kapoor, Anish, British, b. 1954, sculptor
Sculpture (1981), 168
Kiitsu, Suzuki, Japanese, 1796–1858, painter
Reeds and Cranes (one of a pair of screens), 410–411
Kirchner, Ernst Ludwig, German, 1880–1938, painter
Seated Woman, 35
Winter Landscape in Moonlight, 34
Klimt, Gustav, Austrian, 1862–1918, painter
Baby (Cradle), 286, 287
Portrait of Joseph Pembaur, 276
Kollwitz, Käthe, German, 1867–1945, painter, printmaker, graphic artist
Self-Portrait, 374
Krasner, Lee, American, b. 1908, painter
The Springs, 291

L

Lachaise, Gaston, French, 1882–1935, sculptor
Walking Woman, 271, 272
Lange, Dorothea, American, 1895–1965, photojournalist
Migrant Mother, 57
Larraz, Julio, Cuban, b. 1944, painter
Papiamento, 32
Lawrence, Jacob, African American, 1917–2000, painter
Children at Play, 78, 80, 377
Harriet Tubman Series Number 4, 216
Street to M'bari, 66–67
Le Corbusier, Swiss, 1887–1965, architect
Unite d'Habitation, 259

Lee, Doris, American, b. 1905, printmaker, painter
Thanksgiving, 116
Lee-Smith, Hughie, African American, 1915–2000, painter
The Piper, 28, 29
Leonardo Da Vinci, Italian, 1452–1519, painter, sculptor
sketchbook page, 42
Leyster, Judith, Dutch, 1609–1660, painter
The Concert, 178, 256, 257
Lichtenstein, Roy, American, b. 1923, painter
Blam, 379
Liebovitz, Annie, American, 20th century, photographer
Wilt Chamberlain and Willie Shoemaker, 262
Lin, Maya, American, b. 1959, architect, sculptor
The Civil Rights Memorial, 386
The Wave Field, 207

M

Magritte, René, Belgian, 1898–1967, painter
The False Mirror, 375
Manet, Édouard, French, 1832–1883, painter
The Railway, 368–369
Marc, Franz, German, 1880–1916, painter
Yellow Cow, 154
Marisol, Venezuelan (in America since 1950), b. 1930, sculptor
The Family, 268
Matisse, Henri, French, 1869–1954, painter
Interior with Egyptian Curtain, 68, 69
Red Interior Still Life on a Blue Table, 38
Mays, J, American, b. 1955, industrial designer
Volkswagen Beetle, 401
McKie, Judy Kensley, American, b. 1944, furniture artist
Monkey Settee, 53
Michelangelo Buonarroti, Italian, 1475–1564, sculptor, painter
David, 267
Pietà, 356, 357
Mies van der Rohe, Ludwig, American, 1886–1969, architect
Seagram Building (with Johnson), 381–382
Miró, Joan, Spanish, 1893–1983, painter, sculptor
Landscape (The Hare), 235
Mitchell, Joan, American, 1926–1992, painter
Dirty Snow, 179
Mondrian, Piet, Dutch, 1872–1944, painter
Sun, Church in Zeeland, 146
Monet, Claude, French, 1840–1926, painter
Gladioli, 370
Rouen Cathedral, West Facade, 153
Rouen Cathedral, West Facade, Sunlight, 153
Moore, Henry, English, 1898–1986, sculptor
Dallas Piece, 122
Moroles, Jesús Bautista, American, b. 1950, sculptor
Granite Weaving Playscape, 170, 171
Moses, Anna Mary Robertson. See Grandma Moses
Moulthrop, Philip, American, b. 1947, craftsperson
White Pine Mosaic Bowl, 205–206

Munch, Edvard, Norwegian, 1863–1944, painter, printmaker
The Sick Child, 7

Münter, Gabriele, German, 1877–1962, painter
Breakfast of the Birds, 18

Mununggiritj, Yäma, Australian, Aboriginal artist
Yellow Ochre Quarry, 152

Murray, Elizabeth, American, b. 1940, painter
Things to Come, 150

Myron, Greek, c. 480–440 B.C., sculptor
Discobolus (Discus Thrower), 353

N

Namingha, Dan, Native American, b. 1950, painter
Blessing Rain Chant, 75, 77

Naranjo, Michael, Native American, b. 1944, sculptor
Spirits Soaring, 108, 109

Neel, Alice, American, 1900–1984, painter
Still Life, Rose of Sharon, 74

Nevelson, Louise, American, 1899–1988, sculptor
Dawn, 300

O

O'Keeffe, Georgia, American, 1887–1986, painter
Back of Marie's No. 4, 316–317
Cow's Skull: Red, White, and Blue, 30
White Rose With Larkspur, No. 2, 240

Oldenburg, Claes, American, b. 1929, painter, sculptor
Clothespin, 261
Shoestring Potatoes Spilling from a Bag, 96, 97

Oonark, Jessie, Canadian, Inuit, 1906–1986, printmaker
Untitled (1973), 346–347

Orozco, José Clemente, Mexican, 1883–1949, painter
Barricade, 28

P

Paley, Albert Raymond, American, b. 1944, sculptor
Portal Gates, 78

Panini, Giovanni Paolo, Italian, 1691/2–1765, painter
Interior of Saint Peter's Rome, 113

Pei, I. M., Chinese American, b. 1917, architect
Rock-and-Roll Hall of Fame and Museum, 399

Pereira, Irene Rice, American, 1907–1971, painter
Pillar of Fire, 289

Picabia, Francis, French, 1879–1953, painter
Figure Triste, 148, 149

Picasso, Pablo, Spanish, 1881–1973, painter, sculptor
"Ma Jolie" (Woman with a Zither or Guitar), 375
Las Meninas (after Velásquez), 14–15
The Old Guitarist, 270
Studio of "La Californie," 38
The Tragedy, 145

Pinkney, Brian, African American, b. 1961, illustrator
Duke Ellington: The Piano Prince and His Orchestra (cover illustration), 406

Pinkney, Jerry, African American, b. 1939, illustrator
Journeys with Elijah (illustration), 237

Pippin, Horace, African American, 1888–1946, folk artist
Cabin in the Cotton, 234

Pollaiuolo, Italian, c. 1441–1496, painter
Daphne and Apollo, 168

Pollock, Jackson, American, 1912–1956, painter
Cathedral, 13–14, 42

Poons, Larry, American, b.1937, painter
Orange Crush, 379–380

Pootoogook, Napachie, Inuit, b. 1938, printmaker
My Daughter's First Steps, 268–269

Proctor, Mary L., African American, folk artist
Like a Butterfly, 306

R

Rashid, Karim, Egyptian, b. 1960, industrial designer
Chair, 408
Chess set, 408

Rauschenberg, Robert, American, b. 1925, painter
Red Painting, 290

Rembrandt van Rijn, Dutch, 1606-1669, painter
Aristotle with a Bust of Homer, 124, 178, 362

Renoir, Pierre Auguste, French, 1841–1919, painter
Two Sisters (On the Terrace), 177

Ringgold, Faith, African American, b. 1930, painter, soft sculptor
The Men: Mask Face Quilt #2, 198, 199

Rivera, Diego, Mexican, 1886–1957, painter, muralist
Flower Day, 229
Making of a Fresco Showing the Building of a City, The, 254, 255
Self-Portrait, 229

Rothko, Mark, Russian American, 1903–1970, painter
Ochre and Red on Red, 380

Roualt, Georges, French, 1871–1958, painter
The Italian Woman, 74

Royo, Josep, Spanish, b. 1945, textile artist
Woman (after Joan Miró), 86

Rubens, Peter Paul, Flemish, 1577–1640, painter
Daniel in the Lions' Den, 291

Ruiz, Antonio M., Mexican, 1897–1964, painter
The Bicycle Race, 126

Russell, Julia, American, b. 1949, painter
Jaguar Chair, 304

S

Safdie, Moshe, Israeli, b. 1938, architect
Habitat, 382

Samaras, Lucas, American, b. 1936, sculptor, experimental artist
Mirrored Room, 62–63

Sandkühler, Iris, American, b. 1958, jewelry
Viking Net Chain Necklace, 84

Savage, Augusta, African American, 20th century, sculptor
Lift Every Voice and Sing, 209

Schapiro, Miriam, American, b. 1923, painter, sculptor
Father and Daughter, 166–167
In Her Own Image, 180

Scully, Sean, Irish, b. 1945, painter
White Robe, 295

Sewell, Leo, American, found object sculptor
Penguin, 186

Shaughnessy, Arthur, Native American, 1884–1945, sculptor
Dla'ehl Interior House Post: Grizzly Bear Beneath Kolus, 250–251

Shitao, Qing Dynasty, painter *Orchids, Bamboo, and Rock,* 83

Silvers, Robert, American, contemporary, digital artist
Wolf, 188

Siqueiros, David Alfaro, Mexican, 1896–1974, painter
Echo of a Scream, 235
Ethnography, 294
Self-Portrait (El Coronelazo), 264

Smith, David, American, 1906–1965, sculptor
The Royal Bird, 117

Smith, Tony, American, 1912–1980, sculptor
Gracehopper, 101

Solberg, Ramona, American, contemporary, jewelry
Cracker Jack Choo Choo, 214

Stella, Frank, American, b. 1936, painter, sculptor
Agbatana III, 380
St. Michael's Counterguard (Malta Series), 383

Stella, Joseph, Italian American, 1877–1946, painter
Battle of Lights, 212

Straus, Meyer, American, 19th century, painter
Bayou Teche, 6

Sullivan, Louis, American, 1856–1924, architect
Elevator Grille, 204
Wainwright Building, 56

Sutej, Miroslav, Yugoslavian, b. 1936, lithographer
Ultra AB, 288

T

Tamayo, Rufino, Mexican, 1899–1991, painter
Fruit Vendors, 196–197
Girl Attacked by a Strange Bird, 141

Taymor, Julie, American, director, theater artist, puppetry
The Lion King, 224

Thomas, Alma, American, 1891–1978, painter
Iris, Tulips, Jonquils, and Crocuses, 26

Torivio, Dorothy, Native American, b. 1946, ceramicist
Vase, 233

Torres-Garcia, Joaquin, Uruguayan, 1874–1949, painter
New York City: Bird's Eye View, 88

Turner, Joseph M. W., English, 1775–1851, painter
Snowstorm: Steamboat off a Harbours Mouth, 368

Twiggs, Leo, African American, b. 1934, batik painter
East Wind Suite: Door, 10, 42
Single Family Blues, 269

V

van Alen, William, American, 1882–1954, architect
Chrysler Building, 206

van der Weyden, Rogier, Flemish, 1399–1464, painter
Portrait of a Lady, 359

van Eyck, Jan, Flemish, before 1395–1441, painter
The Arnolfi Wedding, 168, 231, 359

van Gogh, Vincent, Dutch, 1853–1890, painter
Café Terrace at Night, 293
The Starry Night, 372–373
Sunflowers, 178

Velázquez, Diego, Spanish, 1599–1660, painter
Las Meninas (The Maids of Honor), 14–15

Vermeer, Jan, Dutch, 1632–1675, painter
The Concert, 350, 351
Girl with the Red Hat, 362

Vigée-Lebrun, Marie-Louise-Élisabeth, French, 1755–1842, painter
Portrait of Princess Belozersky, 268

W

Walkus, George, Kwakiutl, 20th century, maskmaker
Secret Society Mask (Four Headed Cannibal Spirit), 272, 273

Warhol, Andy, American, 1928–1987, painter, printmaker
100 Cans, 20, 21
Self-Portrait, 21

Watteau, Antoine, French, 1684–1721, painter
Embarkation for Cythera, 362–363

Wilkinson, Signe, American, political cartoonist
Self-Portrait, 284
The Thoroughly Modern Medical School, 284

Wilson, Jane, American, b. 1924, painter
Tempest, 302
Winter Wheat, 120, 121

Wood, Grant, American, 1892–1942, painter
American Gothic, 12, 23

Woodruff, Hale, American, b. 1900, painter
Poor Man's Cotton, 202, 203

Wright, Frank Lloyd, American, 1867–1959, architect
Armchair, 118–119
Fallingwater House, 300–301
Taliesin West, 182
Xanadu Gallery, 377

Wyeth, Andrew, American, b. 1917, painter
Winter, 1946, 292

X

Xiong, Chaing, Laotian, b. 1953, craftsperson
Hmong Story Cloth, 211

PREHISTORIC–1 A.D.

Artist Unknown, Altamira Caves, Spain
The Hall of the Bulls, c. 15,000 B.C., 320, Fig. 12.2
Artist Unknown
Statua di Donna, 2700–2600 B.C., 322, Fig. 12.3
Artist Unknown, Egyptian
The Goddess Hathor Places the Magic Collar on Sethos I,
c. 1303–1290 B.C, 323, Fig. 12.5
Artist Unknown, Mexican, Olmec
Colossal Head, 1200 B.C.–A.D. 500, 339, Fig. 12.26
Artist Unknown, Chinese, Shang dynasty
Ritual Wine Container, 1200 B.C., 325, Fig. 12.8
Artist Unknown, Indian
Siva as Lord of the Dance, c. 950, 327, Fig. 12.10
Artist Unknown, Sanchi India
Great Stupa, 1st century B.C., 326, Fig. 12.9
Myron, Greek, c. 480–440 B.C., sculptor
Discobolus (Discus Thrower), c. 450 B.C., 353, Fig. 13.3
Artist Unknown, Roman
Portrait Statue of Boy, 50 B.C., 353, Fig. 13.4

A.D. 1–1399

Artist Unknown, Mexican, Zapotec (from Monte Alban)
Urn, 500–700, 230, Fig. 9.6
Artist Unknown, Kashmir
Crowned Buddha Shakyamuni, 8th century, 318, Fig. 12.1
Artist Unknown, Huari people, Peru
Tunic, 800–1000, 207, Fig. 8.11
Artist Unknown, Byzantine
Virgin and Child, mid 10th–11th century, 354, Fig. 13.5
Artist Unknown, African, Yoruba people
Portrait of a king, 11th–15th century, 332, Fig. 12.17
Artist Unknown, African, Bamana people
Bamana iron figure, 13th century, 334, Fig. 12.19
Artist Unknown, African, Dogon people
Seated Man and Woman, 13th century, 334, Fig. 12.20
Artist Unknown, African, Mali
Equestrian figure, c. 13th century, 334, Fig. 12.18
Artist Unknown, Armenian
Front cover of The Gospels, 13th century, 158, Fig. 6.30
Artist Unknown, Japanese
Great Buddha at Kamakura, 1252, 329, Fig. 12.14
Giotto di Bondone, Italian, c. 1266–1337, painter
Madonna and Child, 1320–30, 263, Fig. 10.13
Artist Unknown
Missal (The Calling of Saints Peter and Andrew), 1389–1404,
391, Fig. 14.4

1400–1499

Leonardo Da Vinci, Italian, 1452–1519, painter, sculptor
sketchbook page, date unknown, 42, Fig. 3.2
Pollaiuolo, Italian, c. 1441–1496, painter
Daphne and Apollo, 15th century, 168
Artist Unknown, Egyptian
Nakht and Wife, c. 1425, 260, Fig. 10.8
Artist Unknown, Ming Dynasty
Chinese pair of vases, 1426–1435, 99, Fig. 5.4

Artist Unknown, (Tsang) Ngor Monastery, Tibet
Four Mandalas of the Vajravali Series, 1429–1456, 226,
Fig. 9.1
Artist Unknown, Valencia, Spain
Dish, 1430, 232, Fig. 9.9
van Eyck, Jan, Flemish, before 1395–1441, painter
The Arnolfi Wedding, 1434, 231, Fig. 9.8
Artist Unknown, Aztec
Plumed Serpent (Quetzalcoatl), last half of the 15th century,
119, Fig. 5.32
van der Weyden, Rogier, Flemish, 1399–1464, painter
Portrait of a Lady, c. 1460, 359, Fig. 13.10
Dürer, Albrecht, German, 1471–1528, painter, printmaker
An Oriental Ruler Seated on His Throne, c. 1495, 76,
Fig. 4.15
Artist Unknown, Shanxi or Henan Province, China
Jar, late 15th century, 297, Fig. 11.15

1500–1599

Artist Unknown, Africa
Queen Idia, 16th century, 348
Artist Unknown, Nigeria
Plaque: Oba or Chief, 16th–17th century, 262, Fig. 10.10
Michelangelo Buonarroti, Italian, 1475–1564, sculptor,
painter
David, 1501–1504, 267, Fig. 10.19
Pietà, c. 1500, 357, Fig. 13.8
Holbein, Hans, German, 1465–1524, painter
Anne of Cleves, 1539, 9, Fig. 1.6
Artist Unknown, African, Edo people
Mounted King with Attendants, c. 16th–17th century, 335,
Fig. 12.21
Anguissola, Sofonisba, Italian, 1527–1625, painter
*A Game of Chess, Involving the Painter's Three Sisters and a
Servant,* 1555, 358, Fig. 13.9
Portrait of the Infanta Isabella Clara Eugenia, c. 1578, 292,
Fig. 11.9
Artist Unknown, India
Stalling Elephant With Two Riders, 1590–1595, 174, Fig. 7.4
El Greco, Spanish, 1541–1614, painter
Saint Martin and the Beggar, 1597/1599, 360, Fig. 13.11

1600–1699

Caravaggio, Michelangelo Merisi da, Italian, 1573–1610,
painter
The Conversion of St. Paul, c. 1601, 361, Fig. 13.12
Rubens, Peter Paul, Flemish, 1577–1640, painter
Daniel in the Lions' Den, 1615, 291, Fig. 11.7
Gentileschi, Artemisia, Italian, c. 1597–after 1651, painter
Judith and Maidservant with the Head of Holofernes, c. 1625,
111, Fig. 5.17
Leyster, Judith, Dutch, 1609–1660, painter
The Concert, c. 1633, 257, Fig. 10.4
Artist Unknown, African, Asante people
Man's cloth (Kente cloth), 17th century, 336, Fig. 12.23
Rembrandt van Rijn, Dutch, 1606–1669, painter
Aristotle with a Bust of Homer, 1653, 124, Fig. 5.36

Velázquez, Diego, Spanish, 1599–1660, painter
  Las Meninas (The Maids of Honor), 1656, 15, Fig. 1.15
Vermeer, Jan, Dutch, 1632–1675, painter
  The Concert, 1658–60, 350, Fig. 13.1
  Girl with the Red Hat, 1665/1666, 362, Fig. 13.13

1700–1799

Shitao, Qing Dynasty
  Orchids, Bamboo, and Rock, c. 1700, 83, Fig. 4.24
Watteau, Antoine, French, 1684–1721, painter
  Embarkment for Cythera, 1717–19, 363, Fig. 13.14
Panini, Giovanni Paolo, Italian, 1691/2–1765, painter
  Interior of Saint Peter's Rome, 1746–1754, 113, Fig. 5.19
Hua Yen, Chinese, c. 1682–1765
  Conversation in Autumn, 1765, 328, Fig. 12.12
Canaletto, Italian, 1697–1768, painter
  *Ascension Day Festival at Venice,*1766, 43, Fig. 3.4
Gainsborough, Thomas, English, 1727–1788, painter
  The Blue Boy, c. 1770, 364, Fig. 13.15
David, Jacques-Louis, French, 1748–1825, painter
  The Death of Socrates, 1787, 366, Fig. 13.17
Vigée-Lebrun, Marie-Louise-Élisabeth, French,
  1755–1842, painter
  Portrait of Princess Belozersky, 1798, 268, Fig. 10.20

1800–1899

Artist Unknown, Himachai Pradesh, India
  Chamba Rumal, early 19th century, 244, Fig. 9.24
Kiitsu, Suzuki, Japanese, 1796–1858, painter
  Reeds and Cranes, (one of a pair of screens), nineteenth
  century, 410–411
Goya, Francisco, Spanish, 1746–1828, painter
  The Third of May, 1808, 1814, 365, Fig. 13.16
Hokusai, Katsushika, Japanese, 1760–1849,
  printmaker, painter
  Shichiri Beach in Sagami Province, 1823–1831, 246, Fig. 9.25
  Ejiri in Suruga Province, 1831, 330, Fig. 12.15
Turner, Joseph M. W., English, 1775–1851, painter
  Snowstorm: Steamboat off a Harbours Mouth, 1842, 368,
  Fig. 13.19
Artist Unknown, African, Akan people
  Necklace, 19th century, 336, Fig. 12.22
Artist Unknown, Inuit
  Mask of Moon Goddess, before 1900, 342, Fig. 12.29
Bonheur, Rosa, French, 1822–1899, painter
  The Horse Fair, 1853–1855, 201, Fig. 8.3
Inness, George, American, 1825–1894, painter
  The Lackawanna Valley, c. 1856, 11, Fig. 1.9
Hiroshige, Utagawa (Andō), Japanese, 1797–1858,
  printmaker
  Plum Garden at Kameido Umeyashiki, 1857, 92, Fig. 4.32
Degas, Edgar, French, 1834–1917, painter, sculptor
  Self-Portrait, c. 1862, 181
Delacroix, Eugène, French, 1798–1863, painter
  Arabs Skirmishing in the Mountains, 1863, 367, Fig. 13.18
Brady, Mathew, American, 1823–1896, photographer
  Civil War, 1865, 369, Fig. 3.21

Artist Unknown, Northwest coast region, Haida
  Haida totem pole, c. 1870, 343, Fig. 12.30
Manet, Édouard, French, 1832–1883, painter
  The Railway, 1873, 369, Fig. 13.20
Monet, Claude, French, 1840–1926, painter
  Gladioli, 1876, 370, Fig. 13.22
Black Hawk, Chief, Native American, 19th century,
  draftsman
  Crow Men in Ceremonial Dress, 1880–1881, 200, Fig 8.2
Degas, Edgar, French, 1834–1917, painter, sculptor
  The Little Fourteen-Year-Old Dancer, c. 1880, 181, Fig. 7.12
Renoir, Pierre Auguste, French, 1841–1919, painter
  Two Sisters (On the Terrace), 1881, 177, Fig. 7.7
Bashkirtseff, Marie, Russian, 1860–1884, painter
  A Meeting, 1884, 301, Fig. 11.21
Beaux, Cecilia, American, 1863–1942, painter
  Ethel Page (Mrs. James Large), 1884, 290, Fig. 11.5
Cézanne, Paul, French, 1839–1906, painter
  The Gulf of Marseilles Seen from L'Estaque, 1885, 371,
  Fig. 13.23
van Gogh, Vincent, Dutch, 1853–1890, painter
  Café Terrace at Night, 1888, 293, Fig. 11.10
  Sunflowers, 1888, 178, Fig. 7.8
  The Starry Night, 1889, 373, Fig. 13.25
Sullivan, Louis, American, 1856–1924, architect
  Wainwright Building, 1890–1891, 56, Fig. 3.17
Artist Unknown, Native American
  Feather Bonnet, c. 1890, 345, Fig. 12.33
Artist Unknown, Native American, Navajo
  Saddle blanket, c. 1890, 344, Fig. 12.32
Degas, Edgar, French, 1834–1917, painter, sculptor
  Before the Ballet, 1890/1892, 238, Fig. 9.18
Klimt, Gustav, Austrian, 1862–1918, painter
  Portrait of Joseph Pembaur, 1890, 276, Fig. 10.29
Gauguin, Paul, French, 1848–1903, painter
  Faaturuma (Melancholic), 1891, 372, Fig. 13.24
  Tahitians, 1891–93, 265, Fig. 10.17
Homer, Winslow, American, 1836–1910, painter
  Hound and Hunter, 1892, 46, Fig. 3.8
  Sketch for 'Hound and Hunter', 1892, 46, Fig. 3.9
Bonnard, Pierre, French, 1867–1947, painter,
  graphic artist
  Family Scene, 1893, 266, Fig. 10.18
Sullivan, Louis, American, 1856–1924, architect
  Elevator Grille, 1893–1894, 204, Fig. 8.7
Monet, Claude, French, 1840–1926, painter
  Rouen Cathedral, West Facade, 1894, 153, Fig. 6.24
  Rouen Cathedral, West Facade, Sunlight, 1894, 153,
  Fig. 6.25
Cézanne, Paul, French, 1839–1906, painter
  The Basket of Apples, c. 1895, 155, Fig 6.27
Church, Frederic Edwin, American, 1826–1900, painter
  The Icebergs, 1861, 2–3
Straus, Meyer, American, 19th century, painter
  Bayou Teche, 1870, 6, Fig. 1.2

1900–1949

Matisse, Henri, French, 1869–1954, painter
Red Interior Still Life on a Blue Table, early twentieth century, 38

Cassatt, Mary, American, 1845–1926, painter
Margot in Blue, 1902, 140, Fig. 6.8

Picasso, Pablo, Spanish, 1881–1973, painter, sculptor
The Old Guitarist, 1903, 270, Fig. 10.24
The Tragedy, 1903, 145, Fig. 6.13

Hodler, Ferdinand, Swiss, 1853–1918, painter
James Vilbert, Sculptor, 1907, 240, Fig. 9.20

Kirchner, Ernst Ludwig, German, 1880–1938, painter
Seated Woman, 1907, 35, Fig. 2.9

Munch, Edvard, Norwegian, 1863–1944, painter, printmaker
The Sick Child, 1907, 7, Fig. 1.3

Shaughnessy, Arthur, Native American, 1884–1945, sculptor
Dla'ehl Interior House Post: Grizzly Bear Beneath Kolus, c. 1907, 250, Fig. 9.30

Brancusi, Constantin, Romanian, 1876–1957, sculptor
The Kiss, c. 1908, 104, Fig. 5.9

Wright, Frank Lloyd, American, 1867–1959, architect
Armchair, c. 1908, 119, Fig. 5.31

Bellows, George, American, 1882–1925, painter, printmaker
Both Members of This Club, 1909, 258, 274, Fig. 10.6, Fig. 10.28

Artist Unknown, Native American, Pueblo
Water jar, 1910, 343, Fig. 12.31

Mondrian, Piet, Dutch, 1872–1944, painter
Sun, Church in Zeeland, 1910, 146, Fig. 6.15

Marc, Franz, German, 1880–1916, painter
Yellow Cow, 1911, 154, Fig. 6.26

Picasso, Pablo, Spanish, 1881–1973, painter, sculptor
"Ma Jolie" (Woman with a Zither or Guitar), 1911–12, 375, Fig. 13.27

Carr, Emily, Canadian, 1871–1945, painter
Cumshewa, c. 1912, 241, Fig. 9.22

Hassam, Childe, American, 1859–1935, painter, printmaker
Jelly Fish, 1912, 157, Fig. 6.29

Huntington, Anna Hyatt, American, 1876–1973, sculptor
Riders to the Sea, 1912, 120, Fig. 5.33

Picabia, Francis, French, 1879–1953, painter
Figure Triste, 1912, 149, Fig. 6.21

Stella, Joseph, Italian American, 1877–1946, painter
Battle of Lights, 1913-1914, 212, Fig. 8.19

Chagall, Marc, Russian, 1887–1985, painter, stained glass artist
Homage to Gogol, 1917, 271, Fig. 10.25

Klimt, Gustav, Austrian, 1862–1918, painter
Baby (Cradle), 1917, 286, Fig. 11.1

Kirchner, Ernst Ludwig, German, 1880–1938, painter
Winter Landscape in Moonlight, 1919, 34, Fig. 2.8

Artist Unknown, New Ireland
Mask, c. 1920, 273, Fig. 10.27

Artist Unknown, Venezuela
Apron, beaded, early twentieth century, 208, Fig. 8.12

Torres-Garcia, Joaquin, Uruguayan, 1874–1949, painter
New York City: Bird's Eye View, 1920, 88, Fig. 4.27

Kollwitz, Käthe, German, 1867–1945, painter, printmaker, graphic artist
Self-Portrait, 1921, 374, Fig. 13.26

Lachaise, Gaston, French, 1882–1935, sculptor
Walking Woman, 1922, 272, Fig. 10.26

Chagall, Marc, Russian, 1887–1985, painter, stained glass artist
The Green Violinist, 1923–24, 282, Fig. 10.35

Rivera, Diego, Mexican, 1886–1957, painter, muralist
Flower Day, 1925, 229, Fig. 9.5

Yoruba people
Headdress for Epa Masquerade, first half of twentieth century, 36, Fig. 2.10

Ernst, Max, German (in America after 1941), 1891–1976, painter
Age of Forests, 1926, 183, Fig. 7.15

Kandinsky, Wassily, Russian, 1866–1944, painter
Tension in Red, 1926, 134, Fig. 6.1

Miró, Joan, Spanish, 1893–1983, painter, sculptor
Landscape (The Hare), 1927, 235, Fig. 9.13

O'Keeffe, Georgia, American, 1887–1986, painter
White Rose With Larkspur, No. 2, 1927, 240, Fig. 9.21

Brancusi, Constantin, Romanian, 1876–1957, sculptor
Bird in Space, 1928, 118, Fig. 5.30

Magritte, René, Belgian, 1898–1967, painter
The False Mirror, 1928, 375, Fig. 13.28

Benton, Thomas Hart, American, 1882–1975, painter
Country Dance, 1929, 79, Fig. 4.18

Hopper, Edward, American, 1882–1967, painter
Railroad Sunset, 1929, 77, Fig. 4.16

van Alen, William, American, 1882–1954, architect
Chrysler Building, completed 1930, 206, Fig. 8.9

Wood, Grant, American, 1892–1942, painter
American Gothic, 1930, 12, Fig. 1.10

O'Keeffe, Georgia, American, 1887–1986, painter
Back of Marie's No. 4, 1931, 316–317
Cow's Skull: Red, White, and Blue, 1931, 30, Fig. 2.5

Orozco, José Clemente, Mexican, 1883–1949, painter
Barricade, 1931, 28, Fig. 2.3

Rivera, Diego, Mexican, 1886–1957, painter, muralist
The Making of a Fresco Showing the Building of a City, 1931, 254, Fig. 10.1

Carr, Emily, Canadian, 1871–1945, painter
A Rushing Sea of Undergrowth, 1932–1935, 236, Fig. 9.15

Münter, Gabriele, German, 1877–1962, painter
Breakfast of the Birds, 1934, 18, Fig. 1.17

Lee, Doris, American, b. 1905, printmaker, painter
Thanksgiving, 1935, 116, Fig. 5.27

Pippin, Horace, African American, 1888–1946, folk artist
Cabin in the Cotton, mid-1930s, 234, Fig. 9.12

Abbott, Berenice, American, b. 1898, photographer
The Night View, 1936, 202, Fig. 8.4

Lange, Dorothea, American, 1895–1965, photojournalist
Migrant Mother, 1936, 57, Fig. 3.18

Wright, Frank Lloyd, American, 1867–1959, architect
Fallingwater House, 1936, 301, Fig. 11.20

Johnson, William H., African American, 1901–1970, painter
Harbor Under the Midnight Sun, 1937, 162, Fig. 6.32

Kahlo, Frida, Mexican, 1907–1954, painter
Self-Portrait Dedicated to Leon Trotsky, 1937, 239, Fig. 9.19

Siqueiros, David Alfaro, Mexican, 1896–1974, painter
Echo of a Scream, 1937, 235, Fig. 9.14

Wright, Frank Lloyd, American, 1867–1959, architect
Taliesin West, 1937, 182, Fig 7.13

Benton, Thomas Hart, American, 1882–1975, painter
Cradling Wheat, 1938, 376, Fig. 13.29

Escher, M. C., Dutch, 1898–1972, printmaker
Day and Night, 1938, 218, Fig. 8.23

Roualt, Georges, French, 1871–1958, painter
The Italian Woman, 1938, 74, Fig. 4.12

Ruiz, Antonio M., Mexican, 1897–1964, painter
The Bicycle Race, 1938, 126, Fig. 5.37

Walkus, George, Kwakiutl, 20th century, maskmaker
Secret Society Mask (Four Headed Cannibal Spirit), 1938, 273, Fig. 10.27

Kahlo, Frida, Mexican, 1907–1954, painter
Self-Portrait with Monkey, 1938, 4, 5, Fig. 1.1

Berman, Eugene, Russian American, 1899–1972, painter, stage designer
Vendeur de Chapeaux, 1939, 43, Fig. 3.3

Lawrence, Jacob, African American, 1917–2000, painter
Harriet Tubman Series Number 4, 1939–1940, 216, Fig. 8.22

Savage, Augusta, African American, 20th century, sculptor
Lift Every Voice and Sing, 1939, 209, Fig. 8.15

Siqueiros, David Alfaro, Mexican, 1896–1974, painter
Ethnography, 1939, 294, Fig. 11.11

Davis, Stuart, American, 1894–1964, painter
Hot Still Scape for Six Colors-7th Avenue Style, 1940, 1940, 156, Fig. 6.28

Rivera, Diego, Mexican, 1886–1957, painter, muralist
Self-Portrait, 1941, 229

Calder, Alexander, American, 1898–1976, sculptor
Untitled, c. 1942, 213, Fig. 8.20

Albright, Ivan, American, 1897–1983, painter
The Picture of Dorian Gray, 1943–1944, 177, Fig. 7.4

Escher, M. C., Dutch, 1898–1972, printmaker
Reptiles, 1943, 210, Fig. 8.17

Woodruff, Hale, American, b. 1900, painter
Poor Man's Cotton, 1944, 202, Fig. 8.6

Siqueiros, David Alfaro, Mexican, 1896–1974, painter
Self-Portrait (El Coronelazo), 1945, 264, Fig. 10.14

Wyeth, Andrew, American, b. 1917, painter
Winter 1946, 1946, 292, Fig. 11.8

Lawrence, Jacob, African-American, b. 1917, painter
Children at Play, 1947, 80, Fig. 4.19

Le Corbusier, Swiss, 1887–1965, architect
Unite d'Habitation, 1947–1952, 259, Fig. 10.7

Pollock, Jackson, American, 1912–1956, painter
Cathedral, 1947, 14, Fig. 1.13

Smith, David, American, 1906–1965, sculptor
The Royal Bird, 1947–1948, 117, Fig. 5.29

Tamayo, Rufino, Mexican, 1899–1991, painter
Girl Attacked by a Strange Bird, 1947, 141, Fig. 6.9

Gwathmey, Robert, American, 1903–1988, painter
Children Dancing, c. 1948, 297, Fig. 11.14

Matisse, Henri, French, 1869–1954, painter
Interior with Egyptian Curtain, 1948, 68, Fig. 4.1

Wright, Frank Lloyd, American, 1867–1959, architect
Xanadu Gallery, 1949, 377, Fig. 13.30

1950–1974

Adla, Ashevak, Canadian, Inuit, sculptor
Walking Bear, 1950, 102, Fig. 5.7

Borsky, David, American, 1950–2000, photographer
Waterfall, 1950–2000, 209, Fig. 8.14

Brice, Jeff, American, 1950–2000, computer artist
Untitled, 1950–2000, 59, Fig. 3.20

Mays, J, American, b. 1955, industrial designer
Volkswagen Beetle, 1950–2000, 401, Fig. 14.20

Moore, Henry, English, 1898–1986, sculptor
Dallas Piece, 1950–2000, 122, Fig. 5.35

Pinkney, Jerry, African American, b. 1939, illustrator
Journeys with Elijah (illustration), 1950–2000, 237, Fig. 9.16

Rashid, Karim, Egyptian, b. 1960, industrial designer
Chair, 1950–2000, 408
Chess set, 1950–2000, 408

Sewell, Leo, American, found object sculptor
Penguin, 1950–2000, 186, Fig. 7.17

Taymor, Julie, American, director, theater artist, puppetry
The Lion King, 1950–2000, 224

Wilkinson, Signe, American
Self-Portrait, 1950–2000, 284

Tamayo, Rufino, Mexican, 1899–1991, painter
Fruit Vendors, 1952, 196–197

Lee-Smith, Hughie, African American, 1915–2000, painter
The Piper, 1953, 29, Fig. 2.4

Rauschenberg, Robert, American, b. 1925, painter
Red Painting, 1953, 290, Fig. 11.4

Rothko, Mark, Russian American, 1903–1970, painter
Ochre and Red on Red, 1954, 380, Fig. 13.34

Picasso, Pablo, Spanish, 1881–1973, painter, sculptor
Studio of "La Californie," 1955, 38

Glarner, Fritz, Swiss American, 1899–1972 painter
Relational Painting, Tondo #40, 1955–1956, 147, Fig. 6.17

Grandma Moses, American, 1860–1961, painter
Sugaring Off, 1955, 110, Fig. 5.15

Pereira, Irene Rice, American, 1907–1971, painter
Pillar of Fire, 1955, 289, Fig. 11.3

Hofmann, Hans, German (born in America), 1880–1966, painter
Flowering Swamp, 1957, 378, Fig. 13.31

Picasso, Pablo, Spanish, 1881–1973, painter, sculptor
Las Meninas (after Velásquez), 1957, 14, Fig. 1.14

Andrews, Benny, African American, b. 1930, painter, printmaker
Thelonious at The Five Spot, 1958, 82, Fig. 4.22

Artist Unknown, Ayacucho, Peru
  Church Quinua, 1958, 107, Fig. 5.12
Flack, Audrey, American, b. 1931, painter, sculptor
  Self-Portrait: The Memory, 1958, 82, Fig. 4.23
Johnson, Philip, American, b. 1906, architect
  Seagram Building (with Mies van der Rohe), 1958, 382,
  Fig. 13.38
Mies van der Rohe, Ludwig, American, 1886–1969,
  architect
  Seagram Building (with Johnson), 1958, 382, Fig. 13.38
Albizu, Olga, Puerto Rican, b. 1924, painter
  Growth, 1960, 148, Fig. 6.20
Artist Unknown, Kuba Group, Congo
  Robe, 1950–1975, 298, Fig. 11.16
Dali, Salvador, Spanish, 1904–1989, painter
  *The Elephants (Design for the Opera La Dama Spagnola e il
  Cavaliere Romano),* 1961, 278, Fig. 10.30
Escher, M. C., Dutch, 1898–1972, printmaker
  Waterfall, 1961, 105, Fig. 5.10
Johns, Jasper, American, b. 1930, painter
  Map, 1961, 296, Fig. 11.13
Mununggiritj, Yäma, Australian, Aboriginal artist
  Yellow Ochre Quarry, 1961, 152, Fig. 6.23
Smith, Tony, American, 1912–1980, sculptor
  Gracehopper, 1961, 101, Fig. 5.6
Lichtenstein, Roy, American, 1923–1997, painter
  Blam, 1962, 379, Fig. 13.32
Marisol, Venezuelan (in America since 1950), b. 1930,
  sculptor
  The Family, 1962, 268, Fig. 10.21
Nevelson, Louise, American, 1899–1988, sculptor
  Dawn, 1962, 300, Fig. 11.19
Warhol, Andy, American, 1928–1987, painter, printmaker
  100 Cans, 1962, 20, Fig. 1.18
Frankenthaler, Helen, American, b. 1928, painter
  The Bay, 1963, 111, Fig. 5.16
Poons, Larry, American, b.1937, painter
  Orange Crush, 1963, 379, Fig. 13.33
Krasner, Lee, American, b. 1908, painter
  The Springs, 1964, 291, Fig. 11.6
Lawrence, Jacob, African American, 1917–2000, painter
  Street to M'bari, 1964, 66–67
Chryssa, Greek American, sculptor, painter
  The Gates to Times Square, 1966, 303, Fig. 11.23
Oldenburg, Claes, American, b. 1929, painter, sculptor
  Shoestring Potatoes Spilling from a Bag, 1966, 96, Fig. 5.1
Samaras, Lucas, American, b. 1936, sculptor,
  experimental artist
  Mirrored Room, 1966, 62, Fig. 3.22
Sutej, Miroslav, Yugoslavian, b. 1936, lithographer
  Ultra AB, 1966, 288, Fig. 11.2
Safdie, Moshe, Israeli, b. 1938, architect
  Habitat, 1967, 382, Fig. 13.39
Stella, Frank, American, b. 1936, painter, sculptor
  Agbatana III, 1968, 380, Fig. 13.35
Thomas, Alma, American, 1891–1978, painter
  Iris, Tulips, Jonquils, and Crocuses, 1969, 26, Fig. 2.2
Artist Unknown, Tapirapé people
  Mask, c. 1970, 182, Fig. 7.14

Catlett, Elizabeth, African American, b. 1915, printmaker,
  sculptor, painter
  Sharecropper, 1970, 48, Fig. 3.10
Andrews, Benny, African American, b. 1930, painter,
  printmaker
  Mom and Us, 1972, 81, Fig. 4.20
Estes, Richard, American, b. 1932, painter
  Paris Street Scene, 1972, 381, Fig. 13.37
Johns, Jasper, American, b. 1930, painter
  Cups 4 Picasso, 1972, 103, Fig. 5.8
Fish, Janet, American, b. 1939, painter
  Oranges, 1973, 176, Fig. 7.5
Neel, Alice, American, 1900–1984, painter
  Still Life, Rose of Sharon, 1973, 74, Fig. 4.13
Oonark, Jessie, Canadian, Inuit, 1906–1986, printmaker
  Untitled, c. 1973, 346, Fig. 12.34
Bearden, Romare, American, 1914–1988, painter,
  printmaker
  In the Garden, 1974, 184, Fig. 7.16
Paley, Albert Raymond, American, b. 1944, sculptor
  Portal Gates, 1974, 78, Fig. 4.17
Artist Unknown, Yup'ik people
  Bird Mask, 1988, 13, Fig. 1.12

1975–

Grooms, Red, American, b. 1937, installation artist
  Ruckus Rodeo, 1975–1976, 24, Fig. 2.1
Bearden, Romare, American, 1914–1988, painter,
  printmaker
  Return of Ulysses, 1976, 12, 13, Fig. 1.11
Johnson, Philip, American, b. 1906, architect
  Water Garden, 1976, 298, Fig. 11.17
Oldenburg, Claes, American, b. 1929, painter, sculptor
  Clothespin, 1976, 261, Fig. 10.9
Chagall, Marc, Russian, 1887–1985, painter, stained-glass
  artist
  The American Windows, 1977, 136, Fig. 6.2
Houser, Allan, Native American, 1914–1994, sculptor
  Coming of Age, 1977, 209, Fig. 8.16
Jimenez, Luis, American, b. 1940, sculptor
  Howl, 1977, 314
Royo, Josep, Spanish, b. 1945, textile artist
  Woman (after Joan Miró), 1977, 86, Fig. 4.26
Goings, Ralph, American, b. 1928, painter, sculptor
  Diner With Red Door, 1979, 112, Fig. 5.18
Cromartie, James H., American, painter
  View of the White House, South Portico, 1980, 230, Fig. 9.7
Jimenez, Luis, American, b. 1940, sculptor
  Vaquero, modeled 1980, cast 1990, 50, Fig. 3.11
Mitchell, Joan, American, 1926–1992, painter
  Dirty Snow, 1980, 179, Fig. 7.9
Fish, Janet, American, b. 1939, painter
  Raspberries and Goldfish, 1981, 17, Fig. 1.16
Hanson, Duane, American, b. 1925, sculptor
  Football Player, 1981, 192, Fig. 7.23
Houser, Allan, Native American, 1914–1994, sculptor
  Reverie, 1981, 299, Fig. 11.18

Kapoor, Anish, British, b. 1954, sculptor
Sculpture, 1981, 168

Graves, Nancy, American, b. 1940, sculptor
Zaga, 1983, 51, Fig. 3.13

Schapiro, Miriam, American, b. 1923, painter, sculptor
In Her Own Image, 1983, 180, Fig. 7.10

Stella, Frank, Italian American, 1877–1946, painter
St. Michael's Counterguard (Malta Series), 1984, 383,
Fig. 13.40

Torivio, Dorothy, Native American, b. 1946, ceramicist
Vase, c. 1984, 233, Fig. 9.11

Artist Unknown, Bwa people, Burkina Faso
Leaf masks, 1985, 337, Fig. 12.24

Naranjo, Michael, Native American, b. 1944, sculptor
Spirits Soaring, 1985, 109, Fig. 5.14

Jimenez, Luis, American, b. 1940, sculptor
Fiesta Jarabel, 1986, 314

Ringgold, Faith, African American, b. 1930, painter, soft
sculptor
The Men: Mask Face Quilt #2, 1986, 198, Fig. 8.1

Warhol, Andy, American, 1928–1987, painter, printmaker
Self-Portrait, 1986, 21

Biggers, John, American, b.1924, painter
Starry Crown, 1987, 99, Fig. 5.3

Larraz, Julio, Cuban, b. 1944, painter
Papiamento, 1987, 32, Fig. 2.6

Liebovitz, Annie, American, 20th century, photographer
Wilt Chamberlain and Willie Shoemaker, 1987, 262,
Fig. 10.11

Xiong, Chaing, Laotian, b. 1953, craftsperson
Hmong Story Cloth, 1987, 211, Fig. 8.18

Butterfield, Deborah, American, sculptor
Woodrow, 1988, 130, Fig. 5.41

Jacquette, Yvonne, American, b. 1934, painter
Town of Skowhegan, Maine V, 1988, 70, Fig. 4.2

Murray, Elizabeth, American, b. 1940, painter
Things to Come, 1988, 150, Fig. 6.22

Arreguin, Alfredo, Mexican American, b. 1935, painter
Nuestra Señora del la Selva, 1989, 222, Fig. 8.28

Twiggs, Leo, African American, b. 1934, batik painter
East Wind Suite: Door, 1989, 10, 42, Fig. 1.7

Brown, Roger, American, b. 1941, muralist
Hurricane Hugo, 1990, 10–11, Fig. 1.8

Dunnigan, John, American, 20th century, furniture
designer
Slipper Chairs, 1990, 33, Fig. 2.7

Pootoogook, Napachie, Inuit, b. 1938, printmaker
My Daughter's First Steps, 1990, 269, Fig. 10.22

Scully, Sean, Irish, b. 1945, painter
White Robe, 1990, 295, Fig. 11.12

Close, Chuck, American, b. 1940, painter
Self-Portrait, 1991, 385

Wilson, Jane, American, b. 1924, painter
Winter Wheat, 1991, 121, Fig. 5.34

Catlett, Elizabeth, African American, b. 1915, printmaker,
sculptor, painter
Singing Their Songs, 1992, 312, Fig. 11.31

Namingha, Dan, Native American, b. 1950, painter
Blessing Rain Chant, 1992, 75, Fig. 4.14

Chihuly, Dale, American, b. 1941, glass artist
Malina Window, 1993, 40, Fig. 3.1

Moulthrop, Philip, American, b. 1947, craftsperson
White Pine Mosaic Bowl, 1993, 205, Fig. 8.8

Wilson, Jane, American, b. 1924, painter
Tempest, 1993, 302, Fig. 11.22

Close, Chuck, American, b. 1940, painter
Paul, 1994, 384, Fig. 13.41

Abrasha, Dutch American, b. 1948, jewelry designer,
goldsmith
Hanukkah Menorah, 1995, 72, Fig. 4.6

Artist Unknown, Kuna people
Mola: Our Environment, 1995, 160, Fig. 6.31

Hanson, Duane, American, b. 1925, sculptor
Old Couple on a Bench, 1995, 381, Fig. 13.36

Lin, Maya, American, b. 1959, architect, sculptor
The Wave Field, 1995, 207, Fig. 8.10

McKie, Judy Kensley, American, b. 1944, furniture artist
Monkey Settee, 1995, 53, Fig. 3.15

Moroles, Jesús Bautista, American, b. 1950, sculptor
Granite Weaving Playscape, 1995, 170, Fig. 7.1

Pei, I. M., Chinese American, b. 1917, architect
Rock-and-Roll Hall of Fame and Museum, 1995, 399,
Fig. 14.16

Solberg, Ramona, American, contemporary, jewelry
Cracker Jack Choo Choo, 1995, 214, Fig. 8.21

Gehry, Frank, American, b. 1929, architect, sculptor
Office complex, two towers (Prague, Czech Republic),
1996, 132

Twiggs, Leo, African American, b. 1934, batik painter
Single Family Blues, 1996, 269, Fig. 10.23

Gehry, Frank, American, b. 1929, architect, sculptor
Guggenheim Museum (Bilbao, Spain), 1997, 388,
Fig. 14.1

Schapiro, Miriam, American, b. 1923, painter, sculptor
Father and Daughter, 1997, 166, Fig. 6.37

Feiss, David, American, b. 1959, animator
Thrown for a Curve, 1998, 308, Fig. 11.26

Pinkney, Brian, African American, b. 1961, illustrator
Duke Ellington: The Piano Prince and His Orchestra (cover
illustration), 1998, 406, Fig. 14.27

Gehry, Frank, American, b. 1929 , architect, sculptor
The Experience Music Project (Seattle, Washington),
1999–2000, 132

Proctor, Mary L., African American, folk artist
Like a Butterfly, 1999, 306, Fig. 11.25

Hoover, John, Native American, Aleut, b. 1919, sculptor
Shaman's Journey, 2000, 180, Fig. 7.11

Sandkühler, Iris, American, b. 1958, jewelry
Viking Net Chain Necklace, 2001, 84, Fig. 4.25

Hirschfeld, Al, American, 1903–2003, illustrator
Self-Portrait at 99, 2002, 94

Russell, Julia, American, b. 1949, painter
Jaguar Chair, 2002, 304, Fig. 11.24

Wilkinson, Signe, American
The Thoroughly Modern Medical School, 2003, 284

This section contains important words and phrases used in *ArtTalk* that may be new to you. You may want to refer to this list of terms as you read the chapters, complete the exercises, and prepare to create your own works of art. You can also use the Glossary to review what you have learned in *ArtTalk*.

A

Abstract art Twentieth-century art containing shapes that simplify shapes of real objects to emphasize form instead of subject matter.

Abstract Expressionism Painting style developed after World War II in New York City that emphasized abstract elements of art rather than recognizable subject matter, and also stressed feelings and emotions (p. 378).

Acrylic paint Pigments mixed with an acrylic vehicle. Available in different degrees of quality: school and artists' acrylics. School acrylics are less expensive than the professional acrylics, can be washed out of brushes and clothes, and are nontoxic.

Action Painting The technique of dripping and splashing paint onto canvases stretched on the floor (p. 13). See *Abstract Expressionism.*

Active Expressing movement. Diagonal and zigzag lines (p. 76) and diagonally slanting shapes and forms (p. 120) are active. Opposite of static.

Aesthetic experience Your personal interaction with a work of art (p. 27).

Aesthetics The philosophy or study of the nature and value of art (p. 26).

Afterimage Weak image of complementary color created by a viewer's brain as a reaction to prolonged looking at a color. After staring at something red, the viewer sees an afterimage of green (p. 137).

Age of Faith See *Middle Ages.*

Air brush Atomizer operated by compressed air used for spraying on paint.

Alternating rhythm Visual rhythm set up by repeating motifs but changing position or content of motifs or spaces between them (p. 208).

• **Analogous colors** Colors that sit side by side on the color wheel and have a common hue (p. 145). Violet, red-violet, and red are analogous colors. Analogous colors can be used as a color scheme.

Analysis In art criticism, the step in which you discover how the principles of art are used to organize the art elements of line, color, shape, form, space, and texture. In art history, the step in which you determine the style of the work (p. 28).

Animators Artists who create moving cartoons (p. 395).

Applied art Art made to be functional as well as visually pleasing (p. 52).

Approximate symmetry Balance that is almost symmetrical (p. 231). This type of symmetry produces the effect of stability, as formal balance does, but small differences make the arrangement more interesting.

Arbitrary color Color chosen by an artist to express his or her feelings (p. 154). Opposite of optical color.

Arch Curved stone structure supporting weight of material over an open space. Doorways and bridges use arches.

Architect A person who designs buildings that are well constructed, aesthetically pleasing, and functional (p. 386).

Architecture Art form of designing and planning construction of buildings, cities, and bridges (p. 54).

Art criticism An organized approach for studying a work of art. It has four stages: description, analysis, interpretation, and judgment (p. 25).

Art history operations A four-step approach for organizing the way you gather information about a work of art (p. 34).

Artistic style See *individual style.*

Artists Creative individuals who use imagination and skill to communicate in visual form (p. 11).

Ashcan School Group of American artists working in the early twentieth century who used city people and city scenes for subject matter (p. 376). Originally called "The Eight," they helped to organize the Armory Show.

Assembling A sculpting technique in which the artist gathers and joins together a variety of different materials to make a sculpture. Also called constructing (p. 186).

Asymmetrical balance Another name for informal balance, in which unlike objects have equal visual weight or eye attraction (p. 234).

Atmospheric perspective Effect of air and light on how an object is perceived by the viewer (p. 114). The more air between the viewer and the object, the more the object seems to fade. A bright object seems closer to the viewer than a dull object.

B

Background Part of the picture plane that seems to be farthest from the viewer.

Balance Principle of art concerned with equalizing visual forces, or elements, in a work of art (p. 228). If a work of art has visual balance, the viewer feels that the elements have been arranged in a satisfying way. Visual imbalance makes the viewer feel that the elements need to be rearranged. The two types of balance are formal (also called symmetrical) and informal (also called asymmetrical).

Baroque Artistic style that emphasized dramatic lighting, movement, and emotional intensity. It developed after the Reformation in the seventeenth century. Artists used movement of forms and figures toward the viewer, dramatic lighting effects, contrast between dark and light, ornamentation, and curved lines to express energy and strong emotions (p. 361).

Bas relief A relief sculpture with positive areas that project slightly from the flat surface.

Binder A liquid that holds together the grains of pigment (p. 45).

Blending Technique of shading through smooth, gradual application of dark value (p .44).

Brayer Roller with a handle used to apply ink to a surface.

Buttress Projecting brick or stone structure that supports an arch or vault. A flying buttress is connected with a wall by an arch. It reaches over the side aisle to support the roof of a cathedral.

Byzantine art Artistic style that developed around Constantinople (now Istanbul, Turkey) in the eastern Roman Empire. It featured very rich colors and heavily outlined figures that appeared flat and stiff (p. 319)

C

Calligraphic lines Flowing lines made with brushstrokes similar to Asian writing (p. 83).

Calligraphy An Asian method of beautiful handwriting (p. 83).

Canvas Rough cloth on which an oil painting is made.

Carving A sculpting technique in which the sculptor cuts, chips, or drills from a solid mass of material to create a sculpture. Material is removed until the sculpture is complete; therefore, carving is referred to as a subtractive process (p. 51).

Casting A sculpting technique in which molten metal or another substance is poured into a mold and allowed to harden. Just as in printmaking, an edition of sculptures can be made from the same mold (p. 51).

Central axis A dividing line that works like the point of balance in the balance scale. The central axis is used to measure visual weight in a work of art. It can be vertical (balance between sides is measured) or horizontal (balance between top and bottom is measured) (p. 228).

Ceramics Art of making objects with clay to produce pottery and sculpture. Pottery is fired in a kiln to make it stronger.

Chiaroscuro The arrangement of light and shadow (p. 112). This technique was introduced by Italian artists during the Renaissance and used widely by Baroque artists. Chiaroscuro is also called modeling or shading.

Classical Referring to the art of ancient Greece and Rome. The Greeks created art based on the ideals of perfect proportion and logic instead of emotion. The Romans adapted Greek art and spread it throughout the civilized world (p. 352).

Clay Stiff, sticky earth that is used in ceramics. It is wet, and it hardens after drying or heating (p. 53).

Clustering Technique for creating a focal point by grouping several different shapes closely together (p. 301).

Coil Long roll joined into a circle or spiral. Clay coils are used to make pottery.

Collage An artwork created by pasting cut or torn materials such as paper, photographs, and fabric to a flat surface (p. 179).

Color An element of art that is derived from reflected light (p. 134). The sensation of color is aroused in the brain by response of the eyes to different wavelengths of light. Color has three properties: hue, value, and intensity.

Color-field painting Twentieth-century art created using only flat fields of color (p. 380).

Color scheme Plan for organizing colors. Types of color schemes include monochromatic, analogous, complementary, triad, split complementary, warm, and cool (p. 144).

Color spectrum The effect that occurs when light passes through a prism; the beam of white light is bent and separated into bands of color. Colors always appear in the same order, by wavelengths, from longest to shortest: red, orange, yellow, green, blue, violet. (p. 136).

Color triad Three colors spaced an equal distance apart on the color wheel (p. 146). The primary color triad is red, yellow, and blue; the secondary color triad is orange, green, and violet. A color triad is a type of color scheme.

Color wheel The spectrum bent into a circle (p. 138).

Compass Instrument used for measuring and drawing arcs and circles.

Complementary colors The colors opposite each other on the color wheel (p. 142). A complement of a color absorbs all the light waves the color reflects and is the strongest contrast to the color. Mixing a hue with its complementary color dulls it. Red and green are complementary colors. Complementary colors can be used as a color scheme.

Composition The way the principles of art are used to organize the elements of art (p. 18).

Content The message the work communicates. The content can relate to the subject matter or be an idea or emotion. Theme is another word for content (p. 19).

Contour drawing Drawing in which only contour lines are used to represent the subject matter (p. 81). Artists keep their eyes on the object they are drawing and concentrate on directions and curves.

Contour line A line that defines the edges and surface ridges of an object (p. 81).

Contrast Technique for creating a focal point by using differences in elements (p. 291).

Convergence Technique for creating a focal point by arranging elements so that many lines or shapes point to one item or area (p. 293).

Cool colors Blue, green, and violet (p. 148). Cool colors suggest coolness and seem to recede from a viewer. Cool colors can be used as a color scheme. Opposite of warm colors.

Crafts Art forms creating works of art that are both beautiful and useful. Crafts include weaving, fabric design, ceramics, and jewelry making (p. 52).

Crayons Pigments held together with wax and molded into sticks.

Credit line A list of important facts about a work of art. A credit line usually includes the artist's name, the title of the work, year completed, medium used, size (height, width, and depth), location (gallery, museum, or collection and city), donors, and date donated (p. 19).

Crewel Loosely twisted yarn used in embroidery.

Criteria Standards of judgment (p. 26).

Crosshatching The technique of using crossed lines for shading (p. 44).

Cubism Twentieth-century art movement that emphasizes structure and design (p. 374). Three-dimensional objects are pictured from many different points of view at the same time.

Culture Behaviors and ideas of a group of people. Studying art objects produced by a group of people is one way to learn about a culture.

Cuneiform The Sumerian writing system made up of wedge-shaped characters (p. 321).

Curved lines Lines that are always bending and change direction gradually (p. 73).

D

Dark Ages See *Middle Ages.*

Decalcomania A technique in which paint is forced into random textured patterns by pulling apart canvases between which blobs of paint have been squeezed (p 183).

Dense Compact; having parts crowded together. Dense materials are solid and heavy. Opposite of soft.

Description A list of all the things you see in the work (p. 27).

Design Plan, organization, or arrangement of elements in a work of art.

Diagonal lines Lines that slant (p. 72)

Digital camera A camera that records images digitally. These images can then be downloaded into computer applications where they can be altered and enhanced (p. 60).

Digital system A system that processes words and images directly as numbers or digits (p. 59).

Dimension The amount of space an object takes up in one direction (p. 70). The three dimensions are height, width, and depth.

Distortion Deviations from expected, normal proportions (p. 268).

Divine Proportion See *Golden Mean.*

Dome Hemispherical vault or ceiling over a circular opening. A dome rises above the center part of a building (p. 326).

Dominant element Element of a work of art noticed first. Elements noticed later are called subordinate (p. 290).

Draw program A computer art application in which images are stored as a series of lines and curves. Objects can be resized without distortion in draw programs (p. 60).

Dyes Pigments that dissolve in liquid. Dye sinks into a material and stains it (p. 151).

Dynasty A period of time during which a single family provided a succession of rulers (p. 324).

E

Edition All the prints made from the same plate or set of plates (p. 48).

Elements of art Basic visual symbols in the language of art. The elements of art are line, shape and form, space, color, value, and texture (p. 16).

Embroidery Method of decorating fabric with stitches.

Emotionalism Theory that requires that a work of art must arouse a response of feelings, moods, or emotions in the viewer. One of the three aesthetic theories of art criticism, the others being Formalism and Imitationalism (p. 32).

Emphasis Principle of art that makes one part of a work dominant over the other parts (p. 290). The element noticed first is called dominant; the elements noticed later are called subordinate

Engraving Method of cutting a design into a material, usually metal, with a sharp tool. A print can be made by inking an engraved surface.

Exaggeration Deviations from expected, normal proportions (p. 268).

Expressionism Twentieth-century art movement. A style that emphasized the expression of innermost feelings (p. 374).

Expressive qualities Those qualities that communicate ideas and moods (p. 31).

F

Fauves French for "wild beasts." A group of early twentieth-century painters who used brilliant colors and bold distortions in an uncontrolled way. Their leader was Henri Matisse.

Fiber Thin, threadlike linear material that can be woven or spun into fabric (p. 52).

Fiberfill Lightweight, fluffy filling material made of synthetic fibers.

Figure Human form in a work of art.

Fine art Art made to be experienced visually. Opposite of applied or functional art (p. 52).

Fire To apply heat to harden pottery.

Flowing rhythm Visual rhythm created by repeating wavy lines (p. 208).

Focal point The first part of a work to attract the attention of the viewer (p. 290). Focal points are created by contrast, location, isolation, convergence, and use of the unusual.

Folk artists Artists who are self-taught and therefore have had little or no formal schooling in artistic methods (p. 10).

Foreground Part of the picture plane that appears closest to the viewer. The foreground is usually at the bottom of the picture.

Foreshortening To shorten an object to make it look as if it extends backward into space (p. 264). This method reproduces proportions a viewer actually sees, which depend on the viewer's distance from the object or person.

Formal balance Way of organizing parts of a design so that equal, or very similar, elements are placed on opposite sides of a central axis (p. 229). Formal balance suggests stability. Symmetry is a type of formal balance. Opposite of informal balance.

Formal qualities How well the work is organized (p. 31). This aesthetic quality is favored by Formalism.

Formalism Theory that places emphasis on the formal qualities. One of the three aesthetic theories of art criticism, the others being Emotionalism and Imitationalism (p. 31).

Forms Objects having three dimensions (p. 101). Like a shape, a form has height and width, but it also has depth. Forms are either geometric or free-form.

Free-form shapes Irregular and uneven shapes (5). Their outlines are curved, or angular, or both. Free-form shapes are often referred to as organic (found in nature). Opposite of geometric shapes.

Freestanding Work of art surrounded on all sides by space. A three-dimensional work of art is freestanding. Opposite of relief (p. 50).

Frottage Designs and textural effects that are created by placing paper over objects that have raised surfaces and rubbing the paper with graphite, wax, or crayon. (p. 183).

Functional art Works of art made to be used instead of only enjoyed. Objects must be judged by how well they work when used (p. 33).

Futurists Early twentieth-century Italian artists who arranged angular forms to suggest motion (p. 212). They called the forces of movement dynamism.

G

Gallery Place for displaying or selling works of art.

Genre painting Paintings that have scenes from everyday life as their subject matter.

Geometric shapes Precise shapes that can be described using mathematical formulas (p. 98). Basic geometric shapes are the circle, the square, and the triangle. Basic geometric forms are the cylinder, the cube, and the pyramid. Opposite of free-form shapes.

Gesture An expressive movement (p. 82).

Gesture drawing Line drawing done quickly to capture movement of the subject's body.

Glaze In ceramics, a thin, glossy coating fired into pottery. In painting, a thin layer of transparent paint.

Golden Mean A line divided into two parts so that the smaller line has the same proportion, or ratio, to the larger line as the larger line has to the whole line (p. 256). Perfect ratio (relationship of parts) discovered by Euclid, a Greek mathematician. Its mathematical expression is 1 to 1.6. It was also called the Golden Section and the Golden Rectangle. The long sides of the Golden Rectangle are a little more than half again as long as the short sides. This ratio was rediscovered in the early sixteenth century and named the Divine Proportion.

Gothic Artistic style developed in western Europe between the twelfth and sixteenth centuries. Featured churches that seemed to soar upward, pointed arches, and stained-glass windows (p. 355).

Gouache Pigments ground in water and mixed with gum to form opaque watercolor. Gouache resembles school tempera or poster paint.

Graphic designer A person who translates ideas into images and arranges them in appealing and memorable ways (p. 392).

Grattage Wet paint is scratched with a variety of tools, such as forks, razors, and combs for the purpose of creating different textures (p. 183).

Grid Pattern of intersecting vertical and horizontal lines (p. 206).

Griots Oral historians who are also musicians and performers (p. 334).

H

Hard-edge In two-dimensional art, shapes with clearly defined outlines. Hard-edge shapes look dense. Opposite of soft-edge.

Harmony The principle of art that creates unity by stressing the similarities of separate but related parts.

Hatching Technique of shading with a series of fine parallel lines (3).

Hierarchical proportion When figures are arranged in a work of art so scale indicates importance (p. 260).

Hieroglyphics Picture writing used by ancient Egyptians (12).

High-key painting Painting using many tints of a color (p. 140). Opposite of low-key painting.

Highlights Small areas of white used to show the very brightest spots (p. 112). Highlights show the surfaces of the subject that reflect the most light. They are used to create the illusion of form. Opposite of shadows.

High relief Sculpture in which areas project far out from a flat surface (p. 106).

High-resolution Producing a sharp image.

Holograms Images in three dimensions created with a laser beam (p. 107).

Horizon Point at which earth and sky seem to meet.

Horizontal line Line parallel to the horizon (p. 72). Horizontal lines lie flat and are parallel to the bottom edge of the paper or canvas.

Hue The name of a color in the color spectrum (p. 138). Hue is related to the wavelength of reflected light. The primary hues are red, yellow, and blue; they are called primary because they cannot be made by mixing other hues together. The secondary hues, made by mixing two primary hues, are orange, violet, and green. Hue is one of the three properties of color.

I

Illustrator A person who creates the visual images that complement written words (p. 393).

Imitationalism An aesthetic theory focusing on realistic presentation. One of the three aesthetic theories of art criticism, the others being Emotionalism and Formalism (p. 31).

Implied lines A series of points that the viewer's eyes automatically connect. Implied lines are suggested, not real (p. 71).

Impressionism Style of painting started in France in the 1860s. It featured everyday subjects and emphasized the momentary effects of light on color (p. 370).

Individual style The artist's personal way of using the elements and principles of art to express feelings and ideas (p. 35).

Informal balance Way of organizing parts of a design involving a balance of unlike objects (p. 234). Asymmetry is another term for informal balance. Opposite of formal balance.

Intaglio (in-**tal**-yo or in-**tal**-ee-o) A printmaking technique in which ink is forced into lines that have been cut or etched on a hard surface such as metal or wood. The plate's surface is then wiped clean and the prints are made (p. 49).

Intensity The brightness or dullness of a hue. A pure hue is called a high-intensity color. A dulled hue (a color mixed with its complement) is called a low-intensity color. Intensity is one of the three properties of color (p. 142).

Interior designer A person who plans the design and decoration of the interior spaces in homes and offices (p. 400).

Intermediate color A color made by mixing a primary color with a secondary color. Red-orange is an intermediate color (p. 138).

International style A style of architecture developed after World War II that emphasizes a plain, austere building style (p. 381).

Interpretation In art criticism, the step in which you explain or tell the meaning or mood of the work. In art history, the step in which you do research about the artist (p. 27).

Invented texture A kind of visual texture that does not represent a real texture but creates a sensation of one by repeating lines and shapes in a two-dimensional pattern (p. 174). Opposite of simulated texture.

Isolation Technique for creating a focal point by putting one object alone to emphasize it (p. 292).

J

Judgment In art criticism, the step in which you determine the degree of artistic merit. In art history, the step in which you determine if the work has made an important contribution to the history of art (p. 27).

K

Kinetic A work of art that moves in space (p. 213).

L

Landscape Painting or drawing in which natural land scenery, such as mountains, trees, rivers, or lakes, is the main feature.

Layout The way items are arranged on the page (p. 454).

Line An element of art that is the path of a moving point through space. Although lines can vary in appearance (they can have different lengths, widths, textures, directions, and degree of curve), they are considered one-dimensional and are measured by length. A line is also used by an artist to control the viewer's eye movement. There are five kinds of lines: vertical, horizontal, diagonal, curved, and zigzag (p. 70).

Linear perspective A graphic system that creates the illusion of depth and volume on a flat surface. In one-point linear perspective, all receding lines meet at a single point. In two-point linear perspective, different sets of lines meet at different points (p. 115).

Literal qualities The realistic qualities that appear in the subject of the work (p. 31).

Lithography A printmaking technique in which the image to be printed is drawn on limestone, zinc, or aluminum with a special greasy pencil or pencil. Ink is attracted to this material (p. 49).

Location The technique of using placement of elements to create a focal point (p. 292). Items near the center of a work of art are usually noticed first.

Logos Symbols or trademarks that are immediately recognizable (p. 392).

Loom Machine or frame for weaving.

Low-key painting Painting using many shades or dark values of a color (p. 140). Opposite of high-key painting.

Low-relief See *bas-relief.*

M

Mannerism European sixteenth-century artistic style featuring highly emotional scenes and elongated figures (p. 360).

Manufactured shapes/forms Shapes or forms made by people either by hand or by machine. Opposite of organic shapes/forms.

Mat To frame a picture or drawing with a cardboard border.

Matte surface Surface that reflects a soft, dull light (p. 175). Paper has a matte surface. Opposite of shiny surface.

Medieval Related to the *Middle Ages.*

Media See *medium.*

Medium Material used to make art. Plural is media (p. 19).

Megaliths Large monuments created from huge stone slabs (p. 321).

Mexican muralists Early twentieth-century artists whose paintings on walls and ceilings used solid forms and powerful colors to express their feelings about the Mexican Revolution. Also called Mexican Expressionists (p. 377).

Middle Ages Period of roughly one thousand years from the destruction of the Roman Empire to the Renaissance. Culture centered around the Catholic Church. The Middle Ages are also called the Dark Ages (because few new ideas developed) and the Age of Faith (because religion was a powerful force) (p. 354).

Middle ground Area in a picture between the foreground and the background.

Minimalism Twentieth-century artistic style that uses a minimum of art elements (p. 380).

Mobile Moving sculpture (p. 213)

Modeling A sculpting technique in which a soft, pliable material is built up and shaped. Because more material is added to build a form, modeling is referred to as an additive process (p. 51).

Module A three-dimensional motif (p. 204).

Monochromatic A color scheme that uses only one hue and the tints and shades of that hue for a unifying effect (p. 145).

Mortar and pestle Ceramic bowl and tool for grinding something into a powder..

Mosaics Pictures made with small cubes of colored marble, glass, or tile and set into cement.

Mosques Muslim places of worship (p. 331).

Motif A unit that is repeated in visual rhythm (p. 202). Units in a motif may or may not be an exact duplicate of the first unit.

Movement See *visual movement.*

Multimedia programs Computer software programs that help users design, organize, and combine text, graphics, video, and sound in one presentation (p. 61).

Mural Painting on a wall or ceiling.

Museum curator Person who oversees the operations of a museum (p. 404).

N

Negative spaces Empty spaces surrounding shapes and forms (p. 103). The shape and size of negative spaces affect the interpretation of positive spaces. Negative spaces are also called ground

Neoclassicism New classicism. French artistic style developed in the nineteenth century after the Rococo style. An approach to art that borrowed subject matter and formal design qualities from the art of Greece and Rome (p. 366).

Neolithic period New Stone Age. A prehistoric period stretching roughly from 7000 B.C. to 2000 B.C. (p. 321).

Neutral colors Black, white, and gray. Black reflects no wavelengths of light, white reflects all wavelengths of light, and gray reflects all wavelengths of light equally but only partially (p. 139).

Nonobjective art Art that has no recognizable subject matter (p. 18).

O

Oil paint Slow-drying paint made by mixing pigments in oil and usually used on canvas (p. 47).

Opaque Quality of a material that does not let any light pass through. Opposite of transparent.

Op Art Optical art. Twentieth-century artistic style in which artists use scientific knowledge about vision to create optical illusions of movement (p. 379).

Optical color Color perceived by the viewer due to the effect of atmosphere or unusual light on the actual color (p. 152). Opposite of arbitrary color.

Organic shapes/forms Shapes or forms made by the forces of nature. Opposite of manufactured shapes/forms (p. 111).

Outline A line that shows or creates the outer edges of a shape (p. 71).

Package designer Person who produces the containers that attract the attention of consumers (p. 402).

Pagoda A tower several stories high with roofs curving slightly upward at the edges (p. 329).

Paint Pigments mixed with oil or water. Pigment particles in paint stick to the surface of the material on which the paint is applied (p. 44).

Paint program A computer art application in which images are stored as bitmaps. Paint programs are capable of producing more lifelike pictures than draw programs (p. 60, 449).

Palette Tray for mixing colors of paint

Papier-mâché French for "mashed paper." Modeling material made of paper and liquid paste and molded over a supporting structure called the armature.

Paleolithic period Old Stone Age. Began about two million years ago and ended with the close of the last ice age about 13,000 B.C. (p. 320).

Parallel lines Lines that move in the same direction and always stay the same distance apart.

Pastels Pigments held together with gum and molded into sticks.

Paste-up Model of a printed page. It is photographed for the purpose of making a plate for the printing process.

Pattern The principle of art that refers to a two-dimensional decorative visual repetition (p. 202). A pattern has no movement and may or may not have rhythm.

Perceive To become deeply aware through the senses of the special nature of a visual object (p. 6).

Perspective A graphic system that creates the illusion of depth and volume on a two-dimensional surface (p. 113). It was developed during the Renaissance by architect Filippo Brunelleschi. Perspective is created by overlapping, size variations, placement, detail, color, and converging lines.

Pharaohs Egyptian rulers who were worshiped as gods and held complete authority over the kingdom (p. 323).

Photography The technique of capturing optical images on light-sensitive surfaces (p. 57).

Photojournalists Visual reporters (p. 395).

Photo-Realism See *Super-Realism.*

Picture plane The surface of a painting or drawing.

Pigments Finely ground, colored powders that form paint when mixed with a liquid (p. 150).

Plaster Mixture of lime, sand, and water that hardens on drying.

Point of view Angle from which the viewer sees an object (p. 108). The shapes and forms a viewer sees depend on his or her point of view.

Polymer medium Liquid used in acrylic painting as a thinning or finishing material (p. 47).

Pop art Artistic style used in the early 1960s in the United States that portrayed images of popular culture (mass media, commercial art, comic strips, advertising) (p. 378).

Portrait Image of a person, especially the face and upper body.

Positive spaces Shapes or forms in two- and three-dimensional art (p. 103). Empty spaces surrounding them are called negative spaces or ground.

Post-and-lintel A method of construction in which one long stone is balanced on top of two posts. Currently referred to as post-and-beam construction (p. 321).

Post-Impressionism French painting style of the late nineteenth century that stressed a more individual approach to painting, unique to each artist working at the time (p. 371).

Post-Modernism An approach to art that incorporates traditional elements and techniques while retaining some characteristics of modern art styles or movements (p. 382).

Pre-Columbian The historical time period before the arrival of Christopher Columbus in the Americas in 1492 (p. 339).

Prehistoric Period before history was written down (p. 320).

Principles of art Rules that govern how artists organize the elements of art. The principles of art are rhythm, movement, pattern, balance, proportion, variety, emphasis, and harmony (p. 18).

Print Impression created by an artist made on paper or fabric from a printing plate, stone, or block and repeated many times to produce identical images (p. 48).

Printing plate Surface containing the impression transferred to paper or fabric to make a print (p. 48).

Printmaking A process in which an artist repeatedly transfers an original image from one prepared surface to another (p. 48).

Prism Wedge-shaped piece of glass that bends white light and separates it into spectral hues.

Profile Side view of a face.

Progressive rhythm Visual rhythm that changes a motif each time it is repeated (p. 209).

Proportion Principle of art concerned with the size relationships of one part to another (p. 256).

Protractor Semicircular instrument used to measure and draw angles.

Proximity Technique for creating unity by limiting negative spaces between shapes (p. 301).

Radial balance Type of balance in which forces or elements of a design come out (radiate) from a central point (p. 232).

Random rhythm Visual rhythm in which a motif is repeated in no apparent order, with no regular spaces (p. 205).

Rasp File with sharp, rough teeth used for cutting into a surface.

Realism Mid-nineteenth-century artistic style in which familiar scenes are presented as they actually appeared (p. 368).

Realists Artists in the nineteenth century who portrayed political, social, and moral issues (p. 368).

Recede To move back or become more distant.

Reformation Religious revolution in western Europe in the sixteenth century. It started as a reform movement in the Catholic Church and led to the beginnings of Protestantism (p. 360).

Regionalists Artists who painted the farmlands and cities of the United States in an optimistic way (p. 376).

Regular rhythm Visual rhythm achieved through repeating identical motifs using the same intervals of space between them (p. 206).

Relief printing A printmaking technique in which the artist cuts away the sections of a surface not meant to hold ink. As a result, the image to be printed is raised from the background (p. 48).

Relief sculpture Type of sculpture in which forms project from a flat background. Opposite of freestanding (p. 50).

Renaissance The name given to the period at the end of the Middle Ages when artists, writers, and philosophers were "re-awakened" to art forms and ideas from ancient Greece and Rome (p. 356).

Repetition Technique for creating rhythm and unity in which a motif or single element appears again and again (p. 308).

Reproduction A copy of a work of art (p. 48).

Rhythm The principle of art that indicates movement by the repetition of elements or objects (p. 200). Visual rhythm is perceived through the eyes and is created by repeating positive spaces separated by negative spaces. There are five types of rhythm: random, regular, alternating, flowing, and progressive.

Rococo Eighteenth-century artistic style that began in the luxurious homes of the French aristocracy and spread to the rest of Europe. It stressed free graceful movement, a playful use of line, and delicate colors (p. 363).

Romanesque Style of architecture and sculpture developed during the Middle Ages in western Europe that featured buildings of massive size; solid, heavy walls; wide use of the rounded Roman arch; and many sculptural decorations (p. 354).

Romanticism Early nineteenth-century artistic style that was a reaction against Neoclassicism. It found its subjects in the world of the dramatic and in cultures foreign to Europe. It emphasized rich color and high emotion (p. 367).

Rough texture Irregular surface that reflects light unevenly (p. 175). Opposite of smooth texture.

Rubbing Technique for transferring textural quality of a surface to paper by placing paper over the surface and rubbing the top of the paper with crayon or pencil (p. 183).

S

Safety labels Labels identifying art products that are safe to use or that must be used with caution.

Scale Size as measured against a standard reference. Scale can refer to an entire work of art or to elements within it (p. 260).

Scanner A device that "reads" a printed image and then translates it into a language the computer can use to make a visual image on the screen (p. 61).

Score To make neat, sharp creases in paper using a cutting tool.

Screen printing A printmaking technique in which a stencil and screen are used as the printing plate. The stencil is placed on a fabric screen stretched across a frame and ink is pressed through the screen where it is not covered by the stencil (p. 49).

Scroll A long roll of parchment or silk (p. 328).

Sculpture Three-dimensional work of art created out of wood, stone, metal, or clay by carving, welding, casting, or modeling (p. 50).

Seascape Painting or drawing in which the sea is the subject.

Shade A dark value of a hue made by adding black to it. Opposite of tint (p. 140).

Shading The use of light and dark values to give the illusion of form (p. 44).

Shadows Shaded areas in a drawing or painting. Shadows show the surfaces of the subject that reflect the least light and are used to create the illusion of form. Opposite of highlights.

Shape A two-dimensional area that is defined in some way. While a form has depth, a shape has only height and width. Shapes are either geometric or free-form (p. 98).

Shiny surface Surface that reflects bright light. Window glass has a shiny surface. Opposite of matte surface (p. 175).

Sighting Technique for determining the proportional relationship of one part of an object to another.

Silhouette Outline drawing of a shape. Originally a silhouette was a profile portrait, filled in with a solid color.

Simplicity Technique for creating unity by limiting the number of variations of an element of art.

Simulated texture A kind of visual texture that imitates real texture by using a two-dimensional pattern to create the illusion of a three-dimensional surface (p. 173). A plastic tabletop can use a pattern to simulate the texture of wood. Opposite of invented texture.

Sketch Quick, rough drawing without much detail that can be used as a plan or reference for later work.

Slip Creamy mixture of clay and water used to fasten pieces of clay together.

Smooth texture Regular surface that reflects light evenly. Opposite of rough texture (p. 175).

Soft edge In two-dimensional art, shapes with fuzzy, blurred outlines. Soft-edge shapes look soft. Opposite of hard-edge.

Soft sculpture Sculpture made with fabric and stuffed with soft material.

Solvent The liquid that controls the thickness or the thinness of the paint (p. 150).

Space The element of art that refers to the emptiness or area between, around, above, below, or within objects. Shapes and forms are defined by space around and within them (p. 103).

Spectral colors Red, orange, yellow, green, blue, violet (p. 136).

Split-complementary colors One hue and the hues on each side of its complement on the color wheel (p. 147). Red-orange, blue, and green are split-complementary colors. Split-complementary colors can be used as a color scheme.

Stained glass Colored glass cut into pieces, arranged in a design, and joined with strips of lead.

Static Inactive (p. 77). Vertical and horizontal lines and horizontal shapes and forms are static. Opposite of active.

Still life Painting or drawing of inanimate (nonmoving) objects.

Stippling Technique of shading using dots (p. 44).

Stitchery Technique for decorating fabric by stitching fibers onto it.

Stone Age Period of history during which stone tools were used (p. 320).

Storyboards A series of still drawings that show a story's progress (p. 395).

Stupas Beehive-shaped domed places of worship (p. 326).

Style See *individual style.*

Subject The image viewers can easily identify in a work of art (p. 18).

Subordinate element Element of a work of art noticed after the dominant element (p. 290).

Super-Realism Twentieth-century artistic style that depicts objects as precisely and accurately as they actually appear (p. 381).

Surrealism Twentieth-century artistic style in which dreams, fantasy, and the subconscious served as inspiration for artists (p. 375).

Symbol Something that stands for, or represents, something else (p. 16).

Symmetry A special type of formal balance in which two halves of a balanced composition are identical, mirror images of each other (p. 230).

Synthetic Made by chemical processes rather than natural processes.

T

Tactile texture Texture that can be perceived through touch. Opposite of visual texture (p. 173).

Tapestry Fabric wall hanging that is woven, painted, or embroidered.

Tempera Paint made by mixing pigments with egg yolk (egg tempera) or another liquid. School poster paint is a type of tempera (p. 47).

Texture The element of art that refers to how things feel, or look as if they might feel if touched. Texture is perceived by touch and sight. Objects can have rough or smooth textures and matte or shiny surfaces (p. 171).

Tint A light value of a hue made by mixing the hue with white. Opposite of shade (p. 140).

Tonality Arrangement of colors in a painting so that one color dominates the work of art (p. 157).

Totem poles Tall posts carved and painted with a series of animal symbols associated with a particular family or clan (p. 343).

Transparent Quality of a material that allows light to pass through. Opposite of opaque.

Trompe l'oeil French for "deceive the eye." Style of painting in which painters try to give the viewer the illusion of seeing a three-dimensional object, so that the viewer wonders whether he or she is seeing a picture or something real.

U

Unity The quality of wholeness or oneness that is achieved through the effective use of the elements and principles of art (p. 296). Unity is created by simplicity, repetition, and proximity.

Unusual Technique for creating a focal point by using the unexpected (p. 295).

V

Value The element of art that describes the darkness or lightness of an object (p. 75). Value depends on how much light a surface reflects. Value is also one of the three properties of color.

Vanishing point Point on the horizon where receding parallel lines seem to meet (p. 115).

Variety Principle of art concerned with difference or contrast (p. 288).

Vault Arched roof, ceiling, or covering made of brick, stone, or concrete (p. 55).

Vehicle Liquid, like water or oil, that pigments are mixed with to make paint or dye (3).

Vertical lines Lines that are straight up and down (p. 72). Vertical lines are at right angles to the bottom edge of the paper or canvas and the horizon, and parallel to the side of the paper or canvas.

Viewing frame A piece of paper with an area cut from the middle. By holding the frame at arm's length and looking through it at the subject, the artist can focus on the area of the subject he or she wants to draw or paint.

Visual arts The arts that produce beautiful objects to look at.

Visual movement The principle of art used to create the look and feeling of action and to guide the viewer's eyes throughout the work of art (p. 211).

Visual rhythm Rhythm you perceive through your eyes rather than through your ears (p. 200).

Visual texture Illusion of a three-dimensional surface based on the memory of how things feel. There are two types of visual texture: invented and simulated (p. 173). Opposite of tactile texture.

Visual weight Attraction that elements in a work of art have for the viewer's eyes. Visual weight is affected by size, contour, intensity of colors, warmth and coolness of colors, contrast in value, texture, and position (p. 228).

W

Warm colors Red, orange, and yellow (p. 148). Warm colors suggest warmth and seem to move toward the viewer. Warm colors can be used as a color scheme. Opposite of cool colors.

Warp In weaving, lengthwise threads held in place on the loom and crossed by weft threads.

Watercolor paint Transparent pigments mixed with water (p. 47).

Weaving Making fabric by interlacing two sets of parallel threads, held at right angles to each other on a loom (p. 52).

Weft In weaving, crosswise threads that are carried over and under the warp threads.

Woodblock printing Making prints by carving images in blocks of wood (p. 330).

Y

Yarn Fibers spun into strands for weaving, knitting, or embroidery.

Z

Ziggurats Stepped mountains made of brick-covered earth (12).

Zigzag lines Lines formed by short, sharp turns (4). Zigzag lines are a combination of diagonal lines. They can change direction suddenly.

Glosario

Esta sección contiene las palabras y frases importantes que se usan en *ArtTalk* y que pueden ser nuevas para ti. Tal vez querrás consultar esta lista de términos mientras lees los capítulos, completas los ejercicios y te preparas para crear tus propias obras de arte. También puedes usar este glosario para revisar lo que has aprendido en *ArtTalk*.

A

Abstract art/arte abstracto Arte del siglo XX que contiene formas bidimensionales que simplifican las formas de objetos reales con tal de recalcar la forma en vez del contenido.

Abstract Expressionism/expresionismo abstracto Estilo de pintura desarrollado en Nueva York después de la Segunda Guerra Mundial. Recalcaba los elementos abstractos del arte en lugar del contenido reconocible. También recalcaba los sentimientos y las emociones (p. 378).

Acrylic paint/pintura acrílica Pigmentos mezclados con vehículo acrílico. Disponibles en varios grados de calidad: para uso escolar y para artistas. Acrílicos para uso escolar son menos costosos que acrílicos profesionales. Se quitan de los pinceles y de la ropa en el lavado y no son tóxicos.

Action Painting/Pintura de acción El método de dejar caer y chapotear gotas de pintura sobre un lienzo. (p. 13) Véase *Abstract Expressionism*.

Active/activo Que expresa movimiento. Son activas las líneas diagonales y en zigzag (p. 76) y las figuras y formas que se inclinan diagonalmente (p. 120). El opuesto de inmóvil.

Aesthetic experience/experiencia estética Tu interacción personal con una obra de arte (p. 27).

Aesthetics/estética La filosofía o el estudio de la naturaleza del arte y de su valor (p. 26).

Afterimage/post-imagen Imagen débil de un color complementario creada por el cerébro del observador como reacción de la observación prolongada de un color. Después de ver algo rojo, el observador ve una post-imagen verde. (p. 137)

Age of Faith/Edad de la Fé Véase *Middle Ages*.

Air brush/pistola de aire Atomizador impulsado por aire comprimido que se usa para rociar la pintura.

Alternating rhythm/ritmo alterno Ritmo visual que se crea al repetir motivos pero cambiar la posición o el contenido de éstos o los espacios entre ellos. (p. 208)

Analogous colors/colores análogos Colores que se ubican uno al lado del otro en el círculo cromático y que tienen en común el mismo color primario o secundario (p. 145). Violeta, rojo-violeta y rojo son colores análogos. Los colores análogos se pueden usar en una combinación de colores.

Analysis/análisis En la crítica del arte, el paso en el que descubres cómo se usan los principios del arte para organizar los elementos del arte: línea, color, formas bi- y tridimensionales, espacio y textura. En la historia del arte, el paso en el que determinas el estilo de la obra (p. 28).

Animators/animadores Artistas que crean dibujos animados (p. 395).

Applied art/artes aplicadas Artes en las que los objetos creados deben ser funcionales tanto como bellos (p. 52).

Approximate symmetry/simetría aproximada Equilibrio que es casi simétrico (p. 231). Este tipo de simetría produce el efecto de la estabilidad, como lo hace el equilibrio formal, pero pequeñas diferencias hacen que el arreglo sea más interesante.

Arbitrary color/color arbitrario Color escogido por el artista para expresar sus sentimientos (p. 154). El opuesto de color óptico.

Arch/arco Estructura de piedra en forma curva que apoya el peso de material sobre un espacio abierto. Las puertas y los puentes usan arcos.

Architect/arquitecto Persona que diseña edificios bien construidos, estéticamente agradables y funcionales (p. 386).

Architecture/arquitectura Forma de arte que consiste en diseñar y planificar la construcción de edificios, ciudades y puentes (p. 54).

Art criticism/crítica del arte Método organizado de estudiar una obra de arte. Tiene cuatro etapas: descripción, análisis, interpretación y opinión (p. 25).

Art history operations/funcionamientos de la historia de arte Un método de cuatro etapas de organizar la manera en que uno puede allegar información sobre una obra de arte. (p. 34)

Artistic style/estilo artístico Véase *individual style*.

Artists/artistas Personas creativas que usan la imaginación y la habilidad para comunicar de forma visual (p. 11).

Artwork/obra de arte La expresión visual de una idea o una experiencia creada con destreza (p. 6).

Ashcan School/escuela cubo de la basura Grupo de artistas estadounidenses que trabajaban a principios del siglo XX y usaban a la gente y las escenas de la ciudad como tema para su obra (p. 376). Originalmente conocidos como "El ocho," ayudaron a organizar la exposición del Armory.

Assembling/juntar Técnica de escultura en la que el artista junta y pega una variedad de materiales distintos para hacer una escultura. Llamado también construcción (p. 186).

Asymmetrical balance/equilibrio asimétrico Otro nombre para el equilibrio informal, en el que objetos no similares tienen igual peso visual o atraen igualmente al ojo (p. 234).

Atmospheric perspective/perspectiva atmosférica Efecto del aire y la luz en cómo se percibe un objeto (p. 114). Más aire entre el observador y el objeto, más parece desvanecerse el objeto. Un objeto brillante parece ser más cerca al observador que un objeto opaco.

B

Background/fondo La parte del plano óptico que parece más lejos del observador.

Balance/equilibrio Principio del arte que se preocupa por igualar las fuerzas visuales, o elementos, en una obra de arte (p. 228). Si una obra tiene equilibrio visual, el observador siente que los elementos han sido distribuidos de una manera satisfactoria. El desequilibrio visual hace que el observador sienta que los elementos deben ser redistribuidos. Los dos tipos de equilibrio son el formal—que también se llama simétrico—e informal, o asimétrico.

Baroque/barroco Estilo artístico que recalcaba la iluminación dramática, el movimiento y la intensidad emocional. Se desarrolló después de la Reforma en el siglo XVII. Los artistas utilizaban formas y figuras que avanzaban hacia el observador, dramáticos efectos de luz, contrastes entre luces y sombras, ornamentación y líneas curvas para expresar energía y emociones fuertes (p. 361).

Bas-relief/bajo relieve Véase *low relief.*

Binder/adhesivo Líquido que mantiene unidos los granos de pigmento (p. 45).

Blending/casar Técnica de sombrear al aplicar gradualmente y de modo uniforme un valor oscuro (p. 44).

Brayer/rodillo Herramienta con mango que se usa para aplicar tinta a una superficie.

Buttress/contrafuerte Estructura proyectante hecha de ladrillo o piedra que apoya un arco o una bóveda. El arbotante es conectado a la pared por un arco. Se extiende por encima de la nave lateral para apoyar el techo de una catedral.

Byzantine art/arte bizantino Estilo artístico que se desenvolvió alrededor de la ciudad de Constantinopla— ahora Estambul, Turquía—en la parte este del imperio romano. Presentaba colores vivos y figuras marcadamente perfiladas que parecían planas y rígidas (p. 319).

C

Calligraphic lines/líneas caligráficas Líneas fluidas hechas con pinceladas similares a las de la escritura asiática (p. 83).

Calligraphy/caligrafía Método asiático de escribir bellamente (p. 83).

Canvas/lienzo Tela basta en el que se pinta un óleo.

Carving/talla Técnica de escultura en el que el escultor corta, cincela o perfora un bulto macizo para crear una escultura. Se quita material hasta que la escultura sea completa; por lo tanto, se refiere a la talla como un procedimiento sustractivo (p. 51).

Casting/fundición Técnica de escultura en la que se vierte metal fundido u otra sustancia a un molde y se lo deja endurecer. Igual como para la imprenta, se puede sacar una edición de esculturas del mismo molde (p. 51).

Central axis/eje central Línea divisora que funciona como el punto de equilibrio en una balanza. El eje central se usa para medir el peso visual en una obra de arte. Puede ser vertical—se mide el equilibrio entre los dos lados —o horizontal— se mide el equilibrio entre la parte de abajo y la parte de arriba (p. 228).

Ceramics/cerámica Arte de hacer objetos con arcilla para producir alfarería y escultura. Se coce la alfarería en un horno para hacerla más fuerte.

Chiaroscuro/claroscuro La distribución de luces y sombras (p. 112). Técnica introducida por artistas italianos durante el Renacimiento que fue utilizado extensamente por artistas barrocos. También se llama modelaje o sombreado.

Classical/clásico Se refiere al arte de la antigua Grecia y de Roma. Los griegos crearon un arte basado en los ideales de la propoción perfecta y en la lógica en vez de la emoción. Los romanos adaptaron el arte griego y lo difundieron por el mundo civilizado (p. 352).

Clay/arcilla Tierra espesa y pegajosa que se usa en la cerámica. Es húmeda y se endurece después de secarse o ser cocida (p. 53).

Clustering/agrupación Técnica de crear un punto focal al agrupar juntamente varias formas diferentes (p. 301).

Coil/rollo Anillo o rosca que se junta en un círculo o en espiral. Los rollos de arcilla se usan para hacer la alfarería.

Collage/collage Obra de arte a la que han sido pegados materiales como papel con textura, fotografías, y tela a una superficie plana (p. 179).

Color/color Elemento del arte que se deriva de la luz reflejada (p. 136). La sensación del color se despierta en el cerébro a la hora que responden los ojos a distintas longitudes de ondas de luz. Aparte del color en sí, las propiedades del color son el valor y la intensidad.

Color-field painting/pintura de campos de color Arte del siglo XX creado al utilizar solamente campos planos de color (p. 380).

Color scheme/combinación de colores Proyecto para organizar colores. Existen combinaciones de colores monocromáticos, análogos, complementarios, de tríada, divididos, cálidos y frescos (p. 144).

Color spectrum/espectro de colores Efecto que ocurre cuando la luz pasa por un prisma; el rayo de luz blanca se dobla y se separa en bandas de color. Los colores siempre aparecen del mismo orden, por longitudes de onda, de la más larga a la más corta: rojo, anaranjado, amarillo, verde, azul, violeta. Un arco iris muestra el espectro (p. 136).

Color triad/tríada de colores Tres colores distribuidos a distancias iguales en el círculo cromático (p. 146). La tríada de colores primarios se consiste en el rojo, el amarillo y el azul; la tríada de colores secundarios se consiste en el anaranjado, el verde y la violeta. Una tríada de colores es un tipo de combinación de colores.

Color wheel/círculo cromático El espectro doblado en forma de un círculo (p. 138).

Compass/compás Instrumento que se usa para medir y trazar arcos y círculos.

Complementary colors/colores complementarios Colores opuestos uno al otro en el círculo cromático (p. 142). El complemento de un color absorbe todas las ondas de luz que refleja el color y es el contraste más fuerte a ese color. Mezclar un color con su complemento lo deslustra. El rojo y el verde son colores complementarios. Los colores complementarios se pueden usar en una combinación de colores.

Composition/composición Modo en que los principios del arte están usados para organizar los elementos del arte (p. 18).

Content/contenido Mensaje que comunica una obra de arte. El contenido puede relacionarse con la materia de la obra o puede ser una idea o emoción. Otra palabra para contenido es tema (p. 19).

Contour drawing/dibujo de nivel Dibujo en el que solamente se utilizan las curvas de nivel para representar el tema (p. 81). El artista mantiene los ojos en el objeto que dibuja y se concentra en las direcciones y en las curvas.

Contour line/curva de nivel Línea que define los contornos y los niveles de superficie de un objeto (p. 81).

Contrast/contraste Técnica de crear un punto focal al utilizar diferencias en elementos (p. 291).

Convergence/convergencia Técnica de crear un punto focal al distribuir los elementos de manera que varias líneas y formas apunten a un objeto o área (p. 293).

Cool colors/colores fríos Azul, verde y violeta (p. 148). Los colores fríos sugieren la frescura y parecen alejarse del observador. Se pueden usar en una combinación de colores. Son el opuesto de los colores cálidos.

Crafts/artesanía Forma de arte que crea obras que son tanto bellas como útiles. La artesanía incluye la tejeduría, el diseño de telas y la fabricación de joyas (p. 52).

Crayons/lapices de colores Pigmentos juntados con cera y moldeados en forma de palitos.

Credit line/leyenda Lista de datos importantes sobre una obra de arte. Una leyenda normalmente incluye el nombre del artista, el título de la obra, el año en que fue completada, el medio, el tamaño—altura, anchura y profundidad, la ubicación—galeria, museo o colección y ciudad, los donantes y la fecha en que fue donada (p. 19).

Crewel/torzal Hilo sueltamente torcido que se usa en el bordado.

Criteria/criterios Valores que se usan para formar una opinión sobre algo (p. 26).

Crosshatching/sombreado cruzado Técnica de usar líneas cruzadas para sombrear (p. 44).

Cubism/cubismo Movimiento artístico del siglo XX que recalca la estructura y el diseño (p. 374). Los objetos tridimensionales se representan de varios puntos de vista diferentes al mismo tiempo.

Culture/cultura Conductas e ideas de un grupo de gente. Se puede estudiar los objetos de arte producidos por un grupo de gente para aprender sobre una cultura.

Cuneiform/escritura cuneiforme Sistema de escritura sumeria compuesto de carácteres de forma de cuña (p. 321).

Curved lines/líneas curvas Líneas que siempre se doblan y cambian de dirección gradualmente (p. 73).

D

Dark Ages/Edades Bárbaras Véase *Middle Ages.*

Decalcomania/decalcomanía Técnica en el que la pintura es forzada a crear diseños y texturas fortuitos al despegar dos lienzos entre los cuales gotas de pintura han sido apretadas (p. 183).

Dense/denso Compacto; que tiene las partes muy juntas. Los materiales densos son sólidos y pesados. El opuesto de ligero.

Description/descripción Una lista de todas las cosas que ves en una obra (p. 27).

Design/diseño Sistema, organización o distribución de los elementos de una obra de arte.

Diagonal lines/líneas diagonales Líneas que se inclinan (p. 72).

Digital camera/cámara digital Una cámara que graba las imágenes de manera digital. Luego estas imágenes se pueden descargar a aplicaciones de computadora donde pueden ser alteradas y realzadas (p. 60).

Digital system/sistema digital Un sistema que procesa palabras e imágenes directamente como números o dígitos (p. 59).

Dimension/dimensión La cantidad de espacio que ocupa un objeto en una dirección (p. 70). Las tres dimensiones son el altura, la anchura y la profundidad.

Distortion/distorción Desviaciones de las proporciones esperadas y/o normales (p. 268).

Divine Proportion/proporción divina Véase *Golden Mean.*

Dome/cúpula Bóveda o techo hemisférico sobre una abertura circular. Una cúpula se levanta sobre la parte central de un edificio (p. 326).

Dominant element/elemento dominante Elemento que se nota primero en una obra de arte. Los elementos que se notan después se conocen como secundarios (p. 290).

Draw program/programa de dibujo Una aplicación de computadora para crear arte en el que las imágenes se guardan como series de líneas y curvas. En programas de dibujo se puede cambiar el tamaño de los objetos sin provocar distorciones (p. 60).

Dyes/tintes Pigmentos que se disuelven en líquido. El tinte penetra un material y lo mancha (p. 151).

Dynamism/dinamismo Término utilizado por los futuristas para referirse a las fuerzas del movimiento.

Dynasty/dinastía Un período de tiempo durante el cual una sola familia proporcionaba una sucesión de gobernantes (p. 324).

E

Edition/edición Todas las estampas hechas de la misma plancha o de la misma serie de planchas (p. 48).

Elements of art/elementos del arte Los más básicos símbolos visuales en el lenguaje del arte. Los elementos del arte son la línea, las formas bi- y tridimensionales, el espacio, el color, el valor y la textura (p. 16).

Embroidery/bordado Técnica de decorar la tela con puntadas.

Emotionalism/sentimentalismo Teoría que requiere que una obra de arte haga reaccionar al observador de una manera sentimental. Una de las tres teorías estéticas dentro de la crítica del arte; las otras son el formalismo y el imitacionalismo (p. 32).

Emphasis/énfasis Principio del arte que hace que parte de una obra domine sobre las otras partes (p. 290). El elemento que se nota primero se conoce como el dominante; los elementos que se notan después se conocen como los secundarios.

Engraving/grabado Técnica de cortar un diseño en un material, normalmente metal, con una herramienta puntiaguda. Se puede sacar una estampa al entintar una superficie grabada.

Exaggeration/exageración Desviación de las proporciones esperadas y/o normales (p. 268).

Expressionism/expresionismo Movimiento artístico del siglo XX. Un estilo que recalcaba la expresión de los sentimientos más íntimos (p. 374).

Expressive qualities/calidades expresivas Esas calidades que comunican las ideas y los sentimientos (p. 31).

F

Fabric/tela Material hecho de fibras. Los tejidos y el fieltro son telas.

Fauves/fauves En francés, "bestias salvajes." Un grupo de pintores al principios del siglo XX que empleaban colores brillantes y distorciones audaces de una manera descontrolada. Su líder fue Henri Matisse.

Fiber/fibra Material delgado y lineal, parecido al hilo, que se puede tejer o hilar para hacer tela (p. 52).

Fiberfill/relleno de fibras Material de relleno ligero y fofo, hecho de fibras sintéticas.

Figure/figura La forma humana en una obra de arte.

Fine art/bellas artes Artes creadas para ser experimentadas de manera visual. El opuesto del arte funcional (p. 52).

Fire/cocer Aplicar calor a la alfarería para endurecerla.

Flowing rhythm/ritmo fluido Ritmo visual creado al repetir líneas onduladas (p. 208).

Focal point/punto focal La primera parte de una obra que atrae la atención del observador (p. 290). Los puntos focales son creados por el contraste, la colocación, el aislamiento, la convergencia y el uso de lo insólito.

Folk artists/artistas de la gente Artistas enseñados por ellos mismos y por lo tanto no han tenido mucha instrucción formal en métodos artísticos (p. 10).

Foreground/primer plano La parte del plano óptico que parece más cerca al observador. El primer plano normalmente se encuentra en la parte de abajo del cuadro.

Foreshortening/escorzo Acortar un objeto para que parezca como si extendiera para atrás en el espacio (p. 264). Esta técnica reproduce las proporciones que ve un observador en la actualidad, las cuales dependen de la distancia entre el observador y el objeto.

Formal balance/equilibrio formal Modo de organizar las partes de un diseño para que elementos iguales o similares estén colocados a lados opuestos de un eje central (p. 229). El equilibrio formal sugiere estabilidad. La simetría es un tipo de equilibrio formal. El opuesto del equilibrio informal.

Formal qualities/calidades de forma Lo bien que está organizada una obra (p. 31). Esta calidad estética es favorecida por el formalismo.

Formalism/formalismo Teoría que recalca las calidades de forma. Una de las tres teorías estéticas dentro de la crítica del arte; las otras son el sentimentalismo y el imitacionalismo (p. 31).

Forms/formas tridimensionales Así como las formas bidimensionales, tienen altura y anchura. Tienen también profundidad. Pueden ser geométricas o de forma libre (p. 101).

Free-form shapes/formas libres Formas irregulares y desiguales (p. 99). Sus perfiles pueden ser curvos, angulares o las dos cosas. A veces, a esas formas se les llaman formas orgánicas (se encuentran en la naturaleza). Son el opuesto de las formas geométricas.

Freestanding/independiente Obra de arte rodeada de espacio por todos lados. Una obra de arte tridimensional es independiente. El opuesto del relieve (p. 50).

Frottage/frottage Se pone un lienzo recientemente pintado boca arriba encima de una textura en relieve y se frota o roza la superficie de la pintura con grafito, cera, o lápiz de color (p. 183).

Functional art/arte funcional Obras de arte hechas para el uso en vez del deleite. Los objetos deben ser juzgados según lo bien que funcionan cuando se usan (p. 33).

Futurists/futuristas Artistas italiano de principios del siglo XX que distribuían las formas angulares de manera que sugerían el movimiento (p. 212). Llamaban a las fuerzas del movimiento el dinamismo.

Gallery/galería Lugar para exponer o vender obras de arte.

Genre painting/pintura de género Pinturas que tienen como tema escenas de la vida diaria.

Geometric shapes/formas geométricas Formas precisas que se pueden describir usando fórmulas matemáticas (p. 98). De las formas geométricas bidimensionales, las básicas son el círculo, el cuadrado y el triángulo. Formas geométricas tridimensionales son el cilindro, el cubo y la pirámide. Las formas geométricas son el opuesto de las formas libres.

Gesture/gesto Un movimiento expresivo (p. 82).

Gesture drawing/dibujo de gestos Dibujo de líneas hecho rápidamente para capturar los movimientos de una persona.

Glaze/barniz En la cerámica, una capa delgada y lustrosa que se coce a la alfarería. En la pintura, una capa delgada de pintura transparente.

Golden Mean/regla de oro Una línea dividida en dos partes de manera que la línea más corta tenga la misma proporción, o razón, con la línea más larga que tiene la línea más larga con la línea entera (p. 256). Razón perfecta—relación de partes—descubierta por Euclid, matemático griego. Su expresión matemática es 1 a 1.6. También se llamaba la sección áurea y el rectángulo de oro. Los lados largos del rectángulo de oro tienen un poco más del doble de la longitud de los lados cortos. Esta razón fue redescubierta a principios del siglo XVI y se llamaba la divina proporción.

Gothic/gótico Estilo artístico que se desenvolvió en el oeste de Europa entre los siglos XII y XVI. Constaba de iglesias que parecían elevarse hacia el cielo, arcos punteados y vidrieras coloreadas (p. 355).

Gouache/gouache Pigmentos molidos en agua y mezclados con goma para forma una acuarela opaca. El gouache se parece a la pintura al temple de uso escolar.

Graphic designer/diseñador gráfico Una persona que traslada ideas a imágenes y las distribuye de modos atractivos y memorables (p. 392).

Grattage/grattage Se raspa pintura húmeda con una variedad de herramientas, como tenedores, navajas y peines, con el fin de crear diferentes texturas (p. 183).

Grid/cuadrícula Diseño de líneas verticales y horizontales que se cruzan (p. 206).

Griots/griots Artistas que cuentan la historia oral y que son músicos y actores (p. 334).

Hard-edge/línea dura En el arte bidimensional, formas que tienen los contornos claramente definidos. Las formas de línea dura parecen densas. El opuesto de la línea suave.

Harmony/armonía El principio del arte que crea unidad al subrayar las similitudes entre partes que son separadas pero relacionadas (p. 295).

Hatching/sombreado rayado Técnica de sombrear usando una serie de finas líneas paralelas (p. 44).

Hierarchical proportion/escala jerárquica Cuando las figuras de una obra de arte están distribuidas de manera que la escala indique importancia (p. 260).

Hieroglyphics/jeroglíficos Escritura con dibujos usada por los antiguos egipcios y en la que se usan figuras o símbolos en vez de letras (p. 323).

High-key painting/pintura de tono alto Pintura en la que se usan muchas tintas de un color (p. 140). El opuesto de la pintura de tono bajo.

Highlights/toques de luz Pequeñas áreas de blanco que se usan para mostrar las partes más claras (p. 112). Los toques de luz muestran las superficies de un objeto que reflejan más luz. Se usan para crear la ilusión de la tridimensionalidad. Son el opuesto de las sombras.

High relief/alto relieve Escultura de la cual áreas sobresalen de una superficie plana (p. 106).

High-resolution/resolución alta Que produce una imagen nítida.

Holograms/hologramas Imágenes de tres dimensiones creadas por un rayo láser (p. 107).

Horizon/horizonte Punto donde parecen juntarse la tierra y el cielo.

Horizontal line/línea horizontal Línea paralela al horizonte (p. 72). Las líneas horizontales son rectas y paralelas al borde inferior de un papel o lienzo.

Hue/color El nombre de un color en el espectro de colores (p. 138). Los colores primarios son el rojo, el amarillo y el azul. Se consideran primarios debido a que no se pueden formar al mezclar diferentes colores. Los colores secundarios son los que se hacen al mezclar dos colores primarios. Son el anaranjado, la violeta y el verde. Cada color figura entre las tres propiedades del color.

Illustrator/ilustrador Persona que crea las imágenes visuales que complementan las palabras escritas (p. 393).

Imitationalism/imitacionalismo Teoría estética que se enfoca en a la representación realística. Una de las tres teorías estéticas dentro de la crítica del arte; las otras son el sentimentalismo y el formalismo (p. 31).

Implied lines/líneas implícitas Una serie de puntos que conectan los ojos del observador automáticamente. Las líneas implícitas son sugeridas, no reales (p. 71).

Impressionism/impresionismo Estilo de pintura que empezó en Francia en los años 1860. Representaba temas de la vida diaria y recalcaba los efectos momentarios de la luz sobre el color (p. 370).

Individual style/estilo individual La forma personal del artista de usar los elementos y principios del arte para expresar sentimientos e ideas (p. 35).

Informal balance/equilibrio informal Modo de organizar las partes de un diseño que crea un equilibrio entre objetos dissimilares (p. 234). La asimetría es otro término para el equilibrio informal. El opuesto del equilibrio formal.

Intaglio/calcografía Técnica de imprenta en la que la tinta es metida dentro de líneas que han sido cortadas o grabadas en una superficie dura como el metal o la madera. Luego se limpia la superficie de la plancha y se hacen las estampas (p. 49).

Intensity/intensidad Lo subido o apagado que es un color. Un color puro se llama un color de alta intensidad. Un color apagado o deslustrado—que ha sido mezclado con su complemento—se llama un color de baja intensidad. La intensidad es una de las tres propiedades del color. (p. 142)

Interior designer/diseñador de interiores Una persona que planifica el diseño y la decoración de espacios interiores de casas y oficinas (p. 400).

Intermediate color/color intermedio Un color hecho al mezclar un color primario con un color secundario. El rojo-anaranjado es un color intermedio (p. 138).

International style/estilo internacional Estilo de arquitectura que se desenvolvió después de la Segunda Guerra Mundial y que recalca los edificios sencillos y adustos (p. 381).

Interpretation/interpretación En la crítica del arte, el paso en el que explicas o cuentas el significado de la obra o lo que expresa. En la historia del arte, el paso en el que haces investigaciones sobre el artista (p. 27).

Invented texture/textura inventada Un tipo de textura visual que no representa una textura verdadera pero que crea la sensación de una textura al repetir líneas y formas en un diseño bidimensional (p. 174). El opuesto de la textura simulada.

Isolation/aislamiento Técnica de crear un punto focal al poner un objeto solo para recalcarlo (p. 292).

Judgment/opinión En la crítica del arte, el paso en el que determinas el grado de mérito artístico. En la historia del arte, el paso en el que determinas si la obra ha hecho una contribución importante a la historia del arte (p. 27).

Kinetic/cinético Una obra de arte que realmente se mueve en el espacio (p. 213).

Landscape/paisaje Pintura o dibujo en el que la naturaleza, incluyendo montañas, arboles, ríos o lagos, es el tema principal.

Layout/composición de la página En la imprenta, la manera en que las formas y las líneas están distribuidas en la página (p. 454).

Line/línea Un elemento del arte que es el camino de un punto que se mueve por el espacio. Aunque las líneas pueden variar en su apariencia—pueden tender longitudes, anchuras, texturas, direcciones y grados de curva diferentes—son consideradas como unidimensionales y se miden por longitud. Un artista usa la línea para controlar el movimiento del ojo del observador. Existen cinco tipos de línea: la vertical, la horizontal, la diagonal, la curva y la línea en zigzag (p. 70).

Linear perspective/perspectiva lineal Un sistema gráfico que crea la ilusión de la profundidad y el volumen en una superficie plana. En la perspectiva lineal de un punto, todas las líneas se retiran hasta un solo punto. En la perspectiva lineal de dos puntos, diferentes grupos de líneas se juntan en puntos diferentes (p. 115).

Literal qualities/calidades literales Las calidades realístas que aparecen en el tema de la obra (p. 31).

Lithography/litografía Una técnica de imprenta en la que la imagen que se quiere imprimir se dibuja en piedra caliza, cinc, o aluminio con un lápiz grasiento especial o con un lápiz. Este material atrae la tinta (p. 49).

Location/colocación La técnica de colocar los elementos para crear un punto focal (p. 292). Los objetos que están cerca del medio de una obra de arte normalmente se notan primero.

Logos/logotipos Símbolos o marcas registradas que se reconocen inmediatamente (p. 392).

Loom/telar Máquina o marco para tejer.

Low-key painting/pintura de tono bajo Tipo de pintura en la que se usan muchos tonos o valores oscuros de un color (p. 140). El opuesto de la pintura de tono alto.

Low-relief/bajo relieve Escultura en relieve con áreas positivas que sobresalen un poquito del superficie plano.

M

Mannerism/manierismo Estilo artístico europeo del siglo XVI que presentaba escenas muy emocionales y figuras alargadas (p. 360).

Manufactured shapes/forms/formas fabricadas Formas bi- o tridimensionales hechas por personas, a mano o a máquina. El opuesto de las formas orgánicas.

Mat/orlar Enmarcar un cuadro o un dibujo con un borde de cartón.

Matte surface/superficie mate Superficie que refleja una luz suave y débil (p. 175). El papel tiene una superficie mate. El opuesto de una superficie lustrosa.

Medieval/medieval Relacionado con la Edad Media. Véase *Middle Ages.*

Medium/medio Material que se usa para hacer arte (p. 19).

Megaliths/megalitos Monumentos grandes creados con bloques masivos de piedra (p. 321).

Mexican muralists/muralistas mexicanos Artistas de principios del siglo XX cuyas pinturas en paredes y techos utilizaban formas sólidas y colores fuertes para expresar sentimientos sobre la Revolución Mexicana. Se llaman también los expresionistas mexicanos (p. 377).

Middle Ages/Edad Media Período de aproximadamente mil años, de la destrucción del imperio romano hasta el Renacimiento. Cultura que tenía por centro la iglesia católica. La Edad Media se llama también las Edades Bárbaras (porque no surgieron muchas ideas nuevas) y la Edad de la Fé (porque la religión era una potencia muy fuerte) (p. 354).

Middle ground/plano medio El área de una imagen entre el primer plano y el fondo.

Minimalism/minimalismo Estilo artístico del siglo XX que usa un mínimo de los elementos del arte (p. 380).

Mobile/móvil Escultura que se mueve (p. 213).

Modeling/modelaje Técnica de escultura en el que se amontona y se le da forma a un material suave y flexible. Como se añade más material para crear una forma, se refiere al modelaje como un proceso aditivo (p. 51).

Module/módulo Un motivo tridimensional (p. 204).

Monochromatic/monocromáticos Una combinación de colores que utiliza solamente un color y las tintas y tonos de ese color. Crea un efecto de unidad (p. 145).

Mortar and pestle/mano y metate Plato cerámico y herramienta que se usan para reducir algo a polvo.

Mosaics/mosaicos Imágenes hechas con cubos pequeños y coloridos de mármol, vidrio o azulejo que se ponen en cemento.

Mosques/mezquitas Edificios de culto musulmanes (p. 331).

Motif/motivo Una unidad que se repite en un ritmo visual (p. 202). Las unidades de un motivo pueden ser duplicados exactos de la primera unidad o pueden variar.

Movement/movimiento Véase *visual movement.*

Multimedia programs/programas de multimedia Programas de computadora software que ayudan a los usuarios a diseñar, organizar y combinar textos, elementos gráficos, vídeos y sonidos en un solo documento (p. 61).

Mural/mural Pintura en una pared o en un techo.

Museum curator/director de museo Persona que superentiende las actividades de un museo (p. 404).

N

Negative spaces/espacios negativos Espacios vacíos que rodean las formas (p. 103). La forma y el tamaño de los espacios negativos afectan la interpretación de los espacios positivos. Los espacios negativos se llaman también el fondo.

Neoclassicism/neoclasicismo Clasicismo nuevo. Estilo artístico francés que surgió en el siglo XIX después del estilo rococó. Una aproximación al arte que adoptaba temas y calidades de diseño del arte de Grecia y de Roma (p. 366).

Neolithic period/período neolítico Edad de la Piedra Nueva. Un período prehistórico que abarcaba aproximadamente los años 7000 A.C. a 2000 A.C. (p. 321).

Neutral colors/colores neutrales El negro, el blanco y el gris. El negro no refleja ninguna longitud de onda de luz, el blanco refleja todas las longitudes de onda de luz y el gris refleja igualmente todas las longitudes de onda de luz, pero solo parcialmente (p. 139).

Nonobjective art/arte no objetivo Arte que no tiene ningún tema reconocible (p. 18).

O

Oil paint/pintura al óleo Pintura que se seca lentamente y que es hecha al mezclar pigmentos en óleo. Normalmente se usa para pintar en un lienzo (p. 47).

Opaque/opaco Calidad de un material que no deja pasar por si nada de luz. El opuesto de transparente.

Op art/art óptico Estilo artístico del siglo XX en el que los artistas usan conocimientos científicos sobre la visión para crear ilusiones ópticas del movimiento (p. 379).

Optical color/color óptico Color percibido por el observador debido al efecto de la atmósfera o de alguna luz anormal en el color verdadero (p. 152). El opuesto del color arbitrario.

Organic shapes/forms/formas orgánicas Formas bi- o tridimensionales hechas por las fuerzas de la naturaleza. El opuesto de las formas fabricadas (p. 111).

Outline/contorno Línea que muestra o crea el perfil de una forma (p. 71).

P

Package designer/diseñador de empaquetadura Persona que produce los envases que atraen la atención del consumidor (p. 402).

Pagoda/pagoda Una torre de varios pisos con tejados cuyos bordes se encorvan un poco hacia arriba (p. 329).

Paint/pintura Pigmentos mezclados con óleo o agua. Los granos de pigmento se adhieren a la superficie del material al que se aplica la pintura (p. 44).

Paint program/programa de pintura Una aplicación de computadora para crear arte en la que las imágenes se guardan como bitmaps. Los programas de pintura son capaces de producir imágenes más naturales que los programas de dibujo (p. 60, 449).

Palette/paleta Bandeja que se usa para mezclar colores de pintura.

Papier-mâché/cartón piedra Material de modelaje hecho de papel y pasta líquida que se moldea sobre un soporte llamado la armadura.

Paleolithic period/período paleolítico Edad de la Piedra Antigua. Empezó hace aproximadamente dos millones de años y terminó con el fin del último período glacial hacia 13,000 A.C. (p. 320).

Parallel lines/líneas paralelas Líneas que se mueven en la misma dirección y que siempre se mantienen separadas de la misma distancia.

Pastels/pasteles Pigmentos juntados con goma y moldeados en forma de palitos.

Paste-up/página pegada Modelo de una página impresa. Se saca fotografías de ésta con el propósito de hacer una plancha para la imprenta.

Pattern/diseño repetido El diseño repetido es un principio del arte que se concentra en el diseño decorativo del superficie. Suele ser una repetición bidimensional visual (p. 202).

Perceive/percibir Por medio de los sentidos, hacerse profundamente conciente de la naturaleza especial de un objeto visual (p. 6).

Perspective/perspectiva Un sistema gráfico que crea la ilusión de la profundidad y el volumen en una superficie bidimensional (p. 113). Durante el Renacimiento lo desarrolló el arquitecto Filippo Brunelleschi. La perspectiva se crea al usar el traslapar, las variaciones de tamaño, la colocación, el detalle, el color y las líneas convergentes.

Pharaohs/faraónes Gobernadores egipcios quienes fueron adorados como dioses y tenían una autoridad completa sobre el reinado (p. 323).

Photogram/fotograma Imagen en papel de cianotipo creada por gases del amoníaco líquido.

Photography/fotografía La técnica de capturar imágenes ópticas en superficies sensibles a la luz (p. 57).

Photojournalists/fotoperiodista Reporteros visuales, que trabajan sacando fotografías (p. 395).

Photo-Realism/fotorrealismo Véase *Super-Realism*.

Picture plane/plano óptico La superficie de una pintura o un dibujo.

Pigments/pigmentos Polvos menudamente molidos y coloridos que forman la pintura cuando se mezclan con un líquido (p. 150).

Plaster/yeso Mezcla de cal, arena y agua que se endurece al secarse.

Point of view/punto de vista Ángulo de que el observador ve un objeto (p. 108). Las formas que ve un observador dependen del punto de vista de este observador.

Polymer medium/medio polímero Líquido que se usa en la pintura acrílica, para hacerla menos densa o como material de acabado (p. 47).

Pop art/arte pop Estilo artístico que se empleaba a principios de los años 60 en los Estados Unidos. Presentaba imágenes de la cultura popular, como de los medios de comunicación, del arte comercial, de las tiras cómicas y de la publicidad (p. 378).

Portrait/retrato Imagen de una persona, especialmente de la cara y la parte superior del cuerpo.

Positive spaces/espacios positivos Formas en el arte bi- y tridimensional (p. 103). Los espacios vacíos que las rodean se llaman espacios negativos o el fondo.

Post-and-lintel/poste y dintel Método de construcción en el que una piedra larga se balancea encima de dos postes. Actualmente se refiere a esto como la construcción de poste y viga (p. 321).

Post-Impressionism/postimpresionismo Estilo de pintura francés que originó al final del siglo XIX. Recalcaba un estilo individual hacia la pintura, que pertenecía sólo a un artista específico de la epoca. (p. 371).

Post-Modernism/posmodernismo Un enfoque hacia el arte que incorpora elementos y técnicas tradicionales mientras conserva algunas características de los estilos y movimientos del arte moderno (p. 382).

Pre-Columbian/precolombino Período de tiempo antes que Cristóbal Colón descubriera las Américas en 1492 (p. 339).

Prehistoric/prehistórico Período anterior a que se escribiera la historia (p. 320).

Principles of art/principios del arte Reglas que determinan cómo los artistas organizan los elementos del arte. Los principios del arte son el ritmo, el movimiento, diseño repetido el equilibrio, la proporción, la variedad, el énfasis, y la armonía (p. 18).

Print/estampa Impresión creada por un artista e impresa en papel o tela de una plancha de grabar, sea de metal, piedra o madera. Se puede repetir la impresión muchas veces para producir imágenes idénticas (p. 48).

Printing plate/plancha de grabar Superficie que contiene una impresión que se traslada a papel o tela para hacer una estampa (p. 48).

Printmaking/imprenta Un proceso en el que un artista traslada repetidamente una imagen original de una superficie preparada a otra (p. 48).

Prism/prisma Pieza de vidrio en forma de cuña que dobla la luz blanca y la separa en matices espectrales.

Profile/perfil Vista lateral de una cara.

Progressive rhythm/ritmo progresivo Ritmo visual que cambia un motivo cada vez que se repite (p. 209).

Proportion/proporción Principio del arte que se preocupa por las relaciones de tamaño entre una parte y otra (p. 256).

Protractor/transportador Instrumento semicircular que se usa para medir y trazar ángulos.

Proximity/proximidad Técnica de crear la unidad al limitar los espacios negativos entre las formas (p. 301).

R

Radial balance/equilibrio radial Tipo de equilibrio en el que las fuerzas o los elementos de un diseño se extienden, o radian, de un punto central (p. 232).

Random rhythm/ritmo aleatorio Ritmo visual en el que un motivo se repite, pero por ningún orden específico y sin espacios regulares (p. 205).

Rasp/escofia Lima con dientes afilados y ásperos que se usa para cortar una superficie.

Realism/realismo Estilo artístico con su origen al mediados del siglo XIX que presentaba escenas familiares como realmente se veían (p. 368).

Realists/realistas Artistas del siglo XIX que representaban cuestiones políticas, sociales y morales (p. 368).

Recede/retirarse Moverse para atrás o alejarse.

Reformation/Reforma Revolución religiosa que ocurrió en el oeste de Europa durante el siglo XVI. Empezó como un movimiento de reforma dentro la iglesia católica y produjo los principios del protestantismo (p. 360).

Regionalists/regionalistas Artistas que pintaban los campos de cultivo y las ciudades de los Estados Unidos de una manera optimista (p. 376).

Regular rhythm/ritmo regular Ritmo visual creado al repetir motivos idénticos usando los mismos intervalos de espacios entre ellos (p. 206).

Relief printing/grabado en relieve Una técnica de imprenta en el que el artista recorta las secciones de una superficie que no deben de retener la tinta. Como resultado, la imagen que se debe imprimir se resalta del fondo (p. 48).

Relief sculpture/escultura en relieve Tipo de escultura en la que las formas sobresalen de un fondo plano. El opuesto de la escultura independiente (p. 50).

Renaissance/Renacimiento Nombre dado al período del final de la Edad Media cuando los artistas, escritores y filósofos se despertaron a las formas artísticas y a las ideas de la antigua Grecia y de Roma (p. 356).

Repetition/repetición Técnica de crear ritmo y unidad en la cual un motivo o un solo elemento aparece una y otra vez (p. 308).

Reproduction/reproducción Una copia de una obra de arte (p. 48).

Rhythm/ritmo El principio del arte que indica el movimiento con la repetición de elementos y objetos (p. 200). El ritmo visual se percibe por los ojos y se crea al repetir espacios positivos separados por espacios negativos. Hay cinco tipos de ritmo: aleatorio, regular, alterno, fluido y progresivo.

Rococo/rococó Estilo artístico del siglo XVIII que comenzó en las casas lujosas de la aristocracia francesa y se difundió por el resto de Europa. Acentuaba el movimiento libre y grácil, el uso alegre de la línea y los colores delicados (p. 363).

Romanesque/arte románico Estilo de arquitectura y escultura que se desarrolló durante la Edad Media en el oeste de Europa. Presentaba edificios de tamaño masivo, paredes sólidas y pesadas, un uso extenso del arco de medio punto romano y muchas decoraciones esculturales (p. 354).

Romanticism/Romanticismo Estilo artístico de principios del siglo XIX que fue una reacción contra el neoclasicismo. Encontraba sus temas en lo dramático y en las culturas foráneas a Europa. Recalcaba colores vivos y emociones exageradas (p. 367).

Rough texture/textura áspera Superficie irregular que refleja desigualmente la luz (p. 175). El opuesto de la textura lisa.

Rubbing/calco Técnica de transferir la calidad de textura de una superficie a un papel al poner el papel encima de la superficie y sombrear el papel con un lápiz (p. 183).

S

Safety labels/avisos de seguridad Etiquetas en productos de arte que avisan si los productos son seguros para usar o si hay que usarlos con precaución.

Scale/escala Tamaño que se mide según un patrón. La escala puede referirse a una obra de arte entera o a elementos dentro de ella (p. 260).

Scanner/escáner Un aparato que "lee" una imagen impresa y luego la traduce a un idioma que puede usar la computadora para hacer una imagen visual en la pantalla (p. 61).

Score/rayar Hacer pliegues limpios y definidos en un papel usando una herramienta de cortar.

Screen printing/serigrafía Técnica de imprenta en la que un patrón picado y un tamiz se usan como la plancha de grabar. El patrón se pone en un tamiz de tela estirada por un marco y se pasa la tinta por el tamiz donde éste no está cubierto por el patrón (p. 49).

Scroll/rollo de pergamino Un rollo largo de pergamino o de seda (p. 328).

Sculpture/escultura Obra de arte tridimensional creada al tallar, soldar, fundir o modelar madera, piedra, metal o arcilla (p. 50).

Seascape/marina Pintura o dibujo que tiene el mar como tema.

Shade/tono Un valor oscuro de un color hecho al añadirle el negro. El opuesto de una tinta (p. 140).

Shading/sombreado El uso de valores claras y oscuras para representar la profundidad y la textura (p. 44).

Shadows/sombras Áreas sombreadas en un dibujo o en una pintura. Las sombras muestran las superficies de un objeto que reflejan menos luz y se usan para crear la ilusión de formas tridimensionales. El opuesto de los toques de luz.

Shape/forma bidimensional Un área que se define de alguna manera. Mientras las formas tridimensionales tienen profundidad, las bidimensionales solamente tienen altura y anchura. Pueden ser geométricas o de forma libre (p. 98).

Shiny surface/superficie lustrosa Superficie que refleja luz brillante. El vidrio de una ventana tiene una superficie lustrosa. El opuesto de una superficie mate (p. 175).

Sighting/poner mira Técnica de determinar la relación entre proporciones entre una parte de un objeto y otra.

Silhouette/silueta Dibujo del contorno de una forma. Originalmente una silueta fue un retrato de perfil, rellenado con un color sólido.

Simplicity/simplicidad Técnica para crear la unidad al limitar el número de variaciones de un elemento del arte.

Simulated texture/textura simulada Un tipo de textura visual que imita la textura real al usar un diseño bidimensional para crear la ilusión de una superficie tridimensional (p. 173). Una mesa de plástico puede tener un diseño que imita la textura de la madera. El opuesto de la textura inventada.

Sketch/bosquejo Dibujo brusco hecho rápidamente sin mucho detalle, que se puede usar como modelo o referencia para una obra posterior.

Slip/barbotina Mezcla cremosa de arcilla y agua que se usa para pegar piezas de arcilla.

Smooth texture/textura lisa Superficie regular que refleja la luz de manera equitativa. El opuesto de una textura áspera (p. 175).

Soft edge/línea suave En el arte bidimensional, formas con los contornos borrosos e imprecisos. Las formas de línea suave parecen suaves. El opuesto de la línea dura.

Soft sculpture/escultura blanda Escultura hecha con tela y rellena con materia blanda.

Solvent/solvente El líquido que controla lo espeso o lo acuoso que sea la pintura (p. 150).

Space/espacio El elemento del arte que se refiere al vacío o al área entre, alrededor de, encima de y debajo de objetos. Las formas se definen por el espacio alrededor y dentro de ellas (p. 103).

Spectral colors/colores espectrales Rojo, anaranjado, amarillo, verde, azul y violeta (p. 136).

Split complementary colors/colores complementarios divididos Un color y los colores a cada lado de su complemento en el círculo cromático (p. 147). El rojo-anaranjado, el azul y el verde son colores complementarios divididos. Los colores complementarios divididos se pueden usar como una combinación de colores.

Stained glass/vidriera Recortes de vidrio colorido, organizados en un diseño y unidos con varillas de plomo.

Static/inmóvil Inactivo (p. 77). Las líneas verticales y horizontales y las formas horizontales son inmóviles. El opuesto de activo.

Still life/naturaleza muerta Pintura o dibujo de objetos inanimados e inmóviles.

Stippling/sombreado punteado Técnica de sombrear usando puntitos (p. 44).

Stitchery/puntadura Técnica de decorar la tela al coserle fibras.

Stone Age/Edad de la Piedra Período de la historia durante el cual se usaban herramientas de piedra (p. 320).

Storyboards/guión gráfico Una serie de dibujos de vista fija que muestran la marcha de una historia (p. 395).

Stupas/stupas Edificios de culto con cupola y en forma de colmena (p. 326).

Style/estilo Véase *individual style.*

Subject/tema La imagen que los observadores pueden reconocer fácilmente en una obra de arte (p. 18).

Subordinate element/elemento secundario Elemento de una obra de arte que se nota después de notar el elemento dominante (p. 290).

Super-Realism/superrealismo Estilo artístico del siglo XX que representa los objetos de modo preciso y exacto, tal cómo parecen en la realidad (p. 381).

Surrealism/surrealismo Estilo artístico del siglo XX en el que los sueños, la fantasía y el subconsciente servían a los artistas como inspiración (p. 375).

Symbol/símbolo Algo que significa, o representa, otra cosa (p. 16).

Symmetry/simetría Un tipo especial de equilibrio formal en el que las dos mitades de una composición equilibrada son reflejos idénticos (p. 230).

Synthetic/sintético Hecho con procesos químicos en vez de procesos naturales.

Tactile texture/textura táctil Textura que se puede percibir por el tacto. El opuesto de la textura visual (p. 173).

Tapestry/tapiz Tela para colgar en la pared que es tejida, pintada o bordada.

Tempera/pintura al temple Pintura hecha al mezclar pigmentos con yema de huevo (temple de huevo) u otro líquido. En las escuelas se usa la pintura al temple de uso escolar (p. 47).

Texture/textura El elemento del arte que se refiere a cómo se sienten las cosas, o cómo parecen que se sentirían si se tocaron. La textura se percibe con el tacto

y la vista. Los objetos pueden tener texturas ásperas o lisas y superficies mates o lustrosas (p. 171).

Tint/tinta Un valor claro de un color hecho al mezclar el color con blanco. El opuesto de un tono (p. 140).

Tonality/tonalidad Arreglo de colores en una pintura en el que un solo color domina (p. 157).

Totem poles/postes totémicos Postes altos tallados y pintados con una serie de símbolos de animales asociados con cierta familia o con cierto clan (p. 343).

Transparent/transparente Calidad de un material que deja pasar la luz por si. El opuesto de opaco.

Trompe l'oiel/trampantojo En frances quiere decir "decepcionar el ojo". Estilo de pintura en el que los pintores tratan de dar al observador la ilusión de ver un objeto tridimensional, para que el observador se pregunte si está viendo una imagen o algo real.

Unity/unidad La calidad de integridad que se logra con el uso eficaz de los elementos y los principios del arte (p. 296). La unidad se crea con la simplicidad, la repetición y la proximidad.

Unusual/insólito Técnica de crear un punto focal al usar lo inesperado (p. 295).

Value/valor El elemento del arte que describe la oscuridad o la claridad de un objeto (p. 75). El valor depende de cuánta luz refleja una superficie. El valor es también una de tres propiedades del color.

Vanishing point/punto de fuga Punto en el horizonte donde parecen juntarse las líneas paralelas que se retiran (p. 115).

Variety/variedad Principio del arte que se preocupa por la diferencia y el contraste (p. 288).

Vault/bóveda Tejado, techo o cubierta en forma de arco hecho con ladrillo, piedra o concreto (p. 55).

Vehicle/vehículo Líquido, como el agua o el óleo, con que se mezclan los pigmentos para hacer pintura o tinte.

Vertical lines/líneas verticales Líneas rectas que corren de arriba para abajo, y de abajo para arriba (p. 72). Las líneas verticales forman ángulos rectos con el borde inferior de un papel o lienzo y con el horizonte, y son paralelas a los bordes laterales de un papel o lienzo.

Viewing frame/marco de observación Una hoja de papel con un área recortada del medio. Al sostener el marco con el brazo extendido y ver un objeto por éste, el artista puede fijarse en el área del objeto que quiere dibujar o pintar.

Visual arts/artes visuales Las artes que producen objetos bellos de ver.

Visual movement/movimiento visual El principio del arte usado para crear la impresión y la sensación de la acción y para guiar los ojos del observador por la obra de arte (p. 211).

Visual rhythm/ritmo visual Ritmo que percibes con los ojos en vez de con los oídos (p. 200).

Visual texture/textura visual Ilusión de una superficie tridimensional basada en la memoria de cómo sienten las cosas. Hay dos tipos de textura visual: la inventada y la simulada (p. 173). El opuesto de la textura táctil.

Visual weight/peso visual La atracción que tienen los elementos en una obra de arte para los ojos del observador. El peso visual es afectado por el tamaño, el contorno, la intensidad de colores, lo cálido y lo frío que son los colores, los contrastes de valor, la textura y la posición (p. 228).

Warm colors/colores cálidos Rojo, anaranjado y amarillo (p. 148). Los colores cálidos sugieren el calor y parecen acercarse al observador. Se puede usar los colores cálidos como una combinación de colores. El opuesto de los colores fríos.

Warp/urdimbre En la tejeduría, hilos de largo sujetados en el telar y cruzados por los hilos de trama.

Watercolor paint/pintura acuarela Pigmentos transparentes mezclados con agua (p. 47).

Weaving/tejeduría El hacer tela al entrelazar dos juegos de hilos paralelos, sujetados a ángulos rectos uno del otro en un telar (p. 52).

Weft/trama En la tejeduría, hilos de cruce que se pasan por encima y por debajo de los hilos de urdimbre.

Woodblock printing/grabado en madera El hacer estampas al tallar imágenes en bloques de madera (p. 330).

Yarn/hilo Fibras hiladas en hebras para la tejeduría, el labor de punto o el bordado.

Ziggurats/zigurats Montañas escalonadas hechas de tierra cubierta con ladrillos (p. 322).

Zigzag lines/líneas en zigzag Líneas formadas por cambios de dirección cortos y fuertes (p. 73). Las líneas en zigzag son una combinación de líneas diagonales. Se pueden cambiar de dirección repentinamente.

INDEX

A

Abbott, Berenice, *The Night View,* 202
Aboriginal bark painting, 152
Abrasha, *Hanukkah Menorah,* 71–72
Abstract Expressionism, 168, 378
Acrylic paint, 47
Action painting, 13–14
Active shapes and forms, 120
Activities
  active and static shapes, 120–121
  aesthetic theories, 33
  alternating pattern, 208
  alternating rhythm, 208
  analyzing ancient art, 325
  analyzing lines in artworks, 73
  animation critique, 396
  architecture, 54, 353
  art history, 353, 355, 365, 373, 381
  balance, 231, 233, 238, 241
  calligraphic lines, 83
  careers in art, 396, 400
  color, 142, 143, 149, 152, 157
  color schemes, 149
  contour lines, 81
  contrast, 175, 289
  credit line, 19
  depth, creating, 115
  display design, 400
  emphasis, 295
  expressive lines, 78
  forms, 102, 112
  geometric and free-form shapes, 100
  gesture drawing, 82
  gothic style, 355
  human proportions, 264, 266
  impressionism, 373
  informal balance, 238
  intensity, 143
  lines, 76, 78, 81–83
  logo design, 392
  masks, 338
  mixing colors, 152
  motifs, 204
  patterns, 204
  perceiving, 7
  point of view, 108
  printing plate, 49
  progressive rhythm, 210
  proportion, 261, 264, 266, 273
  radial balance, 233
  random rhythm, 206
  rhythm, 204, 206, 208, 210
  scale, 261, 264, 266
  shading, 112
  shapes, 100, 108, 120–121
  sketchbook, 15
  sketching events, 345
  space, 104, 107, 115
  symbols, 16
  symmetry, 231
  texture, 174, 175, 183
  traditional and digital media, 60
  unity, 302
  values, 76, 142
  variety and contrast, 290
  watercolor, 47
Adla, Ashevak, *Walking Bear,* 102
Advertising designers, 390, 393
Aesthetic experience, 27
Aestheticians, 31
Aesthetics, 31–33
  activity, 33
  defined, 26
  judging ceremonial objects, 33, 37

judging functional objects, 33
judging installation art, 63
judging your own artwork, 33
qualities of art, 31
theories, 31–32
See also Art criticism; Art Criticism in Action
African American Dance Ensemble, 225, 420
African art, 332–338
  ancient Ife, 332–333
  Asante kingdom, 335–337
  Benin kingdom, 334–335
  Bwa people, 337–338
  Mali empire, 333–334
  role of, 332
  saving, 348
Afterimages, 137–138
Agbatana III **(Stella),** 380
Age of Faith, 354
Age of Forests **(Ernst),** 183
Akan people, 335–336
Albizu, Olga, *Growth,* 148, 149, 169
Albright, Ivan, 177
  The Picture of Dorian Gray, 177
Aleut sculpture, 180
Alternating patterns, 208, 217
Alternating rhythm, 208
American Gothic **(Wood),** 12, 23
American Windows, The **(Chagall),** 41, 136
Analogous colors, 145, 165
Analysis step
  of art criticism, 27–30
  of art history, 34, 35
Ancient Chinese art, 324–325
Ancient Egyptian civilization, 323
Ancient Greece, 352–353
Ancient Ife, 332–333
Ancient Indian civilization, 323–324
Ancient Rome, 353
Anderson, N., *Blue Dome-House Blessing,* 227, 232
Andrews, Benny
  Mom and Us, 81, 82, 95, 315
  Thelonious at the Five Spot, 82, 95
Angkor Wat temple, 327
Anguissola, Sofonisba, 358
  A Game of Chess, Involving the Painter's Three Sisters and a Servant, 358
  Portrait of the Infanta Isabella Clara Eugenia, 292
Animation, 308–309, 451, 452
Animators, 308–309, 395–396
Ankhesenamun, Queen, 107
Anne of Cleves **(Holbein),** 9
Apollo, 276
Applied art
  crafts, 52–53, 182–183
  defined, 52
  fine art vs., 52
  texture in, 182–183
Approximate symmetry, 231, 240
Apron, beaded **(Venezuela),** 208, 210
Arabs Skirmishing in the Mountains **(Delacroix),** 367
Arbitrary color, 154
Architects, 132, 386, 398, 399
  landscape architects, 400
Architecture, 54–56, 132
  activities, 54, 353, 355
  ancient Greek, 352, 353
  ancient Indian, 323–324
  ancient Roman, 353
  formal balance in, 240
  Gothic, 355
  Indian, 326, 327
  informal balance in, 241

International Style, 381–382
Islamic, 331
Japanese, 328–329
media, 57–61
Mesopotamian, 322
Post-Modern, 382–383
pre-Columbian, 340, 341
prehistoric, 321
Romanesque, 354–355
texture in, 182
twentieth century, 376–377, 381–383
Arctic Region Art, 342
Aristotle with a Bust of Homer **(Rembrandt),** 124, 178, 362
Armchair **(Wright),** 118–119
Armory Show of 1913, 376
Arnolfi Wedding, The **(van Eyck),** 168, 231, 359
Arreguin, Alfredo, 223
  Nuestra Señora de la Selva, 222, 223
Art
  as communication, 6–7
  moving, 224
  purposes of, 7–9
Art criticism, 26–30
  aesthetics, 31–33
  criteria, 26
  defined, 25, 26
  judging ceremonial objects, 33, 37
  judging functional objects, 33
  judging installation art, 63
  judging your own artwork, 33
  reasons for studying, 26–27
  steps of, 27–30
  See also Aesthetics; Art Criticism in Action
Art Criticism in Action, *see* table of contents, xv
Art directors, 402–403
Art education careers, 404–405
Art history
  Abstract Expressionism, 378
  activities, 353, 355, 365, 373, 381
  African art, 332–338
  after 1945, 378–383
  ancient Chinese art, 324–325
  ancient Egyptian art, 323
  ancient Greece and Rome, 352–353
  ancient Indian art, 323–324
  Baroque art, 361–362
  Byzantine art, 354
  Chinese art, 327–328
  Color-Field painting, 380
  Cubism, 374–375
  early twentieth century art, 374–377
  eighteenth century art, 363–365
  Expressionism, 374
  Futurists, 212
  Gothic art, 355
  Impressionism, 153, 181, 370, 373
  Indian art, 326–327
  International Style architecture, 381–382
  Islamic art, 331
  Japanese art, 328–330
  Mannerism, 360
  Mesopotamian art, 321–322
  Middle Ages art, 354–355
  Minimalism, 380
  Native American art, 341–345
  Neoclassicism, 366–367
  nineteenth century art, 366–373
  Op art, 379
  Pop art, 378–379
  Post-Impressionism, 371–373
  Post-Modernism, 382–383
  pre-Columbian art, 339–341
  prehistoric art, 320

Realism, 368–370
Regionalism, 376–377
Renaissance art, 356–360
Rococo art, 363–365
Romanesque art, 354–355
Romanticism, 367–368
seventeenth century art, 360–362
Super-Realism, 381
Surrealism, 375
Art history operations, 34–35
Artistic decisions
evaluating in personal artworks, 85, 87, 89, 91, 123, 125, 127, 159, 161, 163, 165, 185, 187, 189, 191, 215, 217–219, 221, 243, 245, 247, 275, 277, 279, 281, 305, 307, 309, 311
interpreting in personal artworks, 85, 87, 89, 97, 123, 125, 127, 159, 161, 163, 185, 187, 189, 215, 217–219, 243, 245, 247, 275, 277, 279, 305, 307, 309
justifying in personal artworks, 85, 87, 123, 127, 187, 189, 218–219, 247, 277, 305
Artists
defined, 11
reasons for creating, 10
sources of ideas, 11–15
as sources of ideas, 14–15
Art Nouveau, 287
Art reviews. *See* Aesthetics; Art criticism; Art Criticism in Action
Artsource® Performing Arts Handbook
African American Dance Ensemble, 225, 420
Ballet Folklorico de Mexico, 95, 416
Cello Man, 285, 422
Cunningham, Merce, 65, 415
"Danza de la Reata," 95, 416
Davis, Chuck, 225, 420
Eth-Noh-Tec, 253, 421
Faustwork Mask Theater, 23, 413
Featherstone, Joanna, 169, 418
Friesen, Eugene, 285, 422
Graham, Martha, 39, 414
Green Table, The, 387, 425
Jooss, Kurt, 387, 425
Korean Classical Music and Dance Company, 349, 424
Lewitzky Dance Company, 133, 417
Ramirez, John, 409, 426
Vocalworks, 315, 423
Winter, Paul, 195, 419
Art teachers, 404
Art therapists, 404
Art trade, illegal, 348
Artworks
basic properties of, 18–19
definition of, 6
Ascension Day Festival at Venice **(Canaletto),** 43
Ashcan School, 376
Asian art
ancient Chinese, 324–325
ancient Indian, 323–324
Chinese, 327–328
folk traditions of music and dance, 349, 424
Indian, 326–327
Japanese, 328–330
Assemblages, 186
Assembling technique, 51
Assistive technology, 391
Assyrian civilization, 322
Asymmetry (informal balance), 234–238, 246–247
Atmospheric perspective, 114
AVI sound files, 452

Avocational opportunities in art, comparing/contrasting, 23, 389, 405
Aztec culture, 119, 340–341
Aztec people, *Sculpture in the form of the deity Quetzalcoatl,* 119

B

Baby (Cradle) **(Klimt),** 286, 287
Babylonian civilization, 322
Background, 113
Back of Marie's No. 4 **(O'Keeffe),** 39, 316–317
Balance, 226–253
activities, 231, 233, 238, 241
asymmetrical, 246–247
central axis, 228–229
comparing/contrasting in artworks of others, 169, 227, 233, 239–241, 248–249, 251, 385
comparing/contrasting in personal artworks, 159, 243
defined, 228
expressive qualities of, 239–241
formal, 248
formal balance, 229, 239–241
informal, 248, 249
informal balance, 234–238, 241
radial balance, 231–233, 240–241
selecting/analyzing exhibitions by peers for, 248–249
selecting/analyzing the use of in personal artworks, 245, 247
student art portfolio, 248–249
symmetry, 230–231, 240
tipping the, 252
visual balance, 228–233
Ball, Philip, 168
Ballet Folklorico de Mexico, 95, 416
Bamana peoples, 334
Bandolier bag **(Ojibwe people),** 208, 210
Bark painting, Aboriginal, 152
Baroque art, 361–362
activity, 365
defined, 361
in Holland, 361–362
in Italy, 361
Barricade **(Orozco),** 28
Bashkirtseff, Marie, *A Meeting,* 301
Basket of Apples, The **(Cézanne),** 155
Bas relief, 106, 107. *See also* Relief sculpture
Battle of Lights, Coney Island Mardi Gras **(Stella),** 212, 213
Bay, The **(Frankenthaler),** 111
Bayou Teche **(Straus),** 6
Bearden, Romare, 184
In the Garden, 184
Return of Ulysses, 12, 13, 133
Beats, 205, 206, 208, 209
Beaux, Cecilia, *Ethel Page (Mrs. James Large),* 290
Before the Ballet **(Degas),** 238
Beliefs as sources of ideas, 12–13
Bellows, George, *Both Members of This Club,* 258, 274
Bell Tower of the Cathedral at Pisa, 228
Bench, ceramic, in Barcelona park **(Guadi),** 194
Benin people, 262, 335
Benton, Thomas Hart, 13
Country Dance, 78, 79, 90
Cradling Wheat, 376, 377
Berman, Eugene, *Vendeur de Chapeaux,* 43
Bicycle Race, The **(Ruiz),** 126
Biggers, John, *Starry Crown,* 99
Binders of paints, 45, 150

Bird in Space **(Brancusi),** 118, 133
Bird Mask **(Yup'ik people),** 13
Bishop, Isabel, *Head #5,* 44, 45
Bitmap, file formats, 449
Black as neutral color, 139
Blackfeet people, 344
Black Hawk, Chief, *Crow Men in Ceremonial Dress,* 200
Blam **(Lichtenstein),** 379, 383
Blanketed Figure Vase **(Qoyawayma),** 50, 51
Blending technique, 44
Blessing Rain Chant **(Naminbha),** 75, 77, 95
Blue Boy, The **(Gainsborough),** 193, 364
Blue Dome-House Blessing **(Anderson),** 227, 232
Blue Rider movement, The, 135
Bondie, Edith, *Porkypine Basket,* 52, 65
Bonheur, Rosa, 201, 225, 369
The Horse Fair, 201, 225, 369
Bonnard, Pierre, *Family Scene,* 266
Book illustrations
for *Duke Ellington: The Piano Prince and His Orchestra* (Pinkney), 406–407
Islamic, 331
for *Journeys with Elijah* (Pinkney), 237
Bookmaking, 64, 158–159
Borsky, David
Wall from the sunken courtyard of Tiwauaku, 55
Waterfall, 209
Both Members of This Club **(Bellows),** 258
Brady, Mathew, 369
Civil War, 369
Brahma, 327
Brancusi, Constantin, 104, 118
Bird in Space, 118, 133
The Kiss, 104, 133, 195
Braque, Georges, 375
Breakfast of the Birds **(Münter),** 18
Brice, Jeff, *Untitled,* 59
Bright Earth **(Ball),** 168
Brown, Roger, *Hurricane Hugo,* 10–11
Buddhism, 227, 297, 318, 319, 326, 327
Buildings, 194
Burkina Faso, 337
Business and industry careers, 390–403. *See also* Careers in art
Bust of Queen Idia **(Africa),** 348
Butterfield, Deborah, 131
Woodrow, 130–131
Bwa people, 337–338
Byzantine art, 319, 354

C

Cabin in the Cotton **(Pippin),** 234
Café Terrace at Night **(van Gogh),** 293
Calder, Alexander, 213, 376
Lobster Trap and Fish Tail, 213
Untitled, 213
Calligraphic drawing, 83
Calligraphy, 83
Cameras, digital, 60
Canaletto, *Ascension Day Festival at Venice,* 43
Caravaggio, Michelangelo Merisi da, 361
The Conversion of St. Paul, 361
Careers in art, 388–409
activities, 396, 400
advertising designer, 393
animator, 395–396
architect, 398, 399
art director, 402–403
art education careers, 404–405
art teacher, 404
art therapist, 404

cartoonist, 394
commercial illustrator, 393
comparing/contrasting, 39, 95, 169, 225, 285, 349, 389, 397, 405, 408, 409
costume designer, 403
environmental planning and development, 398–400
exhibit and display designers, 400
fashion designer, 402
film and video, 395–397
fine artists, 405
game designers, 397
graphic design, 391–393
graphic designer, 392
illustration, 393–394
industrial design, 401–402
interior designer, 400
landscape architect, 400
multimedia designer, 396
museum curator, 39
museum curator and designer, 404
package designer, 402
photographer, 394
photojournalist, 395
product designer, 401–402
special effects designer, 396
technology and, 390–391
thinking about, 405
in three-dimensional art, 398–405
in two-dimensional art, 390–397
urban planner, 399
web designers, 397
Caricatures, 94, 284
Carr, Emily
Cumshewa, 241
A Rushing Sea of Undergrowth, 236
Cartoonists, 272, 284, 394
Carving technique, 51
Cassatt, Mary, *Margot in Blue,* 140, 143
Casting technique, 51, 193
Cathedral **(Pollock),** 13–14, 42
Cathedrals
Chartres, 355
Gothic, 355
at Pisa, Bell Tower, 228
Reims, 106, 194
Catlett, Elizabeth
Sharecropper, 48, 191
Singing Their Songs, 312–313
Cave painting, 320
Cel (animation), 308
Cello Man **(Friesen),** 285, 422
Central axis, 228–229
Ceramics
Chinese, 328
studio projects, 242–243
texture in, 182
See also Clay
Ceremonial Robe, 298
Cézanne, Paul, 162, 255, 371
The Basket of Apples, 155
The Gulf of Marseilles Seen from L'Estaque, 371
Chagall, Marc
The American Windows, 41, 136
The Green Violinist, 282–283
Homage to Gogol, 271
Chair **(Rashid),** 408
Chairs, 304, 408
Chamba Rumal **(Himachai Pradesh, India),** 244
Chamberlain, Wilt, 262
Chartres Cathedrals, 355
Chess set **(Rashid),** 408
Cheyenne people, 344
Chiaroscuro, 112, 124, 125

Chihuly, Dale, 41
Malina Window, 40, 41
Children, proportions of, 263
Children at Play **(Lawrence),** 78, 80, 95, 377
Children Dancing **(Gwathmey),** 297, 303
Chinese art, 327–328
ancient, 324–325
Chinese pair of vases **(Ming Dynasty),** 99
Chrysler Building **(van Alen),** 206
Chryssa, 303
The Gates to Times Square, 303
Church, Frederic Edwin, *The Icebergs,* 2–3
Church Quinua **(Peru),** 107
Cinematographers, 58, 395
Circular forms, 280
Civil Rights Memorial, The **(Lin),** 386
Civil War **(Brady),** 369
Clay
crafts processes, 53
free-form sculpture project, 122–123
texture using, 182
wedged, 123
See also Ceramics
Close, Chuck, 385
Paul, 384–385
Self-Portrait, 385
Closed form, 107
Clothespin **(Oldenburg),** 261
CMYK (Cyan, magenta, yellow and black), 139, 450
Collage, 167, 179–180, 274–275
activity, 261
defined, 179
digital color studio project, 162–163
studio projects, 306–307
tissue paper, 440
Collagraphs, 184–185
Color, 134–169
activities, 142, 143, 149, 152, 157
afterimages, 137–138
analogous colors, 145
arbitrary color, 154
color schemes, 144–149
color spectrum, 136–138
color triads, 146–147
color wheel, 138
comparing/contrasting in artworks of others, 23, 135, 149, 164–165, 167, 169, 283, 310–311, 351
comparing/contrasting in personal artworks, 87, 159, 163, 215, 217, 243, 275, 305, 307
complementary colors, 142–143, 146, 150
defined, 136
expressive qualities, 135, 136, 144–148, 152–157
hue, 138–139
informal balance using, 235–236
intensity, 142–143, 164
mixing colors, 140, 143, 152–154
monochromatic colors, 145
movement and, 155–156
nature and uses of, 150–157
optical color, 152–154
paint, 150–152
perception of, 136–138, 144
perspective technique, 114, 116
pigments, 44–45, 150–152
properties of, 136–143
scheme, 164, 165
seeing, in art, 168
selecting/analyzing the use of in personal artworks, 279
shades, 140–141
simultaneous contrast, 144
space and, 155

split complements, 147
student art portfolio, 164–165
texture and, 178–179
tints, 140
tonality, 157
value, 139–142, 155–156
warm and cool colors, 148–149, 155
Color-Field painting, 380
Color models, 450
Color schemes, 144–149
activity, 149
analogous colors, 145
color triads, 146–147
complementary colors, 146, 150
defined, 144
monochromatic colors, 145
split complements, 147
warm and cool colors, 148–149, 155
Color spectrum, 136–137
color wheel and, 138
star book studio project, 158–159
Color systems, 139, 450
Color triads, 146–147, 165
Color wheel, 138. See also Color schemes
Colossal Head **(Olmec sculpture),** 171, 339
Columbus, Christopher, 341
Coming of Age **(Houser),** 209
Commercial illustrators, 393
Commissions as sources of ideas, 15
Communication, art as, 6–7
Complementary colors, 142–143, 165
in color schemes, 146
defined, 142
intensity and, 143, 150
split complements, 147
Composition of artworks, 18
Computers, 59–61
activity, 60
animators, 396
art tools, 60–61
careers in art and, 390–391
creating art with, 59–60
game designers, 397
monitors, 446
simulators, 397
Concert, The **(Leyster),** 178, 256, 257
Concert, The **(Vermeer),** 350, 351
Constantinople, 354
Constructing technique, 51
Constructive Universalism, 88
Content of artworks, 19
Context clues, 3
Contour, informal balance using, 234–235
Contour drawing, 81
Contour lines, 81
Contrast
activities, 175, 289
for focal point, 291
simultaneous contrast, 144
studio project, 124–125
Convergence for focal point, 293
Converging lines (perspective technique), 113, 115, 116
Conversation in Autumn **(Yen),** 328, 331
Conversion of St. Paul, The **(Caravaggio),** 361
Cool colors, 148–149, 155
Costumes, 224, 403
Country Dance **(Benton),** 78, 79, 90
Court Drummers of the Timi of Ede **(Yoruba people),** 37
Cow's Skull: Red, White, and Blue **(O'Keeffe),** 30
Cracker Jack Choo Choo **(Solberg),** 214
Cradling Wheat **(Benton),** 376, 377
Crafts, 52–53, 182–183

Creating
  reasons for, 10
  sources of ideas, 11–15
Creative techniques as sources of ideas, 13–14
Credit line, 19
Criteria, 26
Critiquing artworks. *See* Aesthetics; Art criticism; Art Criticism in Action
Cromartie, James H., *View of the White House, South Portico,* 230
Crosshatching, 44, 76
Crow Men in Ceremonial Dress **(Chief Black Hawk),** 200
Crowned Buddha Shakyamuni **(Kashmir),** 318, 319
Crow people, 344
Cubism, 86, 374–375
Cumshewa, **(Carr),** 241
Cuneiform writing, 321
Cunningham, Merce, 65, 415
Cups 4 Picasso **(Johns),** 103–104
Curved lines, 73, 77–78. See also Line(s)
Cyan, magenta, yellow and black (CMYK), 139, 450

D

Daguerre, L. J. M., 58
Daguerreotype, 58
Dali, Salvador, 278
  The Elephants, 278
Dallas Piece **(Moore),** 122
Daniel in the Lions' Den **(Rubens),** 291, 295
"Danza de la Reata," 95, 416
David, Jacques-Louis, *The Death of Socrates,* 366
David **(Michelangelo),** 267, 273
da Vinci, Leonardo. *See* Leonardo da Vinci
Davis, Chuck, 225, 420
Davis, Stuart, *Hot Still Scape for Six Colors- 7th Avenue Style, 1940,* 154–156
Dawn **(Nevelson),** 300, 303
Day and Night **(Escher),** 218
Death of Socrates, The **(David),** 366
Decalcomania, 183
Decorated found objects, 304–305
Decorative patterns, 204
Degas, Edgar, 181
  Before the Ballet, 238
  The Little Fourteen-Year-Old Dancer, 180, 181, 195
  Self-Portrait, 181
Delacroix, Eugéne, 367
  Arabs Skirmishing in the Mountains, 367
Density, 118
Depth, illusion of, 113–116
Depth perception, 108
Der Blaue Reiter, 18, 135
Description step
  of art criticism, 27–30
  of art history, 34–35
Detail, illusion of depth and, 114
Diagonal lines, 72, 78. See also Line(s)
Digital cameras, 60, 447
Digital effects, 396
Digital fantasy creature, 278–279
Digital image using line, 88
Digital Media Handbook, 445–454
  digital cameras, 447
  draw software, 450
  frame animation software, 452
  graphics tablets, 448
  multimedia presentation software, 453
  page layout software, 454
  paint software, 449

  scanners, 446
  3-D Graphics software, 451
Digital printmaking, 246–247
Digital studio projects
  animation movie poster, 308–309
  asymmetrical balance painting, 246–247
  digital color collage, 162–163
  digital fantasy creature, 278–279
  digital genre scene, 126–127
  digital image using line, 88
  digital rendering of reflections, 218–219
  layered self-portrait, 188–189
Digital systems, 59
Dimension, 70
Diner With Red Door **(Goings),** 112, 113
Direction of lines, 73
Direct observation
  creating visual solutions by elaborating on, 5, 15, 81, 82, 97, 104, 108, 124, 125, 184–185, 199, 204, 227, 231, 247, 255, 266
  illustrating ideas for artworks from, 7, 82, 87, 124, 125, 129, 158, 231, 247, 277, 353
Directors (theater and film), 224
Dirty Snow **(Mitchell),** 179
Discobolus (Discus Thrower) **(Myron),** 352, 353
Dish **(Valencia, Spain),** 232, 233
Display and exhibit designers, 400
Display techniques, 441–442
Dissolves, 453
Distortion and exaggeration, 268–273
Divine Proportion, 257
Dla'ehl Interior House Post: Grizzly Bear Beneath Kolus **(Shaughnessy),** 250–251
Dogon people, 334
Dominant element, 290
Doors, painted, 306
Drawing
  activities, 15, 104, 112, 115, 231, 241, 264, 266, 345
  calligraphic drawing, 83
  contour drawing, 81
  contrast, 124–125
  gesture drawing, 82
  heads and faces, 264–266
  human figures, 262–264
  media, 43–44
  overview, 42–43
  shading techniques, 44
  sketchbook, 15
  studio projects, 276–277
  techniques, 428–431
Draw programs, 60
Dream Series **(Hines),** 57, 58
Duchamp, Marcel, 213
Dunnigan, John, *Slipper Chair,* 33
Dürer, Albrecht, *An Oriental Ruler Seated on His Throne,* 76
Dutch Baroque art, 361–362
Dutch painters, 350, 351
Dyes, 151–152
Dynamism, 212
Dynasties, 324–325
Dzawada'enuxw people, 250–251

E

East Wind Suite: Door **(Twiggs),** 10, 42
Echoes of Harlem **(quilt),** 199
Echo of a Scream **(Siqueiros),** 235, 253
Editions, 48
Edo people, 335
Educational functions of art, 8–9
Education careers, 404–405

Egyptian art, ancient, 323
Eight, The, 376
Eighteenth century art, 362–365
Ejiri in Suruga Province **(Hokusai),** 330, 335, 349
El Coronelazo (Self-Portrait) **(Siqueiros),** 264
Elements of art
  color, 134–169
  comparing/contrasting in artworks of others, 19
  composition and, 18–19
  defined, 16
  form, 100, 101–102, 111–121
  line, 68–95
  in nonobjective art, 18
  overview, 16–17
  shape, 98–100, 101, 108–121
  space, 103–107, 111–121
  texture, 170–195
  value, 139–142
  See also Symbols; specific elements
Elephants, The (Design for the Opera La Dama Spagnola e il Cavaliere Romano) **(Dali),** 278
Elevator Grille **(Sullivan),** 204
El Greco, 360
  Saint Martin and the Beggar, 360, 365
Elvis Presley, "Blue Suede Shoes" **(Hirschfeld),** 94
Embarkment for Cythera **(Watteau),** 363
Emotionalism, 32
Emphasis, 287, 289–295, 306–307
  activity, 295
  of areas, 290–295
  comparing/contrasting in artworks of others, 287, 295, 351
  comparing/contrasting in personal artworks, 88, 89, 123, 307
  defined, 290
  of elements, 290
  focal point, 290–295
  selecting/analyzing original artworks by peers for, 310–311
  student art portfolio, 310–311
  unity enhanced by, 302–303
England, Rococo style in, 363–364
Environmental planning and development careers, 398–400. *See also* Careers in art
Equestrian figure **(Mali),** 333
Ergonomics, 448
Ernst, Max, 183
  Age of Forests, 183
Escher, M. C., 105, 218
  Day and Night, 218
  Portrait of M. C. Escher, 105
  Reptiles, 210
  Waterfall, 105, 133
Estes, Richard, *Paris Street Scene,* 381, 383
Etchings, 158, 159
Ethel Page (Mrs. James Large) **(Beaux),** 290
Ethnography **(Siqueiros),** 294
Eth-Noh-Tec, 253, 421
Events as sources of ideas, 12
Exaggeration and distortion, 268–273, 278–279, 281, 284
Executable files, 453
Exhibit and display designers, 400
Experience Music Project, The **(Gehry),** 132
Experiences
  creating visual solutions by elaborating on, 16, 127, 160–161
  illustrating ideas for artworks from, 127, 160–161, 244–245
Expressionism, 135, 374

Expressive qualities
  activity, 157
  of balance, 239–241
  of color, 136, 152–157
  of color schemes, 144–149
  defined, 31
  emotionalism and, 32
  exaggeration and distortion, 268–273
  of line, 77–83
  lines, 88, 89
  of shapes and forms, 117–121
  of value, 140–141, 155–156
Extrude command, 450

F

Faaturuma (Melancholic) **(Gauguin),** 372
Faces, 264–266, 272
Fallingwater House **(Wright),** 300–301, 377
False Faces, 345
False Mirror, The **(Magritte),** 375, 377
Family, The **(Marisol),** 268
Family Scene **(Bonnard),** 266
Fashion designers, 402
Father and Daughter **(Schapiro),** 166–167
Faustwork Mask Theater, 23, 413
Fauves ("Wild Beasts"), 69
Feather Bonnet **(Northwestern Plains people),** 345
Featherstone, Joanna, 169, 418
Feiss, David, *Thrown for a Curve,* 308
Femmage, 167
Fiber processes, 53. See also Weavings
Fiesta Jarabel **(Jimenez),** 314
Figure, 103. *See also* Positive space
Figure Triste **(Picabia),** 148, 169
Film, 58, 395–397
Fine art, 52, 278
Fine artists, 15, 405
Fish, Janet
  Oranges, 175, 176
  Raspberries and Goldfish, 16–17
Flack, Audrey, *Self-Portrait: The Memory,* 82
Flash memory, 447
Flower Day **(Rivera),** 229, 253
Flowering Swamp **(Hofmann),** 378
Flowing rhythm, 208–209, 220
Focal point, 290–295
Folk artists, 10
Fonts, 392, 454
Football Player **(Hanson),** 192–193
Foreground, 113
Formal balance, 229, 239–241, 248
Formalism, 31
Formal qualities, 18, 31, 374
  selecting/analyzing exhibitions by others for, 325, 349, 373
  selecting/analyzing exhibitions by peers for, 91, 128, 129, 221, 248–249
  selecting/analyzing original artworks by others for, 21, 37, 63, 93, 313, 347, 407
  selecting/analyzing original artworks by peers for, 128–129
  selecting/analyzing portfolios by peers for, 90–91, 128–129, 164–165, 190–191, 220–221, 248–249, 280–281, 310–311
  See also specific elements, e.g., Color, Line; specific principles, e.g., Rhythm, Movement
Form(s)
  active vs. static, 120–121
  activities, 102, 112
  architectural, 132
  circular, 280
  closed, 107

comparing/contrasting in artworks of others, 65, 97, 102, 128–129, 131, 280, 283, 310–311
comparing/contrasting in personal artworks, 129, 215, 219, 305
creation in space, 111–116
defined, 101
density, 118
depth perception, 108
expression with, 117–121
geometric, 128
illusion of form, 111–112
natural vs. manufactured, 111
openness, 118–119
overview, 101–102
point of view and, 108–110
and proportion, 280
relationship to shapes, 100, 101
relationship to space, 103
student art portfolio, 128–129
surfaces, 117–118
Found objects
  collage, 306–307
  decorated, studio project, 304–305
  jewelry, studio project, 214–215
Four in Block Work Quilt **(Peachey),** 202
Four Mandalas of the Vajravali Series **(Tibet; Tsang, Ngor Monastery),** 226
Frame animation software, 452
Frames, 454
Frankenthaler, Helen, 111
  The Bay, 111
Free-form clay sculpture, 122–123
Free-form forms, 102
Free-form shapes, 99–100
Freestanding works, 50, 106, 107
French Revolution, 366
Friesen, Eugene, 285, 422
  Cello Man, 285, 422
Front cover of The Gospels **(Armenian),** 158
Frottage, 183
Fruit Vendors **(Tamayo),** 196–197
Functional patterns, 204
Futurists, 212

G

Gainsborough, Thomas, 363–364
  The Blue Boy, 193, 364
Game designers, 397
Game of Chess, A, Involving the Painter's Three Sisters and a Servant **(Anguissola),** 358
Gates to Times Square, The **(Chryssa),** 303
Gauguin, Paul, 371, 372
  Faaturuma (Melancholic), 372
  Tahitians, 265–266
Gehry, Frank, 132, 389
  The Experience Music Project, 132
  The Guggenheim Museum, 56, 132, 388, 389, 409
Genre scene, 126–127
Gentileschi, Artemisia, *Judith and Maidservant with the Head of Holofernes,* 111
Geometric form, 128
Geometric shapes
  activity, 100
  defined, 98
  expressiveness, 117–118
  overview, 98–99, 100
German Abstract Expressionism, 18
Gesture drawing, 82
Gestures, 82
GIF file formats, 449
Giotto, *Madonna and Child,* 263

Girl Attacked by a Strange Bird **(Tamayo),** 141, 143, 169
Girl with the Red Hat **(Vermeer),** 362
Gladioli **(Monet),** 370
Glarner, Fritz, *Relational Painting, Tondo #40,* 147
Glassblowing, 40, 41
Glass processes, 53
Goddess Hathor Places the Magic Collar on Sethos I, The **(Egyptian),** 323
Gogol, Nikolay Vasilyevich, 271
Goings, Ralph, *Diner With Red Door,* 112
Golden Mean, 256–259, 274, 275, 280, 281
Golden Rectangle, 256
Gothic art, 355
Gothic ornament, 194
Goya, Francisco, 364
  The Third of May, 364–365
Gracehopper **(Smith),** 101, 102, 104
Graham, Martha, 39, 414
Grandma Moses, *Sugaring Off,* 110
Granite Weaving Playscape **(Moroles),** 170, 171
Graphic design, 391–393
Graphic designers, 15, 392
Graphics tablets, 61, 448
Grattage, 183
Graves, Nancy, *Zaga,* 51, 65
Gray as neutral color, 139–140
Great Buddha at Kamakura **(Japan),** 171, 329
Great Plains Region art, 344
Great Plaza of Tikal, 171, 340
Great Stupa **(Sanchi, India),** 326
Greece, ancient, 352–353
Green Table, The, 387, 425
Green Violinist, The **(Chagall),** 282–283
Griots, 334
Grooms, Red, *Ruckus Rodeo,* 24, 25
Ground, 103. See also Negative space
Growth **(Albizu),** 148, 149, 169
Guadi, Antonio, 194
  ceramic bench in Barcelona park, 194
  Segrada Familia, 194
Guggenheim Museum in Bilbao, Spain, **(Gehry),** 56, 132, 388, 389, 409
Gulf of Marseilles Seen from L'Estaque, The **(Cézanne),** 371
Gwathmey, Robert, *Children Dancing,* 297, 303

H

Habitat **(Safdie),** 382
Haida people, 342–343
Haida totem pole, 249, 343
Hall of the Bulls, The **(cave painting),** 320
Handblown glass, 40, 41
Haniwa Horse, 117
Hanson, Duane, 381
  Football Player, 192–193
  Old Couple on a Bench, 381
Hanukkah Menorah **(Abrasha),** 71–72
Harbor Under the Midnight Sun **(Johnson),** 162, 169
Harmony, 287, 295, 306–309
  comparing/contrasting in artworks of others, 385
  comparing/contrasting in personal artworks, 305, 307, 309
  defined, 295
  and unity, 310
  unity enhanced by, 302–303
  and variety, 311
Harriet Tubman Series Number 4 **(Lawrence),** 216

Hassam, Childe, *Jelly Fish*, 157
Hatching technique, 44
Head #5 (Bishop), 44, 45
Headdress for Epa Masquerade (Yoruba people), 36–37
Heads, 264–266, 272
Hierarchical proportion, 260
High-intensity colors, 142
High-key paintings, 140
Highlights, 112–113
High relief
    African, 335
    collage, 306–307
    defined, 106
    See also Relief sculpture
Himalayas, 244
Hinduism, 326–327
Hines, Jessica, *Dream Series*, 57, 58
Hiroshige, Utagawa (Andō), 93
    Plum Garden at Kameido, 92–93, 349
Hirschfeld, Al, 94
    Elvis Presley, "Blue Suede Shoes," 94
    Self-Portrait at 99, 94
Historical and cultural contexts
    selecting/analyzing original artworks by others for, 84, 86, 88, 122, 124, 126, 158, 160, 162, 184, 188, 214, 216, 218, 242, 244, 246, 274, 276, 278, 304, 306, 308, 314, 339–345, 365
    selecting/analyzing original artworks/portfolios by peers for, 129, 191, 281, 310
Historical/cultural heritage
    comparing/contrasting contemporary styles to identify general themes, 5, 23, 25, 39, 95, 97, 133, 225, 229, 253, 315, 351
    comparing/contrasting contemporary styles to identify general trends, 25, 41, 285, 351, 383, 409
    comparing/contrasting historical styles to identify general themes, 25, 201, 319, 351, 377, 387
    comparing/contrasting historical styles to identify general trends, 25, 65, 195, 319, 331, 349, 351, 365
    describing general characteristics from a variety of cultures, 171, 227, 251, 304–305, 319, 325, 338, 351, 355, 381
Hmong Story Cloth (Xiong), 211, 213, 225
Hodler, Ferdinand, 240
    James Vilbert, Sculptor, 240
Hofmann, Hans, *Flowering Swamp*, 378
Hokusai, Katsushika, 330
    Ejiri in Suruga Province, 330, 335, 349
    Portrait of Hokusai as an Old Man, 330
    Shichiri Beach in Sagami Province, 246
Holbein, Hans, *Anne of Cleves*, 9
Holograms, 107
Homage to Gogol (Chagall), 271
Homer, Winslow, 46, 65
    Hound and Hunter, 46, 47, 65
    Sketch for Hound and Hunter, 46, 47, 65
Hoover, John, *Shaman's Journey*, 180
Hopper, Edward, *Railroad Sunset*, 77
Horizontal lines, 72, 77. See also Line(s)
Horse Fair, The (Bonheur), 201, 225, 369
Hot Still Scape for Six Colors-7th Avenue Style (Davis), 154–156
Hound and Hunter (Homer), 46, 47, 65
Houser, Allan, 299
    Coming of Age, 209
    Reverie, 298, 299, 315, 387
Howl (Jimenez), 314
Huari people, 207
Hue(s), 138–139, 164
    comparing/contrasting the use of in the artworks of others, 135
    defined, 138
    intermediate colors, 138
    primary, 139
    primary hues, 138
    secondary hues, 138
    shades, 140–141
    tints, 140
    value, intensity and, 136
    value and intensity and, 143
Human figure
    activities, 264, 266
    drawing human proportions, 262–266
    Golden Mean and, 256, 257, 259
    heads and faces, 264–266
Humor, 284
Huntington, Anna Hyatt, *Riders to the Sea*, 120
Hurricane Hugo (Brown), 10–11
Hyper-Realism, 381

I

Icebergs, The (Church), 2–3
Ife, ancient, 332–333
Illusion
    of depth, 113–117
    of form, 111–112
    from positive and negative spaces, 103, 105
Illustration, 393–394
Imagination
    creating visual solutions by elaborating on, 16, 78, 97, 115, 122–123, 183, 227, 233, 242–243, 278–279, 295, 325
    illustrating ideas for artworks from, 78, 233, 242–243, 278–279, 325
Imitationalism, 31
Implied lines, 71, 90
Impressionism, 153, 181, 370, 373
In-betweeners, 395
Inca empire, 341
Indian art, 318, 319, 326–327
    ancient, 323–324
Individual style, 35
Indus River Valley, 323
Industrial design, 401–402, 408
Industry and business careers, 390–403.
    See also Careers in art
Infant proportions, 263
Informal balance, 234–238, 241, 248, 249.
    See also Balance
In Her Own Image (Schapiro), 180
Inness, George, 11
    The Lackawanna Valley, 11
Inspiration, sources of, 11–15
Installations, 25, 40, 41, 63
Intaglio, 49
Intensity, 142–143
    activity, 143
    color, 164
    complementary colors, 142–143, 150
    defined, 142
    hue, value and, 136
    hue and value and, 143
    mixing colors, 143, 152–154
    scale, 142
Intent
    selecting/analyzing exhibitions by others for, 349, 373
    selecting/analyzing exhibitions by peers for, 221, 249, 280, 281
    selecting/analyzing original artworks by others for, 4, 9–12, 14, 30, 93, 131, 167, 239–241, 287, 347
    selecting/analyzing original artworks by peers for, 280, 281
    selecting/analyzing portfolios by peers for, 129, 191, 280, 281

Interior designers, 400
Interior of Saint Peter's Rome (Panini), 113
Interior with Egyptian Curtain (Matisse), 68, 69, 95
Intermediate colors, 138
    complements, 142
International Style architecture, 381–382
Interpretation step
    of art criticism, 27, 29
    of art history, 34, 35
In the Garden (Bearden), 184
Inuit people, 102, 342, 347
Invented textures, 174, 183
Iris, Tulips, Jonquils, and Crocuses (Thomas), 26
Iron figure (Mali), 334
Islamic art, 331
Isolation for focal point, 292
Italian Renaissance, 356–358
Italian Woman, The (Roualt), 74

J

Jacquette, Yvonne, *Town of Skowhegan, Maine* V, 70
Jaguar Chair (Russell), 304
James Vilbert, Sculptor (Hodler), 240
Japanese art, 328–330
Jar (Shanxi or Henan Province, China), 297
Jelly Fish (Hassam), 157
Jenne, 334
Jewelry, 84
    Asante people (Africa), 336
    as relief sculpture, 106
    texture in, 182
Jimenez, Luis, 314
    Fiesta Jarabel, 314
    Howl, 314
    Vaquero, 50
Johns, Jasper
    Cups 4 Picasso, 103–104
    Map, 296
Johnson, Philip
    Seagram Building (with Mies van der Rohe), 382
    Water Garden, 298
Johnson, William H., *Harbor Under the Midnight Sun*, 162, 169
Jooss, Kurt, 387, 425
JPEG images, 449
Judgment step
    of art criticism, 27, 29–30
    of art history, 34, 35
Judith and Maidservant with the Head of Holofernes (Gentileschi), 111
Julie Taymor, 224
    The Lion King, 224

K

Kahlo, Frida, 5
    Self Portrait Dedicated to Leon Trotsky, 239, 280
    Self-Portrait with Monkey, 4, 5
Kandinsky, Wassily, 135
    Tension in Red, 134, 135, 154
Kaolin clay, 328
Kapoor, Anish, 168
Kashmir, *Crowned Buddha Shakyamuni*, 318, 319
Kente cloth, 336, 337
Kiitsu, Suzuki, 411
    Reeds and Cranes, 410-411
Kinetic sculpture, 107, 213
King, Martin Luther, Jr., 386

Kirchner, Ernst Ludwig
Seated Woman, 35
Winter Landscape in Moonlight, 34, 39
Kiss, The **(Brancusi)**, 104, 133, 195
Klimt, Gustav, 287
Baby (Cradle), 286, 287
Portrait of Joseph Pembaur, 276
Kollwitz, Käthe, 374
Self-Portrait, 374
Koran, 331
Korean Classical Music and Dance Company, 349, 424
Krasner, Lee, *The Springs*, 291
Kuba people, 242, 298
Kuna people, 160
Kwakiutl art, 342–343

L

Lachaise, Gaston, *Walking Woman*, 271–273
Lackawanna Valley, The **(Inness),** 11
Landscape architects, 400
Landscape (The Hare) **(Miró),** 235
Lange, Dorothea, 57
Migrant Mother, 57
Language of art
composition of artworks, 18–19
content of artworks, 19
credit line, 19
elements of art, 16–17
principles of art, 17–18
subject of artworks, 18
See also Elements of art; Principles of art
Larraz, Julio, *Papiamento*, 32
Las Meninas **(after Velázquez) (Picasso),** 14–15, 23
Las Meninas (The Maids of Honor) **(Velázquez),** 14–15, 23
Lawrence, Jacob, 67, 80, 377
Children at Play, 78, 80, 95, 377
Harriet Tubman Series Number 4, 216
Street to M'bari, 66–67
Layered self-portrait, 188–189
Layout, 454
Leaf masks **(Bwa people),** 337–338
Leaning Tower of Pisa, 228, 252
Le Corbusier, *Unite d'Habitation*, 259
Lee, Doris, *Thanksgiving*, 116
Lee-Smith, Hughie, *The Piper*, 28, 29
Legends as sources of ideas, 12
Length of lines, 73, 75. See also Line(s)
Leonardo da Vinci, 42, 168, 259, 358
sketchbook page, 42, 358
Lewitzky Dance Company, 133, 417
Leyster, Judith, *The Concert*, 178, 256, 257
Libraries (computer), 454
Lichtenstein, Roy, *Blam*, 379, 383
Liebovitz, Annie, *Wilt Chamberlain and Willie Shoemaker*, 262
Lift Every Voice and Sing **(Savage),** 209
Light, primary colors of, 139
Like a Butterfly **(Proctor),** 306
Lin, Maya, 386
The Civil Rights Memorial, 386
National Vietnam Veterans Memorial, 386
The Wave Field, 207
Linear perspective
defined, 115, 356
in Italian Renaissance, 356
Line(s), 68–95
activities, 73, 76, 78, 81, 82, 83
basic kinds, 72–73, 75
calligraphic drawing, 83
caricature, 94
comparing/contrasting in artworks of others, 69, 76, 82, 90, 91, 93, 310–311, 407

comparing/contrasting in personal artworks, 85, 87–89, 217, 305
contour lines, 81
defined, 70
expressive qualities, 77–83
gesture drawing, 82
implied lines, 71, 75
interpreting, 91
meaning of, 70–71
movement, 77–80, 90
outlines, 71
and patterns, 91
perspective technique, 115, 116
selecting/analyzing original artworks by others for, 73, 83
student art portfolio, 90–91
value and, 75–76
variations in appearance, 72–73, 75
Lintels, 321
Lion King, The **(Taymor),** 224
Literal qualities, 31
Lithography, 49, 184, 312–314
Little Fourteen-Year-Old Dancer, The **(Degas),** 180, 181, 195
Lobster Trap and Fish Tail **(Calder),** 213
Location
in credit line, 19
for focal point, 292
placement (perspective technique), 114, 116
See also Position
Logos, 392, 393
Looking Closely, *see* table of contents, xiv
Low-intensity colors, 142, 143
Low-key paintings, 140–141
Low relief, 106, 107. See also Relief sculpture

M

Machu-Picchu **(Peru),** 341
Madonna and Child **(Giotto),** 263
Magritte, René, *The False Mirror*, 375, 377
Maids of Honor, The (Las Meninas) **(Velázquez),** 14–15, 23
"Ma Jolie" (Woman with a Zither or Guitar) **(Picasso),** 375
Making of a Fresco Showing the Building of a City, The **(Rivera),** 254, 255
Mali empire, 333–334
Malina Window **(Chihuly),** 40, 41
Mandalas, 226, 227, 244–245
Manet, Édouard, 368
The Railway, 65, 368–369
Mannerism, 360
Manufactured vs. natural shapes and forms, 111
Manuscript illuminators, 391
Map **(Johns),** 296
Map Still Life with Carnation, Keys, and Glasses **(Zalucha),** 173, 176
Marc, Franz, *Yellow Cow*, 154, 285
Margot in Blue **(Cassatt),** 140, 143
Marisol, *The Family*, 268
Mask **(New Ireland),** 272, 273
Mask of Moon Goddess **(Inuit),** 342
Masks
activity, 338
Bwa people, 337–338
ceramic, 242–243
exaggeration and distortion in, 272–273
False Faces, 345
Inuit people, 342
mukenga, 242
Tapirapé people, 182, 183
Yup'ik people, 13

Matisse, Henri, 69, 374
and Picasso, 38
Interior with Egyptian Curtain, 68, 69, 95
Red Interior Still Life on a Blue Table, 38
Matte surfaces, 175
Mayan culture, 171, 340
Mays, J, 401
Volkswagen Beetle, 401
McKie, Judy Kensley, *Monkey Settee*, 53, 65
Meaning
selecting/analyzing exhibitions by others for, 349, 373
selecting/analyzing exhibitions by peers for, 91, 128, 129, 164, 221, 249
selecting/analyzing original artworks by others for, 21, 63, 69, 83, 88, 93, 131, 135, 157, 167, 171, 183, 223, 251, 283, 313, 385, 407
selecting/analyzing original artworks by peers for, 91, 128, 129, 164
selecting/analyzing portfolios by peers for, 91, 128, 129, 164, 191, 281
Media, 40–65
architecture, 54–56
computers, 59–61
crafts, 52–53
drawing, 42–44
film, 58
multimedia art, 61
painting, 44–47
photography, 58
printmaking, 48–49
sculpture, 50–51
technological, 57–61
three-dimensional, 50–56
two-dimensional, 42–49
video, 59
Media and tools
demonstrating effective use of in design, 54, 100, 120, 135, 149, 208, 238, 302, 338, 392
demonstrating effective use of in drawing, 41, 60, 76, 124–125, 127, 135, 157–161, 175, 216–217, 242–245, 274–277, 308–309
demonstrating effective use of in painting, 41, 47, 126–127, 135, 142, 160–163, 175, 188–189, 216–217, 246, 274–279, 304–305, 308–309
demonstrating effective use of in photography, 88–89
demonstrating effective use of in printmaking, 41, 49, 184–185
demonstrating effective use of in sculpture, 41, 122–123, 186–187, 242
Medium, 19, 42
Meeting, A **(Bashkirtseff),** 301
Meet the Artist, *see* table of contents, xv
Megaliths, 321
Melancholic (Faaturuma) **(Gauguin),** 372
Men: Mask Face Quilt #2, The **(Ringgold),** 198, 199
Merce Cunningham Dance Company, 415
Mesopotamian civilization, 321–322
Message of artworks, 19
Metal processes, 53
Metamorphoses, 218
Mexican art, 254, 255, 314
Mexican Day of the Dead (book), 64
Mexican muralists, 377
Mexican Revolution, 377
Michelangelo Buonarroti, 356–358
David, 267, 273
Pietà, 356, 357, 387
Middle Ages, 354–355

Middle Eastern art
ancient Egyptian, 323
Islamic art, 331
Mesopotamian, 321–322
Mies van der Rohe, Ludwig, *Seagram Building* (with Johnson), 382
Migrant Mother **(Lange),** 57
Ming dynasty, 99, 328
Minimalism, 380
Miró, Joan, 86
Landscape (The Hare), 235
Mirrored Room **(Samaras),** 62–63
Mirror images, 218
Missal (illuminated manuscript), 391
Mitchell, Joan, 179
Dirty Snow, 179
Mixed Media
collage, 306–307
studio projects, 274–275
Mixing colors
activity, 152
changing intensity, 143, 153–154
changing value, 140
Mobiles, 213, 376
Modeling, 51, 112, 451
Modules, 204
Mohenjo-Daro, 323–324
Mola: Our Environment, **Kuna people,** 160
Mom and Us **(Andrews),** 81, 82, 95
Mondrian, Piet, *Sun, Church in Zeeland,* 146, 169
Monet, Claude, 370
Gladioli, 370
Rouen Cathedral, West Facade, 153
Monkey Settee **(McKie),** 53, 65
Monochromatic colors, 145, 157, 165
Mood painting, 160–161
Moore, Henry, 122
Dallas Piece, 122
Moroles, Jesús Bautista, 171
Granite Weaving Playscape, 170, 171
Mosaics, 188
Moses, Anna Mary Robertson. *See* Grandma Moses
Mosques, 331
Motifs, 202, 204–206, 208, 221
Motion pictures (film), 58, 395–397
Moulthrop, Philip, 205–206
Moulthrop, Philip, *White Pine Mosaic Bowl,* 205–206
Mounted King with Attendants **(Edo people, Nigeria),** 335
Movement
color and, 155–156
of lines, 77–80
and patterns, 212
rhythm creating, 211–213
student art portfolio, 220–221
visual movement, 211–213, 224
Movies, 58, 395–397
animation, 308–309
outline for, 309
poster, 308–309
Moving art, 224
MPEG-3 files, 452
Muhammad, 331
Mukenga Mask, **Kuba culture,** 242
Multimedia art, 61
Multimedia designers, 396
Multimedia high-relief collage, 306–307
Multimedia presentation software, 453
Multimedia programs, 61
Munch, Edvard, 7
The Sick Child, 7
Münter, Gabriele, *Breakfast of the Birds,* 18

Mununggiritj, Yäma, *Yellow Ochre Quarry,* 152
Murals, 254, 255, 377
Murray, Elizabeth, 151
Things to Come, 150–151, 169
Museum curators and designers, 404
Museums, virtual art tours of, 22
Music, Korean, 349
My Daughter's First Steps **(Pootoogook),** 269
Myron, *Discobolus (Discus Thrower),* 352, 353
Myths as sources of ideas, 12

N

Nakht and Wife **(Egyptian),** 260
Namingha, Dan, *Blessing Rain Chant,* 75, 77, 95
Naranjo, Michael, *Spirits Soaring,* 108, 109
National Commission for Museums and Monuments (Nigeria), 348
National Vietnam Veterans Memorial **(Lin),** 386
Native American art, 341–345
Natural balance. *See* Formal balance
Natural vs. manufactured shapes and forms, 111
Nature as source of ideas, 11
Nature tapestry, 86–87
Navajo people, 343–344
Necklace, Viking Chain, 84
Necklace **(Akan people, Ghana),** 336
Necklace **(Pardon),** 8, 9
Neel, Alice, *Still Life, Rose of Sharon,* 69, 74
Negatives, 58
Negative space, 128, 246, 247, 277
activity, 107
artists' manipulation of, 103, 105
defined, 103
overview, 103–104
in three-dimensional art, 106–107
Neoclassicism, 366–367
Neolithic period, 321
Neutral colors, 139–140
Nevelson, Louise, 300
Dawn, 300, 303
New Stone Age, 321
New York City—Bird's Eye View **(Torres-Garcia),** 88
Night View, The **(Abbott),** 202
Nineteenth century art, 366–373
Impressionism, 153, 181, 370, 373
Neoclassicism, 366–367
Post-Impressionism, 371–373
Realism, 368–370
Romanticism, 367–368
Nonobjective art, 18
Northern Renaissance, 358–360
Northwest Coast Region art, 342–343
Nuestra Señora de la Selva **(Arreguin),** 222–223

O

Oba, 262, 335
Ochre and Red on Red **(Rothko),** 380
Odyssey, The, 12
Office complex **(Prague, Czech Republic; Gehry),** 132
Oil-based paints, 47, 150
Ojibwe people, *Bandolier bag,* 208, 210
O'Keeffe, Georgia, 30
Back of Marie's No. 4, 39, 316–317
Cow's Skull: Red, White, and Blue, 30
White Rose With Larkspur, No. 2, 240

Old Couple on a Bench **(Hanson),** 381
Oldenburg, Claes, 97
Clothespin, 261
Shoestring Potatoes Spilling from a Bag, 96, 97
Old Guitarist, The **(Picasso),** 270, 285
Old Stone Age, 321
Olmec culture, 171, 294, 339–340
Olmec sculpture, *Colossal Head,* 171, 339
100 Cans **(Warhol),** 20–21, 378
On-screen tools, 61
Oonark, Jessie, 347
Untitled, 346–347
Op art, 379
Openness, 118–119
Optical color, 152–154
Orange Crush **(Poons),** 379
Oranges **(Fish),** 175, 176
Orchids, Bamboo, and Rock **(Shitao, Qing Dynasty),** 83
Oriental Ruler Seated on His Throne, An **(Dürer),** 76
Orozco, José Clemente, *Barricade,* 28
Outlines, 71, 117–118
Overlapping (perspective technique), 114, 116

P

Package designers, 402
Page layout software, 454
Pagoda from the Temple Complex at Horyuji **(Japan),** 329
Paint, 150–152
basic ingredients, 44–45, 150–151
oil-based, 47, 150
pigment sources, 151–152
water-soluble, 47, 150
Painters, 15
Painting
Chinese, 327–328
Golden Mean in, 258
Japanese, 330
media, 44–47
mood, 160–161
rhythm and movement, 214–215
studio projects, 276–279
texture in, 177–180
Paint software, 60, 449
Pakistan, 318, 323
Paleolithic period, 320
Paley, Albert Raymond, *Portal Gates,* 78
Panes (page layout), 454
Panini, Giovanni Paulo, *Interior of Saint Peter's Rome,* 113
Papiamento **(Larraz),** 32
Papier-mâché sculpture, 186–187
Paris Street Scene **(Estes),** 381, 383
Parthenon **(Greece),** 352
Pattern(s), 199–224
alternating, 208, 217
and beats, 205, 206
comparing/contrasting in artworks of others, 91, 199, 208, 210, 407
comparing/contrasting in personal artworks, 204, 217, 220–221
decorative vs. functional, 204
and motifs, 202, 204–206
and movement, 212
random, 205, 206
regular, 206, 207
repetition and, 199, 221
selecting/analyzing original artworks by peers for, 220, 221
student art portfolio, 220–221
visual patterns, 202
Paul **(Close),** 384–385

Peachey, Annie M., *Four in Block Work Quilt,* 202

Pei, I. M., 122, 399, 409
Rock-and-Roll Hall of Fame and Museum, 383, 399, 409

Penguin (**Sewell**), 186

People as sources of ideas, 12

Perceiving
activity, 7
color, 136–138, 144
defined, 6
optical color, 152–154
texture, 172–174

Perception, 6. *See also* Direct observation; Experiences; Imagination

Pereira, Irene Rice, *Pillar of Fire,* 289, 315

Performing Arts Handbook. *See* Artsource® Performing Arts Handbook

Personal functions of art, 7

Perspective, 113–116
atmospheric, 114
defined, 113
in Italian Renaissance, 356
linear, 115, 356
techniques, 114–116

Pharaohs, 323

Photographers, 385, 394

Photography, 57–58, 394–395

Photojournalists, 395

Photomosaics, 188

Photorealism, 276, 381, 385

Physical functions of art, 8

Picabia, Francis, *Figure Triste,* 148, 149, 169

Picasso, Pablo, 255, 270, 374, 375
Las Meninas (after Velázquez), 14–15, 23
"Ma Jolie" (Woman with a Zither or Guitar), 375
and Matisse, 38
The Old Guitarist, 270, 285
Studio of "La Californie," 38
The Tragedy, 145

Picture of Dorian Gray, The (**Albright**), 177

Picture plane, 113

Pietà (**Michelangelo**), 356, 357, 387

Pigments
defined, 150
natural vs. synthetic, 152, 168
in paints, 45, 150–152
sources of, 151–152

Pillar of Fire (**Pereira**), 289, 315

Pinkney, Brian, 407
Book Illustration for *Duke Ellington: The Piano Prince and His Orchestra,* 406–407

Pinkney, Jerry, *Illustration from Journeys with Elijah,* 237

Piper, The (**Lee-Smith**), 28, 29

Pippin, Horace, *Cabin in the Cotton,* 234

Pisa
Bell Tower of Cathedral at, 228
Leaning Tower of, 252

Pixels, 446

Placement (perspective technique), 114, 116. *See also* Location; Position

Plank masks (**Bwa people**), 338

Plaque: Oba or Chief (**Nigeria**), 260, 262, 285

Plum Garden at Kameido (**Hiroshige**), 92–93, 349

Plumed Serpent (**Quetzalcoatl**), 119

PNG (Portable Network Graphics) images, 449

Point of view, 108–110

Pollaiuolo, *Daphne and Apollo,* 168

Pollock, Jackson, 13–14
Cathedral, 13–14, 42

Poons, Larry, *Orange Crush,* 379

Poor Man's Cotton (**Woodruff**), 202, 203, 225

Pootoogook, Napachie, *My Daughter's First Steps,* 268–269

Pop art, 21, 25, 97, 378–379

Porcelain, Chinese, 328

Porkypine Basket (**Bondie**), 52, 65

Portable Network Graphics (PNG) images, 449

Portal Gates (**Paley**), 78

Portfolio. *See* Student art portfolio

Portrait of a king (**Ife, Nigeria**), 332

Portrait of a Lady (**van der Weyden**), 359, 365

Portrait of Hokusai as an Old Man (**Hokusai**), 330

Portrait of M. C. Escher (**Escher**), 105

Portrait of Princess Belozersky (**Vigée-Lebrun**), 268

Portrait of the Infanta Isabella Clara Eugenia (**Anguissola**), 292

Portrait Statue of Boy (**Roman**), 353

Position
informal balance using, 237–238
proximity and unity, 301–302
See also Location

Positive space, 103–104, 105, 128

Post-and-lintel construction, 321

Posters, 308–309

Post-Impressionism, 162, 371–373

Post-Modernism, 382–383

Potlatch, 343

Practical applications, creating designs for, 84–85, 158–159, 214–215, 304–305, 400

Pre-Columbian art, 160, 255, 339–341

Prehistoric art, 320

Presentations, 453

Primary color triad, 147, 165

Primary hues, 138, 139, 142

Principles of art, 287
balance, 226–253
composition and, 18–19
defined, 18
emphasis, 289–295, 302–303
harmony, 295, 302–303
movement, 211–213
overview, 17–18
proportion, 254–285
rhythm, 199–225
unity, 296–302
variety, 288–289, 302–303
See also specific principles

Printer color systems, 139

Printing plates, 48, 49

Printmaking, 48–49, 312, 313
basic steps, 48
defined, 48
digital, 246–247
editions, 48
Japanese woodblock printing, 92, 93, 246, 330
prints vs. reproductions, 48
techniques, 48–49, 433

Prints, 48

Proctor, Mary, 306
Like a Butterfly, 306

Product designers, 401–402

Profile proportions, 265

Programs, computer. *See* Software

Progressive rhythm, 209, 210

Proportion, 254–285
artists' use of, 267–273
comparing/contrasting in artworks of others, 255, 273, 280–281, 283
comparing/contrasting in personal

artworks, 255, 275, 281
defined, 256
exaggeration and distortion, 268–273
Golden Mean, 256–259
human proportions, 262–266
realistic, 267–268
scale, 260–266
student art portfolio, 280–281

Proximity, unity from, 301–302

Pueblo people, 343

Pueblo Scene: Corn Dancers and Church (**Vigil Family, Tesuque Pueblo**), 8

Puppetry, 224

Purposes of art, 7–9

Pythagoras, 256

Q

Qoyawayma, Al, *Blanketed Figure Vase,* 50, 51

Queen Ankhesenamun and King Tutankhamon (**Egypt**), 107

Queen Idia (**Africa**), 348

Quetzalcoatl (*Plumed Serpent*), 119

Quilts, 198, 199

Quipu, 341

R

Radial balance, 244–245
activity, 233
defined, 232
expressive qualities, 240–241
studio project, 244–245

Railroad Sunset (**Hooper**), 77

Railway, The (**Manet**), 65, 368–369

Ramirez, John, 409, 426

Random patterns, 205, 206

Random rhythm, 205

Rashid, Karim, 408
Chair, 408
Chess set, 408

Raspberries and Goldfish (**Fish**), 16–17

Rauschenberg, Robert, *Red Painting,* 290

Realism, 65, 168, 368–370

Recycled materials (in sculpture), 186

Red, green and blue (RGB), 139, 450

Red Interior Still Life on a Blue Table (**Matisse**), 38

Red Painting (**Rauschenberg**), 290

Reeds and Cranes (**Kiitsu**), 410–411

Reflections, 218–219

Regionalists, 376–377

Regular patterns, 206, 207

Regular rhythm, 206–207

Reims Cathedral, 106, 194

Relational Painting, Tondo #40 (**Glarner**), 147

Relief printing, 48–49, 158–159

Relief sculpture
high relief, 106
jewelry as, 106
low relief or bas relief, 106, 107
overview, 50
space in, 106

Religious beliefs as sources of ideas, 12–13

Rembrandt van Rijn, 124, 362
Aristotle with a Bust of Homer, 124, 178, 362

Renaissance, 356

Renaissance art, 356–360
activity, 365
Italian Renaissance, 356–358
Northern Renaissance, 358–360

Rendering, 218–219, 451

Renoir, Pierre Auguste, *Two Sisters (On the Terrace),* 177

Repetition, 308, 309
and motif, 221
and patterns, 199, 221
rhythm from, 202, 204
unity from, 300–301
Reproductions, 48
Reptiles (Escher), 210
Resizing of images, 450
Resolution, computer monitor, 446
Return of Ulysses (Bearden), 12, 13, 133
Reverie (Houser), 298, 299, 387
Reviewing artworks. *See* Aesthetics; Art criticism; Art Criticism in Action
RGB (red, green and blue), 139, 450
Rhythm and movement painting, 216–217
Rhythm(s), 198–225
activities, 204, 206, 208, 210
alternating, 208
and beats, 205, 206
comparing/contrasting in artworks of others, 199, 213, 407
comparing/contrasting in personal artworks, 217, 219–221
defined, 200
flowing, 208–209, 220
modules, 204
motifs, 202, 204
and motifs, 205, 206
movement created by, 211–213
patterns, 202, 204
progressive, 210
random, 205
regular, 206–207
repetition and, 200–204
selecting/analyzing original artworks by peers for, 220, 221
student art portfolio, 220–221
types of, 205–210
visual, 220
visual rhythm, 200–202
Riders to the Sea (Huntington), 120
Ringgold, Faith, 199
The Men: Mask Face Quilt #2, 198, 199
Ritual Wine Container **(Chinese, Shang dynasty),** 325
Rivera, Diego, 229, 255
Flower Day, 229, 253
Making of a Fresco Showing the Building of a City, The, 254, 255
Self-Portrait, 229
Robe **(Kuba Group, Congo),** 298
Rock-and-Roll Hall of Fame and Museum **(Pei),** 399, 409
Rococo art, 363–365
Roman, *Portrait Statue of Boy,* 353
Romanesque architecture, 354–355
Romanticism, 367–368
Rome, ancient, 353
Roots, artistic, 314
Rothko, Mark, *Ochre and Red on Red,* 380
Roualt, Georges, *The Italian Woman,* 74
Rouen Cathedral, West Facade, Sunlight **(Monet),** 153
Rouen Cathedral, West Facade **(Monet),** 153
Rough texture, 175
Royal Bird, The **(Smith),** 117
Royo, Joseph, 86
Woman (after Joan Miró), 86
Rubens, Peter Paul, *Daniel in the Lions' Den,* 291, 295
Ruckus Rodeo **(Grooms),** 24, 25
Ruiz, Antonio, *The Bicycle Race,* 126
Rumal, 244
Rushing Sea of Undergrowth, A **(Carr),** 236
Russell, Julia, *Jaguar Chair,* 304

S

Saddle blanket **(Navajo),** 344
Safdie, Moshe, *Habitat,* 382
Safety, 443–444
Sagrada Familia **(Gaudi),** 194
Saint Martin and the Beggar **(El Greco),** 360, 365
Samaras, Lucas, 63
Mirrored Room, 62–63
Sandkühler, Iris, *Viking Net Chain Necklace,* 84
Savage, Augusta, *Lift Every Voice and Sing,* 209
Scale, 260–266, 281
activities, 261, 264, 266
defined, 260
hierarchical proportion, 260
human proportions, 262–266
photographs of art and, 260
Scanners, 61, 446
Schapiro, Miriam, 180
Father and Daughter, 166–167
Schapiro, Miriam, In Her Own Image, 180
Scratchboards, 407
Screen paintings, Japanese, 330
Screen printing, 49
Scroll, portable **(Thangka),** 226, 227
Scrolls, 328
Scully, Sean, *White Robe,* 295
Sculptors, 15, 314, 386
Sculpture, 50–51, 97
African, 334–335
ancient Greek and Roman, 352–353
Chinese, 328
defined, 50
free-form clay, 122–123
Indian, 326, 327
Japanese, 328
kinetic, 107, 213
media, 50
mobiles, 213, 376
Post-Modern, 383
pre-Columbian, 339–340
relief sculpture, 50, 106–107
sculpture in the round, 50
sculpture of the deity Quetzalcoatl, 119
techniques, 50–51, 433–435
texture in, 180, 182
Seagram Building **(Mies van der Rohe and Johnson),** 382
Seals **(ancient Indian),** 324
Seated Man and Woman **(Dogon people, Mali),** 334
Seated Woman **(Kirchner),** 35
Secondary hues, 138, 142
Secret Society Mask (Four Headed Cannibal Spirit) **(Walkus),** 272, 273
Self-portrait, 184–185, 188–189, 276–277
Self-Portrait: The Memory **(Flack),** 82
Self-Portrait at 99 **(Hirschfeld),** 94
Self-Portrait **(Close),** 385
Self-Portrait Dedicated to Leon Trotsky **(Kahlo),** 239, 280
Self-Portrait **(Degas),** 181
Self-Portrait (El Coronelazo) **(Siqueiros),** 264, 285
Self-Portrait **(Kollwitz),** 374
Self-Portrait **(Rivera),** 229
Self-portrait **(Wilkinson),** 284
Self-Portrait with Monkey **(Kahlo),** 4, 5
Self-Portrait **(Wood),** 12, 23
Serigraphy (screen printing), 49
Set designers, 403
Seventeenth century art, 360–362. *See also* Baroque art

Sewell, Leo, 186
Penguin, 186
Shades, 140–141
Shading, 44, 112
Shaman's Journey **(Hoover),** 180
Shang dynasty wine vessel, 325
Shape(s)
active vs. static, 120–121
activities, 100, 108, 120–121
comparing/contrasting in artworks of others, 63, 128–129
comparing/contrasting in personal artworks, 129
creation in space, 111–116
defined, 98
depth perception, 108
expression with, 117–121
free-form, 99–100
geometric, 98–99, 100, 117–118
identifying, 129
natural vs. manufactured, 111
openness, 118–119
outlines, 117–118
overview, 98–100
point of view and, 108–110
relationship to forms, 100, 101–102
relationship to space, 103
student art portfolio, 128–129
Sharecropper **(Catlett),** 48, 191
Shaughnessy, Arthur, 251
Dla'ehl Interior House Post: Grizzly Bear Beneath Kolus, 250–251
Sheridan, Philip, 344
Shichiri Beach in Sagami Province **(Hokusai),** 246
Shiny surfaces, 175, 176
Shitao, *Orchids, Bamboo, and Rock,* 83
Shoemaker, Willie, 262
Shoestring Potatoes Spilling from a Bag **(Oldenburg),** 96, 97
Sick Child, The **(Munch),** 7
Silvers, Robert, *Wolf,* 188
Simplicity, unity from, 298–299
Simulators, computer, 397
Simultaneous contrast, 144
Singing Their Songs **(Catlett),** 312–313
Single Family Blues **(Twiggs),** 269
Sioux people, 344
Siqueiros, David Alfaro
Echo of a Scream, 235, 253
Ethnography, 294
Self-Portrait (El Coronelazo), 264, 285
Siva as Lord of the Dance **(Tamil Nadu),** 327
Size
in credit line, 19
informal balance using, 235
perspective technique, 113–116
Sketchbooks, 15, 42, 358
Sketch for Hound and Hunter **(Homer),** 46, 47, 65
Slides, 453
Slipper Chair **(Dunnigan),** 33
Smart card, 447
Smith, David, *The Royal Bird,* 117
Smith, Tony, *Gracehopper,* 101, 102, 104
Smooth texture, 175
Snowstorm: Steamboat off a Harbours Mouth **(Turner),** 368
Soapstone seals **(ancient Indian),** 324
Social functions of art, 7
Software, 60–61
draw, 450
frame animation, 452
multimedia presentation, 453
page layout, 454
paint, 449
3-D graphics, 451

Solberg, Ramona, *Cracker Jack Choo Choo*, 214

Solvents of paints, 45, 150–151

Sound, 452

Sources of ideas, 11–15

Southwest Region art, 343–344

Space
activities, 104, 107, 115
beats/motifs and, 206, 208
color and, 15
comparing/contrasting in artworks of others, 97, 107, 126, 128–129, 131
comparing/contrasting in personal artworks, 123, 127
defined, 103
depth perception, 108
expression with, 117–121
illusion of depth, 113–116
overview, 103–107
perspective techniques, 113–116
positive and negative, 103–105, 128
relationship to shape and form, 103
shapes and forms in, 111–116
student art portfolio, 128–129
in three-dimensional art, 106–107

Special effects designers, 395–396

Spectrum of colors, 136–138

Spirits Soaring **(Naranjo),** 108, 109

Spiritual beliefs as sources of ideas, 12–13

Spiritual functions of art, 7–8

Springs, The **(Krasner),** 291

Stage designer, 403

Stalling Elephant with Two Riders **(India),** 174, 225

Starry Crown **(Biggers),** 99

Starry Night, The **(van Gogh),** 372–373

Static lines, 77

Static shapes and forms, 120–121

Statua di Donna **(Sumerian),** 322

Stella, Frank, 380
Abgatuna III, 380
St. Michael's Counterguard, 383

Stella, Joseph, *Battle of Lights, Coney Island Mardi Gras,* 212, 213

Still Life, Rose of Sharon **(Neel),** 69, 74

Stippling technique, 44

Stonehenge, 321

Storage, digital, 447

Storyboards, 395

Straus, Meyer, *Bayou Teche,* 6

Street to M'bari **(Jacob),** 66–67

Student art portfolio
balance, 248–249
color, 164–165
line, 90–91
proportion, 280–281
rhythm, pattern and movement, 220–221
shape, form and space, 128–129
texture, 190–191
variety, emphasis, harmony and unity, 310–311

Studio of "La Californie" **(Picasso),** 38

Studio projects
ceramic mask, 242–243
color spectrum star book, 158–159
contrast drawing, 124–125
decorated found object, 304–305
found objects jewelry, 214–215
free-form clay sculpture, 122–123
golden mean and mixed media, 274–275
mood painting, 160–161
multimedia high-relief collage, 306–307
nature tapestry, 86–87
papier-mâché sculpture, 186–187
radial balance mandala, 244–245
rhythm and movement painting, 216–217

self-portrait collagraph, 184–185
symbolic self-portrait, 276–277
wire jewelry, 84–85

Study (sketch/painting), 125

Stupas, 326

Style, individual, 35

Style sheets, 454

Stylus and graphics tablet, 61

Subject of artworks, 18

Subordinate elements, 290

Sugaring Off **(Grandma Moses),** 110

Sullivan, Louis
Elevator Grille, 204
Wainwright Building, 56

Sumerian civilization, 321–322

Sun, Church in Zeeland **(Mondrian),** 146, 169

Sundiata, king, 333

Sunflowers **(van Gogh),** 40, 178

Sung dynasty, 328

Super-Realism, 381

Surfaces, expressiveness of, 117–118

Surrealism, 278, 375

Sutej, Miroslav, *Ultra AB,* 288, 315

Symbols, 16, 276–277
selecting/analyzing original artworks by others for, 11, 12, 88

Symmetrical balance, 242–243

Symmetry, 230–231, 240

T

Tactile texture, 173, 190

Tahitians **(Gauguin),** 265–266

Taj Mahal **(India),** 331

Tamayo, Rufino, 197
Fruit Vendors, 196–197
Girl Attacked by a Strange Bird, 141, 143, 169

Tapestry, 86–87

Tapirapé people, 182, 183

Techniques
display, 444–442
drawing, 428–431
printmaking, 48–49, 433
sculpting, 50–51, 433–435
shading, 44
as sources of ideas, 13–14

Technological media, 57–61
computers, 59–61
film, 58
multimedia art, 61
photography, 57–58
video, 59
virtual art tours, 22

Technology and careers in art, 390–391

Tempera, 47

Tempest **(Wilson),** 302

Temple at Angkor Wat, 327

Tenochititlán, 340

Tension in Red **(Kandinsky),** 134, 135, 154

Tepees, 344

Texture, 170–195, 276
activities, 174, 175, 183
artists' use of, 177–183
color and, 178–179
comparing/contrasting in artworks of others, 171, 176, 190–191, 193
comparing/contrasting in personal artworks, 123, 171, 185, 187, 189, 215, 243, 307
defined, 171
informal balance using, 236
invented textures, 174, 183
of lines, 73, 75
matte or shiny, 175

perception of, 172–174
rough or smooth, 175
selecting/analyzing original artworks by others for, 183
selecting/analyzing original artworks by peers for, 190–191
selecting/analyzing the use of in personal artworks, 279
student art portfolio, 190–191
tactile, 173, 190
and unity, 191
and value, 190
value and, 175–176
visual, 190–191
visual texture, 173–174, 176

Textured buildings, 194

Thangka **(portable scroll),** 226, 227

Thanksgiving **(Lee),** 116

Theater, 224

Thelonious at The Five Spot **(Andrews),** 82, 95

Therapists, art, 404

Things to Come **(Murray),** 150, 169

Third of May, The **(Goya),** 364–365

Thomas, Alma, *Iris, Tulips, Jonquils, and Crocuses,* 26

Thoroughly Modern Medical School, The **(Wilkinson),** 284

Three-dimensional art, 306–307
careers in, 398–405
space in, 106–107
3-D Graphics software, 451

Three-dimensional media, 50–56
architecture, 54–56
crafts, 52–53
sculpture, 50–51

Throne **(Bamileke),** 170

Thrown for a Curve **(Feiss),** 308

Tibet, *Four Mandalas of the Vajravali Series,* 226

Tikal, 340

Time art scene, see table of contents, xiv

Timeline, animation, 452

Tints, 140–141

Tiwauaku **(Bolivia),** 55

Tonality, 157

Torivio, Dorothy, *Vase,* 233

Torres-Garcia, Joaquin, 88
New York City-Bird's Eye View, 88

Totem poles, 249, 250–251, 343

Town of Skowhegan, Maine V **(Jacquette),** 70

Tragedy, The **(Picasso),** 145

Triads of colors, 146–147

Tunic **(Huari people),** 207

Turner, Joseph M. W., 368
Snowstorm: Steamboat off a Harbours Mouth, 368

Twentieth century art
Abstract Expressionism, 378
after 1945, 378–383
architecture, 377, 381–383
Color-Field painting, 380
Cubism, 374–375
early twentieth century, 374–377
in Europe, 374–375
Expressionism, 374
International Style architecture, 381–382
Minimalism, 380
in North America, 376–377
Op art, 379
Pop art, 378–379
Post-Modernism, 382–383
Regionalism, 376–377
Super-Realism, 381
Surrealism, 375